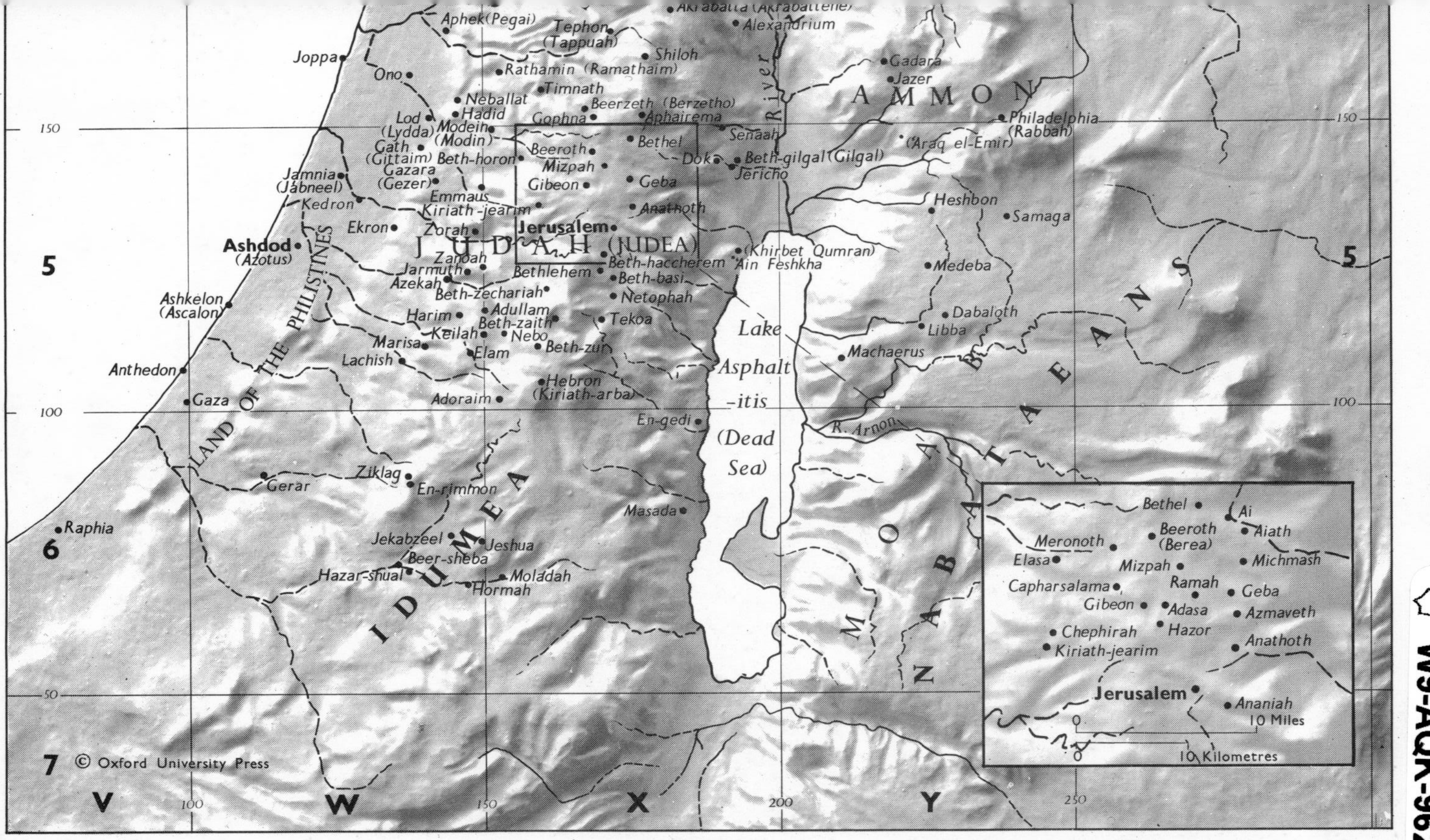
Aphek (Pegai)
Tephon (Tappuah)
Alexandrium
Joppa
Ono
Shiloh
Rathamin (Ramathaim)
Gadara
Jazer
Timnath
Neballat
Beerzeth (Berzetho)
AMMON
Hadid
Lod (Lydda)
Gophna
Aphairema
Philadelphia (Rabbah)
Modein (Modin)
Senaah
River
Gath (Gittaim)
Beth-horon
Beeroth
Bethel
(Araq el-Emir)
Dok
Beth-gilgal (Gilgal)
Jericho
Jamnia (Jabneel)
Gazara (Gezer)
Mizpah
Geba
Gibeon
Emmaus
Heshbon
Kedron
Kiriath-jearim
Anathoth
Samaga
Ekron
Zorah
Jerusalem
Ashdod (Azotus)
JUDAH (JUDEA)
(Khirbet Qumran)
Ain Feshkha
Zanoah
Beth-haccherem
Medeba
Jarmuth
Bethlehem
Beth-basi
Azekah
Beth-zechariah
Netophah
Ashkelon (Ascalon)
Harim
Adullam
Beth-zaith
Tekoa
Dabaloth
Libba
Marisa
Keilah
Nebo
Lake Asphalt-itis (Dead Sea)
Elam
Beth-zur
Machaerus
Lachish
Anthedon
Hebron (Kiriath-arba)
LAND OF THE PHILISTINES
Gaza
Adoraim
En-gedi
R. Arnon
NABATAEANS
Ziklag
Gerar
En-rimmon
Masada
Raphia
IDUMEA
Jekabzeel
Jeshua
Beer-sheba
Hazar-shual
Moladah
Hormah
MOAB
Bethel
Ai
Aiath
Meronoth
Beeroth (Berea)
Elasa
Mizpah
Michmash
Capharsalama
Ramah
Geba
Gibeon
Adasa
Azmaveth
Chephirah
Hazor
Anathoth
Kiriath-jearim
Jerusalem
Ananiah
0 10 Miles
0 10 Kilometres
150
100
50
5
6
7
V
W
X
Y
100
150
200
250

THE OXFORD ANNOTATED APOCRYPHA

THE APOCRYPHA

OF THE OLD TESTAMENT

REVISED STANDARD VERSION

Translated from the Greek and Latin tongues, being the version set forth A.D. *1611*

revised A.D. *1894, compared with the most ancient authorities and revised* A.D. *1957*

WITH

Introductions, comments, cross references, tables of chronology, and index

EDITED BY

BRUCE M. METZGER

NEW YORK · OXFORD UNIVERSITY PRESS · 1965

LIBRARY OF CONGRESS CATALOGUE CARD NUMBER: 65–12463

PRINTED IN THE UNITED STATES OF AMERICA

TABLE OF CONTENTS

TABLE OF CONTENTS

THE BOOKS OF THE APOCRYPHA

THE EDITOR'S PREFACE

THIS ANNOTATED EDITION of the books of the Apocrypha (like the OXFORD ANNOTATED BIBLE, published in 1962) is intended to serve both the general reader and the student of biblical literature. Besides containing the complete text and notes of the Revised Standard Version of the Apocrypha, it supplies the following helps:

1. A general introduction presents information concerning the meanings and usage of the word "apocrypha," the types of literature represented in apocryphal books, divergent attitudes in the Christian Church toward the Apocrypha, and the pervasive influence of the Apocrypha.
2. Each of the fifteen books of the Apocrypha has an introduction dealing with aspects of its composition, date, and contents.
3. Each chapter is provided with annotations which explain literary, historical, geographical, and religious matters in the text. In addition to the comments there are selected cross references to other passages of the Apocrypha and the Bible which shed light upon the verse under consideration. The words in boldface type at the beginning of each section of the annotations serve as an outline of the subject matter.
4. The tables of rulers during the inter-testamental period provide a chronological framework for the history of the period between the Old and the New Testaments.
5. An index to the chief annotations directs attention to comments on important persons, places, and ideas in the Apocrypha.

The following persons contributed to the OXFORD ANNOTATED APOCRYPHA:

The introductions and annotations for individual books of the Apocrypha were written by WALTER J. HARRELSON, The Divinity School, Vanderbilt University, Nashville, Tennessee (1 Esdras); ROBERT C. DENTAN, General Theological Seminary, New York City (Tobit, Judith); FLOYD V. FILSON, McCormick Theological Seminary, Chicago, Illinois (Additions to Esther, Wisdom of Solomon); HERBERT G. MAY, Graduate School of Theology, Oberlin College, Oberlin, Ohio (Baruch, Letter of Jeremiah); and SHERMAN E. JOHNSON, Church Divinity School of the Pacific, Berkeley, California (1 and 2 Maccabees). The editor is responsible for the introductions and annotations for the remaining books of the Apocrypha, as well as for the general introduction and the chronological tables.

The editor expresses his gratitude to those named above, as well as to Father EUGENE H. MALY, Mt. St. Mary's Seminary of the West, Norwood, Ohio, and

LUTHER A. WEIGLE, Sterling Professor of Religious Education and Dean of the Divinity School, Emeritus, Yale University, New Haven, Connecticut, for their willingness to read the introductions and annotations and for their judicious counsel concerning several features of this annotated edition of the Apocrypha. May its varied helps prove useful in bringing about a wider appreciation of the literature that forms a bridge between the Old and New Testaments.

Princeton Theological Seminary
Princeton, New Jersey

BRUCE M. METZGER

PREFACE

IN RESPONSE to the request of the General Convention of the Protestant Episcopal Church, October, 1952, the Division of Christian Education of the National Council of the Churches of Christ in the U.S.A. organized a committee of scholars to undertake revision of the English translation of the Apocrypha; and its publication was authorized by the General Board, NCCCUSA, December 12, 1952. The scholars accepting this assignment were Millar Burrows, Winkley Professor of Biblical Theology, Yale University; Henry J. Cadbury, Hollis Professor of Divinity, Harvard University; Clarence T. Craig, Dean and Professor of New Testament, Drew Theological Seminary; Floyd V. Filson, Dean and Professor of New Testament Literature and History, McCormick Theological Seminary; Frederick C. Grant, Professor of Biblical Theology, Union Theological Seminary; Bruce M. Metzger, Professor of New Testament, Princeton Theological Seminary; Robert H. Pfeiffer, Hancock Professor of Hebrew and other Oriental Languages, Harvard University; Allen P. Wikgren, Professor of New Testament, University of Chicago; and Luther A. Weigle, Sterling Professor of Religious Education and Dean of the Divinity School, Emeritus, Yale University, who was appointed chairman of the Committee. A great loss was sustained in the death, August 20, 1953, of Dean Craig. In 1954, J. Carter Swaim, Professor of New Testament at Western Theological Seminary, Pittsburgh, became Executive Director, Department of the English Bible, in the Division of Christian Education, NCCCUSA, and was added to the membership of the Committee. Roy G. Ross, General Secretary of the National Council of the Churches of Christ in the U.S.A., and Paul C. Payne, Chairman, and Gerald E. Knoff, Executive Secretary, of its Division of Christian Education, have been members of the Committee ex officio.

The work has involved the preparation and circulation of mimeographed drafts of translation, the discussion and resolution of all disputed points in face-to-face conference, the circulation of new drafts embodying the decisions reached in conference, and a final review of each book in the light of written agenda proposed by the members of the Committee and of the Advisory Board made up of representatives appointed by denominations which accepted the invitation to review the drafts. This procedure is similar to that followed by the Committee which prepared the Revised Standard Version of the Bible, containing the Old and New Testaments; and, in general, similar principles of translation have been followed.

The Apocrypha here translated are those books and portions of books which appear in the Latin Vulgate, either as part of the Old Testament or as an appendix, but are not in the Hebrew Bible. With the exception of 2 Esdras these books appear in the Greek version of the Old Testament which is known as the Septuagint, but they are not included in the Hebrew Canon of Holy Scripture.

Because of their inclusion in the Latin Vulgate, the Church throughout the medieval period looked upon these books as belonging to the Scriptures, though not unaware of their lack of canonical status among the Jews. In 1546, the Council of Trent decreed that the Canon of the Old Testament includes them (except the Prayer of Manasseh and

1 and 2 Esdras), and condemned any one who "does not accept these entire books, with all their parts, as they have customarily been read in the Catholic Church and are found in the ancient editions of the Latin Vulgate, as sacred and canonical."

In Luther's German translation of the Bible (1534) the Apocrypha stand between the Old Testament and the New Testament, with the title: "Apocrypha, that is, books which are not held equal to the sacred Scriptures, and nevertheless are useful and good to read." Coverdale's English translation of the Bible (1535) gave them the same position, with the title: "Apocrypha. The books and treatises which among the fathers of old are not reckoned to be of like authority with the other books of the Bible, neither are they found in the Canon of the Hebrew."

The Apocrypha had a place in all the sixteenth century English translations of the Bible, and in the King James Version (1611). The Thirty-nine Articles of the Church of England say concerning the Apocrypha: "And the other books (as Jerome saith) the Church doth read for example of life, and instruction of manners; but yet doth it not apply them to establish any doctrine." The Puritans opposed every use of them that would suggest that they possessed any authority; and the Westminster Confession (1648) declares: "The books commonly called Apocrypha, not being of divine inspiration, are no part of the Canon of Scripture; and therefore are of no authority in the Church of God, nor to be otherwise approved, or made use of, than other human writings."

The basic Greek text of the books of the Apocrypha from which the present translation was made is the edition of the Septuagint prepared by Alfred Rahlfs, published by the Württemberg Bible Society, Stuttgart, 1935. This text is based mainly upon the Codex Vaticanus (4th century A.D.), the Codex Sinaiticus (4th century), and the Codex Alexandrinus (5th century). For the book of Tobit the Greek text found in the codices Vaticanus and Alexandrinus was followed; and for the Additions to Daniel (namely, Susanna, the Prayer of Azariah and the Song of the Three Young Men, and Bel and the Dragon) the translators used the Greek version of Theodotion. In both these cases the Committee's procedure was in accord with general usage.

The basic text followed in the case of 2 Esdras is the Old Latin version edited by Robert L. Bensly. This was supplemented by consulting the Latin text edited by Bruno Violet, as well as the several Oriental versions of 2 Esdras, namely, the Syriac, Ethiopic, Arabic (two forms, referred to as Arabic 1 and Arabic 2), Armenian, and Georgian versions. In addition, account was taken of a few verses of the fifteenth chapter of 2 Esdras which have been preserved in Greek (Oxyrhynchus Papyrus number 1010).

In the translation of Sirach, constant reference was made to the medieval Hebrew fragments of a large part of this book, which were discovered at the end of the nineteenth century. Throughout the work of translating the books of the Apocrypha consideration was given to variant readings, including those in the *apparatus criticus* of Rahlfs as well as those in other editions of the Septuagint or of single books of the Apocrypha. Likewise, a search was made for all portions of the Apocrypha preserved in the Greek papyri from Egypt, and the text of these fragments was collated with that of Rahlfs.

The quarrels over the authority of the Apocrypha are now largely matters of the past. A generation that has witnessed the discovery of the Dead Sea Scrolls will probably agree with the statement by Professor Frank C. Porter, in Hastings' Dictionary of the Bible (1901), that "modern historical interest, on the other hand, is putting the Apocrypha in their true place as significant documents of a most important era in religious history."

INTRODUCTION TO THE APOCRYPHA

1. Meanings and usage of the word "apocrypha."

The word "apocrypha" is used in a variety of ways that can be confusing to the general reader. Confusion arises partly from the ambiguity of the ancient usage of the word, and partly from the modern application of the term to different groups of books. Etymologically the word means "things that are hidden," but why it was chosen to describe certain books is not clear. Some have suggested that the books were "hidden" or withdrawn from common use because they were deemed to contain mysterious or esoteric lore, too profound to be communicated to any except the initiated (compare 2 Esd.14.45–46). Others have suggested that the term was employed by those who held that such books deserved to be "hidden" because they were spurious or heretical. Thus it appears that in antiquity the term had an honorable significance as well as a derogatory one, depending upon the point of view of those who made use of the word.

According to widespread usage today, "the Apocrypha" is the designation applied to a collection of fourteen or fifteen books, or portions of books, written during the last two centuries before Christ and the first century of the Christian era. The following are the titles of these books as given in the Revised Standard Version:

1. The First Book of Esdras
2. The Second Book of Esdras
3. Tobit
4. Judith
5. The Additions to the Book of Esther
6. The Wisdom of Solomon
7. Ecclesiasticus, or the Wisdom of Jesus the Son of Sirach
8. Baruch
9. The Letter of Jeremiah

10. The Prayer of Azariah and the Song of the Three Young Men
11. Susanna
12. Bel and the Dragon
13. The Prayer of Manasseh
14. The First Book of the Maccabees
15. The Second Book of the Maccabees

In most of the previous English editions of the Apocrypha the Letter of Jeremiah is incorporated into the book of Baruch, which stands immediately before it, as the final chapter of that book. In these editions, therefore, there are fourteen books of the Apocrypha.

None of these fifteen books is included in the Hebrew canon of holy Scripture. All of them, however, with the exception of 2 Esdras, are present in copies of the Greek version of the Old Testament known as the Septuagint. The Old Latin translations of the Old Testament, made from the Septuagint, also include them, along with 2 Esdras. As a consequence, many of the early Church Fathers quoted most of these books as authoritative Scripture (see sect. 3 below).

At the end of the fourth century Pope Damasus commissioned Jerome, the most learned biblical scholar of his day, to prepare a standard Latin version of the Scriptures (the Latin Vulgate). In the Old Testament Jerome followed the Hebrew canon and by means of prefaces called the reader's attention to the separate category of the apocryphal books. Subsequent copyists of the Latin Bible, however, were not always careful to transmit Jerome's prefaces, and during the medieval period the Western Church generally regarded these books as part of the holy Scriptures. In 1546 the Council of Trent decreed that the canon of the Old Testament includes them (except the Prayer of Manasseh and 1 and 2 Esdras). Subsequent editions of the Latin Vulgate text, officially approved by the Roman Catholic Church, contain these books incorporated within the sequence of the Old Testament books. Thus Tobit and Judith stand after Nehemiah; the Wisdom of Solomon and Ecclesiasticus stand after the Song of Solomon; Baruch (with the Letter of Jeremiah as chapter 6) stands after Lamentations; and 1 and 2 Maccabees conclude the books of the Old Testament. An appendix after the New Testament contains the Prayer of Manasseh and 1 and 2 Esdras, without implying canonical status.

Editions of the Bible prepared by Protestants have followed the Hebrew canon. The disputed books have generally been placed in a separate section, usually bound between the Old and New Testaments, but occasionally placed after the close of the New Testament.

Modern Roman Catholic scholars commonly employ a distinction introduced by Sixtus of Sienna in 1566 to designate the two groups of books. The terms "protocanonical" and "deuterocanonical" are used to signify respectively those books of Scripture that were received by the entire Church from the beginning as inspired, and those whose inspiration came to be recognized later, after the matter had been disputed by certain Fathers and local churches. Thus Roman

Catholics accept as fully canonical those books and parts of books which Protestants call the Apocrypha (except the Prayer of Manasseh and 1 and 2 Esdras, which both groups regard as apocryphal). In short, as a popular Roman Catholic Catechism puts it, "*Deuterocanonical* does not mean *Apocryphal*, but simply 'later added to the canon.' "

Besides the books that are included in the present edition, many other Jewish and Jewish-Christian works have survived from the period between about 200 B.C. to about A.D. 200. Since most of these profess to have been written by ancient worthies of Israel, who lived long before the books were actually composed, they are generally called "pseudepigrapha" (for a description of several of the more noteworthy pseudepigrapha, see sect. 5 below).

By way of summarizing the preceding paragraphs, it may be said that for a Roman Catholic most of the books which Protestants regard as the Apocrypha (but not the Prayer of Manasseh and 1 and 2 Esdras) are held to be authoritative Scripture and are called deuterocanonical. Other books, which neither Protestants nor Roman Catholics regard as inspired or authoritative, are called apocryphal by Catholics and pseudepigraphical by Protestants.

2. Kinds of literature in the Apocrypha.

The books of the Apocrypha represent several different literary genres, including the historical, novelistic, didactic, devotional, epistolary, and apocalyptic types. Though several of the books combine material belonging to more than one of these genres, most of the books can be classified as predominantly of one type or another. Thus 1 Esdras, 1 Maccabees, and, in a certain sense, 2 Maccabees belong to the genre of historical writing. Second Maccabees, which is characterized by bombastic rhetoric, fiery arguments, exaggerated numbers, and superabundant use of invectives against the enemies of Jewish orthodoxy, falls more precisely into the category, then so popular in the Hellenistic world, known as "pathetic history"—a type of literature that uses all possible means to strike the imagination and move the emotions of the reader.

Ostensibly historical but actually quite imaginative are the books of Tobit, Judith, Susanna, and Bel and the Dragon, which may be called moralistic novels. In fact, the last two are noteworthy as ancient examples of the detective story.

Of a serious and didactic nature are the two treatises on wisdom, the Wisdom of Solomon and Ecclesiasticus, or the Wisdom of Jesus the Son of Sirach. The latter shows particularly close connections with the style and content of the Old Testament book of Proverbs, from which it is a natural development.

The Prayer of Manasseh takes its place with devotional literature of a relatively high order. The psalmody of the Prayer of Azariah and the Song of the Three Young Men is of a decidedly liturgical cast.

The Old Testament contains no books that are in the form of a letter, but twenty-one of the twenty-seven books of the New Testament are in epistolary form. The Letter of Jeremiah, which dates from inter-testamental times, may have provided later writers with an example of how this literary form could be used for religious purposes, a form which offers the possibility of combining profound theological content with a direct personal approach to the reader.

Finally, 2 Esdras, a book which purports to reveal the future, is a specimen of that type of literature called apocalyptic. An apocalypse is literally "an unveiling." Like the last six chapters of Daniel in the Old Testament and the book of Revelation in the New Testament, which also are apocalypses, 2 Esdras includes many symbols involving mysterious numbers, strange beasts, and the disclosure of hitherto hidden truths through angelic visitants.

Despite the diversities of literary form, most of which are parallel to, or developments from, similar genres in the Old Testament, the attentive reader of the Apocrypha will be struck by the absence of the prophetic element. From first to last the apocryphal books bear testimony to the assertion of the Jewish historian Josephus (*Against Apion*, i.8), that "the exact succession of the prophets" had been broken after the close of the Hebrew canon of the Old Testament. Sometimes there is a direct confession that the gift of prophecy had departed (1 Macc.9.27); at other times a hope is expressed that it might one day return (1 Macc.4.46; 14.41). When a writer imitates the prophetic character, as in the book of Baruch, he repeats with slight modifications the language of the older prophets. But the introductory phrase, "Thus says the LORD," which occurs so frequently in the Old Testament, is conspicuous by its absence from the books of the Apocrypha.

3. Divergent attitudes in the Christian Church toward the Apocrypha.

Ecclesiastical opinions concerning the nature and worth of the books of the Apocrypha have varied with age and place.

None of the authors of the books of the New Testament makes a direct quotation from any of the fifteen books of the Apocrypha, although frequent quotations occur from most of the thirty-nine books of the Hebrew canon of the Old Testament. On the other hand, several New Testament writers make occasional allusions to one or more apocryphal books. For example, what seem to be literary echoes from the Wisdom of Solomon are present in Paul's Letter to the Romans (compare Rom.1.20–29 with Wis.13.5,8; 14.24,27; and Rom.9.20–23 with Wis.12.12,20; 15.7) and in his correspondence with the Corinthians (compare 2 Cor.5.1,4 with Wis.9.15). The short Letter of James, a typical bit of "wisdom literature" in the New Testament, contains allusions not only to the Old Testament book of Proverbs but to gnomic sayings in Sirach as well (compare Jas.1.19 with Sir.5.11; and Jas.1.13 with Sir.15.11–12).

During the early Christian centuries most Greek and Latin Church Fathers, such as Irenaeus, Tertullian, Clement of Alexandria, and Cyprian (none of whom knew any Hebrew), quoted passages from the Apocrypha as "Scripture," "divine Scripture," "inspired," and the like. In this period only an occasional Father made an effort to learn the limits of the Palestinian Jewish canon (as

Melito of Sardis) or to distinguish between the Hebrew text of Daniel and the addition of the story of Susanna in the Greek version (as Africanus).

In the fourth century many Greek Fathers (including Eusebius, Athanasius, Cyril of Jerusalem, Gregory of Nazianzus, Amphilochius, and Epiphanius) came to recognize a distinction between the books in the Hebrew canon and the rest, though the latter were still customarily cited as Scripture. During the following centuries usage fluctuated in the East, but at the important Synod of Jerusalem in 1672 the books of Wisdom, Judith, Tobit, Bel and the Dragon, Susanna, Maccabees, and Ecclesiasticus were expressly designated as canonical.

In the Latin Church, on the other hand, though opinion has not been unanimous, a generally high regard for the books of the Apocrypha has prevailed. More than one local synodical council (e.g. Hippo, A.D. 393, and Carthage, 397 and 419) justified and authorized their use as Scripture. The so-called Decretum Gelasianum, a Latin document handed down most frequently under the name of Pope Gelasius (A.D. 492–496), but in some manuscripts as the work of Damasus (366–384) or Hormisdas (514–523), contains, among other material, lists of the books to be read as divine Scripture and of books to be avoided as apocryphal. The former list, which is not present in all the manuscripts, includes among the biblical books Tobit, Judith, Wisdom, Ecclesiasticus, and the two books of Maccabees. Irrespective of the problem of its authorship (many scholars today believe it to be the work of a cleric who lived in south Gaul), the list without doubt reflects the views of the Roman Church at the beginning of the sixth century.

There were, however, occasional voices raised to question the legitimacy of regarding the disputed books as Scripture. At the close of the fourth century, Jerome spoke out decidedly for the Hebrew canon, declaring unreservedly that books which were outside that canon should be classed as apocryphal. When he prepared his celebrated revision of the Latin Bible, the Vulgate, he scrupulously separated the apocryphal Additions to Daniel and Esther, marking them with prefatory notes as absent from the original Hebrew. But, as was remarked above, subsequent scribes were not always careful to transmit Jerome's explanatory material, and during the Middle Ages most readers of the Latin Bible made no distinction between the two classes of books. It is noteworthy, however, that throughout these centuries more than one highly respected ecclesiastical writer (such as Gregory the Great, Walafrid Strabo, Hugh of St. Victor, Hugh of St. Cher, and Nicholas of Lyra), being influenced by the great authority of Jerome, raised theoretical doubts about the disputed books.

Toward the close of the fourteenth century John Wyclif ("the father of English prose") and his disciples, Nicholas of Hereford and John Purvey, produced the first English version of the Bible. This translation, having been rendered from the Latin Vulgate, included all of the disputed books, with the exception of 2 Esdras. In the Prologue to the Old Testament, however, a distinction is made between the books of the Hebrew canon, which are thereupon enumerated, and the others which, the writer says, "shal be set among apocrifa, that is, with outen autorite of bileue." In the case of the books of Esther and Daniel, the translators included a rendering of Jerome's notes calling the reader's attention to the additions.

In the controversies that arose at the time of the Reformation, Protestant leaders soon recognized the need to distinguish between books that were authoritative for the establishment of doctrine and those that were not. Thus, disputes over the doctrines of Purgatory and of the efficacy of prayers and Masses for the dead inevitably involved discussion concerning the authority of 2 Maccabees, which contains what was held to be scriptural warrant for them (12.43–45).

The first extensive discussion of the canon from the Protestant point of view was a treatise in Latin, *De Canonicis Scripturis Libellus*, published at Wittenberg in 1520 by Andreas Bodenstein, who is commonly known as Carlstadt, the name of his birthplace. Besides distinguishing the canonical books of the Hebrew Old Testament from the books of the Apocrypha, Carlstadt classified the latter into two divisions. Of one group, containing Wisdom, Ecclesiasticus, Judith, Tobit, and 1 and 2 Maccabees, he says, "These are Apocrypha, that is, are outside the Hebrew canon; yet they are holy writings" (sect. 114). In explaining his view of the status and worth of such books as Tobit, Wisdom, and Ecclesiasticus, he writes:

> What they contain is not to be despised at once; still it is not right that a Christian should relieve, much less slake, his thirst with them. . . . Before all things the best books must be read, that is, those which are canonical beyond all controversy; afterwards, if one has the time, it is allowed to peruse the controverted books, provided that you have the set purpose of comparing and collating the non-canonical books with those which are truly canonical (sect. 118).

The second group of apocryphal books, namely 1 and 2 Esdras, Baruch, Prayer of Manasseh, and the Additions to Daniel, Carlstadt declared to be filled with ridiculous puerilities worthy of the censor's ban, and therefore to be contemptuously discarded.

The first Bible in a modern vernacular to segregate the apocryphal books from the others was the Dutch Bible published by Jacob van Liesveldt in 1526 at Antwerp. After Malachi there follows a section embodying the Apocrypha, which is entitled, "The books which are not in the canon, that is to say, which one does not find among the Jews in the Hebrew."

The first edition of the Swiss-German Bible, prepared by ministers of the Church in Zurich, was published in six volumes (Zurich, 1527–29), the fifth of which contains the Apocrypha. The title page of this volume states, "These are the books which are not reckoned as biblical by the ancients, nor are found among the Hebrews." A one-volume edition of the Zurich Bible, which appeared in 1530, contains the apocryphal books grouped together after the New Testament. In commenting on the attitude of Protestants respecting the disputed books, Œcolampadius, perhaps on the whole the best representative of the Swiss Reformers, declared in a formal statement issued in 1530: "We do not despise Judith, Tobit, Ecclesiasticus, Baruch, the last two books of Esdras, the three books of Maccabees, the Additions to Daniel; but we do not allow them divine authority with the others."

In reaction to Protestant criticism of the disputed books, on April 8, 1546, the Council of Trent gave what is regarded by Roman Catholics as the first infallible and effectually promulgated declaration on the canon of the holy Scriptures. After enumerating the books, which in the Old Testament include Tobit, Judith, Wisdom, Ecclesiasticus, Baruch, and the two books of Maccabees, the decree pronounces an anathema upon any one who "does not accept as sacred and canonical the aforesaid books in their entirety and with all their parts, as they have been accustomed to be read in the Catholic Church and as they are contained in the old Latin Vulgate Edition" (trans. by Father H. J. Schroeder). The reference to "books in their entirety and with all their parts" is intended to cover the Letter of Jeremiah as chapter 6 of Baruch, the Additions to Esther, and the chapters in Daniel concerning the Song of the Three Young Men, Susanna, and Bel and the Dragon. It is noteworthy, however, that the Prayer of Manasseh and 1 and 2 Esdras, though included in some manuscripts of the Latin Vulgate, were denied canonical status by the Council. In the official edition of the Vulgate, published in 1592, these three are printed as an appendix after the New Testament, "lest they should perish altogether."

In England, though Protestants were unanimous in declaring that the apocryphal books were not to be used to establish any doctrine, differences arose as to the proper use and place of non-canonical books. The milder view prevailed in the Church of England, and the lectionary attached to the Book of Common Prayer, from 1549 onward, has always contained prescribed lessons from the Apocrypha. In reply to those who urged the discontinuance of reading lessons from apocryphal books, as being inconsistent with the sufficiency of Scripture, the bishops at the Savoy Conference, held in 1661, replied that the same objection could be raised against the preaching of sermons, and that it was much to be desired that all sermons should give as useful instruction as did the chapters selected from the Apocrypha.

A more strict point of view was taken by the Puritans, who felt uneasy that there should be any books included within the covers of the Bible besides those which they regarded as authoritative. In time this aversion to associating merely human books with those acknowledged as the only sacred and canonical ones found a natural expression in the publication of editions of the Bible from which the section devoted to the Apocrypha was omitted. The earliest copies of the English Bible which excluded the Apocrypha are certain Geneva Bibles printed in 1599 mainly in the Low Countries. The omission of the sheets containing the Apocrypha was presumably due to those responsible for binding the copies, for the titles of the apocryphal books occur in the table of contents at the beginning of the edition.

It would seem that the practice of issuing copies of the Bible without the Apocrypha continued, for in 1615 George Abbot, Archbishop of Canterbury, who had been one of the translators of the King James Version of 1611, directed public notices to be given that no Bibles were to be bound up and sold without the Apocrypha on pain of a whole year's imprisonment. Despite the severe penalty, however, not a few printings of the King James Version appeared in London and Cambridge without the Apocrypha; copies lacking the disputed books are dated 1616, 1618, 1620, 1622, 1626, 1627, 1629, 1630, and 1633. Like the copies of the Geneva Bible of 1599, these seem to have been the work of publishers who wished to satisfy a growing demand for less bulky and less expensive editions of the Bible.

During subsequent centuries the editions of Bibles that lacked the books of the Apocrypha came to outnumber by far those that included them, and soon it became difficult to obtain ordinary editions of the King James Version containing the Apocrypha.

4. The pervasive influence of the Apocrypha.

Most readers will probably be surprised to learn how pervasive the influence of the Apocrypha has been over the centuries. Not only have these books inspired homilies, meditations, and liturgical forms, but poets, dramatists, composers, and artists have drawn freely upon them for subject matter. Common proverbs and familiar names are derived from their pages. Even the discovery of the New World was due in part to the influence of a passage in 2 Esdras upon Christopher Columbus. In what follows the reader will find a representative selection of such examples, most of them chosen from the editor's book, *An Introduction to the Apocrypha*, and arranged under the headings of (*a*) English Literature, (*b*) Music, (*c*) Art, and (*d*) Miscellaneous.

(*a*) English Literature. Sometime during the ninth or the tenth century an unknown poet, using the West-Saxon dialect, turned the story of Judith into an Old English epic of twelve cantos, transforming at the same time the heroine into a Christian. It is thought that the poem was written to celebrate the prowess of Æthelflæd, "The Lady of the Mercians," who, like the indomitable Judith, delivered her people from the fury of invaders, the heathen Northmen.

During the fourteenth and fifteenth centuries a poem called "The Pistill [i.e. Epistle] of Swete Susan" circulated in Scotland. Written in stanzas of thirteen lines and characterized by an unusual combination of alliteration and rhyme, the ancient apocryphal story was adorned with many imaginative details by the author, thought to have been a certain Huchown (Hugh) of Ayrshire in western Scotland.

How conversant Shakespeare was with the contents of the Bible is a question which, like many another concerning the bard of Avon, has been keenly debated. In any case, it is a fact that two of the poet's daughters bore the names of two of the chief heroines of the Apocrypha—Susanna and Judith—and, what is of greater significance, allusions to about eighty passages from eleven books of the Apocrypha have been identified in his plays.

Noteworthy among American writers who have drawn upon the Apocrypha for themes as well as subject matter is Henry Wadsworth Longfellow. His *New England Tragedies* contains references to 1 and 2 Maccabees, and the chief episodes of the courageous Maccabean uprising are included in his poetic dramatization, *Judas Maccabaeus.*

(*b*) Music. More than one hymn writer has drawn inspiration, as well as, in some cases, the words themselves, from the Apocrypha. For example, the exalted hymn of thanksgiving, "Nun danket alle Gott," written by Pastor Martin Rinkart about 1636 when the devastating Thirty Years War was nearing its end, is dependent upon Luther's translation of Sir.50.22–24. Two stanzas of the hymn, as translated by Catherine Winkworth, will show the amount of borrowing (here printed in italics):

Now thank we all our God
With heart and hands and voices,
Who wondrous things hath done,
In whom His world rejoices;
Who, from our mother's arms,
Hath blessed us on our way
With countless gifts of love,
And still is ours today.

O may this bounteous God
Through all our life be near us,
With ever joyful hearts
And blessed peace to cheer us;
And keep us in His grace,
And guide us when perplexed,
And free us from all ills
In this world and the next.

Strange though it may seem, ideas included in the Christmas hymn, "It Came upon the Midnight Clear," are traceable to the Old Testament Apocrypha. In the New Testament accounts of the Nativity, nothing is said of the exact time of Jesus' birth. The subsequent identification of the hour of his birth as midnight is doubtless due to the influence of a remarkable passage in the Wisdom of Solomon. At an early century in the Christian era the imagination of more than one Church Father was caught by pseudo-Solomon's vivid reference to the time when God's "all-powerful word [the Logos] leaped from heaven, from the royal throne," namely when "night in its swift course was now half gone" (Wis.18.14–15). Despite the context of the passage, which speaks of the destruction of the first-born Egyptians at the time of the Exodus, the words were interpreted as referring to the Incarnation of the eternal Word of God, Jesus Christ. Thus by a curious, not to say ironical, twist of fortune, a passage which tells of a stern warrior with a sharp sword filling a doomed land with death has had a share in fixing popular traditions concerning the time and circumstances of the birth of the Prince of Peace.

The influence of the Apocrypha can also be traced in many an anthem, cantata, oratorio, and opera. Handel's oratorios *Susanna* and *Judas Maccabaeus*, as well as his *Alexander Balus*, an historical sequel to the latter, will occur at once to music lovers. At an early date in operatic history the stirring story of

Judith was found to lend itself admirably to dramatic presentation. Italian and German operas on this theme were written by Andrea Salvadori, Marco da Gangliano, Martin Opitz, and Joachim Beccau. In the nineteenth century the noted Russian pianist and composer, Anton Rubenstein, published *The Maccabees*, an opera of monumental proportions, the libretto of which was written by one of his collaborators, Dr. H. S. von Mosenthal.

(*c*) Art. During the Renaissance and later, many painters chose subjects from the books of the Apocrypha. Almost every large gallery in Europe and America has one or more works of the old masters depicting Judith, Tobit, or Susanna, who were the three most popular subjects from the Apocrypha.

Besides paintings, down through the ages artists in almost every other medium have chosen themes from the Apocrypha. Were space available here for an inventory, examples could be cited from such divergent types of *objets d'art* as mosaics, frescoes, gems, ivories, sarcophagi, enameled plaques, terra cottas, stained glass, manuscript illumination, sculpture, and tapestries.

(*d*) Miscellaneous. The influence of the Apocrypha in everyday life can be observed in the currency of such names as Edna, Susanna (or one of its many derivatives, such as Susan, Suzanne, and Sue), Judith (or Judy), Raphael, and Tobias (or Toby).

The word "macabre," according to the opinion of several lexicographers, may be derived ultimately from "Maccabee," alluding to the grisly and gruesome tortures inflicted upon the Jewish martyrs.

Some of the most common expressions and proverbs have come from the Apocrypha. The sententious sayings, "A good name endures for ever" and "You can't touch pitch without being defiled," are derived from Sir.41.13 and 13.1. The noble affirmation in 1 Esd.4.41, "Great is Truth, and mighty above all things" (King James Version), or its Latin form, *Magna est veritas, et praevalet*, has been used frequently as a motto or maxim in a wide variety of contexts.

A passage from the Apocrypha encouraged Christopher Columbus in the enterprise that resulted in his discovery of the New World. To be sure, the verse in 2 Esdras is an erroneous comment upon the Genesis narrative of creation, and Columbus was mistaken in attributing its authority to the "prophet Ezra" of the Old Testament, but—for all that—it played a significant part in pushing back the earth's horizons, both figuratively and literally. The words of 2 Esd.6.42 concerning God's work of creation ("On the third day thou didst command the waters to be gathered together in the seventh part of the earth; six parts thou didst dry up and keep so that some of them might be planted and cultivated and be of service before thee") led Columbus to reason that, if only one-seventh of the earth's surface is covered with water, the ocean between the west coast of Europe and the east coast of Asia could be no great width and might be navigated in a few days with a fair wind. It was partly by quoting this verse from what was regarded as an authoritative book that Columbus managed to persuade Ferdinand and Isabella of Spain to provide the necessary financial support for his voyage.

5. Other apocryphal and pseudepigraphical literature.

Besides the fifteen books or parts of books which are traditionally called the Apocrypha, there are many other Jewish or Jewish-Christian works, dating from the centuries immediately before and after the beginning of the Christian era, which for a time were popular among certain groups of Jews and in early Eastern Churches. It is customary to classify these writings as Palestinian pseudepigrapha (those composed in Hebrew or Aramaic) and Alexandrian pseudepigrapha (those composed in Greek). Of the scores of such documents which are known to have circulated more or less widely, the following have been chosen as representative examples. (For a definition of pseudepigrapha, see p. xi.)

(*a*) Palestinian pseudepigrapha. The Book of Jubilees is a legendary expansion of Gen.1.1–Ex.12.47, written in Hebrew not long before 100 B.C. by an unknown author of nationalist and rigoristic outlook, who deplored contemporary laxity. It attempts to show that the Mosaic law, with its prescriptions about feasts, the Sabbath offerings, abstinence from blood and from fornication (which for the writer includes intermarriage with Gentiles), was promulgated in patriarchal times, and indeed existed eternally with God in heaven. Events recorded in Genesis are dated exactly (but fictitiously) according to the jubilee (every forty-nine years) and its subdivisions. The book has been transmitted in its entirety in an Ethiopic translation, and portions of the text survive in Greek, Latin, and Syriac versions. At about the middle of the present century five fragmentary manuscripts of Jubilees, written in a good style of Hebrew, were discovered at Qumran by the Dead Sea. These manuscripts, which preserve portions of fifteen of the fifty chapters of the book, show that the Latin and Ethiopic versions are faithful translations of the original.

The Psalms of Solomon is a collection of eighteen songs of generally exalted sentiments, composed in Hebrew during the last century B.C. They are extant today in Greek and Syriac. The author, who is usually thought to reflect Pharisaic polemic against Sadducean dominance in the religious ceremonial of his day, looked forward to the time when the Messiah would reign as king at Jerusalem. According to an extended description of the coming Messiah (chs. 17–18), he is to be sinless, strong through the spirit of holiness, gaining his wisdom from God, shepherding the flock of the Lord with fidelity and righteousness, and conquering the entire heathen world without warfare, "by the word of his mouth."

The book of Enoch, also called 1 Enoch or Ethiopic Enoch, is a heterogeneous collection of apocalypses and other material written by several authors in Aramaic (or Hebrew) during the last two centuries B.C. It embodies a series of revelations, of which Enoch is the professed recipient, on such matters as the origin of evil, the angels and their destinies, the nature of Gehenna and Paradise, and the pre-existent Messiah. Interspersed throughout the lengthy and rambling work are sections which have been called "the book of celestial physics." These sections, which are one of the curiosities of ancient pseudo-scientific literature, set forth contemporary speculations concerning such meteorological and astronomical phenomena as lightning, hail, snow, the twelve winds, the heavenly luminaries, and the like. The entire work is preserved in an Ethiopic translation, which includes what have been thought to be Christian interpolations in chs. 37–71, where the Messiah is called the Son of Man. Portions of the book are extant in Greek and Latin; recently eight manuscripts of part of the work (but not chs. 37–71) have turned up in Aramaic at Qumran. It is of interest that a quotation from the book of Enoch (1.9) occurs in the New Testament letter of Jude (vv. 14–15).

(*b*) Alexandrian pseudepigrapha. Third Maccabees is a religious novel written in Greek by an Alexandrian Jew sometime between 100 B.C. and A.D. 70. The title is a misnomer, for the book has nothing to do with the Maccabees. With many legendary embellishments the author recounts three stories of conflict between Ptolemy IV (221–203 B.C.) and the Jews of Egypt. The most dramatic section describes how the Jews were herded into the hippodrome near Alexandria, to be trampled under the feet of intoxicated elephants. After the king's purpose had been several times providentially delayed, it was finally foiled by a vision of angels which turned the elephants upon the persecutors.

Fourth Maccabees is a Greek philosophical treatise addressed to Jews on the supremacy of devout reason over the passions of body and soul. In the form of a Stoic diatribe, or popular address, the author begins with a philosophical exposition of his theme, which he then illustrates with examples drawn from 2 Maccabees. He describes at length the gruesome tortures that tested the fortitude of Eleazar, the seven brothers, and their mother, all of whom preferred death to committing apostasy. The book was probably written by a Hellenistic Jew of Alexandria at some time later than 2 Maccabees and before A.D. 70.

From what has been said above the reader will be able to form some opinion of the importance of apocryphal and pseudepigraphical literature, both for its own sake as well as for the information it supplies concerning the development of Jewish life and thought just prior to the beginning of the Christian era. The stirring political fortunes of the Jews in the time of the Maccabees; the rise of what has been called normative Judaism, and the emergence of the sects of the Pharisees and the Sadducees; the lush growth of popular belief in the activities of angels and demons, and the use of apotropaic magic to avert the malevolent influence of the latter; the growing preoccupation concerning original sin and its relation to the "evil inclination" present in every person; the blossoming of apocalyptic hopes relating to the coming Messiah, the resurrection of the body, and the vindication of the righteous—all these and many other topics receive welcome light from the books of the Apocrypha.

For further information concerning the history and significance of the Old Testament Apocrypha, reference may be made to Bruce M. Metzger, *An Introduction to the Apocrypha* (New York: Oxford University Press, 1957). For extensive introductions to and commentaries on apocryphal and pseudepigraphical books, the most comprehensive work in English is the two volumes edited by R. H. Charles, *The Apocrypha and Pseudepigrapha of the Old Testament* (Oxford: at the Clarendon Press, 1913).

ALPHABETICAL LIST OF ABBREVIATIONS OF

THE BOOKS OF THE APOCRYPHA

The abbreviations for the books of the Bible are those used in the Oxford Annotated Bible.

MISCELLANEOUS ABBREVIATIONS

Ant.	Josephus, *Antiquities of the Jews*
Arab	Arabic
Arm	Armenian
Arrian	Flavius Arrianus (Greek historian, 2nd cent. A.D.)
Ch., chs.	Chapter, chapters
Cn	Correction; made where the text has suffered in transmission and the versions provide no satisfactory restoration, but where the Standard Bible Committee agrees with the judgment of competent scholars as to the most probable restoration of the original text.
e.g.	for example
Enoch	The Book of Enoch (see pp. xix–xx)
Ethiop	Ethiopic
Georg	Georgian

Gk	Greek
Heb	Hebrew
Her	Herodotus (Greek historian, 5th cent. B.C.)
i.e.	that is
Josephus	Flavius Josephus (Jewish historian, about A.D. 37 to about 100)
Lat	Latin
lit.	literally
3 and 4 Macc.	The Third and Fourth Books of the Maccabees (see p. xx)
Ms(s)	Manuscript(s)
n.	note
Polyb	Polybius (Greek historian, 2nd cent. B.C.)
Syr	Syriac
Vg	Vulgate
v., vv.	Verse, verses

OTHER EXPLANATIONS

In the annotations italics are used to designate the words which are quoted verbatim from the text of the Apocrypha. In the notes belonging to the Revised Standard Version (designated by italic letters and standing at the foot of the second column of the text of the Apocrypha) alternative renderings or readings are printed in italics.

THE FIRST BOOK OF

ESDRAS

The book which is known in the Apocrypha as 1 Esdras is called 3 Esdras in the Latin Vulgate Bible, where it is now placed (since the Council of Trent) in an appendix after the New Testament. None of the other apocryphal books is so intimately connected with the Old Testament. Beginning somewhat abruptly with a description of the great passover held by King Josiah in Jerusalem (about 621 B.C.), the book reproduces the substance of 2 Chr.35.1–36.23, the whole of Ezra, and Neh.7.38–8.12, breaking off in the middle of a sentence after an account of Ezra's reforms (about 398 B.C.). There are numerous minor discrepancies between the apocryphal and canonical accounts, including a rearrangement of the materials; and the story of the three young men in the court of Darius (3.1–5.6) has no parallel in the Old Testament.

The origin of the book is a matter of dispute. It is not a translation of the Masoretic Hebrew text of the Old Testament, though it may represent some other Hebrew or Aramaic original. The book is quite independent of the Septuagint Greek version of the canonical Ezra-Nehemiah. The Jewish historian Josephus followed 1 Esdras rather than the Septuagint as his authority for the history of the period.

The purpose of the unknown author was to emphasize the contribution of Josiah, Zerubbabel, and Ezra to the reform of Israelite worship. The book was written after Daniel (about 165 B.C.) and before Josephus wrote his *Antiquities of the Jewish People* (A.D. 93–94). A date late in the second century B.C. is probable.

JOSIAH KEPT THE PASSOVER TO HIS
Lord in Jerusalem; he killed the
passover lamb on the fourteenth day
of the first month, 2 having placed
the priests according to their divisions, arrayed in their garments, in
the temple of the Lord. 3 And he told
the Levites, the temple servants of
Israel, that they should sanctify themselves to the Lord and put the holy
ark of the Lord in the house which
Solomon the king, the son of David,
had built; 4 and he said, "You need
no longer carry it upon your shoulders. Now worship the Lord your
God and serve his people Israel; and
prepare yourselves by your families
and kindred, 5 in accordance with the
directions of David king of Israel and
the magnificence of Solomon his son.
Stand in order in the temple according to the grouping of the fathers'
houses of you Levites, who minister
before your brethren the people of Israel, 6 and kill the passover lamb and
prepare the sacrifices for your brethren, and keep the passover according
to the commandment of the Lord
which was given to Moses."

7 And Josiah gave to the people
who were present thirty thousand
lambs and kids, and three thousand
calves; these were given from the
king's possessions, as he promised, to
the people and the priests and Levites. 8 And Hilkiah, Zechariah, and
Jehiel,[a] the chief officers of the temple, gave to the priests for the passover two thousand six hundred sheep
and three hundred calves. 9 And Jeconiah and Shemaiah and Nethanel
his brother, and Hashabiah and
Ochiel and Joram, captains over
thousands, gave the Levites for the
passover five thousand sheep and
seven hundred calves.

10 And this is what took place.
The priests and the Levites, properly
arrayed and having the unleavened

a Gk *Esyelus*

1.1–33: Josiah's passover; his effort to intercept the Egyptians at Megiddo, and his death (2 Chr.35.1–27). According to 2 Kg.23.21–23 the passover celebration concluded Josiah's religious reform, the account of which is omitted in 1 Esdras. **7–9:** The list of offerings

bread, stood according to kindred
[11]and the grouping of the fathers'
houses, before the people, to make the
offering to the Lord as it is written in
the book of Moses; this they did in
the morning. [12]They roasted the
passover lamb with fire, as required;
and they boiled the sacrifices in brass
pots and caldrons, with a pleasing
odor, [13]and carried them to all the
people. Afterward they prepared the
passover for themselves and for their
brethren the priests, the sons of
Aaron, [14]because the priests were
offering the fat until night; so the
Levites prepared it for themselves
and for their brethren the priests, the
sons of Aaron. [15]And the temple
singers, the sons of Asaph, were in
their place according to the arrange-
ment made by David, and also Asaph,
Zechariah, and Eddinus, who represented the king. [16]The gatekeepers
were at each gate; no one needed to
depart from his duties, for their
brethren the Levites prepared the
passover for them.
17 So the things that had to do
with the sacrifices to the Lord were
accomplished that day: the passover
was kept [18]and the sacrifices were
offered on the altar of the Lord, according to the command of King
Josiah. [19]And the people of Israel
who were present at that time kept
the passover and the feast of unleavened bread seven days. [20]No passover like it had been kept in Israel
since the times of Samuel the
prophet; [21]none of the kings of Israel had kept such a passover as was
kept by Josiah and the priests and
the Levites and the men of Judah
and all of Israel who were dwelling
in Jerusalem. [22]In the eighteenth
year of the reign of Josiah this passover was kept. [23]And the deeds of
Josiah were upright in the sight of
his Lord, for his heart was full of
godliness. [24]The events of his reign
have been recorded in the past, concerning those who sinned and acted
wickedly toward the Lord beyond any
other people or kingdom, and how
they grieved the Lord[b] deeply, so
that the words of the Lord rose up
against Israel.
25 After all these acts of Josiah,
it happened that Pharaoh, king of
Egypt, went to make war at Car-
chemish on the Euphrates, and
Josiah went out against him. [26]And
the king of Egypt sent word to him
saying, "What have we to do with
each other, king of Judea? [27]I was
not sent against you by the Lord
God, for my war is at the Euphrates.
And now the Lord is with me! The
Lord is with me, urging me on! Stand
aside, and do not oppose the Lord."
28 But Josiah did not turn back to
his chariot, but tried to fight with
him, and did not heed the words
of Jeremiah the prophet from the
mouth of the Lord. [29]He joined
battle with him in the plain of
Megiddo, and the commanders came
down against King Josiah. [30]And
the king said to his servants, "Take
me away from the battle, for I am
very weak." And immediately his
servants took him out of the line of
battle. [31]And he got into his second
chariot; and after he was brought
back to Jerusalem he died, and was
buried in the tomb of his fathers.
[32]And in all Judea they mourned
for Josiah. Jeremiah the prophet
lamented for Josiah, and the principal men, with the women,[c] have
made lamentation for him to this
day; it was ordained that this should
always be done throughout the whole
nation of Israel. [33]These things are
written in the book of the histories

b Gk *him* *c* Or *their wives*

---

differs slightly from that in 2 Chr.35.7–9. **15:** *Zechariah* and *Eddinus* appear in 2 Chr.35.15 as Heman and Jeduthun. **17–33:** 1 Esdras follows the account in 2 Chr.35.16–27 faithfully, apart from the omission of the Pharaoh's name, Josiah's disguising himself, and his being struck by an arrow.

of the kings of Judea; and every one
of the acts of Josiah, and his splendor, and his understanding of the
law of the Lord, and the things that
he had done before and these that are
now told, are recorded in the book of
the kings of Israel and Judah.
34 And the men of the nation took
Jeconiah the son of Josiah, who was
twenty-three years old, and made
him king in succession to Josiah his
father. 35 And he reigned three
months in Judah and Jerusalem.
Then the king of Egypt deposed him
from reigning in Jerusalem, 36 and
fined the nation a hundred talents
of silver and a talent of gold. 37 And
the king of Egypt made Jehoiakim
his brother king of Judea and Jerusalem. 38 Jehoiakim put the nobles
in prison, and seized his brother
Zarius and brought him up out of
Egypt.
39 Jehoiakim was twenty-five years
old when he began to reign in Judea
and Jerusalem, and he did what was
evil in the sight of the Lord. 40 And
Nebuchadnezzar king of Babylon
came up against him, and bound him
with a chain of brass and took him
away to Babylon. 41 Nebuchadnezzar
also took some of the holy vessels of
the Lord, and carried them away,
and stored them in his temple in
Babylon. 42 But the things that are
reported about Jehoiakim[d] and his
uncleanness and impiety are written
in the chronicles of the kings.
43 Jehoiachin[e] his son became
king in his stead; when he was made
king he was eighteen years old, 44 and
he reigned three months and ten days
in Jerusalem. He did what was evil in
the sight of the Lord. 45 So after a
year Nebuchadnezzar sent and removed him to Babylon, with the
holy vessels of the Lord, 46 and made
Zedekiah king of Judea and Jerusalem.
Zedekiah was twenty-one years
old, and he reigned eleven years.
47 He also did what was evil in the
sight of the Lord, and did not heed
the words that were spoken by Jeremiah the prophet from the mouth
of the Lord. 48 And though King
Nebuchadnezzar had made him
swear by the name of the Lord, he
broke his oath and rebelled; and he
stiffened his neck and hardened his
heart and transgressed the laws of
the Lord, the God of Israel. 49 Even
the leaders of the people and of the
priests committed many acts of sacrilege and lawlessness beyond all the
unclean deeds of all the nations, and
polluted the temple of the Lord
which had been hallowed in Jerusalem. 50 So the God of their fathers
sent by his messenger to call them
back, because he would have spared
them and his dwelling place. 51 But
they mocked his messengers, and
whenever the Lord spoke, they
scoffed at his prophets, 52 until in
his anger against his people because
of their ungodly acts he gave command to bring against them the kings
of the Chaldeans. 53 These slew
their young men with the sword
around their holy temple, and did
not spare young man or virgin, old

d Gk *him*
e Gk *Jehoiakim*

1.34–58: The last kings of Judah; Jerusalem's fall to the Babylonians (2 Chr.36.1–21). **34:** The expression *men of the nation* corresponds to the "people of the land" of 2 Chr.36.1; in pre-exilic times these were conservative landowners who often came to the support of reforming kings or who themselves instituted reforms (2 Kg.12.18,20; 21.24; 23.30). *Jeconiah*, also called Jehoahaz (2 Kg.23.30–31; 2 Chr.36.1–2) and Shallum (Jer.22.11). **38:** The author has misunderstood 2 Chr.36.4. Neco of Egypt removed Jehoahaz from the throne and installed Josiah's elder son Eliakim as king, changing his name to Jehoiakim. Jehoahaz was taken to Egypt where presumably he died (Jer.22.10–12). 1 Esdras has *Jehoiakim* bring up his brother *Zarius* from Egypt; the name *Zarius* is apparently an orthographic corruption (through confusion of the Hebrew letters *d* and *r*) of Zedekiah, who was a brother of Jehoiakim (2 Kg.24.17). **39:** 1 Esdras omits the length of Jehoiakim's reign, which was eleven years (2 Chr.36.5). **43:** 1 Esdras mistakenly

man or child, for he gave them all
into their hands. 54 And all the holy
vessels of the Lord, great and small,
and the treasure chests of the Lord,
and the royal stores, they took and
carried away to Babylon. 55 And they
burned the house of the Lord and
broke down the walls of Jerusalem
and burned their towers with fire,
56 and utterly destroyed all its glorious things. The survivors he led away
to Babylon with the sword, 57 and
they were servants to him and to his
sons until the Persians began to
reign, in fulfilment of the word of
the Lord by the mouth of Jeremiah:
58 "Until the land has enjoyed its
sabbaths, it shall keep sabbath all the
time of its desolation until the completion of seventy years."

2 In the first year of Cyrus as king
of the Persians, that the word
of the Lord by the mouth of Jeremiah
might be accomplished, 2 the Lord
stirred up the spirit of Cyrus king of
the Persians, and he made a proclamation throughout all his kingdom and
also put it in writing:

3 "Thus says Cyrus king of the
Persians: The Lord of Israel, the
Lord Most High, has made me king
of the world, 4 and he has commanded me to build him a house at
Jerusalem, which is in Judea. 5 If any
one of you, therefore, is of his people,
may his Lord be with him, and let
him go up to Jerusalem, which is in
Judea, and build the house of the
Lord of Israel—he is the Lord who
dwells in Jerusalem, 6 and let each
man, wherever he may live, be helped
by the men of his place with gold
and silver, 7 with gifts, and with
horses and cattle, besides the other
things added as votive offerings for
the temple of the Lord which is in
Jerusalem."

8 Then arose the heads of families
of the tribes of Judah and Benjamin,
and the priests and the Levites, and
all whose spirit the Lord had stirred
to go up to build the house in Jerusalem for the Lord; 9 and their neighbors helped them with everything,
with silver and gold, with horses and
cattle, and with a very great number
of votive offerings from many whose
hearts were stirred.

10 Cyrus the king also brought out
the holy vessels of the Lord which
Nebuchadnezzar had carried away
from Jerusalem and stored in his
temple of idols. 11 When Cyrus king
of the Persians brought these out, he
gave them to Mithridates his treasurer, 12 and by him they were given
to Sheshbazzar[f] the governor of
Judea. 13 The number of these was:
a thousand gold cups, a thousand
silver cups, twenty-nine silver censers,
thirty gold bowls, two thousand four
hundred and ten silver bowls, and a
thousand other vessels. 14 All the vessels were handed over, gold and silver,
five thousand four hundred and sixty-
nine, 15 and they were carried back
by Sheshbazzar[f] with the returning
exiles from Babylon to Jerusalem.

f Gk *Sanabassarus*

---

gives Jehoiakim (see note *e*) as the name of that king's son and successor, rather than Jehoiachin; but the king's age at the beginning of his reign is correctly given (*eighteen years;* not eight, as in 2 Chr.36.9). **58:** To *keep sabbath* means that the land is to continue in a state of "sabbath" rest (i.e., to lie untended as in the seventh or sabbatical years) until the exiles return (Jer.25.11–12; 29.10; compare Lev.25.1–7; 26.27–39).

2.1–15: Cyrus of Persia permits the exiles to return (Ezra 1.1–11). The text is virtually identical with that in Ezra, although the inventory of the sacred vessels appears to be better preserved in 1 Esdras than in Ezra. **1:** *First year of Cyrus,* i.e. 538 B.C.

2.16–30: Opposition to the rebuilding of the temple and the city walls (Ezra 4.7–24). A misplaced account of opposition to rebuilding the walls of Jerusalem in the time of Artaxerxes I (464–423 B.C.). Cyrus was succeeded by Cambyses (529–521), who was followed by Darius I (521–485). Josephus (*Antiq.* XI. ii.1–3) substitutes Cambyses for Artaxerxes, thus providing the correct sequence of Persian kings. The original location of the passage was probably between

16 But in the time of Artaxerxes
king of the Persians, Bishlam, Mithridates, Tabeel, Rehum, Beltethmus,
Shimshai the scribe, and the rest of
their associates, living in Samaria
and other places, wrote him the following letter, against those who were
living in Judea and Jerusalem:

17 "To King Artaxerxes our lord,
Your servants Rehum the recorder
and Shimshai the scribe and the
other judges of their council in
Coelesyria and Phoenicia: [18]Now be
it known to our lord the king that
the Jews who came up from you to
us have gone to Jerusalem and are
building that rebellious and wicked
city, repairing its market places and
walls and laying the foundations for
a temple. [19]Now if this city is built
and the walls finished, they will not
only refuse to pay tribute but will
even resist kings. [20]And since the
building of the temple is now going
on, we think it best not to neglect
such a matter, [21]but to speak to our
lord the king, in order that, if it
seems good to you, search may be
made in the records of your fathers.
[22]You will find in the chronicles
what has been written about them,
and will learn that this city was rebellious, troubling both kings and
other cities, [23]and that the Jews were
rebels and kept setting up blockades
in it from of old. That is why this
city was laid waste. [24]Therefore we
now make known to you, O lord and
king, that if this city is built and its
walls finished, you will no longer have
access to Coelesyria and Phoenicia."

25 Then the king, in reply to
Rehum the recorder and Beltethmus
and Shimshai the scribe and the
others associated with them and living in Samaria and Syria and Phoenicia, wrote as follows:

26 "I have read the letter which
you sent me. So I ordered search to
be made, and it has been found that
this city from of old has fought
against kings, [27]and that the men in
it were given to rebellion and war,
and that mighty and cruel kings
ruled in Jerusalem and exacted tribute from Coelesyria and Phoenicia.
[28]Therefore I have now issued orders
to prevent these men from building
the city and to take care that nothing
more be done [29]and that such wicked
proceedings go no further to the an-
noyance of kings."

30 Then, when the letter from
King Artaxerxes was read, Rehum
and Shimshai the scribe and their
associates went in haste to Jerusalem,
with horsemen and a multitude in
battle array, and began to hinder the
builders. And the building of the
temple in Jerusalem ceased until the
second year of the reign of Darius king
of the Persians.

3 Now King Darius gave a great
banquet for all that were under
him and all that were born in his
house and all the nobles of Media
and Persia [2]and all the satraps and

Ezra ch. 10 and Neh. ch. 1. **16:** The name *Beltethmus* is a Greek transliteration of the Aramaic title of the office held by *Rehum;* the same mistake occurs in v. 25. **17:** The persons named are officials of the Persian province called "Beyond the River" (Ezra 4.10), which included the lands of Syria, Phoenicia, and Palestine. *Rehum* is designated "the commander" in Ezra 4.8f.; the translation *recorder* is supported by Josephus. **20:** The account differs considerably from that in Ezra 4.14, which contains no reference to the rebuilding of the *temple* at this point (compare Ezra 4.24, however, where work on the *temple* is said to have stopped). **25:** *Rehum* the governor is again identified as the *recorder* rather than as the commander of Persian forces in Samaria (Ezra 4.17). As in v. 16 the name *Beltethmus* is a transliteration of the Aramaic title of *Rehum* and is not the name of a third addressee. **30:** An erroneous reference (as also in Ezra 4.24) to the halting of work on the *temple.*

3.1–5.6: The three young bodyguards in the court of Darius. This famous story, found only in 1 Esdras among the several works attributed to Ezra, provides sufficient reason for the preservation of the book throughout the centuries. The story probably originated outside the Jewish

generals and governors that were under him in the hundred and twenty-
seven satrapies from India to Ethiopia. 3They ate and drank, and when
they were satisfied they departed; and
Darius the king went to his bedroom,
and went to sleep, and then awoke.
4 Then the three young men of the
bodyguard, who kept guard over the
person of the king, said to one another,
5"Let each of us state what one thing
is strongest; and to him whose statement seems wisest, Darius the king
will give rich gifts and great honors of
victory. 6He shall be clothed in purple,
and drink from gold cups, and sleep
on a gold bed, and have a chariot with
gold bridles, and a turban of fine linen,
and a necklace about his neck; 7and
because of his wisdom he shall sit next
to Darius and shall be called kinsman
of Darius."
8 Then each wrote his own statement, and they sealed them and put
them under the pillow of Darius the
king, 9and said, "When the king wakes,
they will give him the writing; and to
the one whose statement the king and
the three nobles of Persia judge to be
wisest the victory shall be given according to what is written." 10The first
wrote, "Wine is strongest." 11The second wrote, "The king is strongest."
12The third wrote, "Women are strongest, but truth is victor over all things."
13 When the king awoke, they took
the writing and gave it to him, and he
read it. 14Then he sent and summoned
all the nobles of Persia and Media and
the satraps and generals and governors
and prefects, 15and he took his seat in
the council chamber, and the writing
was read in their presence. 16And he
said, "Call the young men, and they
shall explain their statements." So
they were summoned, and came in.
17And they said to them, "Explain to
us what you have written."
Then the first, who had spoken of
the strength of wine, began and said:
18"Gentlemen, how is wine the strongest? It leads astray the minds of all
who drink it. 19It makes equal the
mind of the king and the orphan, of the
slave and the free, of the poor and the
rich. 20It turns every thought to feasting and mirth, and forgets all sorrow
and debt. 21It makes all hearts feel
rich, forgets kings and satraps, and
makes every one talk in millions.[g]
22When men drink they forget to be
friendly with friends and brothers, and
before long they draw their swords.
23And when they recover from the
wine, they do not remember what they
have done. 24Gentlemen, is not wine
the strongest, since it forces men to do
these things?" When he had said this,
he stopped speaking.

g Gk *talents*

community as a popular tale praising the relative strength of wine, kings, and women (the original order was perhaps kings, wine, and women). The praise of the strength of truth (4.33–41; compare 3.12) was added later in the transmission of the story, perhaps by a Greek-speaking editor (this part of the story has close parallels to Greek thought and literature). The author of 1 Esdras, adopting the story, needed only to identify the third youth with Zerubbabel (4.13) and to add a sequel to the tale, relating how Darius rewarded Zerubbabel by supporting the rebuilding of Jerusalem and its temple (4.42–5.6). The version of the story found in Josephus (*Antiq.* XI. iii.2–9) differs from the one given here in several particulars.

3.1–17a: The contest planned. 1–3: Apparently Darius' banquet was held at Susa, though the location is not explicitly mentioned. **2:** During Darius' reign (521–485 B.C.) there were actually only about twenty provinces (*satrapies*); this number was increased during Seleucid times (after 312 B.C.), and the total *one hundred twenty-seven* became conventional in later literature (Est.1.1; Josephus, *Antiq.* XI. iii.2). **4–12:** The three bodyguards decide upon a form of entertainment for the king that would bring riches and honor to one of them. According to Josephus (*Antiq.* XI. iii.2) it was the king who proposed the contest. **13–17a:** The entire court is assembled to hear the guardsmen defend their respective answers; such a scene is entirely consonant with court practices in the ancient world.

3.17b–24: In praise of the strength of wine. *Wine* is the great leveler in society; it takes away man's capacity for discernment and remembrance, overpowering king and commoner alike.

4 Then the second, who had spoken
of the strength of the king, began
to speak: 2"Gentlemen, are not men
strongest, who rule over land and sea
and all that is in them? 3But the king
is stronger; he is their lord and master,
and whatever he says to them they
obey. 4If he tells them to make war
on one another, they do it; and if he
sends them out against the enemy, they
go, and conquer mountains, walls, and
towers. 5They kill and are killed, and
do not disobey the king's command;
if they win the victory, they bring everything to the king—whatever spoil they
take and everything else. 6Likewise
those who do not serve in the army or
make war but till the soil, whenever
they sow, reap the harvest and bring
some to the king; and they compel one
another to pay taxes to the king. 7And
yet he is only one man! If he tells them
to kill, they kill; if he tells them to
release, they release; 8if he tells them
to attack, they attack; if he tells them to
lay waste, they lay waste; if he tells
them to build, they build; 9if he
tells them to cut down, they cut down;
if he tells them to plant, they plant.
10All his people and his armies obey
him. Moreover, he reclines, he eats
and drinks and sleeps, 11but they keep
watch around him and no one may go
away to attend to his own affairs, nor
do they disobey him. 12Gentlemen,
why is not the king the strongest, since
he is to be obeyed in this fashion?"
And he stopped speaking.

13 Then the third, that is Zerubbabel,
who had spoken of women and truth,
began to speak: 14"Gentlemen, is not
the king great, and are not men many,
and is not wine strong? Who then is
their master, or who is their lord? Is
it not women? 15Women gave birth
to the king and to every people that
rules over sea and land. 16From women
they came; and women brought up the
very men who plant the vineyards from
which comes wine. 17Women make
men's clothes; they bring men glory;
men cannot exist without women. 18If
men gather gold and silver or any
other beautiful thing, and then see a
woman lovely in appearance and
beauty, 19they let all those things go,
and gape at her, and with open mouths
stare at her, and all prefer her to gold
or silver or any other beautiful thing.
20A man leaves his own father, who
brought him up, and his own country,
and cleaves to his wife. 21With his wife
he ends his days, with no thought of his
father or his mother or his country.
22Hence you must realize that women
rule over you!

"Do you not labor and toil, and
bring everything and give it to women?
23A man takes his sword, and goes out
to travel and rob and steal and to sail
the sea and rivers; 24he faces lions, and
he walks in darkness, and when he
steals and robs and plunders, he brings
it back to the woman he loves. 25A
man loves his wife more than his father
or his mother. 26Many men have lost
their minds because of women, and
have become slaves because of them.
27Many have perished, or stumbled, or
sinned, because of women. 28And now
do you not believe me?

"Is not the king great in his power?
Do not all lands fear to touch him?
29Yet I have seen him with Apame,
the king's concubine, the daughter of
the illustrious Bartacus; she would
sit at the king's right hand 30and take
the crown from the king's head and
put it on her own, and slap the king
with her left hand. 31At this the king

4.1–12: In praise of the strength of kings. The arbitrary power of oriental kings here portrayed is quite true to the actual situation in the ancient world. No polemic against kingship need be seen in the passage.

4.13–32: In praise of the strength of women. The third youth, identified for the first time as *Zerubbabel* (v. 13), depicts the strength of *women*, who give birth to kings, who receive from men the treasures won in warfare and heroic deeds, who can humiliate their masters, including kings, and yet are sought after and fawned upon by those whom they humiliate. **29:** The king's concubine *Apame*, daughter of Bartacus, cannot be identified.

would gaze at her with mouth agape.
If she smiles at him, he laughs; if she
loses her temper with him, he flatters
her, that she may be reconciled to him.
32 Gentlemen, why are not women
strong, since they do such things?"

33 Then the king and the nobles
looked at one another; and he began
to speak about truth: 34 "Gentlemen,
are not women strong? The earth is
vast, and heaven is high, and the sun
is swift in its course, for it makes the
circuit of the heavens and returns to
its place in one day. 35 Is he not great
who does these things? But truth is
great, and stronger than all things.
36 The whole earth calls upon truth,
and heaven blesses her. All God's[h]
works quake and tremble, and with
him there is nothing unrighteous.
37 Wine is unrighteous, the king is unrighteous, women are unrighteous, all
the sons of men are unrighteous,
all their works are unrighteous, and
all such things. There is no truth in
them and in their unrighteousness they
will perish. 38 But truth endures and is
strong for ever, and lives and prevails
for ever and ever. 39 With her there is
no partiality or preference, but she
does what is righteous instead of anything that is unrighteous or wicked.
All men approve her deeds, 40 and there
is nothing unrighteous in her judgment.
To her belongs the strength and the
kingship and the power and the majesty
of all the ages. Blessed be the God of
truth!" 41 He ceased speaking; then all
the people shouted, and said, "Great
is truth, and strongest of all!"

42 Then the king said to him, "Ask
what you wish, even beyond what is
written, and we will give it to you, for
you have been found to be the wisest.
And you shall sit next to me, and be
called my kinsman." 43 Then he said
to the king, "Remember the vow which
you made to build Jerusalem, in the
day when you became king, 44 and to
send back all the vessels that were
taken from Jerusalem, which Cyrus set
apart when he began[i] to destroy Babylon, and vowed to send them back
there. 45 You also vowed to build the
temple, which the Edomites burned
when Judea was laid waste by the
Chaldeans. 46 And now, O lord the
king, this is what I ask and request
of you, and this befits your greatness.
I pray therefore that you fulfil the
vow whose fulfilment you vowed to
the King of heaven with your own
lips."

47 Then Darius the king rose, and
kissed him, and wrote letters for him
to all the treasurers and governors and
generals and satraps, that they should
give escort to him and all who were
going up with him to build Jerusalem.
48 And he wrote letters to all the governors in Coelesyria and Phoenicia and
to those in Lebanon, to bring cedar

h Gk *All the works*
i Cn: Gk *vowed*

4.33–41: In praise of the strength of truth. The strength of *truth,* an addition to the original story probably made prior to the story's adaptation to the Jewish author's purpose, is portrayed in imagery akin to the depiction of truth in Greek literature. The Jewish adapter of the story may have modified the original somewhat to make truth more nearly akin to Hebraic ideas of truth (firmness, reliability). The closing references to truth suggest that it is virtually equivalent to the will of God: "Blessed be the God of truth!" (v. 40). The audience responds (v. 41) with the declaration, "Great is truth, and strongest of all!" The Latin proverb *magna est veritas et praevalet* ("Great is truth, and it prevails") is the most famous line from the Vulgate text of 1 Esdras.

4.42–57: Zerubbabel's reward. Darius authorizes Zerubbabel to return to Jerusalem and rebuild the temple, with generous support from the Persian treasury. **43:** The historically improbable vow of Darius to rebuild Jerusalem and its temple upon his accession to the kingship is not otherwise attested; indeed, the author has already recounted Cyrus' proclamation authorizing the return of the exiles and the restoration of the temple vessels (2.1–15). **45:** *The Edomites* are credited with having burned the temple, contrary to 1.55 (see Ob.11–14). **48–57:** Darius magnificently supports the program outlined by Zerubbabel. The historical background

timber from Lebanon to Jerusalem,
and to help him build the city. 49And
he wrote for all the Jews who were
going up from his kingdom to Judea,
in the interest of their freedom, that
no officer or satrap or governor or
treasurer should forcibly enter their
doors; 50that all the country which
they would occupy should be theirs
without tribute; that the Idumeans
should give up the villages of the Jews
which they held; 51that twenty talents
a year should be given for the building
of the temple until it was completed,
52and an additional ten talents a year
for burnt offerings to be offered on the
altar every day, in accordance with the
commandment to make seventeen
offerings; 53and that all who came from
Babylonia to build the city should have
their freedom, they and their children
and all the priests who came. 54He
wrote also concerning their support
and the priests' garments in which[j]
they were to minister. 55He wrote that
the support for the Levites should be
provided until the day when the temple
should be finished and Jerusalem built.
56He wrote that land and wages should
be provided for all who guarded the
city. 57And he sent back from Babylon all the vessels which Cyrus had
set apart; everything that Cyrus had
ordered to be done, he also commanded to be done and to be sent to
Jerusalem.

58 When the young man went out,
he lifted up his face to heaven toward
Jerusalem, and praised the King of
heaven, saying, 59"From thee is the
victory; from thee is wisdom; and
thine is the glory. I am thy servant.
60Blessed art thou, who hast given
me wisdom; I give thee thanks, O
Lord of our fathers."

61 So he took the letters, and went
to Babylon and told this to all his
brethren. 62And they praised the God
of their fathers, because he had given
them release and permission 63to go
up and build Jerusalem and the temple
which is called by his name; and they
feasted, with music and rejoicing, for
seven days.

5 After this the heads of fathers'
houses were chosen to go up, according to their tribes, with their wives
and sons and daughters, and their menservants and maidservants, and their
cattle. 2And Darius sent with them a
thousand horsemen to take them back
to Jerusalem in safety, with the music
of drums and flutes; 3and all their
brethren were making merry. And he
made them go up with them.

4 These are the names of the men
who went up, according to their fathers'
houses in the tribes, over their groups:
5the priests, the sons of Phinehas, son
of Aaron; Jeshua the son of Jozadak,
son of Seraiah, and Joakim the son of
Zerubbabel, son of Shealtiel, of the
house of David, of the lineage of
Phares, of the tribe of Judah, 6who
spoke wise words before Darius the
king of the Persians, in the second year
of his reign, in the month of Nisan, the
first month.

7 These are the men of Judea who

j Gk *in what priestly garments*

---

is reflected more accurately in the decree issued by Darius after the governor of Samaria had complained about the rebuilding of the temple (Ezra 6.1–13; 1 Esd.6.23–34). The decree of Cyrus allowing the exiles to return and restore the temple and its cult (2.1–15) is no doubt historical, and Darius confirmed this decree (6.23–34); but Zerubbabel's return was hardly supported by Darius in the manner here portrayed.

4.58–60: Zerubbabel's prayer. The language of this prayer is similar to a prayer of Daniel (Dan.2.20–23) and may be dependent upon it.

4.61–5.6: Preparations for the return. Zerubbabel journeys (perhaps from Susa) to Babylon and there recruits leaders for the returning exiles (5.4–6). The list of the leaders is hopelessly confused. *Jeshua* (5.5) is clearly the leading priest, and *Zerubbabel* is the hero of the story, not his son *Joakim.* In Neh.12.10,26, Joakim appears as the son of Jeshua; 1 Chr.3.17–24 gives a different genealogy for Zerubbabel (where he is said to be a grandson of Jehoiachin).

5.7–46: A list of the returning exiles (Ezra 2.1–70 and Neh.7.6–73a). The list in 1 Esdras

came up out of their sojourn in captivity, whom Nebuchadnezzar king of
Babylon had carried away to Babylon
8 and who returned to Jerusalem and
the rest of Judea, each to his own town.
They came with Zerubbabel and
Jeshua, Nehemiah, Seraiah, Resaiah,
Bigvai,[k] Mordecai, Bilshan,[l] Mispar,[m]
Reeliah, Rehum, and Baanah, their
leaders.
9 The number of the men of the nation and their leaders: the sons of
Parosh, two thousand one hundred and
seventy-two. The sons of Shephatiah,
four hundred and seventy-two. 10 The
sons of Arah, seven hundred and fifty-
six. 11 The sons of Pahathmoab, of the
sons of Jeshua and Joab, two thousand
eight hundred and twelve. 12 The sons
of Elam, one thousand two hundred
and fifty-four. The sons of Zattu, nine
hundred and forty-five. The sons of
Chorbe, seven hundred and five. The
sons of Bani, six hundred and forty-
eight. 13 The sons of Bebai, six hundred
and twenty-three. The sons of Azgad,
one thousand three hundred and
twenty-two. 14 The sons of Adonikam,
six hundred and sixty-seven. The sons
of Bigvai, two thousand and sixty-six.
The sons of Adin, four hundred and
fifty-four. 15 The sons of Ater, namely
of Hezekiah, ninety-two. The sons of
Kilan and Azetas, sixty-seven. The
sons of Azaru, four hundred and thirty-
two. 16 The sons of Annias, one hundred and one. The sons of Arom. The
sons of Bezai, three hundred and
twenty-three. The sons of Jorah,[n] one
hundred and twelve. 17 The sons of
Baiterus, three thousand and five. The
sons of Bethlehem,[o] one hundred and
twenty-three. 18 The men of Netophah,
fifty-five. The men of Anathoth, one
hundred and fifty-eight. The men of
Bethasmoth, forty-two. 19 The men of
Kiriatharim, twenty-five. The men of
Chephirah and Beeroth, seven hundred
and forty-three. 20 The Chadiasans and
Ammidians, four hundred and twenty-
two. The men of Ramah[p] and Geba,
six hundred and twenty-one. 21 The
men of Michmas,[q] one hundred and
twenty-two. The men of Bethel,[r] fifty-
two. The sons of Magbish,[s] one
hundred and fifty-six. 22 The sons of
the other Elam[t] and Ono, seven hundred and twenty-five. The sons of
Jericho, three hundred and forty-five.
23 The sons of Senaah, three thousand
three hundred and thirty.
24 The priests: the sons of Jedaiah
the son of Jeshua, of the sons of
Anasib, nine hundred and seventy-two.
The sons of Immer, one thousand and
fifty-two. 25 The sons of Pashhur, one
thousand two hundred and forty-seven.
The sons of Harim, one thousand and
seventeen.
26 The Levites: the sons of Jeshua
and Kadmiel and Bannas and Sudias,
seventy-four. 27 The temple singers:
the sons of Asaph, one hundred and
twenty-eight. 28 The gatekeepers: the
sons of Shallum, the sons of Ater, the
sons of Talmon, the sons of Akkub,
the sons of Hatita, the sons of Shobai,
in all one hundred and thirty-nine.
29 The temple servants: the sons of
Ziha,[u] the sons of Hasupha, the sons of
Tabbaoth, the sons of Keros, the sons
of Siaha,[v] the sons of Padon, the sons
of Lebanah, the sons of Hagabah,
30 the sons of Akkub, the sons of Uthai,
the sons of Ketab, the sons of Hagab,
the sons of Shamlai,[w] the sons of
Hana, the sons of Cathua, the sons of
Gahar,[x] 31 the sons of Reaiah,[y] the
sons of Rezin,[z] the sons of Nekoda,[a]
the sons of Chezib, the sons of Gaz-
zam,[b] the sons of Uzza, the sons of

k Gk *Eneneus* *l* Gk *Beelsarus*
m Gk *Aspharasus* *n* Gk *Arsiphurith*
o Gk *Bethlomon* *p* Gk *Kirama*
q Gk *Macalon* *r* Gk *Betolio*
s Gk *Niphis* *t* Gk *Calamolalus*
u Gk *Esau* *v* Gk *Sua*
w Gk *Subai* *x* Gk *Geddur* *y* Gk *Jairus*
z Gk *Daisan* *a* Gk *Noeba* *b* Gk *Gazera*

---

differs from that in Ezra at many points, both as to names and numbers. The totals, however, are almost identical. The numbers of the priests and Levites are almost identical in the three lists, an indication that priestly and Levitical genealogies were more carefully preserved than the other lists. **24–25:** Only four divisions of priests are given, while in 1 Chr. ch. 24 twenty-four

Paseah,[c] the sons of Hasrah, the sons
of Besai,[d] the sons of Asnah, the sons of
the Meunites,[e] the sons of Nephisim,
the sons of Bakbuk,[f] the sons of Haku-
pha, the sons of Asur, the sons of
Pharakim, the sons of Bazluth, 32the
sons of Mehida, the sons of Cutha,
the sons of Charea, the sons of Barkos,
the sons of Sisera,[g] the sons of Temah,
the sons of Neziah, the sons of Hatipha.
33 The sons of Solomon's servants:
the sons of Hassophereth,[h] the sons
of Peruda, the sons of Jaalah, the
sons of Lozon, the sons of Giddel,[i]
the sons of Shephatiah, 34the sons of
Hattil,[j] the sons of Pochereth-hazze-
baim, the sons of Sarothie, the sons
of Masiah, the sons of Gas, the sons
of Addus, the sons of Subas, the
sons of Apherra, the sons of Barodis,
the sons of Shaphat, the sons of
Ami.[k]
35 All the temple servants and the
sons of Solomon's servants were three
hundred and seventy-two.
36 The following are those who
came up from Telmelah[l] and Tel-
harsha, under the leadership of Cherub,
Addan, and Immer, 37though they
could not prove by their fathers' houses
or lineage that they belonged to Israel:
the sons of Delaiah the son of Tobiah,
the sons of Nekoda, six hundred and
fifty-two.
38 Of the priests the following had
assumed the priesthood but were not
found registered: the sons of Habaiah,
the sons of Hakkoz, the sons of Jaddus
who had married Agia, one of the
daughters of Barzillai, and was called
by his name. 39And when the genealogy
of these men was sought in the register
and was not found, they were excluded
from serving as priests. 40And Nehemiah and Attharias[m] told them not to
share in the holy things until a high
priest should appear wearing Urim and
Thummim.[n]
41 All those of Israel, twelve or more
years of age, besides menservants and
maidservants, were forty-two thousand three hundred and sixty; 42their
menservants and maidservants were
seven thousand three hundred and
thirty-seven; there were two hundred
and forty-five musicians and singers.
43There were four hundred and thirty-
five camels, and seven thousand and
thirty-six horses, two hundred and
forty-five mules, and five thousand five
hundred and twenty-five asses.
44 Some of the heads of families,
when they came to the temple of God
which is in Jerusalem, vowed that they
would erect the house on its site, to the
best of their ability, 45and that they
would give to the sacred treasury for
the work a thousand minas of gold,
five thousand minas of silver, and one
hundred priests' garments.
46 The priests, the Levites, and some
of the people[o] settled in Jerusalem and
its vicinity; and the temple singers, the
gatekeepers, and all Israel in their
towns.
47 When the seventh month came,
and the sons of Israel were each in his
own home, they gathered as one man
in the square before the first gate
toward the east. 48Then Jeshua the
son of Jozadak, with his fellow priests,
and Zerubbabel the son of Shealtiel,

c Gk *Phinoe* *d* Gk *Basthai* *e* Gk *Maani*
f Gk *Acub* or *Acuph* or *Acum* *g* Gk *Serar*
h Gk *Assaphioth* *i* Gk *Isdael*
j Gk *Agia* *k* Gk *Allon* *l* Gk *Thermeleth*
m Or *the governor* *n* Gk *Manifestation and Truth*
o Or *those who were of the people*

divisions appear. **40:** The name *Nehemiah* is not found in the lists in Ezra and Nehemiah; "the governor" (see note *m*) orders the community to await the appearance of a high priest before participating in the holy things. The name is an addition to the text, arising from the circumstance that Nehemiah served as governor of Judah under appointment by Artaxerxes I (Neh.5.14). *Urim and Thummim* are the sacred lots used by the priests to receive oracular decisions (Ex.28.30; Lev.8.8; Dt.33.8; 1 Sam.14.41). **41:** The total exceeds the sum of the several groups listed, it being assumed that others were present who are not specifically mentioned in the list.

5.47–73: Work on the temple commences and is interrupted (Ezra 3.1–4.5; compare Josephus, *Antiq.* XI. iv.1–3). This section is confused because the building of the temple is placed both in

with his kinsmen, took their places and
prepared the altar of the God of Israel,
49 to offer burnt offerings upon it, in
accordance with the directions in the
book of Moses the man of God. 50 And
some joined them from the other
peoples of the land. And they erected
the altar in its place, for all the peoples
of the land were hostile to them and
were stronger than they; and they
offered sacrifices at the proper times
and burnt offerings to the Lord morning and evening. 51 They kept the feast
of booths, as it is commanded in the
law, and offered the proper sacrifices
every day, 52 and thereafter the continual offerings and sacrifices on sabbaths and at new moons and at all the
consecrated feasts. 53 And all who had
made any vow to God began to offer
sacrifices to God, from the new moon
of the seventh month, though the temple of God was not yet built. 54 And
they gave money to the masons and the
carpenters, and food and drink 55 and
carts[p] to the Sidonians and the Tyrians,
to bring cedar logs from Lebanon and
convey them in rafts to the harbor of
Joppa, according to the decree which
they had in writing from Cyrus king of
the Persians.

56 In the second year after their
coming to the temple of God in Jerusalem, in the second month, Zerubbabel the son of Shealtiel and Jeshua
the son of Jozadak made a beginning,
together with their brethren and the
Levitical priests and all who had come
to Jerusalem from the captivity; 57 and
they laid the foundation of the temple
of God on the new moon of the second
month in the second year after they
came to Judea and Jerusalem. 58 And
they appointed the Levites who were
twenty or more years of age to have
charge of the work of the Lord. And
Jeshua arose, and his sons and brethren
and Kadmiel his brother and the sons
of Jeshua Emadabun and the sons of
Joda son of Iliadun, with their sons
and brethren, all the Levites, as one
man pressing forward the work on the
house of God.

So the builders built the temple of
the Lord. 59 And the priests stood
arrayed in their garments, with musical
instruments and trumpets, and the
Levites, the sons of Asaph, with cymbals, 60 praising the Lord and blessing
him, according to the directions of
David king of Israel; 61 and they sang
hymns, giving thanks to the Lord, because his goodness and his glory are
for ever upon all Israel. 62 And all the
people sounded trumpets and shouted
with a great shout, praising the Lord
for the erection of the house of the
Lord. 63 Some of the Levitical priests
and heads of fathers' houses, old men
who had seen the former house, came
to the building of this one with outcries
and loud weeping, 64 while many came
with trumpets and a joyful noise, 65 so
that the people could not hear the trumpets because of the weeping of the
people.

For the multitude sounded the trum-

p The Greek text is uncertain at this point

---

the reign of Cyrus (538–529 B.C.) and that of Darius (521–485 B.C.). A first return of exiles under Sheshbazzar and a second return under Zerubbabel and Jeshua have been merged. The true sequence of events is that Sheshbazzar returned to Judah shortly after 538 B.C., restored the sacrificial altar, resumed the cultic services, and laid the foundation of the temple. The work was halted until the return of additional exiles under Zerubbabel and Jeshua; when the work was resumed, opposition from Samaria, the capital of the province to which Judah belonged, quickly developed. Haggai and Zechariah encouraged the community to complete the temple, and work was begun once more; the temple was finally dedicated in 516 B.C. **47–55:** It is highly doubtful that Zerubbabel and Jeshua were involved in the initial work under Sheshbazzar; the events recorded here belong to the period of rebuilding begun in the second year of Darius, not Cyrus. **51:** The *feast of booths* is observed for one week beginning on the fifteenth day of the seventh month (Lev.23.39). **54:** Minted *money* was in use in the Persian period. **56:** Apparently the *second year* of Cyrus is intended, but the second year of Darius is the correct date. **59–65:** The author erroneously speaks of the temple's being built at this time; the ceremony described

pets loudly, so that the sound was
heard afar; 66and when the enemies of
the tribe of Judah and Benjamin heard
it, they came to find out what the sound
of the trumpets meant. 67And they
learned that those who had returned
from captivity were building the temple
for the Lord God of Israel. 68So they
approached Zerubbabel and Jeshua
and the heads of the fathers' houses
and said to them, "We will build with
you. 69For we obey your Lord just as
you do, and we have been sacrificing
to him ever since the days of Esarhaddon[q] king of the Assyrians, who
brought us here." 70But Zerubbabel
and Jeshua and the heads of the fathers'
houses in Israel said to them, "You
have nothing to do with us in building
the house for the Lord our God, 71for
we alone will build it for the Lord of
Israel, as Cyrus the king of the Persians
has commanded us." 72But the peoples
of the land pressed hard[r] upon those in
Judea, cut off their supplies, and hindered their building; 73and by plots and
demagoguery and uprisings they prevented the completion of the building
as long as King Cyrus lived. And they
were kept from building for two years,
until the reign of Darius.

6 Now in the second year of the
reign of Darius, the prophets
Haggai and Zechariah the son of Iddo
prophesied to the Jews who were in
Judea and Jerusalem; they prophesied
to them in the name of the Lord God
of Israel. 2Then Zerubbabel the son of
Shealtiel and Jeshua the son of Jozadak
arose and began to build the house of
the Lord which is in Jerusalem, with
the help of the prophets of the Lord
who were with them.
3 At the same time Sisinnes the
governor of Syria and Phoenicia and
Sathrabuzanes and their associates
came to them and said, 4"By whose
order are you building this house and
this roof and finishing all the other
things? And who are the builders
that are finishing these things?" 5Yet
the elders of the Jews were dealt with
kindly, for the providence of the Lord
was over the captives; 6and they were
not prevented from building until
word could be sent to Darius concerning them and a report made.
7 A copy of the letter which Sisinnes the governor of Syria and Phoenicia, and Sathrabuzanes, and their
associates the local rulers in Syria
and Phoenicia, wrote and sent to
Darius:
8 "To King Darius, greeting. Let
it be fully known to our lord the king
that, when we went to the country of
Judea and entered the city of Jerusalem, we found the elders of the Jews,
who had been in captivity, 9building in
the city of Jerusalem a great new house
for the Lord, of hewn stone, with costly
timber laid in the walls. 10These operations are going on rapidly, and the
work is prospering in their hands and
being completed with all splendor and
care. 11Then we asked these elders, 'At
whose command are you building this
house and laying the foundations of
this structure?' 12And in order that
we might inform you in writing who
the leaders are, we questioned them
and asked them for a list of the names
of those who are at their head. 13They
answered us, 'We are the servants of
the Lord who created the heaven and

q Gk *Asbasareth*
r The Greek text is uncertain at this point

in Ezra 3.10–13 occurred when the foundation of the temple was laid. **66–73:** Enemies interrupt the work; they hear the sound of celebration, a detail not found in Ezra. **69:** Instead of *Esarhaddon*, Josephus (*Antiq.* XI. iv.3) reads Shalmaneser (as in 2 Kg. ch. 17). **73:** The *two years* from the reign of Cyrus to that of Darius (compare 2.30) is a mistake; Ezra lacks this detail, although in Ezra 4.24 the cessation of work until the time of Darius introduces a similar confusion.

6.1–7.15: The temple completed (Ezra 4.24–6.22). Haggai and Zechariah encourage the resumption of work on the temple and succeed in gaining support for Zerubbabel and Jeshua (= Joshua; compare Hag.1.1–4; 2.1–4; Zech.4.9; 6.15). **6.3:** *Sisinnes* is Tattenai, governor of the province "Beyond the River"; *Sathrabuzanes* is Shetherbozenai (Ezra 5.3). **14:** *A king of*

the earth. 14And the house was built
many years ago by a king of Israel who
was great and strong, and it was
finished. 15But when our fathers
sinned against the Lord of Israel who
is in heaven, and provoked him, he
gave them over into the hands of
Nebuchadnezzar king of Babylon, king
of the Chaldeans; 16and they pulled
down the house, and burned it, and
carried the people away captive to
Babylon. 17But in the first year that
Cyrus reigned over the country of
Babylonia, King Cyrus wrote that this
house should be rebuilt. 18And the
holy vessels of gold and of silver, which
Nebuchadnezzar had taken out of the
house in Jerusalem and stored in his
own temple, these Cyrus the king took
out again from the temple in Babylon,
and they were delivered to Zerubbabel
and Sheshbazzar[s] the governor 19with
the command that he should take all
these vessels back and put them in the
temple at Jerusalem, and that this
temple of the Lord should be rebuilt
on its site. 20Then this Sheshbazzar,[s]
after coming here, laid the foundations
of the house of the Lord which is in
Jerusalem, and although it has been in
process of construction from that time
until now, it has not yet reached completion.' 21Now therefore, if it seems
wise, O king, let search be made in the
royal archives of our lord[t] the king that
are in Babylon; 22and if it is found
that the building of the house of the
Lord in Jerusalem was done with
the consent of King Cyrus, and if it is
approved by our lord the king, let him
send us directions concerning these
things."

23 Then King Darius commanded
that search be made in the royal archives that were deposited in Babylon.
And in Ecbatana, the fortress which is
in the country of Media, a scroll[u] was
found in which this was recorded:
24"In the first year of the reign of
Cyrus, King Cyrus ordered the building
of the house of the Lord in Jerusalem,
where they sacrifice with perpetual fire;
25its height to be sixty cubits and its
breadth sixty cubits, with three courses
of hewn stone and one course of new
native timber; the cost to be paid from
the treasury of Cyrus the king; 26and
that the holy vessels of the house of
the Lord, both of gold and of silver,
which Nebuchadnezzar took out of the
house in Jerusalem and carried away
to Babylon, should be restored to the
house in Jerusalem, to be placed where
they had been."

27 So Darius[v] commanded Sisinnes
the governor of Syria and Phoenicia,
and Sathrabuzanes, and their associates, and those who were appointed
as local rulers in Syria and Phoenicia,
to keep away from the place, and to
permit Zerubbabel, the servant of the
Lord and governor of Judea, and the
elders of the Jews to build this house of
the Lord on its site. 28"And I command
that it be built completely, and that
full effort be made to help the men who
have returned from the captivity of
Judea, until the house of the Lord is
finished; 29and that out of the tribute
of Coelesyria and Phoenicia a portion
be scrupulously given to these men,
that is, to Zerubbabel the governor, for sacrifices to the Lord, for
bulls and rams and lambs, 30and likewise wheat and salt and wine and
oil, regularly every year, without quib-
bling, for daily use as the priests in
Jerusalem may indicate, 31in order that
libations may be made to the Most
High God for the king and his children, and prayers be offered for their
life."

32 And he commanded that if any
should transgress or nullify any of the
things herein written,[w] a beam should

s Gk *Sanabassarus*
t Other authorities read *of Cyrus*
u Other authorities read *passage*
v Gk *he*
w Other authorities read *stated above* or *added in writing*

Israel, namely Solomon. **18:** *Zerubbabel* is an addition; only Sheshbazzar is mentioned in Ezra 5.14 and in Josephus (*Antiq.* XI. iv.4). **23:** *Ecbatana* was the summer residence of Darius. **32:** Ezra 6.11 prescribes that violators of the decree be impaled and their house be made a

be taken out of his house and he should
be hanged upon it, and his property
should be forfeited to the king.
33 "Therefore may the Lord, whose
name is there called upon, destroy
every king and nation that shall stretch
out their hands to hinder or damage
that house of the Lord in Jerusalem.
34 "I, King Darius, have decreed
that it be done with all diligence as
here prescribed."

7 Then Sisinnes the governor of
Coelesyria and Phoenicia, and
Sathrabuzanes, and their associates,
following the orders of King Darius,
2supervised the holy work with very
great care, assisting the elders of the
Jews and the chief officers of the temple. 3And the holy work prospered,
while the prophets Haggai and Zechariah prophesied; 4and they completed
it by the command of the Lord God of
Israel. So with the consent of Cyrus
and Darius and Artaxerxes, kings of
the Persians, 5the holy house was
finished by the twenty-third day of the
month of Adar, in the sixth year of
King Darius. 6And the people of Israel,
the priests, the Levites, and the rest of
those from the captivity who joined
them, did according to what was
written in the book of Moses. 7They
offered at the dedication of the temple
of the Lord one hundred bulls, two
hundred rams, four hundred lambs,
8and twelve he-goats for the sin of all
Israel, according to the number of the
twelve leaders of the tribes of Israel;
9and the priests and the Levites stood
arrayed in their garments, according to
kindred, for the services of the Lord
God of Israel in accordance with the
book of Moses; and the gatekeepers
were at each gate.
10 The people of Israel who came
from the captivity kept the passover
on the fourteenth day of the first
month, after the priests and the Levites
were purified together. 11Not all of
the returned captives were purified,
but the Levites were all purified together,[x] 12and they sacrificed the passover lamb for all the returned captives
and for their brethren the priests and
for themselves. 13And the people of
Israel who came from the captivity ate
it, all those who had separated themselves from the abominations of the
peoples of the land and sought the
Lord. 14And they kept the feast of
unleavened bread seven days, rejoicing
before the Lord, 15because he had
changed the will of the king of the
Assyrians concerning them, to
strengthen their hands for the service
of the Lord God of Israel.

8 After these things, when Artaxerxes the king of the Persians was
reigning, Ezra came, the son of Seraiah,
son of Azariah, son of Hilkiah, son of
Shallum, 2son of Zadok, son of Ahitub,
son of Amariah, son of Uzzi, son of
Bukki, son of Abishua, son of Phineas,
son of Eleazar, son of Aaron the chief
priest. 3This Ezra came up from Babylon as a scribe skilled in the law of
Moses, which was given by the God of
Israel; 4and the king showed him
honor, for he found favor before the
king[y] in all his requests. 5There came
up with him to Jerusalem some of the
people of Israel and some of the priests

x The Greek text of this verse is uncertain *y* Gk *him*

---

dunghill (2 Kg.10.27; Dan.2.5). **7.4:** *Artaxerxes* (see 8.1–9.36 n.) is erroneously named here (as also in Ezra 6.14); the name is omitted by Josephus because of the anachronism. **5:** The date intended is February-March, 516 B.C. **7–8:** Compare the account of the dedication of the first temple (1 Kg.8.5,63). **9:** Compare Ezra 6.18. **13:** Contrary to Ezra 6.21 the account here seems to suggest that only the returned exiles participated in the passover. **15:** The expression *king of the Assyrians* may be used because the Persian empire comprised the former empire of Assyria. Josephus refers to the Persian king (*Antiq.* XI. iv.8).

8.1–9.55: The history of Ezra (Ezra 7.1–10.44 and Neh.7.73–8.12). Ezra, whose name appears as author or central personality in 1 Esdras, is first introduced at this point in the document.

8.1–9.36: Ezra leads a group of exiles from Babylonia. The author ignores the work of Nehemiah (Neh. chs. 1–7), as Sirach ignores the work of Ezra (Sir.49.13). It is probable that

and Levites and temple singers and
gatekeepers and temple servants, 6 in
the seventh year of the reign of Artaxerxes, in the fifth month (this was
the king's seventh year); for they left
Babylon on the new moon of the first
month and arrived in Jerusalem on the
new moon of the fifth month, by the
prosperous journey which the Lord
gave them.[z] 7 For Ezra possessed great
knowledge, so that he omitted nothing
from the law of the Lord or the commandments, but taught all Israel all the
ordinances and judgments.
8 The following is a copy of the
written commission from Artaxerxes
the king which was delivered to Ezra
the priest and reader of the law of the
Lord:
9 "King Artaxerxes to Ezra the
priest and reader of the law of the
Lord, greeting. 10 In accordance with
my gracious decision, I have given orders that those of the Jewish nation
and of the priests and Levites and
others in our realm, who freely choose
to do so, may go with you to Jerusalem. 11 Let as many as are so disposed, therefore, depart with you as
I and the seven friends who are my
counselors have decided, 12 in order to
look into matters in Judea and Jerusalem, in accordance with what is in
the law of the Lord, 13 and to carry to
Jerusalem the gifts for the Lord of
Israel which I and my friends have
vowed, and to collect for the Lord in
Jerusalem all the gold and silver that
may be found in the country of Babylonia, 14 together with what is given by
the nation for the temple of their Lord
which is in Jerusalem, both gold and
silver for bulls and rams and lambs and
what goes with them, 15 so as to offer
sacrifices upon the altar of their Lord
which is in Jerusalem. 16 And whatever
you and your brethren are minded to
do with the gold and silver, perform it
in accordance with the will of your
God; 17 and deliver the holy vessels of
the Lord which are given you for the
use of the temple of your God which
is in Jerusalem. 18 And whatever else
occurs to you as necessary for the temple of your God, you may provide out
of the royal treasury.
19 "And I, Artaxerxes the king, have
commanded the treasurers of Syria and
Phoenicia that whatever Ezra the priest
and reader of the law of the Most High
God sends for, they shall take care to
give him, 20 up to a hundred talents of
silver, and likewise up to a hundred
cors of wheat, a hundred baths of wine,
and salt in abundance. 21 Let all things
prescribed in the law of God be scrupulously fulfilled for the Most High
God, so that wrath may not come upon
the kingdom of the king and his sons.
22 You are also informed that no tribute
or any other tax is to be laid on any of
the priests or Levites or temple singers
or gatekeepers or temple servants or
persons employed in this temple, and
that no one has authority to impose
any tax upon them.
23 "And you, Ezra, according to the
wisdom of God, appoint judges and
justices to judge all those who know
the law of your God, throughout all
Syria and Phoenicia; and those who
do not know it you shall teach. 24 And
all who transgress the law of your God
or the law of the kingdom shall be
strictly punished, whether by death or

z Other authorities add *for him* or *upon him*

Ezra came to Judea under Artaxerxes II (404–358 B.C.) rather than under Artaxerxes I (464–423 B.C.).

8.1–7: Ezra identified. 1–2: The genealogy is briefer than that in Ezra 7.1–5. **6:** *The seventh year* of Artaxerxes II was 398 or 397 B.C. (If Ezra came in the seventh year of Artaxerxes I, the date would be 458 or 457 B.C.). **7:** Ezra comes specifically as a teacher of *the law of the Lord.*

8.8–24: The letter of Artaxerxes to Ezra (Ezra 7.12–26). **11:** *The seven friends* or counselors of the king are referred to in Est.1.14 and Herodotus, *Hist.* III. 84. **20:** The *talent* was 75.5 U.S. pounds; the *cor* 6.5 bushels; and the *bath* about 6 gallons. **22:** Temple personnel are exempt from all taxes. **23–24:** Ezra is given authority to appoint judges throughout the entire province in order to maintain the Jewish law.

some other punishment, either fine or
imprisonment."

25 Blessed be the Lord alone, who
put this into the heart of the king,
to glorify his house which is in Jerusalem, 26and who honored me in the
sight of the king and his counselors
and all his friends and nobles. 27I
was encouraged by the help of the
Lord my God, and I gathered men
from Israel to go up with me.

28 These are the principal men, according to their fathers' houses and
their groups, who went up with me
from Babylon, in the reign of Artaxerxes the king: 29Of the sons of
Phineas, Gershom. Of the sons of
Ithamar, Gamael. Of the sons of
David, Hattush the son of Shecaniah.
30Of the sons of Parosh, Zechariah,
and with him a hundred and fifty men
enrolled. 31Of the sons of Pahathmoab,
Eliehoenai the son of Zerahiah, and
with him two hundred men. 32Of the
sons of Zattu, Shecaniah the son of
Jahaziel, and with him three hundred
men. Of the sons of Adin, Obed the
son of Jonathan, and with him two
hundred and fifty men. 33Of the sons
of Elam, Jeshaiah the son of Gotholiah,
and with him seventy men. 34Of the
sons of Shephatiah, Zeraiah the son of
Michael, and with him seventy men.
35Of the sons of Joab, Obadiah the son
of Jehiel, and with him two hundred
and twelve men. 36Of the sons of Bani,
Shelomith the son of Josiphiah, and
with him a hundred and sixty men.
37Of the sons of Bebai, Zechariah the
son of Bebai, and with him twenty-
eight men. 38Of the sons of Azgad,
Johanan the son of Hakkatan, and with
him a hundred and ten men. 39Of the
sons of Adonikam, the last ones, their
names being Eliphelet, Jeuel, and
Shemaiah, and with them seventy men.
40Of the sons of Bigvai, Uthai the son
of Istalcurus, and with him seventy
men.

41 I assembled them at the river
called Theras, and we encamped there
three days, and I inspected them.
42When I found there none of the sons
of the priests or of the Levites, 43I sent
word to Eliezar, Iduel, Maasmas,
44Elnathan, Shemaiah, Jarib, Nathan,
Elnathan, Zechariah, and Meshullam,
who were leaders and men of understanding; 45and I told them to go to
Iddo, who was the leading man at the
place of the treasury, 46and ordered
them to tell Iddo and his brethren and
the treasurers at that place to send us
men to serve as priests in the house of
our Lord. 47And by the mighty hand
of our Lord they brought us competent
men of the sons of Mahli the son of
Levi, son of Israel, namely Sherebiah[a]
with his sons and kinsmen, eighteen;
48also Hashabiah and Annunus and
Jeshaiah his brother, of the sons of
Hananiah, and their sons, twenty men;
49and of the temple servants, whom
David and the leaders had given for
the service of the Levites, two hundred
and twenty temple servants; the list of
all their names was reported.

50 There I proclaimed a fast for the
young men before our Lord, to seek
from him a prosperous journey for
ourselves and for our children and the
cattle that were with us. 51For I was
ashamed to ask the king for foot
soldiers and horsemen and an escort
to keep us safe from our adversaries;
52for we had said to the king, "The
power of our Lord will be with those
who seek him, and will support them
in every way." 53And again we prayed
to our Lord about these things, and we
found him very merciful.

54 Then I set apart twelve of the

a Gk *Asebebias*

8.25–60: Ezra leads the exiles to Jerusalem (Ezra 7.27–8.30). **28–40:** The list of those who returned differs in a few particulars from that found in Ezra 8.1–14. **41:** *The river . . . Theras* (Ahava in Ezra 8.21) is probably a tributary of the Euphrates. **42–49:** Because neither priests nor Levites were among the group first assembled by Ezra, special measures had to be taken to secure the required number of both. **50:** Fasting prior to an important undertaking was common

leaders of the priests, Sherebiah and
Hashabiah, and ten of their kinsmen
with them; 55 and I weighed out to
them the silver and the gold and the
holy vessels of the house of our Lord,
which the king himself and his counselors and the nobles and all Israel
had given. 56 I weighed and gave to
them six hundred and fifty talents of
silver, and silver vessels worth a hundred talents, and a hundred talents of
gold, 57 and twenty golden bowls, and
twelve bronze vessels of fine bronze
that glittered like gold. 58 And I said
to them, "You are holy to the Lord,
and the vessels are holy, and the silver
and the gold are vowed to the Lord,
the Lord of our fathers. 59 Be watchful
and on guard until you deliver them to
the leaders of the priests and the
Levites, and to the heads of the fathers'
houses of Israel, in Jerusalem, in the
chambers of the house of our Lord."
60 So the priests and the Levites who
took the silver and the gold and the
vessels which had been in Jerusalem
carried them to the temple of the Lord.

61 We departed from the river
Theras on the twelfth day of the first
month; and we arrived in Jerusalem by
the mighty hand of our Lord which
was upon us; he delivered us from
every enemy on the way, and so we
came to Jerusalem. 62 When we had
been there three days, the silver and
the gold were weighed and delivered
in the house of our Lord to Meremoth
the priest, son of Uriah; 63 and with
him was Eleazar the son of Phinehas,
and with them were Jozabad the son of
Jeshua and Moeth the son of Binnui,[b]
the Levites. 64 The whole was counted
and weighed, and the weight of everything was recorded at that very time.
65 And those who had come back from
captivity offered sacrifices to the Lord,
the God of Israel, twelve bulls for all
Israel, ninety-six rams, 66 seventy-two
lambs, and as a thank offering twelve
he-goats—all as a sacrifice to the Lord.
67 And they delivered the king's orders
to the royal stewards and to the governors of Coelesyria and Phoenicia; and
these officials[c] honored the people and
the temple of the Lord.

68 After these things had been done,
the principal men came to me and said,
69 "The people of Israel and the leaders
and the priests and the Levites have
not put away from themselves the alien
peoples of the land and their pollutions,
the Canaanites, the Hittites, the Perizzites, the Jebusites, the Moabites, the
Egyptians, and the Edomites. 70 For
they and their sons have married the
daughters of these people,[d] and the
holy race has been mixed with the alien
peoples of the land; and from the beginning of this matter the leaders and
the nobles have been sharing in this
iniquity."

71 As soon as I heard these things,
I rent my garments and my holy mantle, and pulled out hair from my head
and beard, and sat down in anxiety and
grief. 72 And all who were ever moved

b Gk *Sabannus*
c Gk *they*
d Gk *their daughters*

(2 Chr.20.3; Est.4.16; Jer.36.9). **58:** *Holy* objects could be entrusted only to those who were *holy* themselves.

8.61–67: Arrival in Jerusalem (Ezra 8.31–36). The treasures are placed in the temple storehouses (*chambers*, v. 59), sacrifices are offered to God, and the king's orders delivered to the provincial officers; the latter have no choice but to obey.

8.68–9.36: Mixed marriages in Judah (Ezra 9.1–10.44). No sooner does Ezra arrive than he is presented with evidence that the community has been corrupted by mixed marriages. The older legislation had warned against marriage with the population of Canaan upon entrance into the land (Dt.7.3) but had not expressly forbidden mixed marriages. Strong warnings had been issued, however, against Israel's adopting the abominable practices of the surrounding nations (Lev.18.24–30). During the exile Israel had been able to survive only on the basis of maintaining a relatively high level of racial integrity. The strict separation carried out by Ezra is therefore understandable; in the exile standards were probably higher on this issue than they were in Judah. (Nehemiah also faced the same problem; Neh.10.28–30; 13.3, 23–30).

at[e] the word of the Lord of Israel
gathered round me, as I mourned over
this iniquity, and I sat grief-stricken
until the evening sacrifice. 73Then I
rose from my fast, with my garments
and my holy mantle rent, and kneeling
down and stretching forth my hands
to the Lord 74I said,
"O Lord, I am ashamed and confounded before thy face. 75For our
sins have risen higher than our heads,
and our mistakes have mounted up
to heaven 76from the times of our
fathers, and we are in great sin to
this day. 77And because of our sins
and the sins of our fathers we with our
brethren and our kings and our priests
were given over to the kings of the
earth, to the sword and captivity and
plundering, in shame until this day.
78And now in some measure mercy
has come to us from thee, O Lord, to
leave to us a root and a name in thy
holy place, 79and to uncover a light for
us in the house of the Lord our God,
and to give us food in the time of our
servitude. 80Even in our bondage we
were not forsaken by our Lord, but he
brought us into favor with the kings
of the Persians, so that they have given
us food 81and glorified the temple of
our Lord, and raised Zion from desolation, to give us a stronghold in Judea
and Jerusalem.
82 "And now, O Lord, what shall we
say, when we have these things? For
we have transgressed thy commandments, which thou didst give by thy
servants the prophets, saying, 83'The
land which you are entering to take
possession of it is a land polluted with
the pollution of the aliens of the land,
and they have filled it with their uncleanness. 84Therefore do not give
your daughters in marriage to their
sons, and do not take their daughters
for your sons; 85and do not seek ever
to have peace with them, in order that
you may be strong and eat the good
things of the land and leave it for an
inheritance to your children for ever.'
86And all that has happened to us has
come about because of our evil deeds
and our great sins. For thou, O Lord,
didst lift the burden of our sins 87and
give us such a root as this; but we
turned back again to transgress thy
law by mixing with the uncleanness of
the peoples of the land. 88Wast thou
not angry enough with us to destroy
us without leaving a root or seed or
name? 89O Lord of Israel, thou art
true; for we are left as a root this day.
90Behold, we are now before thee in our
iniquities; for we can no longer stand
in thy presence because of these
things."
91 While Ezra was praying and making his confession, weeping and lying
upon the ground before the temple,
there gathered about him a very great
throng from Jerusalem, men and
women and youths; for there was great
weeping among the multitude. 92Then
Shecaniah the son of Jehiel, one of the
men of Israel, called out, and said to
Ezra, "We have sinned against the
Lord, and have married foreign women
from the peoples of the land; but even
now there is hope for Israel. 93Let us
take an oath to the Lord about this,
that we will put away all our foreign
wives, with their children, 94as seems
good to you and to all who obey the
law of the Lord. 95Arise[f] and take action, for it is your task, and we are
with you to take strong measures."
96Then Ezra arose and had the leaders
of the priests and Levites of all Israel
take oath that they would do this. And
they took the oath.

9 Then Ezra rose and went from the
court of the temple to the chamber

e Or *zealous for*
f Other authorities read *as seems good to you." And all who obeyed the law of the Lord rose and said to Ezra, "Arise*

8.74–90: Ezra's prayer (Ezra 9.6–15). Ezra speaks for the entire community, acknowledging the sin of all and the justice of their punishment by God. **82–85:** The prophetic books contain no such statement; the author may have in mind Lev.18.19–30.

8.91–9.36: The people repent and dismiss their foreign wives (Ezra 10.1–44). **9.4:** *The ruling*

of Jehohanan the son of Eliashib, 2and
spent the night there; and he did not
eat bread or drink water, for he was
mourning over the great iniquities of
the multitude. 3And a proclamation
was made throughout Judea and Jerusalem to all who had returned from the
captivity that they should assemble at
Jerusalem, 4and that if any did not meet
there within two or three days, in accordance with the decision of the ruling
elders, their cattle should be seized for
sacrifice and the men themselves[g] expelled from the multitude of those who
had returned from the captivity.

5 Then the men of the tribe of Judah
and Benjamin assembled at Jerusalem
within three days; this was the ninth
month, on the twentieth day of the
month. 6And all the multitude sat in
the open square before the temple,
shivering because of the bad weather
that prevailed. 7Then Ezra rose and
said to them, "You have broken the
law and married foreign women, and
so have increased the sin of Israel.
8Now then make confession and give
glory to the Lord the God of our
fathers, 9and do his will; separate yourselves from the peoples of the land and
from your foreign wives." 10Then all
the multitude shouted and said with a
loud voice, "We will do as you have
said. 11But the multitude is great and
it is winter, and we are not able to stand
in the open air. This is not a work we
can do in one day or two, for we have
sinned too much in these things. 12So
let the leaders of the multitude stay,
and let all those in our settlements who
have foreign wives come at the time appointed, 13with the elders and judges
of each place, until we are freed from
the wrath of the Lord over this matter."
14Jonathan the son of Asahel and Jah-
zeiah the son of Tikvah[h] undertook the
matter on these terms, and Meshullam
and Levi and Shabbethai served with
them as judges. 15And those who had
returned from the captivity acted in
accordance with all this.

16 Ezra the priest chose for himself
the leading men of their fathers' houses,
all of them by name; and on the new
moon of the tenth month they began
their sessions to investigate the matter.
17And the cases of the men who had
foreign wives were brought to an end
by the new moon of the first month.

18 Of the priests those who were
brought in and found to have foreign
wives were: 19of the sons of Jeshua
the son of Jozadak and his brethren, Maaseiah, Eliezar, Jarib, and
Jodan. 20They pledged themselves to
put away their wives, and to give rams
in expiation of their error. 21Of the
sons of Immer: Hanani and Zeba-
diah and Maaseiah and Shemaiah
and Jehiel and Azariah. 22Of the sons
of Pashhur: Elioenai, Maaseiah, Ish-
mael, and Nathanael, and Gedaliah,
and Elasah.[i]

23 And of the Levites: Jozabad and
Shimei and Kelaiah, who was Kelita,
and Pethahiah and Judah and Jonah.
24Of the temple singers: Eliashib and
Zaccur.[j] 25Of the gatekeepers: Shallum
and Telem.[k]

26 Of Israel: of the sons of Parosh:
Ramiah, Izziah, Malchijah, Mijamin,
and Eleazar, and Asibias, and Benaiah.
27Of the sons of Elam: Mattaniah and

g Gk *he himself* h Gk *Thocanus*
i Gk *Salthas* or *Saloas*
j Gk *Bacchurus*
k Gk *Tolbanes*

elders issue orders for the entire community to assemble within two or three days; Ezra is the religious, not the political, authority in the land. **7:** *The law*, i.e. Dt.7.3. **8:** To *give glory to the Lord* is to acknowledge themselves to be in the wrong (compare Jos.7.19). **11–13:** Because of the severe winter weather, it is agreed that the separation should take place in the local districts, and the multitude is dismissed. **16–17:** Three months are required to settle the cases, from the first of the *tenth month* (Tebet = December-January) to the first of the *first month* (Nisan = March-April). **18–36:** The list of those who put away foreign wives, including priests, Levites, and the laity. The list was probably preserved in the temple archives. **20:** An offering of a ram as a guilt offering (Ezra 10.19) was made *in expiation* of the sin. **22:** *Gedaliah*, Greek "Ocidelos" (the parallel in Ezra 10.22 reads "Jozabad"; compare Ezra 10.18).

Zechariah, Jehiel[l] and Abdi, and Jere-
moth and Elijah. [28]Of the sons of
Zattu:[m] Elioenai,[n] Eliashib, Othoniah,
Jeremoth, and Zabad and Zerdaiah.
[29]Of the sons of Bebai: Jehohanan and
Hananiah and Zabbai and Emathis.
[30]Of the sons of Bani:[o] Meshullam,[p]
Malluch,[q] Adaiah, Jashub, and Sheal
and Jeremoth. [31]Of the sons of Addi:
Naathus and Moossias, Laccunus and
Naidus, and Bescaspasmys and Sesthel,
and Belnuus and Manasseas. [32]Of the
sons of Annan: Elionas and Asaias and
Melchias and Sabbaias and Simon
Chosamaeus. [33]Of the sons of Hash-
um: Mattenai and Mattattah and
Zabad and Eliphelet and Manasseh and
Shimei. [34]Of the sons of Bani: Jeremai,
Maadai,[r] Amram,[s] Joel, Mamdai and
Bedeiah and Vaniah, Carabasion and
Eliashib and Machnadebai,[t] Eliasis,
Binnui, Elialis, Shimei, Shelemiah,
Nethaniah. Of the sons of Ezora:
Shashai, Azarel, Azael, Shemaiah,[u]
Amariah,[v] Joseph. [35]Of the sons of
Nebo:[w] Mattithiah,[x] Zabad, Iddo,
Joel, Benaiah. [36]All these had married
foreign women, and they put them
away with their children.

37 The priests and the Levites and
the men of Israel settled in Jerusalem
and in the country. On the new moon
of the seventh month, when the sons
of Israel were in their settlements, [38]the
whole multitude gathered with one
accord into the open square before the
east gate of the temple; [39]and they told
Ezra the chief priest and reader to bring
the law of Moses which had been given
by the Lord God of Israel. [40]So Ezra
the chief priest brought the law, for all
the multitude, men and women, and all
the priests to hear the law, on the new
moon of the seventh month. [41]And he
read aloud in the open square before
the gate of the temple from early morning until midday, in the presence of
both men and women; and all the multitude gave attention to the law. [42]Ezra
the priest and reader of the law stood
on the wooden platform which had
been prepared; [43]and beside him stood
Mattathiah, Shema, Anaiah,[y] Azariah,
Uriah, Hezekiah, and Baalsamus on
his right hand, [44]and on his left Pe-
daiah, Mishael, Malchijah, Lothasu-
bus, Nabariah, and Zechariah. [45]Then
Ezra took up the book of the law in
the sight of the multitude, for he had
the place of honor in the presence of
all. [46]And when he opened the law,
they all stood erect. And Ezra blessed
the Lord God Most High, the God of
hosts, the Almighty; [47]and all the multitude answered, "Amen." And they
lifted up their hands, and fell to the
ground and worshiped the Lord.
[48]Jeshua and Anniuth and Sherebiah, Jamin,[z] Akkub, Shabbethai,
Hodiah, Maaseiah[a] and Kelita, Azariah and Jozabad, Hanan, Pelaiah,
the Levites, taught the law of the Lord,[b]
at the same time explaining what was
read.

49 Then Attharates[c] said to Ezra
the chief priest and reader, and to the

l Gk *Jezrielus* *m* Gk *Zamoth*
n Gk *Eliadas* *o* Gk *Mani*
p Gk *Olamus* *q* Gk *Mamuchus*
r Gk *Momdius* *s* Gk *Maerus*
t Gk *Mamnitanemus*
u Gk *Samatus* *v* Gk *Zambris*
w Gk *Nooma* *x* Gk *Mazitias*
y Gk *Ananias* *z* Gk *Jadinus*
a Gk *Maiannas*
b Other authorities add *and read the law of the Lord to the multitude*
c Or *the governor*

9.37–55: Ezra's public reading of the law (Neh.7.73–8.12). **37:** *The new moon* or first day *of the seventh month* was a day of holy convocation (Lev.23.23–24; Num.29.1), the day of the New Year. **39:** Ezra is not identified elsewhere as the *chief priest* (in Neh.8.2 he is called the priest). *The law of Moses* is either the present Pentateuch or (more probably) the major legal portions of it. **42:** The *platform* erected for Ezra probably continued the tradition whereby kings would appear before the people to reaffirm the covenant law on the festal occasion at the turn of the year (compare 2 Chr.20.5; 23.13; 29.4). **48:** The Levites explained the law to the people, perhaps translating it (or its difficult portions) into Aramaic for those who may not have been familiar with Hebrew. **49:** *Attharates* is a corruption of *tirshatha*, "governor," in Neh.8.9. 1 Esdras does not intend to indicate that Nehemiah, whom some have identified with Attharates the governor, was a participant in the festivity (in Neh.8.9 the name of Nehemiah is

Levites who were teaching the multitude, and to all, [50]"This day is holy to
the Lord"—now they were all weeping
as they heard the law—[51]"so go your
way, eat the fat and drink the sweet,
and send portions to those who have
none; [52]for the day is holy to the Lord;
and do not be sorrowful, for the Lord
will exalt you." [53]And the Levites
commanded all the people, saying,
"This day is holy; do not be sorrowful." [54]Then they all went their way,
to eat and drink and enjoy themselves,
and to give portions to those who had
none, and to make great rejoicing;
[55]because they were inspired by the
words which they had been taught.
And they came together.[d]

d The Greek text ends abruptly: compare Nehemiah 8.13

an intrusion). **50–55:** The people are to rejoice even though the words of the law cause them to recognize their sin. **55:** The book ends abruptly; originally it may have continued with the story of the great celebration of the feast of booths (Neh.8.13–18). This would have been a fitting conclusion to the work, since it begins with the account of Josiah's great passover celebration.

THE SECOND BOOK OF

ESDRAS

The book commonly known as 2 Esdras differs from the other fourteen books of the Apocrypha in being an apocalypse (for the characteristics of apocalyptic literature, see p. xii above). The main part of 2 Esdras is a series of seven revelations (3.1–5.20; 5.21–6.34; 6.35–9.25; 9.38–10.59; 11.1–12.51; 13.1–58; 14.1–48), in which the seer is instructed by the angel Uriel concerning some of the great mysteries of the moral world.

The problems concerning the composition and transmission of 2 Esdras are extremely complicated. The author of the central portion (chs. 3–14) was an unknown Palestinian Jew who probably wrote in Hebrew or Aramaic near the close of the first century A.D. Subsequently his book was translated into Greek. About the middle of the next century an unknown Christian editor added in Greek an introductory section, which now comprises chs. 1–2. Nearly a century later another unknown Christian appended chs. 15–16, also in Greek.

The Semitic original and almost all of the Greek text have been lost (only 15.57–59 survives on a scrap of Greek papyrus). Before the text of the central section (chs. 3–14) perished, however, translations were made into several other languages, namely Syriac, Coptic, Ethiopic, Arabic (two independent versions), Armenian, and Georgian. In the West the entire book (chs. 1–16) circulated in several Old Latin versions. A later form of the Latin text is printed, since the Council of Trent, as an appendix to the New Testament in the Roman Catholic Vulgate Bible, where it is called the Fourth Book of Esdras.

The purpose of the original author of 2 Esdras was not only to denounce the wickedness of Rome (under the image of "Babylon") and to lament the sorrows that had befallen Jerusalem, but to wrestle with one of the most perplexing of all religious questions, the problem of theodicy, that is the reconciliation of God's justice, wisdom, power, and goodness with the many evils that beset mankind. In spite of the essentially pessimistic outlook of the book, the seer's strong religious faith enabled him to rise above the fires of adversity to high spiritual levels. His agonizing is both honorable and pathetic as he seeks "to justify the ways of God to man."

THE SECOND BOOK OF THE PROPHET
Ezra the son of Seraiah, son of
Azariah, son of Hilkiah, son of Shallum, son of Zadok, son of Ahitub,
2son of Ahijah, son of Phinehas, son of
Eli, son of Amariah, son of Azariah,
son of Meraioth, son of Arna, son of
Uzzi, son of Borith, son of Abishua,
son of Phinehas, son of Eleazar, 3son of
Aaron, of the tribe of Levi, who was a
captive in the country of the Medes in
the reign of Artaxerxes, king of the
Persians.
4 The word of the Lord came to me,
saying, 5"Go and declare to my people
their evil deeds, and to their children
the iniquities which they have committed against me, so that they may
tell their children's children 6that the
sins of their parents have increased in
them, for they have forgotten me and
have offered sacrifices to strange gods.
7Was it not I who brought them out of
the land of Egypt, out of the house of
bondage? But they have angered me
and despised my counsels. 8Pull out
the hair of your head and hurl all evils
upon them, for they have not obeyed
my law—they are a rebellious people.
9How long shall I endure them, on

1.1–2.48: Ezra is commanded to reprove the Jewish people. 1.1–3: The genealogy of Ezra, who is of priestly descent (compare the somewhat different genealogies in Ezra 7.1–5 and 1 Esd.8.1–2). **3:** *Artaxerxes* II, reigned 404–358 B.C.

1.4–11: Ezra receives a prophetic call. 4: The expression, *the word of the Lord came . . .*, so typical of prophetic authorization, is absent from the canonical book of Ezra. **5:** Is.58.1. **8:** The command to *pull out his hair* is to be connected with Ezra's denunciation (*hurl all evils*) of his

whom I have bestowed such great
benefits? 10 For their sake I have overthrown many kings; I struck down
Pharaoh with his servants, and all
his army. 11 I have destroyed all nations before them, and scattered in the
east the people of two provinces, Tyre
and Sidon; I have slain all their enemies.

12 "But speak to them and say,
Thus says the Lord: 13 Surely it was
I who brought you through the sea,
and made safe highways for you where
there was no road; I gave you Moses
as leader and Aaron as priest; 14 I
provided light for you from a pillar
of fire, and did great wonders among
you. Yet you have forgotten me, says
the Lord.

15 "Thus says the Lord Almighty:
The quails were a sign to you; I gave
you camps for your protection, and
in them you complained. 16 You have
not exulted in my name at the destruction of your enemies, but to this day
you still complain. 17 Where are the
benefits which I bestowed on you?
When you were hungry and thirsty in
the wilderness, did you not cry out to
me, 18 saying, 'Why hast thou led us
into this wilderness to kill us? It would
have been better for us to serve the
Egyptians than to die in this wilderness.' 19 I pitied your groanings and
gave you manna for food; you ate the
bread of angels. 20 When you were
thirsty, did I not cleave the rock so that
waters flowed in abundance? Because
of the heat I covered you with the leaves
of trees. 21 I divided fertile lands among
you; I drove out the Canaanites, the
Perizzites, and the Philistines before
you. What more can I do for you? says
the Lord. 22 Thus says the Lord Almighty: When you were in the wilderness, at the bitter stream, thirsty and
blaspheming my name, 23 I did not send
fire upon you for your blasphemies,
but threw a tree into the water and
made the stream sweet.

24 "What shall I do to you, O
Jacob? You would not obey me, O
Judah. I will turn to other nations
and will give them my name, that they
may keep my statutes. 25 Because you
have forsaken me, I also will forsake
you. When you beg mercy of me, I
will show you no mercy. 26 When you
call upon me, I will not listen to you;
for you have defiled your hands with
blood, and your feet are swift to commit murder. 27 It is not as though you
had forsaken me; you have forsaken
yourselves, says the Lord.

28 "Thus says the Lord Almighty:
Have I not entreated you as a father
entreats his sons or a mother her
daughters or a nurse her children,
29 that you should be my people and
I should be your God, and that you
should be my sons and I should be your
father? 30 I gathered you as a hen
gathers her brood under her wings.
But now, what shall I do to you? I
will cast you out from my presence.
31 When you offer oblations to me, I
will turn my face from you; for I have
rejected your feast days, and new
moons, and circumcisions of the flesh.
32 I sent to you my servants the prophets, but you have taken and slain them
and torn their bodies in pieces; their
blood I will require of you, says the
Lord.

33 "Thus says the Lord Almighty:
Your house is desolate; I will drive you
out as the wind drives straw; 34 and
your sons will have no children, be-

---

people. **10:** Ex.14.28. **11:** The author is confused; *Tyre and Sidon*, which were cities, not *provinces*, lay to the west of the land of the Medes (v. 3).

1.12–23: Summary of God's mercies to Israel. 13: Ex.14.29. **14:** Ex.13.21. **15:** Ex.16.13; Ps.105.40. **17–18:** Num.14.3. **19:** *The bread of angels*, Ps. 78.25; Wis.16.20. **20:** Num.20.11; Wis.11.4. **22–23:** Ex.15.22–25.

1.24–32: The casting-off of Israel. 26: Is.1.15; 59.7. **29:** Jer.24.7; Heb.8.10. **30:** The similarity with Mt.23.37 and Lk.13.34 suggests that the author of this part of 2 Esdras was a Jewish Christian. **32:** Compare Mt. 23.34–35.

1.33–40: God will give Israel's houses to another people. 35–36: Gentile Christians are meant

cause with you they have neglected my commandment and have done what is evil in my sight. 35 I will give your houses to a people that will come, who without having heard me will believe. Those to whom I have shown no signs will do what I have commanded. 36 They have seen no prophets, yet will recall their former state.[a] 37 I call to witness the gratitude of the people that is to come, whose children rejoice with gladness; though they do not see me with bodily eyes, yet with the spirit they will believe the things I have said.

38 "And now, father, look with pride and see the people coming from the east; 39 to them I will give as leaders Abraham, Isaac, and Jacob and Hosea and Amos and Micah and Joel and Obadiah and Jonah 40 and Nahum and Habakkuk, Zephaniah, Haggai, Zechariah and Malachi, who is also called the messenger of the Lord.

2 "Thus says the Lord: I brought this people out of bondage, and I gave them commandments through my servants the prophets; but they would not listen to them, and made my counsels void. 2 The mother who bore them says to them, 'Go, my children, because I am a widow and forsaken. 3 I brought you up with gladness; but with mourning and sorrow I have lost you, because you have sinned before the Lord God and have done what is evil in my sight. 4 But now what can I do for you? For I am a widow and forsaken. Go, my children, and ask for mercy from the Lord.' 5 I call upon you, father, as a witness in addition to the mother of the children, because they would not keep my covenant, 6 that you may bring confusion upon them and bring their mother to ruin, so that they may have no offspring. 7 Let them be scattered among the nations, let their names be blotted out from the earth, because they have despised my covenant.

8 "Woe to you, Assyria, who conceal the unrighteous in your midst! O wicked nation, remember what I did to Sodom and Gomorrah, 9 whose land lies in lumps of pitch and heaps of ashes. So will I do to those who have not listened to me, says the Lord Almighty."

10 Thus says the Lord to Ezra: "Tell my people that I will give them the kingdom of Jerusalem, which I was going to give to Israel. 11 Moreover, I will take back to myself their glory, and will give to these others the everlasting habitations, which I had prepared for Israel.[b] 12 The tree of life shall give them fragrant perfume, and they shall neither toil nor become weary. 13 Ask and you will receive; pray that your days may be few, that they may be shortened. The kingdom is already prepared for you; watch! 14 Call, O call heaven and earth to witness, for I left out evil and created good, because I live, says the Lord.

15 "Mother, embrace your sons; bring them up with gladness, as does the dove; establish their feet, because I have chosen you, says the Lord. 16 And I will raise up the dead from their places, and will bring them out from their tombs, because I recognize

a Other authorities read *their iniquities*
b Lat *those*

(compare Rom.10.14–20). **37:** *With bodily eyes*, Jn.20.29. **38:** God is represented as addressing Ezra as *father* of the nation. **39–40:** The three patriarchs and the twelve minor prophets, arranged in the order of the Septuagint.

2.1–9: The Lord's anger against Israel. 2: *The mother who bore them*, Jerusalem (Is.54.1; Gal.4.26–27). *Go . . .*, Bar.4.19. **3:** Bar.4.11. **5:** The writer addresses Ezra as *father*. **6:** *To ruin*, in the fall of Jerusalem, A.D. 70. **8:** By the name *Assyria*, Israel's ancient foe, the author refers cryptically to Rome. *Sodom and Gomorrah*, Gen.19.24.

2.10–14: Israel's habitation to be given to others. 10: *My people*, i.e. the Christians (compare Hos.2.23). **11:** *Everlasting habitations*, Lk.16.9. **12:** Rev.2.7; 22.2,14. **13:** Mt.7.7–8; Lk.11.9–10; Mt.25.34.

2.15–32: Exhortation to good works. 15: *Mother*, probably a reference to the church.

my name in them. 17 Do not fear,
mother of the sons, for I have chosen
you, says the Lord. 18 I will send you
help, my servants Isaiah and Jeremiah.
According to their counsel I have consecrated and prepared for you twelve
trees loaded with various fruits, 19 and
the same number of springs flowing
with milk and honey, and seven mighty
mountains on which roses and lilies
grow; by these I will fill your children
with joy. 20 Guard the rights of the
widow, secure justice for the fatherless,
give to the needy, defend the orphan,
clothe the naked, 21 care for the injured
and the weak, do not ridicule a lame
man, protect the maimed, and let the
blind man have a vision of my splendor.
22 Protect the old and the young within
your walls; 23 when you find any who
are dead, commit them to the grave
and mark it,[c] and I will give you the
first place in my resurrection. 24 Pause
and be quiet, my people, because your
rest will come. 25 Good nurse, nourish
your sons, and strengthen their feet.
26 Not one of the servants whom I have
given you will perish, for I will require
them from among your number. 27 Do
not be anxious, for when the day of
tribulation and anguish comes, others
shall weep and be sorrowful, but you
shall rejoice and have abundance.
28 The nations shall envy you but they
shall not be able to do anything against
you, says the Lord. 29 My hands will
cover you, that your sons may not see
Gehenna. 30 Rejoice, O mother, with
your sons, because I will deliver you,
says the Lord. 31 Remember your sons
that sleep, because I will bring them out
of the hiding places of the earth, and
will show mercy to them; for I am
merciful, says the Lord Almighty.
32 Embrace your children until I come,
and proclaim mercy to them; because
my springs run over, and my grace will
not fail."

33 I, Ezra, received a command from
the Lord on Mount Horeb to go to
Israel. When I came to them they
rejected me and refused the Lord's
commandment. 34 Therefore I say to
you, O nations that hear and understand, "Await your shepherd; he will
give you everlasting rest, because he
who will come at the end of the age is
close at hand. 35 Be ready for the rewards of the kingdom, because the
eternal light will shine upon you for
evermore. 36 Flee from the shadow of
this age, receive the joy of your glory;
I publicly call on my Savior to witness.[d]
37 Receive what the Lord has entrusted
to you and be joyful, giving thanks to
him who has called you to heavenly
kingdoms. 38 Rise and stand, and see
at the feast of the Lord the number of
those who have been sealed. 39 Those
who have departed from the shadow
of this age have received glorious garments from the Lord. 40 Take again
your full number, O Zion, and conclude
the list of your people who are clothed
in white, who have fulfilled the law of
the Lord. 41 The number of your children, whom you desired, is full; beseech
the Lord's power that your people, who
have been called from the beginning,
may be made holy."

42 I, Ezra, saw on Mount Zion a
great multitude, which I could not
number, and they all were praising
the Lord with songs. 43 In their midst
was a young man of great stature, taller
than any of the others, and on the head
of each of them he placed a crown, but
he was more exalted than they. And I

c Or *seal it;* or *mark them and commit them to the grave*
d Other authorities read *I testify that my Savior has been commissioned by the Lord*

18: *Twelve trees,* Rev.22.2. **19:** *Milk and honey,* Dt.31.20. **23:** *Find any . . . dead,* compare Tob.1.17–19. **26:** Jn.17.12. **29:** *Gehenna,* place of torment.

2.33–41: Rejected by Israel, Ezra turns to the Gentiles. **33:** *On Mount Horeb,* like a second Moses (Ex.3.1; 2 Chr.5.10). **35:** *The eternal light,* Is.60.20; Rev.21.23; 22.5. **40:** *Zion,* Heb. 12.22–23. *Clothed in white,* Rev.3.4; 6.11; 7.14. **41:** *The number . . . is full,* see 4.36–37 n.; Rev. 6.11. *Called,* Rom.8.29–30.

2.42–48: Ezra's vision of a great multitude. **42:** Rev.7.9. **43:** *A young man,* compare v. 47 and Enoch 46.1.

was held spellbound. [44]Then I asked
an angel, "Who are these, my lord?"
[45]He answered and said to me, "These
are they who have put off mortal clothing and have put on the immortal, and
they have confessed the name of God;
now they are being crowned, and receive palms." [46]Then I said to the
angel, "Who is that young man who
places crowns on them and puts palms
in their hands?" [47]He answered and
said to me, "He is the Son of God,
whom they confessed in the world."
So I began to praise those who had
stood valiantly for the name of the
Lord. [48]Then the angel said to me,
"Go, tell my people how great and
many are the wonders of the Lord God
which you have seen."

3 In the thirtieth year after the destruction of our city, I Salathiel,
who am also called Ezra, was in Babylon. I was troubled as I lay on my bed,
and my thoughts welled up in my heart,
[2]because I saw the desolation of Zion
and the wealth of those who lived in
Babylon. [3]My spirit was greatly agitated, and I began to speak anxious
words to the Most High, and said, [4]"O
sovereign Lord, didst thou not speak
at the beginning when thou didst form
the earth—and that without help—and
didst command the dust[e] [5]and it gave[f]
thee Adam, a lifeless body? Yet he
was the workmanship of thy hands,
and thou didst breathe into him the
breath of life, and he was made alive
in thy presence. [6]And thou didst
lead him into the garden which thy
right hand had planted before the earth
appeared. [7]And thou didst lay upon
him one commandment of thine; but
he transgressed it, and immediately
thou didst appoint death for him and
for his descendants. From him there
sprang nations and tribes, peoples and
clans, without number. [8]And every
nation walked after its own will and
did ungodly things before thee and
scorned thee, and thou didst not hinder
them. [9]But again, in its time thou didst
bring the flood upon the inhabitants of
the world and destroy them. [10]And the
same fate befell them: as death came
upon Adam, so the flood upon them.
[11]But thou didst leave one of them,
Noah with his household, and all the
righteous who have descended from
him.

12 "When those who dwelt on earth
began to multiply, they produced children and peoples and many nations,
and again they began to be more ungodly than were their ancestors. [13]And
when they were committing iniquity
before thee, thou didst choose for thyself one of them, whose name was
Abraham; [14]and thou didst love him,
and to him only didst thou reveal the
end of the times, secretly by night.
[15]Thou didst make with him an everlasting covenant, and promise him that
thou wouldst never forsake his descendants; and thou gavest to him
Isaac, and to Isaac thou gavest Jacob
and Esau. [16]And thou didst set apart
Jacob for thyself, but Esau thou didst
reject; and Jacob became a great multitude. [17]And when thou didst lead his
descendants out of Egypt, thou didst
bring them to Mount Sinai. [18]Thou

e Syr Ethiop
f Syr

3.1–5.20: The first vision. 3.1–3: Introduction. 1: *The thirtieth year after the destruction* of Jerusalem by Nebuchadnezzar in 587/6 B.C. (2 Kg.25.1ff.) would be 557/6 B.C. The date specified may imply that the author was writing about A.D.100 (i.e. thirty years after the fall of Jerusalem in A.D.70). *Salathiel* is the Greek form of Shealtiel (Ezra 3.2; 5.2; Neh.12.1). The words *who am also called Ezra* are an anachronistic gloss; Ezra lived a century later.

3.4–36: The author raises perplexing questions. Whence comes sin with its consequent misery? How can Israel's continuing affliction be reconciled with God's justice? **4–5:** The creation of Adam. **6–8:** Adam's sin brings death on all mankind. **7:** The words *immediately thou didst appoint death* imply that Adam was not originally intended to be mortal (compare Wis.1.13–14; 2.23–24). **8:** Gen.6.12. **9–11:** The flood (Gen.6.11ff.). **12–16:** The choice of Abraham (Gen. 12.1; 17.5). **14:** *By night*, Gen.15.5,12,17. **17–19:** The Exodus and the giving of the law. **18:**

didst bend down the heavens and
shake[g] the earth, and move the world,
and make the depths to tremble, and
trouble the times. [19]And thy glory
passed through the four gates of fire
and earthquake and wind and ice, to
give the law to the descendants of
Jacob, and thy commandment to the
posterity of Israel.

20 "Yet thou didst not take away
from them their evil heart, so that thy
law might bring forth fruit in them.
[21]For the first Adam, burdened with
an evil heart, transgressed and was
overcome, as were also all who were
descended from him. [22]Thus the dis-
ease became permanent; the law was
in the people's heart along with the evil
root, but what was good departed, and
the evil remained. [23]So the times passed
and the years were completed, and thou
didst raise up for thyself a servant,
named David. [24]And thou didst command him to build a city for thy name,
and in it to offer thee oblations from
what is thine. [25]This was done for
many years; but the inhabitants of the
city transgressed, [26]in everything doing
as Adam and all his descendants had
done, for they also had the evil heart.
[27]So thou didst deliver the city into the
hands of thy enemies.

28 "Then I said in my heart, Are the
deeds of those who inhabit Babylon
any better? Is that why she has gained
dominion over Zion? [29]For when I
came here I saw ungodly deeds without
number, and my soul has seen many
sinners during these thirty years.[h] And
my heart failed me, [30]for I have seen
how thou dost endure those who sin,
and hast spared those who act wickedly,
and hast destroyed thy people, and hast
preserved thy enemies, [31]and hast not
shown to any one how thy way may be
comprehended.[i] Are the deeds of
Babylon better than those of Zion?
[32]Or has another nation known thee
besides Israel? Or what tribes have so
believed thy covenants as these tribes
of Jacob? [33]Yet their reward has not
appeared and their labor has borne no
fruit. For I have traveled widely among
the nations and have seen that they
abound in wealth, though they are
unmindful of thy commandments.
[34]Now therefore weigh in a balance our
iniquities and those of the inhabitants
of the world; and so it will be found
which way the turn of the scale will
incline. [35]When have the inhabitants
of the earth not sinned in thy sight? Or
what nation has kept thy commandments so well? [36]Thou mayest indeed
find individual men who have kept thy
commandments, but nations thou wilt
not find."

4 Then the angel that had been sent
to me, whose name was Uriel,
answered [2]and said to me, "Your understanding has utterly failed regarding
this world, and do you think you can
comprehend the way of the Most
High?" [3]Then I said, "Yes, my lord."
And he replied to me, "I have been sent
to show you three ways, and to put
before you three problems. [4]If you can
solve one of them for me, I also will
show you the way you desire to see,
and will teach you why the heart is
evil."

5 I said, "Speak on, my lord."

And he said to me, "Go, weigh for
me the weight of fire, or measure for

g Syr Ethiop Arab 1 Georg: Lat *didst set fast*
h Ethiop Arab 1 Arm: Lat Syr *in this thirtieth year*
i Syr: Lat *how this way should be forsaken*

Compare Ex.19.16–18; Ps. 68.7–8. **20–27:** The tendency to sin is universal and permanent. **20:** *Evil heart,* the evil *yeṣer* (see Sir.15.14 n.). **28–36:** The deeds of Babylon compared with those of Israel. **28:** *Babylon,* i.e. Rome (Rev.14.8). **29:** *Came here,* to Rome. The first *thirty years* of the Babylonian exile are meant. **30:** Here the author expresses the essence of the problem. **34:** For God's balance, compare Job 31.6; Ps. 62.9; Pr.16.2; Dan.5.27; Enoch 41.1; 61.8. **36:** *Individual men* among the Gentiles.

4.1–5.19: The reply: God's ways are beyond human comprehension.

4.1–12: The limitations of the human mind (Wis.9.16). **1:** The name *Uriel* in Hebrew means "the fire of God." According to Enoch 20.2 Uriel is a watcher over the world and over Tartarus, the lowest part of hell (compare 2 Pet.2.4 marg.).

me a measure[j] of wind, or call back
for me the day that is past."

6 I answered and said, "Who of
those that have been born can do this,
that you ask me concerning these
things?"

7 And he said to me, "If I had asked
you, 'How many dwellings are in the
heart of the sea, or how many streams
are at the source of the deep, or how
many streams are above the firmament,
or which are the exits of hell, or which
are the entrances[k] of paradise?' 8per-
haps you would have said to me, 'I
never went down into the deep, nor as
yet into hell, neither did I ever ascend
into heaven.' 9But now I have asked
you only about fire and wind and the
day, things through which you have
passed and without which you cannot
exist,[l] and you have given me no answer
about them!" 10And he said to me,
"You cannot understand the things
with which you have grown up; 11how
then can your mind comprehend the
way of the Most High? And how can
one who is already worn out[m] by the
corrupt world understand incorruption?"[n] When I heard this, I fell on my
face[o] 12and said to him, "It would be
better for us not to be here than to come
here and live in ungodliness, and to
suffer and not understand why."

13 He answered me and said, "I
went into a forest of trees of the plain,
and they made a plan 14and said,
'Come, let us go and make war against
the sea, that it may recede before us,
and that we may make for ourselves
more forests.' 15And in like manner
the waves of the sea also made a plan
and said, 'Come, let us go up and subdue the forest of the plain so that there
also we may gain more territory for
ourselves.' 16But the plan of the forest
was in vain, for the fire came and consumed it; 17likewise also the plan of
the waves of the sea, for the sand stood
firm and stopped them. 18If now you
were a judge between them, which
would you undertake to justify, and
which to condemn?"

19 I answered and said, "Each has
made a foolish plan, for the land is
assigned to the forest, and to the sea
is assigned a place to carry its waves."

20 He answered me and said, "You
have judged rightly, but why have you
not judged so in your own case? 21For
as the land is assigned to the forest and
the sea to its waves, so also those who
dwell upon earth can understand only
what is on the earth, and he who is
above the heavens can understand what
is above the height of the heavens."

22 Then I answered and said, "I
beseech you, my lord, why[p] have I been
endowed with the power of understanding? 23For I did not wish to
inquire about the ways above, but
about those things which we daily
experience: why Israel has been given
over to the Gentiles as a reproach; why
the people whom you loved has been
given over to godless tribes, and the
law of our fathers has been made of
no effect and the written covenants no
longer exist; 24and why we pass from
the world like locusts, and our life is
like a mist,[q] and we are not worthy to
obtain mercy. 25But what will he do for
his name, by which we are called? It is
about these things that I have asked."

26 He answered me and said, "If
you are alive, you will see, and if you
live long,[r] you will often marvel, because the age is hastening swiftly to
its end. 27For it will not be able to
bring the things that have been promised to the righteous in their appointed
times, because this age is full of sadness

j Syr Ethiop Arab Georg: Lat *a blast*
k Syr Compare Ethiop Arab 2 Arm: Latin omits *of hell, or which are the entrances*
l Other Latin manuscripts read *from which you cannot be separated*
m The text here is uncertain
n Syr Ethiop *the way of the incorruptible?*
o Syr Ethiop Arab 1: Latin is corrupt
p Syr Ethiop Arm: Latin is corrupt
q Syr Ethiop Arab Georg: Lat *a trembling*
r Syr: Lat *live*

4.13–21: Parable of the conflict between the forest and the sea. 21: Is.55.8–9; Jn.3.31; 1 Cor. 2.14.

4.22–32: Additional questions. 26–32: The angel answers that the new age, soon to dawn,

and infirmities. 28For the evil about
which[s] you ask me has been sown, but
the harvest of it has not yet come. 29If
therefore that which has been sown is
not reaped, and if the place where the
evil has been sown does not pass away,
the field where the good has been sown
will not come. 30For a grain of evil
seed was sown in Adam's heart from
the beginning, and how much ungodliness it has produced until now, and will
produce until the time of threshing
comes! 31Consider now for yourself
how much fruit of ungodliness a grain
of evil seed has produced. 32When
heads of grain without number are
sown, how great a threshing floor they
will fill!"

33 Then I answered and said, "How
long[t] and when will these things be?
Why are our years few and evil?" 34He
answered me and said, "You do not
hasten faster than the Most High, for
your haste is for yourself,[u] but the
Highest hastens on behalf of many.
35Did not the souls of the righteous in
their chambers ask about these matters,
saying, 'How long are we to remain
here?[v] And when will come the harvest
of our reward?' 36And Jeremiel the
archangel answered them and said,
'When the number of those like yourselves is completed;[w] for he has weighed
the age in the balance, 37and measured
the times by measure, and numbered
the times by number; and he will not
move or arouse them until that measure
is fulfilled.'"

38 Then I answered and said, "O
sovereign Lord, but all of us also are
full of ungodliness. 39And it is perhaps on account of us that the time of
threshing is delayed for the righteous—
on account of the sins of those who
dwell on earth."

40 He answered me and said, "Go
and ask a woman who is with child if,
when her nine months have been completed, her womb can keep the child
within her any longer."

41 And I said, "No, lord, it cannot."

And he said to me, "In Hades the
chambers of the souls are like the
womb. 42For just as a woman who
is in travail makes haste to escape the
pangs of birth, so also do these places
hasten to give back those things that
were committed to them from the
beginning. 43Then the things that you
desire to see will be disclosed to you."

44 I answered and said, "If I have
found favor in your sight, and if it is
possible, and if I am worthy, 45show
me this also: whether more time is to
come than has passed, or whether for
us the greater part has gone by. 46For
I know what has gone by, but I do not
know what is to come."

47 And he said to me, "Stand at my
right side, and I will show you the
interpretation of a parable."

48 So I stood and looked, and behold, a flaming furnace passed by
before me, and when the flame had
gone by I looked, and behold, the
smoke remained. 49And after this a
cloud full of water passed before me
and poured down a heavy and violent
rain, and when the rainstorm had

s Syr Ethiop: Latin is uncertain
t Syr Ethiop: Latin is uncertain
u Syr Ethiop Arab Arm: the Latin is corrupt
v Syr Ethiop Arab 2 Georg: Lat *How long do I hope thus?*
w Syr Ethiop Arab 2: Lat *number of seeds is completed for you*

---

will solve all problems; but first the evil which is sown must be reaped. **30:** *A grain of evil seed,* the evil *yeṣer* (see Sir.15.14 n.).

4.33–43: The seer asks when the new age will come; he is told that first the predetermined number of the righteous must be completed. **35:** *The righteous,* i.e. the righteous dead. *Chambers,* literally "storehouses" or "garners"; according to rabbinical teaching the souls of the righteous dead are beneath the throne of God (compare Rev.6.9f.). **36:** *Jeremiel,* probably the same as Remiel, the seventh of seven archangels mentioned in Enoch 20.1–8. *Completed,* 2.41; Rev.6.11. **36–37:** *Weighed . . . measured . . . numbered,* God has determined the times and periods of history (see Sir.36.8 n.). **41:** *Chambers,* see v. 35 n.

4.44–50: The seer asks what proportion of time remains; he is told by a parable that the end is near.

passed, drops remained in the cloud.
50 And he said to me, "Consider it
for yourself; for as the rain is more
than the drops, and the fire is greater
than the smoke, so the quantity that
passed was far greater; but drops and
smoke remained."
51 Then I prayed and said, "Do you
think that I shall live until those days?
Or who will be alive in those days?"
52 He answered me and said, "Concerning the signs about which you ask
me, I can tell you in part; but I was not
sent to tell you concerning your life,
for I do not know.

5 "Now concerning the signs: behold, the days are coming when
those who dwell on earth shall be
seized with great terror,[x] and the way
of truth shall be hidden, and the land
shall be barren of faith. 2And unrighteousness shall be increased beyond
what you yourself see, and beyond
what you heard of formerly. 3And the
land which you now see ruling shall be
waste and untrodden,[y] and men shall
see it desolate. 4But if the Most High
grants that you live, you shall see it
thrown into confusion after the third
period;[z]

and the sun shall suddenly shine
forth at night,
and the moon during the day.
5Blood shall drip from wood,
and the stone shall utter its voice;
the peoples shall be troubled,
and the stars shall fall.[a]

6And one shall reign whom those who
dwell on earth do not expect, and the
birds shall fly away together; 7and the
sea of Sodom shall cast up fish; and
one whom the many do not know shall
make his voice heard by night, and all
shall hear his voice.[b] 8There shall be
chaos also in many places, and fire
shall often break out, and the wild
beasts shall roam beyond their haunts,
and menstruous women shall bring
forth monsters. 9And salt waters shall
be found in the sweet, and all friends
shall conquer one another; then shall
reason hide itself, and wisdom shall
withdraw into its chamber, 10and it shall
be sought by many but shall not be
found, and unrighteousness and un-
restraint shall increase on earth. 11And
one country shall ask its neighbor, 'Has
righteousness, or any one who does
right, passed through you?' And it
will answer, 'No.' 12And at that time
men shall hope but not obtain; they
shall labor but their ways shall not
prosper. 13These are the signs which I
am permitted to tell you, and if you
pray again, and weep as you do now,
and fast for seven days, you shall hear
yet greater things than these."
14 Then I awoke, and my body shud-
dered violently, and my soul was so
troubled that it fainted. 15But the angel
who had come and talked with me
held me and strengthened me and set
me on my feet.
16 Now on the second night Phaltiel, a chief of the people, came to me
and said, "Where have you been? And

x Syr: Ethiop *confusion:* Latin is uncertain
y Syr: Latin is corrupt
z Literally *after the third;* Ethiop *after three months;* Arm *after the third vision;* Georg *after the third day*
a Ethiop Compare Syr and Arab: Latin is uncertain
b Cn: Lat *fish; and it shall make its voice heard by night, which the many have not known, but all shall hear its voice.*

4.51–5.13: The seer asks whether the end will come during his own lifetime; he is given a description of the signs which will precede the end (compare Mt.24.4–31; Mk.13.5–27; Lk.21.8–28). **5.2:** Mt.24.12. **3:** *The land which you now see ruling*, i.e. the Roman Empire. **4:** The reference to *the third period* is cryptic (compare 14.11–13). **5:** *The stone shall utter its voice*, Hab.2.11; Lk.19.40. **6:** *The birds*, foreseeing impending disasters, *shall fly away*. **7:** *The sea of Sodom*, i.e. the Dead Sea. **8a:** Syriac, "a fissure shall arise over wide regions" (compare Zech.14.4). *Shall often break out*, or "shall burst forth for a long period." **10–11:** Is.59.14–15. **13:** For the author, fasting prepared one to receive a divine revelation; he refers to three fasts each of seven days (5.20; 6.35; 12.51).

5.14–19: Conclusion of the vision. 14: *Then I awoke*, from the dream-vision. *My soul . . . fainted,* Pss. 84.2; 107.5; Jon.2.7; compare Is.6.5; Dan.10.17b. **16:** *Phaltiel*, the historical reference is uncertain; compare Paltiel in Num.34.26; 2 Sam.3.15.

why is your face sad? 17Or do you not
know that Israel has been entrusted to
you in the land of their exile? 18Rise
therefore and eat some bread, so that
you may not forsake us, like a shepherd
who leaves his flock in the power of
cruel wolves."
19 Then I said to him, "Depart from
me and do not come near me for
seven days, and then you may come
to me."
He heard what I said and left me.
20So I fasted seven days, mourning and
weeping, as Uriel the angel had commanded me.

21 And after seven days the thoughts
of my heart were very grievous to me
again. 22Then my soul recovered the
spirit of understanding, and I began
once more to speak words in the presence of the Most High. 23And I said,
"O sovereign Lord, from every forest
of the earth and from all its trees thou
hast chosen one vine, 24and from all
the lands of the world thou hast chosen
for thyself one region,[c] and from all
the flowers of the world thou hast
chosen for thyself one lily, 25and from
all the depths of the sea thou hast filled
for thyself one river, and from all the
cities that have been built thou hast
consecrated Zion for thyself, 26and
from all the birds that have been
created thou hast named for thyself one
dove, and from all the flocks that have
been made thou hast provided for thyself one sheep, 27and from all the multitude of peoples thou hast gotten for
thyself one people; and to this people,
whom thou hast loved, thou hast given
the law which is approved by all. 28And
now, O Lord, why hast thou given over
the one to the many, and dishonored[d]
the one root beyond the others, and
scattered thine only one among the
many? 29And those who opposed thy
promises have trodden down those who
believed thy covenants. 30If thou dost
really hate thy people, they should be
punished at thy own hands."
31 When I had spoken these words,
the angel who had come to me on a
previous night was sent to me, 32and
he said to me, "Listen to me, and I will
instruct you; pay attention to me, and
I will tell you more."
33 And I said, "Speak, my lord."
And he said to me, "Are you greatly
disturbed in mind over Israel?[e] Or do
you love him more than his Maker
does?"
34 And I said, "No, my lord, but
because of my grief I have spoken; for
every hour I suffer agonies of heart,
while I strive to understand the way of
the Most High and to search out part
of his judgment."
35 And he said to me, "You cannot." And I said, "Why not, my lord?
Why then was I born? Or why did
not my mother's womb become my
grave, that I might not see the travail
of Jacob and the exhaustion of the
people of Israel?"
36 He said to me, "Count up for me
those who have not yet come, and
gather for me the scattered raindrops,
and make the withered flowers bloom
again for me; 37open for me the closed
chambers, and bring forth for me the
winds shut up in them, or show me the
picture of a voice; and then I will
explain to you the travail that you ask
to understand."[f]
38 And I said, "O sovereign Lord,
who is able to know these things except he whose dwelling is not with
men? 39As for me, I am without wis-

c Ethiop: Lat *pit*
d Syr Ethiop Arab: Lat *prepared*
e Or *You are greatly distracted in mind over Israel.*
f Lat *see*

5.21–6.34: The second vision. 5.21–30: The seer reiterates his complaints of divine inequity in dealing with Israel. 23–28: Most of the figures representing Israel have been drawn from the Old Testament: the *vine* (v. 23), Ps. 80.8–15; the *lily* (v. 24), S. of S.2.2 (interpreted allegorically); Hos.14.5; the *river* (v. 25), Is.8.6; the city of *Zion* (v. 25), Ps. 132.13; the *dove* (v. 26), Ps.74.19; the *sheep* (v. 26), Ps. 79.13; Is.53.7; the *root* (v. 28), Enoch 93.8, compare Rom.11.17–18. **33:** It is unthinkable that man should love Israel more than God their *Maker does* (8.47). **35:** Job 3.11; 10.18–19. **36–40:** If the seer cannot understand the things of earth, how can he

dom, and how can I speak concerning
the things which thou hast asked me?"
40 He said to me, "Just as you cannot do one of the things that were
mentioned, so you cannot discover my
judgment, or the goal of the love that
I have promised my people."
41 And I said, "Yet behold, O Lord,
thou dost have charge of those who
are alive at the end, but what will those
do who were before us, or we, or those
who come after us?"
42 He said to me, "I shall liken my
judgment to a circle;[g] just as for those
who are last there is no slowness, so for
those who are first there is no haste."
43 Then I answered and said,
"Couldst thou not have created at one
time those who have been and those
who are and those who will be, that
thou mightest show thy judgment the
sooner?"
44 He replied to me and said, "The
creation cannot make more haste than
the Creator, neither can the world hold
at one time those who have been
created in it."
45 And I said, "How hast thou said
to thy servant that thou[h] wilt certainly
give life at one time to thy creation?
If therefore all creatures will live at one
time[i] and the creation will sustain them,
it might even now be able to support all
of them present at one time."
46 He said to me, "Ask a woman's
womb, and say to it, 'If you bear ten[j]
children, why one after another?' Request it therefore to produce ten at one
time."
47 I said, "Of course it cannot, but
only each in its own time."
48 He said to me, "Even so have I
given the womb of the earth to those
who from time to time are sown in
it. 49 For as an infant does not bring
forth, and a woman who has become
old does not bring forth any longer, so
have I organized the world which I
created."
50 Then I inquired and said, "Since
thou hast now given me the opportunity, let me speak before thee. Is our
mother, of whom thou hast told me,
still young? Or is she now approaching
old age?"
51 He replied to me, "Ask a woman
who bears children, and she will tell
you. 52 Say to her, 'Why are those
whom you have borne recently not like
those whom you bore before, but
smaller in stature?' 53 And she herself
will answer you, 'Those born in the
strength of youth are different from
those born during the time of old age,
when the womb is failing.' 54 Therefore
you also should consider that you and
your contemporaries are smaller in
stature than those who were before you,
55 and those who come after you will be
smaller than you, as born of a creation
which already is aging and passing the
strength of youth."
56 And I said, "O Lord, I beseech
thee, if I have found favor in thy sight,
show thy servant through whom thou
dost visit thy creation."
6 And he said to me, "At the beginning of the circle of the earth,[k]

g Or *crown*
h Syr Ethiop Arab 1: Latin text is uncertain
i Latin omits *If . . . one time*
j Syr Ethiop Arab 2 Arm: Latin text is corrupt
k The text is uncertain: compare Syr *The beginning by the hand of man, but the end by my own hands. For as before the land of the world existed there, and before:* Ethiop: *At first by the Son of Man, and afterwards I myself. For before the earth and the lands were created, and before*

expect to fathom the judgments and purpose of God? **40:** *My . . . I,* the angel speaks in God's name.

5.41–55: The place of successive generations in the divine plan for the world. The seer inquires about the status of those who have died before the messianic age shall begin (v. 41); he is told, in effect, that the last shall be as the first, and the first as the last (v. 42). He inquires why all generations of men could not have lived at the same time, namely at the beginning of the messianic age (v. 43); the reply is that generations must follow one another (vv. 44–49). *Mother* earth has become old and the last generations are inferior to the early ones (vv. 50–55). **52:** *Smaller in stature,* compare Gen.6.4 (the Nephilim, "giants"); Num.13.33.

5.56–6.6: The end of the age. As God alone created the world (without an intermediate agency), so he will bring about its end by himself alone (7.39–44).

before the portals of the world were in
place, and before the assembled winds
blew, 2and before the rumblings of
thunder sounded, and before the flashes
of lightning shone, and before the
foundations of paradise were laid, 3and
before the beautiful flowers were seen,
and before the powers of movement[l]
were established, and before the innumerable hosts of angels were gathered
together, 4and before the heights of
the air were lifted up, and before the
measures of the firmaments were
named, and before the footstool of
Zion was established, 5and before the
present years were reckoned, and before the imaginations of those who
now sin were estranged, and before
those who stored up treasures of faith
were sealed—6then I planned these
things, and they were made through
me and not through another, just as
the end shall come through me and
not through another."

7 And I answered and said, "What
will be the dividing of the times? Or
when will be the end of the first age
and the beginning of the age that
follows?"

8 He said to me, "From Abraham
to Isaac,[m] because from him were born
Jacob and Esau, for Jacob's hand held
Esau's heel from the beginning. 9For
Esau is the end of this age, and Jacob
is the beginning of the age that follows.
10For the beginning of a man is his
hand, and the end of a man is his heel;[n]
between the heel and the hand seek for
nothing else, Ezra!"

11 I answered and said, "O sovereign
Lord, if I have found favor in thy sight,
12show thy servant the end of thy signs
which thou didst show me in part on a
previous night."

13 He answered and said to me,
"Rise to your feet and you will hear a
full, resounding voice. 14And if the
place where you are standing is greatly
shaken 15while the voice is speaking, do not be terrified; because the
word concerns the end, and the foundations of the earth will understand
16that the speech concerns them.
They will tremble and be shaken,
for they know that their end must be
changed."

17 When I heard this, I rose to my
feet and listened, and behold, a voice
was speaking, and its sound was like
the sound of many waters. 18And it
said, "Behold, the days are coming,
and it shall be that when I draw near
to visit the inhabitants of the earth,
19and when I require from the doers
of iniquity the penalty of their iniquity,
and when the humiliation of Zion is
complete, 20and when the seal is placed
upon the age which is about to pass
away, then I will show these signs: the
books shall be opened before the firmament, and all shall see it together.
21Infants a year old shall speak with
their voices, and women with child
shall give birth to premature children
at three or four months, and these shall
live and dance. 22Sown places shall
suddenly appear unsown, and full
storehouses shall suddenly be found to
be empty; 23and the trumpet shall
sound aloud, and when all hear it, they
shall suddenly be terrified. 24At that
time friends shall make war on friends
like enemies, and the earth and those
who inhabit it shall be terrified, and
the springs of the fountains shall stand
still, so that for three hours they shall
not flow.

25 "And it shall be that whoever

l Or *earthquake*
m Other authorities read *Abraham*
n Syr: Latin is defective here

6.7–10: The dividing of the times. In allegorical language the seer is told that the present corrupt age (symbolized by *Esau*) will be followed immediately, without a break, by the glorious age to come (symbolized by *Jacob*).

6.11–28: The signs of the end of the age. 12: *Thou didst show me in part,* 4.51–5.13. **17:** *I rose to my feet,* presumably the author had previously been lying down, experiencing a dream-vision. *Many waters,* Rev.1.15; 14.2; 19.6. **20:** *The books shall be opened,* i.e. the celestial books in which are written the deeds of men (Dan.7.10; 12.1; Mal.3.16; Rev.20.12; compare Ex.32.32; Ps. 69.28; Lk.10.20; Heb.12.23). **23:** *The trumpet,* 1 Cor.15.52; 1 Thess.4.16. **26:** *The men who*

remains after all that I have foretold
to you shall himself be saved and shall
see my salvation and the end of my
world. 26And they shall see the men
who were taken up, who from their
birth have not tasted death; and the
heart of the earth's[o] inhabitants shall be
changed and converted to a different
spirit. 27For evil shall be blotted out,
and deceit shall be quenched; 28faith-
fulness shall flourish, and corruption
shall be overcome, and the truth, which
has been so long without fruit, shall be
revealed."

29 While he spoke to me, behold,
little by little the place where I was
standing began to rock to and fro.[p]
30And he said to me, "I have come to
show you these things this night.[q] 31If
therefore you will pray again and fast
again for seven days, I will again declare to you greater things than these,[r]
32because your voice has surely been
heard before the Most High; for the
Mighty One has seen your uprightness
and has also observed the purity which
you have maintained from your youth.
33Therefore he sent me to show you all
these things, and to say to you: 'Believe
and do not be afraid! 34Do not be
quick to think vain thoughts concerning the former times, lest you be hasty
concerning the last times.' "

35 Now after this I wept again and
fasted seven days as before, in order to
complete the three weeks as I had been
told. 36And on the eighth night my
heart was troubled within me again,
and I began to speak in the presence of
the Most High. 37For my spirit was
greatly aroused, and my soul was in
distress.

38 I said, "O Lord, thou didst speak
at the beginning of creation, and didst
say on the first day, 'Let heaven and
earth be made,' and thy word accomplished the work. 39And then the Spirit
was hovering, and darkness and silence
embraced everything; the sound of
man's voice was not yet there.[s] 40Then
thou didst command that a ray of light
be brought forth from thy treasuries,
so that thy works might then appear.

41 "Again, on the second day, thou
didst create the spirit of the firmament,
and didst command him to divide and
separate the waters, that one part
might move upward and the other part
remain beneath.

42 "On the third day thou didst
command the waters to be gathered
together in the seventh part of the
earth; six parts thou didst dry up and
keep so that some of them might be
planted and cultivated and be of service before thee. 43For thy word went
forth, and at once the work was done.
44For immediately fruit came forth in
endless abundance and of varied appeal to the taste; and flowers of inimi-
table color; and odors of inexpressible
fragrance. These were made on the
third day.

45 "On the fourth day thou didst
command the brightness of the sun,
the light of the moon, and the ar-
rangement of the stars to come into
being; 46and thou didst command them
to serve man, who was about to be
formed.

47 "On the fifth day thou didst
command the seventh part, where the

o Syr Compare Ethiop Arab 1 Arm: Latin omits *earth's*
p Syr Ethiop Compare Arab Arm: Latin is corrupt
q Syr Compare Ethiop: Latin is corrupt
r Syr Ethiop Arab 1 Arm: Latin adds *by day*
s Syr Ethiop: Lat *was not yet from thee*

---

were taken up, such as Enoch (Gen.5.24; Sir.44.16) and Elijah (2 Kg.2.11–12); compare also 14.9. *Shall be . . . converted*, by the preaching of Elijah (Mal.4.6).

6.29–34: Conclusion of the vision. 34: The seer is cautioned against being oversolicitous.

6.35–9.25: The third vision. 6.35–37: Introduction. 35: *I . . . fasted seven days*, see 5.13 n. *The three weeks* (compare Dan.10.2–3), so far only two fasts of seven days have been mentioned (here and at 5.20); presumably the author is thinking also of another fast prior to the first vision (3.1–5.20), not mentioned in the present form of the book.

6.38–59: The seer recounts God's work in creation. If the world was created for Israel (v. 55), why has the nation not possessed its inheritance? **38–54:** Gen. ch. 1. **38:** *Thy word accomplished the work*, Ps. 33.6; Heb.11.3; 2 Pet.3.5. **40:** God's *treasuries* are in heaven. **41:** *The spirit of the*

water had been gathered together, to
bring forth living creatures, birds, and
fishes; and so it was done. [48]The dumb
and lifeless water produced living creatures, as it was commanded,[t] that
therefore the nations might declare
thy wondrous works.

49 "Then thou didst keep in existence two living creatures;[u] the name
of one thou didst call Behemoth and
the name of the other Leviathan. [50]And
thou didst separate one from the other,
for the seventh part where the water
had been gathered together could not
hold them both. [51]And thou didst give
Behemoth one of the parts which had
been dried up on the third day, to live
in it, where there are a thousand mountains; [52]but to Leviathan thou didst
give the seventh part, the watery part;
and thou hast kept them to be eaten
by whom thou wilt, and when thou
wilt.

53 "On the sixth day thou didst
command the earth to bring forth before thee cattle, beasts, and creeping
things; [54]and over these thou didst
place Adam, as ruler over all the works
which thou hadst made; and from him
we have all come, the people whom
thou hast chosen.

55 "All this I have spoken before
thee, O Lord, because thou hast said
that it was for us that thou didst create
this world.[v] [56]As for the other nations
which have descended from Adam,
thou hast said that they are nothing,
and that they are like spittle, and thou
hast compared their abundance to a
drop from a bucket. [57]And now, O
Lord, behold, these nations, which are
reputed as nothing, domineer over us
and devour us. [58]But we thy people,
whom thou hast called thy first-born,
only begotten, zealous for thee,[w] and
most dear, have been given into their
hands. [59]If the world has indeed been
created for us, why do we not possess
our world as an inheritance? How
long will this be so?"

7 When I had finished speaking these
words, the angel who had been
sent to me on the former nights was sent
to me again, [2]and he said to me, "Rise,
Ezra, and listen to the words that I have
come to speak to you."

3 I said, "Speak, my lord." And he
said to me, "There is a sea set in a wide
expanse so that it is broad[x] and vast,
[4]but it has an entrance set in a narrow
place, so that it is like a river. [5]If any
one, then, wishes to reach the sea, to
look at it or to navigate it, how can he
come to the broad part unless he passes
through the narrow part? [6]Another
example: There is a city built and set
on a plain, and it is full of all good
things; [7]but the entrance to it is narrow
and set in a precipitous place, so that
there is fire on the right hand and deep
water on the left; [8]and there is only
one path lying between them, that
is, between the fire and the water,
so that only one man can walk upon
that path. [9]If now that city is given to
a man for an inheritance, how will the
heir receive his inheritance unless he
passes through the danger set before
him?"

10 I said, "He cannot, lord." And
he said to me, "So also is Israel's portion. [11]For I made the world for their
sake, and when Adam transgressed my
statutes, what had been made was

t The text of this verse is uncertain
u Syr Ethiop: Lat *two souls*
v Syr Ethiop Arab 2: Lat *the first-born world* Compare Arab 1 *first world*
w The meaning of the Latin text is obscure
x Syr Compare Ethiop Arab 1: Lat *deep*

---

firmament is an angel (compare the angel with power over fire, Rev.14.18, and the angel of water, Rev.16.5). **46:** Ps. 8.6–8. **49–52:** *Behemoth* and *Leviathan* are two primeval monsters (compare Job 7.12; 26.12–13; Ps.74.12–15; 89.10–11; Is.30.7; 51.9–10). **55:** The idea that the world was created for the sake of Israel (7.11) is not found in the Old Testament, but was deduced by Jewish rabbis from such passages as Ex.4.22; Dt.10.15; 14.2. **56:** *A drop from a bucket*, Is.40.15.

7.1–25: The angel instructs the seer. The wickedness of this world makes the path to the next world narrow and dangerous. **1:** *The former nights*, at the beginning of each vision. **11:** Though *the world* was created for Israel's *sake*, that inheritance was spoiled *when Adam transgressed* (compare Rom.8.18–20). **12** and **13:** *The entrances*, Ethiopic, "the ways," i.e. the paths of life

judged. 12And so the entrances of this
world were made narrow and sorrowful
and toilsome; they are few and evil,
full of dangers and involved in great
hardships. 13But the entrances of the
greater world are broad and safe, and
really yield the fruit of immortality.
14Therefore unless the living pass
through the difficult and vain experiences, they can never receive those
things that have been reserved for them.
15But now why are you disturbed, seeing that you are to perish? And why
are you moved, seeing that you are
mortal? 16And why have you not considered in your mind what is to come,
rather than what is now present?"

17 Then I answered and said, "O
sovereign Lord, behold, thou hast ordained in thy law that the righteous
shall inherit these things, but that the
ungodly shall perish. 18The righteous
therefore can endure difficult circumstances while hoping for easier ones;
but those who have done wickedly have
suffered the difficult circumstances and
will not see the easier ones."

19 And he said to me, "You are not
a better judge than God, or wiser than
the Most High! 20Let many perish who
are now living, rather than that the law
of God which is set before them be disregarded! 21For God strictly commanded those who came into the world,
when they came, what they should do
to live, and what they should observe
to avoid punishment. 22Nevertheless
they were not obedient, and spoke
against him;

they devised for themselves vain
thoughts,
23and proposed to themselves
wicked frauds;
they even declared that the Most
High does not exist,
and they ignored his ways!
24They scorned his law,
and denied his covenants;
they have been unfaithful to his
statutes,
and have not performed his works.

25 "Therefore, Ezra, empty things
are for the empty, and full things are
for the full. 26For behold, the time
will come, when the signs which I have
foretold to you will come to pass, that
the city which now is not seen shall
appear,[y] and the land which now is
hidden shall be disclosed. 27And every
one who has been delivered from the
evils that I have foretold shall see my
wonders. 28For my son the Messiah[z]
shall be revealed with those who are
with him, and those who remain shall
rejoice four hundred years. 29And after
these years my son the Messiah shall
die, and all who draw human breath.
30And the world shall be turned back
to primeval silence for seven days, as
it was at the first beginnings; so that
no one shall be left. 31And after seven
days the world, which is not yet awake,
shall be roused, and that which is corruptible shall perish. 32And the earth
shall give up those who are asleep in it,
and the dust those who dwell silently
in it; and the chambers shall give up
the souls which have been committed
to them. 33And the Most High shall be

y Arm: Lat Syr *that the bride shall appear, even the city appearing*
z Syr Arab 1: Ethiop *my Messiah;* Arab 2 *the Messiah;* Arm *the Messiah of God;* Lat *my son Jesus*

---

here on earth, and in the world of immortality. **13:** *The greater world,* Syriac, "the future world." **14:** *Things . . . reserved for them,* 1 Cor.2.9. **15–16:** The seer should not brood over difficulties and death; though inevitable, they are but preliminary to something better (2 Cor. 4.18). **17–18:** The seer inquires whether the future bliss is only for the righteous Jews, or for all the Jews. **19–25:** The angel replies that those who disregard the Mosaic law will be punished. **25:** Mt.13.12.

7.26–44: The messianic kingdom and the end of the world. 26: *The signs . . . foretold,* 6.20–24. *The city,* the heavenly Jerusalem. *The land,* the heavenly paradise. **28:** *Those who remain,* after the tribulations that will precede the inauguration of the messianic kingdom. *Four hundred years,* so the Latin and Arabic 1; Syriac, "thirty years"; Arabic 2, "one thousand years"; Ethiopic and Armenian omit. **31:** *The world . . . not yet awake,* i.e. the world to come. **32:** Dan.12.2. *Chambers,* see 4.35 n. **33:** *Judgment,* Syriac adds, "and then comes the end." *Away,*

revealed upon the seat of judgment,
and compassion shall pass away, and
patience shall be withdrawn;[a] 34 but
only judgment shall remain, truth shall
stand, and faithfulness shall grow
strong. 35 And recompense shall follow,
and the reward shall be manifested;
righteous deeds shall awake, and unrighteous deeds shall not sleep.[b]
[36]Then the pit[c] of torment shall appear, and opposite it shall be the place
of rest; and the furnace of hell[d] shall be
disclosed, and opposite it the paradise
of delight. [37]Then the Most High will
say to the nations that have been raised
from the dead, 'Look now, and understand whom you have denied, whom
you have not served, whose commandments you have despised! [38]Look on
this side and on that; here are delight
and rest, and there are fire and torments!' Thus he will[e] speak to them on
the day of judgment—[39]a day that has
no sun or moon or stars,[40]or cloud or
thunder or lightning or wind or water
or air, or darkness or evening or morning, [41]or summer or spring or heat or
winter[f] or frost or cold or hail or rain or
dew, [42]or noon or night, or dawn or
shining or brightness or light, but only
the splendor of the glory of the Most
High, by which all shall see what has
been determined for them. [43]For it
will last for about a week of years.
[44]This is my judgment and its prescribed order; and to you alone have I
shown these things."

[45] I answered and said, "O sovereign Lord, I said then and I say
now:[g] Blessed are those who are alive
and keep thy commandments! [46]But
what of those for whom I prayed? For
who among the living is there that has
not sinned, or who among men that
has not transgressed thy covenant?
[47]And now I see that the world to
come will bring delight to few, but
torments to many. [48]For an evil heart
has grown up in us, which has alienated
us from God,[h] and has brought us into
corruption and the ways of death, and
has shown us the paths of perdition
and removed us far from life—and that
not just a few of us but almost all who
have been created!"

[49] He answered me and said,
"Listen to me, Ezra,[i] and I will instruct you, and will admonish you yet
again. [50]For this reason the Most
High has made not one world but two.
[51]For whereas you have said that the
righteous are not many but few, while
the ungodly abound, hear the explanation for this.

[52] "If you have just a few precious
stones, will you add to them lead and
clay?"[j]

[53] I said, "Lord, how could that
be?"

[54] And he said to me, "Not only

a Lat *gather together*
b The passage from verse [36] to verse [105], formerly missing, has been restored to the text
c Syr Ethiop: Lat *place*
d Lat *gehenna*
e Syr Ethiop Arab 1: Lat *thou shalt*
f Or *storm*
g Syr: Lat *And I answered, "I said then, O Lord, and I say now:*
h Cn: Lat Syr Ethiop *from these*
i Syr Arab 1 Georg: Lat Ethiop omit *Ezra*
j Arab 1: Lat Syr Ethiop are corrupt

Syriac adds, "and pity shall be far off." The final judgment will be conducted in strict accord with justice and truth. **34:** *Grow strong*, i.e. triumph. **35:** *Righteous deeds shall awake*, acts of charity hitherto concealed shall be disclosed (compare Mt.25.35–46). **[36–105]:** These verses are lacking from the standard editions of the Latin Vulgate and from the King James version. They are present in the Syriac, Ethiopic, Arabic, and Armenian versions, and in two Latin manuscripts. The section was probably deliberately cut out of an ancestor of most extant Latin manuscripts because of dogmatic reasons, for the passage contains an emphatic denial of the value of prayers for the dead (v. [105]). **[36]:** *Pit*, Rev.9.2. *Opposite*, Lk.16.23–24. **[37]:** Mt. 25.31ff. **[39–43]:** Description of the day of judgment. **[42]:** *Only* the uncreated light *of the Most High* will serve to illuminate the judgment scene (compare Is.60.19–20; Rev.21.23). **[43]:** *A week of years*, seven years.

7.[45–61]: The small number of the saved (contrast Lk.13.23–30). **[48]:** *An evil heart*, see 3.20 n. **[49]:** 5.32. **[52]:** The question implies that the number of the elect cannot be increased by adding base elements.

that, but ask the earth and she will
tell you; defer to her, and she will declare it to you. [55]Say to her, 'You
produce gold and silver and brass, and
also iron and lead and clay; [56]but
silver is more abundant than gold, and
brass than silver, and iron than brass,
and lead than iron, and clay than lead.'
[57]Judge therefore which things are
precious and desirable, those that are
abundant or those that are rare?"

[58] I said, "O sovereign Lord, what
is plentiful is of less worth, for what is
more rare is more precious."

[59] He answered me and said,
"Weigh within yourself[k] what you have
thought, for he who has what is hard
to get rejoices more than he who has
what is plentiful. [60]So also will be
the judgment[l] which I have promised;
for I will rejoice over the few who shall
be saved, because it is they who have
made my glory to prevail now, and
through them my name has now been
honored. [61]And I will not grieve over
the multitude of those who perish; for
it is they who are now like a mist, and
are similar to a flame and smoke—they
are set on fire and burn hotly, and are
extinguished."

[62] I replied and said, "O earth,
what have you brought forth, if the
mind is made out of the dust like the
other created things! [63]For it would
have been better if the dust itself had
not been born, so that the mind might
not have been made from it. [64]But
now the mind grows with us, and therefore we are tormented, because we
perish and know it. [65]Let the human
race lament, but let the beasts of the
field be glad; let all who have been
born lament, but let the four-footed
beasts and the flocks rejoice! [66]For
it is much better with them than with
us; for they do not look for a judgment,
nor do they know of any torment or
salvation promised to them after death.
[67]For what does it profit us that we
shall be preserved alive but cruelly
tormented? [68]For all who have been
born are involved in iniquities, and are
full of sins and burdened with transgressions. [69]And if we were not to
come into judgment after death, perhaps it would have been better for us."

[70] He answered me and said,
"When the Most High made the world
and Adam and all who have come from
him, he first prepared the judgment
and the things that pertain to the judgment. [71]And now understand from
your own words, for you have said
that the mind grows with us. [72]For
this reason, therefore, those who dwell
on earth shall be tormented, because
though they had understanding they
committed iniquity, and though they
received the commandments they did
not keep them, and though they obtained the law they dealt unfaithfully
with what they received. [73]What,
then, will they have to say in the judgment, or how will they answer in the
last times? [74]For how long the time
is that the Most High has been patient
with those who inhabit the world, and
not for their sake, but because of the
times which he has foreordained!"

[75] I answered and said, "If I have
found favor in thy sight, O Lord, show
this also to thy servant: whether after
death, as soon as every one of us yields
up his soul, we shall be kept in rest
until those times come when thou wilt
renew the creation, or whether we shall
be tormented at once?"

[76] He answered me and said, "I
will show you that also, but do not be
associated with those who have shown
scorn, nor number yourself among
those who are tormented. [77]For you

k Syr Ethiop Arab 1: Latin is corrupt here
l Syr Arab 1: Lat *creation*

7.[62–74]: The seer's lament over the human race. [63]: 4.12. **[64]:** The possession of reasoning powers intensifies sufferings. **[67]:** The author identifies himself with sinners (contrast 6.32–34). **[70]:** *Things that pertain to the judgment*, according to rabbinical teaching, before the beginning of the world God created Paradise and Gehenna.

7.[75–101]: The state of the departed after death and before the judgment. [77]: *A treasure of*

have a treasure of works laid up with the Most High; but it will not be shown to you until the last times. [78]Now, concerning death, the teaching is: When the decisive decree has gone forth from the Most High that a man shall die, as the spirit leaves the body to return again to him who gave it, first of all it adores the glory of the Most High. [79]And if it is one of those who have shown scorn and have not kept the way of the Most High, and who have despised his law, and who have hated those who fear God—[80]such spirits shall not enter into habitations, but shall immediately wander about in torments, ever grieving and sad, in seven ways. [81]The first way, because they have scorned the law of the Most High. [82]The second way, because they cannot now make a good repentance that they may live. [83]The third way, they shall see the reward laid up for those who have trusted the covenants of the Most High. [84]The fourth way, they shall consider the torment laid up for themselves in the last days. [85]The fifth way, they shall see how the habitations of the others are guarded by angels in profound quiet. [86]The sixth way, they shall see how some of them will pass over[m] into torments. [87]The seventh way, which is worse[n] than all the ways that have been mentioned, because they shall utterly waste away in confusion and be consumed with shame,[o] and shall wither with fear at seeing the glory of the Most High before whom they sinned while they were alive, and before whom they are to be judged in the last times.

[88] "Now this is the order of those who have kept the ways of the Most High, when they shall be separated from their mortal body.[p] [89]During the time that they lived in it,[q] they laboriously served the Most High, and withstood danger every hour, that they might keep the law of the Lawgiver perfectly. [90]Therefore this is the teaching concerning them: [91]First of all, they shall see with great joy the glory of him who receives them, for they shall have rest in seven orders. [92]The first order, because they have striven with great effort to overcome the evil thought which was formed with them, that it might not lead them astray from life into death. [93]The second order, because they see the perplexity in which the souls of the ungodly wander, and the punishment that awaits them. [94]The third order, they see the witness which he who formed them bears concerning them, that while they were alive they kept the law which was given them in trust. [95]The fourth order, they understand the rest which they now enjoy, being gathered into their chambers and guarded by angels in profound quiet, and the glory which awaits them in the last days. [96]The fifth order, they rejoice that they have now escaped what is corruptible, and shall inherit what is to come; and besides they see the straits and toil[r] from which they have been delivered, and the spacious liberty which they are to receive and enjoy in immortality. [97]The sixth order, when it is shown to them how their face is to shine like the sun, and how they are to be made like the light of the stars, being incorruptible from then on. [98]The seventh order, which is greater than all that have been mentioned, because they shall rejoice with

m Cn: the text of this verse is corrupt
n Lat *greater*
o Syr Ethiop: Latin is corrupt
p Literally *the corruptible vessel*
q Syr Ethiop: Latin is corrupt
r Syr Ethiop: Lat *fulness*

---

works, 8.33,36. *Will not be shown*, see v. 35 n. **[78]**: Ec.12.7. The first act of the departed spirit (whether righteous or wicked) is to adore God. **[80–87]**: Seven kinds of torment for the wicked. **[80]**: *Habitations*, Lk.16.9; elsewhere called "chambers," see 4.35 n. **[83]**: Compare Lk.16.23. **[85]**: *The others*, i.e. the righteous. **[88–99]**: Seven kinds of joyous rest for the righteous. The author implies that the *mortal body* has been merely a prison-house for the spirit (contrast 1 Cor.15.53; 2 Cor.5.2–4). **[92]**: *The evil thought*, the evil *yeṣer* (see Sir.15.14 n.). **[95]**: *Chambers*, see 4.35 n. *In the last days*, better, "at their latter end." **[97]**: *Shine*, v. [125]; Dan.12.3;

boldness, and shall be confident without confusion, and shall be glad without fear, for they hasten to behold the face of him whom they served in life and from whom they are to receive their reward when glorified. [99]This is the order of the souls of the righteous, as henceforth is announced;[s] and the aforesaid are the ways of torment which those who would not give heed shall suffer hereafter."

[100] I answered and said, "Will time therefore be given to the souls, after they have been separated from the bodies, to see what you have described to me?"

[101] He said to me, "They shall have freedom for seven days, so that during these seven days they may see the things of which you have been told, and afterwards they shall be gathered in their habitations."

[102] I answered and said, "If I have found favor in thy sight, show further to me, thy servant, whether on the day of judgment the righteous will be able to intercede for the ungodly or to entreat the Most High for them, [103]fathers for sons or sons for parents, brothers for brothers, relatives for their kinsmen, or friends[t] for those who are most dear."

[104] He answered me and said, "Since you have found favor in my sight, I will show you this also. The day of judgment is decisive[u] and displays to all the seal of truth. Just as now a father does not send his son, or a son his father, or a master his servant, or a friend his dearest friend, to be ill[v] or sleep or eat or be healed in his stead, [105]so no one shall ever pray for another on that day, neither shall any one lay a burden on another;[w] for then every one shall bear his own righteousness or unrighteousness."

36 [106] I answered and said, "How then do we find that first Abraham prayed for the people of Sodom, and Moses for our fathers who sinned in the desert, 37 [107]and Joshua after him for Israel in the days of Achan, 38 [108]and Samuel in the days of Saul,[x] and David for the plague, and Solomon for those in the sanctuary, 39 [109]and Elijah for those who received the rain, and for the one who was dead, that he might live, 40 [110]and Hezekiah for the people in the days of Sennacherib, and many others prayed for many? 41 [111]If therefore the righteous have prayed for the ungodly now, when corruption has increased and unrighteousness has multiplied, why will it not be so then as well?"

42 [112] He answered me and said, "This present world is not the end; the full glory does not[y] abide in it;[z] Therefore those who were strong prayed for the weak. 43 [113]But the day of judgment will be the end of this age and the beginning[a] of the immortal age to come, in which corruption has passed away, 44 [114]sinful indulgence has come to an end, unbelief has been cut off, and righteousness has increased and truth has appeared. 45 [115]Therefore no one will then be able to have mercy on him who has been condemned in the judgment, or to harm[b] him who is victorious."

46 [116] I answered and said, "This is my first and last word, that it would

s Syr: Latin is corrupt here
t Syr Ethiop Arab 1: Lat *kinsmen for their nearest, friends* (literally *the confident*) *for their dearest*
u Lat *bold*
v Syr Ethiop Arm: Lat *understand*
w Syr: Latin omits *on that . . . another*
x Syr Ethiop Arab 1: Latin omits *in the days of Saul*
y Latin omits *not*
z Or *the glory does not continuously abide in it*
a Latin omits *the beginning*
b Syr Ethiop: Lat *overwhelm*

Mt.13.43. **[98]:** *To behold the face* of God (Mt.5.8; Heb.12.14; 1 Jn.3.2; Rev.22.4). *Reward,* 1 Cor.3.14; Rev.22.12. **[101]:** *Habitations,* see v. [80] n.

7.[102–115]: No intercession for the wicked on the day of judgment (compare Dt.24.16; Jer. 31.30). **[106]:** Gen.18.23; Ex.32.11. **[107]:** Jos.7.6–7. **[108]:** *Samuel,* 1 Sam.7.9; 12.23. *David,* 2 Sam.24.17. *Solomon,* 1 Kg.8.22–23,30. **[109]:** 1 Kg.18.42,45; 17.20–21. **[110]:** 2 Kg.19.15–19. **[112–115]:** During the present order intercession *for the weak* is possible, but the day of judgment means the closing of all accounts on the basis of strict justice (see v. 33 n.).

7.[116–131]: The seer laments the fate of the mass of humanity. [116]: *My first . . . word,* 3.5ff.

have been better if the earth had not
produced Adam, or else, when it had
produced him, had restrained him
from sinning. 47[117]For what good is
it to all that they live in sorrow now
and expect punishment after death?
48[118]O Adam, what have you done?
For though it was you who sinned, the
fall was not yours alone, but ours also
who are your descendants. 49[119]For
what good is it to us, if an eternal age
has been promised to us, but we have
done deeds that bring death? 50[120]And
what good is it that an everlasting hope
has been promised us, but we have
miserably failed? 51[121]Or that safe
and healthful habitations have been
reserved for us, but we have lived
wickedly? 52[122]Or that the glory of
the Most High will defend those who
have led a pure life, but we have walked
in the most wicked ways? 53[123]Or
that a paradise shall be revealed, whose
fruit remains unspoiled and in which
are abundance and healing, but we
shall not enter it, 54[124]because we have
lived in unseemly places? 55[125]Or that
the faces of those who practiced self-
control shall shine more than the stars,
but our faces shall be blacker than
darkness? 56[126]For while we lived
and committed iniquity we did not consider what we should suffer after
death."

57 [127] He answered and said, "This
is the meaning of the contest which
every man who is born on earth shall
wage, 58[128]that if he is defeated he
shall suffer what you have said, but if
he is victorious he shall receive what I
have said.[c] 59[129]For this is the way of
which Moses, while he was alive, spoke
to the people, saying, 'Choose for yourself life, that you may live!' 60[130]But
they did not believe him, or the prophets after him, or even myself who have
spoken to them. 61[131]Therefore there
shall not be[d] grief at their destruction,
so much as joy over those to whom
salvation is assured."

62 [132] I answered and said, "I
know, O Lord, that the Most High is
now called merciful, because he has
mercy on those who have not yet come
into the world; 63[133]and gracious, because he is gracious to those who turn
in repentance to his law; 64[134]and
patient, because he shows patience toward those who have sinned, since they
are his own works; 65[135]and bountiful,
because he would rather give than take
away;[e] 66[136]and abundant in compassion, because he makes his com-
passions abound more and more to
those now living and to those who are
gone and to those yet to come, 67[137]for
if he did not make them abound, the
world with those who inhabit it would
not have life; 68[138]and he is called
giver, because if he did not give out of
his goodness so that those who have
committed iniquities might be relieved
of them, not one ten-thousandth of
mankind could have life; 69[139]and
judge, because if he did not pardon
those who were created by his word and
blot out the multitude of their sins,[f]
70[140]there would probably be left only
very few of the innumerable multitude."

8 He answered me and said, "The
Most High made this world for the
sake of many, but the world to come
for the sake of few. 2But I will tell you
a parable, Ezra. Just as, when you ask
the earth, it will tell you that it provides
very much clay from which earthen-

c Syr Ethiop Arab 1: Lat *I say*
d Syr: Lat *was not*
e Or *is ready to give according to requests*
f Lat *contempts*

---

[118]: 4.30–31. **[123]:** *Fruit*, compare Ezek.47.12; Rev.22.2. **[125]:** *Shine more than the stars*, Dan.12.3; compare Mt.13.43. *Darkness*, Mt.8.12; 22.13; Jude 13. **[127–129]:** Man is responsible for his choices (Dt.30.19).

7.[132]–8.3: The seer acknowledges (and implicitly appeals to) God's mercy. Will a merciful God permit so many to perish? He is told that nothing can alter their doom, for *many have been created, but few shall be saved* (8.3). **[132–139]:** For the sevenfold attributes of God, compare Ex.34.6–7. **[132]:** *O Lord*, better, "sir." **[135]:** Acts 20.35. **[138]:** *Life*, i.e. eternal life. **8.2:** *A parable*, an analogous illustration (as in 7.[54–57]). **3:** Mt.22.14.

ware is made, but only a little dust
from which gold comes; so is the
course of the present world. 3Many
have been created, but few shall be
saved."

4 I answered and said, "Then drink
your fill of understanding, O my soul,
and drink wisdom, O my heart![g] 5For
not of your own will did you come into
the world,[h] and against your will you
depart, for you have been given only a
short time to live. 6O Lord who art
over us, grant to thy servant that we
may pray before thee, and give us seed
for our heart and cultivation of our
understanding so that fruit may be produced, by which every mortal who
bears the likeness[i] of a human being
may be able to live. 7For thou alone
dost exist, and we are a work of thy
hands, as thou hast declared. 8And
because thou dost give life to the body
which is now fashioned in the womb,
and dost furnish it with members, what
thou hast created is preserved in fire
and water, and for nine months the
womb[j] which thou hast formed endures
thy creation which has been created in
it. 9But that which keeps and that
which is kept shall both be kept by thy
keeping.[k] And when the womb gives
up again what has been created in it,
10thou hast commanded that from the
members themselves (that is, from the
breasts) milk should be supplied which
is the fruit of the breasts, 11so that
what has been fashioned may be nour-
ished for a time; and afterwards thou
wilt guide him in thy mercy. 12Thou
hast brought him up in thy righteousness, and instructed him in thy law,
and reproved him in thy wisdom.
13Thou wilt take away his life, for he
is thy creation; and thou wilt make him
live, for he is thy work. 14If then thou
wilt suddenly and quickly[l] destroy him
who with so great labor was fashioned
by thy command, to what purpose was
he made? 15And now I will speak out:
About all mankind thou knowest best;
but I will speak about thy people, for
whom I am grieved, 16and about thy
inheritance, for whom I lament, and
about Israel, for whom I am sad, and
about the seed of Jacob, for whom I am
troubled. 17Therefore I will pray before thee for myself and for them, for
I see the failings of us who dwell in the
land, 18and[m] I have heard of the swift-
ness of the judgment that is to come.
19Therefore hear my voice, and understand my words, and I will speak before
thee."

The beginning of the words of Ezra's
prayer, before he was taken up. He
said: 20"O Lord who inhabitest eternity,[n] whose eyes are exalted[o] and
whose upper chambers are in the
air, 21whose throne is beyond measure
and whose glory is beyond comprehension, before whom the hosts of
angels stand trembling 22and at whose
command they are changed to wind
and fire,[p] whose word is sure and
whose utterances are certain, whose
ordinance is strong and whose com-

g Syr: Lat *let it feed on what it understands*
h Syr: Latin is corrupt here i Syr: Lat *place*
j Literally *what thou hast formed*
k Syr: Latin is corrupt here
l Syr: Lat *shalt with a light command*
m Literally *but* n Or *abidest for ever*
o Another Latin text reads *whose are the highest heavens*
p Syr: Lat *they whose service takes the form of wind and fire*

8.4–36: The seer implores God to show mercy upon his creation. 4–19a: Why should God wonderfully fashion and sustain all mankind, only to destroy the great majority? **4–5:** The pre-existence of the soul is implied here (Wis.8.19). **7:** Is.44.6; 45.11; 60.21. **14:** *Was fashioned by thy command*, Ps. 139.14–15. **15–16:** The seer leaves the fate of *mankind* in God's hands, and speaks particularly about Israel, God's *inheritance* (Ps.28.9). **19b–36:** A beautiful and liturgically structured prayer (invocation to God, whose attributes are recalled, vv. 20–23; petitions, interspersed with confession and intercessions, vv. 24–35; concluding ascription of praise, v. 36). This prayer also occurs separately, with the title "Confessio Esdrae," in the section of canticles and hymns contained in many manuscripts of the Latin Vulgate Bible. This circumstance accounts for the presence (in v. 19b) of a superscription in the third person. **19b:** The words, *before he was taken up*, indicate that the belief was current that Ezra, like Enoch and Elijah, was translated to heaven without dying. **22:** *Wind and fire*, Ps.104.4; Heb.1.7.

mand is terrible, 23whose look dries up
the depths and whose indignation
makes the mountains melt away, and
whose truth is established for ever[q]—
24hear, O Lord, the prayer of thy servant, and give ear to the petition of thy
creature; attend to my words. 25For
as long as I live I will speak, and as long
as I have understanding I will answer.
26O look not upon the sins of thy
people, but at those who have served
thee in truth. 27Regard not the endeavors of those who act wickedly, but
the endeavors of those who have kept
thy covenants amid afflictions. 28Think
not on those who have lived wickedly
in thy sight; but remember those who
have willingly acknowledged that thou
art to be feared. 29Let it not be thy
will to destroy those who have had the
ways of cattle; but regard those who
have gloriously taught thy law.[r] 30Be
not angry with those who are deemed
worse than beasts; but love those who
have always put their trust in thy
glory. 31For we and our fathers have
passed our lives in ways that bring
death;[s] but thou, because of us sinners,
art called merciful. 32For if thou hast
desired to have pity on us, who have no
works of righteousness, then thou wilt
be called merciful. 33For the righteous,
who have many works laid up with
thee, shall receive their reward in consequence of their own deeds. 34But
what is man, that thou art angry with
him; or what is a corruptible race, that
thou art so bitter against it? 35For in
truth there is no one among those who
have been born who has not acted
wickedly, and among those who have
existed[t] there is no one who has not
transgressed. 36For in this, O Lord, thy
righteousness and goodness will be declared, when thou art merciful to those
who have no store of good works."

37 He answered me and said, "Some
things you have spoken rightly, and it
will come to pass according to your
words. 38For indeed I will not concern
myself about the fashioning of those
who have sinned, or about their death,
their judgment, or their destruction;
39but I will rejoice over the creation of
the righteous, over their pilgrimage
also, and their salvation, and their
receiving their reward. 40As I have
spoken, therefore, so it shall be.

41 "For just as the farmer sows
many seeds upon the ground and plants
a multitude of seedlings, and yet not
all that have been sown will come up[u]
in due season, and not all that were
planted will take root; so also those
who have been sown in the world will
not all be saved."

42 I answered and said, "If I have
found favor before thee, let me speak.[v]
43 For if the farmer's seed does not
come up, because it has not received
thy rain in due season, or if it has been
ruined by too much rain, it perishes.[w]
44But man, who has been formed by
thy hands and is called thy own image
because he is made like thee, and for
whose sake thou hast formed all things
—hast thou also made him like the

q Arab 2: other authorities read *bears witness*
r Syr *have received the brightness of thy law*
s Syr Ethiop: the Latin text is uncertain
t Syr: the Latin text is uncertain
u Syr Ethiop *will live;* Lat *will be saved*
v Or *If I have found favor, let me speak before thee*
w Cn: Compare Syr Arab 1 Arm Georg 2: the Latin is corrupt

23: *Dries up,* Is.50.2; 51.10. *Mountains melt,* Mic.1.4; Sir.16.18–19. **32:** Rom.3.19–26. **33:** 7.[77].

8.37–40: The divine reply to the seer's prayer: God will rejoice in the righteous and forget the sinners (the central petition of the prayer—mercy on the wicked—is ignored). **39:** *Their pilgrimage,* i.e. their return home to God (compare 2 Cor.5.6–8). **40:** Instead of *I have spoken,* the reading of the Ethiopic, "you have spoken," is to be preferred in view of v. 37 and the irony of the divine reply: "it is to be as you have *spoken,* but not as you had intended" (in vv. 26–36 the seer prayed God to ignore the wicked and their doings and pay attention to the righteous only; this, the Almighty replies, he will do, but in the sense of being unconcerned about the *destruction* of the wicked, v. 38).

8.41–45: Mankind is like the farmer's seed; only a few individuals will escape destruction. **45:** An anguished entreaty: *spare thy people,* Jl.2.17.

farmer's seed? 45 No, O Lord[x] who art over us! But spare thy people and have mercy on thy inheritance, for thou hast mercy on thy own creation."

46 He answered me and said, "Things that are present are for those who live now, and things that are future are for those who will live hereafter. 47 For you come far short of being able to love my creation more than I love it. But you have often compared yourself[y] to the unrighteous. Never do so! 48 But even in this respect you will be praiseworthy before the Most High, 49 because you have humbled yourself, as is becoming for you, and have not deemed yourself to be among the righteous in order to receive[z] the greatest glory. 50 For many miseries will affect those who inhabit the world in the last times, because they have walked in great pride. 51 But think of your own case, and inquire concerning the glory of those who are like yourself, 52 because it is for you that paradise is opened, the tree of life is planted, the age to come is prepared, plenty is provided, a city is built, rest is appointed,[a] goodness is established and wisdom perfected beforehand. 53 The root of evil is sealed up from you, illness is banished from you, and death[b] is hidden; hell has fled and corruption has been forgotten;[c] 54 sorrows have passed away, and in the end the treasure of immortality is made manifest. 55 Therefore do not ask any more questions about the multitude of those who perish. 56 For they also received freedom, but they despised the Most High, and were contemptuous of his law, and forsook his ways. 57 Moreover they have even trampled upon his righteous ones, 58 and said in their hearts that there is no God—though knowing full well that they must die. 59 For just as the things which I have predicted await[d] you, so the thirst and torment which are prepared await them. For the Most High did not intend that men should be destroyed; 60 but they themselves who were created have defiled the name of him who made them, and have been ungrateful to him who prepared life for them. 61 Therefore my judgment is now drawing near; 62 I have not shown this to all men, but only to you and a few like you."

Then I answered and said, 63 "Behold, O Lord, thou hast now shown me a multitude of the signs which thou wilt do in the last times, but thou hast not shown me when thou wilt do them."

9 He answered me and said, "Measure carefully in your mind, and when you see that a certain part of the predicted signs are past, 2 then you will know that it is the very time when the Most High is about to visit the world which he has made. 3 So when there shall appear in the world earthquakes, tumult of peoples, intrigues of nations, wavering of leaders, confusion of princes, 4 then you will know that it was of these that the Most High spoke from the days that were of old, from the beginning. 5 For just as with everything that has occurred in the world,

x Ethiop Arab Compare Syr: Latin omits *O Lord*
y Syr Ethiop: Lat *brought yourself near*
z Or *righteous; so that you will receive*
a Syr: Lat *allowed*
b Syr Ethiop Arm: Latin omits *death*
c Syr: Lat *Hades and corruption have fled into oblivion*, or *corruption has fled into Hades to be forgotten*
d Syr: Lat *will receive*

8.46–62: The final divine reply: The seer is assured that his lot is with the blessed, and is advised to think no more about sinners, who deserve their doom because they have *despised the Most High* (v. 56). **46–47:** The seer's objection (v. 44) is invalid, for the simile of the seeds suits the *present* corruptible order; *the future* has standards of its own. Moreover, God's love for his *creation* far exceeds man's love (see 5.33 n.). **48:** *In this respect*, i.e. the seer's humility (compare Lk.18.13–14). **52:** The future joys of heaven are already in existence and may be contemplated now (1 Pet.1.4). *Tree of life*, 7.[123]; Rev.2.7; 22.2. **53:** *Hell* is personified (as in Rev.6.8). **56:** *Freedom*, i.e. free will. **58:** Ps.14.1; 53.1. **59:** *The things . . . predicted*, in vv. 52–54. *Thirst*, in the fire of hell (Lk.16.24). *The Most High did not intend* man's destruction (Mt.18.14; 1 Tim.2.4). **62:** *A few like you*, i.e. prophets (apocalyptists) like the seer.

8.63–9.13: The end, and the signs which will precede it (4.51–5.13; 6.11–24). **8.63:** *When*, 4.33;

the beginning is evident,[e] and the end
manifest; 6so also are the times of the
Most High: the beginnings are manifest in wonders and mighty works, and
the end in requital[f] and in signs. 7And
it shall be that every one who will be
saved and will be able to escape on
account of his works, or on account of
the faith by which he has believed,
8will survive the dangers that have been
predicted, and will see my salvation in
my land and within my borders, which
I have sanctified for myself from the
beginning. 9Then those who have now
abused my ways shall be amazed, and
those who have rejected them with
contempt shall dwell in torments. 10For
as many as did not acknowledge me
in their lifetime, although they received
my benefits, 11and as many as scorned
my law while they still had freedom,
and did not understand but despised
it[g] while an opportunity of repentance
was still open to them, 12these must in
torment acknowledge it[h] after death.
13Therefore, do not continue to be
curious as to how the ungodly will be
punished; but inquire how the righteous will be saved, those to whom the
age belongs and for whose sake the age
was made."[i]

14 I answered and said, 15"I said
before, and I say now, and will say it
again: there are more who perish than
those who will be saved, 16as a wave is
greater than a drop of water."

17 He answered me and said, "As
is the field, so is the seed; and as are
the flowers, so are the colors; and as
is the work, so is the product; and as
is the farmer, so is the threshing floor.
18For there was a time in this age when
I was preparing for those who now
exist, before the world was made for
them to dwell in, and no one opposed
me then, for no one existed; 19but now
those who have been created in this
world which is supplied both with an
unfailing table and an inexhaustible
pasture,[j] have become corrupt in their
ways. 20So I considered my world, and
behold, it was lost, and my earth, and
behold, it was in peril because of the
devices of those who[k] had come into
it. 21And I saw and spared some[l] with
great difficulty, and saved for myself
one grape out of a cluster, and one
plant out of a great forest.[m] 22So let
the multitude perish which has been
born in vain, but let my grape and my
plant be saved, because with much
labor I have perfected them. 23But if
you will let seven days more pass—do
not fast during them, however; 24but
go into a field of flowers where no
house has been built, and eat only of
the flowers of the field, and taste no
meat and drink no wine, but eat only
flowers, 25and pray to the Most High
continually—then I will come and talk
with you."

26 So I went, as he directed me, into
the field which is called Ardat;[n] and
there I sat among the flowers and ate
of the plants of the field, and the
nourishment they afforded satisfied
me. 27And after seven days, as I lay
on the grass, my heart was troubled
again as it was before. 28And my
mouth was opened, and I began to

e Syr: Ethiop *in the word:* Latin is corrupt
f Syr: Lat Ethiop *in effects*
g Or *me* *h* Or *me*
i Syr: Lat *saved, and whose is the age and for whose sake the age was made and when* *j* Cn: Lat *law*
k Cn: Lat *devices which* *l* Lat *them*
m Syr Ethiop Arab 1: Lat *tribe*
n Syr Ethiop *Arpad:* Arm *Ardab*

contrast Acts 1.7. **9.3:** The messianic woes on earth. **9–12:** The state of the wicked immediately after death. **11:** Opportunity of repentance (Wis.12.10,20; Heb.12.17). **12:** *Acknowledge,* their earlier opportunity of repentance; or the word may be translated "be brought to know."

9.14–25: Recapitulation: The seer again deplores the fate of the wicked, and the small number of the saved is explained a last time. **19:** Restore "law" (see note *j*) to the text: the meaning is that despite God's gracious provision of earthly sustenance and divine law, men *have become corrupt.* **21–22:** The preservation of a small remnant is the result of God's grace. **24:** Likewise Daniel and his companions ate only vegetables (Dan.1.8–16; compare 2 Macc.5.27).

9.26–10.59: The fourth vision. 9.26–28: Introduction. 26: *Ardat,* an unknown location, probably of symbolical or mystic significance.

speak before the Most High, and said,
29"O Lord, thou didst show thyself
among us, to our fathers in the wilderness when they came out from Egypt
and when they came into the untrodden and unfruitful wilderness; 30and
thou didst say, 'Hear me, O Israel,
and give heed to my words, O descendants of Jacob. 31For behold, I sow my
law in you, and it shall bring forth fruit
in you, and you shall be glorified
through it for ever.' 32But though our
fathers received the law, they did not
keep it, and did not observe the statutes; yet the fruit of the law did not
perish—for it could not, because it was
thine. 33Yet those who received it
perished, because they did not keep
what had been sown in them. 34And
behold, it is the rule that, when the
ground has received seed, or the sea a
ship, or any dish food or drink, and
when it happens that what was sown
or what was launched or what was put
in is destroyed, 35they are destroyed,
but the things that held them remain;
yet with us it has not been so. 36For
we who have received the law and
sinned will perish, as well as our heart
which received it; 37the law, however,
does not perish but remains in its
glory."

38 When I said these things in my
heart, I lifted up my eyes[o] and saw a
woman on my right, and behold, she
was mourning and weeping with a loud
voice, and was deeply grieved at heart,
and her clothes were rent, and there
were ashes on her head. 39Then I dismissed the thoughts with which I had
been engaged, and turned to her 40and
said to her, "Why are you weeping,
and why are you grieved at heart?"

41 And she said to me, "Let me
alone, my lord, that I may weep for
myself and continue to mourn, for I
am greatly embittered in spirit and
deeply afflicted."

42 And I said to her, "What has
happened to you? Tell me."

43 And she said to me, "Your
servant was barren and had no child,
though I lived with my husband
thirty years. 44And every hour and
every day during those thirty years I
besought the Most High, night and
day. 45And after thirty years God
heard your handmaid, and looked
upon my low estate, and considered
my distress, and gave me a son. And I
rejoiced greatly over him, I and my
husband and all my neighbors;[p] and
we gave great glory to the Mighty One.
46And I brought him up with much
care. 47So when he grew up and I came
to take a wife for him, I set a day for
the marriage feast.

10 "But it happened that when my
son entered his wedding chamber,
he fell down and died. 2Then we all
put out the lamps, and all my neighbors[q] attempted to console me; and I
remained quiet until evening of the
second day. 3But when they all had
stopped consoling me, that I might be
quiet, I got up in the night and fled,
and came to this field, as you see. 4And
now I intend not to return to the city,
but to stay here, and I will neither eat
nor drink, but without ceasing mourn
and fast until I die."

5 Then I broke off the reflections
with which I was still engaged, and
answered her in anger and said,
6"You most foolish of women, do you
not see our mourning, and what has
happened to us? 7For Zion, the
mother of us all, is in deep grief and
great affliction. 8It is most appropriate to mourn now, because we are all

o Syr Arab Arm: Lat *I looked about me with my eyes*
p Literally *all my fellow-citizens*
q Literally *all my fellow-citizens*

9.29–37: The abiding glory of the Mosaic law, contrasted with Israel. **29:** Ex.19.9; 24.10; Dt.4.12.

9.38–10.24: The seer speaks with a disconsolate woman. 38: *Ashes on her head,* a sign of mourning. **47:** It was customary for the father to arrange for the wedding (see Sir.7.25 n.). **10.2:** *Lamps,* because weddings took place at night. **2:** *I remained quiet,* shows the depth of her grief, for ordinarily there was loud lamentation. **7:** *Zion, the mother of us all,* Gal.4.26.

mourning, and to be sorrowful, because we are all sorrowing; you are
sorrowing for one son, but we, the
whole world, for our mother.[r] 9 Now
ask the earth, and she will tell you that
it is she who ought to mourn over so
many who have come into being upon
her. 10 And from the beginning all
have been born of her, and others will
come; and behold, almost all go to
perdition, and a multitude of them are
destined for destruction. 11 Who then
ought to mourn the more, she[s] who lost
so great a multitude, or you who are
grieving for one? 12 But if you say to
me, 'My lamentation is not like the
earth's, for I have lost the fruit of my
womb, which I brought forth in pain
and bore in sorrow; 13 but it is with the
earth according to the way of the
earth—the multitude that is now in it
goes as it came'; 14 then I say to you,
'As you brought forth in sorrow, so
the earth also has from the beginning
given her fruit, that is, man, to him
who made her.' 15 Now, therefore, keep
your sorrow to yourself, and bear
bravely the troubles that have come
upon you. 16 For if you acknowledge
the decree of God to be just, you
will receive your son back in due time,
and will be praised among women.
17 Therefore go into the city to your
husband."

18 She said to me, "I will not do so;
I will not go into the city, but I will die
here."

19 So I spoke again to her, and
said, 20 "Do not say that, but let yourself be persuaded because of the
troubles of Zion, and be consoled
because of the sorrow of Jerusalem.
21 For you see that our sanctuary has
been laid waste, our altar thrown
down, our temple destroyed; 22 our
harp has been laid low, our song has
been silenced, and our rejoicing has
been ended; the light of our lampstand
has been put out, the ark of our
covenant has been plundered, our holy
things have been polluted, and the
name by which we are called has been
profaned; our free men[t] have suffered
abuse, our priests have been burned to
death, our Levites have gone into captivity, our virgins have been defiled,
and our wives have been ravished; our
righteous men have been carried off,
our little ones have been cast out, our
young men have been enslaved and
our strong men made powerless.
23 And, what is more than all, the seal
of Zion—for she has now lost the seal
of her glory, and has been given over
into the hands of those that hate us.
24 Therefore shake off your great sadness and lay aside your many sorrows,
so that the Mighty One may be merciful
to you again, and the Most High may
give you rest, a relief from your
troubles."

25 While I was talking to her, behold, her face suddenly shone exceedingly, and her countenance flashed like
lightning, so that I was too frightened
to approach her, and my heart was
terrified. While[u] I was wondering what
this meant, 26 behold, she suddenly
uttered a loud and fearful cry, so that
the earth shook at the sound. 27 And I
looked, and behold, the woman was no
longer visible to me, but there was an
established city,[v] and a place of huge
foundations showed itself. Then I
was afraid, and cried with a loud voice
and said, 28 "Where is the angel Uriel,

r Compare Syr: Latin is corrupt
s Syr
t Or *children*
u Syr Ethiop Arab 1: Latin omits *I was too . . . terrified. While*
v Syr Ethiop Arab: Lat *a city was being built*

16: To *acknowledge* the justice of God's *decree* is equivalent to pious submission to his will. *You will receive your son back in due time*, i.e. in the birth of another son, after returning to her husband (v. 17). **21–23:** A pathetic account of the utter ruin of Israel. **22:** *Harp* symbolizes the service of praise. The extinction of the perpetually burning *lamp* marked the cessation of temple services. *Our holy things* are enumerated in 1 Macc.4.49–51. *The name* Israel was bestowed by God (Gen.32.28). **23:** *The seal* of a nation is symbolic of its independence.

10.25–28: A vision of the heavenly Jerusalem. **27:** *An established city*, Heb.11.10; Rev.21.9–21. **28:** *At first*, 4.1.

who came to me at first? For it was
he who brought me into this overpowering bewilderment; my end has
become corruption, and my prayer a
reproach."
29 As I was speaking these words,
behold, the angel who had come to
me at first came to me, and he looked
upon me; 30and behold, I lay there
like a corpse and I was deprived of
my understanding. Then he grasped
my right hand and strengthened me
and set me on my feet, and said to me,
31"What is the matter with you? And
why are you troubled? And why are
your understanding and the thoughts
of your mind troubled?"
32 I said, "Because you have forsaken me! I did as you directed, and
went out into the field, and behold,
I saw, and still see, what I am unable
to explain."
33 He said to me, "Stand up like a
man, and I will instruct you."
34 I said, "Speak, my lord; only do
not forsake me, lest I die before my
time.[w] 35For I have seen what I did
not know, and I have heard what I
do not understand. 36Or is my mind
deceived, and my soul dreaming?
37Now therefore I entreat you to give
your servant an explanation of this
bewildering vision."
38 He answered me and said, "Listen
to me and I will inform you, and tell
you about the things which you fear,
for the Most High has revealed many
secrets to you. 39For he has seen your
righteous conduct, that you have sor-
rowed continually for your people, and
mourned greatly over Zion. 40This
therefore is the meaning of the vision.
41The woman who appeared to you a
little while ago, whom you saw mourning and began to console—42but you
do not now see the form of a woman,
but an established city[x] has appeared
to you—43and as for her telling you
about the misfortune of her son, this
is the interpretation: 44This woman
whom you saw, whom you now behold
as an established city, is Zion.[y] 45And
as for her telling you that she was
barren for thirty years, it is because
there were three thousand[y] years in the
world before any offering was offered
in it.[z] 46And after three thousand[y]
years Solomon built the city, and
offered offerings; then it was that the
barren woman bore a son. 47And as
for her telling you that she brought
him up with much care, that was the
period of residence in Jerusalem. 48And
as for her saying to you, 'When my son
entered his wedding chamber he died,'
and that misfortune had overtaken
her,[a] that was the destruction which
befell Jerusalem. 49And behold, you
saw her likeness, how she mourned for
her son, and you began to console her
for what had happened.[b] 50For now
the Most High, seeing that you are sin-
cerely grieved and profoundly distressed for her, has shown you the
brilliance of her glory, and the loveliness of her beauty. 51Therefore I told
you to remain in the field where no
house had been built, 52for I knew that
the Most High would reveal these
things to you. 53Therefore I told you
to go into the field where there was no
foundation of any building, 54for no
work of man's building could endure in
a place where the city of the Most High
was to be revealed.
55 "Therefore do not be afraid, and
do not let your heart be terrified; but
go in and see the splendor and vastness

w Syr Ethiop Arab: Lat *die to no purpose*
x Syr Ethiop Arab: Lat *a city to be built*
y Syr Ethiop Arab Arm: Latin is corrupt
z Cn: Lat Syr Arab Arm *her* *a* Or *him*
b Most Latin manuscripts and Arab 1 add *these were the things to be opened to you*

10.29–59: Interpretation of the vision. **30:** *Like a corpse*, Rev.1.17; compare Dan.8.18; 10.9. **32:** *And still see*, the vision is still before the seer's eyes. *Unable to explain*, compare 2 Cor.12.3–4 (also of an ecstatic experience). **33:** *Stand up*, 5.15; 6.13,17. **44:** *Zion*, i.e. the heavenly Jerusalem. **45:** *In it*, in the world. **46:** *A son*, i.e. the earthly Jerusalem. **49:** The *likeness*, or model, of the earthly city is the heavenly Zion, who *mourned for her son* (the ruined earthly Jerusalem). For the idea of a heavenly counterpart or model, compare Ex.25.9,40; Heb.8.5. **55–56:** 1 Cor.

of the building, as far as it is possible
for your eyes to see it, 56and afterward
you will hear as much as your ears can
hear. 57For you are more blessed than
many, and you have been called before
the Most High, as but few have been.
58But tomorrow night you shall remain
here, 59and the Most High will show
you in those dream visions what the
Most High will do to those who dwell
on earth in the last days."

So I slept that night and the following one, as he had commanded me.

11 On the second night I had a dream,
and behold, there came up from
the sea an eagle that had twelve feath-
ered wings and three heads. 2And I
looked, and behold, he spread his wings
over[c] all the earth, and all the winds of
heaven blew upon him, and the clouds
were gathered about him.[d] 3And I
looked, and out of his wings there grew
opposing wings; but they became little,
puny wings. 4But his heads were at
rest; the middle head was larger than
the other heads, but it also was at rest
with them. 5And I looked, and behold,
the eagle flew with his wings, to reign
over the earth and over those who
dwell in it. 6And I saw how all things
under heaven were subjected to him,
and no one spoke against him, not even
one creature that was on the earth.
7And I looked, and behold, the eagle
rose upon his talons, and uttered a cry
to his wings, saying, 8"Do not all
watch at the same time; let each sleep
in his own place, and watch in his turn;
9but let the heads be reserved for the
last."

10 And I looked, and behold, the
voice did not come from his heads,
but from the midst of his body. 11And
I counted his opposing wings, and
behold, there were eight of them.
12And I looked, and behold, on the
right side one wing arose, and it reigned
over all the earth. 13And while it was
reigning it came to its end and disappeared, so that its place was not seen.
Then the next wing arose and reigned,
and it continued to reign a long time.
14And while it was reigning its end
came also, so that it disappeared
like the first. 15And behold, a voice
sounded, saying to it, 16"Hear me, you
who have ruled the earth all this time;
I announce this to you before you
disappear. 17After you no one shall
rule as long as you, or even half as
long."

18 Then the third wing raised itself
up, and held the rule like the former
ones, and it also disappeared. 19And
so it went with all the wings; they
wielded power one after another and
then were never seen again. 20And I
looked, and behold, in due course the
wings that followed[e] also rose up on
the right[f] side, in order to rule. There
were some of them that ruled, yet disappeared suddenly; 21and others of
them rose up, but did not hold the rule.

22 And after this I looked and behold, the twelve wings and the two little
wings disappeared; 23and nothing remained on the eagle's body except the
three heads that were at rest and six
little wings. 24And I looked, and
behold, two little wings separated from
the six and remained under the head
that was on the right side; but four
remained in their place. 25And I
looked, and behold, these little wings[g]
planned to set themselves up and hold

c Arab 2 Arm: Lat Syr *in*
d Syr Compare Ethiop Arab: Latin omits *the clouds* and *about him*
e Syr Arab 2 *the little wings*
f Some Ethiopic manuscripts read *left*
g Syr: Lat *underwings*

2.9; 2 Cor.12.4. *Go in and see*, the city is conceived as still standing before Ezra. **57:** *You have been called before the Most High*, Arabic 1, "your name is known [or recognized] before the Most High," i.e. God has singled you out for honor (Is.45.3–4).

11.1–12.51: The fifth vision (the eagle vision). 11.1: *From the sea*, Dan.7.3; Rev.13.1. *An eagle*, symbol of the Roman Empire. **2:** *Spread his wings*, asserted his dominion. *The winds*, 13.2; Dan.7.2. **3:** *Opposing wings*, symbolizing usurpers who revolted against the Roman emperors. *But they became little*, i.e. they were subdued. **4:** *Were at rest*, i.e. were not troubled by the opposing wings. **13:** *It came to its end*, i.e. the ruler perished.

the rule. 26 And I looked, and behold, one was set up, but suddenly disappeared; 27 a second also, and this disappeared more quickly than the first. 28 And I looked, and behold, the two that remained were planning between themselves to reign together; 29 and while they were planning, behold, one of the heads that were at rest (the one which was in the middle) awoke; for it was greater than the other two heads. 30 And I saw how it allied the two heads with itself, 31 and behold, the head turned with those that were with it, and it devoured the two little wings[h] which were planning to reign. 32 Moreover this head gained control of the whole earth, and with much oppression dominated its inhabitants; and it had greater power over the world than all the wings that had gone before.

33 And after this I looked, and behold, the middle head also suddenly disappeared, just as the wings had done. 34 But the two heads remained, which also ruled over the earth and its inhabitants. 35 And I looked, and behold, the head on the right side devoured the one on the left.

36 Then I heard a voice saying to me, "Look before you and consider what you see." 37 And I looked, and behold, a creature like a lion was aroused out of the forest, roaring; and I heard how he uttered a man's voice to the eagle, and spoke, saying, 38 "Listen and I will speak to you. The Most High says to you, 39 'Are you not the one that remains of the four beasts which I had made to reign in my world, so that the end of my times might come through them? 40 You, the fourth that has come, have conquered all the beasts that have gone before; and you have held sway over the world with much terror, and over all the earth with grievous oppression; and for so long you have dwelt on the earth with deceit.[i] 41 And you have judged the earth, but not with truth; 42 for you have afflicted the meek and injured the peaceable; you have hated those who tell the truth, and have loved liars; you have destroyed the dwellings of those who brought forth fruit, and have laid low the walls of those who did you no harm. 43 And so your insolence has come up before the Most High, and your pride to the Mighty One. 44 And the Most High has looked upon his times, and behold, they are ended, and his ages are completed! 45 Therefore you will surely disappear, you eagle, and your terrifying wings, and your most evil little wings, and your malicious heads, and your most evil talons, and your whole worthless body, 46 so that the whole earth, freed from your violence, may be refreshed and relieved, and may hope for the judgment and mercy of him who made it.' "

12 While the lion was saying these words to the eagle, I looked, 2 and behold, the remaining head disappeared. And the two wings that had gone over to it arose[j] and set themselves up to reign, and their reign was brief and full of tumult. 3 And I looked, and behold, they also disappeared, and the whole body of the eagle was burned, and the earth was exceedingly terrified.

Then I awoke in great perplexity of mind and great fear, and I said to my spirit, 4 "Behold, you have brought this upon me, because you search out the ways of the Most High. 5 Behold, I am still weary in mind and very weak in my spirit, and not even a little strength is left in me, because of the great fear with which I have been terrified this night. 6 Therefore I will now beseech the Most High that he may strengthen me to the end."

h Syr: Lat *underwings*
i Syr Arab Arm: Lat Ethiop *The fourth came, however, and conquered . . . and held sway . . . and for so long dwelt*
j Ethiop: Latin omits *arose*

36: *Look before you*, the seer is alerted to the special importance of what follows. **43:** Dan.5.20.

12.3b–39: The interpretation of the vision. 3b–9: The seer awakes and asks for an interpretation of the vision. **11:** *The fourth kingdom* in Daniel's vision (Dan.7.7) symbolized the Greek or

7 And I said, "O sovereign Lord, if I have found favor in thy sight, and if I have been accounted righteous before thee beyond many others, and if my prayer has indeed come up before thy face, 8strengthen me and show me, thy servant, the interpretation and meaning of this terrifying vision, that thou mayest fully comfort my soul. 9For thou hast judged me worthy to be shown the end of the times and the last events of the times."

10 He said to me, "This is the interpretation of this vision which you have seen: 11The eagle which you saw coming up from the sea is the fourth kingdom which appeared in a vision to your brother Daniel. 12But it was not explained to him as I now explain or have explained it to you. 13Behold, the days are coming when a kingdom shall arise on earth, and it shall be more terrifying than all the kingdoms that have been before it. 14And twelve kings shall reign in it, one after another. 15But the second that is to reign shall hold sway for a longer time than any other of the twelve. 16This is the interpretation of the twelve wings which you saw. 17As for your hearing a voice that spoke, coming not from the eagle's[k] heads but from the midst of his body, this is the interpretation: 18In the midst of[l] the time of that kingdom great struggles shall arise, and it shall be in danger of falling; nevertheless it shall not fall then, but shall regain its former power.[m] 19As for your seeing eight little wings[n] clinging to his wings, this is the interpretation: 20Eight kings shall arise in it, whose times shall be short and their years swift; 21and two of them shall perish when the middle of its time draws near; and four shall be kept for the time when its end approaches; but two shall be kept until the end. 22As for your seeing three heads at rest, this is the interpretation: 23In its last days the Most High will raise up three kings,[o] and they[p] shall renew many things in it, and shall rule the earth 24and its inhabitants more oppressively than all who were before them; therefore they are called the heads of the eagle. 25For it is they who shall sum up his wickedness and perform his last actions. 26As for your seeing that the large head disappeared, one of the kings[q] shall die in his bed, but in agonies. 27But as for the two who remained, the sword shall devour them. 28For the sword of one shall devour him who was with him; but he also shall fall by the sword in the last days. 29As for your seeing two little wings[r] passing over to[s] the head which was on the right side, 30this is the interpretation: It is these whom the Most High has kept for the eagle's[t] end; this was the reign which was brief and full of tumult, as you have seen.

31 "And as for the lion whom you saw rousing up out of the forest and roaring and speaking to the eagle and reproving him for his unrighteousness, and as for all his words that you have heard, 32this is the Messiah[u] whom the Most High has kept until the end of days, who will arise from the posterity of David, and will come and speak to

k Lat *his*
l Syr Arm: Lat *After*
m Ethiop Arab 1 Arm: Lat Syr *beginning*
n Syr: Lat *underwings*
o Syr Ethiop Arab Arm: Lat *kingdoms*
p Syr Ethiop Arm: Lat *he*
q Lat *them*
r Arab 1: Lat *underwings*
s Syr Ethiop: Latin omits *to*
t Lat *his*
u Literally *anointed one*

Macedonian Empire; here, however, it is reinterpreted (compare v. 12) to refer to the Roman Empire (see 11.1 n.). **13:** *The days are coming*, the seer is represented as prophesying during the exile. **17:** 11.10; compare 11.15. **18:** There is nothing in the vision which corresponds to what is said in this verse. The author probably refers to *the time* of *great struggles* for power which followed the death of Nero A.D. 68. **19:** *Little wings*, 11.3,11. *Clinging to his wings*, Armenian, "sprouting out around his great wings." **20:** *In it*, within the Roman Empire. **21:** *Its time*, the time of the kingdom. *Its end*, the end of the kingdom. **23:** *Its last days*, the last days of the kingdom. **23–24:** 11.30–32. **28:** *But . . . days*, there is nothing corresponding to this in the vision. **30:** *As you have seen*, v. 3. **31:** *The lion*, 11.37ff. **32:** *Whom the Most High has kept until the end*

them;[v] he will denounce them for their
ungodliness and for their wickedness,
and will cast up before them their contemptuous dealings. 33For first he will
set them living before his judgment
seat, and when he has reproved them,
then he will destroy them. 34But he
will deliver in mercy the remnant of my
people, those who have been saved
throughout my borders, and he will
make them joyful until the end comes,
the day of judgment, of which I spoke
to you at the beginning. 35This is the
dream that you saw, and this is its
interpretation. 36And you alone were
worthy to learn this secret of the Most
High. 37Therefore write all these things
that you have seen in a book, and put
it in a hidden place; 38and you shall
teach them to the wise among your
people, whose hearts you know are able
to comprehend and keep these secrets.
39But wait here seven days more, so
that you may be shown whatever it
pleases the Most High to show you."
Then he left me.

40 When all the people heard that
the seven days were past and I had not
returned to the city, they all gathered
together, from the least to the greatest,
and came to me and spoke to me, saying, 41"How have we offended you,
and what harm have we done you, that
you have forsaken us and sit in this
place? 42For of all the prophets you
alone are left to us, like a cluster of
grapes from the vintage, and like a lamp
in a dark place, and like a haven for a
ship saved from a storm. 43Are not the
evils which have befallen us sufficient?
44Therefore if you forsake us, how
much better it would have been for us
if we also had been consumed in the
burning of Zion! 45For we are no
better than those who died there."
And they wept with a loud voice.

Then I answered them and said,
46"Take courage, O Israel; and do
not be sorrowful, O house of Jacob;
47for the Most High has you in remembrance, and the Mighty One has not
forgotten you in your struggle. 48As
for me, I have neither forsaken you nor
withdrawn from you; but I have come
to this place to pray on account of the
desolation of Zion, and to seek mercy
on account of the humiliation of our[w]
sanctuary. 49Now go, every one of you
to his house, and after these days I will
come to you." 50So the people went
into the city, as I told them to do.
51But I sat in the field seven days, as
the angel[x] had commanded me; and
I ate only of the flowers of the field,
and my food was of plants during
those days.

13 After seven days I dreamed a
dream in the night; 2and behold,
a wind arose from the sea and stirred
up all its waves. 3And I looked, and
behold, this wind made something like
the figure of a man come up out of the
heart of the sea. And I looked, and
behold,[y] that man flew[z] with the clouds
of heaven; and wherever he turned his
face to look, everything under his gaze
trembled, 4and whenever his voice
issued from his mouth, all who heard
his voice melted as wax melts[a] when it
feels the fire.

5 After this I looked, and behold, an
innumerable multitude of men were
gathered together from the four winds

v Syr: Latin omits *of days . . . and speak*
w Syr Ethiop: Lat *your*
x Literally *he*
y Syr: Latin omits *this wind . . . and behold*
z Syr Ethiop Arab Arm: Lat *grew strong*
a Syr: Lat *burned as the earth rests*

---

of days, the pre-existent Messiah in heaven (Dan.7.13–14; Enoch 48.6; 62.7). *He will denounce them*, 13.37. **34:** *He will make them joyful*, 7.28. **35:** *The dream*, 11.1. **37:** The seer is bidden to compose an esoteric book. **37–38:** To *put the book in a hidden place* suggests that it is an apocryphal book, which only the elect (*the wise*) can *comprehend.* **39:** *He*, the angel Uriel (see 4.1 n.).

12.40–51: The seer comforts those who were grieved because of his absence. 40: *The seven days*, 9.23,27. **42:** *A lamp*, 2 Pet.1.19. **49:** *These days*, v. 39. **51:** 9.24–26.

13.1–58: The sixth vision (the man from the sea). 3: *Something like the figure of a man*, the Messiah (Dan.7.13); compare v. 32 "my Son," i.e. the Son of God. *Flew with the clouds*, Is.19.1;

of heaven to make war against the man
who came up out of the sea. 6And I
looked, and behold, he carved out for
himself a great mountain, and flew up
upon it. 7And I tried to see the region
or place from which the mountain was
carved, but I could not.
8 After this I looked, and behold,
all who had gathered together against
him, to wage war with him, were much
afraid, yet dared to fight. 9And behold,
when he saw the onrush of the approaching multitude, he neither lifted
his hand nor held a spear or any
weapon of war; 10but I saw only how
he sent forth from his mouth as it were
a stream of fire, and from his lips a
flaming breath, and from his tongue
he shot forth a storm of sparks.[b] 11All
these were mingled together, the stream
of fire and the flaming breath and the
great storm, and fell on the onrushing
multitude which was prepared to fight,
and burned them all up, so that suddenly nothing was seen of the innumerable multitude but only the dust of
ashes and the smell of smoke. When I
saw it, I was amazed.
12 After this I saw the same man
come down from the mountain and
call to him another multitude which
was peaceable. 13Then many people[c]
came to him, some of whom were joyful and some sorrowful; some of them
were bound, and some were bringing
others as offerings.
Then in great fear I awoke; and I
besought the Most High, and said,
14"From the beginning thou hast shown
thy servant these wonders, and hast
deemed me worthy to have my prayer
heard by thee; 15now show me also
the interpretation of this dream. 16For
as I consider it in my mind, alas for
those who will be left in those days!
And still more, alas for those who are
not left! 17For those who are not left
will be sad, 18because they understand
what is reserved for the last days, but
cannot attain it. 19But alas for those
also who are left, and for that very
reason! For they shall see great dangers and much distress, as these dreams
show. 20Yet it is better[d] to come into
these things,[e] though incurring peril,
than to pass from the world like a
cloud, and not to see what shall happen in the last days."
He answered me and said, 21"I will
tell you the interpretation of the vision,
and I will also explain to you the things
which you have mentioned. 22As for
what you said about those who are left,
this is the interpretation: 23He who
brings the peril at that time will himself protect those who fall into peril,
who have works and have faith in the
Almighty. 24Understand therefore that
those who are left are more blessed
than those who have died. 25This is
the interpretation of the vision: As for
your seeing a man come up from the
heart of the sea, 26this is he whom the
Most High has been keeping for many
ages, who will himself deliver his creation; and he will direct those who are
left. 27And as for your seeing wind and
fire and a storm coming out of his
mouth, 28and as for his not holding a
spear or weapon of war, yet destroying
the onrushing multitude which came to
conquer him, this is the interpretation:
29Behold, the days are coming when the
Most High will deliver those who are
on the earth. 30And bewilderment of

b The text is uncertain
c Lat Syr Arab 2 literally *the faces of many people*
d Ethiop Compare Arab 2: Lat *easier*
e Syr: Lat *this*

Dan.7.13; Rev.1.7. **4:** *As wax melts*, Mic.1.4; Jdt.16.15. **6:** *Carved out*, Dan.2.45. **10:** Is.11.4. **13a:** *Some . . . were bound*, Jews who came from captivity. *Others as offerings*, Is.66.20.

13.13b–20: The seer prays that God will interpret the vision to him. 14: *From the beginning*, when the seer first began to have the visions. *My prayer*, 9.25ff. **19:** *For that very reason*, better, "for this reason—" (the reason follows).

13.21–56: The interpretation of the vision. 21: *Things . . . mentioned*, in vv. 16–20. **22:** *Left*, Syriac and Arabic 1 add, "and of those who do not survive." **23:** *He who brings the peril*, the Messiah, whose advent is preceded by the messianic woes. **26:** *He whom the Most High has been keeping for many ages*, the pre-existent heavenly Messiah (v. 52; 12.32). **27–28:** Vv. 9–11.

mind shall come over those who dwell
on the earth. 31And they shall plan to
make war against one another, city
against city, place against place,
people against people, and kingdom
against kingdom. 32And when these
things come to pass and the signs occur
which I showed you before, then my
Son will be revealed, whom you saw as
a man coming up from the sea.[f] 33And
when all the nations hear his voice,
every man shall leave his own land and
the warfare that they have against one
another; 34and an innumerable multitude shall be gathered together, as you
saw, desiring to come and conquer him.
35But he will stand on the top of Mount
Zion. 36And Zion will come and be
made manifest to all people, prepared
and built, as you saw the mountain
carved out without hands. 37And he,
my Son, will reprove the assembled
nations for their ungodliness (this was
symbolized by the storm), 38and will
reproach them to their face with their
evil thoughts and the torments with
which they are to be tortured (which
were symbolized by the flames), and
will destroy them without effort by the
law[g] (which was symbolized by the
fire). 39And as for your seeing him
gather to himself another multitude
that was peaceable, 40these are the ten
tribes which were led away from their
own land into captivity in the days of
King Hoshea, whom Shalmaneser the
king of the Assyrians led captive; he
took them across the river, and they
were taken into another land. 41But
they formed this plan for themselves,
that they would leave the multitude of
the nations and go to a more distant
region, where mankind had never
lived, 42that there at least they might
keep their statutes which they had
not kept in their own land. 43And
they went in by the narrow passages
of the Euphrates river. 44For at that
time the Most High performed signs
for them, and stopped the channels of
the river until they had passed over.
45Through that region there was a long
way to go, a journey of a year and
a half; and that country is called Arza-
reth.[h]

46 "Then they dwelt there until the
last times; and now, when they are
about to come again, 47the Most High
will stop[i] the channels of the river
again, so that they may be able to pass
over. Therefore you saw the multitude
gathered together in peace. 48But
those who are left of your people, who
are found within my holy borders,
shall be saved.[j] 49Therefore when he
destroys the multitude of the nations
that are gathered together, he will
defend the people who remain. 50And
then he will show them very many
wonders."

51 I said, "O sovereign Lord, explain this to me: Why did I see the man
coming up from the heart of the sea?"

52 He said to me, "Just as no one
can explore or know what is in the
depths of the sea, so no one on earth
can see my Son or those who are with
him, except in the time of his day.[k]
53This is the interpretation of the dream
which you saw. And you alone have
been enlightened about this, 54because
you have forsaken your own ways and
have applied yourself to mine, and have
searched out my law; 55for you have
devoted your life to wisdom, and called

f Syr and most Latin manuscripts omit *from the sea*
g Syr: Lat *and the law*
h That is *Another Land*
i Syr: Lat *stops*
j Syr: Latin omits *shall be saved*
k Syr: Ethiop *except when his time and his day have come.* Latin omits *his*

31: Is.19.2; Mt.24.7. **32:** *Then my son will be revealed,* 7.28; Mt.24.30; Mk.13.26. **34:** Rev.16.16; 19.19. **36:** *Zion,* the heavenly Jerusalem (7.26; Rev.21.2, 9f.). *Without hands,* Dan.2.34,45. **37:** 12.32. **40:** 2 Kg.17.1–6. *The ten tribes,* the Northern Kingdom. *The river,* the Euphrates. **44:** *Stopped . . . the river,* Jos.3.14–16. **45:** *Azareth,* Hebrew for "Another Land" (see note *h*; compare Dt.29.28). **47:** *Will stop . . . the river,* Is.11.15–16. **49:** *The people that remain,* presumably Israel, including the ten tribes who have returned to Palestine (v. 48). **50:** *Then,* in the messianic age. **52:** *Those . . . with him,* perhaps angels (Mt.24.31; 25.31). *Except . . . day,* until the day on which the Messiah appears.

understanding your mother. 56There-
fore I have shown you this, for there is
a reward laid up with the Most High.
And after three more days I will tell
you other things, and explain weighty
and wondrous matters to you."

57 Then I arose and walked in the
field, giving great glory and praise to
the Most High because of his wonders,
which he did from time to time, 58and
because he governs the times and whatever things come to pass in their
seasons. And I stayed there three days.

14 On the third day, while I was
sitting under an oak, behold, a
voice came out of a bush opposite me
and said, "Ezra, Ezra." 2And I said,
"Here I am, Lord," and I rose to my
feet. 3Then he said to me, "I revealed
myself in a bush and spoke to Moses,
when my people were in bondage in
Egypt; 4and I sent him and led[l] my
people out of Egypt; and I led him up
on Mount Sinai, where I kept him with
me many days; 5and I told him many
wondrous things, and showed him the
secrets of the times and declared to
him[m] the end of the times. Then I
commanded him, saying, 6'These words
you shall publish openly, and these you
shall keep secret.' 7And now I say to
you: 8Lay up in your heart the signs
that I have shown you, the dreams that
you have seen, and the interpretations
that you have heard; 9for you shall be
taken up from among men, and henceforth you shall live with my Son and
with those who are like you, until the
times are ended. 10For the age has lost
its youth, and the times begin to grow
old. 11For the age is divided into
twelve parts, and nine[n] of its parts
have already passed, 12as well as half
of the tenth part; so two of its parts
remain, besides half of the tenth part.[o]
13Now therefore, set your house in
order, and reprove your people; comfort the lowly among them, and instruct those that are wise.[p] And now
renounce the life that is corruptible,
14and put away from you mortal
thoughts; cast away from you the
burdens of man, and divest yourself
now of your weak nature, 15and lay
to one side the thoughts that are most
grievous to you, and hasten to escape
from these times. 16For evils worse
than those which you have now seen
happen shall be done hereafter. 17For
the weaker the world becomes through
old age, the more shall evils be multiplied among[q] its inhabitants. 18For
truth shall go farther away, and false-
hood shall come near. For the eagle[r]
which you saw in the vision is already
hastening to come."

19 Then I answered and said, "Let
me speak in thy presence, Lord.[s] 20For
behold, I will go, as thou hast commanded me, and I will reprove the
people who are now living; but who
will warn those who will be born
hereafter? For the world lies in darkness, and its inhabitants are without
light. 21For thy law has been burned,
and so no one knows the things which
have been done or will be done by
thee. 22If then I have found favor before thee, send the Holy Spirit into me,
and I will write everything that has
happened in the world from the
beginning, the things which were written in thy law, that men may be able to
find the path, and that those who wish
to live in the last days may live."

l Other authorities read *he led*
m Syr Ethiop Arab Arm: Latin omits *declared to him*
n Cn: Lat Ethiop *ten*
o Syr omits verses 11, 12: Ethiop *For the world is divided into ten parts, and has come to the tenth, and half of the tenth remains. Now . . .*
p Latin omits *and . . . wise*
q Literally *upon*
r Syr Ethiop Arab Arm: Latin is corrupt
s Most Latin manuscripts omit *Let me speak*

14.1–48: The seventh vision (the legend of Ezra and the holy Scriptures). 1–18: God speaks to Ezra. **1:** *A bush,* compare Ex.3.4. **4:** *Many days,* forty days (Ex.34.28). **9:** *My son,* the pre-existent heavenly Messiah (7.28; 13.32,52). **10:** 5.50–55. **13:** *House,* of Israel. **14:** 2 Cor.5.4. **16:** Mt.24.8. **18:** *The eagle,* ch. 11.

14.19–26: Ezra's prayer for inspiration to restore the holy Scriptures. 20: *Without light,* without the light of God's law (Ps.19.8b). **21:** 4.23. **22:** *The Holy Spirit* will guide Ezra in

23 He answered me and said, "Go and gather the people, and tell them not to seek you for forty days. [24]But prepare for yourself many writing tablets, and take with you Sarea, Dabria, Selemia, Ethanus, and Asiel—these five, because they are trained to write rapidly; [25]and you shall come here, and I will light in your heart the lamp of understanding, which shall not be put out until what you are about to write is finished. [26]And when you have finished, some things you shall make public, and some you shall deliver in secret to the wise; tomorrow at this hour you shall begin to write."

27 Then I went as he commanded me, and I gathered all the people together, and said, [28]"Hear these words, O Israel. [29]At first our fathers dwelt as aliens in Egypt, and they were delivered from there, [30]and received the law of life, which they did not keep, which you also have transgressed after them. [31]Then land was given to you for a possession in the land of Zion; but you and your fathers committed iniquity and did not keep the ways which the Most High commanded you. [32]And because he is a righteous judge, in due time he took from you what he had given. [33]And now you are here, and your brethren are farther in the interior.[t] [34]If you, then, will rule over your minds and discipline your hearts, you shall be kept alive, and after death you shall obtain mercy. [35]For after death the judgment will come, when we shall live again; and then the names of the righteous will become manifest, and the deeds of the ungodly will be disclosed. [36]But let no one come to me now, and let no one seek me for forty days."

37 So I took the five men, as he commanded me, and we proceeded to the field, and remained there. [38]And on the next day, behold, a voice called me, saying, "Ezra, open your mouth and drink what I give you to drink." [39]Then I opened my mouth, and behold, a full cup was offered to me; it was full of something like water, but its color was like fire. [40]And I took it and drank; and when I had drunk it, my heart poured forth understanding, and wisdom increased in my breast, for my spirit retained its memory; [41]and my mouth was opened, and was no longer closed. [42]And the Most High gave understanding to the five men, and by turns they wrote what was dictated, in characters which they did not know.[u] They sat forty days, and wrote during the daytime, and ate their bread at night. [43]As for me, I spoke in the daytime and was not silent at night. [44]So during the forty days ninety-four[v] books were written. [45]And when the forty days were ended, the Most High spoke to me, saying, "Make public the twenty-four[w] books that you wrote first and let the worthy and the unworthy read them; [46]but keep

t Syr Ethiop Arm: Lat *are among you*
u Syr Compare Ethiop Arab 2 Arm: Latin is corrupt
v Syr Ethiop Arab 1 Arm: Latin is corrupt
w Syr Arab 1: Latin omits *twenty-four*

---

rewriting the law, which has been burned (v. 21). **23:** *Forty days,* Ex.24.18; 34.28; Dt.9.9,18. **24:** *Many,* compare v. 44. **26:** *Some things . . . make public,* namely, the rewritten books of the Old Testament. *Some . . . deliver in secret,* namely, the apocalypses (see 12.37–38 n.).

14.27–36: The last words of Ezra. 29: *Aliens,* Gen.47.4. **30:** *The law,* which, if observed, would confer *life.* **33:** *Farther,* 13.45. **34:** *Kept alive,* i.e. spiritually alive. **36:** *Forty days,* v. 23.

14.37–48: The restoration of the holy Scriptures. 37: *The five men,* v. 24. **39:** *A full cup* of inspiration, containing the fire of the Spirit (v. 22). **41:** *Was opened,* in fluent speech. **42:** *In characters which they did not know,* in a new Hebrew script, the (modern) square characters. **45:** *The twenty-four books* of the Hebrew canon comprise the five books of the Law (Gen., Ex., Lev., Num., Dt.), eight books of the Prophets (the former prophets, Jos., Jg., 1 and 2 Sam. [as one book], 1 and 2 Kg. [as one book]; the latter prophets, Is., Jer., Ezek., and the Twelve [counted as one book]), and eleven books of the Writings (Ps., Pr., Job, S. of S., Ru., Lam., Ec., Est., Dan., Ezra-Neh. [as one book], 1 and 2 Chr. [as one book]). **46:** *The seventy* are esoteric, apocalyptic books (see 12.37–38 n.).

the seventy that were written last, in order to give them to the wise among your people. 47For in them is the spring of understanding, the fountain of wisdom, and the river of knowledge." 48And I did so.[x]

15[y] The Lord says, "Behold, speak in the ears of my people the words of the prophecy which I will put in your mouth, 2and cause them to be written on paper; for they are trustworthy and true. 3Do not fear the plots against you, and do not be troubled by the unbelief of those who oppose you. 4For every unbeliever shall die in his unbelief."

5 "Behold," says the Lord, "I bring evils upon the world, the sword and famine and death and destruction. 6For iniquity has spread throughout every land, and their harmful deeds have reached their limit. 7Therefore," says the Lord, 8"I will be silent no longer concerning their ungodly deeds which they impiously commit, neither will I tolerate their wicked practices. Behold, innocent and righteous blood cries out to me, and the souls of the righteous cry out continually. 9I will surely avenge them," says the Lord, "and will receive to myself all the innocent blood from among them. 10Behold, my people is led like a flock to the slaughter; I will not allow them to live any longer in the land of Egypt, 11but I will bring them out with a mighty hand and with an uplifted arm, and will smite Egypt with plagues, as before, and will destroy all its land."

12 Let Egypt mourn, and its foundations, for the plague of chastisement and punishment that the Lord will bring upon it. 13Let the farmers that till the ground mourn, because their seed shall fail and their trees shall be ruined by blight and hail and by a terrible tempest. 14Alas for the world and for those who live in it! 15For the sword and misery draw near them, and nation shall rise up to fight against nation, with swords in their hands. 16For there shall be unrest among men; growing strong against one another, they shall in their might have no respect for their king or the chief of their leaders. 17For a man will desire to go into a city, and shall not be able. 18For because of their pride the cities shall be in confusion, the houses shall be destroyed, and people shall be afraid. 19A man shall have no pity upon his neighbors, but shall make an assault upon their houses with the sword, and plunder their goods, because of hunger for bread and because of great tribulation.

20 "Behold," says God, "I call together all the kings of the earth to fear me, from the rising sun and from the south, from the east and from Lebanon; to turn and repay what they have given them. 21Just as they have done to my elect until this day, so I will do, and will repay into their bosom." Thus says the Lord God: 22"My right hand will not spare the sinners, and my sword will not cease from those who shed innocent blood on the earth." 23And a fire will go forth from his wrath, and will consume the foundations of the earth, and the sinners, like straw that is kindled. 24"Woe to those

x Syr adds *in the seventh year of the sixth week, five thousand years and three months and twelve days after creation.*
At that time Ezra was caught up, and taken to the place of those who are like him, after he had written all these things. And he was called the Scribe of the knowledge of the Most High for ever and ever. Ethiop Arab 1 Arm have a similar ending

y Chapters 15 and 16 (except 15:57–59 which has been found in Greek) are extant only in Latin

15.1–16.78: An appendix. 15.1–4: The certainty of this prophecy. **1:** *Which I will put in your mouth*, Is.51.16; Jer.1.9.

15.5–11: God will take vengeance upon the wicked. 9: *All the innocent blood*, i.e. all the souls of the righteous (compare Rev.6.10; 19.2). **10:** Ps.44.22; Is.53.7. **11:** *Will smite Egypt . . . as before*, perhaps an allusion to the occurrence during the reign of Gallienus (A.D. 260–268) of a terrible famine, followed by a plague, which killed two-thirds of the population of Alexandria.

15.12–27: The signs of the end. 15: *Nation . . . against nation*, Mt.24.7; Mk.13.8; Lk.21.10. **18:** Lk.21.26.

who sin and do not observe my commandments," says the Lord; 25"I will
not spare them. Depart, you faithless
children! Do not pollute my sanctuary." 26For the Lord knows all who
transgress against him; therefore he
will hand them over to death and
slaughter. 27For now calamities have
come upon the whole earth, and you
shall remain in them; for God will not
deliver you, because you have sinned
against him.

28 Behold, a terrifying sight, appearing from the east! 29The nations
of the dragons of Arabia shall come
out with many chariots, and from
the day that they set out, their hissing
shall spread over the earth, so that all
who hear them fear and tremble.
30Also the Carmonians, raging in
wrath, shall go forth like wild boars
of the forest, and with great power
they shall come, and engage them
in battle, and shall devastate a portion
of the land of the Assyrians with their
teeth. 31And then the dragons, remembering their origin, shall become
still stronger; and if they combine in
great power and turn to pursue them,
32then these shall be disorganized and
silenced by their power, and shall turn
and flee. 33And from the land of the
Assyrians an enemy in ambush shall
beset them and destroy one of them,
and fear and trembling shall come upon
their army, and indecision upon their
kings.

34 Behold, clouds from the east,
and from the north to the south; and
their appearance is very threatening,
full of wrath and storm. 35They shall
dash against one another and shall
pour out a heavy tempest upon the
earth, and their own tempest; and
there shall be blood from the sword
as high as a horse's belly 36and a man's
thigh and a camel's hock. 37And there
shall be fear and great trembling upon
the earth; and those who see that
wrath shall be horror-stricken, and they
shall be seized with trembling. 38And,
after that, heavy storm clouds shall be
stirred up from the south, and from the
north, and another part from the west.
39And the winds from the east shall
prevail over the cloud that was[z] raised
in wrath, and shall dispel it; and the
tempest that was to cause destruction
by the east wind shall be driven violently toward the south and west.
40And great and mighty clouds, full
of wrath and tempest, shall rise, to
destroy all the earth and its inhabitants,
and shall pour out upon every high
and lofty place[a] a terrible tempest,
41fire and hail and flying swords and
floods of water, that all the fields and
all the streams may be filled with the
abundance of those waters. 42And
they shall destroy cities and walls,
mountains and hills, trees of the forests, and grass of the meadows, and
their grain. 43And they shall go on
steadily to Babylon, and shall destroy
her. 44They shall come to her and
surround her; they shall pour out the
tempest and all its wrath upon her;
then the dust and smoke shall go up
to heaven, and all who are about her
shall wail over her. 45And those who
survive shall serve those who have destroyed her.

46 And you, Asia, who share in the
glamour of Babylon and the glory of
her person—47woe to you, miserable
wretch! For you have made yourself
like her; you have decked out your
daughters in harlotry to please and
glory in your lovers, who have always
lusted after you. 48You have imitated
that hateful harlot in all her deeds
and devices; therefore God says, 49"I

z Literally *that he*
a Or *eminent person*

15.28–63: A vision of warfare. This section is thought to reflect events of the third century A.D., including the attack of King Sapor I of Persia (A.D. 240–273) upon the Roman province of Syria. **30:** *The Carmonians,* from Carmania (Kirman), the southern province of the Parthian empire. *Like wild boars,* Ps.8.13. **35:** *As high as . . .*, Rev.14.20. **43:** *Babylon,* i.e. Rome. **47–48:** Rev.14.8; 17.4–5. **49:** Rev.18.7–8.

will send evils upon you, widowhood,
poverty, famine, sword, and pestilence, to lay waste your houses and
bring you to destruction and death.
50And the glory of your power shall
wither like a flower, when the heat
rises that is sent upon you. 51You
shall be weakened like a wretched
woman who is beaten and wounded,
so that you cannot receive your
mighty lovers. 52Would I have dealt
with you so violently," says the Lord,
53"if you had not always killed my
chosen people, exulting and clapping
your hands and talking about their
death when you were drunk? 54Trick
out the beauty of your face! 55The
reward of a harlot is in your bosom,
therefore you shall receive your recompense. 56As you will do to my
chosen people," says the Lord, "so
God will do to you, and will hand
you over to adversities. 57Your children shall die of hunger, and you shall
fall by the sword, and your cities shall
be wiped out, and all your people who
are in the open country shall fall by
the sword. 58And those who are in the
mountains and highlands[b] shall perish
of hunger, and they shall eat their own
flesh in hunger for bread and drink
their own blood in thirst for water.
59Unhappy above all others, you shall
come and suffer fresh afflictions. 60And
as they pass they shall wreck the hateful[c] city, and shall destroy a part of
your land and abolish a portion of your
glory, as they return from devastated
Babylon. 61And you shall be broken
down by them like stubble, and they
shall be like fire to you. 62And they
shall devour you and your cities, your
land and your mountains; they shall
burn with fire all your forests and your
fruitful trees. 63They shall carry your
children away captive, and shall plunder your wealth, and abolish the glory
of your countenance."

16 Woe to you, Babylon and Asia!
Woe to you, Egypt and Syria!
2Gird yourselves with sackcloth and
haircloth, and wail for your children,
and lament for them; for your destruction is at hand. 3The sword has been
sent upon you, and who is there to turn
it back? 4A fire has been sent upon
you, and who is there to quench it?
5Calamities have been sent upon you,
and who is there to drive them away?
6Can one drive off a hungry lion in the
forest, or quench a fire in the stubble,
when once it has begun to burn? 7Can
one turn back an arrow shot by a strong
archer? 8The Lord God sends calamities, and who will drive them away?
9Fire will go forth from his wrath, and
who is there to quench it? 10He will
flash lightning, and who will not be
afraid? He will thunder, and who will
not be terrified? 11The Lord will
threaten, and who will not be utterly
shattered at his presence? 12The earth
and its foundations quake, the sea is
churned up from the depths, and its
waves and the fish also shall be
troubled at the presence of the Lord
and before the glory of his power.
13For his right hand that bends the bow
is strong, and his arrows that he shoots
are sharp and will not miss when they
begin to be shot to the ends of the
world. 14Behold, calamities are sent
forth and shall not return until they
come over the earth. 15The fire is
kindled, and shall not be put out until
it consumes the foundations of the
earth. 16Just as an arrow shot by a
mighty archer does not return, so the
calamities that are sent upon the earth
shall not return. 17Alas for me! Alas
for me! Who will deliver me in those
days?

18 The beginning of sorrows, when
there shall be much lamentation; the
beginning of famine, when many shall
perish; the beginning of wars, when
the powers shall be terrified; the beginning of calamities, when all shall

b Gk: Latin omits *and highlands*
c Another reading is *idle* or *unprofitable*

16.1–34: Denunciation of Babylon, Asia, Egypt, and Syria. 1: *Babylon,* i.e. Rome. **2:** *Sackcloth and haircloth,* signs of mourning. **12:** Ps.18.15. **15:** *Until it consumes . . . the earth,* an

tremble. What shall they do in these
circumstances, when the calamities
come? [19]Behold, famine and plague,
tribulation and anguish are sent as
scourges for the correction of men.
[20]Yet for all this they will not turn
from their iniquities, nor be always
mindful of the scourges. [21]Behold,
provisions will be so cheap upon earth
that men will imagine that peace is
assured for them, and then the calamities shall spring up on the earth—the
sword, famine, and great confusion.
[22]For many of those who live on the
earth shall perish by famine; and those
who survive the famine shall die by
the sword. [23]And the dead shall be
cast out like dung, and there shall be
no one to console them; for the earth
shall be left desolate, and its cities shall
be demolished. [24]No one shall be left
to cultivate the earth or to sow it.
[25]The trees shall bear fruit, and who
will gather it? [26]The grapes shall ripen,
and who will tread them? For in all
places there shall be great solitude;
[27]one man will long to see another, or
even to hear his voice. [28]For out of a
city, ten shall be left; and out of the
field, two who have hidden themselves
in thick groves and clefts in the rocks.
[29]As in an olive orchard three or four
olives may be left on every tree, [30]or
as when a vineyard is gathered some
clusters may be left by those who
search carefully through the vineyard,
[31]so in those days three or four shall be
left by those who search their houses
with the sword. [32]And the earth shall
be left desolate, and its fields shall be
for briers, and its roads and all its paths
shall bring forth thorns, because no
sheep will go along them. [33]Virgins
shall mourn because they have no
bridegrooms; women shall mourn because they have no husbands; their
daughters shall mourn, because they
have no helpers. [34]Their bridegrooms
shall be killed in war, and their husbands shall perish of famine.

35 Listen now to these things, and
understand them, O servants of the
Lord. [36]Behold the word of the Lord,
receive it; do not disbelieve what the
Lord says.[d] [37]Behold, the calamities
draw near, and are not delayed. [38]Just
as a woman with child, in the ninth
month, when the time of her delivery
draws near, has great pains about her
womb for two or three hours beforehand, and when the child comes forth
from the womb, there will not be a
moment's delay, [39]so the calamities
will not delay in coming forth upon the
earth, and the world will groan, and
pains will seize it on every side.

40 "Hear my words, O my people;
prepare for battle, and in the midst of
the calamities be like strangers on the
earth. [41]Let him that sells be like one
who will flee; let him that buys be like
one who will lose; [42]let him that does
business be like one who will not make
a profit; and let him that builds a house
be like one who will not live in it; [43]let
him that sows be like one who will not
reap; so also him that prunes the vines,
like one who will not gather the grapes;
[44]them that marry, like those who will
have no children; and them that do
not marry, like those who are widowed.
[45]Because those who labor, labor in
vain; [46]for strangers shall gather their
fruits, and plunder their goods, and
overthrow their houses, and take their
children captive; for in captivity and
famine they will beget their children.
[47]Those who conduct business, do it
only to be plundered; the more they
adorn their cities, their houses and possessions, and their persons, [48]the more
angry I will be with them for their sins,"
says the Lord. [49]Just as a respectable
and virtuous woman abhors a harlot,
[50]so righteousness shall abhor iniquity,
when she decks herself out, and shall
accuse her to her face, when he comes
who will defend him who searches out
every sin on earth.

d Cn: Lat *do not believe the gods of whom the Lord speaks*

---

apocalyptic idea from Persian eschatology (compare 2 Pet.3.10). **19:** Heb.12.5–11. **29:** Is.17.6.
16.35–50: God's people are warned of impending disasters. **38:** 4.40. **41:** 1 Cor.7.29–31.

51 Therefore do not be like her or
her works. 52For behold, just a little
while, and iniquity will be removed
from the earth, and righteousness will
reign over us. 53Let no sinner say that
he has not sinned; for God[e] will burn
coals of fire on the head of him who
says, "I have not sinned before God
and his glory." 54Behold, the Lord
knows all the works of men, their
imaginations and their thoughts and
their hearts. 55He said, "Let the earth
be made," and it was made; "Let the
heaven be made," and it was made.
56At his word the stars were fixed, and
he knows the number of the stars. 57It
is he who searches the deep and its
treasures, who has measured the sea
and its contents; 58who has enclosed
the sea in the midst of the waters, and
by his word has suspended the earth
over the water; 59who has spread out
the heaven like an arch, and founded it
upon the waters; 60who has put springs
of water in the desert, and pools on the
tops of the mountains, to send rivers
from the heights to water the earth;
61who formed man, and put a heart in
the midst of his body, and gave him
breath and life and understanding 62and
the spirit of Almighty God; who made
all things and searches out hidden
things in hidden places. 63Surely he
knows your imaginations and what you
think in your hearts! Woe to those
who sin and want to hide their sins!
64Because the Lord will strictly examine
all their works, and will make a public
spectacle of all of you. 65And when
your sins come out before men, you
shall be put to shame; and your own
iniquities shall stand as your accusers
in that day. 66What will you do? Or
how will you hide your sins before God
and his angels? 67Behold, God is the
judge, fear him! Cease from your sins,
and forget your iniquities, never to
commit them again; so God will lead
you forth and deliver you from all
tribulation.

68 For behold, the burning wrath
of a great multitude is kindled over
you, and they shall carry off some of
you and shall feed you what was sacrificed to idols. 69And those who consent to eat shall be held in[f] derision
and contempt, and be trodden under
foot. 70For in many places[g] and in
neighboring cities there shall be a great
insurrection against those who fear the
Lord. 71They shall be like mad men,
sparing no one, but plundering and
destroying those who continue to fear
the Lord. 72For they shall destroy and
plunder their goods, and drive them
out of their houses. 73Then the tested
quality of my elect shall be manifest,
as gold that is tested by fire.

74 "Hear, my elect," says the Lord.
"Behold, the days of tribulation are at
hand, and I will deliver you from them.
75Do not fear or doubt, for God is your
guide. 76You who keep my commandments and precepts," says the Lord
God, "do not let your sins pull you
down, or your iniquities prevail over
you." 77Woe to those who are choked
by their sins and overwhelmed by their
iniquities, as a field is choked with
underbrush and its path[h] overwhelmed
with thorns, so that no one can pass
through! 78It is shut off and given up
to be consumed by fire.

e Literally *he*
f Literally *consent to them shall be for these in*
g The Latin is uncertain
h Another reading is *seed*

16.51–67: The impossibility of hiding sin from God.
16.68–78: Though persecuted, God's elect will be delivered. 73: Zech.13.9; 1 Pet.1.7.

TOBIT

A fascinating amalgam of *Arabian Nights* romance, kindly Jewish piety, and sound moral teaching, Tobit is one of the most popular of the books of the Apocrypha. Originally composed in Hebrew or Aramaic, probably sometime during the second century B.C., its author is unknown, as is also the place where he wrote it, although Jerusalem, Antioch, and Alexandria have all been suggested as possibilities.

Besides the intrinsic interest of the tale, which is compounded in large part of themes derived from ancient folklore, the book's principal value lies in the picture it gives of Jewish culture and religious life in an age not too remote, either in time or temper, from that of the New Testament.

The ostensible setting of the story is the Assyrian capital, Nineveh, where the people of Northern Israel had been taken captive in the latter part of the eighth century B.C. (2 Kg.17.1–6). There, it is said, dwelt the pious Tobit, who, despite his many charitable deeds, became blind and poor (chs. 1–2). But God heard his prayer, as well as the prayer of demon-haunted Sarah in faraway Media, and sent the angel Raphael to save them both (ch. 3). When Tobit commissioned his son Tobias to collect a deposit of money he had made long before in Media, the angel accompanied him and revealed magic formulas which would heal his father's blindness and exorcise Sarah's demon-lover, Asmodeus (chs. 4–6). Tobias successfully completed his mission and married Sarah (chs. 7–14).

The book exists in numerous recensions and versions which differ considerably from one another in matters of detail.

THE BOOK OF THE ACTS[a] OF TOBIT
the son of Tobiel, son of Ananiel,
son of Aduel, son of Gabael, of the
descendants of Asiel and the tribe
of Naphtali, 2 who in the days of
Shalmaneser,[b] king of the Assyrians,
was taken into captivity from Thisbe,
which is to the south of Kedesh
Naphtali in Galilee above Asher.
3 I, Tobit, walked in the ways of
truth and righteousness all the days
of my life, and I performed many acts
of charity to my brethren and countrymen who went with me into the land of
the Assyrians, to Nineveh. 4 Now when
I was in my own country, in the land of
Israel, while I was still a young man,
the whole tribe of Naphtali my forefather deserted the house of Jerusalem.
This was the place which had been
chosen from among all the tribes of
Israel, where all the tribes should sacrifice and where the temple of the
dwelling of the Most High was consecrated and established for all generations for ever.
5 All the tribes that joined in apostasy used to sacrifice to the calf[c]
Baal, and so did the house of Naphtali
my forefather. 6 But I alone went often
to Jerusalem for the feasts, as it is
ordained for all Israel by an everlasting
decree. Taking the first fruits and the
tithes of my produce and the first
shearings, I would give these to the
priests, the sons of Aaron, at the altar.
7 Of all my produce I would give a tenth
to the sons of Levi who ministered at
Jerusalem; a second tenth I would sell,

a Gk *words*
b Gk *Enemessarus*
c Other authorities read *heifer*

1.1–2: Title. 2: *Shalmaneser* (or rather Sargon; see v. 15 n.) took Samaria, the capital of Israel, in 722 B.C. and transported a large part of the population to Assyria (2 Kg.17.1–6). *Thisbe* is unidentified. *Kedesh Naphtali*, 2 Kg.15.29. *Asher* is probably Hazor.

1.3–3.6: Tobit's own account of his virtuous life and unhappy fate.

1.3–22: Tobit's piety brings him into conflict with the king. 3: *Nineveh* was the capital of Assyria. **4:** Since the rebellion of the northern tribes against Jerusalem (1 Kg.12.19–20) occurred about 922 B.C., Tobit could not have been *still a young man*, or even born, when it happened. Such chronological, and other historical, difficulties make it clear that the story is fiction (compare v. 15 n., 6.1 n., 9.2 n., 14.15 n.). **5:** *Calf*, 1 Kg.12.28–29. **6–8:** During the apostasy, Tobit alone remains loyal to the divinely-appointed temple in Jerusalem. **6:** *An everlasting decree*, Dt.12.11,

and I would go and spend the proceeds
each year at Jerusalem; 8 the third
tenth I would give to those to whom
it was my duty, as Deborah my father's
mother had commanded me, for I was
left an orphan by my father. 9 When I
became a man I married Anna, a
member of our family, and by her I
became the father of Tobias.

10 Now when I was carried away
captive to Nineveh, all my brethren
and my relatives ate the food of the
Gentiles; 11 but I kept myself from
eating it, 12 because I remembered God
with all my heart. 13 Then the Most
High gave me favor and good appearance in the sight of Shalmaneser,[b] and
I was his buyer of provisions. 14 So I
used to go into Media, and once at
Rages in Media I left ten talents of
silver in trust with Gabael, the brother
of Gabrias. 15 But when Shalmaneser[b]
died, Sennacherib his son reigned in
his place; and under him the highways
were unsafe, so that I could no longer
go into Media.

16 In the days of Shalmaneser[b] I
performed many acts of charity to my
brethren. 17 I would give my bread to
the hungry and my clothing to the
naked; and if I saw any one of my
people dead and thrown out behind
the wall of Nineveh, I would bury him.
18 And if Sennacherib the king put to
death any who came fleeing from
Judea, I buried them secretly. For in
his anger he put many to death. When
the bodies were sought by the king,
they were not found. 19 Then one of
the men of Nineveh went and informed
the king about me, that I was burying
them; so I hid myself. When I learned
that I was being searched for, to be put
to death, I left home in fear. 20 Then all
my property was confiscated and nothing was left to me except my wife Anna
and my son Tobias.

21 But not fifty[d] days passed before
two of Sennacherib's[e] sons killed him,
and they fled to the mountains of
Ararat. Then Esarhaddon,[f] his son,
reigned in his place; and he appointed
Ahikar, the son of my brother Anael,
over all the accounts of his kingdom
and over the entire administration.
22 Ahikar interceded for me, and I returned to Nineveh. Now Ahikar was
cupbearer, keeper of the signet, and in
charge of administration of the accounts, for Esarhaddon[f] had appointed
him second to himself.[g] He was my
nephew.

2 When I arrived home and my wife
Anna and my son Tobias were
restored to me, at the feast of Pentecost,
which is the sacred festival of the seven
weeks, a good dinner was prepared for
me and I sat down to eat. 2 Upon seeing
the abundance of food I said to my son,
"Go and bring whatever poor man of
our brethren you may find who is mindful of the Lord, and I will wait for
you." 3 But he came back and said,
"Father, one of our people has been
strangled and thrown into the market

b Gk *Enemessarus*
d Other authorities read *fifty-five*
e Gk *his* *f* Gk *Sacherdonus*
g Or *a second time*

13–14. **10–12:** Even in captivity among Gentiles Tobit refuses to violate the dietary laws. **14:** *Media* is the northern part of modern Iran, east of Assyria. *Rages* was an important city whose ruins are located about five miles southeast of modern Teheran. *Ten talents,* at least $10,000. **15–20:** Tobit arouses Sennacherib's wrath and flees the country. **15:** *Shalmaneser* actually died before the fall of Samaria, which was taken by Sargon. *Sennacherib* succeeded his father Sargon in 705 B.C. **17:** It was for the Jews a great calamity that a dead body should lie unburied. **21–22:** Under a new king, *Esarhaddon* (681–669 B.C.), Tobit is able to return. **21:** *Ahikar* was a legendary ancient wise man whose story survives in several oriental languages. An Aramaic version of his adventures, dating from the fifth century B.C., was found among the Jewish papyri at Elephantine in upper Egypt (see also 14.10 n.).

2.1–14: Another act of charity results in Tobit's blindness and impoverishment. **1:** *Pentecost . . . seven weeks,* approximately, after Passover (Lev.23.15–21; Dt.16.9–11). **2:** Generosity toward the poor is one of the virtues taught by this book (4.7–11,16). **3:** *Strangled,* presumably executed (compare 1.18). Leaving the body unburied was intended as additional punishment, so

place.” 4So before I tasted anything
I sprang up and removed the body[h] to
a place of shelter until sunset. 5And
when I returned I washed myself and
ate my food in sorrow. 6Then I remembered the prophecy of Amos, how he
said,

“Your feasts shall be turned into
mourning,
and all your festivities into
lamentation.”

And I wept.

7 When the sun had set I went and
dug a grave and buried the body.[h]
8And my neighbors laughed at me
and said, “He is no longer afraid that
he will be put to death for doing this;
he once ran away, and here he is burying the dead again!” 9On the same
night I returned from burying him,
and because I was defiled I slept by the
wall of the courtyard, and my face was
uncovered. 10I did not know that
there were sparrows on the wall and
their fresh droppings fell into my open
eyes and white films formed on my
eyes. I went to physicians, but they
did not help me. Ahikar, however,
took care of me until he[i] went to Elymais.

11 Then my wife Anna earned money
at women’s work. 12She used to send
the product to the owners. Once when
they paid her wages, they also gave her
a kid; 13and when she returned to me
it began to bleat. So I said to her,
“Where did you get the kid? It is not
stolen, is it? Return it to the owners;
for it is not right to eat what is stolen.”
14And she said, “It was given to me as
a gift in addition to my wages.” But I
did not believe her, and told her to
return it to the owners; and I blushed
for her. Then she replied to me,
“Where are your charities and your
righteous deeds? You seem to know
everything!”

3 Then in my grief I wept, and I
prayed in anguish, saying, 2“Righteous art thou, O Lord; all thy deeds
and all thy ways are mercy and truth,
and thou dost render true and righteous
judgment for ever. 3Remember me
and look favorably upon me; do not
punish me for my sins and for my
unwitting offenses and those which my
fathers committed before thee. 4For
they disobeyed thy commandments,
and thou gavest us over to plunder,
captivity, and death; thou madest us a
byword of reproach in all the nations
among which we have been dispersed.
5And now thy many judgments are
true in exacting penalty from me for
my sins and those of my fathers, because we did not keep thy commandments. For we did not walk in truth
before thee. 6And now deal with me
according to thy pleasure; command
my spirit to be taken up, that I may depart and become dust. For it is better
for me to die than to live, because I
have heard false reproaches, and great
is the sorrow within me. Command
that I now be released from my distress
to go to the eternal abode; do not turn
thy face away from me.”

7 On the same day, at Ecbatana in
Media, it also happened that Sarah,
the daughter of Raguel, was reproached
by her father’s maids, 8because she had
been given to seven husbands, and the
evil demon Asmodeus had slain each
of them before he had been with her as
his wife. So the maids[j] said to her,
“Do you not know that you strangle
your husbands? You already have had
seven and have had no benefit[k] from
any of them. 9Why do you beat us? If
they are dead, go with them! May we
never see a son or daughter of yours!”

h Gk *him* *i* Other authorities read *I* *j* Gk *they*
k Other authorities read *have not borne the name of*

Tobit’s act of charity was an act of defiance toward the king. **5:** *Washed myself*, ceremonially, after touching a corpse (Num.19.11–13). **9:** *Defiled*, from handling the corpse. **10:** *Elymais*, a city, or possibly a region, in Persia (1 Macc.6.1).

3.1–6: Tobit’s prayer.

3.7–17: God hears the prayer of Tobit, and also of Sarah, plagued by a demon-lover. From this point on the story is told in the third person. **7–10:** Sarah contemplates suicide. **7:** *Ecbatana*,

10 When she heard these things she
was deeply grieved, even to the thought
of hanging herself. But she said, "I am
the only child of my father; if I do this,
it will be a disgrace to him, and I shall
bring his old age down in sorrow to the
grave."[l] 11So she prayed by her win-
dow and said, "Blessed art thou, O
Lord my God, and blessed is thy holy
and honored name for ever. May all
thy works praise thee for ever. 12And
now, O Lord, I have turned my eyes
and my face toward thee. 13Command
that I be released from the earth and
that I hear reproach no more. 14Thou
knowest, O Lord, that I am innocent
of any sin with man, 15and that I did
not stain my name or the name of my
father in the land of my captivity. I am
my father's only child, and he has no
child to be his heir, no near kinsman
or kinsman's[m] son for whom I should
keep myself as wife. Already seven
husbands of mine are dead. Why
should I live? But if it be not pleasing
to thee to take my life, command that
respect be shown to me and pity be
taken upon me, and that I hear reproach no more."

16 The prayer of both was heard in
the presence of the glory of the great
God. 17And Raphael[n] was sent to heal
the two of them: to scale away the
white films from Tobit's eyes; to give
Sarah the daughter of Raguel in marriage to Tobias the son of Tobit, and
to bind Asmodeus the evil demon,
because Tobias was entitled to possess
her. At that very moment Tobit returned and entered his house and Sarah
the daughter of Raguel came down
from her upper room.

4 On that day Tobit remembered
the money which he had left in
trust with Gabael at Rages in Media,
and he said to himself: 2"I have asked
for death. Why do I not call my son
Tobias so that I may explain to him
about the money[o] before I die?" 3So
he called him and said, "My son, when
I die, bury me, and do not neglect your
mother. Honor her all the days of your
life; do what is pleasing to her, and do
not grieve her. 4Remember, my son,
that she faced many dangers for you
while you were yet unborn. When she
dies, bury her beside me in the same
grave.

5 "Remember the Lord our God all
your days, my son, and refuse to sin or
to transgress his commandments. Live
uprightly all the days of your life, and
do not walk in the ways of wrongdoing.
6For if you do what is true, your ways
will prosper through your deeds. 7Give
alms from your possessions to all who
live uprightly, and do not let your eye
begrudge the gift when you make it.
Do not turn your face away from any
poor man, and the face of God will
not be turned away from you. 8If you
have many possessions, make your gift
from them in proportion; if few, do
not be afraid to give according to the
little you have. 9So you will be laying
up a good treasure for yourself against
the day of necessity. 10For charity delivers from death and keeps you from entering the darkness; 11and for all who
practice it charity is an excellent offering
in the presence of the Most High.

12 "Beware, my son, of all immo-

l Gk *to Hades* *m* Gk *his*
n Other authorities read *the great Raphael. And he*
o Other authorities omit *about the money*

capital of Media, in Persia. **8:** The name *Asmodeus* means "destroyer." **11–15:** Sarah's prayer. **11:** *Blessed art thou* is the traditional beginning of a Jewish prayer (compare 8.5, 15 and see Jdt.13.17 n.). **16–17:** The angel Raphael is sent in answer to both the prayers. **17:** The name *Raphael* means "God heals." *Entitled to possess her*, 6.11. The phrase *at that very moment* is a dramatic device which heightens the interest of the story.

4.1–21: Preparing to send his son for the trust-money, Tobit imparts his philosophy of life. **1:** *The money . . . at Rages*, 1.14. **5–19:** This section of general ethical counsel epitomizes the moral teaching of the book. There are many close parallels with other books of wisdom, such as Proverbs and Sirach. **6:** Morality guarantees prosperity; a dogma of orthodox Hebrew wisdom (Ps.1.1–3, Pr.10.27–30). **7–11:** The value of almsgiving; the emphasis is typical of the period (12.8–9; 14.10–11; Sir.3.30; 35.2; Mt.6.2–4). **12–13:** One should marry within his own

rality. First of all take a wife from
among the descendants of your fathers
and do not marry a foreign woman,
who is not of your father's tribe; for
we are the sons of the prophets. Remember, my son, that Noah, Abraham,
Isaac, and Jacob, our fathers of old,
all took wives from among their brethren. They were blessed in their children, and their posterity will inherit
the land. [13]So now, my son, love your
brethren, and in your heart do not disdain your brethren and the sons and
daughters of your people by refusing
to take a wife for yourself from among
them. For in pride there is ruin and
great confusion; and in shiftlessness
there is loss and great want, because
shiftlessness is the mother of famine.
[14]Do not hold over till the next day
the wages of any man who works for
you, but pay him at once; and if you
serve God you will receive payment.
"Watch yourself, my son, in everything you do, and be disciplined in all
your conduct. [15]And what you hate,
do not do to any one. Do not drink
wine to excess or let drunkenness go
with you on your way. [16]Give of your
bread to the hungry, and of your
clothing to the naked. Give all your
surplus to charity, and do not let your
eye begrudge the gift when you make
it. [17]Place your bread on the grave of
the righteous, but give none to sinners.
[18]Seek advice from every wise man, and
do not despise any useful counsel.
[19]Bless the Lord God on every occasion; ask him that your ways may be
made straight and that all your paths
and plans may prosper. For none of
the nations has understanding; but the
Lord himself gives all good things, and
according to his will he humbles whom-
ever he wishes.
"So, my son, remember my commands, and do not let them be blotted
out of your mind. [20]And now let me
explain to you about the ten talents of
silver which I left in trust with Gabael
the son of Gabrias at Rages in Media.
[21]Do not be afraid, my son, because
we have become poor. You have great
wealth if you fear God and refrain from
every sin and do what is pleasing in his
sight."

5 Then Tobias answered him,
"Father, I will do everything that
you have commanded me; [2]but how
can I obtain the money when I do not
know the man?" [3]Then Tobit gave
him the receipt, and said to him, "Find
a man to go with you and I will pay
him wages as long as I live; and go and
get the money." [4]So he went to look
for a man; and he found Raphael, who
was an angel, [5]but Tobias[p] did not
know it. Tobias[p] said to him, "Can
you go with me to Rages in Media?
Are you acquainted with that region?"
[6]The angel replied, "I will go with you;
I am familiar with the way, and I have
stayed with our brother Gabael."
[7]Then Tobias said to him, "Wait for
me, and I shall tell my father." [8]And
he said to him, "Go, and do not
delay." So he went in and said to his
father, "I have found some one to go
with me." He said, "Call him to me,
so that I may learn to what tribe he
belongs, and whether he is a reliable
man to go with you."
9 So Tobias[p] invited him in; he
entered and they greeted each other.
[10]Then Tobit said to him, "My

p Gk *he*

family group; this is a keynote of the book (1.9; 3.15; 6.11–12). **13:** *Pride*, Pr.16.18. *Shiftlessness*, Pr.19.15; Sir.22.1–2. **14:** Lev.19.13. **15:** *What you hate, do not do*, the Golden Rule (Mt.7.12) in negative form, which was enunciated also by the great Jewish teacher, Hillel (flourished in the time of Herod the Great, 37–4 B.C.). *Wine*, Pr.23.29–35; Sir.31.29–31. **16:** Compare vv. 7–11. **17:** Placing food on graves was a pagan practice, forbidden in the Old Testament (Dt.26.14) and deprecated by many Jews (compare Sir.30.18). Some interpret the verse as a reference to the meals provided the mourners at funerals (compare Jer.16.7; Ezek.24.17). **19:** A sound moral life needs to be sustained by prayer.

5.1–21: Raphael, in the disguise of Azarias, is employed as Tobias' guide. 5: *Tobias did not know it*, as frequently in folklore, where angels (or gods) traveling in disguise are a favorite

brother, to what tribe and family do
you belong? Tell me." 11But he answered, "Are you looking for a tribe
and a family or for a man whom you
will pay to go with your son?" And
Tobit said to him, "I should like to
know, my brother, your people and
your name." 12He replied, "I am
Azarias the son of the great Ananias,
one of your relatives." 13Then Tobit
said to him, "You are welcome, my
brother. Do not be angry with me
because I tried to learn your tribe and
family. You are a relative of mine, of
a good and noble lineage. For I used
to know Ananias and Jathan, the sons
of the great Shemaiah, when we went
together to Jerusalem to worship and
offered the first-born of our flocks and
the tithes of our produce. They did
not go astray in the error of our brethren. My brother, you come of good
stock. 14But tell me, what wages
am I to pay you—a drachma a day,
and expenses for yourself as for
my son? 15And besides, I will add to
your wages if you both return safe
and sound." So they agreed to these
terms.

16 Then he said to Tobias, "Get
ready for the journey, and good success to you both." So his son made
the preparations for the journey. And
his father said to him, "Go with this
man; God who dwells in heaven will
prosper your way, and may his angel
attend you." So they both went out
and departed, and the young man's
dog was with them.

17 But Anna,[q] his mother, began to
weep, and said to Tobit, "Why have
you sent our child away? Is he not the
staff of our hands as he goes in and out
before us? 18Do not add money to
money, but consider it rubbish as compared to our child. 19For the life that
is given to us by the Lord is enough for
us." 20And Tobit said to her, "Do not
worry, my sister; he will return safe
and sound, and your eyes will see him.
21For a good angel will go with him;
his journey will be successful, and he
will come back safe and sound." So
she stopped weeping.

6 Now as they proceeded on their
way they came at evening to the
Tigris river and camped there. 2Then
the young man went down to wash
himself. A fish leaped up from the river
and would have swallowed the young
man; 3and the angel said to him,
"Catch the fish." So the young man
seized the fish and threw it up on the
land. 4Then the angel said to him,
"Cut open the fish and take the heart
and liver and gall and put them away
safely." 5So the young man did as the
angel told him; and they roasted and
ate the fish.

And they both continued on their
way until they came near to Ecbatana.
6Then the young man said to the angel,
"Brother Azarias, of what use is
the liver and heart and gall of the
fish?" 7He replied, "As for the heart
and the liver, if a demon or evil
spirit gives trouble to any one, you
make a smoke from these before the
man or woman, and that person will
never be troubled again. 8And as for
the gall, anoint with it a man who has
white films in his eyes, and he will be
cured."

9 When they approached Ecbatana,[r]
10the angel said to the young man,
"Brother, today we shall stay with
Raguel. He is your relative, and he has

q Other authorities omit *Anna*
r Other authorities read *Rages*

theme (compare Gen. ch. 18; Heb.13.2). **12:** In Hebrew *Azarias* means "God helps." **14:** A *drachma* was the normal day's wage for an artisan, about sixteen cents. **16:** The *dog* is a surprising feature of the story, but plays no special role (see 11.4 n.). **21:** Pleasing irony; Tobit does not know that Raphael is the *good angel.*

6.1–8: On the journey, Raphael instructs Tobias in obtaining magical medicines from a man-eating fish. **1:** *The Tigris* is actually west of Nineveh, so they would not have crossed it going to Persia (see 1.4 n.). **6–8:** Belief in the healing properties of the fish's organs is typical of folklore.

6.9–17: Raphael prepares Tobias to seek the hand of Sarah. **12:** *According to the law of Moses,*

an only daughter named Sarah. I will
suggest that she be given to you in
marriage, 11because you are entitled to
her and to her inheritance, for you are
her only eligible kinsman. 12The girl
is also beautiful and sensible. Now
listen to my plan. I will speak to her
father, and as soon as we return from
Rages we will celebrate the marriage.
For I know that Raguel, according to
the law of Moses, cannot give her to
another man without incurring the
penalty of death, because you rather
than any other man are entitled to the
inheritance."

13 Then the young man said to the
angel, "Brother Azarias, I have heard
that the girl has been given to seven
husbands and that each died in the
bridal chamber. 14Now I am the only
son my father has, and I am afraid that
if I go in I will die as those before me
did, for a demon is in love with her,
and he harms no one except those who
approach her. So now I fear that I may
die and bring the lives of my father and
mother to the grave in sorrow on my
account. And they have no other son
to bury them."

15 But the angel said to him, "Do
you remember the words with which
your father commanded you to take
a wife from among your own people?
Now listen to me, brother, for she will
become your wife; and do not worry
about the demon, for this very night
she will be given to you in marriage.
16When you enter the bridal chamber,
you shall take live ashes of incense and
lay upon them some of the heart and
liver of the fish so as to make a smoke.
17Then the demon will smell it and flee
away, and will never again return. And
when you approach her, rise up, both
of you, and cry out to the merciful
God, and he will save you and have
mercy on you. Do not be afraid, for
she was destined for you from eternity.
You will save her, and she will go with
you, and I suppose that you will have
children by her." When Tobias heard
these things, he fell in love with her and
yearned deeply for her.

7 When they reached Ecbatana and
arrived at the house of Raguel,
Sarah met them and greeted them.
They returned her greeting, and she
brought them into the house. 2Then
Raguel said to his wife Edna, "How
much the young man resembles my
cousin Tobit!" 3And Raguel asked
them, "Where are you from, brethren?" They answered him, "We belong
to the sons of Naphtali, who are captives in Nineveh." 4So he said to them,
"Do you know our brother Tobit?"
And they said, "Yes, we do." And he
asked them, "Is he in good health?"
5They replied, "He is alive and in good
health." And Tobias said, "He is my
father." 6Then Raguel sprang up and
kissed him and wept. 7And he blessed
him and exclaimed, "Son of that good
and noble man!" When he heard that
Tobit had lost his sight, he was stricken
with grief and wept. 8And his wife
Edna and his daughter Sarah wept.
They received them very warmly; and
they killed a ram from the flock
and set large servings of food before
them.

Then Tobias said to Raphael,
"Brother Azarias, speak of those
things which you talked about on the
journey, and let the matter be settled."
9So he communicated the proposal to
Raguel. And Raguel said to Tobias,
"Eat, drink, and be merry; 10for it is
your right to take my child. But let me

---

presumably Num.36.6–8, although there is no mention of a death penalty. **14:** *To bury them*, one of the chief concerns of this book (see 1.17 n.; 4.3–4; 14.10). **17:** *Cry out . . . to God*, magic is not enough, prayer is necessary too. *From eternity*, "marriages are made in heaven" (compare Gen.24.14).

7.1–8a: Tobias and Raphael arrive at the home of Sarah's father. 1: *Ecbatana*, 3.7. The following conversation implies that Sarah and her family had not previously been aware of Tobias' existence. **4–5:** The Syriac and Latin Vulgate omit the conversation about Tobit's health, probably on account of his blindness.

explain the true situation to you. 11I
have given my daughter to seven husbands, and when each came to her he
died in the night. But for the present
be merry." And Tobias said, "I will
eat nothing here until you make a binding agreement with me." 12So Raguel
said, "Take her right now, in accordance with the law. You are her relative,
and she is yours. The merciful God
will guide you both for the best."
13Then he called his daughter Sarah,
and taking her by the hand he gave her
to Tobias to be his wife, saying, "Here
she is; take her according to the law of
Moses, and take her with you to your
father." And he blessed them. 14Next
he called his wife Edna, and took a
scroll and wrote out the contract; and
they set their seals to it. 15Then they
began to eat.

16 And Raguel called his wife Edna
and said to her, "Sister, make up the
other room, and take her into it."
17So she did as he said, and took her
there; and the girl[s] began to weep.
But the mother[s] comforted her daughter in her tears, and said to her, 18"Be
brave, my child; the Lord of heaven
and earth grant you joy[t] in place of this
sorrow of yours. Be brave, my
daughter."

8 When they had finished eating,
they escorted Tobias in to her. 2As
he went he remembered the words of
Raphael, and he took the live ashes of
incense and put the heart and liver of
the fish upon them and made a smoke.
3And when the demon smelled the odor
he fled to the remotest parts of Egypt,
and the angel bound him. 4When the
door was shut and the two were alone,
Tobias got up from the bed and said,
"Sister, get up, and let us pray that the
Lord may have mercy upon us." 5And
Tobias began to pray,

"Blessed art thou, O God of our
fathers,
and blessed be thy holy and
glorious name for ever.
Let the heavens and all of thy
creatures bless thee.
6Thou madest Adam and gavest him
Eve his wife
as a helper and support.
From them the race of mankind
has sprung.
Thou didst say, 'It is not good that
the man should be alone;
let us make a helper for him like
himself.'

7And now, O Lord, I am not taking
this sister of mine because of lust, but
with sincerity. Grant that I may find
mercy and may grow old together
with her." 8And she said with him,
"Amen." 9Then they both went to
sleep for the night.

But Raguel arose and went and dug
a grave, 10with the thought, "Perhaps
he too will die." 11Then Raguel went
into his house 12and said to his wife
Edna, "Send one of the maids to see
whether he is alive; and if he is not, let
us bury him without any one knowing
about it." 13So the maid opened the
door and went in, and found them both
asleep. 14And she came out and told
them that he was alive. 15Then Raguel
blessed God and said,

"Blessed art thou, O God, with
every pure and holy blessing.
Let thy saints and all thy creatures
bless thee;
let all thy angels and thy chosen
people bless thee for ever.

s Gk *she*
t Other authorities read *favor*

7.8b–18: Tobias proposes and the wedding takes place. 13: *Taking her by the hand*, like a modern father "giving away the bride," he marries her to Tobias. **14:** Signing *the contract* was the only other ceremony required.

8.1–9a: On the wedding night, Tobias routs the demon. 3: *Egypt* was the traditional home of magic and witchcraft (compare Ex.7.11). **4:** See 6.17 n. **5–8:** Tobias and Sarah join in prayer before consummating the marriage. **5:** *Blessed art thou*, see 3.11 n.

8.9b–21: Raguel's fears are happily disappointed and he provides an extended wedding feast. 9b: *Dug a grave*, because he did not, of course, know that Tobias was provided with an effective means to drive away the demon. **19:** For joy Raguel doubles the usual length of a wedding

16Blessed art thou, because thou hast
made me glad.
It has not happened to me as I
expected;
but thou hast treated us according
to thy great mercy.
17Blessed art thou, because thou hast
had compassion on two only
children.
Show them mercy, O Lord;
and bring their lives to fulfilment
in health and happiness and
mercy."
18Then he ordered his servants to fill in
the grave.
19 After this he gave a wedding feast
for them which lasted fourteen days.
20And before the days of the feast were
over, Raguel declared by oath to
Tobias[u] that he should not leave until
the fourteen days of the wedding feast
were ended, 21that then he should take
half of Raguel's[v] property and return
in safety to his father, and that the
rest would be his "when my wife and I
die."
9 Then Tobias called Raphael and
said to him, 2"Brother Azarias,
take a servant and two camels with you
and go to Gabael at Rages in Media
and get the money for me; and bring
him to the wedding feast. 3For Raguel
has sworn that I should not leave; 4but
my father is counting the days, and if
I delay long he will be greatly distressed."
5So Raphael made the journey
and stayed overnight with Gabael.
He gave him the receipt, and Gabael[w]
brought out the money bags with their
seals intact and gave them to him. 6In
the morning they both got up early
and came to the wedding feast.
And Gabael blessed Tobias and his
wife.[x]
10 Now his father Tobit was counting
each day, and when the days
for the journey had expired and they
did not arrive, 2he said, "Is it possible
that he has been detained?[y] Or is it
possible that Gabael has died and there
is no one to give him the money?"
3And he was greatly distressed. 4And
his wife said to him, "The lad has
perished; his long delay proves it."
Then she began to mourn for him, and
said, 5"Am I not distressed, my child,
that I let you go, you who are the light
of my eyes?" 6But Tobit said to her,
"Be still and stop worrying; he is well."
7And she answered him, "Be still and
stop deceiving me; my child has
perished." And she went out every day
to the road by which they had left;
she ate nothing in the daytime, and
throughout the nights she never stopped
mourning for her son Tobias, until
the fourteen days of the wedding feast
had expired which Raguel had sworn
that he should spend there.
At that time Tobias said to Raguel,
"Send me back, for my father and
mother have given up hope of ever
seeing me again." 8But his father-in-law
said to him, "Stay with me, and I
will send messengers to your father,
and they will inform him how things
are with you." 9Tobias replied, "No,
send me back to my father." 10So
Raguel arose and gave him his wife

u Gk *him* *v* Gk *his* *w* Gk *he*
x Cn: Gk *And Tobias blessed his wife*
y One Gk Ms Lat: Gk *they are put to shame* or *they are disappointed*

feast (11.19; Jg.14.12). The oath complicates Tobias' affairs and makes necessary Raphael's solitary mission in the next chapter.

9.1–6: Raphael goes to Rages and obtains the money from Gabael. 2: From Ecbatana to *Rages* was a journey which, according to the ancient historian Arrian (*Anabasis*, III. 19–20), took Alexander's army eleven days of forced marches; the author evidently supposed it to be much shorter (see 1.4 n.). **3:** *Has sworn*, 8.20. **4:** Tobias' tender concern for his father is typical of the spirit of the book. The son's unwillingness to prolong his visit is thoroughly justified by the touching description of his parent's uneasiness in 10.1–7.

10.1–7a: Tobias' father and mother grow anxious at their son's absence. 1: In *counting each day*, Tobit had naturally made no allowance for a two-week wedding celebration. **4:** *The lad has perished*, the mother's feminine tendency to suspect the worst and her husband's courageous attempts to console her illustrate the author's fine sensitivity to human feeling.

Sarah and half of his property in slaves,
cattle, and money. 11 And when he had
blessed them he sent them away, saying, "The God of heaven will prosper
you, my children, before I die." 12 He
said also to his daughter, "Honor your
father-in-law and your mother-in-law;
they are now your parents. Let me
hear a good report of you." And he
kissed her. And Edna said to Tobias,
"The Lord of heaven bring you back
safely, dear brother, and grant me to
see your children by my daughter
Sarah, that I may rejoice before the
Lord. See, I am entrusting my daughter
to you; do nothing to grieve her."

11 After this Tobias went on his way,
praising God because he had made
his journey a success. And he blessed
Raguel and his wife Edna.
So he continued on his way until
they came near to Nineveh. 2 Then
Raphael said to Tobias, "Are you not
aware, brother, of how you left your
father? 3 Let us run ahead of your wife
and prepare the house. 4 And take the
gall of the fish with you." So they
went their way, and the dog went along
behind them.
5 Now Anna sat looking intently
down the road for her son. 6 And she
caught sight of him coming, and said
to his father, "Behold, your son is
coming, and so is the man who went
with him!"
7 Raphael said, "I know, Tobias,
that your father will open his eyes.
8 You therefore must anoint his eyes
with the gall; and when they smart he
will rub them, and will cause the white
films to fall away, and he will see you."
9 Then Anna ran to meet them, and
embraced her son, and said to him, "I
have seen you, my child; now I am
ready to die." And they both wept.
10 Tobit started toward the door, and
stumbled. But his son ran to him 11 and
took hold of his father, and he sprinkled
the gall upon his father's eyes, saying,
"Be of good cheer, father." 12 And
when his eyes began to smart he rubbed
them, 13 and the white films scaled off
from the corners of his eyes. 14 Then he
saw his son and embraced him, and he
wept and said, "Blessed art thou, O
God, and blessed is thy name for ever,
and blessed are all thy holy angels.
15 For thou hast afflicted me, but thou
hast had mercy upon me; here I see
my son Tobias!" And his son went in
rejoicing, and he reported to his father
the great things that had happened to
him in Media.
16 Then Tobit went out to meet his
daughter-in-law at the gate of Nineveh,
rejoicing and praising God. Those who
saw him as he went were amazed because he could see. 17 And Tobit gave
thanks before them that God had been
merciful to him. When Tobit came
near to Sarah his daughter-in-law, he
blessed her, saying, "Welcome, daughter! Blessed is God who has brought
you to us, and blessed are your father
and your mother." So there was rejoicing among all his brethren in
Nineveh. 18 Ahikar and his nephew
Nadab[z] came, 19 and Tobias' marriage
was celebrated for seven days with great
festivity.

12 Tobit then called his son Tobias
and said to him, "My son, see to
the wages of the man who went with
you; and he must also be given more."
2 He replied, "Father, it would do me

z Other authorities read *Nasbas*

10.7b–12: Tobias and Sarah start for home. 11: *The God of heaven* was a favorite name for Israel's God in the Persian period and later (Jdt.5.8; Ezra 1.2).

11.1–15: Tobias and Raphael precede Sarah into the city and heal Tobit's blindness. 4: *The dog* appears again for the first time since 5.16; perhaps his presence in the story is a survival from an older folk tale, in which he had a real function. **14:** *Blessed be God*, see 3.11 n.

11.16–19: Tobit meets his daughter-in-law and celebrates the marriage. 18: *Ahikar . . . Nadab*, see 14.10 n. **19:** *Seven days*, apparently the normal period of a wedding celebration (see 8.19 n.).

12.1–22: Raphael, being offered his wages, gives good advice and discloses his true identity. 1–5: Tobias generously wishes to reward Raphael far beyond the amount agreed upon (5.14).

no harm to give him half of what I have brought back. 3 For he has led me back to you safely, he cured my wife, he obtained the money for me, and he also healed you." 4 The old man said, "He deserves it." 5 So he called the angel and said to him, "Take half of all that you two have brought back."

6 Then the angel[a] called the two of them privately and said to them: "Praise God and give thanks to him; exalt him and give thanks to him in the presence of all the living for what he has done for you. It is good to praise God and to exalt his name, worthily declaring the works of God. Do not be slow to give him thanks. 7 It is good to guard the secret of a king, but gloriously to reveal the works of God. Do good, and evil will not overtake you. 8 Prayer is good when accompanied by fasting, almsgiving, and righteousness. A little with righteousness is better than much with wrongdoing. It is better to give alms than to treasure up gold. 9 For almsgiving delivers from death, and it will purge away every sin. Those who perform deeds of charity and of righteousness will have fulness of life; 10 but those who commit sin are the enemies of their own lives.

11 "I will not conceal anything from you. I have said, 'It is good to guard the secret of a king, but gloriously to reveal the works of God.' 12 And so, when you and your daughter-in-law Sarah prayed, I brought a reminder of your prayer before the Holy One; and when you buried the dead, I was likewise present with you. 13 When you did not hesitate to rise and leave your dinner in order to go and lay out the dead, your good deed was not hidden from me, but I was with you. 14 So now God sent me to heal you and your daughter-in-law Sarah. 15 I am Raphael, one of the seven holy angels who present the prayers of the saints and enter into the presence of the glory of the Holy One."

16 They were both alarmed; and they fell upon their faces, for they were afraid. 17 But he said to them, "Do not be afraid; you will be safe. But praise God for ever. 18 For I did not come as a favor on my part, but by the will of our God. Therefore praise him for ever. 19 All these days I merely appeared to you and did not eat or drink, but you were seeing a vision. 20 And now give thanks to God, for I am ascending to him who sent me. Write in a book everything that has happened." 21 Then they stood up; but they saw him no more. 22 So they confessed the great and wonderful works of God, and acknowledged that the angel of the Lord had appeared to them.

13 Then Tobit wrote a prayer of rejoicing, and said:

"Blessed is God who lives for ever,
and blessed is his kingdom.
2 For he afflicts, and he shows mercy;
he leads down to Hades, and
brings up again,
and there is no one who can
escape his hand.

a Gk *he*

6–10: In the style of a Jewish teacher of wisdom, Raphael delivers a brief exhortation on the good life, similar to that of Tobit in ch. 4. **8:** *Prayer . . . fasting, almsgiving, and righteousness* ("piety") are mentioned together also in Mt.6.1–18 (on almsgiving, compare 4.7–11 and see Sir.3.30 n.). **11:** V. 7. **12–15:** Raphael reveals himself as an angelic intercessor who brings the prayers of men into the presence of God. From v. 15 we learn that there are six others. "Uriel" is named in 2 Esd.4.1; "Gabriel" and "Michael," respectively, in Dan.9.21 and 10.13. The growth of angelology was characteristic of the Judaism of the period; this was partly due to an increasing sense of God's transcendence and partly, perhaps, to Persian influences. **17:** *Do not be afraid,* compare Mt.28.5,10.

13.1–18: Tobit's hymn of praise. Some scholars believe that chs. 13 and 14 were added to the book much later in order to give substance to the words of 12.22a and to round out the account of Tobit's life. The hymn contains numerous echoes of Old Testament passages and has no particular appropriateness to Tobit's personal situation. **1–6:** Exhortation to the exiles. **2:**

3 Acknowledge him before the nations,
O sons of Israel;
for he has scattered us among
them.
4 Make his greatness known there,
and exalt him in the presence of
all the living;
because he is our Lord and God,
he is our Father for ever.
5 He will afflict us for our iniquities;
and again he will show mercy,
and will gather us from all the
nations
among whom you[b] have been
scattered.
6 If you turn to him with all your heart
and with all your soul,
to do what is true before him,
then he will turn to you
and will not hide his face from
you.
But see what he will do with you;
give thanks to him with your
full voice.
Praise the Lord of righteousness,
and exalt the King of the ages.
I give him thanks in the land of my
captivity,
and I show his power and majesty
to a nation of sinners.
Turn back, you sinners, and do
right before him;
who knows if he will accept you
and have mercy on you?
7 I exalt my God;
my soul exalts the King of heaven,
and will rejoice in his majesty.
8 Let all men speak,
and give him thanks in
Jerusalem.
9 O Jerusalem, the holy city,
he will afflict you for the deeds
of your sons,
but again he will show mercy to
the sons of the righteous.
10 Give thanks worthily to the Lord,
and praise the King of the ages,
that his tent may be raised for
you again with joy.
May he cheer those within you who
are captives,
and love those within you who
are distressed,
to all generations for ever.
11 Many nations will come from afar
to the name of the Lord God,
bearing gifts in their hands, gifts
for the King of heaven.
Generations of generations will give
you joyful praise.
12 Cursed are all who hate you;
blessed for ever will be all who
love you.
13 Rejoice and be glad for the sons of
the righteous;
for they will be gathered together,
and will praise the Lord of the
righteous.
14 How blessed are those who love
you!
They will rejoice in your peace.
Blessed are those who grieved over
all your afflictions;
for they will rejoice for you upon
seeing all your glory,
and they will be made glad for
ever.
15 Let my soul praise God the great
King.
16 For Jerusalem will be built with
sapphires and emeralds,
her[c] walls with precious stones,
and her towers and battlements
with pure gold.
17 The streets of Jerusalem will be
paved[d] with beryl and ruby and
stones of Ophir;
18 all her lanes will cry 'Hallelujah!'
and will give praise,
saying, 'Blessed is God, who has
exalted you for ever.' "

14 Here Tobit ended his words of
praise. 2 He was fifty-eight years
old when he lost his sight, and after
eight years he regained it. He gave

b Other authorities read *we*
c Gk *your*
d Or *inlaid*

1 Sam.2.6–8; Lk.1.52–53. **4:** *Our Father*, Is.63.16; 64.8; Sir.23.1,4; Mt.6.9. **7:** The psalmist offers his own praise. **8–18:** God's favor to Jerusalem. **10:** *Tent*, temple. **16–18:** That *Jerusalem will be built* with precious stones is an echo of Is.54.11–12 (compare Rev.21.18–21).

alms, and he continued to fear the
Lord God and to praise him. 3 When
he had grown very old he called his son
and grandsons, and said to him, "My
son, take your sons; behold, I have
grown old and am about to depart this
life. 4 Go to Media, my son, for I fully
believe what Jonah the prophet said
about Nineveh, that it will be overthrown. But in Media there will be
peace for a time. Our brethren will be
scattered over the earth from the good
land, and Jerusalem will be desolate.
The house of God in it will be burned
down and will be in ruins for a time.
5 But God will again have mercy on
them, and bring them back into their
land; and they will rebuild the house
of God,[e] though it will not be like the
former one until the times of the age
are completed. After this they will
return from the places of their captivity, and will rebuild Jerusalem in
splendor. And the house of God will
be rebuilt there with a glorious building for all generations for ever, just as
the prophets said of it. 6 Then all the
Gentiles will turn to fear the Lord God
in truth, and will bury their idols.
7 All the Gentiles will praise the Lord,
and his people will give thanks to God,
and the Lord will exalt his people. And
all who love the Lord God in truth and
righteousness will rejoice, showing
mercy to our brethren.
8 "So now, my son, leave Nineveh,
because what the prophet Jonah said
will surely happen. 9 But keep the law
and the commandments, and be merciful and just, so that it may be well with
you. 10 Bury me properly, and your
mother with me. And do not live in
Nineveh any longer. See, my son,
what Nadab[f] did to Ahikar who had
reared him, how he brought him from
light into darkness, and with what he
repaid him. But Ahikar was saved, and
the other received repayment as he
himself went down into the darkness.
Ahikar[g] gave alms and escaped the
deathtrap which Nadab[h] had set for
him; but Nadab[f] fell into the trap and
perished. 11 So now, my children, consider what almsgiving accomplishes
and how righteousness delivers." As
he said this he died in his bed. He was
a hundred and fifty-eight years old;
and Tobias[h] gave him a magnificent
funeral. 12 And when Anna died he
buried her with his father.

Then Tobias returned with his wife
and his sons to Ecbatana, to Raguel
his father-in-law. 13 He grew old with
honor, and he gave his father-in-law
and mother-in-law magnificent funerals. He inherited their property and
that of his father Tobit. 14 He died in
Ecbatana of Media at the age of a
hundred and twenty-seven years. 15 But
before he died he heard of the destruction of Nineveh, which Nebuchadnezzar and Ahasuerus had captured. Before his death he rejoiced over Nineveh.

e Gk *house*
f Other authorities read *Aman*
g Other authorities read *Manasses*
h Gk *he*

14.1–12: Tobit's final counsel, and death. 3–8: He advises his son to leave Nineveh, which is to be destroyed, and predicts the future course of Israel's history. **4:** *What Jonah the prophet said,* Jon.3.4 (Jonah's prophecy, however, was not fulfilled, Jon.3.10). **6:** That *the Gentiles will turn* to Judaism was a characteristic belief of the post-exilic age (e.g. Zech.8.20–23). **10:** *Bury me properly,* see 6.14 n. *Nadab* (also Nasbas or Nadin) is the villain of the *Ahikar* story (see 1.21 n.). *Gave alms,* 4.7–11. **15:** *Nebuchadnezzar . . . Ahasuerus,* i.e. Xerxes (Est.1.1). Both names are anachronistic; Nineveh's conquerors were Nabopolassar and Cyaxares (see 1.4 n.).

JUDITH

Rising slowly to a climax of unforgettable horror, the plot of Judith is a masterpiece of ancient Jewish narrative art. Although obviously a work of fiction, the atmosphere of the tale is entirely realistic, untouched by the aura of the marvelous which envelops such books as Jonah and Tobit. This is not to say that it is irreligious, but that its religion is of a national, legal, and practical type which tends to equate piety with patriotism and to encourage the belief that God helps those who help themselves. In mood and theme the book is closely akin to the book of Esther in the canonical Old Testament, but the character of its heroine is far more positive than Esther's. Judith observes the Mosaic law with scrupulous devotion; she does not, like Esther, demur when duty calls; the impulse to save her people is her own, and the grim stratagem which brings deliverance is of her own devising.

The first part of the book (chs. 1–7) describes at somewhat wearisome length how Nebuchadnezzar's general, Holofernes, invaded the west and at length laid siege to the Jewish town of Bethulia, hoping to starve it into submission. Judith, a beautiful and pious widow, is introduced in ch. 8, and the rest of the story relates how she beguiled Holofernes into entertaining her in his tent, where, when he had become thoroughly drunk, she decapitated him.

The story was probably written in Hebrew during the latter part of the second century B.C. It has been transmitted to us today in three slightly different Greek versions, two Latin versions, a Syriac version, as well as several later Hebrew recensions. The stirring narrative has inspired numerous works of painting, sculpture, and literature, notably an Anglo-Saxon epic of which extensive fragments survive.

IN THE TWELFTH YEAR OF THE REIGN of Nebuchadnezzar, who ruled over the Assyrians in the great city of Nineveh, in the days of Arphaxad, who ruled over the Medes in Ecbatana—[2]he is the king who built walls about Ecbatana with hewn stones three cubits thick and six cubits long; he made the walls seventy cubits high and
fifty cubits wide; [3]at the gates he built towers a hundred cubits high and sixty cubits wide at the foundations;
[4]and he made its gates, which were seventy cubits high and forty cubits wide, so that his armies could march out in force and his infantry form their
ranks—[5]it was in those days that King Nebuchadnezzar made war against King Arphaxad in the great plain
which is on the borders of Ragae. [6]He
was joined by all the people of the hill country and all those who lived along the Euphrates and the Tigris and the Hydaspes and in the plain where Arioch ruled the Elymaeans. Many nations joined the forces of the Chaldeans.

7 Then Nebuchadnezzar king of the Assyrians sent to all who lived in Persia and to all who lived in the west, those who lived in Cilicia and Damascus and Lebanon and Antilebanon and

---

1.1–6: Nebuchadnezzar declares war on Arphaxad, king of Media. 1: *Nebuchadnezzar* (605 [or 604]–562 B.C.) was second ruler over the Neo-Babylonian Empire (not *over the Assyrians*). It was he who destroyed Jerusalem in 587–86 B.C. and carried the Jews off into their Babylonian Exile (2 Kg.24.1–25.26). The author of the book of Judith, in complete disregard of history, represents him as flourishing after the Exile (4.3; 5.19). Some scholars believe that the historical confusion of the book, of which this is but one example, is deliberate, intended to stamp the work unmistakably as fiction. *Arphaxad* is unknown. *The Medes* inhabited the northern part of modern Iran and had their capital at *Ecbatana* (Tob.3.7). **5:** *Ragae*, called Rages in Tob.1.14 (see note there). **6:** *Euphrates . . . Tigris*, the principal rivers of Mesopotamia (modern Iraq). *Hydaspes*, a river in India, but here evidently placed in Mesopotamia. *Arioch*, unknown. *Elymaeans*, Elamites. *Chaldeans*, the Neo-Babylonians (see v. 1 n.).

1.7–11: The Persians and the western nations refuse Nebuchadnezzar's plea for help. 7–10: The nations enumerated correspond to modern Syria, Lebanon, Palestine, and Egypt. **7:** *Persia*, the south of modern Iran.

all who lived along the seacoast, [8]and
those among the nations of Carmel
and Gilead, and Upper Galilee and the
great Plain of Esdraelon, [9]and all who
were in Samaria and its surrounding
towns, and beyond the Jordan as far as
Jerusalem and Bethany and Chelous
and Kadesh and the river of Egypt,
and Tahpanhes and Raamses and the
whole land of Goshen, [10]even beyond
Tanis and Memphis, and all who lived
in Egypt as far as the borders of
Ethiopia. [11]But all who lived in the
whole region disregarded the orders of
Nebuchadnezzar king of the Assyrians,
and refused to join him in the war; for
they were not afraid of him, but looked
upon him as only one man,[a] and they
sent back his messengers empty-handed
and shamefaced.

12 Then Nebuchadnezzar was very
angry with this whole region, and
swore by his throne and kingdom that
he would surely take revenge on the
whole territory of Cilicia and Damascus
and Syria, that he would kill them by
the sword, and also all the inhabitants
of the land of Moab, and the people of
Ammon, and all Judea, and every one
in Egypt, as far as the coasts of the two
seas. [13]In the seventeenth year he led
his forces against King Arphaxad, and
defeated him in battle, and overthrew
the whole army of Arphaxad, and all
his cavalry and all his chariots. [14]Thus
he took possession of his cities, and
came to Ecbatana, captured its towers,
plundered its markets, and turned its
beauty into shame. [15]He captured
Arphaxad in the mountains of Ragae
and struck him down with hunting
spears; and he utterly destroyed him,
to this day. [16]Then he returned with
them to Nineveh, he and all his com-
bined forces, a vast body of troops;
and there he and his forces rested and
feasted for one hundred and twenty
days.

2 In the eighteenth year, on the
twenty-second day of the first
month, there was talk in the palace of
Nebuchadnezzar king of the Assyrians
about carrying out his revenge on the
whole region, just as he had said. [2]He
called together all his officers and all
his nobles and set forth to them his
secret plan and recounted fully, with
his own lips, all the wickedness of the
region;[b] [3]and it was decided that every
one who had not obeyed his command
should be destroyed. [4]When he had
finished setting forth his plan, Nebuchadnezzar king of the Assyrians
called Holofernes, the chief general of
his army, second only to himself, and
said to him,

5 "Thus says the Great King, the
lord of the whole earth: When you
leave my presence, take with you men
confident in their strength, to the number of one hundred and twenty thousand foot soldiers and twelve thousand
cavalry. [6]Go and attack the whole
west country, because they disobeyed
my orders. [7]Tell them to prepare
earth and water, for I am coming
against them in my anger, and will
cover the whole face of the earth with
the feet of my armies, and will hand
them over to be plundered by my
troops,[c] [8]till their wounded shall fill
their valleys, and every brook and river
shall be filled with their dead, and over-
flow; [9]and I will lead them away captive to the ends of the whole earth.
[10]You shall go and seize all their terri-

a Or *a man*
b The meaning of the Greek of the last clause of this verse is uncertain *c* Gk *them*

1.12–16: Angry at the western nations, Nebuchadnezzar defeats Arphaxad without their assistance. 12: *The two seas*, presumably the Red and the Mediterranean.

2.1–13: Nebuchadnezzar orders Holofernes to lead a punitive expedition against the West. 4: Next to Judith, *Holofernes* is the principal character of the book. So far as is known, Nebuchadnezzar had no such general, but the name is found in classical authors of a much later period. His career may have been suggested by memories of a Persian general of similar name who was a leader in the expedition which invaded the West under Artaxerxes III about 350 B.C. (Diodorus Siculus, *Hist.* XXXI. 19; see 12.11 n.). **7:** *Earth and water* were characteristic signs of submission demanded by Persian (not Assyrian or Babylonian) kings (Herodotus, *Hist.* VI. 48).

tory for me in advance. They will yield themselves to you, and you shall hold them for me till the day of their punishment. 11But if they refuse, your eye shall not spare and you shall hand them over to slaughter and plunder throughout your whole region. 12For as I live, and by the power of my kingdom, what I have spoken my hand will execute. 13And you—take care not to transgress any of your sovereign's commands, but be sure to carry them out just as I have ordered you; and do not delay about it."

14 So Holofernes left the presence of his master, and called together all the commanders, generals, and officers of the Assyrian army, 15and mustered the picked troops by divisions as his lord had ordered him to do, one hundred and twenty thousand of them, together with twelve thousand archers on horseback, 16and he organized them as a great army is marshaled for a campaign. 17He collected a vast number of camels and asses and mules for transport, and innumerable sheep and oxen and goats for provision; 18also plenty of food for every man, and a huge amount of gold and silver from the royal palace. 19So he set out with his whole army, to go ahead of King Nebuchadnezzar and to cover the whole face of the earth to the west with their chariots and horsemen and picked troops of infantry. 20Along with them went a mixed crowd like a swarm of locusts, like the dust of the earth—a multitude that could not be counted.

21 They marched for three days from Nineveh to the plain of Bectileth, and camped opposite Bectileth near the mountain which is to the north of Upper Cilicia. 22From there Holofernes[d] took his whole army, his infantry, cavalry, and chariots, and went up into the hill country 23and ravaged Put and Lud, and plundered all the people of Rassis and the Ishmaelites who lived along the desert, south of the country of the Chelleans. 24Then he followed[e] the Euphrates and passed through Mesopotamia and destroyed all the hilltop cities along the brook Abron, as far as the sea. 25He also seized the territory of Cilicia, and killed every one who resisted him, and came to the southern borders of Japheth, fronting toward Arabia. 26He surrounded all the Midianites, and burned their tents and plundered their sheepfolds. 27Then he went down into the plain of Damascus during the wheat harvest, and burned all their fields and destroyed their flocks and herds and sacked their cities and ravaged their lands and put to death all their young men with the edge of the sword.

28 So fear and terror of him fell upon all the people who lived along the seacoast, at Sidon and Tyre, and those who lived in Sur and Ocina and all who lived in Jamnia. Those who lived in Azotus and Ascalon feared him exceedingly.

3 So they sent messengers to sue for peace, and said, "Behold, we the servants of Nebuchadnezzar, the Great King, lie prostrate before you. Do with us whatever you will. 3Behold, our buildings, and all our land, and all

d Gk *he* *e* Or *crossed*

2.14–27: Holofernes brings an enormous army to Damascus. 21: The *three days* march is impossible, since *Nineveh*, the capital of Assyria, is at least three hundred miles from *Bectileth* (an unidentified site), which is described as *north of Upper Cilicia.* Cilicia is in southeastern Asia Minor. **23:** *Put and Lud*, probably in Asia Minor. *Rassis*, unknown. *Ishmaelites*, Arabs (Gen. 16.11–12). *Chelleans*, unknown. **24:** The geography here is confused. *Abron*, unknown. The natural line of march would be directly south from Cilicia to Damascus. **26:** *Midianites*, archaic for Arabs (Jg.6.1–6). **27:** *Damascus*, the ancient and beautiful capital of Syria, was noted for its fertile surroundings.

2.28–3.8: Through fear the people of the seacoast submit voluntarily. 2.28: *Sidon and Tyre*, on the Phoenician coast, west of Damascus. *Sur and Ocina*, unknown. *Jamnia*, just north of *Azotus* (Ashdod) *and Ascalon* (Ashkelon), important Philistine cities in southwest Palestine.

our wheat fields, and our flocks and
herds, and all our sheepfolds with their
tents, lie before you; do with them
whatever you please. 4Our cities also
and their inhabitants are your slaves;
come and deal with them in any way
that seems good to you."
5 The men came to Holofernes and
told him all this. 6Then he went down
to the seacoast with his army and
stationed garrisons in the hilltop cities
and took picked men from them as his
allies. 7And these people and all in the
country round about welcomed him
with garlands and dances and tambourines. 8And he demolished all
their shrines[f] and cut down their sacred
groves; for it had been given to him to
destroy all the gods of the land, so that
all nations should worship Nebuchadnezzar only, and all their tongues and
tribes should call upon him as god.
9 Then he came to the edge of
Esdraelon, near Dothan, fronting the
great ridge of Judea; 10here he camped
between Geba and Scythopolis, and
remained for a whole month in order
to assemble all the supplies for his
army.

4 By this time the people of Israel
living in Judea heard of everything that Holofernes, the general of
Nebuchadnezzar the king of the Assyrians, had done to the nations, and how
he had plundered and destroyed all
their temples; 2they were therefore very
greatly terrified at his approach, and
were alarmed both for Jerusalem and
for the temple of the Lord their God.
3For they had only recently returned
from the captivity, and all the people
of Judea were newly gathered together,
and the sacred vessels and the altar and
the temple had been consecrated after
their profanation. 4So they sent to
every district of Samaria, and to Kona
and Beth-horon and Belmain and
Jericho and to Choba and Aesora and
the valley of Salem, 5and immediately
seized all the high hilltops and fortified
the villages on them and stored up food
in preparation for war—since their
fields had recently been harvested.
6And Joakim, the high priest, who was
in Jerusalem at that time, wrote to the
people of Bethulia and Betomesthaim,
which faces Esdraelon opposite the
plain near Dothan, 7ordering them to
seize the passes up into the hills, since
by them Judea could be invaded, and
it was easy to stop any who tried to
enter, for the approach was narrow,
only wide enough for two men at the
most.
8 So the Israelites did as Joakim the
high priest and the senate of the whole
people of Israel, in session at Jerusalem,
had given order. 9And every man of
Israel cried out to God with great

f Syr: Gk *borders*

3.8: Holofernes seems here to go beyond his original commission, which was merely punitive; now he seeks to impose religious unity by forcing all men to worship Nebuchadnezzar alone. The language is suggested directly by such passages as Dan. chs. 3 and 6, and indirectly by the persecutions of Antiochus Epiphanes as related in 1 Macc.1.10–2.26 and 2 Macc. chs. 6–7. Holofernes' invasion thus becomes a threat to Israel's religious integrity as well as her national security.

3.9–4.15: When Holofernes reaches the soil of Palestine, the Jews prepare to resist. 3.9: *Esdraelon* is the great plain which cuts across Palestine just north of Mt. Carmel. *Dothan* is a short distance south of the plain. *Scythopolis* is identical with Beth-shan, located at the junction of Esdraelon and the Jordan Valley. **4.3:** The statement that *they had only recently returned from the captivity* is flagrantly anachronistic, since it was Nebuchadnezzar who had begun the captivity (compare 1.1 n.), and the return took place nearly fifty years later under the Persian Empire, which had succeeded the Babylonian (Ezra 1.1–3). **4:** The inclusion of *Samaria* is quite unrealistic, since the people of Judea (v. 1) and the Samaritans were separate and increasingly hostile communities in the post-exilic era. **6:** The name of the high priest, *Joakim*, is no doubt derived from Neh.12.26. The identification of *Bethulia*, the center of the story's action, is one of the major puzzles of the book; the most probable suggestion is that it is a pseudonym for Shechem (see 6.11 n.; 7.18 n.; and 10.10 n.). **8:** *Senate*, an anachronism of the author (see 1.1 n. and 1 Macc.12.6 n.).

fervor, and they humbled themselves
with much fasting. 10They and their
wives and their children and their
cattle and every resident alien and hired
laborer and purchased slave—they all
girded themselves with sackcloth.
11And all the men and women of Israel,
and their children, living at Jerusalem,
prostrated themselves before the temple and put ashes on their heads and
spread out their sackcloth before the
Lord. 12They even surrounded the
altar with sackcloth and cried out in
unison, praying earnestly to the God
of Israel not to give up their infants as
prey and their wives as booty, and the
cities they had inherited to be destroyed, and the sanctuary to be profaned and desecrated to the malicious
joy of the Gentiles. 13So the Lord
heard their prayers and looked upon
their affliction; for the people fasted
many days throughout Judea and in
Jerusalem before the sanctuary of the
Lord Almighty. 14And Joakim the
high priest and all the priests who stood
before the Lord and ministered to the
Lord, with their loins girded with
sackcloth, offered the continual burnt
offerings and the vows and freewill
offerings of the people. 15With ashes
upon their turbans, they cried out to
the Lord with all their might to look
with favor upon the whole house of
Israel.

5 When Holofernes, the general of
the Assyrian army, heard that the
people of Israel had prepared for war
and had closed the passes in the hills
and had fortified all the high hilltops
and set up barricades in the plains, 2he
was very angry. So he called together
all the princes of Moab and the commanders of Ammon and all the governors of the coastland, 3and said to
them, "Tell me, you Canaanites, what
people is this that lives in the hill
country? What cities do they inhabit?
How large is their army, and in what
does their power or strength consist?
Who rules over them as king, leading
their army? 4And why have they alone,
of all who live in the west, refused to
come out and meet me?"

5 Then Achior, the leader of all the
Ammonites, said to him, "Let my lord
now hear a word from the mouth of
your servant, and I will tell you the
truth about this people that dwells in
the nearby mountain district. No false-
hood shall come from your servant's
mouth. 6This people is descended from
the Chaldeans. 7At one time they lived
in Mesopotamia, because they would
not follow the gods of their fathers who
were in Chaldea. 8For they had left
the ways of their ancestors, and they
worshiped the God of heaven, the God
they had come to know; hence they
drove them out from the presence of
their gods; and they fled to Mesopotamia, and lived there for a long time.
9Then their God commanded them to
leave the place where they were living
and go to the land of Canaan. There
they settled, and prospered, with much
gold and silver and very many cattle.
10When a famine spread over Canaan
they went down to Egypt and lived
there as long as they had food; and

14: *The continual burnt offerings* were the prescribed daily sacrifices (Ex.29.38–42); the *freewill offerings* were presented voluntarily as occasion required (Lev.22.18–30).

5.1–24: Holofernes is advised by Achior that the Jews are invincible as long as they keep God's law. **2:** *Moab* was the region directly east of the Dead Sea, while *Ammon* lay north and east of it. Both nations were traditional enemies of the Jews (Jg.3.12–30; 2 Sam.10–12; 2 Kg.3.4–27; 24.2). **3:** The circumstance that Israel inhabited the rugged *hill country* had often helped her to preserve her independence in the past. **5–21:** To explain the character of the Jews, Achior summarizes their entire history from Abraham to the return from exile. **6–9:** The migration of Abraham and the prosperity of his descendants (Gen.11.27–37.1). **6:** *Chaldeans*, Abraham came from Ur of the Chaldees (Gen.11.27–31). **7:** *Mesopotamia* here is the region in the north around Haran (Gen.11.31). Late Jewish tradition ascribed the migration of Abraham's family to a desire to escape the influence of polytheism. **8:** *The God of heaven* was a favorite name for Israel's God during the Persian period and later (Tob.10.11; Ezra 1.2). **10–13:** The descent into

there they became a great multitude—
so great that they could not be counted.
11 So the king of Egypt became hostile
to them; he took advantage of them
and set them to making bricks, and
humbled them and made slaves of
them. 12 Then they cried out to their
God, and he afflicted the whole land of
Egypt with incurable plagues; and so
the Egyptians drove them out of their
sight. 13 Then God dried up the Red
Sea before them, 14 and he led them by
the way of Sinai and Kadesh-barnea,
and drove out all the people of the
wilderness. 15 So they lived in the land
of the Amorites, and by their might
destroyed all the inhabitants of Heshbon; and crossing over the Jordan they
took possession of all the hill country.
16 And they drove out before them the
Canaanites and the Perizzites and the
Jebusites and the Shechemites and all
the Gergesites, and lived there a long
time. 17 As long as they did not sin
against their God they prospered, for
the God who hates iniquity is with
them. 18 But when they departed from
the way which he had appointed for
them, they were utterly defeated in
many battles and were led away captive to a foreign country; the temple of
their God was razed to the ground, and
their cities were captured by their
enemies. 19 But now they have returned to their God, and have come
back from the places to which they
were scattered, and have occupied
Jerusalem, where their sanctuary is,
and have settled in the hill country,
because it was uninhabited. 20 Now
therefore, my master and lord, if there
is any unwitting error in this people
and they sin against their God and we
find out their offense, then we will go
up and defeat them. 21 But if there is
no transgression in their nation, then
let my lord pass them by; for their
Lord will defend them, and their
God will protect them, and we shall
be put to shame before the whole
world."

22 When Achior had finished saying
this, all the men standing around the
tent began to complain; Holofernes'
officers and all the men from the seacoast and from Moab insisted that he
must be put to death. 23 "For," they
said, "we will not be afraid of the
Israelites; they are a people with no
strength or power for making war.
24 Therefore let us go up, Lord Holofernes, and they will be devoured by
your vast army."

6 When the disturbance made by
the men outside the council died
down, Holofernes, the commander of
the Assyrian army, said to Achior and
all the Moabites in the presence of all
the foreign contingents:

2 "And who are you, Achior, and
you hirelings of Ephraim, to prophesy
among us as you have done today and
tell us not to make war against the
people of Israel because their God will
defend them? Who is God except
Nebuchadnezzar? 3 He will send his
forces and will destroy them from
the face of the earth, and their God
will not deliver them—we the king's[f]
servants will destroy them as one
man. They cannot resist the might
of our cavalry. 4 We will burn them
up,[g] and their mountains will be drunk
with their blood, and their fields will
be full of their dead. They[h] cannot
withstand us, but will utterly perish.
So says King Nebuchadnezzar, the
lord of the whole earth. For he has
spoken; none of his words shall be in
vain.

f Gk *his*
g Other authorities add *with it*
h Gk *the track of their feet*

Egypt and the Exodus (Gen.37.2–Ex.18.27). **14:** *Sinai*, Ex.19.1–Num.10.10. *Kadesh-barnea*, Num.20.1. **15–16:** The conquests in Transjordan and Canaan (Num.20.14–Jos.11.23). **15:** *Amorites . . . Heshbon*, Num.21.21–32. **17:** *They prospered*, the philosophy of Deuteronomy (28.1–14). **18:** The exile (see 1.1 n.). **19:** The return from exile (Ezra chs. 1–3); see 4.3 n. **22–24:** Holofernes' other advisers oppose the view of Achior.

6.1–21: For his presumption, Achior is handed over to the Jews to perish with them in the fall of Bethulia. **1–9:** Holofernes' denunciation of Achior. **2:** By calling Achior and his Ammonite

5 "But you, Achior, you Ammonite
hireling, who have said these words
on the day of your iniquity, you shall
not see my face again from this day
until I take revenge on this race that
came out of Egypt. 6 Then the sword
of my army and the spear[i] of my
servants shall pierce your sides, and
you shall fall among their wounded,
when I return. 7 Now my slaves are
going to take you back into the hill
country and put you in one of the
cities beside the passes, 8 and you will
not die until you perish along with
them. 9 If you really hope in your
heart that they will not be taken, do
not look downcast! I have spoken
and none of my words shall fail."
10 Then Holofernes ordered his
slaves, who waited on him in his tent,
to seize Achior and take him to
Bethulia and hand him over to the
men of Israel. 11 So the slaves took
him and led him out of the camp into
the plain, and from the plain they
went up into the hill country and came
to the springs below Bethulia. 12 When
the men of the city saw them,[j] they
caught up their weapons and ran out of
the city to the top of the hill, and all
the slingers kept them from coming up
by casting stones at them. 13 However,
they got under the shelter of the hill
and they bound Achior and left him
lying at the foot of the hill, and returned to their master.
14 Then the men of Israel came
down from their city and found him;
and they untied him and brought him
into Bethulia and placed him before
the magistrates of their city, 15 who in
those days were Uzziah the son of
Micah, of the tribe of Simeon, and
Chabris the son of Gothoniel, and
Charmis the son of Melchiel. 16 They
called together all the elders of the city,
and all their young men and their
women ran to the assembly; and they
set Achior in the midst of all their
people, and Uzziah asked him what
had happened. 17 He answered and told
them what had taken place at the council of Holofernes, and all that he had
said in the presence of the Assyrian
leaders, and all that Holofernes had
said so boastfully against the house of
Israel. 18 Then the people fell down
and worshiped God, and cried out to
him, and said,
19 "O Lord God of heaven, behold
their arrogance, and have pity on the
humiliation of our people, and look
this day upon the faces of those who are
consecrated to thee."
20 Then they consoled Achior, and
praised him greatly. 21 And Uzziah
took him from the assembly to his own
house and gave a banquet for the
elders; and all that night they called
on the God of Israel for help.

7 The next day Holofernes ordered
his whole army, and all the allies
who had joined him, to break camp
and move against Bethulia, and to
seize the passes up into the hill country
and make war on the Israelites. 2 So
all their warriors moved their camp
that day; their force of men of war was
one hundred and seventy thousand
infantry and twelve thousand cavalry,
together with the baggage and the foot
soldiers handling it, a very great multitude. 3 They encamped in the valley
near Bethulia, beside the spring, and
they spread out in breadth over Dothan
as far as Balbaim and in length from
Bethulia to Cyamon, which faces
Esdraelon.

i Lat Syr: Gk *people*
j Other authorities add *on the top of the hill*

---

friends *hirelings of Ephraim* (i.e. Israel), Holofernes may intend to say that Achior has been corrupted by Jewish money. **10–13:** Achior is left bound in sight of the men of Bethulia. **11:** With whatever place the mysterious Bethulia may be identified (see 4.6 n.), it is clearly pictured as a city on a hill *with springs* below it. **14–21:** The Jews bring Achior inside the city, which then hears the story of Holofernes' arrogance.

7.1–7: Holofernes and his allies advance to Bethulia and survey the situation. 1–3: The line of march is south from Esdraelon. **3:** *Beside the spring*, see 6.11 n. *Dothan*, see 3.9 n. *Balbaim* and *Cyamon* are unknown. *Esdraelon*, see 3.9 n.

4 When the Israelites saw their vast
numbers they were greatly terrified,
and every one said to his neighbor,
"These men will now lick up the face
of the whole land; neither the high
mountains nor the valleys nor the
hills will bear their weight." [5]Then
each man took up his weapons, and
when they had kindled fires on their
towers they remained on guard all that
night.
6 On the second day Holofernes led
out all his cavalry in full view of the
Israelites in Bethulia, [7]and examined
the approaches to the city, and visited
the springs that supplied their water,
and seized them and set guards of
soldiers over them, and then returned
to his army.
8 Then all the chieftains of the
people of Esau and all the leaders of
the Moabites and the commanders of
the coastland came to him and said,
[9]"Let our lord hear a word, lest his
army be defeated. [10]For these people,
the Israelites, do not rely on their
spears but on the height of the mountains where they live, for it is not easy
to reach the tops of their mountains.
[11]Therefore, my lord, do not fight
against them in battle array, and not a
man of your army will fall. [12]Remain
in your camp, and keep all the men in
your forces with you; only let your
servants take possession of the spring
of water that flows from the foot of the
mountain—[13]for this is where all the
people of Bethulia get their water. So
thirst will destroy them, and they will
give up their city. We and our people
will go up to the tops of the nearby
mountains and camp there to keep
watch that not a man gets out of the
city. [14]They and their wives and children will waste away with famine, and
before the sword reaches them they
will be strewn about in the streets
where they live. [15]So you will pay them
back with evil, because they rebelled
and did not receive you peaceably."
16 These words pleased Holofernes
and all his servants, and he gave orders
to do as they had said. [17]So the army
of the Ammonites moved forward,
together with five thousand Assyrians,
and they encamped in the valley and
seized the water supply and the springs
of the Israelites. [18]And the sons of
Esau and the sons of Ammon went up
and encamped in the hill country opposite Dothan; and they sent some of
their men toward the south and the
east, toward Acraba, which is near
Chusi beside the brook Mochmur.
The rest of the Assyrian army encamped in the plain, and covered the
whole face of the land, and their tents
and supply trains spread out in great
number, and they formed a vast
multitude.
19 The people of Israel cried out
to the Lord their God, for their courage failed, because all their enemies
had surrounded them and there was
no way of escape from them. [20]The
whole Assyrian army, their infantry,
chariots, and cavalry, surrounded them
for thirty-four days, until all the vessels
of water belonging to every inhabitant
of Bethulia were empty; [21]their cisterns
were going dry, and they did not have
enough water to drink their fill for a
single day, because it was measured
out to them to drink. [22]Their children
lost heart, and the women and young
men fainted from thirst and fell
down in the streets of the city and
in the passages through the gates;
there was no strength left in them any
longer.
23 Then all the people, the young
men, the women, and the children,

7.8–18: They cut off the city's water supply by seizing the springs. 8: *Esau* means Edom, southeast of the Dead Sea. These people have not previously been mentioned, but were also traditional enemies of the Jews (see e.g. Ob.18). **18:** The localities of *Acraba* and *Chusi* and the valley of *Mochmur* have all been identified with sites in the neighborhood of Shechem (see 4.6 n.).

7.19–28: Driven to desperation, the citizens of Bethulia urge their leaders to capitulate. 23: *Uzziah*, 6.15.

gathered about Uzziah and the rulers
of the city and cried out with a loud
voice, and said before all the elders,
24 “God be judge between you and us!
For you have done us a great injury
in not making peace with the Assyrians.
25 For now we have no one to help us;
God has sold us into their hands, to
strew us on the ground before them
with thirst and utter destruction.
26 Now call them in and surrender the
whole city to the army of Holofernes
and to all his forces, to be plundered.
27 For it would be better for us to be
captured by them;[k] for we will be
slaves, but our lives will be spared,
and we shall not witness the death of
our babes before our eyes, or see our
wives and children draw their last
breath. 28 We call to witness against
you heaven and earth and our God,
the Lord of our fathers, who punishes
us according to our sins and the sins
of our fathers. Let him not do this
day the things which we have described!”

29 Then great and general lamentation arose throughout the assembly,
and they cried out to the Lord God
with a loud voice. 30 And Uzziah said
to them, “Have courage, my brothers!
Let us hold out for five more days; by
that time the Lord our God will restore to us his mercy, for he will not
forsake us utterly. 31 But if these days
pass by, and no help comes for us, I
will do what you say.”

32 Then he dismissed the people to
their various posts, and they went up
on the walls and towers of their city.
The women and children he sent home.
And they were greatly depressed in
the city.

8 At that time Judith heard about
these things: she was the daughter
of Merari the son of Ox, son of Joseph,
son of Oziel, son of Elkiah, son of
Ananias, son of Gideon, son of
Raphaim, son of Ahitub, son of Elijah,
son of Hilkiah, son of Eliab, son of
Nathanael, son of Salamiel, son of
Sarasadai, son of Israel. 2 Her husband
Manasseh, who belonged to her tribe
and family, had died during the barley
harvest. 3 For as he stood overseeing
the men who were binding sheaves in
the field, he was overcome by the burning heat, and took to his bed and died
in Bethulia his city. So they buried him
with his fathers in the field between
Dothan and Balamon. 4 Judith had
lived at home as a widow for three
years and four months. 5 She set up a
tent for herself on the roof of her house,
and girded sackcloth about her loins
and wore the garments of her widowhood. 6 She fasted all the days of her
widowhood, except the day before the
sabbath and the sabbath itself, the day
before the new moon and the day of
the new moon, and the feasts and days
of rejoicing of the house of Israel.
7 She was beautiful in appearance, and
had a very lovely face; and her husband Manasseh had left her gold and
silver, and men and women slaves,
and cattle, and fields; and she maintained this estate. 8 No one spoke ill
of her, for she feared God with great
devotion.

9 When Judith heard the wicked
words spoken by the people against
the ruler, because they were faint for
lack of water, and when she heard all
that Uzziah said to them, and how he
promised them under oath to surrender the city to the Assyrians after
five days, 10 she sent her maid, who was
in charge of all she possessed, to summon[l] Chabris and Charmis, the elders

k Other authorities add *than to die of thirst*
l Some authorities add *Uzziah and* (See verses 28 and 35)

7.29–32: Uzziah advises a delay of five days.

8.1–8: The character of Judith. 1: The name *Judith* means “Jewess.” Her ancestors cannot be identified: some of the names are unparalleled in the Old Testament. **2–3:** Her husband had died of sunstroke (compare 2 Kg.4.18–20). **6:** The rigorous piety which is her outstanding quality is of the rabbinical or Pharisaical type. She omits fasting only on days when it is forbidden. **7:** Beauty and wealth are normal elements in the character of a romantic heroine.

8.9–27: Judith presents sound theological arguments against Uzziah's proposal. 12: Note the

of her city. 11They came to her, and
she said to them,
"Listen to me, rulers of the people
of Bethulia! What you have said to
the people today is not right; you have
even sworn and pronounced this oath
between God and you, promising to
surrender the city to our enemies unless
the Lord turns and helps us within so
many days. 12Who are you, that have
put God to the test this day, and are
setting yourselves up in the place of[m]
God among the sons of men? 13You
are putting the Lord Almighty to the
test—but you will never know anything! 14You cannot plumb the depths
of the human heart, nor find out what
a man is thinking; how do you expect
to search out God, who made all these
things, and find out his mind or comprehend his thought? No, my brethren,
do not provoke the Lord our God to
anger. 15For if he does not choose to
help us within these five days, he has
power to protect us within any time he
pleases, or even to destroy us in the
presence of our enemies. 16Do not try
to bind the purposes of the Lord our
God; for God is not like man, to be
threatened, nor like a human being,
to be won over by pleading. 17There-
fore, while we wait for his deliverance,
let us call upon him to help us, and
he will hear our voice, if it pleases
him.

18 "For never in our generation, nor
in these present days, has there been
any tribe or family or people or city of
ours which worshiped gods made with
hands, as was done in days gone by—
19and that was why our fathers were
handed over to the sword, and to be
plundered, and so they suffered a great
catastrophe before our enemies. 20But
we know no other god but him, and
therefore we hope that he will not disdain us or any of our nation. 21For if
we are captured all Judea will be captured and our sanctuary will be plundered; and he will exact of us[n] the
penalty for its desecration. 22And the
slaughter of our brethren and the
captivity of the land and the desolation
of our inheritance—all this he will
bring upon our heads among the
Gentiles, wherever we serve as slaves;
and we shall be an offense and a reproach in the eyes of those who acquire
us. 23For our slavery will not bring us
into favor, but the Lord our God will
turn it to dishonor.

24 "Now therefore, brethren, let us
set an example to our brethren, for
their lives depend upon us, and the
sanctuary and the temple and the altar
rest upon us. 25In spite of everything
let us give thanks to the Lord our God,
who is putting us to the test as he did
our forefathers. 26Remember what he
did with Abraham, and how he tested
Isaac, and what happened to Jacob in
Mesopotamia in Syria, while he was
keeping the sheep of Laban, his
mother's brother. 27For he has not
tried us with fire, as he did them, to
search their hearts, nor has he taken
revenge upon us; but the Lord scourges
those who draw near to him, in order
to admonish them."

28 Then Uzziah said to her, "All
that you have said has been spoken
out of a true heart, and there is no one
who can deny your words. 29Today is
not the first time your wisdom has been
shown, but from the beginning of your
life all the people have recognized your
understanding, for your heart's disposition is right. 30But the people were
very thirsty, and they compelled us to
do for them what we have promised,
and made us take an oath which we
cannot break. 31So pray for us, since

m Or *above*
n Gk *our blood*

---

neat balance of her antitheses: it is not for us to *put God to the test* (Dt.6.16); he is (v. 25) putting us to the test. **16:** *God is not like man,* Num.23.19; 1 Sam.15.29. **18:** The people are safe because they have been entirely loyal to God (compare 5.21). Judith's optimistic judgment of her contemporaries stands in sharp contrast to the attitude of the great prophets, but is similar to that of Ps.44.17–18. **27:** Their present sufferings are not punitive, but educative.

8.28–35: Answering Uzziah's plea, she personally pledges to deliver the city. 30–31: The vow,

you are a devout woman, and the Lord
will send us rain to fill our cisterns and
we will no longer be faint."
32 Judith said to them, "Listen to
me. I am about to do a thing which
will go down through all generations
of our descendants. [33]Stand at the city
gate tonight, and I will go out with my
maid; and within the days after which
you have promised to surrender the
city to our enemies, the Lord will
deliver Israel by my hand. [34]Only, do
not try to find out what I plan; for I
will not tell you until I have finished
what I am about to do."
35 Uzziah and the rulers said to her,
"Go in peace, and may the Lord God
go before you, to take revenge upon
our enemies." [36]So they returned from
the tent and went to their posts.

9 Then Judith fell upon her face,
and put ashes on her head, and uncovered the sackcloth she was wearing;
and at the very time when that evening's
incense was being offered in the house
of God in Jerusalem, Judith cried out
to the Lord with a loud voice, and said,
2 "O Lord God of my father Simeon, to whom thou gavest a sword to
take revenge on the strangers who had
loosed the girdle[o] of a virgin to defile
her, and uncovered her thigh to put her
to shame, and polluted her womb to
disgrace her; for thou hast said, 'It
shall not be done'—yet they did it. [3]So
thou gavest up their rulers to be slain,
and their bed, which was ashamed of
the deceit they had practiced, to be
stained with blood, and thou didst
strike down slaves along with princes,
and princes on their thrones; [4]and thou
gavest their wives for a prey and their
daughters to captivity, and all their
booty to be divided among thy beloved
sons, who were zealous for thee, and
abhorred the pollution of their blood,
and called on thee for help—O God,
my God, hear me also, a widow.
5 "For thou hast done these things
and those that went before and those
that followed; thou hast designed the
things that are now, and those that are
to come. Yea, the things thou didst
intend came to pass, [6]and the things
thou didst presented themselves and
said, 'Lo, we are here'; for all thy ways
are prepared in advance, and thy judgment is with foreknowledge.
7 "Behold now, the Assyrians are
increased in their might; they are
exalted, with their horses and riders;
they glory in the strength of their foot
soldiers; they trust in shield and spear,
in bow and sling, and know not that
thou art the Lord who crushest wars;
the Lord is thy name. [8]Break their
strength by thy might, and bring down
their power in thy anger; for they
intend to defile thy sanctuary, and to
pollute the tabernacle where thy glorious name rests, and to cast down the
horn of thy altar with the sword.
[9]Behold their pride, and send thy
wrath upon their heads; give to me, a
widow, the strength to do what I plan.
[10]By the deceit of my lips strike down
the slave with the prince and the prince
with his servant; crush their arrogance
by the hand of a woman.
11 "For thy power depends not upon
numbers, nor thy might upon men of
strength; for thou art God of the lowly,
helper of the oppressed, upholder of
the weak, protector of the forlorn,
savior of those without hope. [12]Hear,

o Cn: Gk *womb*

though wrong, as Judith said, had been made and its consequences could be avoided only by an act of God. **33:** Judith promises that God will act through her.

9.1–14: Judith's prayer. 1: *Evening's incense*, Ex.30.8; Ps.141.2. It may have become customary to offer prayer regularly at this time of day. **2:** *My father Simeon*, the patriarch, son of Jacob, who, with Levi, avenged their sister Dinah (Gen.34.25–26). **4:** God's special care for the *widow* was an article of Israel's faith (Dt.10.18; Ps.146.9). **5–6:** God's absolute foreknowledge and control of history, both past and future (Is.44.6–8). **10:** The author of the book apparently feels no moral inconsistency in having Judith pray for divine help in practicing *deceit* (see v. 13 n.). That an enemy should be destroyed *by the hand of a woman* would be not only remarkable, but particularly ignominious (Jg.9.54). **11:** *Thy power depends not upon*

O hear me, God of my father, God of
the inheritance of Israel, Lord of
heaven and earth, Creator of the
waters, King of all thy creation, hear
my prayer! 13 Make my deceitful words
to be their wound and stripe, for they
have planned cruel things against thy
covenant, and against thy consecrated
house, and against the top of Zion, and
against the house possessed by thy
children. 14 And cause thy whole nation and every tribe to know and understand that thou art God, the God of all
power and might, and that there is no
other who protects the people of Israel
but thou alone!"

10 When Judith[p] had ceased crying
out to the God of Israel, and had
ended all these words, 2 she rose from
where she lay prostrate and called her
maid and went down into the house
where she lived on sabbaths and on her
feast days; 3 and she removed the sackcloth which she had been wearing, and
took off her widow's garments, and
bathed her body with water, and a-
nointed herself with precious ointment,
and combed her hair and put on a
tiara, and arrayed herself in her gayest
apparel, which she used to wear while
her husband Manasseh was living.
4 And she put sandals on her feet, and
put on her anklets and bracelets and
rings, and her earrings and all her
ornaments, and made herself very beautiful, to entice the eyes of all men who
might see her. 5 And she gave her maid
a bottle of wine and a flask of oil, and
filled a bag with parched grain and a
cake of dried fruit and fine bread; and
she wrapped up all her vessels and gave
them to her to carry.

6 Then they went out to the city gate
of Bethulia, and found Uzziah standing
there with the elders of the city, Chabris
and Charmis. 7 When they saw her, and
noted how her face was altered and her
clothing changed, they greatly admired
her beauty, and said to her, 8 "May the
God of our fathers grant you favor and
fulfil your plans, that the people of
Israel may glory and Jerusalem may be
exalted." And she worshiped God.

9 Then she said to them, "Order the
gate of the city to be opened for me,
and I will go out and accomplish the
things about which you spoke with
me." So they ordered the young men
to open the gate for her, as she had said.
10 When they had done this, Judith went
out, she and her maid with her; and
the men of the city watched her until
she had gone down the mountain and
passed through the valley and they
could no longer see her.

11 The women[q] went straight on
through the valley; and an Assyrian
patrol met her 12 and took her into
custody, and asked her, "To what
people do you belong, and where are
you coming from, and where are you
going?" She replied, "I am a daughter
of the Hebrews, but I am fleeing from
them, for they are about to be handed
over to you to be devoured. 13 I am on

p Gk *she* q Gk *They*

---

numbers, Jg.7.2; 1 Sam.14.6. **12:** *King of all thy creation*, a favorite late Jewish title for God. **13:** This prayer for God's blessing on a lie has been frequently criticized as a serious, and basic, moral blemish in the book. While Judith's conduct may, in the abstract, seem indefensible, it has often been imitated by both Jews and Christians in similar circumstances of crisis; the moral question is complex and the practical solution sometimes agonizing.

10.1–5: Judith beautifies herself. 2: *Went down into the house*, from the roof where she apparently lived (presumably in a tent) except on the sabbath and festivals. **4:** The Latin version states that God gave her a supernatural beauty because her motive in adorning herself was virtuous, not lustful. **5:** *Vessels*, for cooking her food in accordance with the Jewish dietary laws.

10.6–10: She leaves the city with the elders' blessing. 8: *She worshiped God*, prayer and acts of piety accompany every one of her decisive acts. **10:** *Down the mountain . . . through the valley*, the geographical location of Bethulia, on the mountain with the "Assyrian" camp at the entrance of the valley leading up to it, could hardly be described more clearly.

10.11–23: Arriving at the enemy lines, she is brought into Holofernes' presence. 13: *I will*

my way to the presence of Holofernes
the commander of your army, to give
him a true report; and I will show him
a way by which he can go and capture
all the hill country without losing one
of his men, captured or slain."
14 When the men heard her words,
and observed her face—she was in
their eyes marvelously beautiful—they
said to her, 15"You have saved your
life by hurrying down to the presence
of our lord. Go at once to his tent;
some of us will escort you and hand
you over to him. 16And when you
stand before him, do not be afraid
in your heart, but tell him just what
you have said, and he will treat you
well."
17 They chose from their number a
hundred men to accompany her and
her maid, and they brought them to
the tent of Holofernes. 18There was
great excitement in the whole camp,
for her arrival was reported from tent
to tent, and they came and stood
around her as she waited outside the
tent of Holofernes while they told him
about her. 19And they marveled at her
beauty, and admired the Israelites,
judging them by her, and every one
said to his neighbor, "Who can despise
these people, who have women like
this among them? Surely not a man of
them had better be left alive, for if we
let them go they will be able to ensnare
the whole world!"
20 Then Holofernes' companions
and all his servants came out and led
her into the tent. 21Holofernes was
resting on his bed, under a canopy
which was woven with purple and gold
and emeralds and precious stones.
22When they told him of her he came
forward to the front of the tent, with
silver lamps carried before him. 23And
when Judith came into the presence of
Holofernes[r] and his servants, they all
marveled at the beauty of her face;
and she prostrated herself and made
obeisance to him, and his slaves raised
her up.

11 Then Holofernes said to her, "Take
courage, woman, and do not be
afraid in your heart, for I have never
hurt any one who chose to serve
Nebuchadnezzar, the king of all the
earth. 2And even now, if your people
who live in the hill country had not
slighted me, I would never have lifted
my spear against them; but they have
brought all this on themselves. 3And
now tell me why you have fled from
them and have come over to us—since
you have come to safety. 4Have
courage; you will live, tonight and from
now on. No one will hurt you, but all
will treat you well, as they do the
servants of my lord King Nebuchadnezzar."
5 Judith replied to him, "Accept the
words of your servant, and let your
maidservant speak in your presence,
and I will tell nothing false to my lord
this night. 6And if you follow out the
words of your maidservant, God will
accomplish something through you,
and my lord will not fail to achieve his
purposes. 7Nebuchadnezzar the king
of the whole earth lives, and as his
power endures, who has sent you to
direct every living soul, not only do
men serve him because of you, but also
the beasts of the field and the cattle and
the birds of the air will live by your
power under Nebuchadnezzar and all
his house. 8For we have heard of your
wisdom and skill, and it is reported

r Gk *him*

---

show him a way. The first of her "deceitful words" (see 9.13 n.). **21:** The *canopy* was some kind of decorated mosquito net. The Anglo-Saxon poem of Judith describes it thus: "There was hung|All golden a fair fly-net round the bed|Of the folk-leader, that the baleful one,|The chief of warriors, might look through on each|Child of the brave who came therein, and none|Might look on him . . . ."

11.1–4: Holofernes graciously receives her.

11.5–23: Judith's explanation of her flight commends her to the general and his advisers. 6: The idea that God can work through heathen kings and their armies is fairly common in the Old Testament (Is.10.5; 44.28; Jer.25.9). **7:** This verse is as obscure in the Greek as in the English.

throughout the whole world that you
are the one good man in the whole
kingdom, thoroughly informed and
marvelous in military strategy.
9 "Now as for the things Achior said
in your council, we have heard his
words, for the men of Bethulia spared
him and he told them all he had said
to you. 10Therefore, my lord and
master, do not disregard what he said,
but keep it in your mind, for it is true:
our nation cannot be punished, nor can
the sword prevail against them, unless
they sin against their God.
11 "And now, in order that my lord
may not be defeated and his purpose
frustrated, death will fall upon them,
for a sin has overtaken them by which
they are about to provoke their God
to anger when they do what is wrong.
12Since their food supply is exhausted
and their water has almost given out,
they have planned to kill their cattle
and have determined to use all that
God by his laws has forbidden them
to eat. 13They have decided to consume the first fruits of the grain and
the tithes of the wine and oil, which
they had consecrated and set aside for
the priests who minister in the presence
of our God at Jerusalem—although it
is not lawful for any of the people so
much as to touch these things with
their hands. 14They have sent men to
Jerusalem, because even the people
living there have been doing this, to
bring back to them permission from
the senate. 15When the word reaches
them and they proceed to do this, on
that very day they will be handed over
to you to be destroyed.
16 "Therefore, when I, your servant,
learned all this, I fled from them; and
God has sent me to accomplish with
you things that will astonish the whole
world, as many as shall hear about
them. 17For your servant is religious,
and serves the God of heaven day and
night; therefore, my lord, I will remain
with you, and every night your servant
will go out into the valley, and I will
pray to God and he will tell me when
they have committed their sins. 18And
I will come and tell you, and then you
shall go out with your whole army, and
not one of them will withstand you.
19Then I will lead you through the middle of Judea, till you come to Jerusalem; and I will set your throne[s] in the
midst of it; and you will lead them like
sheep that have no shepherd, and not
a dog will so much as open its mouth
to growl at you. For this has been told
me, by my foreknowledge; it was announced to me, and I was sent to tell
you."
20 Her words pleased Holofernes
and all his servants, and they marveled
at her wisdom and said, 21"There is
not such a woman from one end of the
earth to the other, either for beauty of
face or wisdom of speech!" 22And
Holofernes said to her, "God has done
well to send you before the people, to
lend strength to our hands and to
bring destruction upon those who have
slighted my lord. 23You are not only
beautiful in appearance, but wise in
speech; and if you do as you have said,
your God shall be my God, and you
shall live in the house of King Nebuchadnezzar and be renowned throughout the whole world."
12 Then he commanded them to
bring her in where his silver
dishes were kept, and ordered them to
set a table for her with some of his own
food and to serve her with his own
wine. 2But Judith said, "I cannot eat

s Or *chariot*

9: *The things Achior said*, compare 5.5–21. **11–15:** She declares that the imminent fall of Bethulia is due to the circumstance that its citizens are about to appropriate to common use food which the Mosaic law assigned to God and the temple. **13:** *First fruits*, Ex.23.19. *Tithes*, Lev.27.30. **14:** *Senate*, the Sanhedrin, the supreme religious authority of later Judaism. **17:** *God of heaven*, see 5.8 n. By telling him that *every night* she *will go out into the valley* Judith is preparing a ruse for her eventual escape (13.10). The Anglo-Saxon poem, no doubt for moral reasons, omits this element in the story.

12.1–9: For three days Judith remains and establishes a pattern of conduct. 2: Once again

it, lest it be an offense; but I will
be provided from the things I have
brought with me." 3Holofernes said
to her, "If your supply runs out,
where can we get more like it for
you? For none of your people is
here with us." 4Judith replied, "As
your soul lives, my lord, your servant
will not use up the things I have with
me before the Lord carries out by
my hand what he has determined to
do."
5 Then the servants of Holofernes
brought her into the tent, and she slept
until midnight. Along toward the
morning watch she arose 6and sent to
Holofernes and said, "Let my lord now
command that your servant be permitted to go out and pray." 7So Holofernes commanded his guards not to
hinder her. And she remained in the
camp for three days, and went out each
night to the valley of Bethulia, and
bathed at the spring in the camp.[t]
8When she came up from the spring
she prayed the Lord God of Israel to
direct her way for the raising up of her
people. 9So she returned clean and
stayed in the tent until she ate her food
toward evening.
10 On the fourth day Holofernes
held a banquet for his slaves only, and
did not invite any of his officers. 11And
he said to Bagoas, the eunuch who had
charge of all his personal affairs, "Go
now and persuade the Hebrew woman
who is in your care to join us and eat
and drink with us. 12For it will be a
disgrace if we let such a woman go
without enjoying her company, for if
we do not embrace her she will laugh
at us." 13So Bagoas went out from the
presence of Holofernes, and approached her and said, "This beautiful
maidservant will please come to my
lord and be honored in his presence,
and drink wine and be merry with us,
and become today like one of the
daughters of the Assyrians who serve
in the house of Nebuchadnezzar."
14And Judith said, "Who am I, to refuse my lord? Surely whatever pleases
him I will do at once, and it will be a
joy to me until the day of my death!"
15So she got up and arrayed herself in
all her woman's finery, and her maid
went and spread on the ground for her
before Holofernes the soft fleeces which
she had received from Bagoas for her
daily use, so that she might recline on
them when she ate.
16 Then Judith came in and lay
down, and Holofernes' heart was
ravished with her and he was moved
with great desire to possess her; for he
had been waiting for an opportunity
to deceive her, ever since the day he
first saw her. 17So Holofernes said to
her, "Drink now, and be merry with
us!" 18Judith said, "I will drink now,
my lord, because my life means more
to me today than in all the days since
I was born." 19Then she took and ate
and drank before him what her maid
had prepared. 20And Holofernes was
greatly pleased with her, and drank a
great quantity of wine, much more
than he had ever drunk in any one day
since he was born.

t Other authorities omit *in the camp*

---

the narrative stresses Judith's meticulous observance of the Jewish dietary laws, even in the presence of the Gentiles. Her behavior contrasts markedly with that of Esther (Est.2.20; compare Dan.1.8). **6–7:** Since she had gone out every night, her departure after Holofernes' assassination would occasion no surprise. **8:** Her prayer was genuine enough, but not for the purpose previously announced (11.17).

12.10–20: Judith invited to Holofernes' banquet. **11:** *Bagoas* is a well-known Persian name, spelled "Bigvai" in Ezra 2.2 and the Elephantine papyri. Diodorus Siculus (*Hist.* XVI. 47) mentions an officer Bagoas in the army of Artaxerxes III (see 2.4 n.). In oriental kingdoms the officer in charge of the women was normally a *eunuch;* eunuchs often attained also to positions of considerable responsibility in the state (Dan.1.3; Acts 8.27). **14:** Judith pretends to be pleased by his obviously dishonorable intentions toward her. Her real thoughts are paraphrased in the Anglo-Saxon poem as follows: ". . . the Saviour's handmaid then|Gloried, intently mindful how she might|Take from the hateful one most easily|His life. . . ."

13 When evening came, his slaves
quickly withdrew, and Bagoas
closed the tent from outside and shut
out the attendants from his master's
presence; and they went to bed, for
they all were weary because the banquet
had lasted long. 2So Judith was left
alone in the tent, with Holofernes
stretched out on his bed, for he was
overcome with wine.
3 Now Judith had told her maid to
stand outside the bedchamber and to
wait for her to come out, as she did
every day; for she said she would be
going out for her prayers. And she
had said the same thing to Bagoas.
4So every one went out, and no one,
either small or great, was left in the
bedchamber. Then Judith, standing
beside his bed, said in her heart, "O
Lord God of all might, look in this
hour upon the work of my hands for
the exaltation of Jerusalem. 5For now
is the time to help thy inheritance, and
to carry out my undertaking for the
destruction of the enemies who have
risen up against us."
6 She went up to the post at the end
of the bed, above Holofernes' head,
and took down his sword that hung
there. 7She came close to his bed and
took hold of the hair of his head, and
said, "Give me strength this day, O
Lord God of Israel!" 8And she struck
his neck twice with all her might, and
severed his head from his body. 9Then
she tumbled his body off the bed and
pulled down the canopy from the posts;
after a moment she went out, and gave
Holofernes' head to her maid, 10who
placed it in her food bag.
Then the two of them went out together, as they were accustomed to go
for prayer; and they passed through
the camp and circled around the valley and went up the mountain to
Bethulia and came to its gates. 11Ju-
dith called out from afar to the watchmen at the gates, "Open, open the
gate! God, our God, is still with us,
to show his power in Israel, and his
strength against our enemies, even as
he has done this day!"
12 When the men of her city heard
her voice, they hurried down to the city
gate and called together the elders of
the city. 13They all ran together, both
small and great, for it was unbelievable
that she had returned; they opened the
gate and admitted them, and they
kindled a fire for light, and gathered
around them. 14Then she said to them
with a loud voice, "Praise God, O
praise him! Praise God, who has not
withdrawn his mercy from the house of
Israel, but has destroyed our enemies
by my hand this very night!"
15 Then she took the head out of the
bag and showed it to them, and said,
"See, here is the head of Holofernes,
the commander of the Assyrian army,
and here is the canopy beneath which
he lay in his drunken stupor. The Lord
has struck him down by the hand of a
woman. 16As the Lord lives, who has
protected me in the way I went, it was
my face that tricked him to his destruction, and yet he committed no act of
sin with me, to defile and shame me."
17 All the people were greatly astonished, and bowed down and worshiped God, and said with one accord,
"Blessed art thou, our God, who hast
brought into contempt this day the
enemies of thy people."
18 And Uzziah said to her, "O

13.1–10a: Judith beheads Holofernes. 4–7: Judith's prayer before she decapitates the enemy of her people is both the most dramatic and most horrifying moment of the story. In the Anglo-Saxon version, the prayer becomes an invocation of the Holy Trinity. **9:** *Pulled down the canopy* (10.21) and carried it off as a trophy (v. 15). **10a:** Even the bag in which she brought her food (10.5) is now seen to have been part of a well-laid plan.

13.10b–20: She escapes and returns to her own people. 10b: Her established habit of leaving the camp each night for prayer (11.17; 12.7) permits her an easy escape. **17:** *Blessed art thou, our God,* is the most common formula of late Jewish prayers (see Tob.3.11 n.). **18:** Uzziah's words are reminiscent of those spoken concerning Jael under similar circumstances (Jg.5.24); also of Melchizedek's greeting to Abraham (Gen.14.19–20).

daughter, you are blessed by the Most
High God above all women on earth;
and blessed be the Lord God, who
created the heavens and the earth, who
has guided you to strike the head of
the leader of our enemies. 19 Your hope
will never depart from the hearts of
men, as they remember the power of
God. 20 May God grant this to be a
perpetual honor to you, and may he
visit you with blessings, because you
did not spare your own life when our
nation was brought low, but have
avenged our ruin, walking in the
straight path before our God." And
all the people said, "So be it, so be it!"

14 Then Judith said to them, "Listen
to me, my brethren, and take this
head and hang it upon the parapet of
your wall. 2 And as soon as morning
comes and the sun rises, let every
valiant man take his weapons and go
out of the city, and set a captain over
them, as if you were going down to the
plain against the Assyrian outpost;
only do not go down. 3 Then they will
seize their arms and go into the camp
and rouse the officers of the Assyrian
army; and they will rush into the tent
of Holofernes, and will not find him.
Then fear will come over them, and
they will flee before you, 4 and you and
all who live within the borders of Israel
shall pursue them and cut them down
as they flee. 5 But before you do all this,
bring Achior the Ammonite to me, and
let him see and recognize the man who
despised the house of Israel and sent
him to us as if to his death."

6 So they summoned Achior from
the house of Uzziah. And when he
came and saw the head of Holofernes
in the hand of one of the men at the
gathering of the people, he fell down
on his face and his spirit failed him.
7 And when they raised him up he fell
at Judith's feet, and knelt before her,
and said, "Blessed are you in every
tent of Judah! In every nation those
who hear your name will be alarmed.
8 Now tell me what you have done
during these days."

Then Judith described to him in the
presence of the people all that she had
done, from the day she left until the
moment of her speaking to them.
9 And when she had finished, the people
raised a great shout and made a joyful
noise in their city. 10 And when Achior
saw all that the God of Israel had done,
he believed firmly in God, and was circumcised, and joined the house of
Israel, remaining so to this day.

11 As soon as it was dawn they hung
the head of Holofernes on the wall,
and every man took his weapons, and
they went out in companies to the
passes in the mountains. 12 And when
the Assyrians saw them they sent word
to their commanders, and they went to
the generals and the captains and to
all their officers. 13 So they came to
Holofernes' tent and said to the
steward in charge of all his personal
affairs, "Wake up our lord, for the
slaves have been so bold as to come
down against us to give battle, in order
to be destroyed completely."

14 So Bagoas went in and knocked
at the door of the tent, for he supposed
that he was sleeping with Judith. 15 But
when no one answered, he opened it
and went into the bedchamber and
found him thrown down on the platform dead, with his head cut off and
missing. 16 And he cried out with a

14.1–10: Achior identifies the head of Holofernes and is converted to Judaism. 1–4: Judith suggests tactics which will put the enemy to flight with minimum effort by the Jewish forces. In the Latin version, v. 5 is omitted and vv. 6–7, more logically, precede vv. 1–4. **5:** *Achior*, the Ammonite leader whom Holofernes had left to be destroyed with the Jews (5.5–6.21). The full irony of the situation is evident when one remembers that Achior had been told he would see that face again only on the day of Holofernes' vengeance (6.5). **10:** The author seems to have forgotten that the conversion of an Ammonite to Judaism is strictly forbidden by the law (Dt.23.3).

14.11–19: The enemy discovers Holofernes' death. 11–13: As Judith had planned, the threatening movements of the Jews lead to the discovery of Holofernes' body.

loud voice and wept and groaned and
shouted, and rent his garments. [17]Then
he went to the tent where Judith had
stayed, and when he did not find her
he rushed out to the people and
shouted, [18]"The slaves have tricked us!
One Hebrew woman has brought disgrace upon the house of King Nebuchadnezzar! For look, here is Holofernes lying on the ground, and his
head is not on him!"

19 When the leaders of the Assyrian
army heard this, they rent their tunics
and were greatly dismayed, and their
loud cries and shouts arose in the midst
of the camp.

15 When the men in the tents heard
it, they were amazed at what had
happened. [2]Fear and trembling came
over them, so that they did not wait for
one another, but with one impulse all
rushed out and fled by every path
across the plain and through the hill
country. [3]Those who had camped in
the hills around Bethulia also took to
flight. Then the men of Israel, every
one that was a soldier, rushed out upon
them. [4]And Uzziah sent men to Betomasthaim and Bebai and Choba and
Kola, and to all the frontiers of Israel,
to tell what had taken place and to
urge all to rush out upon their enemies
to destroy them. [5]And when the
Israelites heard it, with one accord they
fell upon the enemy,[u] and cut them
down as far as Choba. Those in Jerusalem and all the hill country also
came, for they were told what had
happened in the camp of the enemy;
and those in Gilead and in Galilee out-
flanked them with great slaughter, even
beyond Damascus and its borders.
[6]The rest of the people of Bethulia fell
upon the Assyrian camp and plundered
it, and were greatly enriched. [7]And
the Israelites, when they returned from
the slaughter, took possession of what
remained, and the villages and towns
in the hill country and in the plain got
a great amount of booty, for there was
a vast quantity of it.

8 Then Joakim the high priest, and
the senate of the people of Israel who
lived at Jerusalem, came to witness the
good things which the Lord had done
for Israel, and to see Judith and to
greet her. [9]And when they met her
they all blessed her with one accord
and said to her, "You are the exaltation of Jerusalem, you are the great
glory of Israel, you are the great pride
of our nation! [10]You have done all
this singlehanded; you have done great
good to Israel, and God is well pleased
with it. May the Almighty Lord bless
you for ever!" And all the people said,
"So be it!"

11 So all the people plundered the
camp for thirty days. They gave Judith
the tent of Holofernes and all his silver
dishes and his beds and his bowls
and all his furniture; and she took
them and loaded her mule and hitched
up her carts and piled the things on
them.

12 Then all the women of Israel
gathered to see her, and blessed her,
and some of them performed a dance
for her; and she took branches in her
hands and gave them to the women
who were with her; [13]and they crowned

u Gk *them*

15.1–7: The Assyrians, fleeing in panic, are slaughtered and despoiled by the Jews. 3: *Those who had camped in the hills* were the Edomites and Ammonites (7.18). **4:** As with so many place names in this book, *Betomasthaim and Bebai and Choba and Kola* have never been satisfactorily identified. **5:** *Gilead,* which was situated in the northern part of Transjordan, and *Galilee,* in the north of Palestine proper, lay on either flank of the enemy's northeastward flight through *Damascus* and back toward Assyria.

15.8–13: Judith is led in triumph to Jerusalem. 11: The *thirty days* of plundering is obviously unrealistic. While the people apparently intend that Judith herself shall have Holofernes' treasure, she accepts the gifts only with the intention of dedicating them to God (16.19). **12:** *A dance,* compare 1 Sam.18.6; Ps.149.3–9. *Branches,* Ps.118.27; 1 Macc.13.51; 2 Macc.10.7. **13:** The reference to *olive wreaths* seems to indicate a late date for the book, for the custom is Greek, not Jewish. The destination of the procession is the temple in Jerusalem (16.18).

themselves with olive wreaths, she and
those who were with her; and she went
before all the people in the dance, leading all the women, while all the men of
Israel followed, bearing their arms and
wearing garlands and with songs on
their lips.

16 Then Judith began this thanksgiving before all Israel, and all
the people loudly sang this song of
praise. 2 And Judith said,

Begin a song to my God with
tambourines,
sing to my Lord with cymbals.
Raise to him a new psalm;[v]
exalt him, and call upon his
name.
3 For God is the Lord who crushes
wars;
for he has delivered me out of
the hands of my pursuers,
and brought me into his camp,
in the midst of the people.

4 The Assyrian came down from the
mountains of the north;
he came with myriads of his
warriors;
their multitude blocked up the
valleys,
their cavalry covered the hills.
5 He boasted that he would burn up
my territory,
and kill my young men with the
sword,
and dash my infants to the
ground
and seize my children as prey,
and take my virgins as booty.

6 But the Lord Almighty has foiled
them
by the hand of a woman.
7 For their mighty one did not fall
by the hands of the young
men,
nor did the sons of the Titans
smite him,
nor did tall giants set upon him;
but Judith the daughter of Merari
undid him
with the beauty of her
countenance.

8 For she took off her widow's
mourning
to exalt the oppressed in Israel.
She anointed her face with ointment
and fastened her hair with a
tiara
and put on a linen gown to
deceive him.
9 Her sandal ravished his eyes,
her beauty captivated his mind,
and the sword severed his
neck.
10 The Persians trembled at her
boldness,
the Medes were daunted at her
daring.

11 Then my oppressed people shouted
for joy;
my weak people shouted[w] and
the enemy[x] trembled;
they lifted up their voices, and the
enemy[x] were turned back.
12 The sons of maidservants have
pierced them through;
they were wounded like the
children of fugitives,
they perished before the army of
my Lord.

13 I will sing to my God a new song:
O Lord, thou art great and
glorious,
wonderful in strength, invincible.

v Other authorities read *a psalm and praise*
w Other authorities read *feared*
x Gk *they*

16.1–17: Judith's thanksgiving psalm. In the book of Tobit (ch. 13) a prayer composed by Tobit occupies a similar position at the end of the story. It is Israel, personified as a woman, who sings the hymn; Judith herself is referred to only in the third person (v. 7). **2–3:** A call to praise (compare Ex.15.21; Jg.5.2). **2:** The phrase "a new" psalm (compare v. 13) is a cliché drawn from the Psalter (e.g. Pss.96.1; 98.1). **4–12:** Description of the victory. **7:** *Sons of the Titans* is Greek; perhaps the original had "sons of Rephaim" (compare Dt.3.11). **13–16:** A general hymn of praise. **13:** *I will sing . . . a new song*, Ps.144.9. The hymn begins in the next

[14]Let all thy creatures serve thee,
for thou didst speak, and they were made.
Thou didst send forth thy Spirit,[y]
and it formed them;
there is none that can resist thy voice.
[15]For the mountains shall be shaken
to their foundations with the waters;
at thy presence the rocks shall melt like wax,
but to those who fear thee
thou wilt continue to show mercy.
[16]For every sacrifice as a fragrant
offering is a small thing,
and all fat for burnt offerings to
thee is a very little thing,
but he who fears the Lord shall be
great for ever.

[17]Woe to the nations that rise up
against my people!
The Lord Almighty will take
vengeance on them in the day
of judgment;
fire and worms he will give to their
flesh;
they shall weep in pain for ever.

18 When they arrived at Jerusalem
they worshiped God. As soon as the
people were purified, they offered
their burnt offerings, their freewill
offerings, and their gifts. [19]Judith
also dedicated to God all the vessels
of Holofernes, which the people had
given her; and the canopy which she
took for herself from his bedchamber
she gave as a votive offering to the
Lord. [20]So the people continued feasting in Jerusalem before the sanctuary
for three months, and Judith remained
with them.

21 After this every one returned
home to his own inheritance, and
Judith went to Bethulia, and remained
on her estate, and was honored in her
time throughout the whole country.
[22]Many desired to marry her, but she
remained a widow all the days of her
life after Manasseh her husband died
and was gathered to his people. [23]She
became more and more famous, and
grew old in her husband's house, until
she was one hundred and five years old.
She set her maid free. She died in
Bethulia, and they buried her in the
cave of her husband Manasseh, [24]and
the house of Israel mourned for her
seven days. Before she died she distributed her property to all those who
were next of kin to her husband
Manasseh, and to her own nearest
kindred. [25]And no one ever again
spread terror among the people of
Israel in the days of Judith, or for a
long time after her death.

y Or *breath*

line. **14:** Pss.33.6; 104.30. **16:** *Every sacrifice . . . is a small thing;* to compare sacrifice unfavorably with moral obedience ("to fear the Lord") is a commonplace of Old Testament religion, especially in later times (1 Sam.15.22; Pss.40.6–8; 50.8–15; 51.16–17; Hos.6.6; compare Sir.34.18–19). **17:** Concluding anathema on Israel's enemies (compare Jg.5.31). *Fire and worms,* Is.66.24; Sir.7.17. As in Dan.12.2, the punishment of the wicked is eternal.

16.18–20: A victory celebration in Jerusalem. **20:** *Three months,* Syriac, "a month of days."

16.21–25: Judith remains a widow and dies at a ripe old age. **24:** She *distributed her property,* according to the Mosaic law (Num.27.11).

THE ADDITIONS TO THE BOOK OF

ESTHER

Translated in the order of the Greek version of Esther but with the chapter and verse numbers of the King James Version

After the book of Esther had been translated from Hebrew into Greek, six Additions totaling 107 verses were incorporated at various points in the narrative. These supplementary sections were also included in the Old Latin translation, which was based on the Greek. In the fourth century A.D. Jerome, when making the Latin Vulgate Bible, removed all of the Additions and placed them at the end of the book of Esther. Rearranged in their proper chronological order, and with chapter and verse numbering which reflects Jerome's order, the six Additions are: 11.2–12.6, Mordecai saves the king's life; 13.1–7, The king's letter ordering the massacre of the Jews; 13.8–14, The prayers of Mordecai and Esther; 15.1–16, Esther risks her life to appeal to the king; 16.1–24, The king's second letter, denouncing Haman and directing his subjects to help the Jews; 10.4–11.1, Mordecai's dream interpreted and the book of Esther attested as genuine.

Some of the Additions were probably introduced by Lysimachus, an Alexandrian Jew who lived at Jerusalem and who translated the canonical book of Esther about 114 B.C. (11.1). Other Additions appear to have been inserted several years later, either by Lysimachus or by another person.

The purpose of the Additions is partly to make the story more vivid but chiefly to supply a religious element that is lacking in the canonical book of Esther, which never mentions God or religious practices. The Additions make frequent reference to God, emphasize his choice of Abraham and Israel, and give prominence to prayer. They occasionally contradict the canonical book of Esther, and have little or no historical value.

---

11 [2]In the second year of the reign
of Artaxerxes the Great, on the
first day of Nisan, Mordecai the son of
Jair, son of Shimei, son of Kish, of
the tribe of Benjamin, had a dream.
[3]He was a Jew, dwelling in the city of
Susa, a great man, serving in the court
of the king. [4]He was one of the captives
whom Nebuchadnezzar king of Babylon had brought from Jerusalem with
Jeconiah king of Judea. And this was
his dream:

5 Behold, noise[a] and confusion,
thunders and earthquake, tumult upon
the earth! [6]And behold, two great
dragons came forward, both ready to
fight, and they roared terribly. [7]And
at their roaring every nation prepared
for war, to fight against the nation of
the righteous. [8]And behold, a day of
darkness and gloom, tribulation and
distress, affliction and great tumult
upon the earth! [9]And the whole righteous nation was troubled; they feared
the evils that threatened them, and
were ready to perish. [10]Then they cried
to God; and from their cry, as though
from a tiny spring, there came a great
river, with abundant water; [11]light
came, and the sun rose, and the lowly
were exalted and consumed those held
in honor.

12 Mordecai saw in this dream what

[a] Or *voices*

11.2–12: Mordecai's dream of impending conflict between two *dragons* (Mordecai and Haman; compare 10.7) pictures how the *righteous nation* Israel, threatened with annihilation, is delivered by God. **2:** *Artaxerxes* is Xerxes I (486 [or 485]–465 B.C.). His *second year* was 485 [or 484] B.C. **4:** This verse dates Mordecai's captivity in 597 B.C. (2 Kg.24.15); v. 2 dates his dream 112 years later. **7:** *Nation of the righteous*, that is, the Jews. **10:** The expressions *tiny spring* and *great river* refer to Esther (10.6). **12:** Mordecai knows that the *dream* forecasts God's action, but does not yet grasp the interpretation given in 10.6–12.

God had determined to do, and after
he awoke he had it on his mind and
sought all day to understand it in every
detail.

12 Now Mordecai took his rest in
the courtyard with Gabatha and
Tharra, the two eunuchs of the king
who kept watch in the courtyard. [2]He
overheard their conversation and inquired into their purposes, and learned
that they were preparing to lay hands
upon Artaxerxes the king; and he informed the king concerning them.
[3]Then the king examined the two
eunuchs, and when they confessed they
were led to execution. [4]The king made
a permanent record of these things, and
Mordecai wrote an account of them.
[5]And the king ordered Mordecai to
serve in the court and rewarded him
for these things. [6]But Haman, the son
of Hammedatha, a Bougaean, was in
great honor with the king, and he
sought to injure Mordecai and his
people because of the two eunuchs of
the king.

Esther 1.1–3.13 follows here in the Greek

13 This is a copy of the letter: "The
Great King, Artaxerxes, to the
rulers of the hundred and twenty-seven
provinces from India to Ethiopia and
to the governors under them, writes
thus:

2 "Having become ruler of many
nations and master of the whole world,
not elated with presumption of authority but always acting reasonably and
with kindness, I have determined to
settle the lives of my subjects in lasting
tranquillity and, in order to make my
kingdom peaceable and open to travel
throughout all its extent, to re-establish
the peace which all men desire.

3 "When I asked my counselors how
this might be accomplished, Haman,
who excels among us in sound judgment, and is distinguished for his un-
changing good will and steadfast
fidelity, and has attained the second
place in the kingdom, [4]pointed out to
us that among all the nations in the
world there is scattered a certain hostile
people, who have laws contrary to
those of every nation and continually
disregard the ordinances of the kings,
so that the unifying of the kingdom
which we honorably intend cannot be
brought about. [5]We understand that
this people, and it alone, stands constantly in opposition to all men, per-
versely following a strange manner of
life and laws, and is ill-disposed to our
government, doing all the harm they
can so that our kingdom may not
attain stability.

6 "Therefore we have decreed that
those indicated to you in the letters
of Haman, who is in charge of affairs
and is our second father, shall all, with
their wives and children, be utterly
destroyed by the sword of their
enemies, without pity or mercy, on the
fourteenth day of the twelfth month,
Adar, of this present year, [7]so that
those who have long been and are now
hostile may in one day go down in
violence to Hades, and leave our
government completely secure and
untroubled hereafter."

12.1–6: Mordecai saves the king's life when two eunuchs posted to protect the king plot instead to kill him. **5:** The king rewards Mordecai (in Est.6.3, however, it is said later that "nothing has been done for him"). **6:** It is implied that Haman shared in the plot and so resented Mordecai's action. *Bougaean* represents a Greek word which in Est.3.1 translates the Hebrew word Agagite (compare 1 Sam.15.8).

13.1–7: The king's letter ordering the massacre of the Jews. This addition follows Est.3.1–13, in which Haman has induced Artaxerxes to send a letter to all provinces of his kingdom, ordering complete annihilation of *a certain hostile people*, the Jews, because they observe *a strange manner of life and laws;* they observe the Mosaic law. **6:** *Our second father* implies that Haman ranked second only to the king. *Fourteenth day*, according to 16.20 (and Est.3.13; 8.12; 9.1) it was the thirteenth day. *Adar*, February-March.

Esther 3.14–4.17 follows
here in the Greek

8 Then Mordecai[b] prayed to the
Lord, calling to remembrance all the
works of the Lord. He said:
9 "O Lord, Lord, King who rulest
over all things, for the universe is in
thy power and there is no one who
can oppose thee if it is thy will to save
Israel. 10For thou hast made heaven
and earth and every wonderful thing
under heaven, 11and thou art Lord of
all, and there is no one who can resist
thee, who art the Lord. 12Thou knowest all things; thou knowest, O Lord,
that it was not in insolence or pride or
for any love of glory that I did this, and
refused to bow down to this proud
Haman. 13For I would have been willing to kiss the soles of his feet, to save
Israel! 14But I did this, that I might
not set the glory of man above the
glory of God, and I will not bow down
to any one but to thee, who art my
Lord; and I will not do these things
in pride. 15And now, O Lord God and
King, God of Abraham, spare thy
people; for the eyes of our foes are
upon us[c] to annihilate us, and they
desire to destroy the inheritance that
has been thine from the beginning.
16Do not neglect thy portion, which
thou didst redeem for thyself out of
the land of Egypt. 17Hear my prayer,
and have mercy upon thy inheritance;
turn our mourning into feasting, that
we may live and sing praise to thy
name, O Lord; do not destroy the
mouth of those who praise thee."
18 And all Israel cried out mightily,
for their death was before their eyes.

14 And Esther the queen, seized
with deathly anxiety, fled to the
Lord; 2she took off her splendid
apparel and put on the garments of
distress and mourning, and instead of
costly perfumes she covered her head
with ashes and dung, and she utterly
humbled her body, and every part that
she loved to adorn she covered with
her tangled hair. 3And she prayed to
the Lord God of Israel, and said:
"O my Lord, thou only art our King;
help me, who am alone and have no
helper but thee, 4for my danger is in
my hand. 5Ever since I was born I
have heard in the tribe of my family
that thou, O Lord, didst take Israel out
of all the nations, and our fathers from
among all their ancestors, for an everlasting inheritance, and that thou didst
do for them all that thou didst promise.
6And now we have sinned before thee,
and thou hast given us into the hands
of our enemies, 7because we glorified
their gods. Thou art righteous, O
Lord! 8And now they are not satisfied
that we are in bitter slavery, but they
have covenanted with their idols 9to
abolish what thy mouth has ordained
and to destroy thy inheritance, to stop
the mouths of those who praise thee
and to quench thy altar and the glory
of thy house, 10to open the mouths of
the nations for the praise of vain idols,
and to magnify for ever a mortal king.
11O Lord, do not surrender thy scepter
to what has no being; and do not let
them mock at our downfall; but turn
their plan against themselves, and make
an example of the man who began this
against us. 12Remember, O Lord;

b Gk *he* *c* Gk *for they are looking upon us*

13.8–14.19: The prayers of Mordecai and Esther. The canonical book of Esther never mentions God or prayer or calls Israel God's chosen people. These prayers are added to give the book a deeply religious tone. They call God *Lord* and *King* and *Lord God of Abraham.* He is righteous, has created and rules all things, has redeemed his people Israel from Egypt, answers prayer, and can save them now. **13.12–14:** Mordecai did not *bow down* to Haman, as the king's other servants did (Est.3.2), because such homage is due only to God. **18:** All Israel echoed Mordecai's prayer.

14.1–19: Esther joins in her people's prayer for deliverance. 1–2: She discards every trace of queenly attire and elegance and prays as an unworthy member of Israel. **6–7:** Her people's captivity is due to their sinfulness and idolatry while living in Palestine (Dan.9.16); Israel does not deserve to be saved. **11:** Esther begs God not to let pagan idols, that have no real existence,

make thyself known in this time of our
affliction, and give me courage, O King
of the gods and Master of all dominion!
13Put eloquent speech in my mouth
before the lion, and turn his heart to
hate the man who is fighting against
us, so that there may be an end of him
and those who agree with him. 14But
save us by thy hand, and help me, who
am alone and have no helper but thee,
O Lord. 15Thou hast knowledge of all
things; and thou knowest that I hate
the splendor of the wicked and abhor
the bed of the uncircumcised and of
any alien. 16Thou knowest my necessity—that I abhor the sign of my proud
position, which is upon my head on the
days when I appear in public. I abhor
it like a menstruous rag, and I do not
wear it on the days when I am at
leisure. 17And thy servant has not
eaten at Haman's table, and I have
not honored the king's feast or drunk
the wine of the libations. 18Thy servant
has had no joy since the day that I was
brought here until now, except in thee,
O Lord God of Abraham. 19O God,
whose might is over all, hear the voice
of the despairing, and save us from the
hands of evildoers. And save me from
my fear!"

15 On the third day, when she
ended her prayer, she took off
the garments in which she had worshiped, and arrayed herself in splendid
attire. 2Then, majestically adorned,
after invoking the aid of the all-seeing
God and Savior, she took her two
maids with her, 3leaning daintily on
one, 4while the other followed carrying
her train. 5She was radiant with perfect beauty, and she looked happy, as
if beloved, but her heart was frozen
with fear. 6When she had gone through
all the doors, she stood before the king.
He was seated on his royal throne,
clothed in the full array of his majesty,
all covered with gold and precious
stones. And he was most terrifying.
7 Lifting his face, flushed with
splendor, he looked at her in fierce
anger. And the queen faltered, and
turned pale and faint, and collapsed
upon the head of the maid who went
before her. 8Then God changed the
spirit of the king to gentleness, and in
alarm he sprang from his throne and
took her in his arms until she came to
herself. And he comforted her with
soothing words, and said to her,
9"What is it, Esther? I am your
brother. Take courage; 10you shall not
die, for our law applies only to the
people.[d] Come near."
11 Then he raised the golden scepter
and touched it to her neck; 12and he
embraced her, and said, "Speak to
me." 13And she said to him, "I saw
you, my lord, like an angel of God,
and my heart was shaken with fear at
your glory. 14For you are wonderful,
my lord, and your countenance is full
of grace." 15But as she was speaking,
she fell fainting. 16And the king was
agitated, and all his servants sought to
comfort her.

Esther 5.3–8.12 follows
here in the Greek

16 The following is a copy of this
letter:
"The Great King, Artaxerxes, to
the rulers of the provinces from India

d The meaning of the Greek text of this clause is obscure

---

rule the world. **16–18:** Esther says she hates her position as queen and wife of the king, and has never *eaten at Haman's table* or *honored the king's feast* (but compare Est.2.18, as well as Est.5.5 and 7.1).

15.1–16: Esther risks her life to appeal to the king. This passage expands and exaggerates Est.5.1–2. Any one who entered the king's presence without his summons or permission was put to death, unless the king forgave the intrusion (Est.4.11). To avoid personal danger and to induce the king to reverse his decree, Esther enhanced her charm by splendid attire; then with fearful heart she entered the king's presence. The king's initial anger was changed to tender concern by her fright and fainting; she then could plead for her people.

16.1–24: The king's second letter, denouncing Haman and directing his subjects to help the

to Ethiopia, one hundred and twenty-
seven satrapies, and to those who are
loyal to our government, greeting.
2 "The more often they are honored
by the too great kindness of their
benefactors, the more proud do many
men become. 3They not only seek to
injure our subjects, but in their inability to stand prosperity they even
undertake to scheme against their own
benefactors. 4They not only take away
thankfulness from among men, but,
carried away by the boasts of those who
know nothing of goodness, they suppose that they will escape the evil-
hating justice of God, who always sees
everything. 5And often many of those
who are set in places of authority have
been made in part responsible for the
shedding of innocent blood, and have
been involved in irremediable calamities, by the persuasion of friends who
have been entrusted with the administration of public affairs, 6when these
men by the false trickery of their evil
natures beguile the sincere good will
of their sovereigns.
7 "What has been wickedly accomplished through the pestilent behavior
of those who exercise authority un-
worthily, can be seen not so much
from the more ancient records which
we hand on as from investigation of
matters close at hand. 8For the future
we will take care to render our kingdom
quiet and peaceable for all men, 9by
changing our methods and always
judging what comes before our eyes
with more equitable consideration.
10For Haman, the son of Hammedatha,
a Macedonian (really an alien to the
Persian blood, and quite devoid of our
kindliness), having become our guest,
11so far enjoyed the good will that we
have for every nation that he was called
our father and was continually bowed
down to by all as the person second to
the royal throne. 12But, unable to
restrain his arrogance, he undertook
to deprive us of our kingdom and our
life, 13and with intricate craft and
deceit asked for the destruction of
Mordecai, our savior and perpetual
benefactor, and of Esther, the blameless partner of our kingdom, together
with their whole nation. 14He thought
that in this way he would find us
undefended and would transfer the
kingdom of the Persians to the
Macedonians.
15 "But we find that the Jews, who
were consigned to annihilation by this
thrice accursed man, are not evildoers
but are governed by most righteous
laws 16and are sons of the Most High,
the most mighty living God, who has
directed the kingdom both for us and
for our fathers in the most excellent
order.
17 "You will therefore do well not
to put in execution the letters sent by
Haman the son of Hammedatha,
18because the man himself who did
these things has been hanged at the
gate of Susa, with all his household.
For God, who rules over all things, has
speedily inflicted on him the punishment he deserved.
19 "Therefore post a copy of this
letter publicly in every place, and permit the Jews to live under their own
laws. 20And give them reinforcements,
so that on the thirteenth day of the
twelfth month, Adar, on that very day
they may defend themselves against
those who attack them at the time of
their affliction. 21For God, who rules
over all things, has made this day to
be a joy to his chosen people instead
of a day of destruction for them.
22 "Therefore you shall observe
this with all good cheer as a notable
day among your commemorative festivals, 23so that both now and hereafter
it may mean salvation for us and the
loyal Persians, but that for those who

Jews. 10–14: Haman, already executed (Est.7.6–10), is (falsely) called a *Macedonian* trying to overthrow Persian rule. **15–16:** The king commends the Mosaic *laws*, praises the Jews, and recognizes God's rule. All Persian subjects are commanded to ignore Haman's letter (according to 13.1–6 it was really the king's letter) and help the Jews defend themselves on the thirteenth

plot against us it may be a reminder of
destruction.
24 "Every city and country, without
exception, which does not act accordingly, shall be destroyed in wrath with
spear and fire. It shall be made not
only impassable for men, but also
most hateful for all time to beasts and
birds."

This is followed in the Greek by 8.13–10.3, where the Hebrew Esther ends. The Greek version adds the following:

10 [4]And Mordecai said, "These
things have come from God.
[5]For I remember the dream that I had
concerning these matters, and none of
them has failed to be fulfilled. [6]The
tiny spring which became a river, and
there was light and the sun and
abundant water—the river is Esther,
whom the king married and made
queen. [7]The two dragons are Haman
and myself. [8]The nations are those
that gathered to destroy the name of
the Jews. [9]And my nation, this is Israel,
who cried out to God and were saved.
The Lord has saved his people; the
Lord has delivered us from all these
evils; God has done great signs and
wonders, which have not occurred
among the nations. [10]For this purpose
he made two lots, one for the people
of God and one for all the nations.
[11]And these two lots came to the hour
and moment and day of decision before
God and among all the nations. [12]And
God remembered his people and vindicated his inheritance. [13]So they will
observe these days in the month of
Adar, on the fourteenth and fifteenth
of that month, with an assembly and
joy and gladness before God, from
generation to generation for ever
among his people Israel."

11 [1]In the fourth year of the reign of
Ptolemy and Cleopatra, Dositheus,
who said that he was a priest and a
Levite,[e] and Ptolemy his son brought
to Egypt[f] the preceding Letter of
Purim, which they said was genuine
and had been translated by Lysimachus
the son of Ptolemy, one of the residents
of Jerusalem.

e Or *priest, and Levitas*
f Cn: Gk *brought in*

---

day of Adar, the prescribed day of annihilation. **24:** Destruction faces every place which does not defend and respect the Jews.

10.4–11.1: Mordecai's dream interpreted and the book of Esther attested as genuine. This passage interprets the dream of 11.5–11. The threat to Israel is here ascribed not to one man, Haman, as in the canonical Esther, but to a general anti-Semitic hostility against the Jews. **13:** As in Est.9.20–22, Israel is to celebrate this deliverance annually. **11.1:** *Fourth year*, that is 114–113 B.C. *Letter of Purim*, a reference not merely to Mordecai's letter (Est.9.20–22) but to the entire book of Esther. *Lysimachus* is a Greek name; on his work of translating the Hebrew book of Esther into Greek, see the Introduction.

THE WISDOM OF SOLOMON

The Wisdom of Solomon, which the Latin Vulgate Bible entitles simply the book of Wisdom, professes to have been written by Solomon (7.1–14 and 8.17–9.18 recall Solomon's prayer for wisdom in 1 Kg.3.6–9 and 2 Chr.1.8–10). Internal evidence, however, indicates that the book was composed in Greek by an unknown Hellenistic Jew, probably at Alexandria during the latter part of the first century B.C. He no doubt used traditional wisdom material, which perhaps included for the earlier chapters material originally written in Hebrew and then translated into Greek. Such a supposition helps to account for the fact that the word "wisdom" occurs twenty-nine times in the first ten chapters, where the concept of wisdom is personified, while in the last nine chapters the word appears only twice and with a much vaguer meaning. Whatever oral or written sources were used, however, it is probable that one man wrote the entire book.

The literary style of the book varies from poetic patches of high lyrical quality to plodding and pedestrian prose. Impersonating King Solomon, the author promises reward and immortality to the righteous and warns the wicked of judgment (chs. 1–5); praises wisdom and describes her nature and works (chs. 6–9); illustrates wisdom's guidance of God's people from Adam to Moses and recalls God's judgment on the Egyptians and Canaanites (chs. 10–12); explains the origin and folly of idolatry (chs. 13–15); and contrasts God's plagues on the Egyptians and his kindness to his people (chs. 16–19).

LOVE RIGHTEOUSNESS, YOU RULERS OF
the earth,
think of the Lord with uprightness,
and seek him with sincerity of
heart;
2 because he is found by those who do
not put him to the test,
and manifests himself to those who
do not distrust him.
3 For perverse thoughts separate men
from God,
and when his power is tested, it
convicts the foolish;
4 because wisdom will not enter a
deceitful soul,
nor dwell in a body enslaved to sin.
5 For a holy and disciplined spirit will
flee from deceit,
and will rise and depart from foolish
thoughts,
and will be ashamed at the approach
of unrighteousness.

6 For wisdom is a kindly spirit and
will not free a blasphemer from the
guilt of his words;
because God is witness of his inmost
feelings,
and a true observer of his heart, and
a hearer of his tongue.
7 Because the Spirit of the Lord has
filled the world,
and that which holds all things
together knows what is said;
8 therefore no one who utters
unrighteous things will escape
notice,
and justice, when it punishes, will
not pass him by.
9 For inquiry will be made into the
counsels of an ungodly man,
and a report of his words will come
to the Lord,
to convict him of his lawless deeds;
10 because a jealous ear hears all things,
and the sound of murmurings does
not go unheard.
11 Beware then of useless murmuring,
and keep your tongue from slander;
because no secret word is without
result,[a]

[a] Or *will go unpunished*

1.1–5.23: Commendation of wisdom as guide to happiness and immortality. 1.1–5: *Rulers* (compare 6.1) are urged to *love righteousness* and seek God. *Wisdom* dwells only in a sincere, holy, and disciplined soul.

1.6–11: The ungodly will not escape punishment; God knows their unrighteous thoughts, words, and deeds and will judge them. **6:** *A kindly spirit*, literally "a spirit that loves man"; wisdom's concern for man's welfare will not tolerate blasphemous or unrighteous words.

and a lying mouth destroys the soul.

[12]Do not invite death by the error of
your life,
nor bring on destruction by the
works of your hands;
[13]because God did not make death,
and he does not delight in the death
of the living.
[14]For he created all things that they
might exist,
and the generative forces[b] of the
world are wholesome,
and there is no destructive poison in
them;
and the dominion[c] of Hades is not
on earth.
[15]For righteousness is immortal.

[16]But ungodly men by their words and
deeds summoned death;[d]
considering him a friend, they pined
away,
and they made a convenant with
him,
because they are fit to belong to his
party.

2 For they reasoned unsoundly,
saying to themselves,
"Short and sorrowful is our life,
and there is no remedy when a
man comes to his end,
and no one has been known to
return from Hades.
[2]Because we were born by mere
chance,
and hereafter we shall be as though
we had never been;
because the breath in our nostrils is
smoke,
and reason is a spark kindled by the
beating of our hearts.
[3]When it is extinguished, the body
will turn to ashes,
and the spirit will dissolve like
empty air.
[4]Our name will be forgotten in time,
and no one will remember our
works;
our life will pass away like the traces
of a cloud,
and be scattered like mist
that is chased by the rays of the sun
and overcome by its heat.
[5]For our allotted time is the passing
of a shadow,
and there is no return from our
death,
because it is sealed up and no one
turns back.

[6]"Come, therefore, let us enjoy the
good things that exist,
and make use of the creation to the
full as in youth.
[7]Let us take our fill of costly wine
and perfumes,
and let no flower of spring pass by
us.
[8]Let us crown ourselves with
rosebuds before they wither.
[9]Let none of us fail to share in our
revelry,
everywhere let us leave signs of
enjoyment,
because this is our portion, and this
our lot.
[10]Let us oppress the righteous poor
man;
let us not spare the widow
nor regard the gray hairs of the
aged.
[11]But let our might be our law of
right,
for what is weak proves itself to be
useless.

[12]"Let us lie in wait for the righteous
man,
because he is inconvenient to us
and opposes our actions;

b Or *the creatures* *c* Or *palace* *d* Gk *him*

1.12–15: God has made man for immortality. 15: Righteous living leads to immortality.
1.16–2.24: The reasoning of the materialist or sensualist. 2.1–5: The ungodly say that life is *short*, birth the result of *mere chance*, life without real meaning, and physical death the end of existence. **6–9:** They encourage one another to live lives of sensual satisfaction before death snuffs out existence. **10–20:** They urge one another to oppress *righteous*, helpless folk, whose godly words and lives reproach them, and to persecute, torture, and kill those who call *God*

he reproaches us for sins against
the law,
and accuses us of sins against our
training.
13 He professes to have knowledge of
God,
and calls himself a child[e] of the
Lord.
14 He became to us a reproof of our
thoughts;
15 the very sight of him is a burden
to us,
because his manner of life is unlike
that of others,
and his ways are strange.
16 We are considered by him as
something base,
and he avoids our ways as
unclean;
he calls the last end of the
righteous happy,
and boasts that God is his father.
17 Let us see if his words are true,
and let us test what will happen at
the end of his life;
18 for if the righteous man is God's
son, he will help him,
and will deliver him from the hand
of his adversaries.
19 Let us test him with insult and
torture,
that we may find out how gentle
he is,
and make trial of his forbearance.
20 Let us condemn him to a shameful
death,
for, according to what he says, he
will be protected."

21 Thus they reasoned, but they were
led astray,
for their wickedness blinded them,
22 and they did not know the secret
purposes of God,
nor hope for the wages of holiness,
nor discern the prize for blameless
souls;
23 for God created man for
incorruption,
and made him in the image of his
own eternity,[f]
24 but through the devil's envy death
entered the world,
and those who belong to his party
experience it.

3 But the souls of the righteous
are in the hand of God,
and no torment will ever touch
them.
2 In the eyes of the foolish they
seemed to have died,
and their departure was thought to
be an affliction,
3 and their going from us to be their
destruction;
but they are at peace.
4 For though in the sight of men they
were punished,
their hope is full of immortality.
5 Having been disciplined a little,
they will receive great good,
because God tested them and found
them worthy of himself;
6 like gold in the furnace he tried
them,
and like a sacrificial burnt offering
he accepted them.
7 In the time of their visitation they
will shine forth,
and will run like sparks through
the stubble.
8 They will govern nations and rule
over peoples,
and the Lord will reign over them
for ever.
9 Those who trust in him will
understand truth,

e Or *servant*
f Other ancient authorities read *nature*

their *father*. **21–24:** Such false reasoning arises from *wickedness* and consequent failure to know God. God made man in his image to be immortal, but *the devil's envy* (compare 1.16) brought *death* into *the world.*

3.1–9: The blessed estate of the righteous. Though affliction, suffering, and the early death of *the righteous* may seem to be divine punishment, after death their *souls* are forever safe and at *peace* with God; they enjoy sure *immortality.* **7–9:** Their discipline and testing will be followed by a divine *visitation;* God will vindicate them, let them share in his rule over all peoples, and give them understanding of his ways.

and the faithful will abide with him
in love,
because grace and mercy are upon
his elect,
and he watches over his holy ones.[g]

10 But the ungodly will be punished
as their reasoning deserves,
who disregarded the righteous
man[h]
and rebelled against the Lord;
11 for whoever despises wisdom and
instruction is miserable.
Their hope is vain, their labors are
unprofitable,
and their works are useless.
12 Their wives are foolish, and their
children evil;
13 their offspring are accursed.
For blessed is the barren woman
who is undefiled,
who has not entered into a sinful
union;
she will have fruit when God
examines souls.
14 Blessed also is the eunuch whose
hands have done no lawless
deed,
and who has not devised wicked
things against the Lord;
for special favor will be shown him
for his faithfulness,
and a place of great delight in the
temple of the Lord.
15 For the fruit of good labors is
renowned,
and the root of understanding does
not fail.
16 But children of adulterers will not
come to maturity,
and the offspring of an unlawful
union will perish.
17 Even if they live long they will be
held of no account,
and finally their old age will be
without honor.
18 If they die young, they will have
no hope
and no consolation in the day of
decision.
19 For the end of an unrighteous
generation is grievous.

4 Better than this is childlessness
with virtue,
for in the memory of virtue[i] is
immortality,
because it is known both by God
and by men.
2 When it is present, men imitate[j]
it,
and they long for it when it has
gone;
and throughout all time it marches
crowned in triumph,
victor in the contest for prizes that
are undefiled.
3 But the prolific brood of the
ungodly will be of no use,
and none of their illegitimate
seedlings will strike a deep root
or take a firm hold.
4 For even if they put forth boughs
for a while,
standing insecurely they will be
shaken by the wind,
and by the violence of the winds
they will be uprooted.
5 The branches will be broken off
before they come to maturity,
and their fruit will be useless,
not ripe enough to eat, and good
for nothing.
6 For children born of unlawful
unions
are witnesses of evil against their
parents when God examines
them.[k]

g The text of this line is uncertain, and it is omitted here by some ancient authorities. Compare 4.15
h Or *what is right* *i* Gk *it*
j Other ancient authorities read *honor*
k Gk *at their examination*

3.10–4.6: The punishment of the ungodly. The ungodly will meet a sad end, because disregarding what *the righteous* could teach them *they rebelled against the Lord* (v. 10). In Israel the possession of many children and a long life were often considered proof of God's favor. But the *barren woman* and the *eunuch* are also blessed by God (vv. 13–14); a virtuous life is what counts, for it alone assures *immortality*. The wicked, even if they *live long* (v. 17) and have many children (4.3), have *no* justified *hope* for the future; their children usually die early, are *of no account*, and attest their parents' wickedness (3.16–18).

[7]But the righteous man, though he
die early, will be at rest.
[8]For old age is not honored for
length of time,
nor measured by number of years;
[9]but understanding is gray hair for
men,
and a blameless life is ripe old age.

[10]There was one who pleased God
and was loved by him,
and while living among sinners he
was taken up.
[11]He was caught up lest evil change
his understanding
or guile deceive his soul.
[12]For the fascination of wickedness
obscures what is good,
and roving desire perverts the
innocent mind.
[13]Being perfected in a short time, he
fulfilled long years;
[14]for his soul was pleasing to the
Lord,
therefore he took him quickly from
the midst of wickedness.
[15]Yet the peoples saw and did not
understand,
nor take such a thing to heart,
that God's grace and mercy are
with his elect,
and he watches over his holy ones.

[16]The righteous man who has died
will condemn the ungodly who
are living,
and youth that is quickly perfected[l]
will condemn the prolonged old
age of the unrighteous man.
[17]For they will see the end of the wise
man,
and will not understand what the
Lord purposed for him,
and for what he kept him safe.
[18]They will see, and will have
contempt for him,
but the Lord will laugh them to
scorn.
After this they will become
dishonored corpses,
and an outrage among the dead
for ever;
[19]because he will dash them
speechless to the ground,
and shake them from the
foundations;
they will be left utterly dry and
barren,
and they will suffer anguish,
and the memory of them will
perish.

[20]They will come with dread when
their sins are reckoned up,
and their lawless deeds will convict
them to their face.
5 Then the righteous man will
stand with great confidence
in the presence of those who have
afflicted him,
and those who make light of his
labors.
[2]When they see him, they will be
shaken with dreadful fear,
and they will be amazed at his
unexpected salvation.
[3]They will speak to one another in
repentance,
and in anguish of spirit they will
groan, and say,
[4]"This is the man whom we once
held in derision
and made a byword of reproach—
we fools!
We thought that his life was
madness
and that his end was without honor.

l Or *ended*

4.7–19: The blessedness of the righteous despite premature death. The righteous man who dies young has three advantages: he *will be at rest* with God (v. 7); *a blameless life* means more than long years; and early death ends the danger of falling into evil. **10–15:** Enoch is an example of a good man *perfected in a short time;* he lived 365 years, several hundred years less than any other listed in Gen. ch. 5. **14–15:** *The peoples . . . did not understand* that God was good to Enoch in removing him *from the midst of wickedness.* The wicked, who have contempt for such good men, will be judged by God for their sins.

4.20–5.14: The confusion and remorse of the ungodly at the judgment. 5.3–14: The wicked who have persecuted the righteous will repent; they will see that their lawless, godless way has done

5 Why has he been numbered among
the sons of God?
And why is his lot among the
saints?
6 So it was we who strayed from the
way of truth,
and the light of righteousness did
not shine on us,
and the sun did not rise upon
us.
7 We took our fill of the paths of
lawlessness and destruction,
and we journeyed through
trackless deserts,
but the way of the Lord we have
not known.
8 What has our arrogance profited
us?
And what good has our boasted
wealth brought us?
9 "All those things have vanished
like a shadow,
and like a rumor that passes
by;
10 like a ship that sails through the
billowy water,
and when it has passed no trace
can be found,
nor track of its keel in the waves;
11 or as, when a bird flies through the
air,
no evidence of its passage is found;
the light air, lashed by the beat of
its pinions
and pierced by the force of its
rushing flight,
is traversed by the movement of its
wings,
and afterward no sign of its coming
is found there;
12 or as, when an arrow is shot at a
target,
the air, thus divided, comes
together at once,
so that no one knows its pathway.
13 So we also, as soon as we were born,
ceased to be,
and we had no sign of virtue to
show,
but were consumed in our
wickedness."
14 Because the hope of the ungodly
man is like chaff[m] carried by
the wind,
and like a light hoarfrost[n] driven
away by a storm;
it is dispersed like smoke before
the wind,
and it passes like the remembrance
of a guest who stays but a day.

15 But the righteous live for ever,
and their reward is with the Lord;
the Most High takes care of them.
16 Therefore they will receive a
glorious crown
and a beautiful diadem from the
hand of the Lord,
because with his right hand he will
cover them,
and with his arm he will shield
them.
17 The Lord[o] will take his zeal as his
whole armor,
and will arm all creation to repel[p]
his enemies;
18 he will put on righteousness as a
breastplate,
and wear impartial justice as a
helmet;
19 he will take holiness as an
invincible shield,
20 and sharpen stern wrath for a
sword,
and creation will join with him to
fight against the madmen.
21 Shafts of lightning will fly with
true aim,

m Or *dust*
n Other authorities read *spider's web*
o Gk *He*
p Or *punish*

them no good. **5:** *Sons of God*, either angels, or God's holy people. **6–7:** *Way of truth . . . way of the Lord*, the way which the righteous chose and followed. **9:** *All those things*, namely their wealth and pleasure in tormenting the righteous, give no permanent pleasure or benefit; they vanish without a trace.

5.15–23: The future bliss of the righteous and the misery of the ungodly at the judgment. 17–23: The Lord will put on his full armor (*breastplate, helmet, shield, sword;* compare Eph.6.11–17), and with *lightning*, hail, raging waves, rushing rivers, and mighty winds will fight and overwhelm

and will leap to the target as from a
well-drawn bow of clouds,
22and hailstones full of wrath will be
hurled as from a catapult;
the water of the sea will rage
against them,
and rivers will relentlessly
overwhelm them;
23a mighty wind will rise against them,
and like a tempest it will winnow
them away.
Lawlessness will lay waste the
whole earth,
and evil-doing will overturn the
thrones of rulers.

6 Listen therefore, O kings, and
understand;
learn, O judges of the ends of the
earth.
2Give ear, you that rule over
multitudes,
and boast of many nations.
3For your dominion was given you
from the Lord,
and your sovereignty from the Most
High,
who will search out your works and
inquire into your plans.
4Because as servants of his kingdom
you did not rule rightly,
nor keep the law,
nor walk according to the purpose
of God,
5he will come upon you terribly and
swiftly,
because severe judgment falls on
those in high places.
6For the lowliest man may be
pardoned in mercy,
but mighty men will be mightily
tested.
7For the Lord of all will not stand
in awe of any one,
nor show deference to greatness;
because he himself made both small
and great,
and he takes thought for all alike.
8But a strict inquiry is in store for
the mighty.
9To you then, O monarchs, my
words are directed,
that you may learn wisdom and not
transgress.
10For they will be made holy who
observe holy things in holiness,
and those who have been taught
them will find a defense.
11Therefore set your desire on my
words;
long for them, and you will be
instructed.

12Wisdom is radiant and unfading,
and she is easily discerned by those
who love her,
and is found by those who seek her.
13She hastens to make herself known
to those who desire her.
14He who rises early to seek her will
have no difficulty,
for he will find her sitting at his
gates.
15To fix one's thought on her is
perfect understanding,
and he who is vigilant on her
account will soon be free from
care,
16because she goes about seeking
those worthy of her,
and she graciously appears to them
in their paths,
and meets them in every thought.

17The beginning of wisdom[q] is the
most sincere desire for
instruction,

q Gk *Her beginning*

---

the wicked. **23:** The statement that *evil-doing* overthrows *thrones* recalls 1.1 and prepares for 6.1–11.

6.1–9.18: Commendation of wisdom as the guide of life. 6.1–11: Further admonition to rulers, who receive their authority from God and must answer to him for lawless, godless acts; for he treats alike lowly and *mighty, small and great* (vv. 6–7). *Monarchs* need *wisdom,* and will receive it if they desire it (vv. 9–11).

6.12–16: Wisdom is easily found; for she seeks out those who desire to know her, and gives them understanding (compare Pr. ch. 8, which also refers to rulers).

6.17–20: The steps from the love of wisdom to immortality. A sorites (a form of logic much

and concern for instruction is love
of her,
18and love of her is the keeping of her
laws,
and giving heed to her laws is
assurance of immortality,
19and immortality brings one near to
God;
20so the desire for wisdom leads to a
kingdom.

21Therefore if you delight in thrones
and scepters, O monarchs over
the peoples,
honor wisdom, that you may reign
for ever.
22I will tell you what wisdom is and
how she came to be,
and I will hide no secrets from
you,
but I will trace her course from the
beginning of creation,
and make the knowledge of her
clear,
and I will not pass by the truth;
23neither will I travel in the company
of sickly envy,
for envy[r] does not associate with
wisdom.
24A multitude of wise men is the
salvation of the world,
and a sensible king is the stability
of his people.
25Therefore be instructed by my
words, and you will profit.

7 I also am mortal, like all men,
a descendant of the first-formed
child of earth;
and in the womb of a mother I was
molded into flesh,
2within the period of ten months,
compacted with blood,
from the seed of a man and the
pleasure of marriage.
3And when I was born, I began to
breathe the common air,
and fell upon the kindred earth,
and my first sound was a cry, like
that of all.
4I was nursed with care in swaddling
cloths.
5For no king has had a different
beginning of existence;
6there is for all mankind one
entrance into life, and a common
departure.

7Therefore I prayed, and
understanding was given me;
I called upon God, and the spirit
of wisdom came to me.
8I preferred her to scepters and
thrones,
and I accounted wealth as nothing
in comparison with her.
9Neither did I liken to her any
priceless gem,
because all gold is but a little sand
in her sight,
and silver will be accounted as clay
before her.
10I loved her more than health and
beauty,
and I chose to have her rather than
light,
because her radiance never ceases.
11All good things came to me along
with her,
and in her hands uncounted wealth.
12I rejoiced in them all, because
wisdom leads them;
but I did not know that she was
their mother.
13I learned without guile and I impart

r Gk *this*

used by the Stoics), tracing the path from desire for *wisdom* to its results in *immortality* and fellowship with God. **20:** *A kingdom,* God's eternal kingdom, in which rulers and others who truly desire wisdom participate.

6.21–25: A promise of instruction in the nature of wisdom. The writer speaks in the name of Solomon. **24:** The beneficial results of wisdom: *wise men* save *the world;* rulers guided by wisdom give *stability* to their *people.*

7.1–22a: Solomon received wisdom from God. 1–10: Recognizing his need for wisdom, Solomon *prayed* for and received it, and valued it above every other gift (1 Kg.3.5–15). **11–22a:** With the gift of wisdom Solomon received *all good things, friendship with God,* and *unerring knowledge* of the world, the heavenly bodies, and plant and animal life.

without grudging;
I do not hide her wealth,
14for it is an unfailing treasure for men;
those who get it obtain friendship with God,
commended for the gifts that come from instruction.

15May God grant that I speak with judgment
and have thoughts worthy of what I have received,
for he is the guide even of wisdom
and the corrector of the wise.
16For both we and our words are in his hand,
as are all understanding and skill in crafts.
17For it is he who gave me unerring knowledge of what exists,
to know the structure of the world and the activity of the elements;
18the beginning and end and middle of times,
the alternations of the solstices and the changes of the seasons,
19the cycles of the year and the constellations of the stars,
20the natures of animals and the tempers of wild beasts,
the powers of spirits[s] and the reasonings of men,
the varieties of plants and the virtues of roots;
21I learned both what is secret and what is manifest,
22for wisdom, the fashioner of all things, taught me.

For in her there is a spirit that is intelligent, holy,
unique, manifold, subtle,
mobile, clear, unpolluted,
distinct, invulnerable, loving the good, keen,
irresistible, 23beneficent, humane,
steadfast, sure, free from anxiety,
all-powerful, overseeing all,
and penetrating through all spirits
that are intelligent and pure and most subtle.
24For wisdom is more mobile than any motion;
because of her pureness she pervades and penetrates all things.
25For she is a breath of the power of God,
and a pure emanation of the glory of the Almighty;
therefore nothing defiled gains entrance into her.
26For she is a reflection of eternal light,
a spotless mirror of the working of God,
and an image of his goodness.
27Though she is but one, she can do all things,
and while remaining in herself, she renews all things;
in every generation she passes into holy souls
and makes them friends of God, and prophets;
28for God loves nothing so much as the man who lives with wisdom.
29For she is more beautiful than the sun,
and excels every constellation of the stars.
Compared with the light she is found to be superior,
30for it is succeeded by the night,
but against wisdom evil does not prevail.

8 She reaches mightily from one end of the earth to the other,
and she orders all things well.

s Or *winds*

7.22b–8.1: The nature and beneficial works of wisdom. 22b–23: Wisdom's twenty-one (3 × 7) attributes. **24:** She is a pure, freely moving, and all-penetrating *spirit*. **25–26:** She emanates from God; his *power*, *glory*, purity, *light*, and *goodness* are expressed through her (compare Jn.1.1–14; Heb.1.1–3). **7.27–8.1:** She is everywhere, *orders all things well*, and *can do all things*. Her greatest work is to enter *holy souls* and make them *friends of God, and prophets*. *Evil* cannot defeat her.

[2]I loved her and sought her from
my youth,
and I desired to take her for my
bride,
and I became enamored of her
beauty.
[3]She glorifies her noble birth by
living with God,
and the Lord of all loves her.
[4]For she is an initiate in the
knowledge of God,
and an associate in his works.
[5]If riches are a desirable possession
in life,
what is richer than wisdom who
effects all things?
[6]And if understanding is effective,
who more than she is fashioner of
what exists?
[7]And if any one loves righteousness,
her labors are virtues;
for she teaches self-control and
prudence,
justice and courage;
nothing in life is more profitable
for men than these.
[8]And if any one longs for wide
experience,
she knows the things of old, and
infers the things to come;
she understands turns of speech
and the solutions of riddles;
she has foreknowledge of signs and
wonders
and of the outcome of seasons and
times.
[9]Therefore I determined to take
her to live with me,
knowing that she would give me
good counsel
and encouragement in cares and
grief.
[10]Because of her I shall have glory
among the multitudes
and honor in the presence of the
elders, though I am young.
[11]I shall be found keen in judgment,
and in the sight of rulers I shall be
admired.
[12]When I am silent they will wait
for me,
and when I speak they will give
heed;
and when I speak at greater length
they will put their hands on their
mouths.
[13]Because of her I shall have
immortality,
and leave an everlasting
remembrance to those who
come after me.
[14]I shall govern peoples,
and nations will be subject to me;
[15]dread monarchs will be afraid of
me when they hear of me;
among the people I shall show
myself capable, and courageous
in war.
[16]When I enter my house, I shall
find rest with her,
for companionship with her has
no bitterness,
and life with her has no pain, but
gladness and joy.
[17]When I considered these things
inwardly,
and thought upon them in my mind,
that in kinship with wisdom there
is immortality,
[18]and in friendship with her, pure
delight,
and in the labors of her hands,
unfailing wealth,
and in the experience of her
company, understanding,
and renown in sharing her words,
I went about seeking how to get
her for myself.
[19]As a child I was by nature
well-endowed,

8.2–16: Solomon desires to take wisdom as his bride. 4–6: She is *God's associate in his works*, and his agent in making all things (Pr.8.22–30; compare Jn.1.3; Col.1.16; Heb.1.2). **7:** She *teaches self-control, prudence, justice*, and *courage*, which (according to Plato and the Stoics) are the four cardinal virtues. **8:** She knows the past and the future, and so can give good counsel. **10–16:** *Because of her* Solomon receives *honor* and respect, *immortality*, a great empire, *rest* and *joy*.

8.17–21: Considering all the benefits conferred by wisdom, Solomon prays to God to grant her to him. 19–20: The Platonic view of the soul as pre-existent.

and a good soul fell to my lot;
[20]or rather, being good, I entered an undefiled body.
[21]But I perceived that I would not possess wisdom unless God gave her to me—
and it was a mark of insight to know whose gift she was—
so I appealed to the Lord and besought him,
and with my whole heart I said:

9 "O God of my fathers and Lord of mercy,
who hast made all things by thy word,
[2]and by thy wisdom hast formed man,
to have dominion over the creatures thou hast made,
[3]and rule the world in holiness and righteousness,
and pronounce judgment in uprightness of soul,
[4]give me the wisdom that sits by thy throne,
and do not reject me from among thy servants.
[5]For I am thy slave and the son of thy maidservant,
a man who is weak and short-lived,
with little understanding of judgment and laws;
[6]for even if one is perfect among the sons of men,
yet without the wisdom that comes from thee he will be regarded as nothing.
[7]Thou hast chosen me to be king of thy people
and to be judge over thy sons and daughters.
[8]Thou hast given command to build a temple on thy holy mountain,
and an altar in the city of thy habitation,
a copy of the holy tent which thou didst prepare from the beginning.
[9]With thee is wisdom, who knows thy works
and was present when thou didst make the world,
and who understands what is pleasing in thy sight
and what is right according to thy commandments.
[10]Send her forth from the holy heavens,
and from the throne of thy glory send her,
that she may be with me and toil,
and that I may learn what is pleasing to thee.
[11]For she knows and understands all things,
and she will guide me wisely in my actions
and guard me with her glory.
[12]Then my works will be acceptable,
and I shall judge thy people justly,
and shall be worthy of the throne[t] of my father.
[13]For what man can learn the counsel of God?
Or who can discern what the Lord wills?
[14]For the reasoning of mortals is worthless,
and our designs are likely to fail,
[15]for a perishable body weighs down the soul,
and this earthy tent burdens the thoughtful[u] mind.
[16]We can hardly guess at what is on earth,
and what is at hand we find with labor;
but who has traced out what is in the heavens?
[17]Who has learned thy counsel,
unless thou hast given wisdom

t Gk *thrones* *u* Or *anxious*

9.1–18: Solomon's prayer for wisdom (1 Kg.3.6–9). **1–2:** God *made all things* by his *word* and *wisdom* (compare Jn.1.1–3); here "word" and "wisdom" are synonyms. **6–9:** The *king* needs *wisdom* to learn God's will and to know what is right. **10–12:** Only by wisdom's presence and guidance can the king govern well. **13–15:** Man's *perishable body*, though not called evil (compare 8.20), *burdens* and *hampers* the mind. **16–17:** Man knows even earthly things imperfectly; only through *wisdom*, also called *the holy Spirit*, can he learn heavenly things (1 Cor.2.7–12).

and sent thy holy Spirit from on
high?
18 And thus the paths of those on
earth were set right,
and men were taught what pleases
thee,
and were saved by wisdom."

10 Wisdom[v] protected the
first-formed father of the
world, when he alone had been
created;
she delivered him from his
transgression,
2 and gave him strength to rule all
things.
3 But when an unrighteous man
departed from her in his anger,
he perished because in rage he slew
his brother.
4 When the earth was flooded
because of him, wisdom again
saved it,
steering the righteous man by a
paltry piece of wood.

5 Wisdom[w] also, when the nations
in wicked agreement had been
confounded,
recognized the righteous man and
preserved him blameless before
God,
and kept him strong in the face
of his compassion for his child.

6 Wisdom[w] rescued a righteous man
when the ungodly were
perishing;
he escaped the fire that descended
on the Five Cities.[x]
7 Evidence of their wickedness still
remains:
a continually smoking wasteland,
plants bearing fruit that does not
ripen,
and a pillar of salt standing as a
monument to an unbelieving
soul.
8 For because they passed wisdom
by,
they not only were hindered from
recognizing the good,
but also left for mankind a
reminder of their folly,
so that their failures could never
go unnoticed.

9 Wisdom rescued from troubles
those who served her.
10 When a righteous man fled from
his brother's wrath,
she guided him on straight paths;
she showed him the kingdom of
God,
and gave him knowledge of
angels;[y]
she prospered him in his labors,
and increased the fruit of his toil.
11 When his oppressors were covetous,
she stood by him and made him
rich.
12 She protected him from his
enemies,
and kept him safe from those who
lay in wait for him;
in his arduous contest she gave him
the victory,
so that he might learn that godliness
is more powerful than anything.

13 When a righteous man was sold,
wisdom[z] did not desert him,
but delivered him from sin.
She descended with him into the
dungeon,
14 and when he was in prison she did
not leave him,
until she brought him the scepter
of a kingdom

v Gk *She* w Gk *She*
x Or *Pentapolis*
y Or *of holy things*
z Gk *she*

18: *Wisdom* guides, teaches, and saves men. The remaining chapters of the book tell how wisdom saved Israel and her ancestors, though references to wisdom by name almost disappear after ch. 10.

10.1–12.27: Historical illustrations of the power of wisdom. 10.1–11.4: From Adam to Moses. 10.1–2: Adam (Gen.1.26–5.5). **3:** Cain (Gen.4.1–16). *Perished*, spiritual death. **4:** Noah (Gen. 5.28–9.29). **5:** Abraham (Gen.11.26–25.10). *Nations*, Gen.11.1–9. **6–8:** *A righteous man*, Lot (Gen. ch. 19). **9–12:** Jacob (Gen.25.19–49.33, especially ch. 28). **13–14:** Joseph (Gen. chs.

and authority over his masters.
Those who accused him she showed
to be false,
and she gave him everlasting honor.

15 A holy people and blameless race
wisdom[a] delivered from a nation
of oppressors.
16 She entered the soul of a servant
of the Lord,
and withstood dread kings with
wonders and signs.
17 She gave to holy men the reward
of their labors;
she guided them along a marvelous
way,
and became a shelter to them by
day,
and a starry flame through the
night.
18 She brought them over the Red Sea,
and led them through deep waters;
19 but she drowned their enemies,
and cast them up from the depth
of the sea.
20 Therefore the righteous plundered
the ungodly;
they sang hymns, O Lord, to thy
holy name,
and praised with one accord thy
defending hand,
21 because wisdom opened the mouth
of the dumb,
and made the tongues of babes
speak clearly.

11 Wisdom[a] prospered their works
by the hand of a holy prophet.
2 They journeyed through an
uninhabited wilderness,
and pitched their tents in untrodden
places.
3 They withstood their enemies and
fought off their foes.
4 When they thirsted they called
upon thee,
and water was given them out of
flinty rock,
and slaking of thirst from hard
stone.
5 For through the very things by
which their enemies were
punished,
they themselves received benefit
in their need.
6 Instead of the fountain of an
ever-flowing river,
stirred up and defiled with blood
7 in rebuke for the decree to slay the
infants,
thou gavest them abundant water
unexpectedly,
8 showing by their thirst at that time
how thou didst punish their
enemies.
9 For when they were tried, though
they were being disciplined in
mercy,
they learned how the ungodly were
tormented when judged in wrath.
10 For thou didst test them as a father
does in warning,
but thou didst examine the
ungodly[b] as a stern king does in
condemnation.
11 Whether absent or present, they
were equally distressed,
12 for a twofold grief possessed them,
and a groaning at the memory of
what had occurred.
13 For when they heard that through
their own punishments
the righteous[c] had received benefit,
they perceived it was the
Lord's doing.
14 For though they had mockingly
rejected him who long before

a Gk *She* *b* Gk *those* *c* Gk *they*

37–50). **15–21:** Through Moses wisdom delivered Israel from Egypt (Ex.1.1–15.21, especially chs. 12–15).

11.1–12.2: The contrast between the fortunes of Israel and Egypt. 11.1–4: Wisdom guided Israel through the wilderness (Ex.15.22–17.16). **1:** *A holy prophet*, that is, Moses (Dt.18.15,18).

11.5–14: How water was used to bless the Israelites and to punish the Egyptians. Israel's thirst was God's discipline in *mercy* (v. 9); *water* from the *rock* (vv. 4, 7) showed that God could help in every need. But the Egyptians were *judged in wrath;* the Nile was turned to *blood* (vv. 6–9). They suffered *twofold grief:* the *memory* of their own punishment and the knowledge that through it Israel had been blessed and Moses vindicated (vv. 11–14).

had been cast out and exposed,
at the end of the events they
marveled at him,
for their thirst was not like that of
the righteous.

15 In return for their foolish and
wicked thoughts,
which led them astray to worship
irrational serpents and worthless
animals,
thou didst send upon them a
multitude of irrational creatures
to punish them,
16 that they might learn that one is
punished by the very things by
which he sins.
17 For thy all-powerful hand,
which created the world out of
formless matter,
did not lack the means to send
upon them a multitude of bears,
or bold lions,
18 or newly created unknown beasts
full of rage,
or such as breathe out fiery
breath,
or belch forth a thick pall of
smoke,
or flash terrible sparks from their
eyes;
19 not only could their damage
exterminate men,[d]
but the mere sight of them could
kill by fright.
20 Even apart from these, men[e] could
fall at a single breath
when pursued by justice
and scattered by the breath of thy
power.
But thou hast arranged all things
by measure and number and
weight.

21 For it is always in thy power to
show great strength,
and who can withstand the might
of thy arm?
22 Because the whole world before
thee is like a speck that tips the
scales,
and like a drop of morning dew
that falls upon the ground.
23 But thou art merciful to all, for
thou canst do all things,
and thou dost overlook men's sins,
that they may repent.
24 For thou lovest all things that
exist,
and hast loathing for none of the
things which thou hast made,
for thou wouldst not have made
anything if thou hadst hated
it.
25 How would anything have endured
if thou hadst not willed it?
Or how would anything not called
forth by thee have been
preserved?
26 Thou sparest all things, for they
are thine, O Lord who lovest the
living.

12 For thy immortal spirit is in
all things.
2 Therefore thou dost correct little
by little those who trespass,
and dost remind and warn them
of the things wherein they sin,
that they may be freed from
wickedness and put their trust
in thee, O Lord.

3 Those who dwelt of old in thy holy
land
4 thou didst hate for their detestable
practices,
their works of sorcery and unholy
rites,

d Gk *them*
e Gk *they*

11.15–20: The plague of frogs and lice. The wicked man is *punished by the very things by which he sins;* the Egyptians worshiped *irrational creatures*, and were punished by frogs, flies, lice, locusts (Ex. chs. 8 and 10). But God was merciful; he could have sent *bears, lions,* or newly created fierce *beasts*, or killed the Egyptians by *a single breath.*

11.21–12.2: God's universal love. God is almighty, but he is *merciful to all*, withholding punishment to give time to *repent.* He loves and preserves *all*, and corrects *little by little those who trespass* in order to lead them to repentance.

12.3–11: An example of God's patience and mercy. He hated the pagan peoples of Canaan

[5]their merciless slaughter[f] of
children,
and their sacrificial feasting on
human flesh and blood.
These initiates from the midst of
a heathen cult,[g]
[6]these parents who murder helpless
lives,
thou didst will to destroy by the
hands of our fathers,
[7]that the land most precious of all
to thee
might receive a worthy colony of
the servants[h] of God.
[8]But even these thou didst spare,
since they were but men,
and didst send wasps[i] as
forerunners of thy army,
to destroy them little by little,
[9]though thou wast not unable to
give the ungodly into the hands
of the righteous in battle,
or to destroy them at one blow by
dread wild beasts or thy stern
word.
[10]But judging them little by little
thou gavest them a chance to
repent,
though thou wast not unaware
that their origin[j] was evil
and their wickedness inborn,
and that their way of thinking
would never change.
[11]For they were an accursed race
from the beginning,
and it was not through fear of any
one that thou didst leave them
unpunished for their sins.

[12]For who will say, "What hast thou
done?"
Or who will resist thy judgment?
Who will accuse thee for the
destruction of nations which
thou didst make?
Or who will come before thee to
plead as an advocate for
unrighteous men?
[13]For neither is there any god
besides thee, whose care is for
all men,[k]
to whom thou shouldst prove that
thou hast not judged unjustly;
[14]nor can any king or monarch
confront thee about those whom
thou hast punished.
[15]Thou art righteous and rulest all
things righteously,
deeming it alien to thy power
to condemn him who does not
deserve to be punished.
[16]For thy strength is the source of
righteousness,
and thy sovereignty over all causes
thee to spare all.
[17]For thou dost show thy strength
when men doubt the
completeness of thy power,
and dost rebuke any insolence
among those who know it.[l]
[18]Thou who art sovereign in strength
dost judge with mildness,
and with great forebearance thou
dost govern us;
for thou hast power to act whenever
thou dost choose.

[19]Through such works thou hast
taught thy people
that the righteous man must be
kind,
and thou hast filled thy sons with
good hope,
because thou givest repentance for
sins.
[20]For if thou didst punish with such
great care and indulgence[m]

f Cn: Gk *slaughterers*
g The Greek text of this line is uncertain
h Or *children* *i* Or *hornets*
j Or *nature* *k* Or *all things*
l The Greek text of this line is uncertain
m Some ancient authorities omit *and indulgence;* others read *and entreaty*

(Ex.23.23; Dt.7.1) for their evil *practices;* but he judged them *little by little* (v. 8; compare Ex.23.29–30), giving them *a chance to repent* (v. 10; compare 2 Esd.9.11; Heb.12.17).

12.12–18: God's supreme power delights in benevolence. God, *sovereign*, all-powerful, is answerable to no one; he is *righteous*, condemns no man unjustly, and judges with *mildness* and *forbearance*. He cares *for all men* (v. 13) and rules *all things* (v. 15).

12.19–22: God's mercy is an example to Israel. Israel may think that God has *judged* them

the enemies of thy servants[n] and
those deserving of death,
granting them time and opportunity
to give up their wickedness,
21 with what strictness thou hast
judged thy sons,
to whose fathers thou gavest oaths
and covenants full of good
promises!
22 So while chastening us thou
scourgest our enemies ten
thousand times more,
so that we may meditate upon thy
goodness when we judge,
and when we are judged we may
expect mercy.

23 Therefore those who in folly of
life lived unrighteously
thou didst torment through their
own abominations.
24 For they went far astray on the
paths of error,
accepting as gods those animals
which even their enemies[o]
despised;
they were deceived like foolish
babes.
25 Therefore, as to thoughtless
children,
thou didst send thy judgment to
mock them.
26 But those who have not heeded
the warning of light rebukes
will experience the deserved
judgment of God.
27 For when in their suffering they
became incensed
at those creatures which they had
thought to be gods, being
punished by means of them,
they saw and recognized as the true
God him whom they had before
refused to know.
Therefore the utmost condemnation
came upon them.

13 For all men who were ignorant
of God were foolish by nature;
and they were unable from the
good things that are seen to
know him who exists,
nor did they recognize the craftsman
while paying heed to his
works;
2 but they supposed that either fire
or wind or swift air,
or the circle of the stars, or
turbulent water,
or the luminaries of heaven were
the gods that rule the world.
3 If through delight in the beauty
of these things men[p] assumed
them to be gods,
let them know how much better
than these is their Lord,
for the author of beauty created
them.
4 And if men[p] were amazed at their
power and working,
let them perceive from them
how much more powerful is he
who formed them.
5 For from the greatness and beauty
of created things
comes a corresponding perception
of their Creator.
6 Yet these men are little to be
blamed,
for perhaps they go astray
while seeking God and desiring to
find him.
7 For as they live among his works
they keep searching,
and they trust in what they see,
because the things that are seen
are beautiful.

n Or *children* *o* Gk *they* *p* Gk *they*

strictly (v. 21), but he *scourges* Israel's *enemies* far *more;* he chastens Israel in *mercy* and for their own good.

12.23–27: Further comments on the punishment of the Egyptians (in accord with the principle set forth in 11.16). The Egyptians were tormented by the *animals* that they worshiped. **27:** Though the Egyptians *recognized* Israel's God as *the true God,* they refused to let Israel go. *The utmost condemnation,* i.e. the death of their first-born sons.

13.1–15.17: The origin and folly of idolatry. 13.1–9: Nature-worship is the least culpable form of false worship. *Ignorant, foolish* men, misled by the *beauty* and *power* of *created things,* thought them *gods.* **6–7:** The author partly excuses such idolatry as arising from honest search for God.

8Yet again, not even they are to be
excused;
9for if they had the power to know
so much
that they could investigate the
world,
how did they fail to find sooner
the Lord of these things?
10But miserable, with their hopes set
on dead things, are the men
who give the name "gods" to the
works of men's hands,
gold and silver fashioned with
skill,
and likenesses of animals,
or a useless stone, the work of an
ancient hand.
11A skilled woodcutter may saw down
a tree easy to handle
and skilfully strip off all its bark,
and then with pleasing workmanship
make a useful vessel that serves
life's needs,
12and burn the castoff pieces of his
work
to prepare his food, and eat his fill.
13But a castoff piece from among
them, useful for nothing,
a stick crooked and full of knots,
he takes and carves with care in his
leisure,
and shapes it with skill gained in
idleness;[q]
he forms it like the image of a man,
14or makes it like some worthless
animal,
giving it a coat of red paint and
coloring its surface red
and covering every blemish in it
with paint;
15then he makes for it a niche that
befits it,
and sets it in the wall, and fastens
it there with iron.
16So he takes thought for it, that it
may not fall,
because he knows that it cannot
help itself,
for it is only an image and has
need of help.
17When he prays about possessions
and his marriage and children,
he is not ashamed to address a
lifeless thing.
18For health he appeals to a thing
that is weak;
for life he prays to a thing that is
dead;
for aid he entreats a thing that is
utterly inexperienced;
for a prosperous journey, a thing
that cannot take a step;
19for money-making and work and
success with his hands
he asks strength of a thing whose
hands have no strength.

14 Again, one preparing to sail
and about to voyage over
raging waves
calls upon a piece of wood more
fragile than the ship which
carries him.
2For it was desire for gain that
planned that vessel,
and wisdom was the craftsman who
built it;
3but it is thy providence, O Father,
that steers its course,
because thou hast given it a path
in the sea,
and a safe way through the waves,
4showing that thou canst save from
every danger,
so that even if a man lacks skill, he
may put to sea.
5It is thy will that the works of thy
wisdom should not be without
effect;
therefore men trust their lives even
to the smallest piece of wood,
and passing through the billows on

q Other authorities read *with intelligent skill*

8–9: Yet it cannot be *excused;* such idolaters should have discerned *the Lord* of created things.

13.10–19: The folly of image-worship (compare the Letter of Jeremiah). A *woodcutter* fells a *tree*, makes of some knotty *castoff* piece an *image* of *man* or *animal,* and calls it his god, although it cannot stand or act and has no life.

14.1–7: The folly of the seafarer who trusts in a wooden image on a ship's prow. Though men

a raft they come safely to land.
[6]For even in the beginning, when
arrogant giants were perishing,
the hope of the world took refuge
on a raft,
and guided by thy hand left to the
world the seed of a new
generation.
[7]For blessed is the wood by which
righteousness comes.

[8]But the idol made with hands is
accursed, and so is he who made
it;
because he did the work, and the
perishable thing was named a
god.
[9]For equally hateful to God are the
ungodly man and his
ungodliness,
[10]for what was done will be punished
together with him who did it.
[11]Therefore there will be a visitation
also upon the heathen idols,
because, though part of what God
created, they became an
abomination,
and became traps for the souls of
men
and a snare to the feet of the
foolish.

[12]For the idea of making idols was
the beginning of fornication,
and the invention of them was the
corruption of life,
[13]for neither have they existed from
the beginning
nor will they exist for ever.
[14]For through the vanity of men
they entered the world,
and therefore their speedy end has
been planned.
[15]For a father, consumed with grief
at an untimely bereavement,
made an image of his child, who
had been suddenly taken from
him;
and he now honored as a god
what was once a dead human
being,
and handed on to his dependents
secret rites and initiations.
[16]Then the ungodly custom, grown
strong with time, was kept as a
law,
and at the command of monarchs
graven images were worshiped.
[17]When men could not honor
monarchs[r] in their presence,
since they lived at a distance,
they imagined their appearance
far away,
and made a visible image of the
king whom they honored,
so that by their zeal they might
flatter the absent one as though
present.
[18]Then the ambition of the craftsman
impelled
even those who did not know the
king to intensify their worship.
[19]For he, perhaps wishing to please
his ruler,
skilfully forced the likeness to take
more beautiful form,
[20]and the multitude, attracted by the
charm of his work,
now regarded as an object of
worship the one whom shortly
before they had honored as a
man.
[21]And this became a hidden trap for
mankind,
because men, in bondage to
misfortune or to royal authority,
bestowed on objects of stone or
wood the name that ought not
to be shared.

r Gk *them*

---

planned the vessel, a safe voyage is God's doing. **6:** God saved Noah and his family in the ark (Gen. chs. 6–8). **7:** *The wood* refers not (as some have thought) to the cross of Christ but to Noah's ark, which carried forward God's righteous will.

14.8–11: Idolaters will be punished. 9: Contrast 11.24–26.

14.14–21: The origins of idolatry. A grief-stricken *father* made and *worshiped* an *image* of his *dead* child (vv. 15–16). Subjects living at a distance made and worshiped images of their king (v. 17); moreover skilled craftsmen made the image *more beautiful* than the king (vv. 18–20). (Euhemerus, about 300 B.C., taught that all gods were deified mortals.)

[22]Afterward it was not enough for
them to err about the knowledge
of God,
but they live in great strife due to
ignorance,
and they call such great evils
peace.
[23]For whether they kill children in
their initiations, or celebrate
secret mysteries,
or hold frenzied revels with strange
customs,
[24]they no longer keep either their
lives or their marriages pure,
but they either treacherously kill
one another, or grieve one
another by adultery,
[25]and all is a raging riot of blood and
murder, theft and deceit,
corruption, faithlessness, tumult,
perjury,
[26]confusion over what is good,
forgetfulness of favors,
pollution of souls, sex perversion,
disorder in marriage, adultery, and
debauchery.
[27]For the worship of idols not to be
named
is the beginning and cause and end
of every evil.
[28]For their worshipers[s] either rave
in exultation, or prophesy lies,
or live unrighteously, or readily
commit perjury;
[29]for because they trust in lifeless
idols
they swear wicked oaths and
expect to suffer no harm.
[30]But just penalties will overtake
them on two counts:
because they thought wickedly of
God in devoting themselves to
idols,
and because in deceit they swore
unrighteously through contempt
for holiness.
[31]For it is not the power of the things
by which men swear,[t]
but the just penalty for those who
sin,
that always pursues the
transgression of the unrighteous.

15 But thou, our God, art kind
and true,
patient, and ruling all things[u] in
mercy.
[2]For even if we sin we are thine,
knowing thy power;
but we will not sin, because we
know that we are accounted
thine.
[3]For to know thee is complete
righteousness,
and to know thy power is the root
of immortality.
[4]For neither has the evil intent of
human art misled us,
nor the fruitless toil of painters,
a figure stained with varied colors,
[5]whose appearance arouses yearning
in fools,
so that they desire[v] the lifeless
form of a dead image.
[6]Lovers of evil things and fit for
such objects of hope[w]
are those who either make or
desire or worship them.

[7]For when a potter kneads the soft
earth
and laboriously molds each vessel
for our service,
he fashions out of the same clay
both the vessels that serve clean uses
and those for contrary uses, making
all in like manner;
but which shall be the use of each
of these
the worker in clay decides.

s Gk *they* *t* Or *of the oaths men swear*
u Or *ruling the universe*
v Gk *and he desires* *w* Gk *such hopes*

14.22–31: The evil results of idolatry (Rom.1.24–32). Ignorance of God, *strife*, moral wrong, and perversion (v. 27), will bring sure punishment.

15.1–17: The contrast between the worshipers of the true God and idolaters. 1–5: The purifying influence of the worship of the true God on the life of Israel. **3:** *To know* God is *righteousness* and true life (compare Jn.17.3). **6–17:** The folly and wickedness of making and worshiping clay idols. For financial profit *a potter* molds from one mass of *clay* both useful *vessels* and

8With misspent toil, he forms a
futile god from the same clay—
this man who was made of earth
a short time before
and after a little while goes to the
earth from which he was taken,
when he is required to return the
soul that was lent him.
9But he is not concerned that he is
destined to die
or that his life is brief,
but he competes with workers in
gold and silver,
and imitates workers in copper;
and he counts it his glory that he
molds counterfeit gods.
10His heart is ashes, his hope is
cheaper than dirt,
and his life is of less worth than
clay,
11because he failed to know the one
who formed him
and inspired him with an active
soul
and breathed into him a living
spirit.
12But he[x] considered our existence
an idle game,
and life a festival held for profit,
for he says one must get money
however one can, even by base
means.
13For this man, more than all others,
knows that he sins
when he makes from earthy matter
fragile vessels and graven images.

14But most foolish, and more
miserable than an infant,
are all the enemies who oppressed
thy people.
15For they thought that all their
heathen idols were gods,
though these have neither the use
of their eyes to see with,
nor nostrils with which to draw
breath,
nor ears with which to hear,
nor fingers to feel with,
and their feet are of no use for
walking.
16For a man made them,
and one whose spirit is borrowed
formed them;
for no man can form a god which
is like himself.
17He is mortal, and what he makes
with lawless hands is dead,
for he is better than the objects he
worships,
since[y] he has life, but they never
have.

18The enemies of thy people[z] worship
even the most hateful animals,
which are worse than all others,
when judged by their lack of
intelligence;
19and even as animals they are not
so beautiful in appearance that
one would desire them,
but they have escaped both the
praise of God and his blessing.

16 Therefore those men were
deservedly punished through
such creatures,
and were tormented by a multitude
of animals.
2Instead of this punishment thou
didst show kindness to thy
people,
and thou didst prepare quails to
eat,
a delicacy to satisfy the desire of
appetite;
3in order that those men, when
they desired food,
might lose the least remnant of
appetite[a]
because of the odious creatures
sent to them,

x Other authorities read *they*
y Other authorities read *of which*
z Gk *They*
a Gk *loathed the necessary appetite*

---

counterfeit gods; cheap imitations of gold, silver, and copper *images*. **14–17:** The stupidity of Israel's *enemies*, who worship useless, lifeless images.

15.18–19.22: The contrast between God's treatment of the Egyptians and of the Israelites (compare 11.1–14). **16.1–4:** The Egyptians, *tormented* by the *animals* they worshiped (Ex. chs. 8 and 10), lost all appetite (v. 3); the Israelites, after brief hunger, enjoyed *quails* (Num. ch. 11).

while thy people,[b] after suffering
want a short time,
might partake of delicacies.
4For it was necessary that upon
those oppressors inexorable want
should come,
while to these it was merely shown
how their enemies were being
tormented.

5For when the terrible rage of wild
beasts came upon thy people[c]
and they were being destroyed by
the bites of writhing serpents,
thy wrath did not continue to the
end;
6they were troubled for a little
while as a warning,
and received a token of deliverance
to remind them of thy law's
command.
7For he who turned toward it was
saved, not by what he saw,
but by thee, the Savior of all.
8And by this also thou didst
convince our enemies
that it is thou who deliverest from
every evil.
9For they were killed by the bites
of locusts and flies,
and no healing was found for them,
because they deserved to be
punished by such things;
10but thy sons were not conquered
even by the teeth of venomous
serpents,
for thy mercy came to their help
and healed them.
11To remind them of thy oracles
they were bitten,
and then were quickly delivered,
lest they should fall into deep
forgetfulness
and become unresponsive[d] to thy
kindness.
12For neither herb nor poultice cured
them,
but it was thy word, O Lord,
which heals all men.
13For thou hast power over life and
death;
thou dost lead men down to the
gates of Hades and back again.
14A man in his wickedness kills
another,
but he cannot bring back the
departed spirit,
nor set free the imprisoned soul.

15To escape from thy hand is
impossible;
16for the ungodly, refusing to know
thee,
were scourged by the strength of
thy arm,
pursued by unusual rains and hail
and relentless storms,
and utterly consumed by fire.
17For—most incredible of all—in
the water, which quenches all
things,
the fire had still greater effect,
for the universe defends the
righteous.
18At one time the flame was
restrained,
so that it might not consume the
creatures sent against the
ungodly,
but that seeing this they might
know
that they were being pursued by
the judgment of God;
19and at another time even in the
midst of water it burned more
intensely than fire,
to destroy the crops of the
unrighteous land.
20Instead of these things thou didst
give thy people the food of
angels,
and without their toil thou didst
supply them from heaven with
bread ready to eat,

b Gk *they* *c* Gk *them*
d The meaning of the Greek is obscure

5–14: The Egyptians were killed by *bites of locusts and flies* (not mentioned in Exodus); Israel, bitten by serpents (Num.21.6–9), suffered briefly as a *warning* (vv. 6,11), and were *quickly* healed by God's *word* (vv. 11–12). God has *power over life and death* (vv. 13–14).
16.15–29: How fire from God punished the Egyptians. 20: The food of angels is manna,

providing every pleasure and suited
to every taste.
21 For thy sustenance manifested thy
sweetness toward thy children;
and the bread, ministering[e] to the
desire of the one who took it,
was changed to suit every one's
liking.
22 Snow and ice withstood fire without
melting,
so that they might know that the
crops of their enemies
were being destroyed by the fire
that blazed in the hail
and flashed in the showers of
rain;
23 whereas the fire,[f] in order that the
righteous might be fed,
even forgot its native power.

24 For the creation, serving thee who
hast made it,
exerts itself to punish the
unrighteous,
and in kindness relaxes on behalf
of those who trust in thee.
25 Therefore at that time also, changed
into all forms,
it served thy all-nourishing bounty,
according to the desire of those
who had need,[g]
26 so that thy sons, whom thou didst
love, O Lord, might learn
that it is not the production of
crops that feeds man,
but that thy word preserves those
who trust in thee.
27 For what was not destroyed by fire
was melted when simply warmed
by a fleeting ray of the sun,
28 to make it known that one must rise
before the sun to give thee
thanks,
and must pray to thee at the
dawning of the light;
29 for the hope of an ungrateful man
will melt like wintry frost,
and flow away like waste water.

17 Great are thy judgments and
hard to describe;
therefore uninstructed souls have
gone astray.
2 For when lawless men supposed
that they held the holy nation
in their power,
they themselves lay as captives of
darkness and prisoners of long
night,
shut in under their roofs, exiles
from eternal providence.
3 For thinking that in their secret
sins they were unobserved
behind a dark curtain of
forgetfulness,
they were scattered, terribly[h]
alarmed,
and appalled by specters.
4 For not even the inner chamber
that held them protected them
from fear,
but terrifying sounds rang out
around them,
and dismal phantoms with gloomy
faces appeared.
5 And no power of fire was able to
give light,
nor did the brilliant flames of the
stars
avail to illumine that hateful
night.
6 Nothing was shining through to
them
except a dreadful, self-kindled
fire,
and in terror they deemed the
things which they saw
to be worse than that unseen
appearance.

e Gk *and it, ministering*
f Gk *this*
g Or *who made supplication*
h Or, with other authorities, *unobserved, they were darkened behind a dark curtain of forgetfulness, terribly*

---

suited to the taste of each Israelite (vv. 20–21,25). **22–27:** The *fire* God sent executed his judgment; now he kept fire from melting *snow and ice* (a poetical expression for the manna; compare 19.21); now *a fleeting ray of the sun* melted it (Ex.16.21). **28–29:** Man should *rise* at dawn to thank God, for God's blessing escapes the *ungrateful man* as fast as the rising sun melts *wintry frost.*

17.1–18.4: The contrast between the Egyptians and the Israelites during the plague of darkness. God's judgment made *lawless men* (the Egyptians) terrified *captives of darkness,* unaided by

7 The delusions of their magic art
lay humbled,
and their boasted wisdom was
scornfully rebuked.
8 For those who promised to drive
off the fears and disorders of a
sick soul
were sick themselves with ridiculous
fear.
9 For even if nothing disturbing
frightened them,
yet, scared by the passing of beasts
and the hissing of serpents,
10 they perished in trembling fear,
refusing to look even at the air,
though it nowhere could be
avoided.
11 For wickedness is a cowardly thing,
condemned by its own
testimony;[i]
distressed by conscience, it has
always exaggerated[j] the
difficulties.
12 For fear is nothing but surrender
of the helps that come from
reason;
13 and the inner expectation of help,
being weak,
prefers ignorance of what causes
the torment.
14 But throughout the night, which
was really powerless,
and which beset them from the
recesses of powerless Hades,
they all slept the same sleep,
15 and now were driven by monstrous
specters,
and now were paralyzed by their
souls' surrender,
for sudden and unexpected fear
overwhelmed them.
16 And whoever was there fell down,
and thus was kept shut up in a
prison not made of iron;
17 for whether he was a farmer or a
shepherd
or a workman who toiled in the
wilderness,
he was seized, and endured the
inescapable fate;
for with one chain of darkness they
all were bound.
18 Whether there came a whistling
wind,
or a melodious sound of birds in
wide-spreading branches,
or the rhythm of violently rushing
water,
19 or the harsh crash of rocks hurled
down,
or the unseen running of leaping
animals,
or the sound of the most savage
roaring beasts,
or an echo thrown back from a
hollow of the mountains,
it paralyzed them with terror.
20 For the whole world was illumined
with brilliant light,
and was engaged in unhindered
work,
21 while over those men alone heavy
night was spread,
an image of the darkness that was
destined to receive them;
but still heavier than darkness
were they to themselves.

18 But for thy holy ones there
was very great light.
Their enemies[k] heard their voices
but did not see their forms,
and counted them happy for not
having suffered,
2 and were thankful that thy holy
ones,[l] though previously wronged,
were doing them no injury;
and they begged their pardon for
having been at variance with
them.[l]
3 Therefore thou didst provide a
flaming pillar of fire
as a guide for thy people's[m]
unknown journey,
and a harmless sun for their
glorious wandering.

i The Greek text of this line is uncertain and probably corrupt
j Other ancient authorities read *anticipated* *k* Gk *they*
l The meaning of the Greek of this line is uncertain
m Gk *their*

---

their *magic art* or *boasted wisdom* (Ex.10.21–23). **18.1:** *Thy holy ones*, the Israelites. **3:** *Pillar of fire . . . a harmless sun* (Ex.13.21–22). Most details here come from the author's imagination or from Jewish tradition.

4For their enemies[n] deserved to be
deprived of light and imprisoned
in darkness,
those who had kept thy sons
imprisoned,
through whom the imperishable
light of the law was to be given
to the world.

5When they had resolved to kill the
babes of thy holy ones,
and one child had been exposed
and rescued,
thou didst in punishment take
away a multitude of their
children;
and thou didst destroy them all
together by a mighty flood.
6That night was made known
beforehand to our fathers,
so that they might rejoice in sure
knowledge of the oaths in which
they trusted.
7The deliverance of the righteous
and the destruction of their
enemies
were expected by thy people.
8For by the same means by which
thou didst punish our enemies
thou didst call us to thyself and
glorify us.
9For in secret the holy children of
good men offered sacrifices,
and with one accord agreed to the
divine law,
that the saints would share alike
the same things,
both blessings and dangers;
and already they were singing the
praises of the fathers.[o]
10But the discordant cry of their
enemies echoed back,
and their piteous lament for their
children was spread abroad.
11The slave was punished with the
same penalty as the master,
and the common man suffered the
same loss as the king;
12and they all together, by the one
form of death,
had corpses too many to count.
For the living were not sufficient
even to bury them,
since in one instant their most
valued children had been
destroyed.
13For though they had disbelieved
everything because of their
magic arts,
yet, when their first-born were
destroyed, they acknowledged
thy people to be God's son.
14For while gentle silence enveloped
all things,
and night in its swift course was
now half gone,
15thy all-powerful word leaped from
heaven, from the royal throne,
into the midst of the land that was
doomed,
a stern warrior 16carrying the sharp
sword of thy authentic command,
and stood and filled all things
with death,
and touched heaven while standing
on the earth.
17Then at once apparitions in dreadful
dreams greatly troubled them,
and unexpected fears assailed them;
18and one here and another there,
hurled down half dead,
made known why they were dying;
19for the dreams which disturbed
them forewarned them of this,
so that they might not perish
without knowing why they
suffered.

20The experience of death touched
also the righteous,
and a plague came upon the
multitude in the desert,

n Gk *those men*
o Other authorities read *dangers, the fathers already leading the songs of praise*

18.5–25: The contrast between the visitation of death on the Egyptians and on the Israelites. **5:** *Resolved*, Ex.1.16. *Exposed and rescued*, Ex.2.1–10. *A multitude of their children*, the Egyptian first-born (Ex.12.29). *Didst destroy them*, Ex.14.27–28. **6:** *That night*, the first Passover. **15:** God's *all-powerful word*, as a *stern warrior*, *leaped from heaven* and carried out God's judgment (this recalls Rev.19.13 rather than Jn.1.1–18). **20–25:** When *a plague* struck Israel *in the desert*,

but the wrath did not long
continue.
21 For a blameless man was quick to
act as their champion;
he brought forward the shield of
his ministry,
prayer and propitiation by incense;
he withstood the anger and put an
end to the disaster,
showing that he was thy servant.
22 He conquered the wrath[p] not by
strength of body,
and not by force of arms,
but by his word he subdued the
punisher,
appealing to the oaths and
covenants given to our fathers.
23 For when the dead had already
fallen on one another in heaps,
he intervened and held back the
wrath,
and cut off its way to the living.
24 For upon his long robe the whole
world was depicted,
and the glories of the fathers were
engraved on the four rows of
stones,
and thy majesty on the diadem
upon his head.
25 To these the destroyer yielded,
these he[q] feared;
for merely to test the wrath was
enough.

19 But the ungodly were assailed
to the end by pitiless anger,
for God[r] knew in advance even
their future actions,
2 that, though they themselves had
permitted[s] thy people to depart
and hastily sent them forth,
they would change their minds
and pursue them.
3 For while they were still busy at
mourning,
and were lamenting at the graves
of their dead,
they reached another foolish
decision,
and pursued as fugitives those
whom they had begged and
compelled to depart.
4 For the fate they deserved drew
them on to this end,
and made them forget what had
happened,
in order that they might fill up the
punishment which their torments
still lacked,
5 and that thy people might
experience[t] an incredible journey,
but they themselves might meet a
strange death.

6 For the whole creation in its nature
was fashioned anew,
complying with thy commands,
that thy children[u] might be kept
unharmed.
7 The cloud was seen overshadowing
the camp,
and dry land emerging where water
had stood before,
an unhindered way out of the Red
Sea,
and a grassy plain out of the raging
waves,
8 where those protected by thy hand
passed through as one nation,
after gazing on marvelous wonders.
9 For they ranged like horses,
and leaped like lambs,
praising thee, O Lord, who didst
deliver them.
10 For they still recalled the events
of their sojourn,
how instead of producing animals
the earth brought forth gnats,
and instead of fish the river spewed
out vast numbers of frogs.
11 Afterward they saw also a new

p Cn: Gk *multitude* q Other authorities read *they*
r Gk *he*
s Other authorities read *had changed their minds to permit*
t Other authorities read *accomplish* u Or *servants*

Aaron stopped the destroying angel of God from inflicting further death (Num.16.41–50). **24:** From Ex. ch. 28 and Jewish tradition.

19.1–21: God judged the Egyptians and delivered Israel at the Red Sea. 1–5: The Egyptians' foolish decision to pursue Israel and enslave them again. **6–12:** God worked changes in nature to deliver Israel. **7:** *Cloud,* Ex.13.21–22. *Dry land,* Ex.14.21–22. **10:** Ex. ch. 8. **11–12:** Num.

kind[v] of birds,
when desire led them to ask for
luxurious food;
12 for, to give them relief, quails came
up from the sea.

13 The punishments did not come
upon the sinners
without prior signs in the violence
of thunder,
for they justly suffered because of
their wicked acts;
for they practiced a more bitter
hatred of strangers.
14 Others had refused to receive
strangers when they came to
them,
but these made slaves of guests
who were their benefactors.
15 And not only so, but punishment
of some sort will come upon the
former
for their hostile reception of the
aliens;
16 but the latter, after receiving them
with festal celebrations,
afflicted with terrible sufferings
those who had already shared the
same rights.
17 They were stricken also with loss
of sight—
just as were those at the door of
the righteous man—
when, surrounded by yawning
darkness,
each tried to find the way through
his own door.

18 For the elements changed[w] places
with one another,
as on a harp the notes vary the
nature of the rhythm,
while each note remains the same.[x]
This may be clearly inferred from
the sight of what took place.
19 For land animals were transformed
into water creatures,
and creatures that swim moved
over to the land.
20 Fire even in water retained its
normal power,
and water forgot its fire-quenching
nature.
21 Flames, on the contrary, failed to
consume
the flesh of perishable creatures
that walked among them,
nor did they melt[y] the crystalline,
easily melted kind of heavenly
food.

22 For in everything, O Lord, thou
hast exalted and glorified thy
people;
and thou hast not neglected to
help them at all times and in all
places.

v Or *production*
w Gk *changing*
x The meaning of this verse is uncertain
y Cn: Gk *nor could be melted*

ch. 11; compare Ex.16.13. **13–17:** The Egyptians treated *strangers* worse than did the men of Sodom, and so deserved greater *punishment*. **14:** *Others*, men of Sodom (Gen.19.1–11). *These*, the Egyptians. *Guests*, Israel was invited to Egypt (Gen.45.16–20). **17:** Gen.19.11; Ex.10.21–23. **18–21:** In the plagues and at the Red Sea nature and *animals* changed their customary action to effect God's redemptive purpose. **19:** *Land animals*, apparently a reference to Israel and their cattle crossing the Red Sea. *Creatures that swim*, frogs (Ex.8.1–7). **20–21:** 16.17. *Heavenly food*, the manna. **22:** The lesson of the preceding historical survey.

ECCLESIASTICUS, OR THE WISDOM OF JESUS THE SON OF

SIRACH

Ecclesiasticus, or the Wisdom of Jesus the Son of Sirach, is the only book in the Apocrypha of which the name of the author is known (50.27). From internal hints we may infer that Joshua ben Sira (which is Hebrew for "Jesus the son of Sirach") was a Jewish scribe, that is, a professional teacher of the Old Testament law. The invitation in 51.23 suggests that the author conducted an academy, probably in Jerusalem, where he lectured to young men on ethical and religious subjects. About 180 B.C. this seasoned scribe and sage committed to writing the distilled wisdom that he had been accustomed to impart orally. Though the material is loosely arranged and the author almost desultory in passing from one subject to another, it appears that he intended to compose a work in two volumes (chs. 1–23 and 24–51), each of which commences with an encomium on wisdom.

Soon after 132 B.C. Ben Sira's grandson (see the Prologue) translated the original Hebrew text into Greek. About three or four centuries later a Syriac translation was made from a Hebrew text that differed considerably from that which underlies the Greek translation. Five fragmentary Hebrew manuscripts, which date from the medieval period, preserve a little more than two-thirds of the book. In the relatively few places where they overlap, these Hebrew manuscripts sometimes present quite different readings, and not infrequently a word in one manuscript is represented by a synonym in another. There is no unanimity of opinion concerning the importance of these Hebrew manuscripts; some scholars maintain that they are secondary, having been translated from an inferior form of the Greek, while others believe that they derive from Ben Sira's original Hebrew text, though embodying certain modifications adopted from the Greek and Syriac versions. In 1952 several tiny fragments of the Hebrew text, dating from about the time of Christ, were discovered in a cave near Qumran by the Dead Sea. This new evidence confirms the antiquity of the corresponding readings in the medieval Hebrew manuscripts.

In the Latin Church during the third century A.D. the book of Sirach came to be known as Ecclesiasticus, which means "The Church Book." This rather nondescript title was apparently meant to suggest that the book is the most important of the several deuterocanonical books which, though not in the Palestinian Jewish canon of the Scriptures, are accepted as inspired by the Roman Catholic Church.

Sirach is a significant link in the history of the development of ancient Jewish thought. It is the last great example of the type of wisdom literature represented in the Old Testament book of Proverbs, and the first specimen of that form of Judaism which subsequently developed into the rabbinical schools of the Pharisees and the Sadducees.

The Prologue

WHEREAS MANY GREAT TEACHINGS have been given to us through the law and the prophets and the others that followed them, on account of which we should praise Israel for instruction and wisdom; and since it is necessary not only that the readers themselves should acquire understanding but also that those who love learning should be able to help the outsiders by both speaking and writing, my grandfather Jesus, after devoting himself especially to the reading of the law and the prophets and the other books of our fathers, and after acquiring considerable proficiency in them, was himself also led to write something pertaining to instruction and wisdom, in order that, by becoming conversant with this also, those who love learning should make even greater progress in living according to the law.

You are urged therefore to read

with good will and attention, and to be indulgent[a] in cases where, despite our diligent labor in translating, we may seem to have rendered some phrases imperfectly. For what was originally expressed in Hebrew does not have exactly the same sense when translated into another language. Not only this work, but even the law itself, the prophecies, and the rest of the books differ not a little as originally expressed.

When I came to Egypt in the thirty-eighth year of the reign of Euergetes and stayed for some time, I found opportunity for no little instruction.[b] It seemed highly necessary that I should myself devote some pains and labor to the translation of the following book, using in that period of time great watchfulness and skill in order to complete and publish the book for those living abroad who wished to gain learning, being prepared in character to live according to the law.

1 All wisdom comes from the Lord
and is with him for ever.
2 The sand of the sea, the drops of rain,
and the days of eternity—who can count them?
3 The height of heaven, the breadth of the earth,
the abyss, and wisdom—who can search them out?
4 Wisdom was created before all things,
and prudent understanding from eternity.[c]
6 The root of wisdom—to whom has it been revealed?
Her clever devices—who knows them?[d]
8 There is One who is wise, greatly to be feared,
sitting upon his throne.
9 The Lord himself created wisdom;[e]
he saw her and apportioned her,
he poured her out upon all his works.
10 She dwells with all flesh according to his gift,
and he supplied her to those who love him.

11 The fear of the Lord is glory and exultation,
and gladness and a crown of rejoicing.
12 The fear of the Lord delights the heart,
and gives gladness and joy and long life.
13 With him who fears the Lord it will go well at the end;
on the day of his death he will be blessed.

14 To fear the Lord is the beginning of wisdom;
she is created with the faithful in the womb.
15 She made[f] among men an eternal foundation,
and among their descendants she will be trusted.

a Or *Please read therefore with good will and attention, and be indulgent*
b Other authorities read *a copy affording no little instruction*
c Other authorities add as verse 5, *The source of wisdom is God's word in the highest heaven, and her ways are the eternal commandments.*
d Other authorities add as verse 7, *The knowledge of wisdom—to whom was it manifested? And her abundant experience—who has understood it?*
e Gk *her*
f Gk *made as nest*

1.1–10: The origin of wisdom. 1: The opening statement, *all wisdom comes from the Lord,* serves as a text on which the author's discourse is based (compare Pr.3.13–20). **2–3:** Illustrations of the impossibility of fathoming the depths of divine wisdom (18.5; Rom.11.33). **3:** *Height of heaven,* Ps.103.11. **8:** *Sitting upon his throne,* Ps.47.8; Is.6.1. **9:** *The Lord . . . created wisdom,* Pr.8.22–31. **10:** *All flesh,* mankind in general. *According to his gift,* i.e. in measured quantity, but *to those who love him,* i.e. to Israel, he gave wisdom unstintedly.

1.11–20: The fear of the Lord leads to obedience of the divine law. In the wisdom literature the fear of the Lord is roughly equivalent to religion and piety (Job 28.28; Ps.111.10; Pr.1.7; 9.10). **12:** *Long life,* v. 20; Pr.3.16. **15a:** Syriac, "With faithful men is she, and she has been established

[16]To fear the Lord is wisdom's full
measure;
she satisfies[g] men with her
fruits;
[17]she fills their whole house with
desirable goods,
and their storehouses with her
produce.
[18]The fear of the Lord is the crown
of wisdom,
making peace and perfect health
to flourish.
[19]He saw her and apportioned her;
he rained down knowledge and
discerning comprehension,
and he exalted the glory of those
who held her fast.
[20]To fear the Lord is the root of
wisdom,
and her branches are long life.[h]

[22]Unrighteous anger cannot be
justified,
for a man's anger tips the scale
to his ruin.
[23]A patient man will endure until
the right moment,
and then joy will burst forth for
him.
[24]He will hide his words until the
right moment,
and the lips of many will tell of
his good sense.
[25]In the treasuries of wisdom are
wise sayings,
but godliness is an abomination
to a sinner.
[26]If you desire wisdom, keep the
commandments,
and the Lord will supply it for
you.
[27]For the fear of the Lord is wisdom
and instruction,
and he delights in fidelity and
meekness.
[28]Do not disobey the fear of the
Lord;
do not approach him with a
divided mind.
[29]Be not a hypocrite in men's sight,[i]
and keep watch over your lips.
[30]Do not exalt yourself lest you fall,
and thus bring dishonor upon
yourself.
The Lord will reveal your secrets
and cast you down in the midst
of the congregation,
because you did not come in the
fear of the Lord,
and your heart was full of deceit.

2 My son, if you come forward
to serve the Lord,
prepare yourself for temptation.[j]
[2]Set your heart right and be
steadfast,
and do not be hasty in time of
calamity.
[3]Cleave to him and do not depart,
that you may be honored at the
end of your life.
[4]Accept whatever is brought upon
you,
and in changes that humble you
be patient.
[5]For gold is tested in the fire,
and acceptable men in the
furnace of humiliation.
[6]Trust in him, and he will help you;

g Gk *intoxicates*
h Other authorities add as verse 21, *The fear of the Lord drives away sins; and where it abides, it will turn away all anger.*
i Syr: Gk *in the mouths of men* *j* Or *trials*

---

from eternity." **16:** *Her fruits,* Pr.8.19; 11.30. **17:** Wis.7.11. **20:** *Long life,* v. 12; Pr.4.10.
1.22–30: Wisdom is shown in the exercise of patience, self-control, and humility. 22: Pr.29.22. **24:** *Will hide his words,* a patient man is not hasty to speak. **26:** 19.20; Ec.12.13. **27:** Pr.15.33. **28:** Obedience is the result of trust. *A divided mind,* 2.12; Jas.1.6–8; 4.8. **29:** *Hypocrite,* 32.15; 33.2. **30:** *Do not exalt yourself,* Mt.23.12. *In the . . . congregation,* 4.7; 7.7; Pr.5.14. *Full of deceit,* 19.26.

2.1–6: Serving God faithfully. 1: *My son,* the usual mode of a Jewish teacher's address to his pupil (7.3; Pr.2.1; 3.1). *Prepare . . . for temptation,* Jas.1.2–4 and 12–15. **2:** *Do not be hasty,* i.e. do not be impatient and fearful, but calm and self-possessed (Is.52.12; 1 Pet.4.12). **3:** *Cleave to him,* to God (Dt.10.20). *At the end of your life,* 1.13. **4:** *Accept* divinely appointed adversities (Job 2.10; Jas.1.2). *Be patient,* Jas.5.7–8. **5:** Pr.17.3; 27.21; Wis.3.6; Jas.1.12; 1 Pet.1.7. **6:** Ps.37.3,5.

make your ways straight, and
hope in him.

7You who fear the Lord, wait for
his mercy;
and turn not aside, lest you fall.
8You who fear the Lord, trust in
him,
and your reward will not fail;
9you who fear the Lord, hope for
good things,
for everlasting joy and mercy.
10Consider the ancient generations
and see:
who ever trusted in the Lord
and was put to shame?
Or who ever persevered in the fear
of the Lord[k] and was
forsaken?
Or who ever called upon him
and was overlooked?
11For the Lord is compassionate and
merciful;
he forgives sins and saves in
time of affliction.

12Woe to timid hearts and to slack
hands,
and to the sinner who walks
along two ways!
13Woe to the faint heart, for it has
no trust!
Therefore it will not be sheltered.
14Woe to you who have lost your
endurance!
What will you do when the
Lord punishes you?
15Those who fear the Lord will not
disobey his words,
and those who love him will
keep his ways.
16Those who fear the Lord will seek
his approval,
and those who love him will be
filled with the law.
17Those who fear the Lord will
prepare their hearts,
and will humble themselves
before him.
18Let us fall[l] into the hands of the
Lord,
but not into the hands of men;
for as his majesty is,
so also is his mercy.

3

Listen to me your father, O
children;
and act accordingly, that you
may be kept in safety.
2For the Lord honored the father
above the children,
and he confirmed the right of
the mother over her sons.
3Whoever honors his father atones
for sins,
4 and whoever glorifies his mother
is like one who lays up
treasure.
5Whoever honors his father will be
gladdened by his own children,
and when he prays he will be
heard.
6Whoever glorifies his father will
have long life,
and whoever obeys the Lord
will refresh his mother;
7 he will serve his parents as his
masters.[m]
8Honor your father by word and
deed,

k Gk *of him* *l* Gk *We shall fall*
m In other authorities this line is preceded by *Whoever fears the Lord will honor his father*

2.7–11: The reward of those who fear the Lord. 7: *Wait for his mercy*, Jdt.8.17. **9:** *Everlasting joy*, Is.35.10; 51.11; 61.7. **10:** Ps.37.25. **11:** *Compassionate and merciful*, Ex.34.6–7; Ps.103.8–9; 145.8; Jon.4.2.

2.12–14: A threefold woe against the unfaithful. 12: *Timid hearts*, 22.18; Dt.20.8. *Slack hands*, 25.23; Heb.12.12. **14:** *Endurance*, compare v. 1.

2.15–18: Characteristics of those who fear the Lord. 15: Jn.14.15; 15.10. **16:** *Will be filled with the law*, will be in heart and mind saturated with the Mosaic statutes (32.15). **17:** *Will humble themselves*, 3.18; 7.17; 18.21. **18:** 2 Sam.24.14.

3.1–16: Filial duty and its reward (Ex.20.12; Dt.5.16; Eph.6.1–3). In accord with the Jewish doctrine that the observance of the Mosaic law is meritorious, Sirach teaches that the keeping of the commandment to honor one's parents (Ex.20.12) *atones for sins* (vv. 14–15); contrast the teaching in Lk.17.10. **4:** *Lays up treasure*, Mt.6.20. **6:** *Will refresh*, will give rest from

that a blessing from him may
come upon you.
[9]For a father's blessing strengthens
the houses of the children,
but a mother's curse uproots
their foundations.

[10]Do not glorify yourself by
dishonoring your father,
for your father's dishonor is no
glory to you.
[11]For a man's glory comes from
honoring his father,
and it is a disgrace for children
not to respect their mother.
[12]O son, help your father in his old
age,
and do not grieve him as long
as he lives;
[13]even if he is lacking in
understanding, show
forbearance;
in all your strength do not
despise him.
[14]For kindness to a father will not
be forgotten,
and against your sins it will be
credited to you;
[15]in the day of your affliction it will
be remembered in your favor;
as frost in fair weather, your sins
will melt away.
[16]Whoever forsakes his father is like
a blasphemer,
and whoever angers his mother
is cursed by the Lord.

[17]My son, perform your tasks in
meekness;
then you will be loved by those
whom God accepts.
[18]The greater you are, the more you
must humble yourself;
so you will find favor in the sight
of the Lord.[n]
[20]For great is the might of the Lord;
he is glorified by the humble.
[21]Seek not what is too difficult for
you,
nor investigate what is beyond
your power.
[22]Reflect upon what has been
assigned to you,
for you do not need what is
hidden.
[23]Do not meddle in what is beyond
your tasks,
for matters too great for human
understanding have been shown
you.
[24]For their hasty judgment has led
many astray,
and wrong opinion has caused
their thoughts to slip.[o]

[26]A stubborn mind will be afflicted
at the end,
and whoever loves danger will
perish by it.
[27]A stubborn mind will be burdened
by troubles,
and the sinner will heap sin
upon sin.
[28]The affliction of the proud has no
healing,
for a plant of wickedness has
taken root in him.
[29]The mind of the intelligent man
will ponder a parable,
and an attentive ear is the wise
man's desire.

n Other authorities add as verse 19, *Many are lofty and renowned, but to the meek he reveals his secrets.*
o Other authorities add as verse 25, *If you have no eyes you will be without light; if you lack knowledge do not profess to have it.*

---

anxieties (Pr.29.17). **9:** Hebrew, "The blessing of a father establishes the root, but the curse of a mother uproots the young plant." **10:** *Your father's dishonor*, i.e. the dishonor brought upon a father by his son. **13:** Or, "Even if his mind fail, be considerate with him." **14–15:** Compare v. 3. *Will not be forgotten . . . will be credited . . . will be remembered* by God. **16:** Lev.20.9; Dt.27.16; Pr.19.26; 30.11,17. *Forsakes*, Hebrew and Syriac, "despises."

3.17–24: On humility. 17: Hebrew, "My son, when in prosperity walk with humility, and you will be loved more than a giver of gifts." **18:** Mt.20.26–28; Phil.2.3–8; 1 Pet.5.5–6. **21:** Ps.131.1; Jer.45.5; Rom.12.16. **22:** Dt.29.29. **23:** 1 Cor.2.9. **24:** Or, "their conceit has misled many," referring perhaps to speculations of Greek philosophers.

3.26–31: Retribution and reward. 26: Pr.28.14; Rom.2.5. **28:** *Has no healing*, i.e. adversity works no reformation in *the proud.* **29:** Hebrew, "the ear that listens to wisdom rejoices."

[30]Water extinguishes a blazing fire:
so almsgiving atones for sin.
[31]Whoever requites favors gives
thought to the future;
at the moment of his falling he
will find support.

4 My son, deprive not the poor
of his living,
and do not keep needy eyes
waiting.
[2]Do not grieve the one who is
hungry,
nor anger a man in want.
[3]Do not add to the troubles of an
angry mind,
nor delay your gift to a beggar.
[4]Do not reject an afflicted suppliant,
nor turn your face away from
the poor.
[5]Do not avert your eye from the
needy,
nor give a man occasion to
curse you;
[6]for if in bitterness of soul he calls
down a curse upon you,
his Creator will hear his
prayer.

[7]Make yourself beloved in the
congregation;
bow your head low to a great
man.
[8]Incline your ear to the poor,
and answer him peaceably and
gently.
[9]Deliver him who is wronged from
the hand of the wrongdoer;
and do not be fainthearted in
judging a case.
[10]Be like a father to orphans,
and instead of a husband to
their mother;
you will then be like a son of the
Most High,
and he will love you more than
does your mother.

[11]Wisdom exalts her sons
and gives help to those who
seek her.
[12]Whoever loves her loves life,
and those who seek her early
will be filled with joy.
[13]Whoever holds her fast will obtain
glory,
and the Lord will bless the place
she[p] enters.
[14]Those who serve her will minister
to the Holy One;[q]
the Lord loves those who love
her.
[15]He who obeys her will judge the
nations,
and whoever gives heed to her
will dwell secure.
[16]If he has faith in her he will obtain
her;
and his descendants will remain
in possession of her.
[17]For at first she will walk with him
on tortuous paths,
she will bring fear and cowardice
upon him,
and will torment him by her
discipline
until she trusts him,
and she will test him with her
ordinances.
[18]Then she will come straight
back to him and gladden
him,
and will reveal her secrets to
him.
[19]If he goes astray she will forsake
him,
and hand him over to his
ruin.

p Or *he*
q Or *at the holy place*

30: That *almsgiving atones for sin* accords with the Jewish doctrine of the efficacy of good works (Tob.4.7–11; contrast Gal.2.16; Eph.2.9); see also 7.10 n.; 29.11 n.

4.1–10: Duties toward the poor (7.32–36; 29.8–13; Dt.15.7–11). **1:** *Do not keep needy eyes waiting*, when they look for help. **4:** Mt.5.42. **6:** Ex.22.23; Dt.15.9; Pr.17.5. **7:** *Make yourself beloved*, by giving alms to the poor. **7:** *A great man*, Hebrew, "the ruler of the city." **10:** Job 29.10; 31.18; Ps.82.3; Is.1.17; Jas.1.27.

4.11–19: The rewards of wisdom. 11: 6.27. **12:** Pr.3.16–17; 8.17; Wis.8.17–18. **14–15:** The disciples of wisdom are like priests and judges. **18:** *Secrets*, 39.7; Job 11.6; Dan.2.21–22.

20 Observe the right time, and beware
of evil;[r]
and do not bring shame on
yourself.
21 For there is a shame which brings
sin,
and there is a shame which is
glory and favor.
22 Do not show partiality, to your
own harm,
or deference, to your downfall.
23 Do not refrain from speaking at
the crucial time,[s]
and do not hide your wisdom.[t]
24 For wisdom is known through
speech,
and education through the words
of the tongue.
25 Never speak against the truth,
but be mindful of your
ignorance.
26 Do not be ashamed to confess your
sins,
and do not try to stop the current
of a river.
27 Do not subject yourself to a foolish
fellow,
nor show partiality to a ruler.
28 Strive even to death for the truth
and the Lord God will fight for
you.

29 Do not be reckless in your speech,
or sluggish and remiss in your
deeds.
30 Do not be like a lion in your home,
nor be a faultfinder with your
servants.
31 Let not your hand be extended to
receive,
but withdrawn when it is time
to repay.

5 Do not set your heart on your
wealth,
nor say, "I have enough."
2 Do not follow your inclination and
strength,
walking according to the desires
of your heart.
3 Do not say, "Who will have power
over me?"
for the Lord will surely punish
you.

4 Do not say, "I sinned, and what
happened to me?"
for the Lord is slow to anger.
5 Do not be so confident of
atonement
that you add sin to sin.
6 Do not say, "His mercy is great,
he will forgive[u] the multitude of
my sins,"
for both mercy and wrath are with
him,
and his anger rests on sinners.
7 Do not delay to turn to the Lord,
nor postpone it from day to
day;
for suddenly the wrath of the Lord
will go forth,
and at the time of punishment
you will perish.

8 Do not depend on dishonest
wealth,
for it will not benefit you in the
day of calamity.
9 Do not winnow with every wind,
nor follow every path:
the double-tongued sinner does
that.
10 Be steadfast in your understanding,
and let your speech be consistent.

r Or *an evil man*
s Cn: Gk *at a time of salvation*
t So some Gk Mss and Heb Syr Vg: other Gk Mss omit *and do not hide your wisdom*
u Heb: Gk *he* (or *it*) *will atone for*

4.20–5.3: Precepts for everyday life. 22: That is, a man should not be afraid of offending another so long as he does what is right; even if it results in his *own harm*, he will have no cause for shame. **26:** That is, it is as futile to hide one's sins from God as to try to stop a river from flowing. **30:** *Like a lion*, wild, hasty, relentless, destructive. **31:** Compare Acts 20.35. **5.1:** *Enough*, Hebrew, "the power." **3:** Ps.12.4.

5.4–7: Warnings against presuming on God's mercy. 4: Ec.8.11. **5:** That is, do not continue sinning, *confident of* God's forgiveness. **6:** God's *mercy and wrath*, 16.11–12. **7:** *Postpone it*, i.e. postpone repentance.

5.8–6.1: Honesty and sincerity. 5.8: Pr.10.2; 11.4; Ezek.7.19. **9:** A condemnation of time-

[11]Be quick to hear,
and be deliberate in answering.
[12]If you have understanding, answer
your neighbor;
but if not, put your hand on
your mouth.
[13]Glory and dishonor come from
speaking,
and a man's tongue is his
downfall.

[14]Do not be called a slanderer,
and do not lie in ambush with
your tongue;
for shame comes to the thief,
and severe condemnation to the
double-tongued.
[15]In great or small matters do not
act amiss,
and do not become an enemy
instead of a friend;
6 for a bad name incurs shame
and reproach:
so fares the double-tongued
sinner.

[2]Do not exalt yourself through your
soul's counsel,
lest your soul be torn in pieces
like a bull.[v]
[3]You will devour your leaves and
destroy your fruit,
and will be left like a withered
tree.
[4]An evil soul will destroy him who
has it,
and make him the laughingstock
of his enemies.

[5]A pleasant voice multiplies friends,
and a gracious tongue multiplies
courtesies.
[6]Let those that are at peace with
you be many,
but let your advisers be one in a
thousand.
[7]When you gain a friend, gain him
through testing,
and do not trust him hastily.
[8]For there is a friend who is such
at his own convenience,
but will not stand by you in
your day of trouble.
[9]And there is a friend who changes
into an enemy,
and will disclose a quarrel to
your disgrace.
[10]And there is a friend who is a table
companion,
but will not stand by you in
your day of trouble.
[11]In your prosperity he will make
himself your equal,
and be bold with your
servants;
[12]but if you are brought low he will
turn against you,
and will hide himself from your
presence.
[13]Keep yourself far from your
enemies,
and be on guard toward your
friends.

[14]A faithful friend is a sturdy shelter:
he that has found one has found
a treasure.
[15]There is nothing so precious as a
faithful friend,
and no scales can measure his
excellence.
[16]A faithful friend is an elixir of
life;
and those who fear the Lord will
find him.
[17]Whoever fears the Lord directs his
friendship aright,

[v] The meaning of the Greek of this verse is obscure

servers, who speak according to expediency rather than truth. **11:** Jas.1.19. **12:** *Hand on . . mouth*, Job 21.5; 29.9; 30.32. **13:** Pr.18.21; Mt.12.37.

6.2–4: Self-control; a warning against lustful passions. Hebrew (freely), "Be not a slave to your passions, lest they consume your strength; they will eat up your leaves [figurative for youth], and destroy your fruit [offspring], and leave you as a dried-up tree. For unbridled passion destroys its possessor, and makes him the sport of his enemies."

6.5–17: True and false friendship. 5: 20.13; Pr.15.1. **6–7:** Care in choosing friends. **8–13:** False friendship. **9:** Pr.25.9–10. **10:** 37.5. **11b:** Hebrew (one manuscript) and Syriac, "and when you are in adversity, he will desert you." **13:** *Friends*, i.e. false friends. **14–17:** True

for as he is, so is his neighbor also.

18 My son, from your youth up choose
instruction,
and until you are old you will
keep finding wisdom.
19 Come to her like one who plows
and sows,
and wait for her good harvest.
For in her service you will toil a
little while,
and soon you will eat of her
produce.
20 She seems very harsh to the
uninstructed;
a weakling will not remain with
her.
21 She will weigh him down like a
heavy testing stone,
and he will not be slow to cast
her off.
22 For wisdom is like her name,
and is not manifest to many.

23 Listen, my son, and accept my
judgment;
do not reject my counsel.
24 Put your feet into her fetters,
and your neck into her collar.
25 Put your shoulder under her and
carry her,
and do not fret under her bonds.
26 Come to her with all your soul,
and keep her ways with all your
might.
27 Search out and seek, and she will
become known to you;
and when you get hold of her,
do not let her go.
28 For at last you will find the rest
she gives,
and she will be changed into joy
for you.
29 Then her fetters will become for
you a strong protection,
and her collar a glorious robe.
30 Her yoke[w] is a golden ornament,
and her bonds are a cord of blue.
31 You will wear her like a glorious robe,
and put her on like a crown of
gladness.

32 If you are willing, my son, you will
be taught,
and if you apply yourself you
will become clever.
33 If you love to listen you will gain
knowledge,
and if you incline your ear you
will become wise.
34 Stand in the assembly of the elders.
Who is wise? Cleave to him.
35 Be ready to listen to every[x]
narrative,
and do not let wise proverbs
escape you.
36 If you see an intelligent man, visit
him early;
let your foot wear out his
doorstep.
37 Reflect on the statutes of the Lord,
and meditate at all times on his
commandments.
It is he who will give insight to[y]
your mind,
and your desire for wisdom will
be granted.

7 Do no evil, and evil will never
befall you.
2 Stay away from wrong, and it
will turn away from you.
3 My son, do not sow the furrows of
injustice,

w Heb: Gk *Upon her*
x Heb: Gk adds *divine*
y Heb: Gk *will confirm*

---

friends are beyond value, and are the gift of God. **17b:** That is, *his neighbor* is as dear to him as he is to himself.

6.18–37: The blessings of wisdom. 18: 22.6. **19:** *Wait for the harvest*, Jas.5.7–8. **22:** *Wisdom is like her name*, Hebrew, "Discipline [*musar*] is like her name," perhaps a play on the Hebrew participle *musar*, meaning "removed, withdrawn"; hence the path of discipline *is not manifest to many*. **25:** *Put your shoulder under her*, wisdom is like a yoke. *Under her hands*, Hebrew, "at her counsels." **27:** *Do not let her go*, Pr.4.13. **28:** *Rest*, compare Mt.11.29. **30:** *A cord of blue*, Num.15.38. **31:** *A crown of gladness*, 1.11; 15.6; Pr.4.9; 16.31. **34:** 8.9. **37:** The law (*statutes, commandments*) is the source of wisdom. *Meditate*, Jos.1.8; Ps.1.2.

7.1–3: The avoidance of sin. 3: Job 4.8; Pr.22.8; Gal.6.8. *Sevenfold*, 35.11.

and you will not reap a sevenfold
crop.
4Do not seek from the Lord the
highest office,
nor the seat of honor from the
king.
5Do not assert your righteousness
before the Lord,
nor display your wisdom before
the king.
6Do not seek to become a judge,
lest you be unable to remove
iniquity,
lest you be partial to a powerful man,
and thus put a blot on your
integrity.
7Do not offend against the public,
and do not disgrace yourself
among the people.

8Do not commit a sin twice;
even for one you will not go
unpunished.
9Do not say, "He will consider the
multitude of my gifts,
and when I make an offering to
the Most High God he will
accept it."
10Do not be fainthearted in your
prayer,
nor neglect to give alms.

11Do not ridicule a man who is bitter
in soul,
for there is One who abases and
exalts.
12Do not devise[z] a lie against your
brother,
nor do the like to a friend.
13Refuse to utter any lie,
for the habit of lying serves no
good.
14Do not prattle in the assembly of
the elders,
nor repeat yourself in your prayer.

15Do not hate toilsome labor,
or farm work, which were
created by the Most High.
16Do not count yourself among the
crowd of sinners;
remember that wrath does not
delay.
17Humble yourself greatly,
for the punishment of the
ungodly is fire and worms.[a]

18Do not exchange a friend for money,
or a real brother for the gold of
Ophir.
19Do not deprive yourself of a wise
and good wife,
for her charm is worth more
than gold.
20Do not abuse a servant who
performs his work faithfully,
or a hired laborer who devotes
himself to you.
21Let your soul love[b] an intelligent
servant;
do not withhold from him his
freedom.

22Do you have cattle? Look after them;
if they are profitable to you, keep
them.
23Do you have children? Discipline
them,

z Heb: Gk *plow*
a The Hebrew text reads *for the expectation of man is worms*
b The Hebrew text reads *Love like yourself*

7.4–7: Conduct in public life. 4: Pr.25.6–7. **6:** *A judge*, Hebrew, "a ruler."

7.8–10: A warning against presuming upon God's forgiveness without amendment of life. **10:** According to Jewish teaching, *to give alms* is the highest form of righteousness (see 3.30 n. and 29.11 n.; compare Mt.6.1).

7.11–17: Precepts for right conduct of life. 11: *Bitter in soul*, because of poverty (4.2; Pr.17.5). *Abases and exalts*, 1 Sam.2.7; Lk.1.52–53. **14:** Mt.6.7. **15:** Pr.24.27. **16:** *Wrath*, 6.7. **17:** *Humble*, 2.17. A motive for humility is the thought that the body is destined to corruption. *Fire and worms*, Is.66.24; Jdt.16.17; Mk.9.48.

7.18–21: Duties to a friend, a wife, and a servant. 18: *Ophir*, 1 Kg.9.28; Job 22.24; 28.16. **19:** *Do not deprive*, Hebrew, "reject not," referring to divorce (v. 26). **21:** After six years of service a Hebrew slave was entitled to *freedom* (Ex.21.2; Lev.25.39–43; Dt.15.12–15).

7.22–25: Duties to cattle, and to children. 23: Hebrew (one manuscript) and Syriac, "Do

and make them obedient[c] from
their youth.
24Do you have daughters? Be
concerned for their chastity,[d]
and do not show yourself too
indulgent with them.
25Give a daughter in marriage; you
will have finished a great task.
But give her to a man of
understanding.

26If you have a wife who pleases
you,[e] do not cast her out;
but do not trust yourself to one
whom you detest.
27With all your heart honor your
father,
and do not forget the birth pangs
of your mother.
28Remember that through your
parents[f] you were born;
and what can you give back to
them that equals their gift to
you?

29With all your soul fear the Lord,
and honor his priests.
30With all your might love your Maker,
and do not forsake his ministers.
31Fear the Lord and honor the priest,
and give him his portion, as is
commanded you:
the first fruits, the guilt offering,
the gift of the shoulders,
the sacrifice of sanctification,
and the first fruits of the holy
things.

32Stretch forth your hand to the poor,
so that your blessing may be
complete.
33Give graciously to all the living,
and withhold not kindness from
the dead.
34Do not fail those who weep,
but mourn with those who
mourn.
35Do not shrink from visiting a sick
man,
because for such deeds you will
be loved.
36In all you do, remember the end
of your life,
and then you will never sin.

8 Do not contend with a powerful
man,
lest you fall into his hands.
2Do not quarrel with a rich man,
lest his resources outweigh yours;
for gold has ruined many,
and has perverted the minds of
kings.
3Do not argue with a chatterer,
nor heap wood on his fire.

4Do not jest with an ill-bred person,
lest your ancestors be disgraced.
5Do not reproach a man who is
turning away from sin;
remember that we all deserve
punishment.
6Do not disdain a man when he is old,
for some of us are growing old.
7Do not rejoice over any one's death;
remember that we all must die.

c Gk *bend their necks* d Gk *body*
e Heb Syr omit *who pleases you* f Gk *them*

---

you have sons? Correct them, and choose wives for them while they are young." **24:** 26.10–11; 42.9–11. **25:** Marriages were arranged by the father (see v. 23 n. and 36.21 n.).

7.26–28: Duties to one's wife and parents. 26: *Do not cast her out*, see v. 19 n. **27–28:** An expansion of Ex.20.12.

7.29–31: Duties to God and to the priesthood. In supporting and showing honor to God's ministers one indirectly honors God himself. **31:** *As is commanded*, Ex.29.27; Lev.7.31–34; Num.18.8–20; Dt.18.3.

7.32–36: Various duties: to give alms, respect the dead, comfort mourners, visit the sick. **32:** Dt.14.28–29. **33b:** Hebrew, "deny not respect to the dead," by providing honorable burial (38.16–18; Tob.1.17) and showing solicitude for their dependents. **34:** Rom.12.15. **35:** Mt. 25.36. **36:** Ec.11.9–12.7.

8.1–19: Warnings concerning various kinds of men. 1–3: A prudent man will avoid quarreling with the *powerful*, the *rich*, and the *chatterer*. **2:** *Lest his resources outweigh yours*, as a bribe in perverting *the minds of kings*. **4:** *Be disgraced*, by his railing. **5–7:** Have respect for the penitent,

[8]Do not slight the discourse of the sages,
but busy yourself with their maxims;
because from them you will gain instruction
and learn how to serve great men.
[9]Do not disregard the discourse of the aged,
for they themselves learned from their fathers;
because from them you will gain understanding
and learn how to give an answer in time of need.

[10]Do not kindle the coals of a sinner,
lest you be burned in his flaming fire.
[11]Do not get up and leave an insolent fellow,
lest he lie in ambush against your words.
[12]Do not lend to a man who is stronger than you;
but if you do lend anything, be as one who has lost it.
[13]Do not give surety beyond your means,
but if you give surety, be concerned as one who must pay.

[14]Do not go to law against a judge,
for the decision will favor him because of his standing.
[15]Do not travel on the road with a foolhardy fellow,
lest he be burdensome to you;
for he will act as he pleases,
and through his folly you will perish with him.
[16]Do not fight with a wrathful man,
and do not cross the wilderness with him;
because blood is as nothing in his sight,
and where no help is at hand,
he will strike you down.
[17]Do not consult with a fool,
for he will not be able to keep a secret.
[18]In the presence of a stranger do nothing that is to be kept secret,
for you do not know what he will divulge.[g]
[19]Do not reveal your thoughts to every one,
lest you drive away your good luck.[h]

9 Do not be jealous of the wife of your bosom,
and do not teach her an evil lesson to your own hurt.
[2]Do not give yourself to a woman
so that she gains mastery over your strength.
[3]Do not go to meet a loose woman,
lest you fall into her snares.
[4]Do not associate with a woman singer,
lest you be caught in her intrigues.
[5]Do not look intently at a virgin,
lest you stumble and incur penalties for her.
[6]Do not give yourself to harlots
lest you lose your inheritance.
[7]Do not look around in the streets of a city,
nor wander about in its deserted sections.
[8]Turn away your eyes from a shapely woman,
and do not look intently at beauty belonging to another;
many have been misled by a woman's beauty,
and by it passion is kindled like a fire.
[9]Never dine with another man's wife,

g Or *it will bring forth*
h Heb: Gk *let him not return a favor to you*

---

the aged, and the departed. **8–9:** Learn from men of experience. **10–11:** Warnings against associating with sinners. **12–13:** Warnings concerning lending, and giving *surety*. **14–19:** Warnings concerning various social relationships.

9.1–9: Warnings concerning women. 1: *Jealous*, Num.5.14–15. **2:** Pr.31.3. **3:** Pr.23.27. **5:** Job 31.1; Mt.5.28. **6:** Pr.29.3; Lk.15.13. **8:** *Belonging to another* man's wife. **9:** *Into destruction* refers to the adulterer's punishment (Lev.20.10; Dt.22.22).

nor revel with her at wine;
lest your heart turn aside to her,
and in blood[i] you be plunged
into destruction.

10Forsake not an old friend,
for a new one does not compare
with him.
A new friend is like new wine;
when it has aged you will drink
it with pleasure.

11Do not envy the honors of a
sinner,
for you do not know what his
end will be.
12Do not delight in what pleases the
ungodly;
remember that they will not be
held guiltless as long as they
live.

13Keep far from a man who has the
power to kill,
and you will not be worried by
the fear of death.
But if you approach him, make no
misstep,
lest he rob you of your life.
Know that you are walking in the
midst of snares,
and that you are going about
on the city battlements.

14As much as you can, aim to know
your neighbors,
and consult with the wise.
15Let your conversation be with men
of understanding,
and let all your discussion be
about the law of the Most
High.
16Let righteous men be your dinner
companions,
and let your glorying be in the
fear of the Lord.
17A work will be praised for the skill
of the craftsmen;
so a people's leader is proved
wise by his words.
18A babbler is feared in his city,
and the man who is reckless in
speech will be hated.

10 A wise magistrate will educate
his people,
and the rule of an understanding
man will be well ordered.
2Like the magistrate of the people,
so are his officials;
and like the ruler of the city, so
are all its inhabitants.
3An undisciplined king will ruin his
people,
but a city will grow through the
understanding of its rulers.
4The government of the earth is in
the hands of the Lord,
and over it he will raise up the
right man for the time.
5The success of a man is in the
hands of the Lord,
and he confers his honor upon
the person of the scribe.[j]

6Do not be angry with your neighbor
for any injury,
and do not attempt anything by
acts of insolence.
7Arrogance is hateful before the
Lord and before men,
and injustice is outrageous to
both.
8Sovereignty passes from nation to
nation
on account of injustice and
insolence and wealth.
9How can he who is dust and ashes
be proud?
for even in life his bowels
decay.[k]
10A long illness baffles the physician;[l]
the king of today will die
tomorrow.

i Heb: Gk *by your spirit*
j Or *the official*
k Heb: Gk is obscure
l Heb Vg: Gk is uncertain

9.10–18: Precepts concerning various kinds of persons. 11: Ps.37.1; 73.3 and 17. **15b:** Ps.1.2. **16b:** 10.22.

10.1–5: Concerning rulers. 4: Pr.8.15–16; Wis.6.1–3. *For the* right *time.*

10.6–18: Concerning arrogance and pride, especially in rulers (Pr.16.18). **6:** Lev.19.17;

[11]For when a man is dead,
he will inherit creeping things,
and wild beasts, and worms.
[12]The beginning of man's pride is to
depart from the Lord;
his heart has forsaken his
Maker.
[13]For the beginning of pride is sin,
and the man who clings to it
pours out abominations.
Therefore the Lord brought upon
them extraordinary afflictions,
and destroyed them utterly.
[14]The Lord has cast down the thrones
of rulers,
and has seated the lowly in their
place.
[15]The Lord has plucked up the roots
of the nations,[m]
and has planted the humble in
their place.
[16]The Lord has overthrown the lands
of the nations,
and has destroyed them to the
foundations of the earth.
[17]He has removed some of them and
destroyed them,
and has extinguished the memory
of them from the earth.
[18]Pride was not created for men,
nor fierce anger for those born of
women.

[19]What race is worthy of honor?
The human race.
What race is worthy of honor?
Those who fear the Lord.
What race is unworthy of honor?
The human race.
What race is unworthy of honor?
Those who transgress the
commandments.
[20]Among brothers their leader is
worthy of honor,
and those who fear the Lord are
worthy of honor in his eyes.[n]
[22]The rich, and the eminent, and the
poor—
their glory is the fear of the
Lord.
[23]It is not right to despise an
intelligent poor man,
nor is it proper to honor a sinful
man.
[24]The nobleman, and the judge, and
the ruler will be honored,
but none of them is greater than
the man who fears the Lord.
[25]Free men will be at the service of
a wise servant,
and a man of understanding will
not grumble.

[26]Do not make a display of your wisdom when you do your work,
nor glorify yourself at a time
when you are in want.
[27]Better is a man who works and has
an abundance of everything,
than one who goes about
boasting, but lacks bread.
[28]My son, glorify yourself with
humility,
and ascribe to yourself honor
according to your worth.
[29]Who will justify the man that sins
against himself?
And who will honor the man
that dishonors his own life?
[30]A poor man is honored for his
knowledge,
while a rich man is honored for
his wealth.
[31]A man honored in poverty, how
much more in wealth!
And a man dishonored in wealth,
how much more in poverty!
‖ The wisdom of a humble man
will lift up his head,

m Some authorities read *proud nations*
n Other authorities add as verse 21, *The fear of the Lord is the beginning of acceptance; obduracy and pride are the beginning of rejection.*

Mt.18.21. **11:** Job 17.14; Is.14.11. **12:** Dt.8.14. **14:** 1 Sam.2.8; Lk.1.52. **16:** Is.40.15–17; Wis.11.21–22.

10.19–25: True honor. 19: Jer.9.23–24; 1 Cor.1.26–31; 2 Cor.10.17; Jas.1.9. **23:** Jas.2.1–4. **25:** Pr.17.2.

10.26–11.1: Wrong and right estimation of self. 27: Pr.12.9. **11.1:** 39.4; compare Gen.41.40; Dan.6.3.

and will seat him among the
great.
[2]Do not praise a man for his good
looks,
nor loathe a man because of his
appearance.
[3]The bee is small among flying
creatures,
but her product is the best of
sweet things.
[4]Do not boast about wearing fine
clothes,
nor exalt yourself in the day that
you are honored;
for the works of the Lord are
wonderful,
and his works are concealed
from men.
[5]Many kings have had to sit on the
ground,
but one who was never thought
of has worn a crown.
[6]Many rulers have been greatly
disgraced,
and illustrious men have been
handed over to others.

[7]Do not find fault before you
investigate;
first consider, and then
reprove.
[8]Do not answer before you have
heard,
nor interrupt a speaker in the
midst of his words.
[9]Do not argue about a matter which
does not concern you,
nor sit with sinners when they
judge a case.

[10]My son, do not busy yourself with
many matters;
if you multiply activities you will
not go unpunished,
and if you pursue you will not
overtake,
and by fleeing you will not
escape.
[11]There is a man who works, and
toils, and presses on,
but is so much the more in want.
[12]There is another who is slow and
needs help,
who lacks strength and abounds
in poverty;
but the eyes of the Lord look upon
him for his good;
he lifts him out of his low estate
[13]and raises up his head,
so that many are amazed at him.

[14]Good things and bad, life and
death,
poverty and wealth, come from
the Lord.[o]
[17]The gift of the Lord endures for
those who are godly,
and what he approves will have
lasting success.
[18]There is a man who is rich through
his diligence and self-denial,
and this is the reward allotted to
him:
[19]when he says, "I have found rest,
and now I shall enjoy[p] my
goods!"
he does not know how much time
will pass
until he leaves them to others
and dies.
[20]Stand by your covenant[q] and
attend to it,
and grow old in your work.

[21]Do not wonder at the works of a
sinner,
but trust in the Lord and keep at
your toil;

o Other authorities add as verses 15 and 16, [15]*Wisdom, understanding, and knowledge of the law come from the Lord; affection and the ways of good works come from him.* [16]*Error and darkness were created with sinners; evil will grow old with those who take pride in malice.*
p Gk *eat of*
q Heb *task*

11.2–9: Warnings against hasty judgments, based on *looks* (v. 2), size (v. 3), or *clothes* (v. 4); compare 1 Sam.16.7. **6:** 1 Sam.15.28; Est.7.10. **8:** Pr.18.13. **9b:** Ps.1.1.
11.10–13: Discretion in conduct. **11:** Pr.10.3; Ec.9.11. **12b:** Ps.34.15.
11.14–28: All things come from God. **14:** A summary of the following section (1 Sam.2.7; Job 1.21; Is.45.7). **19:** Lk.12.19. **21:** 9.11; Pr.3.31; 23.17. *Keep at your toil,* Hebrew and Syriac, "abide in his light."

for it is easy in the sight of the Lord
to enrich a poor man quickly
and suddenly.
22The blessing of the Lord is[r] the
reward of the godly,
and quickly God causes his
blessing to flourish.
23Do not say, "What do I need,
and what prosperity could be
mine in the future?"
24Do not say, "I have enough,
and what calamity could
happen to me in the future?"
25In the day of prosperity, adversity
is forgotten,
and in the day of adversity,
prosperity is not remembered.
26For it is easy in the sight of the
Lord
to reward a man on the day of
death according to his
conduct.
27The misery of an hour makes one
forget luxury,
and at the close of a man's life
his deeds will be revealed.
28Call no one happy before his
death;
a man will be known through
his children.

29Do not bring every man into your
home,
for many are the wiles of the
crafty.
30Like a decoy partridge in a cage,
so is the mind of a proud man,
and like a spy he observes your
weakness;[s]
31for he lies in wait, turning good
into evil,
and to worthy actions he will
attach blame.
32From a spark of fire come many
burning coals,
and a sinner lies in wait to shed
blood.
33Beware of a scoundrel, for he
devises evil,
lest he give you a lasting
blemish.
34Receive a stranger into your home
and he will upset you with
commotion,
and will estrange you from your
family.

12 If you do a kindness, know to
whom you do it,
and you will be thanked for your
good deeds.
2Do good to a godly man, and you
will be repaid—
if not by him, certainly by the
Most High.
3No good will come to the man who
persists in evil
or to him who does not give
alms.
4Give to the godly man, but do not
help the sinner.
5 Do good to the humble, but do
not give to the ungodly;
hold back his bread, and do not
give it to him,
lest by means of it he subdue
you;
for you will receive twice as much
evil
for all the good which you do to
him.
6For the Most High also hates
sinners
and will inflict punishment on
the ungodly.[t]
7Give to the good man, but do not
help the sinner.

r Gk *is in*
s Heb: Gk *downfall*
t Other authorities add *and he is keeping them for the mighty day of their punishment*

26–27: Sirach's theology does not include a future life. **28:** *Through his children*, Hebrew, "by his latter end," i.e. a man's circumstances at the time of his death indicate the kind of life he has lived.

11.29–34: Care in choosing companions. 31: Hebrew, "The backbiter turns good to evil." **32:** Pr.1.11.

12.1–7: The need of discretion in almsgiving (Mt.7.6). **3:** Hebrew, "No good comes to him who helps the wicked, nor is it an act of benevolence which he has done." **4–5:** Contrast Lk.6.27–31; Gal.6.10.

[8]A friend will not be known[u] in
prosperity,
nor will an enemy be hidden in
adversity.
[9]A man's enemies are grieved when
he prospers,
and in his adversity even his
friend will separate from him.
[10]Never trust your enemy,
for like the rusting of copper, so
is his wickedness.
[11]Even if he humbles himself and
goes about cringing,
watch yourself, and be on your
guard against him;
and you will be to him like one
who has polished a mirror,
and you will know that it was
not hopelessly tarnished.
[12]Do not put him next to you,
lest he overthrow you and take
your place;
do not have him sit at your right,
lest he try to take your seat of
honor,
and at last you will realize the
truth of my words,
and be stung by what I have
said.

[13]Who will pity a snake charmer
bitten by a serpent,
or any who go near wild beasts?
[14]So no one will pity a man who
associates with a sinner
and becomes involved in his sins.
[15]He will stay with you for a time,
but if you falter, he will not
stand by you.

[16]An enemy will speak sweetly with
his lips,
but in his mind he will plan to
throw you into a pit;
an enemy will weep with his eyes,
but if he finds an opportunity
his thirst for blood will be
insatiable.
[17]If calamity befalls you, you will
find him there ahead of you;
and while pretending to help
you, he will trip you by the
heel;
[18]he will shake his head, and clap
his hands,
and whisper much, and change
his expression.

13 Whoever touches pitch will
be defiled,
and whoever associates with a
proud man will become like
him.
[2]Do not lift a weight beyond your
strength,
nor associate with a man
mightier and richer than
you.
How can the clay pot associate
with the iron kettle?
The pot will strike against it,
and will itself be broken.
[3]A rich man does wrong, and he
even adds reproaches;
a poor man suffers wrong, and
he must add apologies.
[4]A rich man[v] will exploit you if you
can be of use to him,
but if you are in need he will
forsake you.
[5]If you own something, he will live
with you;
he will drain your resources and
he will not care.
[6]When he needs you he will deceive
you,
he will smile at you and give you
hope.
He will speak to you kindly and
say, "What do you need?"

u Other authorities read *punished*
v Gk *He*

12.8–18: False friends (compare 6.5–17). **9a:** Hebrew, "When a man is prosperous, even his enemy is friendly" (Pr.19.4,6). **11c,d:** As one can prevent tarnish on a metal mirror by constantly polishing it, so the dangers of false friendship can be avoided by constant watchfulness. **18:** *Shake his head*, a gesture of derisive triumph (13.7; Job 16.4; Ps.22.7; Mt.27.39). *Whisper*, secretly conspiring (Ps.41.7). *Change his expression*, openly showing his enmity.

13.1–20: Warnings concerning associates. 1: A summary of what follows. **3:** *He must add*

[7]He will shame you with his foods,
until he has drained you two or
three times;
and finally he will deride you.
Should he see you afterwards, he
will forsake you,
and shake his head at you.

[8]Take care not to be led astray,
and not to be humiliated in your
feasting.[w]
[9]When a powerful man invites you,
be reserved;
and he will invite you the more
often.
[10]Do not push forward, lest you be
repulsed;
and do not remain at a distance,
lest you be forgotten.
[11]Do not try to treat him as an equal,
nor trust his abundance of words;
for he will test you through much
talk,
and while he smiles he will be
examining you.
[12]Cruel is he who does not keep
words to himself;
he will not hesitate to injure or
to imprison.
[13]Keep words to yourself and be very
watchful,
for you are walking about with
your own downfall.[x]

[15]Every creature loves its like,
and every person his neighbor;
[16]all living beings associate by species,
and a man clings to one like
himself.
[17]What fellowship has a wolf with a
lamb?
No more has a sinner with a
godly man.
[18]What peace is there between a
hyena and a dog?
And what peace between a rich
man and a poor man?
[19]Wild asses in the wilderness are
the prey of lions;
likewise the poor are pastures
for the rich.
[20]Humility is an abomination to a
proud man;
likewise a poor man is an
abomination to a rich one.

[21]When a rich man totters, he is
steadied by friends,
but when a humble man falls, he
is even pushed away by friends.
[22]If a rich man slips, his helpers are
many;
he speaks unseemly words, and
they justify him.
If a humble man slips, they even
reproach him;
he speaks sensibly, and receives
no attention.
[23]When the rich man speaks all are
silent,
and they extol to the clouds what
he says.
When the poor man speaks they
say, "Who is this fellow?"
And should he stumble, they
even push him down.

[24]Riches are good if they are free
from sin,
and poverty is evil in the
opinion of the ungodly.
[25]A man's heart changes his
countenance,
either for good or for evil.[y]
[26]The mark of a happy heart is a
cheerful face,
but to devise proverbs requires
painful thinking.

14 Blessed is the man who does
not blunder with his lips
and need not suffer grief for sin.
[2]Blessed is he whose heart does

w Other authorities read *folly*
x Other authorities add *When you hear these things in your sleep, wake up!* [14]*During all your life love the Lord, and call on him for your salvation.*
y Other authorities add *and a glad heart makes a cheerful countenance*

---

apologies, as though it were he who committed the wrong. **7:** Compare Pr.23.1–3. *Shake his head*, see 12.18 n. **15:** 27.9. **17:** 2 Cor.6.14. **19:** Job 24.5. **20:** Pr.29.27.

13.21–14.2: The rich and the poor. 21–23: Pr.14.20; 19.4,7. **26a:** Pr.15.13. **26b:** Ec.12.12. **14.2:** Rom.14.22; 1 Jn.3.21.

not condemn him,
and who has not given up his hope.

3 Riches are not seemly for a stingy man;
and of what use is property to an envious man?
4 Whoever accumulates by depriving himself, accumulates for others;
and others will live in luxury on his goods.
5 If a man is mean to himself, to whom will he be generous?
He will not enjoy his own riches.
6 No one is meaner than the man who is grudging to himself,
and this is the retribution for his baseness;
7 even if he does good, he does it unintentionally,
and betrays his baseness in the end.
8 Evil is the man with a grudging eye;
he averts his face and disregards people.
9 A greedy man's eye is not satisfied with a portion,
and mean injustice withers the soul.
10 A stingy man's eye begrudges bread,
and it is lacking at his table.

11 My son, treat yourself well, according to your means,
and present worthy offerings to the Lord.
12 Remember that death will not delay,
and the decree[z] of Hades has not been shown to you.
13 Do good to a friend before you die,
and reach out and give to him as much as you can.
14 Do not deprive yourself of a happy day;
let not your share of desired good pass by you.
15 Will you not leave the fruit of your labors to another,
and what you acquired by toil to be divided by lot?
16 Give, and take, and beguile yourself,
because in Hades one cannot look for luxury.
17 All living beings become old like a garment,
for the decree[a] from of old is, "You must surely die!"
18 Like flourishing leaves on a spreading tree
which sheds some and puts forth others,
so are the generations of flesh and blood:
one dies and another is born.
19 Every product decays and ceases to exist,
and the man who made it will pass away with it.

20 Blessed is the man who meditates on[b] wisdom
and who reasons intelligently.
21 He who reflects in his mind on her ways
will also ponder her secrets.
22 Pursue wisdom[c] like a hunter,
and lie in wait on her paths.
23 He who peers through her windows
will also listen at her doors;
24 he who encamps near her house
will also fasten his tent peg to her walls;
25 he will pitch his tent hear her,
and will lodge in an excellent lodging place;
26 he will place his children under her shelter,
and will camp under her boughs;

z Gk *covenant* *a* Gk *covenant*
b Other authorities read *dies in* *c* Gk *her*

14.3–19: Envy and avarice. 4: 11.19–20; Job 27.16–17; Pr.13.22; Ec.6.2; Lk.12.16–21. **8:** *Averts his face*, 4.4; Tob.4.11. **10:** Pr.23.6–7. The Hebrew and Syriac add, "A good eye [i.e. a liberal man] causes bread to increase, and 'A dry spring sends forth water' [this appears to be a proverb] upon his table." **11–16:** Wealth should be used wisely during life, for it must be left behind at death. **13:** Tob.4.7; Lk.14.13. **14:** Ec.5.18. **15:** V. 4. **16:** Ec.9.10. *Hades*, Hebrew "sheol." **17:** *Like a garment*, Ps.102.26; compare Is.40.6; Jas.1.10; 1 Pet.1.24. **18:** Ec.1.4. **19:** Contrast Rev.14.13.

14.20–15.10: The search for wisdom and its blessings (Pr.8.32–35). **26a:** Hebrew, "He builds

27 he will be sheltered by her from
the heat,
and will dwell in the midst of her
glory.

15 The man who fears the Lord
will do this,
and he who holds to the law will
obtain wisdom.[d]
2 She will come to meet him like a
mother,
and like the wife of his youth
she will welcome him.
3 She will feed him with the bread
of understanding,
and give him the water of
wisdom to drink.
4 He will lean on her and will not
fall,
and he will rely on her and will
not be put to shame.
5 She will exalt him above his
neighbors,
and will open his mouth in the
midst of the assembly.
6 He will find gladness and a crown
of rejoicing,
and will acquire an everlasting
name.
7 Foolish men will not obtain her,
and sinful men will not see
her.
8 She is far from men of pride,
and liars will never think of
her.

9 A hymn of praise is not fitting on
the lips of a sinner,
for it has not been sent from the
Lord.
10 For a hymn of praise should be
uttered in wisdom,
and the Lord will prosper it.
11 Do not say, "Because of the Lord
I left the right way";
for he[e] will not do what he hates.
12 Do not say, "It was he who led me
astray";
for he has no need of a sinful
man.
13 The Lord hates all abominations,
and they are not loved by those
who fear him.
14 It was he who created man in the
beginning,
and he left him in the power of
his own inclination.
15 If you will, you can keep the
commandments,
and to act faithfully is a matter
of your own choice.
16 He has placed before you fire and
water:
stretch out your hand for
whichever you wish.
17 Before a man[f] are life and death,
and whichever he chooses will be
given to him.
18 For great is the wisdom of the
Lord;
he is mighty in power and sees
everything;
19 his eyes are on those who fear him,
and he knows every deed of
man.
20 He has not commanded any one
to be ungodly,
and he has not given any one
permission to sin.

d Gk *her*
e Heb: Gk *you* *f* Gk *men*

---

his nest in her foliage." **15.1:** Hebrew prefixes "For," connecting 14.20–27 (telling how wisdom must be sought) with 15.1–8 (telling how wisdom will welcome those who seek her). *The law* is identified with wisdom (1.26; 19.20; 21.11; 24.23). **2b:** Hebrew, "Like a young bride she will embrace him." **3:** Pr.9.2,5. **9–10:** Compare Pr.27.21b.

15.11–20: Free will and responsibility for sin (17.1–12). **11–12:** Jas.1.13. **13b:** Hebrew, "and he does not let them come near those who fear him." **14:** Gen.1.27. *Inclination,* the Hebrew word *yeṣer* is a technical term, used here in a neutral sense meaning "free will." Elsewhere *yeṣer* is sometimes used in a good sense (Is.26.3; 1 Chr.29.18); but usually it refers to an evil tendency or inclination toward sin (Gen.6.5; 8.21; compare 2 Esd.4.30–31). In post-biblical times the doctrine arose of a good and an evil *yeser* which every person possesses. **16:** *Fire and water,* representing opposite extremes. *Fire* here has no eschatological significance. **17:** Dt.30.19; Jer.21.8. **18–19:** Ps.33.13,18; 34.15; Heb.4.13.

16 Do not desire a multitude
of useless children,
nor rejoice in ungodly sons.
2If they multiply, do not rejoice in
them,
unless the fear of the Lord is in
them.
3Do not trust in their survival,
and do not rely on their
multitude;
for one is better than a thousand,[g]
and to die childless is better
than to have ungodly children.
4For through one man of
understanding a city will be
filled with people,
but through a tribe of lawless
men it will be made desolate.
5Many such things my eye has seen,
and my ear has heard things
more striking than these.

6In an assembly of sinners a fire will
be kindled,
and in a disobedient nation
wrath was kindled.
7He was not propitiated for the
ancient giants
who revolted in their might.
8He did not spare the neighbors of
Lot,
whom he loathed on account of
their insolence.
9He showed no pity for a nation
devoted to destruction,
for those destroyed in their sins;
10nor for the six hundred thousand
men on foot,
who rebelliously assembled in
their stubbornness.
11Even if there is only one stiff-necked
person,
it will be a wonder if he remains
unpunished.
For mercy and wrath are with the
Lord;[h]
he is mighty to forgive, and he
pours out wrath.
12As great as his mercy, so great is
also his reproof;
he judges a man according to
his deeds.
13The sinner will not escape with his
plunder,
and the patience of the godly
will not be frustrated.
14He will make room for every act
of mercy;
every one will receive in
accordance with his deeds.[i]

17Do not say, "I shall be hidden from
the Lord,
and who from on high will
remember me?
Among so many people I shall not
be known,
for what is my soul in the
boundless creation?
18Behold, heaven and the highest
heaven,
the abyss and the earth, will
tremble at his visitation.
19The mountains also and the
foundations of the earth
shake with trembling when he
looks upon them.
20And no mind will reflect on this.
Who will ponder his ways?
21Like a tempest which no man can
see,
so most of his works are
concealed.

g The text of this line is uncertain
h Gk *him*
i Other authorities add 15*The Lord hardened Pharaoh so that he did not know him; in order that his works might be known under heaven.* 16*His mercy is manifest to the whole of creation, and he divided his light and darkness with a plumb line.*

16.1–5: The misfortune of having ungodly children. 3c: Hebrew and Syriac, "For better is one who does the will [of the Lord] than a thousand [godless children]."

16.6–23: The certainty of punishment for sin. 6: *A fire will be kindled,* 21.9; compare Num. 16.35. **7:** *Ancient giants,* Gen.6.4; Wis.14.6; Bar.3.26–28. **8:** Gen.19.14–25. **10:** 46.8; Num. 11.21. **11:** *Mercy and wrath,* 5.6. **12b:** Ps.62.12. **16b** (in note *i*): Hebrew, "and his light and his darkness he has apportioned to the children of men." **17d:** Hebrew, "and what is my soul among the multitudes of spirits of all the children of men?" **18–19:** A parenthetical meditation on the supreme power of God. **20–22:** Hebrew, continuing the thought of v. 17, "In truth, he [God] does not set his heart on me [pays no attention to me]; and as for my ways, who will

22Who will announce his acts of
justice?
Or who will await them? For
the covenant is far off."
23This is what one devoid of
understanding thinks;
a senseless and misguided man
thinks foolishly.

24Listen to me, my son, and acquire
knowledge,
and pay close attention to my
words.
25I will impart instruction by weight,
and declare knowledge accurately.

26The works of the Lord have existed
from the beginning by his
creation,[j]
and when he made them, he
determined their divisions.
27He arranged his works in an eternal
order,
and their dominion[k] for all[l]
generations;
they neither hunger nor grow weary,
and they do not cease from their
labors.
28They do not crowd one another
aside,
and they will never disobey his
word.
29After this the Lord looked upon
the earth,
and filled it with his good things;
30with all kinds of living beings he
covered its surface,
and to it they return.

17 The Lord created man out of
earth,
and turned him back to it again.
2He gave to men[m] few days, a
limited time,
but granted them authority over
the things upon the earth.[n]
3He endowed them with strength
like his own,[o]
and made them in his own image.
4He placed the fear of them[p] in all
living beings,
and granted them dominion
over beasts and birds.[q]
6He made for them[r] tongue and eyes;
he gave them ears and a mind
for thinking.
7He filled them with knowledge
and understanding,
and showed them good and evil.
8He set his eye upon their hearts
to show them the majesty of his
works.[s]
10And they will praise his holy name,
to proclaim the grandeur of his
works.
11He bestowed knowledge upon them,
and allotted to them the law of life.
12He established with them an eternal
covenant,
and showed them his judgments.
13Their eyes saw his glorious majesty,
and their ears heard the glory of
his voice.
14And he said to them, "Beware of
all unrighteousness."[t]
And he gave commandment to
each of them concerning his
neighbor.

j Heb: Gk *judgment* *k* Or *elements*
l Gk *their* *m* Gk *them* *n* Gk *it*
o Cn: Gk *proper to them* *p* Syr: Gk *him*
q Other authorities add 5*They obtained the use of the five operations of the Lord; as sixth he distributed to them the gift of mind, and as seventh reason, the interpreter of his operations.* *r* Syr: Gk *Inclination and*
s Other authorities add 9*and he gave them to boast of his marvels for ever* *t* Or *every unrighteous man*

---

mark them? 21 If I sin, no eye will see me, or if I deal untruly in all secrecy, who will know it? 22 My righteous dealing, who shall declare it? And what hope is there? For the decree is distant" (i.e. the decreed reward for righteousness is remote and uncertain). **23:** Sirach's own view of the ideas expressed in vv. 17–22.

16.24–17.14: Divine wisdom seen in creation. 16.27–28: 43.10; Is.40.26. **29:** *After this*, compare Gen.1.20–31. **30:** *To it*, the earth (Gen.3.19; Ps.104.29). **17.1:** Gen.2.7; 3.19; Ps.146.4. **2a:** Literally, "He granted them days by number, and a set time" (Gen.6.3; Ps.90.10). **3:** Gen. 1.26–27. **4:** Gen.1.28; Ps.8.6–8. **5** (in note *q*): *The five operations*, or "powers" (i.e. the five senses). **7:** Gen.2.17. **11:** Syriac, "He set before them the covenant" (Dt.4.44). *The law of life*, the law which gives life (45.5; Bar.4.1). **12:** *Eternal covenant*, Ex.19.16–24.18. **14:** A summary of all the prohibitory commandments.

15Their ways are always before him,
they will not be hid from his eyes.[u]
17He appointed a ruler for every nation,
but Israel is the Lord's own portion.[v]
19All their works are as the sun before him,
and his eyes are continually upon their ways.
20Their iniquities are not hidden from him,
and all their sins are before the Lord.[w]
22A man's almsgiving is like a signet with the Lord,[x]
and he will keep a person's kindness like the apple of his eye.
23Afterward he will arise and requite them,
and he will bring their recompense on their heads.
24Yet to those who repent he grants a return,
and he encourages those whose endurance is failing.

25Turn to the Lord and forsake your sins;
pray in his presence and lessen your offenses.
26Return to the Most High and turn away from iniquity,[y]
and hate abominations intensely.
27Who will sing praises to the Most High in Hades,
as do those who are alive and give thanks?
28From the dead, as from one who does not exist, thanksgiving has ceased;
he who is alive and well sings the Lord's praises.
29How great is the mercy of the Lord,
and his forgiveness for those who turn to him!
30For all things cannot be in men,[z]
since a son of man is not immortal.
31What is brighter than the sun? Yet its light fails.[a]
So flesh and blood devise evil.
32He marshals the host of the height of heaven;
but all men are dust and ashes.

18 He who lives for ever created the whole universe;
2 the Lord alone will be declared righteous.[b]
4To none has he given power to proclaim his works;
and who can search out his mighty deeds?
5Who can measure his majestic power?
And who can fully recount his mercies?
6It is not possible to diminish or increase them,
nor is it possible to trace the wonders of the Lord.
7When a man has finished, he is just beginning,
and when he stops, he will be at a loss.
8What is man, and of what use is he?
What is his good and what is his evil?

u Other authorities add 16*Their ways from youth tend toward evil, and they are unable to make for themselves hearts of flesh in place of their stony hearts.* 17*For in the division of the nations of the whole earth*
v Other authorities add 18*whom, being his first-born, he brings up with discipline, and allotting to him the light of his love, he does not neglect him.*
w Other authorities add 21*But the Lord, who is gracious and knows his creatures, has neither left nor abandoned them, but spared them.*
x Gk *him*
y Other authorities add *for he will lead you out of darkness to the light of health*
z The Greek text of this line is uncertain
a Or *suffers eclipse*
b Other authorities add *and there is no other beside him;* 3*he steers the world with the span of his hand, and all things obey his will; for he is king of all things, by his power separating among them the holy things from the profane.*

17.15–24: The divine judge. 17: Dt.32.8–9. **22:** *Almsgiving*, 29.12–13. *Apple of his eye*, Dt.32.10; Ps.17.8; Pr.7.2. **23:** *Arise*, in judgment. **24:** *A return*, to God's favor.

17.25–32: Exhortation to turn to God. 25–26: Jer.3.12. **27–28:** Ps.6.5; 115.17; Is.38.18; Bar.2.17. **30:** Syriac, "For it is not like this in man [i.e. only God has such mercy and forgiveness (18.13)], nor is his [i.e. God's] thought like the thoughts of the children of men." **31b:** Syriac, "So is man who has the inclination [see 15.14 n.] of flesh and blood."

18.1–14: The majesty of God. 4b: Ps.106.2. **8:** Ps.8.4. **9:** Compare Ps.90.10.

[9]The number of a man's days is
great if he reaches a hundred
years.
[10]Like a drop of water from the sea
and a grain[c] of sand
so are a few years in the day of
eternity.
[11]Therefore the Lord is patient with
them
and pours out his mercy upon
them.
[12]He sees and recognizes that their
end will be evil;
therefore he grants them
forgiveness in abundance.
[13]The compassion of man is for his
neighbor,
but the compassion of the Lord
is for all living beings.
He rebukes and trains and teaches
them,
and turns them back, as a
shepherd his flock.
[14]He has compassion on those who
accept his discipline
and who are eager for his
judgments.

[15]My son, do not mix reproach with
your good deeds,
nor cause grief by your words
when you present a gift.
[16]Does not the dew assuage the
scorching heat?
So a word is better than a gift.
[17]Indeed, does not a word surpass a
good gift?
Both are to be found in a
gracious man.
[18]A fool is ungracious and abusive,
and the gift of a grudging man
makes the eyes dim.

[19]Before you speak, learn,
and before you fall ill, take care
of your health.
[20]Before judgment, examine yourself,
and in the hour of visitation
you will find forgiveness.
[21]Before falling ill, humble yourself,
and when you are on the point
of sinning, turn back.
[22]Let nothing hinder you from
paying a vow promptly,
and do not wait until death to
be released from it.
[23]Before making a vow,[d] prepare
yourself;
and do not be like a man who
tempts the Lord.
[24]Think of his wrath on the day of
death,
and of the moment of vengeance
when he turns away his face.
[25]In the time of plenty think of the
time of hunger;
in the days of wealth think of
poverty and need.
[26]From morning to evening
conditions change,
and all things move swiftly
before the Lord.

[27]A wise man is cautious in
everything,
and in days of sin he guards
against wrongdoing.
[28]Every intelligent man knows
wisdom,
and he praises the one who finds
her.
[29]Those who understand sayings
become skilled themselves,
and pour forth apt proverbs.

[30]Do not follow your base desires,
but restrain your appetites.
[31]If you allow your soul to take
pleasure in base desire,
it will make you the
laughingstock of your enemies.
[32]Do not revel in great luxury,

c Gk *pebble*
d Or *offering a prayer*

18.15–18: The right spirit in giving alms. **15:** Do not humiliate the receiver of charity (41.22). **16b:** Syriac, "So a [kindly] word changes [the character of] a gift." **17a:** Syriac, "For there is a good word which is better than a gift."

18.19–29: The need of foresight. **22:** Dt.23.21; Ec.5.4. **24:** 7.36.

18.30–19.3: An exhortation to self-control. **33:** Hebrew, "Do not be a squanderer and a

lest you become impoverished
by its expense.
33Do not become a beggar by feasting
with borrowed money,
when you have nothing in your
purse.

19 A workman who is a drunkard
will not become rich;
he who despises small things
will fail little by little.
2Wine and women lead intelligent
men astray,
and the man who consorts with
harlots is very reckless.
3Decay and worms will inherit him,
and the reckless soul will be
snatched away.

4One who trusts others too quickly
is lightminded,
and one who sins does wrong to
himself.
5One who rejoices in wickedness[e]
will be condemned,[f]
6 and for one who hates gossip
evil is lessened.
7Never repeat a conversation,
and you will lose nothing at
all.
8With friend or foe do not report
it,
and unless it would be a sin for
you, do not disclose it;
9for some one has heard you and
watched you,
and when the time comes he
will hate you.
10Have you heard a word? Let it die
with you.
Be brave! It will not make you
burst!
11With such a word a fool will suffer
pangs
like a woman in labor with a
child.
12Like an arrow stuck in the flesh of
the thigh,
so is a word inside a fool.

13Question a friend, perhaps he did
not do it;
but if he did anything, so that
he may do it no more.
14Question a neighbor, perhaps he
did not say it;
but if he said it, so that he may
not say it again.
15Question a friend, for often it is
slander;
so do not believe everything you
hear.
16A person may make a slip without
intending it.
Who has never sinned with his
tongue?
17Question your neighbor before you
threaten him;
and let the law of the Most
High take its course.[g]

20All wisdom is the fear of the
Lord,
and in all wisdom there is the
fulfilment of the law.[h]
22But the knowledge of wickedness
is not wisdom,
nor is there prudence where
sinners take counsel.
23There is a cleverness which is
abominable,
but there is a fool who merely
lacks wisdom.

e Other authorities read *heart*

f Other authorities add *but he who withstands pleasures crowns his life.* [6]*He who controls his tongue will live without strife,*

g Other authorities add *and do not be angry.* [18]*The fear of the Lord is the beginning of acceptance, and wisdom obtains his love.* [19]*The knowledge of the Lord's commandments is life-giving discipline; and those who do what is pleasing to him enjoy the fruit of the tree of immortality.*

h Other authorities add, *and the knowledge of his omnipotence.* [21]*When a servant says to his master, "I will not act as you wish," even if later he does it, he angers the one who supports him.*

---

drunkard, else there will be nothing in your purse." **19.1:** *Will fail . . . little*, Hebrew, "will become altogether naked," i.e. destitute.

19.4–12: A warning against too much talking. 7b: Syriac, "then no one will reproach you" (Pr.25.9–10). **8:** *Unless* by keeping silent *it would be a sin.* **9:** Pr.25.10.

19.13–17: On administering reproof. 16: Jas.3.2. **17:** Lev.19.17; Mt.18.15; Lk.17.3.

19.20–30: Wisdom and craftiness contrasted. 20: Jas.1.25. **21** (in note *h*): Mt.21.28–32. **23:** *Who merely lacks wisdom*, and is guileless.

24 Better is the God-fearing man who
lacks intelligence,
than the highly prudent man
who transgresses the law.
25 There is a cleverness which is
scrupulous but unjust,
and there are people who distort
kindness to gain a verdict.
26 There is a rascal bowed down in
mourning,[i]
but inwardly he is full of deceit.
27 He hides his face and pretends not
to hear;
but where no one notices, he
will forestall you.
28 And if by lack of strength he is
prevented from sinning,
he will do evil when he finds an
opportunity.
29 A man is known by his appearance,
and a sensible man is known
by his face, when you meet
him.
30 A man's attire and open-mouthed
laughter,
and a man's manner of walking,
show what he is.

20 There is a reproof which is
not timely;
and there is a man who keeps
silent but is wise.
2 How much better it is to reprove
than to stay angry!
And the one who confesses his
fault will be kept from loss.[j]
4 Like a eunuch's desire to violate a
maiden
is a man who executes
judgments by violence.
5 There is one who by keeping silent
is found wise,
while another is detested for
being too talkative.
6 There is one who keeps silent
because he has no answer,
while another keeps silent
because he knows when to
speak.
7 A wise man will be silent until the
right moment,
but a braggart and fool goes
beyond the right moment.
8 Whoever uses too many words will
be loathed,
and whoever usurps the right to
speak will be hated.

9 There may be good fortune for a
man in adversity,
and a windfall may result in a
loss.
10 There is a gift that profits you
nothing,
and there is a gift that brings a
double return.
11 There are losses because of glory,
and there are men who have
raised their heads from humble
circumstances.
12 There is a man who buys much for
a little,
but pays for it seven times over.
13 The wise man makes himself
beloved through his words,
but the courtesies of fools are
wasted.
14 A fool's gift will profit you nothing,
for he has many eyes instead of
one.
15 He gives little and upbraids much,
he opens his mouth like a
herald;
today he lends and tomorrow he
asks it back;
such a one is a hateful man.
16 A fool will say, "I have no friend,
and there is no gratitude for my
good deeds;
those who eat my bread speak
unkindly."

i Gk *blackness*
j Other authorities add [3]*How good it is to show repentance when you are reproved, for so you will escape deliberate sin!*

30: Instead of *and . . . laughter*, the Syriac reads, "proclaims his deeds," i.e. his occupation.

20.1–26: Use and abuse of the tongue. 1–8: Proper times for speech and for silence. 2: Syriac, "He that reproves a sinner gets no thanks, but let him that makes confession be kept back from hurt" (i.e. be spared humiliation). **5:** Pr.17.28. **7:** V. 20b; Ec.3.7.

20.9–17: Paradoxes. 13: 6.5. *Are wasted*, are thrown away. **14:** Syriac, "for he looks for sevenfold repayment."

17How many will ridicule him, and
how often!
18A slip on the pavement is better
than a slip of the tongue;
so the downfall of the wicked
will occur speedily.
19An ungracious man is like a story
told at the wrong time,
which is continually on the lips
of the ignorant.
20A proverb from a fool's lips will
be rejected,
for he does not tell it at its
proper time.

21A man may be prevented from
sinning by his poverty,
so when he rests he feels no
remorse.
22A man may lose his life through
shame,
or lose it because of his foolish
look.
23A man may for shame make
promises to a friend,
and needlessly make him an
enemy.

24A lie is an ugly blot on a man;
it is continually on the lips of
the ignorant.
25A thief is preferable to a habitual
liar,
but the lot of both is ruin.
26The disposition of a liar brings
disgrace,
and his shame is ever with him.

27He who speaks wisely will advance
himself,
and a sensible man will please
great men.
28Whoever cultivates the soil will
heap up his harvest,
and whoever pleases great men
will atone for injustice.
29Presents and gifts blind the eyes of
the wise;
like a muzzle on the mouth they
avert reproofs.
30Hidden wisdom and unseen treasure,
what advantage is there in either
of them?
31Better is the man who hides his folly
than the man who hides his
wisdom.[k]

21 Have you sinned, my son?
Do so no more,
but pray about your former sins.
2Flee from sin as from a snake;
for if you approach sin, it will
bite you.
Its teeth are lion's teeth,
and destroy the souls of men.
3All lawlessness is like a two-edged
sword;
there is no healing for its wound.

4Terror and violence will lay waste
riches;
thus the house of the proud will
be laid waste.
5The prayer of a poor man goes from
his lips to the ears of God,[l]
and his judgment comes speedily.
6Whoever hates reproof walks in
the steps of the sinner,
but he that fears the Lord will
repent in his heart.
7He who is mighty in speech is
known from afar;

k Other authorities add 32*Unwearied patience in seeking the Lord is better than a masterless charioteer of one's own life.* l Gk *his ears*

20.18–20: Concerning inappropriate speech. 19: Syriac, "As the fat tail of a sheep [Ex.29.22], eaten without salt, so is a word spoken out of season."

20.21–23: Sin unintentionally avoided, and intentionally committed. 22: 4.20–21. **23:** *Make him an enemy*, because of inability to fulfil the promises.

20.24–26: Lying. Ps.5.6; Pr.12.22; 13.5.

20.27–31: The reward of the wise. 27: *Will please*, Syriac, "will rule." **28:** Pr.12.11. **29:** *Presents and gifts*, i.e. bribes (Dt.16.19; Pr.17.8). **30:** 41.14–15.

21.1–10: Warnings against sin. 2–3: The characteristics of sin are subtlety, strength, and deadliness. **5:** 35.17–19. **5b:** Syriac, "and it ascends unto the presence of the eternal Judge." **7:** Syriac, "The wise man recognizes him that is before him, and discerns the sinner in a mo-

but the sensible man, when he
slips, is aware of it.

[8]A man who builds his house with
other people's money
is like one who gathers stones
for his burial mound.[m]
[9]An assembly of the wicked is like
tow gathered together,
and their end is a flame of fire.
[10]The way of sinners is smoothly
paved with stones,
but at its end is the pit of Hades.

[11]Whoever keeps the law controls
his thoughts,
and wisdom is the fulfilment of
the fear of the Lord.
[12]He who is not clever cannot be
taught,
but there is a cleverness which
increases bitterness.
[13]The knowledge of a wise man will
increase like a flood,
and his counsel like a flowing
spring.
[14]The mind of a fool is like a broken
jar;
it will hold no knowledge.

[15]When a man of understanding
hears a wise saying,
he will praise it and add to it;
when a reveler hears it, he dislikes
it
and casts it behind his back.
[16]A fool's narration is like a burden
on a journey,
but delight will be found in the
speech of the intelligent.
[17]The utterance of a sensible man
will be sought in the assembly,
and they will ponder his words
in their minds.

[18]Like a house that has vanished, so
is wisdom to a fool;
and the knowledge of the
ignorant is unexamined talk.
[19]To a senseless man education is
fetters on his feet,
and like manacles on his right
hand.
[20]A fool raises his voice when he
laughs,
but a clever man smiles quietly.
[21]To a sensible man education is like
a golden ornament,
and like a bracelet on the right
arm.

[22]The foot of a fool rushes into a
house,
but a man of experience stands
respectfully before it.
[23]A boor peers into the house from
the door,
but a cultivated man remains
outside.
[24]It is ill-mannered for a man to
listen at a door,
and a discreet man is grieved by
the disgrace.
[25]The lips of strangers will speak of
these things,[n]
but the words of the prudent
will be weighed in the balance.
[26]The mind of fools is in their mouth,
but the mouth of wise men is
in[o] their mind.
[27]When an ungodly man curses his
adversary,[p]
he curses his own soul.
[28]A whisperer defiles his own soul
and is hated in his neighborhood.

22 The indolent may be compared
to a filthy stone,
and every one hisses at his disgrace.
[2]The indolent may be compared to
the filth of dunghills;

m Other authorities read *for the winter*
n The Greek text of this line is uncertain
o Other authorities omit *in*
p Or *curses Satan*

ment." **8:** That is, he prepares for his own destruction. **9:** 16.6. **10:** *Smoothly paved,* Pr.14.12; 16.25; Mt.7.13.

21.11–28: The contrast between the wise man and the fool. 15: *Dislikes,* Syriac, "mocks at." **18a:** Syriac, "As a prison-house is wisdom to a fool." **21:** This verse should follow v. 19. **20:** 19.30; Ec.7.6. **22:** Pr.25.17. **28:** 5.14; 28.13.

22.1–18: Concerning laziness and foolishness. 1b: Syriac, "Everyone flees from the stench

any one that picks it up will
shake it off his hand.
3It is a disgrace to be the father of
an undisciplined son,
and the birth of a daughter is a
loss.
4A sensible daughter obtains her
husband,
but one who acts shamefully
brings grief to her father.
5An impudent daughter disgraces
father and husband,
and will be despised by both.
6Like music in mourning is a tale
told at the wrong time,
but chastising and discipline are
wisdom at all times.

7He who teaches a fool is like
one who glues potsherds
together,
or who rouses a sleeper from
deep slumber.
8He who tells a story to a fool tells
it to a drowsy man;
and at the end he will say,
"What is it?"[q]
11Weep for the dead, for he lacks
the light;
and weep for the fool, for he
lacks intelligence;
weep less bitterly for the dead, for
he has attained rest;
but the life of the fool is worse
than death.
12Mourning for the dead lasts seven
days,
but for a fool or an ungodly man
it lasts all his life.

13Do not talk much with a foolish
man,
and do not visit an unintelligent
man;
guard yourself from him to escape
trouble,
and you will not be soiled when
he shakes himself off;
avoid him and you will find rest,
and you will never be wearied by
his madness.
14What is heavier than lead?
And what is its name except
"Fool"?
15Sand, salt, and a piece of iron
are easier to bear than a stupid
man.

16A wooden beam firmly bonded
into a building
will not be torn loose by an
earthquake;
so the mind firmly fixed on a
reasonable counsel
will not be afraid in a crisis.
17A mind settled on an intelligent
thought
is like the stucco decoration on
the wall of a colonnade.[r]
18Fences set on a high place
will not stand firm against the
wind;
so a timid heart with a fool's
purpose
will not stand firm against any
fear.

19A man who pricks an eye will
make tears fall,
and one who pricks the heart
makes it show feeling.
20One who throws a stone at birds
scares them away,
and one who reviles a friend will
break off the friendship.
21Even if you have drawn your sword
against a friend,
do not despair, for a renewal of
friendship is possible.
22If you have opened your mouth
against your friend,
do not worry, for reconciliation
is possible;
but as for reviling, arrogance,

q Other authorities add 9*Children who are brought up in a good life, conceal the lowly birth of their parents.* 10*Children who are disdainfully and boorishly haughty stain the nobility of their kindred.*
r Or *on a smooth wall*

thereof." **3–6:** 16.1–5. **4:** *Obtains*, Hebrew, "becomes a treasure to." **5:** 42.11. **6:** Pr.25.20. **7:** A thankless task. **12:** *Seven days*, Gen.50.10; Jdt.16.24. **13b:** *An unintelligent man*, Syriac, "a pig in the way" (compare v. 13d). **15:** *Sand*, Job 6.3; Pr.27.3.

disclosure of secrets, or a
treacherous blow—
in these cases any friend will
flee.

23 Gain the trust of your neighbor in
his poverty,
that you may rejoice with him
in his prosperity;
stand by him in time of affliction,
that you may share with him in
his inheritance.[s]
24 The vapor and smoke of the
furnace precede the fire;
so insults precede bloodshed.
25 I will not be ashamed to protect
a friend,
and I will not hide from him;
26 but if some harm should happen
to me because of him,
whoever hears of it will beware
of him.

27 O that a guard were set over my
mouth,
and a seal of prudence upon my
lips,
that it may keep me from falling,
so that my tongue may not
destroy me![t]

23 O Lord, Father and Ruler
of my life,
do not abandon me to their
counsel,
and let me not fall because of
them!
2 O that whips were set over my
thoughts,
and the discipline of wisdom
over my mind![u]
That they may not spare me in my
errors,
and that it may not pass by my[v]
sins;
3 in order that my mistakes may not
be multiplied,
and my sins may not abound;
then I will not fall before my
adversaries,
and my enemy will not rejoice
over me.
4 O Lord, Father and God of my life,
do not give me haughty eyes,
and remove from me evil desire.
6 Let neither gluttony nor lust
overcome me,
and do not surrender me to a
shameless soul.

7 Listen, my children, to instruction
concerning speech;
the one who observes it will
never be caught.
8 The sinner is overtaken through
his lips,
the reviler and the arrogant are
tripped by them.
9 Do not accustom your mouth to
oaths,
and do not habitually utter the
name of the Holy One;
10 for as a servant who is continually
examined under torture
will not lack bruises,
so also the man who always swears
and utters the Name
will not be cleansed from sin.
11 A man who swears many oaths will
be filled with iniquity,
and the scourge will not leave
his house;
if he offends, his sin remains on
him,
and if he disregards it, he sins
doubly;
if he has sworn needlessly, he will
not be justified,
for his house will be filled with
calamities.

12 There is an utterance which is
comparable to death;[w]
may it never be found in the
inheritance of Jacob!

s Other authorities add *For one should not always despise restricted circumstances, nor admire a rich man who is stupid.*
t Or *Who will set a guard . . . destroy me?*
u Or *Who will set whips . . . my mind* *v* Gk *their*
w Other authorities read *clothed about with death*

22.19–26: The preservation of friendship. 25: *A friend,* Syriac adds, "who becomes poor."
22.27–23.6: A prayer for self-control. 27: Ps.141.3.
23.7–15: The proper use of the tongue (compare Jas.3.5–12). **11:** Lev.5.4. **12a:** Lev.24.15–16.

For all these errors will be far from
the godly,
and they will not wallow in
sins.
13Do not accustom your mouth to
lewd vulgarity,
for it involves sinful speech.
14Remember your father and
mother
when[x] you sit among great
men;
lest you be forgetful in their
presence,
and be deemed a fool on
account of your habits;
then you will wish that you had
never been born,
and you will curse the day of
your birth.
15A man accustomed to use insulting
words
will never become disciplined
all his days.

16Two sorts of men multiply sins,
and a third incurs wrath.
The soul heated like a burning fire
will not be quenched until it is
consumed;
a man who commits fornication
with his near of kin[y]
will never cease until the fire
burns him up.
17To a fornicator all bread tastes
sweet;
he will never cease until he dies.
18A man who breaks his marriage
vows
says to himself, "Who sees me?
Darkness surrounds me, and the
walls hide me,
and no one sees me. Why should
I fear?
The Most High will not take notice
of my sins."
19His fear is confined to the eyes of
men,
and he does not realize that the
eyes of the Lord
are ten thousand times brighter
than the sun;
they look upon all the ways of
men,
and perceive even the hidden
places.
20Before the universe was created, it
was known to him;
so it was also after it was
finished.
21This man will be punished in the
streets of the city,
and where he least suspects it,
he will be seized.
22So it is with a woman who leaves
her husband
and provides an heir by a
stranger.
23For first of all, she has disobeyed
the law of the Most High;
second, she has committed
an offense against her
husband;
and third, she has committed
adultery through harlotry
and brought forth children by
another man.
24She herself will be brought before
the assembly,
and punishment will fall on her
children.
25Her children will not take root,
and her branches will not bear
fruit.
26She will leave her memory for a
curse,
and her disgrace will not be
blotted out.
27Those who survive her will
recognize
that nothing is better than the
fear of the Lord,
and nothing sweeter than to heed
the commandments of the
Lord.[z]

x Gk *for*
y Gk *in the body of his flesh*
z Other authorities add [28]*It is a great honor to follow God, and to be received by him is long life.*

23.16–27: Sins of the flesh. 16: *The fire*, of passion. **17:** *All bread*, a euphemism (Syriac, "all flesh"). **18:** Job 24.15. **19:** 15.19; Pr.15.3. **21–22:** Lev.20.10; Dt.22.21–23. **24–25:** Dt.23.2; Wis.3.16–19; 4.3–6.

24 Wisdom will praise herself,
and will glory in the midst
of her people.[a]
[2]In the assembly of the Most High
she will open her mouth,
and in the presence of his host
she will glory:
[3]"I came forth from the mouth of
the Most High,
and covered the earth like a mist.
[4]I dwelt in high places,
and my throne was in a pillar of
cloud.
[5]Alone I have made the circuit of
the vault of heaven
and have walked in the depths
of the abyss.
[6]In the waves of the sea, in the
whole earth,
and in every people and nation
I have gotten a possession.
[7]Among all these I sought a resting
place;
I sought in whose territory I
might lodge.

[8]"Then the Creator of all things
gave me a commandment,
and the one who created me
assigned a place for my tent.
And he said, 'Make your dwelling
in Jacob,
and in Israel receive your
inheritance.'
[9]From eternity, in the beginning,
he created me,
and for eternity I shall not cease
to exist.
[10]In the holy tabernacle I ministered
before him,
and so I was established in Zion.
[11]In the beloved city likewise he
gave me a resting place,
and in Jerusalem was my
dominion.
[12]So I took root in an honored people,
in the portion of the Lord, who
is their inheritance.

[13]"I grew tall like a cedar in Lebanon,
and like a cypress on the heights
of Hermon.
[14]I grew tall like a palm tree in
En-ge'di,[b]
and like rose plants in Jericho;
like a beautiful olive tree in the
field,
and like a plane tree I grew
tall.
[15]Like cassia and camel's thorn I
gave forth the aroma of spices,
and like choice myrrh I spread
a pleasant odor,
like galbanum, onycha, and stacte,
and like the fragrance of
frankincense in the tabernacle.
[16]Like a terebinth I spread out my
branches,
and my branches are glorious
and graceful.
[17]Like a vine I caused loveliness to
bud,
and my blossoms became
glorious and abundant
fruit.[c]

[19]"Come to me, you who desire
me,
and eat your fill of my produce.
[20]For the remembrance of me is
sweeter than honey,
and my inheritance sweeter than
the honeycomb.
[21]Those who eat me will hunger for
more,
and those who drink me will
thirst for more.
[22]Whoever obeys me will not be put
to shame,
and those who work with my
help will not sin."

[23]All this is the book of the covenant
of the Most High God,
the law which Moses
commanded us

a Or *will glorify herself in the midst of the people.*
b Other authorities read *on the beaches*
c Other authorities add [18]*I am the mother of beautiful love, of fear, of knowledge, and of holy hope; being eternal, I therefore am given to all my children, to those who are named by him.*

24.1–34: Praise of wisdom. 3–22: Pr.8.22–9.12. **6:** *Have gotten a possession*, Syriac and Latin, "have ruled." **4:** Ex.33.9–10. **19:** Is.55.1. **20:** Ps.19.10.

as an inheritance for the
congregations of Jacob.[d]
25It fills men with wisdom, like the
Pishon,
and like the Tigris at the time
of the first fruits.
26It makes them full of understanding,
like the Euphrates,
and like the Jordan at harvest
time.
27It makes instruction shine forth
like light,
like the Gihon at the time of
vintage.
28Just as the first man did not know
her perfectly,
the last one has not fathomed
her;
29for her thought is more abundant
than the sea,
and her counsel deeper than the
great abyss.

30I went forth like a canal from a
river
and like a water channel into a
garden.
31I said, "I will water my orchard
and drench my garden
plot";
and lo, my canal became a
river,
and my river became a sea.
32I will again make instruction shine
forth like the dawn,
and I will make it shine afar;
33I will again pour out teaching like
prophecy,
and leave it to all future
generations.
34Observe that I have not labored
for myself alone,
but for all who seek instruction.[e]

25 My soul takes pleasure in
three things,
and they are beautiful in the
sight of the Lord and of men:[f]
agreement between brothers,
friendship between neighbors,
and a wife and husband who
live in harmony.
2My soul hates three kinds of
men,
and I am greatly offended at
their life:
a beggar who is proud, a rich man
who is a liar,
and an adulterous old man who
lacks good sense.

3You have gathered nothing in your
youth;
how then can you find anything
in your old age?
4What an attractive thing is judgment
in gray-haired men,
and for the aged to possess good
counsel!
5How attractive is wisdom in the
aged,
and understanding and counsel
in honorable men!
6Rich experience is the crown of the
aged,
and their boast is the fear of the
Lord.

7With nine thoughts I have gladdened
my heart,
and a tenth I shall tell with my
tongue:
a man rejoicing in his children;
a man who lives to see the
downfall of his foes;
8happy is he who lives with an
intelligent wife,

d Other authorities add 24"*Do not cease to be strong in the Lord, cleave to him so that he may strengthen you; the Lord Almighty alone is God, and besides him there is no savior.*"
e Gk *it*
f Syr Vg: Gk *In three things I was beautified and I stood in beauty before the Lord and men*

25: Gen.2.11,14. **26:** Jos.3.15. **30–34:** The author compares himself to an irrigation canal leading off from the great river of wisdom. **34:** 33.17.

25.1–2: Three beautiful and three hateful things.

25.3–6: The attractiveness of wisdom in the aged.

25.7–11: Ten happy thoughts. 8a: Hebrew and Syriac add, "and does not plow with ox and ass" (compare Dt.22.10).

and he who has not made a slip
with his tongue,
and he who has not served a
man inferior to himself;
9happy is he who has gained good
sense,
and he who speaks to attentive
listeners.
10How great is he who has gained
wisdom!
But there is no one superior to
him who fears the Lord.
11The fear of the Lord surpasses
everything;
to whom shall be likened the
one who holds it fast?[g]

13Any wound, but not a wound of
the heart!
Any wickedness, but not the
wickedness of a wife!
14Any attack, but not an attack from
those who hate!
And any vengeance, but not the
vengeance of enemies!
15There is no venom[h] worse than a
snake's venom,[h]
and no wrath worse than an
enemy's wrath.

16I would rather dwell with a lion
and a dragon
than dwell with an evil wife.
17The wickedness of a wife changes
her appearance,
and darkens her face like that of
a bear.
18Her husband takes his meals among
the neighbors,
and he cannot help sighing[i]
bitterly.
19Any iniquity is insignificant
compared to a wife's iniquity;
may a sinner's lot befall her!
20A sandy ascent for the feet of the
aged—
such is a garrulous wife for a
quiet husband.
21Do not be ensnared by a woman's
beauty,
and do not desire a woman for
her possessions.[j]
22There is wrath and impudence and
great disgrace
when a wife supports her
husband.
23A dejected mind, a gloomy face,
and a wounded heart are caused
by an evil wife.
Drooping hands and weak knees
are caused by the wife who
does not make her husband
happy.
24From a woman sin had its
beginning,
and because of her we all die.
25Allow no outlet to water,
and no boldness of speech in an
evil wife.
26If she does not go as you
direct,
separate her from yourself.

26 Happy is the husband of a
good wife;
the number of his days will be
doubled.
2A loyal wife rejoices her husband,
and he will complete his years
in peace.
3A good wife is a great blessing;
she will be granted among the
blessings of the man who fears
the Lord.
4Whether rich or poor, his heart is
glad,
and at all times his face is
cheerful.

g Other authorities add 12*The fear of the Lord is the beginning of love for him, and faith is the beginning of clinging to him.*
h Cn: Gk *head*
i Other authorities read *and listening he sighs*
j Heb Syr: Some Gk authorities read *for her beauty*

25.13–26: Wicked and virtuous women. 15: *An enemy's*, Syriac, "a woman's." **16:** Pr.21.19; 25.24. **20a:** It is tedious and wearisome. **21:** 42.12. **24:** Gen.3.6; 2 Cor.11.3; 1 Tim.2.14. **26b:** Literally, "cut her off from your flesh," that is, divorce her (Dt.24.1); hitherto they had been "one flesh" (Gen.2.24).

26.1–4: The happiness of the husband of a good wife (Pr.31.10–31). **2:** *Rejoices*, Hebrew, "makes fat" (v.13). **3:** 36.24; Pr.12.4.

5Of three things my heart is afraid,
and of a fourth I am frightened:[k]
The slander of a city, the gathering
of a mob,
and false accusation—all these
are worse than death.
6There is grief of heart and sorrow
when a wife is envious of a
rival,
and a tongue-lashing makes it
known to all.
7An evil wife is an ox yoke which
chafes;
taking hold of her is like grasping
a scorpion.
8There is great anger when a wife
is drunken;
she will not hide her shame.
9A wife's harlotry shows in her
lustful eyes,
and she is known by her eyelids.
10Keep strict watch over a headstrong
daughter,
lest, when she finds liberty, she
use it to her hurt.
11Be on guard against her impudent
eye,
and do not wonder if she sins
against you.
12As a thirsty wayfarer opens his
mouth
and drinks from any water near
him,
so will she sit in front of every post
and open her quiver to the arrow.

13A wife's charm delights her husband,
and her skill puts fat on his bones.
14A silent wife is a gift of the Lord,
and there is nothing so precious
as a disciplined soul.
15A modest wife adds charm to charm,
and no balance can weigh the
value of a chaste soul.
16Like the sun rising in the heights
of the Lord,
so is the beauty of a good wife in
her well-ordered home.
17Like the shining lamp on the holy
lampstand,
so is a beautiful face on a stately
figure.
18Like pillars of gold on a base of
silver,
so are beautiful feet with a
steadfast heart.[l]

28At two things my heart is grieved,
and because of a third anger
comes over me:
a warrior in want through poverty,
and intelligent men who are
treated contemptuously;
a man who turns back from
righteousness to sin—
the Lord will prepare him for the
sword!

29A merchant can hardly keep from
wrongdoing,
and a tradesman will not be
declared innocent of sin.

27 Many have committed sin
for a trifle,[m]
and whoever seeks to get rich
will avert his eyes.
2As a stake is driven firmly into a
fissure between stones,

k The Greek of this line is uncertain
l Other authorities add verses 19–27:
19*My son, keep sound the bloom of your youth,*
and do not give your strength to strangers.
20*Seek a fertile field within the whole plain,*
and sow it with your own seed, trusting in your fine stock.
21*So your offspring will survive*
and, having confidence in their good descent, will grow great.
22*A harlot is regarded as spittle,*
and a married woman as a tower of death to her lovers,
23*A godless wife is given as a portion to a lawless man,*
but a pious wife is given to the man who fears the Lord.
24*A shameless woman constantly acts disgracefully,*
but a modest daughter will even be embarrassed before her husband.
25*A headstrong wife is regarded as a dog,*
but one who has a sense of shame will fear the Lord.
26*A wife honoring her husband will seem wise to all,*
but if she dishonors him in her pride she will be known to all as ungodly.
Happy is the husband of a good wife;
for the number of his years will be doubled.
27*A loud-voiced and garrulous wife is regarded as a war trumpet for putting the enemy to flight,*
and every person like this lives in the anarchy of war.
m One ancient authority reads *gain*

26.5–12: A wicked wife. 10: 42.11.
26.13–18: A good wife. 18: *With . . . heart,* other witnesses read, "upon firm heels."
26.28–27.3: Miscellaneous observations. 26.28: *A warrior,* Syriac, "a wealthy man." **27.1:** Pr.28.21.

so sin is wedged in between
selling and buying.
[3]If a man is not steadfast and zealous
in the fear of the Lord,
his house will be quickly
overthrown.

[4]When a sieve is shaken, the refuse
remains;
so a man's filth remains in his
thoughts.
[5]The kiln tests the potter's vessels;
so the test of a man is in his
reasoning.
[6]The fruit discloses the cultivation
of a tree;
so the expression of a thought
discloses the cultivation of a
man's mind.
[7]Do not praise a man before you
hear him reason,
for this is the test of men.

[8]If you pursue justice, you will
attain it
and wear it as a glorious robe.
[9]Birds flock with their kind;
so truth returns to those who
practice it.
[10]A lion lies in wait for prey;
so does sin for the workers of
iniquity.

[11]The talk of the godly man is
always wise,
but the fool changes like the
moon.
[12]Among stupid people watch for a
chance to leave,
but among thoughtful people
stay on.
[13]The talk of fools is offensive,
and their laughter is wantonly
sinful.
[14]The talk of men given to swearing
makes one's hair stand on end,
and their quarrels make a man
stop his ears.
[15]The strife of the proud leads to
bloodshed,
and their abuse is grievous to
hear.

[16]Whoever betrays secrets destroys
confidence,
and he will never find a
congenial friend.
[17]Love your friend and keep faith
with him;
but if you betray his secrets, do
not run after him.
[18]For as a man destroys his enemy,
so you have destroyed the
friendship of your neighbor.
[19]And as you allow a bird to escape
from your hand,
so you have let your neighbor
go, and will not catch him
again.
[20]Do not go after him, for he is too
far off,
and has escaped like a gazelle
from a snare.
[21]For a wound may be bandaged,
and there is reconciliation after
abuse,
but whoever has betrayed secrets is
without hope.

[22]Whoever winks his eye plans evil
deeds,
and no one can keep him from
them.
[23]In your presence his mouth is all
sweetness,
and he admires your words;
but later he will twist his speech
and with your own words he
will give offense.
[24]I have hated many things, but none
to be compared to him;
even the Lord will hate him.

27.4–7: Tests in life. 6: Mt.7.17.
27.8–10: Reward and retribution.
27.11–15: Kinds of talk.
27.16–21: Against disclosing secrets (Pr.20.19; 25.9). **18:** *Enemy*, Syriac, "inheritance." **21:** *Without hope*, of reconciliation (22.22).
27.22–24: Hypocrisy. 22: *Winks*, with insincerity (Ps.35.19; Pr.6.13; 10.10).

25 Whoever throws a stone straight
up throws it on his own head;
and a treacherous blow opens up
wounds.
26 He who digs a pit will fall into it,
and he who sets a snare will be
caught in it.
27 If a man does evil, it will roll back
upon him,
and he will not know where it
came from.
28 Mockery and abuse issue from the
proud man,[n]
but vengeance lies in wait for
him like a lion.
29 Those who rejoice in the fall of the
godly will be caught in a
snare,
and pain will consume them
before their death.

30 Anger and wrath, these also are
abominations,
and the sinful man will possess
them.

28 He that takes vengeance will
suffer vengeance from the
Lord,
and he will firmly establish[o] his
sins.
2 Forgive your neighbor the wrong
he has done,
and then your sins will be
pardoned when you pray.
3 Does a man harbor anger against
another,
and yet seek for healing from
the Lord?
4 Does he have no mercy toward a
man like himself,
and yet pray for his own sins?
5 If he himself, being flesh, maintains
wrath,
who will make expiation for his
sins?
6 Remember the end of your life, and
cease from enmity,
remember destruction and death,
and be true to the
commandments.
7 Remember the commandments,
and do not be angry with your
neighbor;
remember the covenant of the
Most High, and overlook
ignorance.

8 Refrain from strife, and you will
lessen sins;
for a man given to anger will
kindle strife,
9 and a sinful man will disturb
friends
and inject enmity among those
who are at peace.
10 In proportion to the fuel for the
fire, so will be the burning,
and in proportion to the
obstinacy of strife will be
the burning;[p]
in proportion to the strength of the
man will be his anger,
and in proportion to his wealth
he will heighten his wrath.
11 A hasty quarrel kindles fire,
and urgent strife sheds blood.
12 If you blow on a spark, it will glow;
if you spit on it, it will be put out;
and both come out of your mouth.

13 Curse the whisperer and deceiver,
for he has destroyed many who
were at peace.
14 Slander[q] has shaken many,
and scattered them from nation
to nation,
and destroyed strong cities,
and overturned the houses of
great men.
15 Slander[q] has driven away
courageous women,

n Other authorities read *proud men*
o Other authorities read *closely observe*
p Other authorities place this line at the end of the verse, or omit it
q Gk *a third tongue*

27.25–29: Retribution (Ps.7.14–16; 9.15–16; Pr.26.27; Ec.10.8).
27.30–28.7: Vengeance. 1: Dt.32.35; Rom.12.19. **2:** Mt.6.14; Mk.11.25. **3:** Mt.18.23–35. **4:** Mt.5.7. **6:** 7.36.
28.8–12: Strife and quarrels. 8: Pr.15.18. **10:** 26.20–21; Jas.3.5. **12:** Pr.15.1.
28.13–26: Slander and an evil tongue (51.2–6; Jas.3.5–12). **15:** *Has driven away*, from their

and deprived them of the fruit
of their toil.
16Whoever pays heed to slander[r]
will not find rest,
nor will he settle down in peace.
17The blow of a whip raises a welt,
but a blow of the tongue crushes
the bones.
18Many have fallen by the edge of
the sword,
but not so many as have fallen
because of the tongue.
19Happy is the man who is protected
from it,
who has not been exposed to its
anger,
who has not borne its yoke,
and has not been bound with its
fetters;
20for its yoke is a yoke of iron,
and its fetters are fetters of
bronze;
21its death is an evil death,
and Hades is preferable to it.
22It will not be master over the
godly,
and they will not be burned in its
flame.
23Those who forsake the Lord will
fall into its power;
it will burn among them and
will not be put out.
It will be sent out against them like
a lion;
like a leopard it will mangle
them.
24See that you fence in your property
with thorns,
lock up your silver and gold,
25make balances and scales for your
words,
and make a door and a bolt for
your mouth.
26Beware lest you err with your
tongue,[s]
lest you fall before him who lies
in wait.

29 He that shows mercy will
lend to his neighbor,
and he that strengthens him with
his hand keeps the
commandments.
2Lend to your neighbor in the time
of his need;
and in turn, repay your neighbor
promptly.
3Confirm your word and keep faith
with him,
and on every occasion you will
find what you need.
4Many persons regard a loan as a
windfall,
and cause trouble to those who
help them.
5A man will kiss another's hands
until he gets a loan,
and will lower his voice in
speaking of his neighbor's
money;
but at the time for repayment he
will delay,
and will pay in words of
unconcern,
and will find fault with the
time.
6If the lender[t] exerts pressure, he
will hardly get back half,
and will regard that as a
windfall.
If he does not, the borrower[u] has
robbed him of his money,
and he has needlessly made him
his enemy;
he will repay him with curses and
reproaches,
and instead of glory will repay
him with dishonor.
7Because of such wickedness,
therefore,[v] many have refused
to lend;
they have been afraid of being
defrauded needlessly.

8Nevertheless, be patient with a
man in humble circumstances,

r Gk *it*
s Gk *with it*
t Gk *he*
u Gk *he*
v Other authorities read *It is not because of wickedness that*

homes. **16:** The statement refers primarily to the husband. **17:** Pr.25.15. **25b:** 22.27; Ps.141.3.
29.1–13: Concerning loans (Ex.22.25; Lev.25.36; Mt.5.42; Lk.6.35). **2:** Pr.19.17. **4:** 8.12.

and do not make him wait for
your alms.
9Help a poor man for the
commandment's sake,
and because of his need do not
send him away empty.
10Lose your silver for the sake of a
brother or a friend,
and do not let it rust under a
stone and be lost.
11Lay up your treasure according to
the commandments of the
Most High,
and it will profit you more than
gold.
12Store up almsgiving in your
treasury,
and it will rescue you from all
affliction;
13more than a mighty shield and
more than a heavy spear,
it will fight on your behalf
against your enemy.

14A good man will be surety for his
neighbor,
but a man who has lost his
sense of shame will fail him.
15Do not forget all the kindness of
your surety,
for he has given his life for you.
16A sinner will overthrow the
prosperity of his surety,
17 and one who does not feel grateful will abandon his rescuer.
18Being surety has ruined many men
who were prosperous,
and has shaken them like a wave
of the sea;
it has driven men of power into exile,
and they have wandered among
foreign nations.
19The sinner who has fallen into
suretyship
and pursues gain will fall into
lawsuits.
20Assist your neighbor according to
your ability,
but take heed to yourself lest
you fall.

21The essentials for life are water
and bread
and clothing and a house to
cover one's nakedness.
22Better is the life of a poor man
under the shelter of his roof
than sumptuous food in another
man's house.
23Be content with little or much.[w]
24It is a miserable life to go from
house to house,
and where you are a stranger you
may not open your mouth;
25you will play the host and provide
drink without being thanked,
and besides this you will hear
bitter words:
26"Come here, stranger, prepare the
table,
and if you have anything at
hand, let me have it to eat."
27"Give place, stranger, to an
honored person;
my brother has come to stay
with me; I need my house."
28These things are hard to bear for
a man who has feeling:
scolding about lodging[x] and
the reproach of the
moneylender.

30 He who loves his son will
whip him often,
in order that he may rejoice at
the way he turns out.
2He who disciplines his son will
profit by him,
and will boast of him among
acquaintances.

w Other authorities add *and you will not hear reproach for your sojourning.*
x Or *from the household,* or (Syr) *from the host*

10: *Rust,* Mt.6.19; Jas.5.3. **11:** Syriac, "Lay up for yourself a treasure of righteousness [i.e. through almsgiving] and love, and it shall profit you more than all that you have" (see 3.30 n. and compare Mt.19.21; Lk.12.33).

29.14–20: Concerning suretyship. 14: Contrast Pr.6.1–5; 17.18. **20:** 8.13.

29.21–28: On contentment and hospitality. 21: 39.26. **23:** Phil.4.11; 1 Tim.6.8; Heb.13.5. **28:** Syriac adds, "Give very freely to the poor, and feed him from that which is at hand; if he is

[3]He who teaches his son will make
his enemies envious,
and will glory in him in the
presence of friends.
[4]The[y] father may die, and yet he
is not dead,
for he has left behind him one
like himself;
[5]while alive he saw and rejoiced,
and when he died he was not
grieved;
[6]he has left behind him an avenger
against his enemies,
and one to repay the kindness
of his friends.

[7]He who spoils his son will bind up
his wounds,
and his feelings will be troubled
at every cry.
[8]A horse that is untamed turns out
to be stubborn,
and a son unrestrained turns out
to be wilful.
[9]Pamper a child, and he will frighten
you;
play with him, and he will give
you grief.
[10]Do not laugh with him, lest you
have sorrow with him,
and in the end you will gnash
your teeth.
[11]Give him no authority in his
youth,
and do not ignore his errors.
[12]Bow down his neck in his
youth,[z]
and beat his sides while he is
young,
lest he become stubborn and
disobey you,
and you have sorrow of soul
from him.[a]
[13]Discipline your son and take pains
with him,
that you may not be offended by
his shamelessness.

[14]Better off is a poor man who is well
and strong in constitution
than a rich man who is severely
afflicted in body.
[15]Health and soundness are better
than all gold,
and a robust body than countless
riches.
[16]There is no wealth better than
health of body,
and there is no gladness above
joy of heart.
[17]Death is better than a miserable
life,
and eternal rest[b] than chronic
sickness.

[18]Good things poured out upon a
mouth that is closed
are like offerings of food placed
upon a grave.
[19]Of what use to an idol is an
offering of fruit?
For it can neither eat nor smell.
So is he who is afflicted by the
Lord;
[20]he sees with his eyes and groans,
like a eunuch who embraces a
maiden and groans.

[21]Do not give yourself over to sorrow,
and do not afflict yourself
deliberately.
[22]Gladness of heart is the life of man,
and the rejoicing of a man is
length of days.
[23]Delight your soul and comfort your
heart,
and remove sorrow far from you,

y Gk *His*
z Other authorities omit this line and the preceding line
a Other authorities omit this line
b Some authorities omit *eternal rest*

---

naked, clothe him; thus you will be lending unto God, and he will repay you sevenfold" (compare Is.58.7; Mt.25.35–36).

30.1–13: On bringing up children. 1: Pr.13.24; 23.13–14; 29.15. **2:** Pr.29.17. **11:** 7.23. **13:** *Take pains with him*, Hebrew, "make his yoke heavy."

30:14–20: Concerning health. 18: Tob.4.17. **19:** Let.Jer.27–28; Bel 3 (compare Ps.115.5–7). **20:** *Groans*, with regret.

30.21–25: Gladness of heart (Ec.11.9–10). **21:** 38.20; Pr.12.25. **22:** 15.13; 17.22. **23:** 38.18–19.

for sorrow has destroyed many,
and there is no profit in it.
24 Jealousy and anger shorten life,
and anxiety brings on old age
too soon.
25 A man of cheerful and good heart
will give heed to the food he
eats.

31 Wakefulness over wealth
wastes away one's flesh,
and anxiety about it removes
sleep.
2 Wakeful anxiety prevents slumber,
and a severe illness carries off
sleep.[c]
3 The rich man toils as his wealth
accumulates,
and when he rests he fills himself
with his dainties.
4 The poor man toils as his livelihood
diminishes,
and when he rests he becomes
needy.

5 He who loves gold will not be
justified,
and he who pursues money will
be led astray[d] by it.
6 Many have come to ruin because
of gold,
and their destruction has met
them face to face.
7 It is a stumbling block to those
who are devoted to it,
and every fool will be taken
captive by it.
8 Blessed is the rich man who is
found blameless,
and who does not go after gold.
9 Who is he? And we will call him
blessed,
for he has done wonderful things
among his people.
10 Who has been tested by it and
been found perfect?
Let it be for him a ground for
boasting.
Who has had the power to
transgress and did not
transgress,
and to do evil and did not do it?
11 His prosperity will be established,
and the assembly will relate his
acts of charity.

12 Are you seated at the table of a
great man?[e]
Do not be greedy[f] at it,
and do not say, "There is
certainly much upon it!"
13 Remember that a greedy[g] eye is
a bad thing.
What has been created more
greedy[g] than the eye?
Therefore it sheds tears from
every face.
14 Do not reach out your hand for
everything you see,
and do not crowd your neighbor[h]
at the dish.
15 Judge your neighbor's feelings by
your own,
and in every matter be
thoughtful.
16 Eat like a human being what is set
before you,
and do not chew greedily, lest
you be hated.
17 Be the first to stop eating, for the
sake of good manners,
and do not be insatiable, lest
you give offense.
18 If you are seated among many
persons,
do not reach out your hand
before they do.

19 How ample a little is for a well
disciplined man!
He does not breathe heavily
upon his bed.

c Other authorities read *sleep carries off a severe illness*
d Heb Syr: Gk *will be filled*
e Heb Syr: Gk *at a great table*
f Gk *open your throat*
g Gk *evil* *h* Gk *him*

31.1–11: The right attitude toward wealth. **1:** 1 Tim.6.9–10. **4:** The opposite of v. 3 (compare 11.11).

31.12–30: Temperance in food and drink. **12:** Pr.23.1–3. **15b:** Hebrew, "and keep in mind your own dislikes." **16:** *Like a human being*, and not like an animal. **17:** 37.29.

[20]Healthy sleep depends on moderate
eating;
he rises early, and feels fit.[i]
The distress of sleeplessness and
of nausea
and colic are with the glutton.
[21]If you are overstuffed with food,
get up in the middle of the
meal, and you will have relief.
[22]Listen to me, my son, and do not
disregard me,
and in the end you will appreciate
my words.
In all your work be industrious,
and no sickness will overtake you.

[23]Men will praise the one who is
liberal with food,
and their testimony to his
excellence is trustworthy.
[24]The city will complain of the one
who is niggardly with food,
and their testimony to his
niggardliness is accurate.

[25]Do not aim to be valiant over wine,
for wine has destroyed many.
[26]Fire and water prove[j] the temper
of steel,
so wine tests hearts in the strife
of the proud.
[27]Wine is like life to men,
if you drink it in moderation.
What is life to a man who is
without wine?
It has been created to make men
glad.
[28]Wine drunk in season and
temperately
is rejoicing of heart and gladness
of soul.
[29]Wine drunk to excess is bitterness
of soul,
with provocation and stumbling.
[30]Drunkenness increases the anger
of a fool to his injury,
reducing his strength and adding
wounds.
[31]Do not reprove your neighbor at
a banquet of wine,
and do not despise him in his
merrymaking;
speak no word of reproach to him,
and do not afflict him by making
demands of him.

32 If they make you master of
the feast, do not exalt
yourself;
be among them as one of
them;
take good care of them and then
be seated;
2 when you have fulfilled your
duties, take your place,
that you may be merry on their
account
and receive a wreath for your
excellent leadership.

[3]Speak, you who are older, for it is
fitting that you should,
but with accurate knowledge,
and do not interrupt the
music.
[4]Where there is entertainment, do
not pour out talk;
do not display your cleverness
out of season.
[5]A ruby seal in a setting of gold
is a concert of music at a
banquet of wine.
[6]A seal of emerald in a rich setting
of gold
is the melody of music with
good wine.

[7]Speak, young man, if there is need
of you,
but no more than twice, and
only if asked.
[8]Speak concisely, say much in few
words;
be as one who knows and yet
holds his tongue.

i Gk *his soul is with him*
j Gk *The furnace by dipping proves*

22: *Be industrious*, Hebrew, "be moderate," which suits the context better. **23:** Pr.22.9. **25:** Is.5.22. **27:** Ps.104.15; Pr.31.6–7.

31.31–32.13: Etiquette at a banquet. 2: *A wreath*, Syriac, "honor." **7–9:** Advice for younger guests.

[9]Among the great do not act as
their equal;
and when another is speaking,
do not babble.

[10]Lightning speeds before the
thunder,
and approval precedes a modest
man.
[11]Leave in good time and do not be
the last;
go home quickly and do not
linger.
[12]Amuse yourself there, and do what
you have in mind,
but do not sin through proud
speech.
[13]And for these things bless him who
made you
and satisfies you with his good
gifts.

[14]He who fears the Lord will accept
his discipline,
and those who rise early to seek
him[k] will find favor.
[15]He who seeks the law will be filled
with it,
but the hypocrite will stumble
at it.
[16]Those who fear the Lord will form
true judgments,
and like a light they will kindle
righteous deeds.
[17]A sinful man will shun reproof,
and will find a decision according
to his liking.

[18]A man of judgment will not
overlook an idea,
and an insolent[l] and proud
man will not cower in
fear.[m]
[19]Do nothing without deliberation;
and when you have acted, do not
regret it.
[20]Do not go on a path full of
hazards,
and do not stumble over stony
ground.
[21]Do not be overconfident on a
smooth[n] way,
[22] and give good heed to your
paths.[o]
[23]Guard[p] yourself in every act,
for this is the keeping of the
commandments.
[24]He who believes the law gives heed
to the commandments,
and he who trusts the Lord will
not suffer loss.

33 No evil will befall the man
who fears the Lord,
but in trial he will deliver him
again and again.
[2]A wise man will not hate the law,
but he who is hypocritical about
it is like a boat in a storm.
[3]A man of understanding will trust
in the law;
for him the law is as dependable
as an inquiry by means of
Urim.

[4]Prepare what to say, and thus you
will be heard;
bind together your instruction,
and make your answer.
[5]The heart of a fool is like a cart
wheel,
and his thoughts like a turning
axle.
[6]A stallion is like a mocking
friend;
he neighs under every one who
sits on him.

k Other authorities omit *to seek him*
l Heb: Gk *alien*
m The meaning of this line is uncertain. Other authorities add the phrases *and after acting, with him, without deliberation*
n Or *an unexplored*
o Syr Vg: Gk *and beware of your children*
p Heb Syr: Gk *Trust*

32.14–33.6: The God-fearing man contrasted with the sinner. 32.14: 18.14; Job 5.17; Heb. 12.5–7. **17:** *A decision*, i.e. an interpretation (of the law). **20b:** Hebrew and Syriac, "Do not trip over the same obstacle twice." **24a:** Hebrew and Syriac, "He who observes the law preserves himself" (Pr.19.16). **33.1:** Pr.12.21; 1 Pet.3.13. **2:** Hebrew, "He that hates the law is not wise, and is tossed about like a boat in a storm." **3:** *Urim*, 45.10; Ex.28.30; Num.27.21; 1 Sam. 14.41–42.

7 Why is any day better than
another,
when all the daylight in the
year is from the sun?
8 By the Lord's decision they were
distinguished,
and he appointed the different
seasons and feasts;
9 some of them he exalted and
hallowed,
and some of them he made
ordinary days.
10 All men are from the ground,
and Adam was created of the
dust.
11 In the fulness of his knowledge
the Lord distinguished them
and appointed their different
ways;
12 some of them he blessed and
exalted,
and some of them he made
holy and brought near to
himself;
but some of them he cursed and
brought low,
and he turned them out of their
place.
13 As clay in the hand of the potter—
for all his ways are as he
pleases—
so men are in the hand of him
who made them,
to give them as he decides.

14 Good is the opposite of evil,
and life the opposite of death;
so the sinner is the opposite of
the godly.
15 Look upon all the works of the
Most High;
they likewise are in pairs, one
the opposite of the other.

16 I was the last on watch;
I was like one who gleans after
the grape-gatherers;
by the blessing of the Lord I
excelled,
and like a grape-gatherer I filled
my wine press.
17 Consider that I have not labored
for myself alone,
but for all who seek instruction.
18 Hear me, you who are great among
the people,
and you leaders of the
congregation, hearken.

19 To son or wife, to brother or
friend,
do not give power over yourself,
as long as you live;
and do not give your property to
another,
lest you change your mind and
must ask for it.
20 While you are still alive and have
breath in you,
do not let any one take your
place.
21 For it is better that your children
should ask from you
than that you should look to the
hand of your sons.
22 Excel in all that you do;
bring no stain upon your honor.
23 At the time when you end the days
of your life,
in the hour of death, distribute
your inheritance.

24 Fodder and a stick and burdens
for an ass;
bread and discipline and work
for a servant.
25 Set your slave to work, and you
will find rest;
leave his hands idle, and he will
seek liberty.

33.7–15: Divinely ordained diversities in nature. **10:** Gen.2.7; Job 10.9. **11:** *Ways*, destinies. **12:** *Blessed*, Gen.9.1; 12.2. *Made holy*, ordained to the priesthood (Num.16.5,10; Ezek.40.46; 42.13; 45.4). *Cursed*, Gen.9.25. **13:** Is.29.16; 45.9; 64.8; Jer.18.4,6; Wis.15.7–8; Rom.9.21. **15:** 42.24 (compare Ec.3.2–8).

33.16–18: The author's qualifications as a teacher (24.30–34). **17:** 24.34; Wis.6.1–2.

33.19–23: On preserving one's financial independence.

33.24–31: On the treatment of slaves (7.20–21). The rights of slaves were defined in the

26Yoke and thong will bow the neck,
and for a wicked servant there
are racks and tortures.
27Put him to work, that he may not
be idle,
for idleness teaches much evil.
28Set him to work, as is fitting for
him,
and if he does not obey, make
his fetters heavy.
29Do not act immoderately toward
anybody,
and do nothing without
discretion.

30If you have a servant, let him be
as yourself,
because you have bought him
with blood.
31If you have a servant, treat him as
a brother,
for as your own soul you will
need him.
If you ill-treat him, and he leaves
and runs away,
which way will you go to seek
him?

34 A man of no understanding
has vain and false hopes,
and dreams give wings to fools.
2As one who catches at a shadow
and pursues the wind,
so is he who gives heed to
dreams.
3The vision of dreams is this against
that,
the likeness of a face confronting
a face.
4From an unclean thing what will
be made clean?
And from something false what
will be true?
5Divinations and omens and dreams
are folly,
and like a woman in travail the
mind has fancies.
6Unless they are sent from the Most
High as a visitation,
do not give your mind to them.
7For dreams have deceived many,
and those who put their hope in
them have failed.
8Without such deceptions the law
will be fulfilled,
and wisdom is made perfect in
truthful lips.

9An educated[q] man knows many
things,
and one with much experience
will speak with understanding.
10He that is inexperienced knows
few things,
but he that has traveled acquires
much cleverness.
11I have seen many things in my
travels,
and I understand more than I
can express.
12I have often been in danger of
death,
but have escaped because of
these experiences.

13The spirit of those who fear the
Lord will live,
for their hope is in him who
saves them.
14He who fears the Lord will not be
timid,
nor play the coward, for he is
his hope.
15Blessed is the soul of the man who
fears the Lord!
To whom does he look? And
who is his support?
16The eyes of the Lord are upon
those who love him,

q Other authorities read *A traveled*

Mosaic law (Ex.21.2–6,20–21,26–27; Lev.25.46; Dt.15.12–18). **30** and **31:** Syriac, "If you have (only) one servant. . . ."

34.1–8: The vanity of dreams and omens (Dt.13.2–5; 18.9–14; Ec.5.7; Jer.29.8). **3a:** Syriac, "A dream of the night is like a mirror," i.e. the image in each is insubstantial. **4:** Job 14.4. **6:** Allowance is made for God-given dreams (Gen.37.5ff.; Jg.7.13ff.; Job 33.15–18).

34.9–12: Experience as a teacher.

34.13–17: The blessedness of those who fear God. 14: Ps.112.6–7; Pr.3.23–26; 28.1. **16:** *Eyes*, Ps.33.18; 34.15. *Shelter*, Ps.61.2–4; 91.1–4; Is.25.4.

a mighty protection and strong support,
a shelter from the hot wind and a shade from noonday sun,
a guard against stumbling and a defense against falling.
17 He lifts up the soul and gives light to the eyes;
he grants healing, life, and blessing.

18 If one sacrifices from what has been wrongfully obtained, the offering is blemished;[r]
the gifts[s] of the lawless are not acceptable.
19 The Most High is not pleased with the offerings of the ungodly;
and he is not propitiated for sins by a multitude of sacrifices.
20 Like one who kills a son before his father's eyes
is the man who offers a sacrifice from the property of the poor.
21 The bread of the needy is the life of the poor;
whoever deprives them of it is a man of blood.
22 To take away a neighbor's living is to murder him;
to deprive an employee of his wages is to shed blood.

23 When one builds and another tears down,
what do they gain but toil?
24 When one prays and another curses,
to whose voice will the Lord listen?
25 If a man washes after touching a dead body, and touches it again,
what has he gained by his washing?
26 So if a man fasts for his sins,
and goes again and does the same things,
who will listen to his prayer?
And what has he gained by humbling himself?

35 He who keeps the law makes many offerings;
he who heeds the commandments sacrifices a peace offering.
2 He who returns a kindness offers fine flour,
and he who gives alms sacrifices a thank offering.
3 To keep from wickedness is pleasing to the Lord,
and to forsake unrighteousness is atonement.
4 Do not appear before the Lord empty-handed,
5 for all these things are to be done because of the commandment.
6 The offering of a righteous man anoints the altar,
and its pleasing odor rises before the Most High.
7 The sacrifice of a righteous man is acceptable,
and the memory of it will not be forgotten.
8 Glorify the Lord generously,
and do not stint the first fruits of your hands.
9 With every gift show a cheerful face,
and dedicate your tithe with gladness.
10 Give to the Most High as he has given,
and as generously as your hand has found.
11 For the Lord is the one who repays,
and he will repay you sevenfold.

r Other authorities read *is made in mockery*
s Other authorities read *mockeries*

34.18–26: Unacceptable sacrifices (1 Sam.15.22; Ps.51.16–19; Pr.15.8; 21.3; Hos.6.6; Am.5.21–24; Mt.23.23). **21:** Lev.19.13; Dt.24.14–15; Tob.4.14. **25:** Num.19.11–13; 2 Pet.2.22.
35.1–11: Acceptable sacrifices (Is.1.11–18; Mic.6.6–8; Mk.12.33). **1:** *Peace offering*, Lev.3.1–17. **2:** *Fine flour*, Lev.2.1–16. *Thank offering*, Lev.7.12. **3:** Dan.4.27. **4:** Ex.23.15; Dt.16.16. **8:** 7.31; Pr.3.9; 22.9. **9:** 2 Cor.9.7. **10:** Tob.4.8. **11:** Pr.19.17; 2 Cor.9.8.

12 Do not offer him a bribe, for he
will not accept it;
and do not trust to an
unrighteous sacrifice;
for the Lord is the judge,
and with him is no partiality.
13 He will not show partiality in the
case of a poor man;
and he will listen to the prayer
of one who is wronged.
14 He will not ignore the supplication
of the fatherless,
nor the widow when she pours
out her story.
15 Do not the tears of the widow run
down her cheek
as she cries out against him
who has caused them to
fall?
16 He whose service is pleasing to the
Lord will be accepted,
and his prayer will reach to the
clouds.
17 The prayer of the humble pierces
the clouds,
and he will not be consoled until
it reaches the Lord;[t]
he will not desist until the Most
High visits him,
and does justice for the righteous,
and executes judgment.
18 And the Lord will not delay,
neither will he be patient with
them,
till he crushes the loins of the
unmerciful
and repays vengeance on the
nations;
till he takes away the multitude of
the insolent,
and breaks the scepters of the
unrighteous;
19 till he repays man according to his
deeds,
and the works of men according
to their devices;
till he judges the case of his people
and makes them rejoice in his
mercy.
20 Mercy is as welcome when he
afflicts them
as clouds of rain in the time of
drought.

36 Have mercy upon us, O
Lord, the God of all, and
look upon us,
2 and cause the fear of thee to fall
upon all the nations.
3 Lift up thy hand against foreign
nations
and let them see thy might.
4 As in us thou hast been sanctified
before them,
so in them be thou magnified
before us;
5 and let them know thee, as we
have known
that there is no God but thee,
O Lord.
6 Show signs anew, and work further
wonders;
make thy hand and thy right
arm glorious.
7 Rouse thy anger and pour out thy
wrath;
destroy the adversary and wipe
out the enemy.
8 Hasten the day, and remember the
appointed time,[u]
and let people recount thy
mighty deeds.
9 Let him who survives be consumed
in the fiery wrath,
and may those who harm thy
people meet destruction.

t Or *until the Lord draws near*
u Other authorities read *remember thy oath*

35.12–20: God's mercy and justice. 12: *Unrighteous sacrifice*, Hebrew and Syriac, "sacrifice of violence (or extortion)," i.e. derived from unjust dealing (34.20). *No partiality*, Dt.10.17; Job 34.19; Wis.6.7; Acts 10.34; Gal.2.6. **14–15:** Ex.22.22. **18:** *Will not delay*, in executing judgment (2 Pet.3.9). Here and in vv. 19–20 the author has in mind the pagan oppressors of God's chosen people.

36.1–17: A prayer for the deliverance and restoration of Israel. 2–3: Ps.79.6; Is.19.16; Jer. 10.25. **4:** Ezek.20.41; 28.25. **5:** 1 Kg.8.43,60. **7:** Ps.79.6. **8a:** Hebrew and Syriac, "Hasten the end" (of the present age). **8b:** Hebrew and Syriac, "For who may say to thee, 'What dost thou?'" i.e. God has *appointed* the *time* of the coming of the Messianic era (see 2 Esd.4.36–37 n.;

10Crush the heads of the rulers of
the enemy,
who say, "There is no one but
ourselves."
11Gather all the tribes of Jacob,
and give[v] them their inheritance,
as at the beginning.
12Have mercy, O Lord, upon the
people called by thy name,
upon Israel, whom thou hast
likened to a[w] first-born son.
13Have pity on the city of thy
sanctuary,[x]
Jerusalem, the place of thy
rest.
14Fill Zion with the celebration of
thy wondrous deeds,
and thy temple[y] with thy
glory.
15Bear witness to those whom thou
didst create in the beginning,
and fulfil the prophecies spoken
in thy name.
16Reward those who wait for thee,
and let thy prophets be found
trustworthy.
17Hearken, O Lord, to the prayer of
thy servants,
according to the blessing of
Aaron for thy people,
and all who are on the earth will
know
that thou art the Lord, the God
of the ages.

18The stomach will take any food,
yet one food is better than
another.
19As the palate tastes the kinds of
game,
so an intelligent mind detects
false words.
20A perverse mind will cause grief,
but a man of experience will pay
him back.
21A woman will accept any man,
but one daughter is better than
another.
22A woman's beauty gladdens the
countenance,
and surpasses every human
desire.
23If kindness and humility mark her
speech,
her husband is not like other
men.
24He who acquires a wife gets his
best possession,[z]
a helper fit for him and a pillar
of support.[a]
25Where there is no fence, the
property will be plundered;
and where there is no wife, a
man will wander about and
sigh.
26For who will trust a nimble
robber
that skips from city to city?
So who will trust a man that has
no home,
and lodges wherever night finds
him?

37 Every friend will say, "I too
am a friend";
but some friends are friends
only in name.
2Is it not a grief to the death
when a companion and friend
turns to enmity?
3O evil imagination, why were you
formed
to cover the land with deceit?
4Some companions rejoice in the
happiness of a friend,
but in time of trouble are
against him.

v Other authorities read *gave*
w Other authorities read *hast named thy*
x Or *on thy holy city*
y Heb Syr: Gk Vg *people*
z Heb: Gk *enters upon a possession*
a Heb: Gk *rest*

Acts 1.7–8). **11:** Jer.31.10. **12:** Dan.9.18–19. **13:** Ps.132.14. **17:** *The blessing of Aaron for thy people*, Num.6.23–26; Hebrew and Syriac, "thy good favor toward thy people." *The God of the ages*, the eternal God (Gen.21.33; Is.40.28).

36.18–26: Concerning discrimination (vv. 18–20, in general; vv. 21–26, in choosing a wife). **19:** Job 12.11; 34.3. **21a:** *Will accept*, because the marriage was arranged by her father (see 7.25 n.). **24:** *A helper fit for him*, Gen.2.18. **26:** *Home*, literally "nest."

37.1–6: False friends (6.7–13). **3:** *Evil imagination*, the evil *yeṣer* (see 15.14 n.). **4:** *Happi-*

[5]Some companions help a friend
for their stomachs' sake,
and in the face of battle take up
the shield.
[6]Do not forget a friend in your heart,
and be not unmindful of him in
your wealth.

[7]Every counselor praises counsel,
but some give counsel in their
own interest.
[8]Be wary of a counselor,
and learn first what is his
interest—
for he will take thought for
himself—
lest he cast the lot against you
[9] and tell you, "Your way is
good,"
and then stand aloof to see what
will happen to you.
[10]Do not consult with one who looks
at you suspiciously;
hide your counsel from those
who are jealous of you.
[11]Do not consult with a woman
about her rival
or with a coward about war,
with a merchant about barter
or with a buyer about selling,
with a grudging man about
gratitude
or with a merciless man about
kindness,
with an idler about any work
or with a man hired for a year
about completing his work,
with a lazy servant about a big
task—
pay no attention to these in any
matter of counsel.
[12]But stay constantly with a godly
man
whom you know to be a keeper
of the commandments,
whose soul is in accord with your
soul,
and who will sorrow with you if
you fail.
[13]And establish the counsel of your
own heart,
for no one is more faithful to
you than it is.
[14]For a man's soul sometimes keeps
him better informed
than seven watchmen sitting
high on a watchtower.
[15]And besides all this pray to the
Most High
that he may direct your way in
truth.

[16]Reason is the beginning of every
work,
and counsel precedes every
undertaking.
[17]As a clue to changes of heart
[18] four turns of fortune appear,
good and evil, life and death;
and it is the tongue that
continually rules them.
[19]A man may be shrewd and the
teacher of many,
and yet be unprofitable to
himself.
[20]A man skilled in words may be
hated;
he will be destitute of all
food,
[21]for grace was not given him by the
Lord,
since he is lacking in all wisdom.
[22]A man may be wise to his own
advantage,
and the fruits of his
understanding may be
trustworthy on his lips.
[23]A wise man will instruct his own
people,
and the fruits of his
understanding will be
trustworthy.
[24]A wise man will have praise heaped
upon him,

---

ness, arising from feasting (see v. 5). **6:** *In your heart*, Hebrew, "in war." *In your wealth*, Hebrew, "when you take the spoil."

37.7–15: Concerning counselors. 14: *Watchmen*, probably astrologers are meant.

37.16–26: True and false wisdom. 17–18: Hebrew, "The roots of the heart's counsels send out four branches." **18:** Pr.18.21. **21:** *Grace*, graciousness.

and all who see him will call him
happy.
25 The life of a man is numbered by
days,
but the days of Israel are
without number.
26 He who is wise among his people
will inherit confidence,[b]
and his name will live for ever.

27 My son, test your soul while you
live;
see what is bad for it and do not
give it that.
28 For not everything is good for
every one,
and not every person enjoys
everything.
29 Do not have an insatiable appetite
for any luxury,
and do not give yourself up to
food;
30 for overeating brings sickness,
and gluttony leads to nausea.
31 Many have died of gluttony,
but he who is careful to avoid
it prolongs his life.

38 Honor the physician with
the honor due him,[c] according to your need of him,
for the Lord created him;
2 for healing comes from the Most
High,
and he will receive a gift from
the king.
3 The skill of the physician lifts up
his head,
and in the presence of great
men he is admired.
4 The Lord created medicines from
the earth,
and a sensible man will not
despise them.
5 Was not water made sweet with a
tree
in order that his[d] power might
be known?
6 And he gave skill to men
that he[e] might be glorified in
his marvelous works.
7 By them he heals and takes away
pain;
8 the pharmacist makes of them
a compound.
His works will never be finished;
and from him health[f] is upon
the face of the earth.

9 My son, when you are sick do not
be negligent,
but pray to the Lord, and he
will heal you.
10 Give up your faults and direct your
hands aright,
and cleanse your heart from all
sin.
11 Offer a sweet-smelling sacrifice,
and a memorial portion of
fine flour,
and pour oil on your offering,
as much as you can afford.[g]
12 And give the physician his place,
for the Lord created him;
let him not leave you, for there
is need of him.
13 There is a time when success lies
in the hands of physicians,[h]
14 for they too will pray to the Lord
that he should grant them success
in diagnosis[i]
and in healing, for the sake of
preserving life.
15 He who sins before his Maker,

b Other authorities read *honor*
c Other authorities omit *with the honor due him*
d Or *its* *e* Or *they* *f* Or *peace*
g Heb: Vulgate omits *as much as you can afford;* Greek is obscure
h Gk *in their hands* *i* Heb: Gk *rest*

25: *Is numbered by days,* i.e. is of limited duration, contrasted with the nation of *Israel* (39.9; 44.13–14; 2 Macc. 14.15).

37.27–31: Temperance (31.16–22).

38.1–15: Concerning physicians. 1: *Created him,* i.e. established his profession. **5:** Ex.15.23–25. **8:** *His works,* God's works. **9–14:** In sickness turn first to God, by prayer, repentance, and sacrifice (contrast 2 Chr.16.12); then call the physician. **12:** *Created,* see v. 1 n. **15:** Severe illness, according to Jewish ideas, is divine judgment for sin (Job 5.17–18; 1 Cor.11.30). The Hebrew text, however, reads, "He who sins before his Maker will behave himself proudly before the physician."

may he fall into the care[j] of a
physician.

16My son, let your tears fall for the
dead,
and as one who is suffering
grievously begin the lament.
Lay out his body with the honor
due him,
and do not neglect his burial.
17Let your weeping be bitter and
your wailing fervent;
observe the mourning according
to his merit,
for one day, or two, to avoid
criticism;
then be comforted for your
sorrow.
18For sorrow results in death,
and sorrow of heart saps one's
strength.
19In calamity sorrow continues,
and the life of the poor man
weighs down his heart.
20Do not give your heart to
sorrow;
drive it away, remembering the
end of life.
21Do not forget, there is no coming
back;
you do the dead[k] no good, and
you injure yourself.
22"Remember my doom, for yours is
like it:
yesterday it was mine, and
today it is yours."
23When the dead is at rest, let his
remembrance cease,
and be comforted for him when
his spirit has departed.

24The wisdom of the scribe depends
on the opportunity of
leisure;
and he who has little business
may become wise.
25How can he become wise who
handles the plow,
and who glories in the shaft of
a goad,
who drives oxen and is occupied
with their work,
and whose talk is about[l] bulls?
26He sets his heart on plowing
furrows,
and he is careful about fodder
for the heifers.
27So too is every craftsman and
master workman
who labors by night as well as
by day;
those who cut the signets of
seals,
each is diligent in making a
great variety;
he sets his heart on painting a
lifelike image,
and he is careful to finish his
work.
28So too is the smith sitting by the
anvil,
intent upon his handiwork in
iron;
the breath of the fire melts his
flesh,
and he wastes away in[m] the heat
of the furnace;
he inclines his ear to the sound of
the hammer,[n]
and his eyes are on the pattern
of the object.
He sets his heart on finishing his
handiwork,
and he is careful to complete its
decoration.
29So too is the potter sitting at his
work
and turning the wheel with his
feet;
he is always deeply concerned over
his work,
and all his output is by
number.
30He moulds the clay with his arm

j Gk *hands* *k* Gk *him* *l* Or *among*
m Cn Compare Syr: Gk *contends with*
n Cn: Gk *the sound of the hammer renews his ear*

38.16–23: On mourning for the dead (22.11–12). **16d:** Hebrew, "and do not hide yourself when he has become a corpse." **18:** *Death,* Hebrew "harm." **22:** Lugubrious counsel from the dead man. **23:** 2 Sam.12.20.

38.24–39.11: Various craftsmen contrasted with the scribe, a student of divine wisdom.

and makes it pliable with his
feet;
he sets his heart to finish the
glazing,
and he is careful to clean the
furnace.

31 All these rely upon their hands,
and each is skilful in his own
work.
32 Without them a city cannot be
established,
and men can neither sojourn nor
live there.
33 Yet they are not sought out for
the council of the people,
nor do they attain eminence in
the public assembly.
They do not sit in the judge's
seat,
nor do they understand the
sentence of judgment;
they cannot expound discipline or
judgment,
and they are not found using
proverbs.
34 But they keep stable the fabric of
the world,
and their prayer is in the practice
of their trade.

39 On the other hand he who
devotes himself
to the study of the law of the
Most High
will seek out the wisdom of all the
ancients,
and will be concerned with
prophecies;
2 he will preserve the discourse of
notable men
and penetrate the subtleties of
parables;
3 he will seek out the hidden meanings
of proverbs
and be at home with the
obscurities of parables.
4 He will serve among great men
and appear before rulers;
he will travel through the lands of
foreign nations,
for he tests the good and the evil
among men.
5 He will set his heart to rise early
to seek the Lord who made
him,
and will make supplication
before the Most High;
he will open his mouth in
prayer
and make supplication for his
sins.

6 If the great Lord is willing,
he will be filled with the spirit
of understanding;
he will pour forth words[o] of
wisdom
and give thanks to the Lord in
prayer.
7 He will direct his counsel and
knowledge aright,
and meditate on his secrets.
8 He will reveal instruction in his
teaching,
and will glory in the law of the
Lord's covenant.
9 Many will praise his understanding,
and it will never be blotted
out;
his memory will not disappear,
and his name will live through
all generations.
10 Nations will declare his wisdom,
and the congregation will
proclaim his praise;
11 if he lives long, he will leave a
name greater than a
thousand,
and if he goes to rest, it is
enough[p] for him.

o Other authorities read *his words*
p Cn: the meaning of the Greek is uncertain

38.32: Craftsmen are necessary for the well-being of the social structure. **39.1:** The threefold division of the Hebrew canon: the law, wisdom (= the writings), and the prophets (given third place here in deference to wisdom; compare the Prologue to Sirach and see 2 Esd.14.45 n.). **2–3:** These verses refer to the oral traditions of the sages. *He will preserve*, in his memory (Pr.4.21; 22.17–18). **4:** *Will travel*, 51.13. **6:** Jas.4.15. **9:** *It*, Syriac, "his name." **11:** *It*, i.e. his name, which survives him and keeps him in remembrance.

12 I have yet more to say, which I
have thought upon,
and I am filled, like the moon
at the full.
13 Listen to me, O you holy sons,
and bud like a rose growing by
a stream of water;
14 send forth fragrance like
frankincense,
and put forth blossoms like a lily.
Scatter the fragrance, and sing a
hymn of praise;
bless the Lord for all his works;
15 ascribe majesty to his name
and give thanks to him with
praise,
with songs on your lips, and with
lyres;
and this you shall say in
thanksgiving:
16 "All things are the works of the
Lord, for they are very good,
and whatever he commands will
be done in his time."

17 No one can say, "What is this?"
"Why is that?"
for in God's[q] time all things
will be sought after.
At his word the waters stood in a
heap,
and the reservoirs of water at
the word of his mouth.
18 At his command whatever pleases
him is done,
and none can limit his saving
power.
19 The works of all flesh are before him,
and nothing can be hid from his
eyes.
20 From everlasting to everlasting he
beholds them,
and nothing is marvelous to him.
21 No one can say, "What is this?"
"Why is that?"
for everything has been created
for its use.

22 His blessing covers the dry land
like a river,
and drenches it like a flood.
23 The nations will incur his wrath,
just as he turns fresh water into
salt.
24 To the holy his ways are straight,
just as they are obstacles to the
wicked.
25 From the beginning good things
were created for good people,
just as evil things for sinners.
26 Basic to all the needs of man's
life
are water and fire and iron and
salt
and wheat flour and milk and
honey,
the blood of the grape, and oil
and clothing.
27 All these are for good to the
godly,
just as they turn into evils for
sinners.

28 There are winds that have been
created for vengeance,
and in their anger they scourge
heavily;
in the time of consummation they
will pour out their strength
and calm the anger of their
Maker.
29 Fire and hail and famine and
pestilence,
all these have been created for
vengeance;
30 the teeth of wild beasts, and
scorpions and vipers,
and the sword that punishes the
ungodly with destruction;
31 they will rejoice in his commands,
and be made ready on earth for
their service,
and when their times come they
will not transgress his word.

q Gk *his*

39.12–35: In praise of God the creator. 12–15: Introduction to Sirach's eulogy. **15:** *In thanksgiving*, Hebrew, "with a shout." **16:** Gen.1.31; 1 Tim.4.4. **17a:** Rom.9.20. **17c:** Ps.33.6–7; 147.15,18. **18:** Ps.135.6. **19:** 16.17–19; Heb.4.13. **22:** *A river*, the Nile is meant. *A flood*, the Euphrates is meant. **23b:** Ps.107.33. **24:** Hos.14.9. **25b:** 40.10. **26:** 29.21. **29:** 40.9; Ex.9.32. **30:** Dt.32.24; Wis.16.5. **31:** *They*, the previously mentioned instruments appointed

[32]Therefore from the beginning I
have been convinced,
and have thought this out and
left it in writing:
[33]The works of the Lord are all
good,
and he will supply every need in
its hour.
[34]And no one can say, "This is worse
than that,"
for all things will prove good in
their season.
[35]So now sing praise with all your
heart and voice,
and bless the name of the Lord.

40 Much labor was created for
every man,
and a heavy yoke is upon the
sons of Adam,
from the day they come forth from
their mother's womb
till the day they return to[r] the
mother of all.
[2]Their perplexities and fear of
heart—
their anxious thought is the day
of death,
[3]from the man who sits on a
splendid throne
to the one who is humbled in
dust and ashes,
[4]from the man who wears purple
and a crown
to the one who is clothed in
burlap;
[5]there is anger and envy and trouble
and unrest,
and fear of death, and fury and
strife.
And when one rests upon his bed,
his sleep at night confuses his
mind.
[6]He gets little or no rest,
and afterward in his sleep, as
though he were on watch,
he is troubled by the visions of his
mind
like one who has escaped from
the battle-front;
[7]at the moment of his rescue he
wakes up,
and wonders that his fear came
to nothing.
[8]With all flesh, both man and beast,
and upon sinners seven times
more,
[9]are death and bloodshed and strife
and sword,
calamities, famine and affliction
and plague.
[10]All these were created for the
wicked,
and on their account the flood
came.
[11]All things that are from the earth
turn back to the earth,
and what is from the waters
returns to the sea.

[12]All bribery and injustice will be
blotted out,
but good faith will stand for
ever.
[13]The wealth of the unjust will dry
up like a torrent,
and crash like a loud clap of
thunder in a rain.
[14]A generous man will be made glad;
likewise transgressors will
utterly fail.
[15]The children of the ungodly will
not put forth many branches;
they are unhealthy roots upon
sheer rock.
[16]The reeds by any water or river bank
will be plucked up before any
grass.
[17]Kindness is like a garden of
blessings,
and almsgiving endures for ever.

r Other authorities read *are buried in*

---

to execute God's wrath. **33a:** V. 16. **34:** *In their season*, compare Ec.3.1–8. **35:** Ps.145.21.

40.1–11: The miseries of mankind. 1: Gen.3.19; Job 7.1–2; 14.1; Ec.1.3; 2.23. **4:** *Purple*, Hebrew, "a turban," which was worn by the high priest (Ex.28.37). **8:** *Seven times*, 35.11. **11b:** Hebrew and Syriac, "and what is from above (returns) on high" (Ec.12.7).

40.12–17: Injustice will be blotted out. 17: *Almsgiving*, see 7.10 n. The verse in Hebrew reads, "But kindness shall never be moved, and righteousness abides forever."

18 Life is sweet for the self-reliant and
the worker,[s]
but he who finds treasure is
better off than both.
19 Children and the building of a
city establish a man's name,
but a blameless wife is accounted
better than both.
20 Wine and music gladden the
heart,
but the love of wisdom is better
than both.
21 The flute and the harp make
pleasant melody,
but a pleasant voice is better
than both.
22 The eye desires grace and
beauty,
but the green shoots of grain
more than both.
23 A friend or a companion never
meets one amiss,
but a wife with her husband is
better than both.
24 Brothers and help are for a time
of trouble,
but almsgiving rescues better
than both.
25 Gold and silver make the foot
stand sure,
but good counsel is esteemed
more than both.
26 Riches and strength lift up the
heart,
but the fear of the Lord is
better than both.
There is no loss in the fear of the
Lord,
and with it there is no need to
seek for help.
27 The fear of the Lord is like a
garden of blessing,
and covers a man[t] better than
any glory.

28 My son, do not lead the life of a
beggar;
it is better to die than to
beg.
29 When a man looks to the table of
another,
his existence cannot be
considered as life.
He pollutes himself with another
man's food,
but a man who is intelligent and
well-instructed guards against
that.
30 In the mouth of the shameless
begging is sweet,
but in his stomach a fire is
kindled.

41 O death, how bitter is the
reminder of you
to one who lives at peace among
his possessions,
to a man without distractions, who
is prosperous in everything,
and who still has the vigor to
enjoy his food!
2 O death, how welcome is your
sentence
to one who is in need and is
failing in strength,
very old and distracted over
everything;
to one who is contrary, and has
lost his patience!
3 Do not fear the sentence of
death;
remember your former days and
the end of life;
this is the decree from the Lord
for all flesh,
4 and how can you reject the
good pleasure of the Most
High?
Whether life is for ten or a hundred
or a thousand years,
there is no inquiry about it in
Hades.

s Cn: Gk *self-reliant worker*
t Gk *him*

40.18–27: The joys of life. 23b: *A wife with her husband,* Hebrew, "a prudent wife." **27a:** V. 17a.

40.28–30: A beggar's life is no life at all (29.24).

41.1–42.14: A series of contrasts. 41.1–7: *Death*—bitter to some, welcome to others. **3–4:** 38.20–23. **3b:** Hebrew, "Remember that the former and the latter (share it) with you."

5The children of sinners are
abominable children,
and they frequent the haunts of
the ungodly.
6The inheritance of the children of
sinners will perish,
and on their posterity will be a
perpetual reproach.
7Children will blame an ungodly
father,
for they suffer reproach because
of him.
8Woe to you, ungodly men,
who have forsaken the law of the
Most High God!
9When you are born, you are born
to a curse;
and when you die, a curse is your
lot.
10Whatever is from the dust returns
to dust;
so the ungodly go from curse to
destruction.

11The mourning of men is about their
bodies,
but the evil name of sinners will
be blotted out.
12Have regard for your name, since
it will remain for you
longer than a thousand great
stores of gold.
13The days of a good life are
numbered,
but a good name endures for ever.

14My children, observe instruction
and be at peace;
hidden wisdom and unseen treasure,
what advantage is there in either
of them?
15Better is the man who hides his
folly
than the man who hides his
wisdom.
16Therefore show respect for my
words:
For it is not good to retain every
kind of shame,
and not everything is confidently
esteemed by every one.
17Be ashamed of immorality, before
your father or mother;
and of a lie, before a prince or a
ruler;
18of a transgression, before a judge
or magistrate;
and of iniquity, before a
congregation or the people;
of unjust dealing, before your
partner or friend;
19 and of theft, in the place where
you live.
Be ashamed before the truth of
God and his covenant.
Be ashamed of selfish behavior
at meals,[u]
of surliness in receiving and giving,
20 and of silence, before those who
greet you;
of looking at a woman who is a
harlot,
21 and of rejecting the appeal of a
kinsman;
of taking away some one's portion
or gift,
and of gazing at another man's
wife;
22of meddling with his maidservant—
and do not approach her bed;
of abusive words, before friends—
and do not upbraid after making
a gift;
23of repeating and telling what you
hear,
and of revealing secrets.
Then you will show proper shame,
and will find favor with every
man.

42 Of the following things do
not be ashamed,
and do not let partiality lead
you to sin:
2of the law of the Most High and
his covenant,

u Gk *of fixing the elbow on the bread*

5–13: A contrast between the memorials left by the ungodly and the just. **10:** 40.11. **12:** Pr.22.1. **41.14–42.14: True and false shame. 41.14–16:** Introductory section. **17–23:** Things to be ashamed of. **21:** Pr.6.29; Mt.5.28. **22:** 18.15. **23:** 27.16. **42.1–8:** Things of which one must

and of rendering judgment to
acquit the ungodly;
3of keeping accounts with a partner
or with traveling companions,
and of dividing the inheritance
of friends;
4of accuracy with scales and
weights,
and of acquiring much or little;
5of profit from dealing with
merchants,
and of much discipline of
children,
and of whipping a wicked
servant severely.[v]
6Where there is an evil wife, a seal
is a good thing;
and where there are many hands,
lock things up.
7Whatever you deal out, let it be
by number and weight,
and make a record of all that you
give out or take in.
8Do not be ashamed to instruct the
stupid or foolish
or the aged man who quarrels
with the young.
Then you will be truly instructed,
and will be approved before all
men.

9A daughter keeps her father secretly
wakeful,
and worry over her robs him of
sleep;
when she is young, lest she do not
marry,
or if married, lest she be hated;
10while a virgin, lest she be defiled
or become pregnant in her
father's house;
or having a husband, lest she prove
unfaithful,
or, though married, lest she be
barren.
11Keep strict watch over a headstrong
daughter,
lest she make you a laughingstock
to your enemies,
a byword in the city and notorious[w]
among the people,
and put you to shame before the
great multitude.

12Do not look upon any one for
beauty,
and do not sit in the midst of
women;
13for from garments comes the moth,
and from a woman comes
woman's wickedness.
14Better is the wickedness of a man
than a woman who does
good;
and it is a woman who brings
shame and disgrace.

15I will now call to mind the works
of the Lord,
and will declare what I have
seen.
By the words of the Lord his works
are done.
16The sun looks down on everything
with its light,
and the work of the Lord is full
of his glory.
17The Lord has not enabled his holy
ones
to recount all his marvelous
works,
which the Lord the Almighty has
established
that the universe may stand firm
in his glory.
18He searches out the abyss, and the
hearts of men,[x]
and considers their crafty devices.

v Gk *making the side of a wicked servant bleed*
w Gk *called out*
x Gk *and the heart*

---

not be ashamed. **1:** Lev.19.15; Dt.1.17; Pr.24.23. **5c:** 33.26–29. **6:** *Many hands*, in the household.

42.9–11: A father's concern for his daughter (7.24–25; 26.10–12).

42.12–14: Concerning women (9.1–9). **12:** 25.21. Hebrew, "Let her not parade her charms before men, or spend her time conversing with married women."

42.15–43.33: In praise of God, the Creator.

42.15–25: The omnipotence and omniscience of God. 17: *Holy ones*, the angels; Sirach means that even the angels lack sufficient power to declare all the wonders of his mighty works.

For the Most High knows all that
may be known,
and he looks into the signs[y] of
the age.
19He declares what has been and
what is to be,
and he reveals the tracks of
hidden things.
20No thought escapes him,
and not one word is hidden from
him.
21He has ordained the splendors of
his wisdom,
and he is from everlasting and to
everlasting.
Nothing can be added or taken
away,
and he needs no one to be his
counselor.
22How greatly to be desired are all
his works,
and how sparkling they are to
see![z]
23All these things live and remain
for ever
for every need, and are all
obedient.
24All things are twofold, one opposite
the other,
and he has made nothing
incomplete.
25One confirms the good things of
the other,
and who can have enough of
beholding his glory?

43 The pride of the heavenly
heights is the clear
firmament,
the appearance of heaven in a
spectacle of glory.
2The sun, when it appears, making
proclamation as it goes
forth,
is a marvelous instrument, the
work of the Most High.
3At noon it parches the land;
and who can withstand its
burning heat?
4A man tending[a] a furnace works
in burning heat,
but the sun burns the mountains
three times as much;
it breathes out fiery vapors,
and with bright beams it blinds
the eyes.
5Great is the Lord who made it;
and at his command it hastens
on its course.

6He made the moon also, to serve
in its season[b]
to mark the times and to be an
everlasting sign.
7From the moon comes the sign for
feast days,
a light that wanes when it has
reached the full.
8The month is named for the moon,
increasing marvelously in its
phases,
an instrument of the hosts on
high
shining forth in the firmament
of heaven.

9The glory of the stars is the beauty
of heaven,
a gleaming array in the heights
of the Lord.
10At the command of the Holy One
they stand as ordered,
they never relax in their
watches.
11Look upon the rainbow, and
praise him who made it,
exceedingly beautiful in its
brightness.
12It encircles the heaven with its
glorious arc;
the hands of the Most High
have stretched it out.

y Gk *sign* *z* The Greek of this line is uncertain
a Other authorities read *blowing*
b The Greek text of this line is uncertain

20: Job.42.2; Is.29.15. **21:** *His counselor*, Hebrew, "his instructor" (see Is.40.13–14). **24:** 33.15.

43.1–5: The splendor of the firmament and the sun. 1: Ex.24.10. **2:** Ps.19.1–5.

43.6–8: The splendor of the moon. 6: Gen.1.16. The Hebrews followed a lunar calendar.

43.9–12: The glory of the stars and the rainbow. 10: *They stand* like sentinels on high. **11–12:** 50.7; Gen.9.13; Ezek.1.28.

[13]By his command he sends the
driving snow
and speeds the lightnings of his
judgment.
[14]Therefore the storehouses are
opened,
and the clouds fly forth like
birds.
[15]In his majesty he amasses the
clouds,
and the hailstones are broken in
pieces.
[16]At his appearing the mountains
are shaken;
at his will the south wind blows.
[17]The voice of his thunder rebukes
the earth;
so do the tempest from the
north and the whirlwind.
He scatters the snow like birds
flying down,
and its descent is like locusts
alighting.
[18]The eye marvels at the beauty of
its whiteness,
and the mind is amazed at its
falling.
[19]He pours the hoarfrost upon the
earth like salt,
and when it freezes, it becomes
pointed thorns.
[20]The cold north wind blows,
and ice freezes over the water;
it rests upon every pool of water,
and the water puts it on like a
breastplate.
[21]He consumes the mountains and
burns up the wilderness,
and withers the tender grass like
fire.
[22]A mist quickly heals all things;
when the dew appears, it
refreshes from the heat.

[23]By his counsel he stilled the great
deep
and planted islands in it.
[24]Those who sail the sea tell of its
dangers,
and we marvel at what we hear.
[25]For in it are strange and marvelous
works,
all kinds of living things, and
huge creatures of the sea.
[26]Because of him his messenger finds
the way,
and by his word all things hold
together.

[27]Though we speak much we cannot
reach the end,
and the sum of our words is:
"He is the all."
[28]Where shall we find strength to
praise him?
For he is greater than all his
works.
[29]Terrible is the Lord and very
great,
and marvelous is his power.
[30]When you praise the Lord, exalt
him as much as you can;
for he will surpass even that.
When you exalt him, put forth all
your strength,
and do not grow weary, for you
cannot praise him enough.
[31]Who has seen him and can describe
him?
Or who can extol him as he is?
[32]Many things greater than these lie
hidden,
for we have seen but few of his
works.
[33]For the Lord has made all things,
and to the godly he has granted
wisdom.

44 Let us now praise famous
men,
and our fathers in their
generations.

43.13–26: Marvels of nature. 13: *Snow*, Hebrew, "lightning." **14:** Job 38.22; Jer.51.16. **20:** *Blows*, Hebrew, "he causes to blow." **23:** Ps.104.25–26. **26b:** Col.1.17.

43.27–33: God is greater than all his works. 27: *He is the all*, not to be taken in a pantheistic sense. **28a:** Hebrew, "Let us praise him the more, since we cannot fathom (him)" (Job 11.7; Ps.145.3).

44.1–50.24: In praise of famous men. 44.1–15: Introduction. **1:** *Famous men*, Hebrew and Syriac, "men of piety." *Generations*, i.e. historical sequence.

2The Lord apportioned to them[c]
great glory,
his majesty from the beginning.
3There were those who ruled in
their kingdoms,
and were men renowned for
their power,
giving counsel by their
understanding,
and proclaiming prophecies;
4leaders of the people in their
deliberations
and in understanding of
learning for the people,
wise in their words of instruction;
5those who composed musical tunes,
and set forth verses in writing;
6rich men furnished with resources,
living peaceably in their
habitations—
7all these were honored in their
generations,
and were the glory of their times.
8There are some of them who have
left a name,
so that men declare their praise.
9And there are some who have no
memorial,
who have perished as though
they had not lived;
they have become as though they
had not been born,
and so have their children after
them.
10But these were men of mercy,
whose righteous deeds have not
been forgotten;
11their prosperity will remain with
their descendants,
and their inheritance to their
children's children.[d]
12Their descendants stand by the
covenants;
their children also, for their sake.
13Their posterity will continue for ever,
and their glory will not be
blotted out.
14Their bodies were buried in peace,
and their name lives to all
generations.
15Peoples will declare their wisdom,
and the congregation proclaims
their praise.

16Enoch pleased the Lord, and was
taken up;
he was an example of repentance
to all generations.

17Noah was found perfect and
righteous;
in the time of wrath he was
taken in exchange;
therefore a remnant was left to the
earth
when the flood came.
18Everlasting covenants were made
with him
that all flesh should not be
blotted out by a flood.

19Abraham was the great father of
a multitude of nations,
and no one has been found like
him in glory;
20he kept the law of the Most High,
and was taken into covenant
with him;
he established the covenant in his
flesh,
and when he was tested he was
found faithful.
21Therefore the Lord[e] assured him
by an oath
that the nations would be blessed
through his posterity;
that he would multiply him like
the dust of the earth,
and exalt his posterity like the
stars,
and cause them to inherit from
sea to sea
and from the River to the ends
of the earth.

c Heb: Gk *created*
d Heb Compare Vg Syr: The Greek of this verse is uncertain *e* Gk *he*

44.16–18: Enoch and Noah. 16: 49.14; Gen.5.24; Heb.11.5. **17a:** Gen.6.9; Heb.11.7. **18:** Gen.8.20–22; 9.12–17.

44.19–23: Abraham, Isaac, and Jacob. 19: *Father*, Gen.17.4; Mt.3.9. **20:** *Kept the law*, Gen.26.5. *In his flesh*, Gen.17.10–14. *Tested*, Gen.22.1–14; 1 Macc.2.52; Heb.11.17. **21:** Gen.

22 To Isaac also he gave the same assurance
for the sake of Abraham his father.

23 The blessing of all men and the covenant
he made to rest upon the head of Jacob;
he acknowledged him with his blessings,
and gave him his inheritance;[f]
he determined his portions,
and distributed them among twelve tribes.

45 From his descendants the Lord[g] brought forth a man of mercy,
who found favor in the sight of all flesh
and was beloved by God and man,
Moses, whose memory is blessed.
2 He made him equal in glory to the holy ones,
and made him great in the fears of his enemies.
3 By his words he caused signs to cease;
the Lord[g] glorified him in the presence of kings.
He gave him commands for his people,
and showed him part of his glory.
4 He sanctified him through faithfulness and meekness;
he chose him out of all mankind.
5 He made him hear his voice,
and led him into the thick darkness,
and gave him the commandments face to face,
the law of life and knowledge,
to teach Jacob the covenant,
and Israel his judgments.

6 He exalted Aaron, the brother of Moses,[h]
a holy man like him, of the tribe of Levi.
7 He made an everlasting covenant with him,
and gave him the priesthood of the people.
He blessed him with splendid vestments,
and put a glorious robe upon him.
8 He clothed him with superb perfection,
and strengthened him with the symbols of authority,
the linen breeches, the long robe, and the ephod.
9 And he encircled him with pomegranates,
with very many golden bells round about,
to send forth a sound as he walked,
to make their ringing heard in the temple
as a reminder to the sons of his people;
10 with a holy garment, of gold and blue and purple, the work of an embroiderer;
with the oracle of judgment, Urim and Thummim;
11 with twisted scarlet, the work of a craftsman;
with precious stones engraved like signets,
in a setting of gold, the work of a jeweler,
for a reminder, in engraved letters,
according to the number of the tribes of Israel;
12 with a gold crown upon his turban,
inscribed like a signet with "Holiness,"
a distinction to be prized, the work of an expert,
the delight of the eyes, richly adorned.

f Heb: Gk *by inheritance*
g Gk *he* *h* Gk *him*

22.16–18; Gal.3.8. *River*, the Euphrates. **22:** Gen.17.19; 26.3–5. **23:** Gen.27.28; 28.14.
45.1–5: Moses. 1: Ex.11.3. **2:** *Holy ones*, the angels. **3:** Ex.7–10. *Part*, Ex.34.6. **4:** *Meekness*, Num.12.3. **5:** Ex.19.7; 24.18; Dt.6.1–2.
45.6–22: Aaron. 6: Ex.4.14. **7:** Ex.28.1–4. **8–13:** Ex. ch. 28. **10:** *Urim*, see 33.3 n.

[13]Before his time there never were
such beautiful things.
No outsider ever put them on,
but only his sons
and his descendants perpetually.
[14]His sacrifices shall be wholly burned
twice every day continually.
[15]Moses ordained him,
and anointed him with holy
oil;
it was an everlasting covenant for
him
and for his descendants all the
days of heaven,
to minister to the Lord[i] and serve
as priest
and bless his people in his
name.
[16]He chose him out of all the living
to offer sacrifice to the Lord,
incense and a pleasing odor as a
memorial portion,
to make atonement for the
people.[j]
[17]In his commandments he gave him
authority in statutes and[k]
judgments,
to teach Jacob the testimonies,
and to enlighten Israel with his
law.
[18]Outsiders conspired against him,
and envied him in the wilderness,
Dathan and Abiram and their men
and the company of Korah, in
wrath and anger.
[19]The Lord saw it and was not
pleased,
and in the wrath of his anger
they were destroyed;
he wrought wonders against them
to consume them in flaming
fire.
[20]He added glory to Aaron
and gave him a heritage;
he allotted to him the first of the
first fruits,
he prepared bread of first fruits
in abundance;
[21]for they eat the sacrifices to the
Lord,
which he gave to him and his
descendants.
[22]But in the land of the people he
has no inheritance,
and he has no portion among
the people;
for the Lord[l] himself is his[m]
portion and inheritance.

[23]Phinehas the son of Eleazar is the
third in glory,
for he was zealous in the fear of
the Lord,
and stood fast, when the people
turned away,
in the ready goodness of his soul,
and made atonement for Israel.
[24]Therefore a covenant of peace was
established with him,
that he should be leader of the
sanctuary and of his people,
that he and his descendants should
have
the dignity of the priesthood for
ever.
[25]A covenant was also established
with David,
the son of Jesse, of the tribe of
Judah:
the heritage of the king is from
son to son only;
so the heritage of Aaron is for
his descendants.
[26]May the Lord[n] grant you wisdom
in your heart
to judge his people in
righteousness,
so that their prosperity may not
vanish,
and that their glory may endure
throughout their generations.[o]

i Gk *him*
j Other authorities read *thy people*
k Heb: Gk *in covenants of*
l Gk *he*
m Other authorities read *your*
n Gk *he*
o The Greek of this line is obscure

14: Num.28.3–4. **15:** Lev. ch. 8. *Bless,* Num. 6.23–27. **18:** Num. ch. 16. *Outsiders,* as in v. 13, those who were not of the family of Aaron. **22:** Num.18.20; Dt.12.12.

45.23–26: Phinehas (Num.25.10–13; Ps.106.30; 1 Macc.2.54). **25:** 2 Sam.7.12. **26:** *You . . . your,* the reference is to Simon, son of Onias (see 50.1 n.), and his successors.

46 Joshua the son of Nun was
mighty in war,
and was the successor of Moses
in prophesying.
He became, in accordance with his
name,
a great savior of God's[p] elect,
to take vengeance on the enemies
that rose against them,
so that he might give Israel its
inheritance.
2 How glorious he was when he lifted
his hands
and stretched out his sword
against the cities!
3 Who before him ever stood so firm?
For he waged the wars of the
Lord.
4 Was not the sun held back by his
hand?
And did not one day become as
long as two?
5 He called upon the Most High,
the Mighty One,
when enemies pressed him on
every side,
6 and the great Lord answered him
with hailstones of mighty power.
He hurled down war upon that
nation,
and at the descent of Beth-horon[q]
he destroyed those who resisted,
so that the nations might know
his armament,
that he was fighting in the sight
of the Lord;
for he wholly followed the
Mighty One.
7 And in the days of Moses he did
a loyal deed,
he and Caleb the son of
Jephunneh:
they withstood the congregation,[r]
restrained the people from sin,
and stilled their wicked
murmuring.
8 And these two alone were preserved
out of six hundred thousand
people on foot,
to bring them into their inheritance,
into a land flowing with milk
and honey.
9 And the Lord gave Caleb strength,
which remained with him to
old age,
so that he went up to the hill
country,
and his children obtained it for
an inheritance;
10 so that all the sons of Israel might see
that it is good to follow the Lord.

11 The judges also, with their
respective names,
those whose hearts did not fall
into idolatry
and who did not turn away from
the Lord—
may their memory be blessed!
12 May their bones revive from where
they lie,
and may the name of those who
have been honored
live again in their sons!

13 Samuel, beloved by his Lord,
a prophet of the Lord, established
the kingdom
and anointed rulers over his
people.
14 By the law of the Lord he judged
the congregation,
and the Lord watched over
Jacob.
15 By his faithfulness he was proved
to be a prophet,
and by his words he became
known as a trustworthy seer.
16 He called upon the Lord, the
Mighty One,

p Gk *his*
q Compare Joshua 10.11: Greek lacks *of Beth-horon*
r Other authorities read *the enemy*

46.1–10: Joshua and Caleb. 1: *His name* means "Jehovah is salvation." **2–8:** Jos. chs. 6–11. **4:** Jos.10.12–14. **6:** Jos.10.11. **7:** Num.14.6–10; 1 Macc.2.55–56. **8:** Num.11.21; 14.38; 26.65. **9:** Jos.14.6–11.

46.11–12: The judges. 12: *Bones revive* (49.10), the meaning is to be interpreted in the light of the last line of the verse.

46.13–20: Samuel. 13: *Anointed rulers,* 1 Sam.10.1; 16.13. **15:** 1 Sam.3.19–20. **16–18:** 1 Sam. 7.9–11. **19:** 1 Sam.12.3. **20:** 1 Sam.28.18–19.

when his enemies pressed him on
every side,
and he offered in sacrifice a
sucking lamb.
17Then the Lord thundered from
heaven,
and made his voice heard with
a mighty sound;
18and he wiped out the leaders of the
people of Tyre
and all the rulers of the Philistines.
19Before the time of his eternal sleep,
Samuel[s] called men to witness
before the Lord and his
anointed:
"I have not taken any one's
property,
not so much as a pair of shoes."
And no man accused him.
20Even after he had fallen asleep he
prophesied
and revealed to the king his
death,
and lifted up his voice out of the
earth in prophecy,
to blot out the wickedness of
the people.

47 And after him Nathan rose
up
to prophesy in the days of David.
2As the fat is selected from the
peace offering,
so David was selected from the
sons of Israel.
3He played with lions as with young
goats,
and with bears as with lambs of
the flock.
4In his youth did he not kill a giant,
and take away reproach from
the people,
when he lifted his hand with a
stone in the sling
and struck down the boasting of
Goliath?
5For he appealed to the Lord, the
Most High,
and he gave him strength in his
right hand
to slay a man mighty in war,
to exalt the power[t] of his people.
6So they glorified him for his ten
thousands,
and praised him for the blessings
of the Lord,
when the glorious diadem was
bestowed upon him.
7For he wiped out his enemies on
every side,
and annihilated his adversaries
the Philistines;
he crushed their power[t] even
to this day.
8In all that he did he gave thanks
to the Holy One, the Most High,
with ascriptions of glory;
he sang praise with all his heart,
and he loved his Maker.
9He placed singers before the altar,
to make sweet melody with their
voices.
10He gave beauty to the feasts,
and arranged their times
throughout the year,[u]
while they praised God's[v] holy
name,
and the sanctuary resounded
from early morning.
11The Lord took away his sins,
and exalted his power[w] for ever;
he gave him the covenant of kings
and a throne of glory in Israel.
12After him rose up a wise son
who fared amply[x] because of him;
13Solomon reigned in days of peace,
and God gave him rest on every
side,
that he might build a house for
his name
and prepare a sanctuary to stand
for ever.
14How wise you became in your youth!

s Gk *he* *t* Gk *horn*
u Gk *to completion* *v* Gk *his*
w Gk *horn* *x* Gk *lived in a broad place*

47.1–11: David. 1: 2 Sam.7.2–3; 12.1; 1 Chr.17.1. **2:** *The fat*, the portion reserved for sacrifice (Lev.3.3–5). **3:** 1 Sam.17.34. **4:** 1 Sam.17.49–51. **6:** 1 Sam.18.7. **7:** 2 Sam.5.7; 8.1. **9:** 1 Chr.16.4. **11:** 2 Sam.12.13.

47.12–22: Solomon. 13–17: 1 Kg.4.21–32. **14:** Compare the address to Elijah in 48.4–11.

You overflowed like a river with
understanding.
15Your soul covered the earth,
and you filled it with parables
and riddles.
16Your name reached to far-off
islands,
and you were loved for your
peace.
17For your songs and proverbs and
parables,
and for your interpretations, the
countries marveled at you.
18In the name of the Lord God,
who is called the God of Israel,
you gathered gold like tin
and amassed silver like lead.
19But you laid your loins beside
women,
and through your body you were
brought into subjection.
20You put a stain upon your honor,
and defiled your posterity,
so that you brought wrath upon
your children
and they were grieved[y] at your
folly,
21so that the sovereignty was divided
and a disobedient kingdom arose
out of Ephraim.
22But the Lord will never give up
his mercy,
nor cause any of his works to
perish;
he will never blot out the
descendants of his chosen one,
nor destroy the posterity of him
who loved him;
so he gave a remnant to Jacob,
and to David a root of his stock.

23Solomon rested with his fathers,
and left behind him one of his
sons,
ample in[z] folly and lacking in
understanding,
Rehoboam, whose policy caused
the people to revolt.
Also Jeroboam the son of Nebat,
who caused Israel to sin
and gave to Ephraim a sinful
way.
24Their sins became exceedingly many,
so as to remove them from their
land.
25For they sought out every sort of
wickedness,
till vengeance came upon them.

48 Then the prophet Elijah
arose like a fire,
and his word burned like a torch.
2He brought a famine upon them,
and by his zeal he made them
few in number.
3By the word of the Lord he shut
up the heavens,
and also three times brought
down fire.
4How glorious you were, O Elijah,
in your wondrous deeds!
And who has the right to boast
which you have?
5You who raised a corpse from
death
and from Hades, by the word
of the Most High;
6who brought kings down to
destruction,
and famous men from their beds;
7who heard rebuke at Sinai
and judgments of vengeance at
Horeb;
8who anointed kings to inflict
retribution,
and prophets to succeed you.[a]
9You who were taken up by a
whirlwind of fire,
in a chariot with horses of fire;

y Other authorities read *I was grieved*
z Heb (with a play on the name Rehoboam) Syr: Gk *the people's*
a Heb: Gk *him*

18: 1 Kg.10.21,27. **19:** 1 Kg.11.1. **21:** 1 Kg.12.15–20. **22:** 2 Sam.7.15; Ps.89.33. *Nor . . . perish*, Hebrew, "He will let none of his words fall to the ground."

47.23–25: Solomon's successors. 23: *Rehoboam*, 1 Kg.11.43; 12.10–14. *Jeroboam*, 1 Kg.12.28–30. **24:** 2 Kg.17.6,18.

48.1–11: Elijah. 1: 1 Kg.17.1. *Torch*, Hebrew, "furnace." **2:** Jas.5.17. **3:** 1 Kg.18.38; 2 Kg.1.10–12. **5:** 1 Kg.17.21–22. **6:** 2 Kg.1.16. **7:** 1 Kg.19.8. **8:** 1 Kg.19.15–16. **9:** 2 Kg.2.11. **10:** Mal. 4.5–6.

10you who are ready[b] at the
appointed time, it is written,
to calm the wrath of God before
it breaks out in fury,
to turn the heart of the father to
the son,
and to restore the tribes of
Jacob.
11Blessed are those who saw you,
and those who have been
adorned[c] in love;
for we also shall surely live.[d]

12It was Elijah who was covered by
the whirlwind,
and Elisha was filled with his
spirit;
in all his days he did not tremble
before any ruler,
and no one brought him into
subjection.
13Nothing was too hard for him,
and when he was dead his body
prophesied.
14As in his life he did wonders,
so in death his deeds were
marvelous.

15For all this the people did not
repent,
and they did not forsake their
sins,
till they were carried away captive
from their land
and were scattered over all the
earth;
the people were left very few in
number,
but with rulers from the house
of David.
16Some of them did what was
pleasing to God,[e]
but others multiplied sins.

17Hezekiah fortified his city,
and brought water into the
midst of it;
he tunneled the sheer rock with iron
and built pools for water.
18In his days Sennacherib came up,
and sent the Rabshakeh;[f]
he lifted up his hand against
Zion
and made great boasts in his
arrogance.
19Then their hearts were shaken and
their hands trembled,
and they were in anguish, like
women in travail.
20But they called upon the Lord who
is merciful,
spreading forth their hands
toward him;
and the Holy One quickly heard
them from heaven,
and delivered them by the hand
of Isaiah.
21The Lord[g] smote the camp of the
Assyrians,
and his angel wiped them
out.
22For Hezekiah did what was
pleasing to the Lord,
and he held strongly to the ways
of David his father,
which Isaiah the prophet
commanded,
who was great and faithful in
his vision.
23In his days the sun went backward,
and he lengthened the life of
the king.
24By the spirit of might he saw the
last things,
and comforted those who
mourned in Zion.
25He revealed what was to occur to
the end of time,
and the hidden things before
they came to pass.

b Heb: Gk *are for reproofs*
c Other authorities read *who have died*
d The text and meaning of this verse are uncertain
e Gk lacks *to God*
f Other authorities add *and departed*
g Gk *he*

48.12–16: Elisha and subsequent generations. 12: 2 Kg.2.9,13. **13:** 2 Kg.13.20–21. **15:** 2 Kg. 18.11–12.

48.17–25: Hezekiah and Isaiah. 17: 2 Kg.20.20. **18:** 2 Kg.18.13,17; Is.36.1. *Made . . . boasts,* Hebrew and Syriac, "blasphemed God." **20:** 2 Kg.19.15–20. **21:** 2 Kg.19.35; Is.37.36; 1 Macc.7.41. **22:** 2 Kg.18.3. **23:** 2 Kg.20.10–11; Is.38.8. **24–25:** Is.40.1; 42.9.

49 The memory of Josiah is like
a blending of incense
prepared by the art of the
perfumer;
it is sweet as honey to every
mouth,
and like music at a banquet of
wine.
2He was led aright in converting
the people,
and took away the abominations
of iniquity.
3He set his heart upon the Lord;
in the days of wicked men he
strengthened godliness.

4Except David and Hezekiah and
Josiah
they all sinned greatly,
for they forsook the law of the
Most High;
the kings of Judah came to an
end;
5for they gave their power to others,
and their glory to a foreign
nation,
6who set fire to the chosen city of
the sanctuary,
and made her streets desolate,
according to the word[h] of
Jeremiah.
7For they had afflicted him;
yet he had been consecrated in
the womb as prophet,
to pluck up and afflict and destroy,
and likewise to build and to
plant.

8It was Ezekiel who saw the vision
of glory
which God[i] showed him above
the chariot of the cherubim.
9For God[i] remembered his enemies
with storm,
and did good to those who
directed their ways aright.[j]
10May the bones of the twelve
prophets
revive from where they lie,
for they comforted the people of
Jacob
and delivered them with
confident hope.

11How shall we magnify Zerubbabel?
He was like a signet on the right
hand,
12 and so was Jeshua the son of
Jozadak;
in their days they built the house
and raised a temple[k] holy to
the Lord,
prepared for everlasting glory.
13The memory of Nehemiah also is
lasting;
he raised for us the walls that
had fallen,
and set up the gates and bars
and rebuilt our ruined houses.

14No one like Enoch has been
created on earth,
for he was taken up from the
earth.
15And no man like Joseph[l] has been
born,
and his bones are cared for.
16Shem and Seth were honored
among men,
and Adam above every living
being in the creation.

50 The leader of his brethren
and the pride of his
people[m]
was Simon the high priest, son
of Onias,
who in his life repaired the house,

h Gk *by the hand* i Gk *he*
j The text and meaning of this verse are uncertain
k Other authorities read *people*
l Heb Syr: Gk adds *the leader of his brothers, the support of the people*
m Heb Syr: Gk lacks this line. Compare 49.15

49.1–3: Josiah (2 Kg.22.1). **2a:** Hebrew, "For he was grieved over our backslidings" (2 Kg. 22.11–13). **3:** 2 Kg.23.3,25.

49.4–10: The last kings and the last prophets. 5–6: 2 Chr.36.17–19. *Jeremiah,* Jer.1.5–10; 39.8. **8–9:** Ezek.1.3–15; 13.11; 38.9,16,22. **10:** *Bones,* see 46.12 n.

49.11–16: Zerubbabel, Jeshua, Nehemiah, and others. 11: Ezra 3.2; Hag.2.23. **12:** Ezra 3.2; Hag.1.12; 2.2; Zech.3.1. **13:** Neh.7.1. **14:** 44.16. **15:** Gen.39.1ff.; 50.25–26. **16:** Gen.5.3,32.

50.1–24: Simon, son of Onias (see 45.26 n.). **1:** Simon II was high priest about 219–196 B.C.

and in his time fortified the
temple.
[2]He laid the foundations for the
high double walls,[n]
the high retaining walls for the
temple enclosure.
[3]In his days a cistern for water was
quarried out,[o]
a reservoir like the sea in
circumference.
[4]He considered how to save his
people from ruin,
and fortified the city to
withstand a siege.
[5]How glorious he was when the
people gathered round him
as he came out of the inner
sanctuary![p]
[6]Like the morning star among the
clouds,
like the moon when it is full;
[7]like the sun shining upon the
temple of the Most High,
and like the rainbow gleaming
in glorious clouds;
[8]like roses in the days of the first
fruits,
like lilies by a spring of water,
like a green shoot on Lebanon[q]
on a summer day;
[9]like fire and incense in the censer,
like a vessel of hammered gold
adorned with all kinds of
precious stones;
[10]like an olive tree putting forth its
fruit,
and like a cypress towering in
the clouds.
[11]When he put on his glorious robe
and clothed himself with superb
perfection
and went up to the holy altar,
he made the court of the
sanctuary glorious.
[12]And when he received the portions
from the hands of the priests,
as he stood by the hearth of the
altar
with a garland of brethren around
him,
he was like a young cedar on
Lebanon;
and they surrounded him like the
trunks of palm trees,
13 all the sons of Aaron in their
splendor
with the Lord's offering in their
hands,
before the whole congregation
of Israel.
[14]Finishing the service at the altars,
and arranging the offering to the
Most High, the Almighty,
[15]he reached out his hand to the cup
and poured a libation of the
blood of the grape;
he poured it out at the foot of the
altar,
a pleasing odor to the Most
High, the King of all.
[16]Then the sons of Aaron shouted,
they sounded the trumpets of
hammered work,
they made a great noise to be heard
for remembrance before the
Most High.
[17]Then all the people together made
haste
and fell to the ground upon their
faces
to worship their Lord,
the Almighty, God Most High.
[18]And the singers praised him with
their voices
in sweet and full-toned melody.[r]
[19]And the people besought the Lord
Most High
in prayer before him who is
merciful,
till the order of worship of the
Lord was ended;
so they completed his service.
[20]Then Simon[s] came down, and
lifted up his hands
over the whole congregation of
the sons of Israel,

n The meaning of this phrase is obscure
o Cn Compare Heb: Gk *was diminished*
p Gk *the house of the veil*
q Or *a sprig of frankincense*
r Other authorities read *in sweet melody throughout the house*
s Gk *he*

(Josephus, *Antiquities*, XII.iv.10). *Onias* is the Greek form of Johanan. *The house*, of God. **16:** *Trumpets*, Num.10.2; 31.6. **20:** *The blessing*, namely Num.6.24–27. *His name*, only the high

to pronounce the blessing of the
Lord with his lips,
and to glory in his name;
21 and they bowed down in worship
a second time,
to receive the blessing from the
Most High.

22 And now bless the God of all,
who in every way does great things;
who exalts our days from birth,
and deals with us according to
his mercy.
23 May he give us[t] gladness of heart,
and grant that peace may be in
our days in Israel,
as in the days of old.
24 May he entrust to us his mercy!
And let him deliver us in our[u] days!

25 With two nations my soul is vexed,
and the third is no nation:
26 Those who live on Mount Seir,[v]
and the Philistines,
and the foolish people that dwell
in Shechem.

27 Instruction in understanding and
knowledge
I have written in this book,
Jesus the son of Sirach, son of
Eleazar,[w] of Jerusalem,
who out of his heart poured
forth wisdom.
28 Blessed is he who concerns himself
with these things,
and he who lays them to heart
will become wise.
29 For if he does them, he will be
strong for all things,
for the light of the Lord is his path.

51 I will give thanks to thee, O
Lord and King,
and will praise thee as God my
Savior.
I give thanks to thy name,
2 for thou hast been my protector
and helper
and hast delivered my body from
destruction
and from the snare of a
slanderous tongue,
from lips that utter lies.
Before those who stood by
thou wast my helper, 3 and didst
deliver me,
in the greatness of thy mercy
and of thy name,
from the gnashings of teeth about
to devour me,[x]
from the hand of those who
sought my life,
from the many afflictions that I
endured,
4 from choking fire on every side
and from the midst of fire which
I did not kindle,
5 from the depths of the belly of Hades,
from an unclean tongue and
lying words—
6 the slander of an unrighteous
tongue to the king.
My soul drew near to death,
and my life was very near to
Hades beneath.
7 They surrounded me on every side,
and there was no one to help me;
I looked for the assistance of men,
and there was none.
8 Then I remembered thy mercy, O
Lord,
and thy work from of old,
that thou dost deliver those who
wait for thee

t Other authorities read *you*
u Other authorities read *his*
v Heb Vg: Gk *on the mountain of Samaria*
w The text of this line is uncertain
x Cn Compare Vg: Gk *when I was about to be devoured*

priest (and only once a year, on the Day of Atonement), could utter the ineffable name "Yahweh." **22–24:** Doxology. **24:** Hebrew, "May his love abide upon Simon, and may he keep in him the covenant of Phinehas; may one never be cut off from him; and as for his offspring, (may it be) as the days of heaven."

50.25–26: A fragment. 26: *Those ... on Mount Seir*, Edomites. *People ... in Shechem*, Samaritans.

50.27–29: The author's epilogue.

51.1–30: Appendix. 1–12: A hymn of thanksgiving for deliverance. **10a:** Hebrew, "Yea, I exalted Jehovah (saying), 'Thou art my Father [Ps.89.26], for thou art the Mighty One of my

and dost save them from the
hand of their enemies.
9And I sent up my supplication
from the earth,
and prayed for deliverance from
death.
10I appealed to the Lord, the Father
of my lord,
not to forsake me in the days
of affliction,
at the time when there is no
help against the proud.
11I will praise thy name continually,
and will sing praise with
thanksgiving.
My prayer was heard,
12 for thou didst save me from
destruction
and rescue me from an evil plight.
Therefore I will give thanks to
thee and praise thee,
and I will bless the name of the
Lord.

13While I was still young, before I
went on my travels,
I sought wisdom openly in my
prayer.
14Before the temple I asked for her,
and I will search for her to the last.
15From blossom to[y] ripening grape
my heart delighted in her;
my foot entered upon the straight
path;
from my youth I followed her steps.
16I inclined my ear a little and
received her,
and I found for myself much
instruction.
17I made progress therein;
to him who gives me wisdom I
will give glory.
18For I resolved to live according to
wisdom,[z]
and I was zealous for the good;
and I shall never be put to shame.
19My soul grappled with wisdom,[z]
and in my conduct I was strict;[a]
I spread out my hands to the
heavens,
and lamented my ignorance of her.
20I directed my soul to her,
and through purification I
found her.
I gained understanding[b] with her
from the first,
therefore I will not be forsaken.
21My heart was stirred to seek her,
therefore I have gained a good
possession.
22The Lord gave me a tongue as my
reward,
and I will praise him with it.

23Draw near to me, you who are
untaught,
and lodge in my school.
24Why do you say you are lacking
in these things,[c]
and why are your souls very
thirsty?
25I opened my mouth and said,
Get these things[d] for yourselves
without money.
26Put your neck under the yoke,
and let your souls receive
instruction;
it is to be found close by.
27See with your eyes that I have
labored little
and found for myself much rest.
28Get instruction with a large sum
of silver,
and you will gain by it much gold.
29May your soul rejoice in his mercy,
and may you not be put to
shame when you praise him.
30Do your work before the appointed
time,
and in God's[e] time he will give
you your reward.

y Other authorities read *As from* *z* Gk *her*
a The Greek text of this line is uncertain *b* Gk *heart*
c Cn Compare Heb Syr: The Greek text of this line is uncertain
d Greek lacks *these things* *e* Gk *his*

---

salvation.'" **13–30:** A concluding poem (serving the purpose of a modern preface) in which the author tells how he acquired wisdom and sought to impart it to others. The poem (like Ps.25 and Pr.31.10–31) is an acrostic; the verses begin with the successive letters of the Hebrew alphabet. **13:** *Travels*, 34.11; 39.4. **22:** *Tongue*, eloquence. **26:** *The yoke*, of wisdom (compare Mt.11.29–30). **30:** *Your work*, of learning wisdom.

BARUCH

The book which goes under the name of Baruch purports to have been written during the Babylonian captivity by Baruch, the companion and secretary of the prophet Jeremiah (Jer. 32.12; 36.4), and sent to Jerusalem to be read on feast days as a confession of sins (1.14). The first part, which is in prose, comprises an introduction (1.1–14) and a confession of Israel's guilt (1.15–3.8). The second part is made up of two poems, one lauding wisdom as God's special gift to Israel (3.9–4.4) and the other dealing with the themes of comfort and restoration (4.5–5.9). Diverse authorship of the two parts is indicated by differing viewpoints, literary forms, and diction. For example, God is spoken of in quite different ways in the two parts; the word "Lord" appears forty-nine times in the first part but not once in the second part, where it is replaced by the word "God." Furthermore, only in the second part does one find the expressions "the Everlasting," "everlasting Savior," and "the Holy One."

That the book was written originally in Hebrew is suggested by the decidedly Hebraic cast of many sentences. In fact, the Greek text, particularly in the first part, is often incomprehensible without re-translating it back into Hebrew. Today the book is extant in Greek, from which a number of other ancient versions were made, including two in Latin, two in Syriac, and others in Coptic, Armenian, Ethiopic, and Arabic.

The date at which the several component parts of the book were brought together is disputed. According to a widely held opinion its final redaction took place sometime between about 150 and 60 B.C.

THESE ARE THE WORDS OF THE BOOK
which Baruch the son of Neraiah,
son of Mahseiah, son of Zedekiah, son
of Hasadiah, son of Hilkiah, wrote in
Babylon, 2 in the fifth year, on the
seventh day of the month, at the time
when the Chaldeans took Jerusalem
and burned it with fire. 3 And Baruch
read the words of this book in the hearing of Jeconiah the son of Jehoiakim,
king of Judah, and in the hearing of all
the people who came to hear the book,
4 and in the hearing of the mighty men
and the princes, and in the hearing of
the elders, and in the hearing of all the
people, small and great, all who dwelt
in Babylon by the river Sud.
5 Then they wept, and fasted, and
prayed before the Lord; 6 and they
collected money, each giving what he
could; 7 and they sent it to Jerusalem
to Jehoiakim the high priest,[a] the son
of Hilkiah, son of Shallum, and to the
priests, and to all the people who were
present with him in Jerusalem. 8 At the
same time, on the tenth day of Sivan,
Baruch[b] took the vessels of the house
of the Lord, which had been carried
away from the temple, to return them
to the land of Judah—the silver vessels
which Zedekiah the son of Josiah, king
of Judah, had made, 9 after Nebuchadnezzar king of Babylon had carried
away from Jerusalem Jeconiah and the
princes and the prisoners and the
mighty men and the people of the land,
and brought them to Babylon.
10 And they said: "Herewith we send
you money; so buy with the money
burnt offerings and sin offerings and
incense, and prepare a cereal offering,
and offer them upon the altar of the
Lord our God; 11 and pray for the life

a Gk *the priest* *b* Gk *he*

1.1–14: Historical introduction. 1–2: Authorship and date. **1:** *Baruch*, Jeremiah's secretary (Jer.36.4). **2:** *Fifth year*, after the fall of Jerusalem in 587/6 B.C. **3–4:** The book is read before the exiles. **3:** *Jeconiah*, also called Jehoiachin (2 Kg.24.15; Jer.24.1). **4:** *Sud*, unknown. **5–14:** A gift of money, the temple vessels, and the book are sent to Jerusalem. **5:** The word *Lord* occurs only in the first part of the book (1.1–3.8). **7:** *Jehoiakim the high priest*, otherwise unknown. **8:** *Sivan*, the third month (May-June). For the return of gold and *silver vessels*, see Ezra 1.7–11. **9:** Jer.24.1. **11:** Jer.29.7. *Belshazzar* was actually the son of Nabonidus. *Like the days of heaven*, without end (Dt.11.21).

of Nebuchadnezzar king of Babylon,
and for the life of Belshazzar his son,
that their days on earth may be like
the days of heaven. 12And the Lord
will give us strength, and he will give
light to our eyes, and we shall live
under the protection[c] of Nebuchadnezzar king of Babylon, and under the
protection[c] of Belshazzar his son, and
we shall serve them many days and find
favor in their sight. 13And pray for us
to the Lord our God, for we have
sinned against the Lord our God, and
to this day the anger of the Lord and
his wrath have not turned away from
us. 14And you shall read this book
which we are sending you, to make your
confession in the house of the Lord on
the days of the feasts and at appointed
seasons.
15 "And you shall say: 'Righteousness belongs to the Lord our God, but
confusion of face, as at this day, to us,
to the men of Judah, to the inhabitants
of Jerusalem, 16and to our kings and
our princes and our priests and our
prophets and our fathers, 17because
we have sinned before the Lord, 18and
have disobeyed him, and have not
heeded the voice of the Lord our God,
to walk in the statutes of the Lord
which he set before us. 19From the day
when the Lord brought our fathers out
of the land of Egypt until today, we
have been disobedient to the Lord our
God, and we have been negligent, in
not heeding his voice. 20So to this day
there have clung to us the calamities
and the curse which the Lord declared
through Moses his servant at the time
when he brought our fathers out of the
land of Egypt to give to us a land flowing with milk and honey. 21We did not
heed the voice of the Lord our God in
all the words of the prophets whom he
sent to us, but we each followed the
intent of his own wicked heart by
serving other gods and doing what
is evil in the sight of the Lord our
God.

2 " 'So the Lord confirmed his
word, which he spoke against us,
and against our judges who judged
Israel, and against our kings and
against our princes and against the
men of Israel and Judah. 2Under the
whole heaven there has not been done
the like of what he has done in Jerusalem, in accordance with what is written
in the law of Moses, 3that we should
eat, one the flesh of his son and another
the flesh of his daughter. 4And he gave
them into subjection to all the kingdoms around us, to be a reproach and
a desolation among all the surrounding
peoples, where the Lord has scattered
them. 5They were brought low and not
raised up, because we sinned against
the Lord our God, in not heeding his
voice.
6 " 'Righteousness belongs to the
Lord our God, but confusion of face
to us and our fathers, as at this day.
7All those calamities with which the
Lord threatened us have come upon us.
8Yet we have not entreated the favor of
the Lord by turning away, each of us,
from the thoughts of his wicked heart.
9And the Lord has kept the calamities
ready, and the Lord has brought them
upon us, for the Lord is righteous in all
his works which he has commanded us
to do. 10Yet we have not obeyed his
voice, to walk in the statutes of the
Lord which he set before us.
11 " 'And now, O Lord God of
Israel, who didst bring thy people out
of the land of Egypt with a mighty hand
and with signs and wonders and with
great power and outstretched arm, and
hast made thee a name, as at this day,
12we have sinned, we have been ungodly, we have done wrong, O Lord our

c Gk *in the shadow*

1.15–3.8: Confession of sin, for the Jerusalem community (1.15–2.5), and for the exiles (2.6–3.8); compare 1.15 and 2.6. **1.15–2.5:** Disobedience brought the judgment of exile. **1.15–18:** Based on Dan.9.7–10. **15:** Ezra 9.7. **20:** Dt. ch. 28; Jer.11.3–5. **21:** Jer.7.25–26; Dan.9.5. **2.1–2:** Dan.9.12–13. **3:** Lev.26.29; Dt.28.53; Jer.19.9; Lam.4.10. **5:** Dt.28.13. **2.6–10:** Confession of guilt. **8:** Dan.9.13. **9:** Dan.9.14. **11–26:** Supplication and confession. **11–14:** Dan.

God, against all thy ordinances. [13]Let
thy anger turn away from us, for we
are left, few in number, among the
nations where thou hast scattered us.
[14]Hear, O Lord, our prayer and our
supplication, and for thy own sake
deliver us, and grant us favor in the
sight of those who have carried us into
exile; [15]that all the earth may know
that thou art the Lord our God, for
Israel and his descendants are called by
thy name. [16]O Lord, look down from
thy holy habitation, and consider us.
Incline thy ear, O Lord, and hear;
[17]open thy eyes, O Lord, and see; for
the dead who are in Hades, whose
spirit has been taken from their bodies,
will not ascribe glory or justice to the
Lord, [18]but the person that is greatly
distressed,[d] that goes about bent over
and feeble, and the eyes that are failing,
and the person that hungers, will ascribe to thee glory and righteousness,
O Lord. [19]For it is not because of any
righteous deeds of our fathers or our
kings that we bring before thee our
prayer for mercy, O Lord our God.
[20]For thou hast sent thy anger and thy
wrath upon us, as thou didst declare by
thy servants the prophets, saying:
[21]“Thus says the Lord: Bend your
shoulders and serve the king of Babylon, and you will remain in the land
which I gave to your fathers. [22]But if
you will not obey the voice of the Lord
and will not serve the king of Babylon,
[23]I will make to cease from the cities of
Judah and from the region about
Jerusalem the voice of mirth and the
voice of gladness, the voice of the
bridegroom and the voice of the bride,
and the whole land will be a desolation
without inhabitants.”

24 “ ‘But we did not obey thy voice, to
serve the king of Babylon; and thou hast
confirmed thy words, which thou didst
speak by thy servants the prophets, that
the bones of our kings and the bones of
our fathers would be brought out of
their graves;[e] [25]and behold, they have
been cast out to the heat of day and the
frost of night. They perished in great
misery, by famine and sword and pestilence. [26]And the house which is called
by thy name thou hast made as it is today, because of the wickedness of the
house of Israel and the house of Judah.

27 “ ‘Yet thou hast dealt with us, O
Lord our God, in all thy kindness and
in all thy great compassion, [28]as thou
didst speak by thy servant Moses on
the day when thou didst command him
to write thy law in the presence of the
people of Israel, saying, [29]“If you will
not obey my voice, this very great
multitude will surely turn into a small
number among the nations, where I will
scatter them. [30]For I know that they
will not obey me, for they are a stiff-
necked people. But in the land of their
exile they will come to themselves,
[31]and they will know that I am the Lord
their God. I will give them a heart that
obeys and ears that hear; [32]and they
will praise me in the land of their exile,
and will remember my name, [33]and
will turn from their stubbornness and
their wicked deeds; for they will remember the ways of their fathers, who
sinned before the Lord. [34]I will bring
them again into the land which I swore
to give to their fathers, to Abraham and
to Isaac and to Jacob, and they will
rule over it; and I will increase them,
and they will not be diminished. [35]I
will make an everlasting covenant with
them to be their God and they shall be
my people; and I will never again remove my people Israel from the land
which I have given them.”

3 “ ‘O Lord Almighty, God of
Israel, the soul in anguish and the

d The meaning of the Greek is uncertain
e Gk *their place*

9.15–17. **13:** Dt.4.27; Jer.42.2. **16:** Dt.26.15. **17:** Pss.6.5; 30.9; Is.38.18; Sir.17.27–28. *Hades*, Sheol. **21:** Jer.27.11–12. **23:** Jer.7.34. **25:** Jer.36.30. **26:** Jer.7.14. **27–35:** Repentance and restoration under an everlasting covenant. **28–29:** Dt.28.58,62. **30:** 1 Kg.8.47. **31:** Jer.24.7. **33:** Dt.9.6. **34:** Lev.26.42; Dt.6.10; Jer.32.37. **35:** Jer.32.38–40; Ezek.36.26–29; Am.9.15. **3.1–8:** Impassioned plea of repentant exiles (“though penitent we are still in exile!”).

wearied spirit cry out to thee. 2Hear,
O Lord, and have mercy, for we have
sinned before thee. 3For thou art
enthroned for ever, and we are perishing for ever. 4O Lord Almighty, God
of Israel, hear now the prayer of the
dead of Israel and of the sons of those
who sinned before thee, who did not
heed the voice of the Lord their God,
so that calamities have clung to us.
5Remember not the iniquities of our
fathers, but in this crisis remember thy
power and thy name. 6For thou art
the Lord our God, and thee, O Lord,
will we praise. 7For thou hast put the
fear of thee in our hearts in order that
we should call upon thy name; and we
will praise thee in our exile, for we
have put away from our hearts all the
iniquity of our fathers who sinned
before thee. 8Behold, we are today in
our exile where thou hast scattered us,
to be reproached and cursed and
punished for all the iniquities of our
fathers who forsook the Lord our
God.'"

9Hear the commandments of life,
O Israel;
give ear, and learn wisdom!
10Why is it, O Israel, why is it that
you are in the land of your
enemies,
that you are growing old in a
foreign country,
that you are defiled with the
dead,
11 that you are counted among
those in Hades?
12You have forsaken the fountain of
wisdom.
13If you had walked in the way of
God,
you would be dwelling in peace
for ever.
14Learn where there is wisdom,
where there is strength,
where there is understanding,
that you may at the same time
discern
where there is length of days,
and life,
where there is light for the eyes,
and peace.

15Who has found her place?
And who has entered her
storehouses?
16Where are the princes of the
nations,
and those who rule over the
beasts on the earth;
17those who have sport with the
birds of the air,
and who hoard up silver and
gold,
in which men trust,
and there is no end to their
getting;
18those who scheme to get silver,
and are anxious,
whose labors are beyond
measure?
19They have vanished and gone down
to Hades,
and others have arisen in their
place.

20Young men have seen the light of
day,
and have dwelt upon the
earth;
but they have not learned the way
to knowledge,
nor understood her paths,
nor laid hold of her.
21Their sons have strayed far from
her[f] way.
22She has not been heard of in
Canaan,
nor seen in Teman;

f Other authorities read *their*

4: *The dead of Israel,* the Israelites in exile (v. 11; Is.59.10b; Lam.3.6). **7:** Jer.32.40b. **8:** The fathers' sins (2.33; 3.4–5) are visited on the sons (Lam.5.7).

3.9–4.4: Wisdom, found by God, was given to Israel and is the law. 3.9–14: Introduction to the poem. **10:** *Growing old,* the exile has been long (contrast 1.2). **11:** Pss.28.1; 88.4. **12:** Pr.18.4; Jer.2.13. **14:** Pr.3.16; 8.14. **15–28:** The rulers of the world and the mighty have not found wisdom. **15:** Job 28.12. **16b–17a:** Jer.27.6; Dan.2.38; Jdt.11.7. **22:** *Canaan,* Ezek.28.3–5 associates Tyre (in Canaan) with wisdom. *Teman,* in Edom, was reputed for its wisdom (Jer.49.7;

[23]the sons of Hagar, who seek for
understanding on the earth,
the merchants of Merran and
Teman,
the story-tellers and the seekers
for understanding,
have not learned the way to
wisdom,
nor given thought to her paths.

[24]O Israel, how great is the house
of God!
And how vast the territory that
he possesses!
[25]It is great and has no bounds;
it is high and immeasurable.
[26]The giants were born there, who
were famous of old,
great in stature, expert in war.
[27]God did not choose them,
nor give them the way to
knowledge;
[28]so they perished because they had
no wisdom,
they perished through their
folly.

[29]Who has gone up into heaven,
and taken her,
and brought her down from the
clouds?
[30]Who has gone over the sea, and
found her,
and will buy her for pure gold?
[31]No one knows the way to her,
or is concerned about the path
to her.
[32]But he who knows all things knows
her,
he found her by his
understanding.
He who prepared the earth for all
time
filled it with four-footed
creatures;
[33]he who sends forth the light, and
it goes,
called it, and it obeyed him in
fear;
[34]the stars shone in their watches,
and were glad;
he called them, and they said,
"Here we are!"
They shone with gladness for
him who made them.
[35]This is our God;
no other can be compared to
him!
[36]He found the whole way to
knowledge,
and gave her to Jacob his
servant
and to Israel whom he loved.
[37]Afterward she appeared upon earth
and lived among men.

4 She is the book of the
commandments of God,
and the law that endures for
ever.
All who hold her fast will live,
and those who forsake her will
die.
[2]Turn, O Jacob, and take her;
walk toward the shining of her
light.
[3]Do not give your glory to another,
or your advantages to an alien
people.
[4]Happy are we, O Israel,
for we know what is pleasing to
God.

[5]Take courage, my people,
O memorial of Israel!
[6]It was not for destruction
that you were sold to the nations,
but you were handed over to your
enemies
because you angered God.

Ob.8–9). **23:** *Merran,* probably a corruption which arose in the Hebrew text for "Midian," a son of Keturah (Gen.25.2). **24:** *House of God,* the created world. **26:** Gen.6.4; Wis.14.6; compare the book of Enoch 7.1–6. **29–37:** God found wisdom and gave her to Israel (Sir.24.1–12). **29–30:** Dt.30.12–13; Job 28.13–14. **32–34:** Job 28.23–26; Pr.8.22–31. **33:** *Light,* Gen.1.3. **34:** *Stars . . . were glad,* Job 38.7. **37:** Many church fathers took this as an allusion to the Incarnation. **4.1–3:** Wisdom is *the law* (the Torah). **1:** Sir.24.23. **2:** Is.60.3.

4.5–5.9: Poem of comfort and restoration. 4.5–20: Israel provoked God, and Zion now mourns for her captive children. **5:** *Take courage, my people* (compare vv. 21,27,30), inspired

7 For you provoked him who made
you,
by sacrificing to demons and
not to God.
8 You forgot the everlasting God,
who brought you up,
and you grieved Jerusalem, who
reared you.
9 For she saw the wrath that came
upon you from God,
and she said:
"Hearken, you neighbors of Zion,
God has brought great sorrow
upon me;
10 for I have seen the captivity of my
sons and daughters,
which the Everlasting brought
upon them.
11 With joy I nurtured them,
but I sent them away with
weeping and sorrow.
12 Let no one rejoice over me, a widow
and bereaved of many;
I was left desolate because of the
sins of my children,
because they turned away from
the law of God.
13 They had no regard for his statutes;
they did not walk in the ways
of God's commandments,
nor tread the paths of discipline
in his righteousness.
14 Let the neighbors of Zion come;
remember the capture of my
sons and daughters,
which the Everlasting brought
upon them.
15 For he brought against them a
nation from afar,
a shameless nation, of a strange
language,
who had no respect for an old man,
and had no pity for a child.
16 They led away the widow's
beloved sons,
and bereaved the lonely woman
of her daughters.

17 "But I, how can I help you?
18 For he who brought these calamities
upon you
will deliver you from the hand
of your enemies.
19 Go, my children, go;
for I have been left desolate.
20 I have taken off the robe of peace
and put on the sackcloth of my
supplication;
I will cry to the Everlasting all
my days.

21 "Take courage, my children, cry
to God,
and he will deliver you from the
power and hand of the enemy.
22 For I have put my hope in the
Everlasting to save you,
and joy has come to me from
the Holy One,
because of the mercy which soon
will come to you
from your everlasting Savior.[g]
23 For I sent you out with sorrow and
weeping,
but God will give you back to
me with joy and gladness for
ever.
24 For as the neighbors of Zion have
now seen your capture,
so they soon will see your
salvation by God,
which will come to you with great
glory
and with the splendor of the
Everlasting.
25 My children, endure with patience
the wrath that has come upon
you from God.
Your enemy has overtaken you,
but you will soon see their
destruction
and will tread upon their necks.
26 My tender sons have traveled
rough roads;

g Or *from the Everlasting, your Savior*

by Is.40.1. **7:** *Demons*, Dt.32.16–17; Ps.106.37; 1 Cor.10.20. **9b–16:** Jerusalem speaks to her *neighbors* (i.e. neighboring cities). **12:** *Widow*, Lam.1.1. **15:** Dt.28.49–50; Jer.6.15. **17–29:** Jerusalem encourages her exiled children. **17–18:** Only God can help. **20:** *Robe of peace*, garment worn in time of prosperity. *Sackcloth of my supplication*, garment worn by a suppliant. **23:** Ps.126.6; Jer.31.12–13. **24:** Is.60.1–3. **25:** *The wrath* is only temporary (Is.54.7–8).

they were taken away like a
flock carried off by the enemy.

27"Take courage, my children, and
cry to God,
for you will be remembered by
him who brought this upon you.
28For just as you purposed to go
astray from God,
return with tenfold zeal to seek
him.
29For he who brought these calamities
upon you
will bring you everlasting joy
with your salvation."

30Take courage, O Jerusalem,
for he who named you will
comfort you.
31Wretched will be those who
afflicted you
and rejoiced at your fall.
32Wretched will be the cities which
your children served as slaves;
wretched will be the city which
received your sons.
33For just as she rejoiced at your fall
and was glad for your ruin,
so she will be grieved at her own
desolation.
34And I will take away her pride in
her great population,
and her insolence will be turned
to grief.
35For fire will come upon her from
the Everlasting for many days,
and for a long time she will be
inhabited by demons.

36Look toward the east, O Jerusalem,
and see the joy that is coming
to you from God!
37Behold, your sons are coming,
whom you sent away;
they are coming, gathered from
east and west,
at the word of the Holy One,
rejoicing in the glory of God.

5 Take off the garment of your sorrow and affliction, O Jerusalem,
and put on for ever the beauty
of the glory from God.
2Put on the robe of the righteousness
from God;
put on your head the diadem of
the glory of the Everlasting.
3For God will show your splendor
everywhere under heaven.
4For your name will for ever be
called by God,
"Peace of righteousness and
glory of godliness."

5Arise, O Jerusalem, stand upon the
height
and look toward the east,
and see your children gathered
from west and east,
at the word of the Holy One,
rejoicing that God has
remembered them.
6For they went forth from you on
foot,
led away by their enemies;
but God will bring them back to you,
carried in glory, as on a royal
throne.
7For God has ordered that every
high mountain and the
everlasting hills be made low
and the valleys filled up, to
make level ground,
so that Israel may walk safely in
the glory of God.
8The woods and every fragrant tree
have shaded Israel at God's
command.
9For God will lead Israel with joy,
in the light of his glory,
with the mercy and righteousness
that come from him.

4.30–5.9: Jerusalem encouraged with promises concerning the destruction of her enemy and the return of her children. **30:** *He who named you*, see 5.4 n. **31–35:** Contrast the attitude toward Babylon in 1.11–12. **35:** *Fire*, Jer.51.58. *Demons*, Is.13.21. **36:** Is.40.9–11. **37:** Is.43.5. **5.1–9:** Glorification of Jerusalem and return of the exiles. **1–2:** Is.61.3,10. **4:** Is.60.14; 62.4; Jer.33.16; Ezek.48.35. *Peace of righteousness*, Is.32.17. **5:** Is.49.18; 60.4. **6:** Is.49.22; 66.20. **7:** Is.42.16–17.

THE LETTER OF JEREMIAH

The so-called Letter of Jeremiah, which professes to be a copy of a letter sent by Jeremiah in 597 B.C. to those Jews who were about to be taken as captives to Babylon (v. 1), is an earnest though rambling discourse against the folly of idolatry. It can be characterized as an impassioned sermon on Jer.10.11, a verse (in Aramaic) which provides the exiled Jews with a response when invited to participate in the worship of idols: "Thus shall you say to them: 'The gods who did not make the heavens and the earth shall perish from the earth and from under the heavens.'" Elaborating upon this text, the author draws upon Jer.10.3–9,14 and Ps.115.4–8 (compare also Is.40.18–20; 41.6–7) for a variety of arguments to prove the utter impotence, whether for good or ill, of gods of wood and silver and gold. The style of the tractate is florid and declamatory, with no logical connection in the sequence of its statements. In a mechanical way the author divides his homily into sections by a refrain repeated with slight variations, insisting that "this shows that they are no gods" (vv. 16, 23, 29b, 40a, 44b, 52, 56b, 65, 69).

On the basis of linguistic and historical considerations most scholars date the Letter of Jeremiah in the Hellenistic period. The seven generations of exile mentioned in v. 3, at forty years for a generation, would imply a date 280 years after the exile in 597, that is 317 B.C. Others think that the Letter is still later, dating it in the Maccabean period. The original language was most probably Hebrew (see, for example, v. 72 n.), though some think that it was written in either Aramaic or Greek. The oldest manuscript remains of the book is a tiny fragment of Greek papyrus containing several words from vv. 43–44; it was discovered in Cave VII at Qumran by the Dead Sea, and is thought to date from about 100 B.C.

The Letter stands at different places in various manuscripts and versions. It appears as a separate book between Lamentations and Ezekiel in two ancient Greek manuscripts of the Old Testament (the fourth century codex Vaticanus and the fifth century codex Alexandrinus), in the Syriac Hexaplar manuscript at Milan, and in the Arabic version. In other Greek and Syriac manuscripts, as well as the Latin version, it is attached to the apocryphal book of Baruch, and consequently many English translations include it as the final (sixth) chapter of that book. Since, however, the Letter is an independent composition and has nothing to do with Baruch, the Revised Standard Version prints it as a separate book.

---

6 [h]A COPY OF A LETTER WHICH JEREMIAH
sent to those who were to be taken
to Babylon as captives by the king of
the Babylonians, to give them the
message which God had commanded
him.
2 Because of the sins which you have
committed before God, you will be
taken to Babylon as captives by Nebuchadnezzar, king of the Babylonians.
3Therefore when you have come to
Babylon you will remain there for many
years, for a long time, up to seven
generations; after that I will bring you
away from there in peace. 4Now in
Babylon you will see gods made of
silver and gold and wood, which are
carried on men's shoulders and inspire
fear in the heathen. 5So take care not
to become at all like the foreigners
or to let fear for these gods[i] possess
you, when you see the multitude before
and behind them worshiping them.
6But say in your heart, "It is thou,
O Lord, whom we must worship."
7For my angel is with you, and he is
watching your lives.

h The King James Version prints *The Epistle of Jeremy* as Chapter 6 of the book of Baruch, and the chapter and verse numbers are here retained
i Gk *for them*

6.1–7: Historical introduction. 1: The exile of 597 B.C. (2 Kg.24.10–17). *Letter*, according to Jer.29.1 a letter is sent to Babylon. *King of the Babylonians*, but "king of Babylon" in the book of Jeremiah (Jer.20.4; 21.2; etc.). **2:** Jer.16.10. **3:** *Seven generations*, contrast seventy years in Jer.29.10, forty years in Ezek.4.6, seventy weeks of years in Dan.9.24. **4:** *Silver and gold*, overlaid on wood (v. 55; Is.40.19; Jer.10.3–4). *Carried on men's shoulders*, perhaps an allusion to the Babylonian New Year procession, or a reflection of Is.46.7; Jer.10.5. **5:** *Like the foreigners*, Jer.10.2. **7:** *My angel*, Ex.23.23; 32.34.

8 Their tongues are smoothed by
the craftsman, and they themselves
are overlaid with gold and silver; but
they are false and cannot speak.
9People[j] take gold and make crowns
for the heads of their gods, as they
would for a girl who loves ornaments;
10and sometimes the priests secretly
take gold and silver from their gods
and spend it upon themselves, 11and
even give some of it to the harlots in
the brothel. They deck their gods[k]
out with garments like men—these
gods of silver and gold and wood,
12which cannot save themselves from
rust and corrosion. When they have
been dressed in purple robes, 13their
faces are wiped because of the dust
from the temple, which is thick upon
them. 14Like a local ruler the god[l]
holds a scepter, though unable to
destroy any one who offends it. 15It
has a dagger in its right hand, and has
an axe; but it cannot save itself from
war and robbers. 16Therefore they
evidently are not gods; so do not fear
them.

17 For just as one's dish is useless
when it is broken, so are the gods of
the heathen,[m] when they have been set
up in the temples. Their eyes are full
of the dust raised by the feet of those
who enter. 18And just as the gates are
shut on every side upon a man who has
offended a king, as though he were
sentenced to death, so the priests make
their temples secure with doors and
locks and bars, in order that they may
not be plundered by robbers. 19They
light lamps, even more than they light
for themselves, though their gods[n] can
see none of them. 20They are[o] just like
a beam of the temple, but men say
their hearts have melted, when worms
from the earth devour them and their
robes. They do not notice 21when
their faces have been blackened by
the smoke of the temple. 22Bats,
swallows, and birds light on their
bodies and heads; and so do cats.
23From this you will know that they
are not gods; so do not fear them.

24 As for the gold which they wear
for beauty—they will not shine unless
some one wipes off the rust; for even
when they were being cast, they had
no feeling. 25They are bought at any
cost, but there is no breath in them.
26Having no feet, they are carried on
men's shoulders, revealing to mankind
their worthlessness. 27And those
who serve them are ashamed because
through them these gods[n] are made to
stand, lest they fall to the ground. If
any one sets one of them upright, it
cannot move of itself; and if it is
tipped over, it cannot straighten itself;
but gifts are placed before them just as
before the dead. 28The priests sell the
sacrifices that are offered to these gods[p]
and use the money; and likewise their
wives preserve some with salt, but give
none to the poor or helpless. 29Sacri-
fices to them may be touched by women
in menstruation or at childbirth. Since
you know by these things that they are
not gods, do not fear them.

j Gk *They*
k Gk *them*
l Gk *he*
m Gk *of them*
n Gk *they*
o Gk *It is*
p Gk *to them*

8–73: Condemnation of idolatry. 8–16: Idols are decked out like people. 8: *Craftsman,* Is.40.20. **11:** *Harlots,* probably cult prostitutes. *In the brothel,* alternate translation, "on the roof." **12:** *Purple robes,* Jer.10.9. **14:** *Scepter,* Est.5.2. *Destroy,* put to death. **15:** *Dagger,* the Hebrew word behind the Greek could also mean "sword." Archaeologists have found representations of deities bearing scepters, swords, daggers, and battle-axes.

17–23: Uselessness and helplessness of idols. 17: *Dish . . . broken,* Jer.19.11; 22.28. **18:** *Gates* of the palace or doors of courtyard prison (Jer.32.2). **19:** Ps.115.5. *Lamps* have been found in excavated temples. **22:** This is the earliest Jewish reference to *cats,* which were first domesticated in Egypt.

24–29: Idols are unable to feel or move. 25: *Any cost,* great cost. *No breath,* Ps.135.17; Jer.10.14; Hab.2.19. **26:** Is.46.7. **27:** *Cannot move,* Is.46.7; Jer.10.4. *Gifts* for *the dead,* Ps. 106.28; Sir.30.18–19. **29:** Lev.12.1–8.

30 For why should they be called
gods? Women serve meals for gods
of silver and gold and wood; 31and
in their temples the priests sit with
their clothes rent, their heads and
beards shaved, and their heads uncovered. 32They howl and shout before their gods as some do at a funeral
feast for a man who has died. 33The
priests take some of the clothing of
their gods[q] to clothe their wives and
children. 34Whether one does evil to
them or good, they will not be able to
repay it. They cannot set up a king or
depose one. 35Likewise they are not
able to give either wealth or money; if
one makes a vow to them and does not
keep it, they will not require it. 36They
cannot save a man from death or rescue
the weak from the strong. 37They
cannot restore sight to a blind man;
they cannot rescue a man who is in
distress. 38They cannot take pity on
a widow or do good to an orphan.
39These things that are made of wood
and overlaid with gold and silver are
like stones from the mountain, and
those who serve them will be put to
shame. 40Why then must any one
think that they are gods, or call them
gods?

Besides, even the Chaldeans themselves dishonor them; 41for when they
see a dumb man, who cannot speak,
they bring him and pray Bel[r] that the
man may speak, as though Bel[s] were
able to understand. 42Yet they themselves cannot perceive this and abandon
them, for they have no sense. 43And
the women, with cords about them, sit
along the passageways, burning bran
for incense; and when one of them is
led off by one of the passers-by and is
lain with, she derides the woman next
to her, because she was not as attractive as herself and her cord was not
broken. 44Whatever is done for them
is false. Why then must any one think
that they are gods, or call them gods?

45 They are made by carpenters and
goldsmiths; they can be nothing but
what the craftsmen wish them to be.
46The men that make them will certainly not live very long themselves;
how then can the things that are made
by them be gods? 47They have left only
lies and reproach for those who come
after. 48For when war or calamity
comes upon them, the priests consult
together as to where they can hide
themselves and their gods.[t] 49How
then can one fail to see that these are
not gods, for they cannot save themselves from war or calamity? 50Since
they are made of wood and overlaid
with gold and silver, it will afterward
be known that they are false. 51It will
be manifest to all the nations and kings
that they are not gods but the work of
men's hands, and that there is no work
of God in them. 52Who then can fail to
know that they are not gods?[u]

53 For they cannot set up a king
over a country or give rain to men.
54They cannot judge their own cause or
deliver one who is wronged, for they
have no power; they are like crows
between heaven and earth. 55When
fire breaks out in a temple of wooden

q Gk *them*
r Or *they bring Bel and pray*
s Gk *he*
t Gk *them*
u The Greek text of this verse is uncertain

30–40a: Idols cannot repay good or evil, or help mankind. 30: *Women*, there were only male ministrants in the Jewish temple. **31–32:** Ritual lamentations for dying gods (such as Tammuz, Ezek.8.14; compare Lev.21.5,10; Ezek.24.17). **34b:** Job 12.18; Dan.2.21. **35b:** Dt.23.21. **36:** On the contrary, the Lord can do this (Dt.32.39; Ps.49.15). **37:** Ps.146.8. **38:** Dt.10.18; Ps. 146.9; Jer.7.6. **39:** Hab.2.19.

40b–44: The Chaldeans dishonor their own idols. 41: *Bel*, Marduk (Is.46.1). **43:** A similar Babylonian practice is described by Herodotus (*Hist.* I. 199), according to which cult prostitutes sat among roped-off passageways.

45–52: Idols are but the work of man's hands. 45: Ps.115.4; Is.40.19; Jer.10.9. **47:** Idolaters bequeath lies and reproach, not real gods, to posterity. **50:** *Afterward*, when the veneer has been exposed for what it is. *False*, a fraud.

53–56: The impotence of idols. 53: V. 34b. *Give rain*, Dt.11.14; 28.12; Ps.147.8.

gods overlaid with gold or silver, their
priests will flee and escape, but the
gods[v] will be burnt in two like beams.
[56]Besides, they can offer no resistance
to a king or any enemies. Why then
must any one admit or think that they
are gods?

57 Gods made of wood and overlaid
with silver and gold are not able to
save themselves from thieves and
robbers. [58]Strong men will strip them
of their gold and silver and of the robes
they wear, and go off with this booty,
and they will not be able to help themselves. [59]So it is better to be a king who
shows his courage, or a household
utensil that serves its owner's need,
than to be these false gods; better even
the door of a house that protects its
contents, than these false gods; better
also a wooden pillar in a palace, than
these false gods.

60 For sun and moon and stars,
shining and sent forth for service, are
obedient. [61]So also the lightning, when
it flashes, is widely seen; and the wind
likewise blows in every land. [62]When
God commands the clouds to go over
the whole world, they carry out his
command. [63]And the fire sent from
above to consume mountains and
woods does what it is ordered. But
these idols[w] are not to be compared
with them in appearance or power.
[64]Therefore one must not think that
they are gods nor call them gods, for
they are not able either to decide a case
or to do good to men. [65]Since you
know then that they are not gods, do
not fear them.

66 For they can neither curse nor
bless kings; [67]they cannot show signs
in the heavens and[x] among the nations,
or shine like the sun or give light like
the moon. [68]The wild beasts are better
than they are, for they can flee to cover
and help themselves. [69]So we have no
evidence whatever that they are gods;
therefore do not fear them.

70 Like a scarecrow in a cucumber
bed, that guards nothing, so are their
gods of wood, overlaid with gold and
silver. [71]In the same way, their gods
of wood, overlaid with gold and silver,
are like a thorn bush in a garden, on
which every bird sits; or like a dead
body cast out in the darkness. [72]By
the purple and linen[y] that rot upon
them you will know that they are not
gods; and they will finally themselves
be consumed, and be a reproach in the
land. [73]Better therefore is a just man
who has no idols, for he will be far
from reproach.

v Gk *they* *w* Gk *these things*
x Other ancient authorities omit *and*
y Cn: Gk *marble*, Syr *silk*

57–65: Idols are helpless, useless, and not to be compared with celestial phenomena. 60: Gen.1.14–18. **61–62:** Job 38.24–27; Ps.97.4. **63:** *Fire*, lightning. **64:** *Decide a case*, the true God does this (Ex.18.19; Ps.43.1).

66–69: The helplessness of idols. 67: *Signs*, portents (Jer.10.2; Jl.2.30; Mt.16.1).

70–73: Idols are compared with a scarecrow, thorn bush, and corpse. 70: *Scarecrow*, Jer.10.5. **71:** *Thorn bush*, an ordinary, useless shrub (compare Jg.9.14–15). **72:** The Greek text (*marble*, see note *y*) is a misinterpretation of the Hebrew word *shesh*, which means both "linen" and "marble" ("alabaster"). **73:** The conclusion of the matter.

THE PRAYER OF AZARIAH AND THE

SONG OF THE THREE YOUNG MEN

Additions to Daniel, inserted between 3.23 and 3.24

The ancient Greek and Latin versions of the book of Daniel contain a number of additions which are not present in the original Hebrew and Aramaic text. Besides many minor accretions throughout the book there are three lengthy Additions, now included among the Apocrypha as separate books under the respective titles: The Prayer of Azariah and the Song of the Three Young Men; Susanna; Bel and the Dragon.

The date when these Additions were composed is probably sometime in the second or first century B.C. Whether they were written originally in Hebrew, Aramaic, or Greek has been debated by scholars. Of the three Additions the Prayer of Azariah and the Song of the Three Young Men has the best claim to have been composed in Hebrew.

According to the book of Daniel, three Jewish captives in Babylon, named Shadrach, Meshach, and Abednego, refused to worship the golden image which Nebuchadnezzar had set up. By way of punishment for their refusal they were bound and thrown into the burning fiery furnace (Dan.3.23). Then follows the interpolation, which has three sections: vv. 1–22, the prayer of Azariah (Azariah is his Hebrew name; Abednego, his pagan name; see Dan.1.7); vv. 23–27, details about the furnace; vv. 28–68, the song of the three. This song is in two parts: the first is a liturgy addressed to God (vv. 29–34), and the second is a series of exhortations addressed to all creatures, animate and inanimate, to praise the Lord (vv. 35–68). Both parts of the song possess a certain solemnity and majestic rhythm owing to the presence of a regularly recurring refrain, which may have been used as the response of the congregation. The unknown hymnwriter derived much of his inspiration from the antiphonal liturgies in Pss. 136 and 148.

AND THEY WALKED ABOUT IN THE midst of the flames, singing hymns to God and blessing the Lord.
2Then Azariah stood and offered this prayer; in the midst of the fire he opened his mouth and said:
3"Blessed art thou, O Lord, God of
our fathers, and worthy of
praise;
and thy name is glorified for
ever.
4For thou art just in all that thou
hast done to us,
and all thy works are true and
thy ways right,
and all thy judgments are truth.
5Thou hast executed true judgments
in all that thou hast brought
upon us
and upon Jerusalem, the holy
city of our fathers,
for in truth and justice thou hast
brought all this upon us
because of our sins.
6For we have sinfully and lawlessly
departed from thee,
and have sinned in all things
and have not obeyed thy
commandments;
7we have not observed them or done
them,
as thou hast commanded us that
it might go well with us.
8So all that thou hast brought upon
us,
and all that thou hast done to
us,
thou hast done in true judgment.
9Thou hast given us into the hands
of lawless enemies, most
hateful rebels,
and to an unjust king, the most
wicked in all the world.
10And now we cannot open our mouths;

1–22: The prayer of Azariah. 1: *They,* the three men mentioned in Dan.3.23. **3:** 1 Chr. 29.10,20. **4:** Neh.9.33; Rev.16.7; 19.2. **6–7:** Is.59.12–13; Dan.9.5–8; Bar.1.17–18. **8–10:**

shame and disgrace have befallen
thy servants and worshipers.
11 For thy name's sake do not give us
up utterly,
and do not break thy covenant,
12 and do not withdraw thy mercy
from us,
for the sake of Abraham thy beloved
and for the sake of Isaac thy
servant
and Israel thy holy one,
13 to whom thou didst promise
to make their descendants as
many as the stars of heaven
and as the sand on the shore of
the sea.
14 For we, O Lord, have become
fewer than any nation,
and are brought low this day in all
the world because of our sins.
15 And at this time there is no prince,
or prophet, or leader,
no burnt offering, or sacrifice, or
oblation, or incense,
no place to make an offering
before thee or to find mercy.
16 Yet with a contrite heart and a
humble spirit may we be
accepted,
as though it were with burnt
offerings of rams and bulls,
and with tens of thousands of
fat lambs;
17 such may our sacrifice be in thy
sight this day,
and may we wholly follow thee,
for there will be no shame for
those who trust in thee.
18 And now with all our heart we
follow thee,
we fear thee and seek thy face.
19 Do not put us to shame,
but deal with us in thy forbearance
and in thy abundant mercy.
20 Deliver us in accordance with thy
marvelous works,
and give glory to thy name, O
Lord!
Let all who do harm to thy servants
be put to shame;
21 let them be disgraced and
deprived of all power and
dominion,
and let their strength be broken.
22 Let them know that thou art the
Lord, the only God,
glorious over the whole world."

23 Now the king's servants who
threw them in did not cease feeding
the furnace fires with naphtha, pitch,
tow, and brush. 24 And the flame
streamed out above the furnace forty-
nine cubits, 25 and it broke through and
burned those of the Chaldeans whom
it caught about the furnace. 26 But the
angel of the Lord came down into the
furnace to be with Azariah and his
companions, and drove the fiery flame
out of the furnace, 27 and made the
midst of the furnace like a moist
whistling wind, so that the fire did not
touch them at all or hurt or trouble
them.
28 Then the three, as with one
mouth, praised and glorified and
blessed God in the furnace, saying:
29 "Blessed art thou, O Lord, God of
our fathers,
and to be praised and highly
exalted for ever;
30 And blessed is thy glorious, holy
name
and to be highly praised and
highly exalted for ever;
31 Blessed art thou in the temple of
thy holy glory
and to be extolled and highly
glorified for ever.
32 Blessed art thou, who sittest upon
cherubim and lookest upon
the deeps,

Lev.26.14,38; Dt.28.15,63–64. **12:** *Abraham thy beloved,* 2 Chr.20.7; Is.41.8; Jas.2.23. **13:** Gen.15.5; 22.17. **14:** Dt.28.63; Jer.42.2; Bar.2.13. **15:** Lam.2.9; Hos.3.4; 2 Esd.10.21–22. **16:** Ps.51.16–17; Hos.6.6. **19:** Ps.25.3. **21:** Ps.35.26. **22:** Ps.83.18.

23–27: The continued stoking of the furnace, and the descent of the angel of the Lord. 23: *Naphtha,* a natural petroleum.

28–69: Song of the three young men. 32–37: Ps.148. **35:** Pss.103.22; 145.10.

and to be praised and highly
exalted for ever.
33 Blessed art thou upon the throne
of thy kingdom
and to be extolled and highly
exalted for ever.
34 Blessed art thou in the firmament
of heaven
and to be sung and glorified for
ever.

35 "Bless the Lord, all works of the
Lord,
sing praise to him and highly
exalt him for ever.
36 Bless the Lord, you heavens,
sing praise to him and highly
exalt him for ever.
37 Bless the Lord, you angels of the
Lord,
sing praise to him and highly
exalt him for ever.
38 Bless the Lord, all waters above
the heaven,
sing praise to him and highly
exalt him for ever.
39 Bless the Lord, all powers,
sing praise to him and highly
exalt him for ever.
40 Bless the Lord, sun and moon,
sing praise to him and highly
exalt him for ever.
41 Bless the Lord, stars of heaven,
sing praise to him and highly
exalt him for ever.
42 Bless the Lord, all rain and
dew,
sing praise to him and highly
exalt him for ever.
43 Bless the Lord, all winds,
sing praise to him and highly
exalt him for ever.
44 Bless the Lord, fire and heat,
sing praise to him and highly
exalt him for ever.
45 Bless the Lord, winter cold and
summer heat,
sing praise to him and highly
exalt him for ever.
46 Bless the Lord, dews and snows,
sing praise to him and highly
exalt him for ever.
47 Bless the Lord, nights and days,
sing praise to him and highly
exalt him for ever.
48 Bless the Lord, light and darkness,
sing praise to him and highly
exalt him for ever.
49 Bless the Lord, ice and cold,
sing praise to him and highly
exalt him for ever.
50 Bless the Lord, frosts and snows,
sing praise to him and highly
exalt him for ever.
51 Bless the Lord, lightnings and
clouds,
sing praise to him and highly
exalt him for ever.
52 Let the earth bless the Lord;
let it sing praise to him and
highly exalt him for ever.
53 Bless the Lord, mountains and
hills,
sing praise to him and highly
exalt him for ever.
54 Bless the Lord, all things that
grow on the earth,
sing praise to him and highly
exalt him for ever.
55 Bless the Lord, you springs,
sing praise to him and highly
exalt him for ever.
56 Bless the Lord, seas and rivers,
sing praise to him and highly
exalt him for ever.
57 Bless the Lord, you whales and all
creatures that move in the
waters,
sing praise to him and highly
exalt him for ever.
58 Bless the Lord, all birds of the air,
sing praise to him and highly
exalt him for ever.
59 Bless the Lord, all beasts and
cattle,
sing praise to him and highly
exalt him for ever.
60 Bless the Lord, you sons of men,
sing praise to him and highly
exalt him for ever.

37: Pss.103.20; 148.2. **38:** Ps.148.4. **39:** *All powers*, i.e. with heavenly bodies or angels. **40:** Ps.148.3. **44:** Ps.148.8. **53:** Ps.148.9. **58–59:** Ps.148.10.

61 Bless the Lord, O Israel,
sing praise to him and highly
exalt him for ever.
62 Bless the Lord, you priests of the
Lord,
sing praise to him and highly
exalt him for ever.
63 Bless the Lord, you servants of the
Lord,
sing praise to him and highly
exalt him for ever.
64 Bless the Lord, spirits and souls of
the righteous,
sing praise to him and highly
exalt him for ever.
65 Bless the Lord, you who are holy
and humble in heart,
sing praise to him and highly
exalt him for ever.
66 Bless the Lord, Hananiah, Azariah,
and Mishael,
sing praise to him and highly
exalt him for ever;
for he has rescued us from Hades
and saved us from the hand
of death,
and delivered us from the midst
of the burning fiery furnace;
from the midst of the fire he has
delivered us.
67 Give thanks to the Lord, for he is
good,
for his mercy endures for ever.
68 Bless him, all who worship the
Lord, the God of gods,
sing praise to him and give
thanks to him,
for his mercy endures for ever."

61–62: Ps.135.19. **63:** Ps.134.1. **65:** *Holy and humble in heart*, Pss.18.25,27; 86.1–2; Zeph.2.3. **67–68:** Pss.106.1; 136.1–2.

SUSANNA

Of the cycle of traditions concerning Daniel which were added to the book of Daniel when it was translated into Greek the story of Susanna is undoubtedly the gem. One of the finest short stories in world literature, it is based on the familiar motif of the triumph of virtue over villainy, the narrow escape from death of an innocent victim. While inculcating lessons of morality and trust in God, the story is a model of artistic fiction. Plot, surprise, struggle, and unfolding character are present in just the right proportion, and the whole is told succinctly and pungently.

In Hebrew the name Susanna means "a lily" and the name Daniel means "God has judged." Both are obviously appropriate names for the heroine and hero in a story that tells how Susanna was cleared of a false charge of adultery through the timely intervention of a sagacious and brave youth.

The position of this addition in the book of Daniel varies in the manuscripts. In the Septuagint and the Latin Vulgate the account of Susanna follows the last chapter of Daniel (which in Hebrew is ch. 12), and is numbered ch. 13. In the Greek text of Theodotion, however, as well as the Old Latin, Coptic, and Arabic versions the story of Susanna forms the introduction to the book of Daniel, being prefixed to ch. 1. It may be that this latter position was thought more appropriate because the addition describes Daniel as "a young lad" (v. 45).

Concerning date and original language, see the first part of the Introduction to the Prayer of Azariah and the Song of the Three Young Men.

THERE WAS A MAN LIVING IN BABY-
lon whose name was Joakim.
2And he took a wife named Susanna,
the daughter of Hilkiah, a very beautiful woman and one who feared
the Lord. 3Her parents were righteous, and had taught their daughter
according to the law of Moses. 4Jo-
akim was very rich, and had a spacious garden adjoining his house;
and the Jews used to come to him
because he was the most honored of
them all.

5 In that year two elders from the
people were appointed as judges.
Concerning them the Lord had said:
"Iniquity came forth from Babylon,
from elders who were judges, who
were supposed to govern the people."
6These men were frequently at Joakim's
house, and all who had suits at law
came to them.

7 When the people departed at
noon, Susanna would go into her
husband's garden to walk. 8The two
elders used to see her every day, going
in and walking about, and they began
to desire her. 9And they perverted
their minds and turned away their eyes
from looking to Heaven or remembering righteous judgments. 10Both were
overwhelmed with passion for her, but
they did not tell each other of their
distress, 11for they were ashamed to
disclose their lustful desire to possess
her. 12And they watched eagerly, day
after day, to see her.

13 They said to each other, "Let us
go home, for it is mealtime." 14And
when they went out, they parted from
each other. But turning back, they
met again; and when each pressed the
other for the reason, they confessed
their lust. And then together they arranged for a time when they could find
her alone.

1–4: Introduction. The setting of the story is Babylon during the exile. **1:** The name *Joakim* means "the Lord will establish." **2:** The names *Susanna* and *Hilkiah* mean respectively "lily" and "the Lord is my portion." **4:** Some Jews prospered during the exile (Jer.29.5).

5–14: The two lustful elders. **5:** *In that year*, apparently the year of Joakim's marriage (v. 2). The *two elders* are identified by Jewish tradition to be the two false prophets mentioned in Jer. 29.21–23. The quotation ("*Iniquity . . . people*") is either an unwritten prophetic saying or an allusion to Jer.23.14–15. **9:** *Heaven*, a metonym for God (see 1 Macc.3.18 n. and compare Lk.15.18).

15 Once, while they were watching for an opportune day, she went in as before with only two maids, and wished to bathe in the garden, for it was very hot. [16]And no one was there except the two elders, who had hid themselves and were watching her. [17]She said to her maids, "Bring me oil and ointments, and shut the garden doors so that I may bathe." [18]They did as she said, shut the garden doors, and went out by the side doors to bring what they had been commanded; and they did not see the elders, because they were hidden.

19 When the maids had gone out, the two elders rose and ran to her, and said: [20]"Look, the garden doors are shut, no one sees us, and we are in love with you; so give your consent, and lie with us. [21]If you refuse, we will testify against you that a young man was with you, and this was why you sent your maids away."

22 Susanna sighed deeply, and said, "I am hemmed in on every side. For if I do this thing, it is death for me; and if I do not, I shall not escape your hands. [23]I choose not to do it and to fall into your hands, rather than to sin in the sight of the Lord."

24 Then Susanna cried out with a loud voice, and the two elders shouted against her. [25]And one of them ran and opened the garden doors. [26]When the household servants heard the shouting in the garden, they rushed in at the side door to see what had happened to her. [27]And when the elders told their tale, the servants were greatly ashamed, for nothing like this had ever been said about Susanna.

28 The next day, when the people gathered at the house of her husband Joakim, the two elders came, full of their wicked plot to have Susanna put to death. [29]They said before the people, "Send for Susanna, the daughter of Hilkiah, who is the wife of Joakim." [30]So they sent for her. And she came, with her parents, her children, and all her kindred.

31 Now Susanna was a woman of great refinement, and beautiful in appearance. [32]As she was veiled, the wicked men ordered her to be unveiled, that they might feast upon her beauty. [33]But her family and friends and all who saw her wept.

34 Then the two elders stood up in the midst of the people, and laid their hands upon her head. [35]And she, weeping, looked up toward heaven, for her heart trusted in the Lord. [36]The elders said, "As we were walking in the garden alone, this woman came in with two maids, shut the garden doors, and dismissed the maids. [37]Then a young man, who had been hidden, came to her and lay with her. [38]We were in a corner of the garden, and when we saw this wickedness we ran to them. [39]We saw them embracing, but we could not hold the man, for he was too strong for us, and he opened the doors and dashed out. [40]So we seized this woman and asked her who the young man was, but she would not tell us. These things we testify."

41 The assembly believed them, because they were elders of the people and judges; and they condemned her to death.

42 Then Susanna cried out with a loud voice, and said, "O eternal God, who dost discern what is secret, who art aware of all things before they come to be, [43]thou knowest that these men have borne false witness against me. And now I am to die! Yet I have

---

15–27: The attempted seduction. **17:** *Oil and* (perfumed) *ointments* were used after bathing. **22:** The Mosaic law prescribed *death* as punishment for the unfaithful wife (Lev.20.10; Dt.22.22). **23:** Compare Joseph's reply to his tempter (Gen.39.9).

28–43: Susanna falsely accused and condemned to death. **34:** The judges play the part of witnesses by laying their hands on the head of the accused (Lev.24.14). **35:** *She . . . looked up toward heaven*, appealing her cause to a higher tribunal (vv. 42–43). **41:** Since, according to Jewish law, a witness could not be the judge, the sentence of death is passed by the credulous *assembly*. **42:** *God, who dost discern what is secret*, Ps.33.13–15; Pr.15.11; Heb.4.13.

done none of the things that they have
wickedly invented against me!"
44 The Lord heard her cry. [45]And
as she was being led away to be
put to death, God aroused the holy
spirit of a young lad named Daniel;
[46]and he cried with a loud voice, "I
am innocent of the blood of this
woman."
47 All the people turned to him,
and said, "What is this that you have
said?" [48]Taking his stand in the midst
of them, he said, "Are you such fools,
you sons of Israel? Have you condemned a daughter of Israel without
examination and without learning the
facts? [49]Return to the place of judgment. For these men have borne false
witness against her."
50 Then all the people returned in
haste. And the elders said to him,
"Come, sit among us and inform us,
for God has given you that right."
[51]And Daniel said to them, "Separate
them far from each other, and I will
examine them."
52 When they were separated from
each other, he summoned one of them
and said to him, "You old relic of
wicked days, your sins have now come
home, which you have committed in
the past, [53]pronouncing unjust judgments, condemning the innocent and
letting the guilty go free, though the
Lord said, 'Do not put to death an
innocent and righteous person.' [54]Now
then, if you really saw her, tell me this:
Under what tree did you see them
being intimate with each other?" He
answered, "Under a mastic tree."[a]
[55]And Daniel said, "Very well! You
have lied against your own head, for
the angel of God has received the sentence from God and will immediately
cut[a] you in two."
56 Then he put him aside, and commanded them to bring the other. And
he said to him, "You offspring of
Canaan and not of Judah, beauty has
deceived you and lust has perverted
your heart. [57]This is how you both
have been dealing with the daughters
of Israel, and they were intimate with
you through fear; but a daughter of
Judah would not endure your wickedness. [58]Now then, tell me: Under
what tree did you catch them being
intimate with each other?" He answered, "Under an evergreen oak."[b]
[59]And Daniel said to him, "Very well!
You also have lied against your own
head, for the angel of God is waiting
with his sword to saw[b] you in two,
that he may destroy you both."
60 Then all the assembly shouted
loudly and blessed God, who saves
those who hope in him. [61]And they
rose against the two elders, for out of
their own mouths Daniel had con-
victed them of bearing false witness;
[62]and they did to them as they had
wickedly planned to do to their neighbor; acting in accordance with the law
of Moses, they put them to death.
Thus innocent blood was saved that
day.
63 And Hilkiah and his wife praised
God for their daughter Susanna, and
so did Joakim her husband and all her
kindred, because nothing shameful was
found in her. [64]And from that day
onward Daniel had a great reputation
among the people.

a The Greek words for *mastic tree* and *cut* are so similar that the use of *cut* is ironic wordplay
b The Greek words for *evergreen oak* and *saw* are so similar that the use of *saw* is ironic wordplay

44–59: Susanna acquitted. 50: Here *the elders* are obviously not the two who had testified, but their colleagues on the bench. **53:** Ex.23.7. **54–59:** The wordplay of the original (see notes *a* and *b*) may be represented in English by the paraphrase, "Under a *clove* tree . . . the angel will *cleave* you"; "under a *yew* tree . . . the angel will *hew* you asunder."

60–62: The two elders condemned to death. 62: *The law of Moses*, concerning false witnesses (Dt.19.16–21).

BEL AND THE DRAGON

This addition to the Greek text of the book of Daniel comprises two popular tales, both designed to ridicule the folly of idolatry and to discredit heathen priestcraft. The first story tells of the great statue of Bel, the patron deity of Babylon, which every night devours huge quantities of food and drink and thus proves itself to be a living god. By clever detective work Daniel unmasks the chicanery of Bel's priests. The second story tells of Daniel's refusal to worship a monstrous dragon as a god, and his killing it with a ridiculous concoction of pitch, fat, and hair. The Babylonians, enraged by the death of their god, demand that Daniel be thrown into the lions' den. He is kept safe among the lions for six days, and is provided with food brought from Judea by the prophet Habakkuk. On the seventh day the king removes Daniel and throws into the den his enemies, who are immediately devoured.

The religious teaching of these stories, bizarre and fantastic as they appear to us today, is that those who worship the true and living God will be sustained in every kind of trial.

In the Greek manuscripts of Daniel the account of Bel and the Dragon is added at the close of ch. 12 of Daniel. In the Latin Vulgate it forms ch. 14, the story of Susanna being ch. 13. Concerning date and original language, see the first part of the Introduction to the Prayer of Azariah and the Song of the Three Young Men.

When King Astyages was laid
with his fathers, Cyrus the
Persian received his kingdom. 2And
Daniel was a companion of the king,
and was the most honored of his
friends.

3 Now the Babylonians had an idol
called Bel, and every day they spent
on it twelve bushels of fine flour and
forty sheep and fifty gallons of wine.
4The king revered it and went every
day to worship it. But Daniel worshiped his own God.

5 And the king said to him, "Why
do you not worship Bel?" He answered, "Because I do not revere manmade idols, but the living God, who
created heaven and earth and has
dominion over all flesh."

6 The king said to him, "Do you
not think that Bel is a living God? Do
you not see how much he eats and
drinks every day?" 7Then Daniel
laughed, and said, "Do not be deceived, O king; for this is but clay
inside and brass outside, and it never
ate or drank anything."

8 Then the king was angry, and he
called his priests and said to them,
"If you do not tell me who is eating
these provisions, you shall die. 9But
if you prove that Bel is eating them,
Daniel shall die, because he blasphemed against Bel." And Daniel said
to the king, "Let it be done as you have
said."

10 Now there were seventy priests
of Bel, besides their wives and children. And the king went with Daniel
into the temple of Bel. 11And the
priests of Bel said, "Behold, we are
going outside; you yourself, O king,
shall set forth the food and mix and
place the wine, and shut the door and
seal it with your signet. 12And when
you return in the morning, if you do
not find that Bel has eaten it all, we
will die; or else Daniel will, who is
telling lies about us." 13They were
unconcerned, for beneath the table
they had made a hidden entrance,
through which they used to go in regularly and consume the provisions.
14When they had gone out, the king

1–2: Introduction. **1:** *Cyrus the Persian* (Dan.6.28) became king of Babylon in 538 B.C.
3–22: The story of Bel. **3:** *Bel*, or Bel-Marduk (compare Merodach, Jer.50.2), was the chief god in the Babylonian pantheon. Several ancient sources testify to the enormous quantities of sacrifices presented to Marduk in the daily ritual. **7:** Daniel ridicules the king's argument: clay and brass do not eat (Sir.30.19). **11:** Dan.6.17. Archaeologists have found great numbers of Babylonian signets.

set forth the food for Bel. Then Daniel
ordered his servants to bring ashes
and they sifted them throughout the
whole temple in the presence of the
king alone. Then they went out,
shut the door and sealed it with the
king's signet, and departed. 15 In
the night the priests came with their
wives and children, as they were accustomed to do, and ate and drank
everything.
16 Early in the morning the king
rose and came, and Daniel with him.
17 And the king said, "Are the seals
unbroken, Daniel?" He answered,
"They are unbroken, O king." 18 As
soon as the doors were opened, the
king looked at the table, and shouted
in a loud voice, "You are great, O
Bel; and with you there is no deceit,
none at all."
19 Then Daniel laughed, and restrained the king from going in, and
said, "Look at the floor, and notice
whose footsteps these are." 20 The
king said, "I see the footsteps of men
and women and children."
21 Then the king was enraged, and
he seized the priests and their wives
and children; and they showed him
the secret doors through which they
were accustomed to enter and devour
what was on the table. 22 Therefore
the king put them to death, and gave
Bel over to Daniel, who destroyed it
and its temple.

23 There was also a great dragon,
which the Babylonians revered. 24 And
the king said to Daniel, "You cannot
deny that this is a living god; so worship him." 25 Daniel said, "I will worship the Lord my God, for he is the
living God. 26 But if you, O king, will
give me permission, I will slay the
dragon without sword or club." The
king said, "I give you permission."
27 Then Daniel took pitch, fat, and
hair, and boiled them together and
made cakes, which he fed to the
dragon. The dragon ate them, and
burst open. And Daniel said, "See
what you have been worshiping!"
28 When the Babylonians heard it,
they were very indignant and conspired against the king, saying, "The
king has become a Jew; he has destroyed Bel, and slain the dragon, and
slaughtered the priests." 29 Going to
the king, they said, "Hand Daniel over
to us, or else we will kill you and your
household." 30 The king saw that they
were pressing him hard, and under
compulsion he handed Daniel over to
them.
31 They threw Daniel into the
lions' den, and he was there for six
days. 32 There were seven lions in the
den, and every day they had been given
two human bodies and two sheep; but
these were not given to them now, so
that they might devour Daniel.
33 Now the prophet Habakkuk was
in Judea. He had boiled pottage and
had broken bread into a bowl, and was
going into the field to take it to the
reapers. 34 But the angel of the Lord
said to Habakkuk, "Take the dinner
which you have to Babylon, to Daniel,
in the lions' den." 35 Habakkuk said,
"Sir, I have never seen Babylon, and I
know nothing about the den." 36 Then
the angel of the Lord took him by the
crown of his head, and lifted him by
his hair and set him down in Babylon,
right over the den, with the rushing
sound of the wind itself.
37 Then Habakkuk shouted,

16–22: The fraud detected (compare Dan.2.12; 6.24). **22:** According to ancient historians it was Xerxes who destroyed Bel's temple.

23–42: The story of the dragon. 23: *A great dragon*, that is, a live serpent worshiped as a god (compare Num.21.8–9; 2 Kg.18.4). **26:** *Permission* was granted because the king believed in the immortality of the serpent-god. **31–32:** The second time that Daniel is put in *the lions' den* (Dan.6.16–24).

33–39: The intervention of Habakkuk. 33: The author intends to identify this Habakkuk with the Minor Prophet of that name; chronologically, however, such an identification is impossible. **36:** *Hair*, Ezek.8.3. **37:** 1 Kg.17.4.

"Daniel! Daniel! Take the dinner
which God has sent you." [38]And
Daniel said, "Thou hast remembered
me, O God, and hast not forsaken
those who love thee." [39]So Daniel
arose and ate. And the angel of God
immediately returned Habakkuk to
his own place.
40 On the seventh day the king came
to mourn for Daniel. When he came
to the den he looked in, and there sat
Daniel. [41]And the king shouted with a
loud voice, "Thou art great, O Lord
God of Daniel, and there is no other
besides thee." [42]And he pulled
Daniel[a] out, and threw into the den the
men who had attempted his destruction, and they were devoured immediately before his eyes.

a Gk *him*

40–42: Daniel's liberation. 41: Compare Dan.6.26–27.

THE PRAYER OF MANASSEH

One of the finest pieces in the Apocrypha is the little classic of penitential devotion known as the Prayer of Manasseh. Constructed in accord with the best liturgical forms and full without being protracted, this beautiful prayer breathes throughout a spirit of deep and genuine religious feeling.

According to 2 Chr.33.11–13, Manasseh, the wicked king of Judah, while in exile composed a prayer entreating divine forgiveness for his many sins. The Old Testament account also refers to two literary works that contained Manasseh's prayer (2 Chr.33.18–19). Since neither of these has survived, it is not surprising that some devout Jew undertook to remedy the loss by drawing up such a prayer as might have been used by the wicked though now repentant king. Henceforth the name Manasseh was associated in Jewish tradition not only with the grossest acts of idolatry (2 Chr.33.1–9), but also with the efficacy of genuine repentance in securing divine forgiveness. It may be that the unknown author also had in mind the practical use of the prayer in providing a suitable penitential devotion for those of his countrymen who, having fallen into idolatry, could be reclaimed from the error of their way.

The date of composition of the Prayer is difficult to determine. Though there is no positive evidence, many scholars place it sometime during the last two centuries B.C. Whether it was composed originally in Hebrew, Aramaic, or Greek is disputed; today it survives in Greek, Latin, Syriac, Armenian, and Ethiopic. The Latin translation of the Prayer in the Vulgate Bible (which since the Council of Trent has been put into an Appendix) is entirely different from the Old Latin translation, and is of much more recent origin.

O LORD ALMIGHTY,
God of our fathers,
of Abraham and Isaac and Jacob
and of their righteous posterity;
[2]thou who hast made heaven and earth
with all their order;
[3]who hast shackled the sea by thy word of command,
who hast confined the deep
and sealed it with thy terrible and glorious name;
[4]at whom all things shudder,
and tremble before thy power,
[5]for thy glorious splendor cannot be borne,
and the wrath of thy threat to sinners is irresistible;
[6]yet immeasurable and unsearchable is thy promised mercy,
[7] for thou art the Lord Most High,
of great compassion, long-suffering, and very merciful,
and repentest over the evils of men.
Thou, O Lord, according to thy great goodness
hast promised repentance and forgiveness
to those who have sinned against thee;
and in the multitude of thy mercies
thou hast appointed repentance for sinners,
that they may be saved.
[8]Therefore thou, O Lord, God of the righteous,
hast not appointed repentance for the righteous,
for Abraham and Isaac and Jacob, who did not sin against thee,
but thou hast appointed repentance for me, who am a sinner.

1–8: Invocation and ascription of praise to God, whose majesty is displayed in creation (vv. 1–4), and whose mercy grants repentance to sinners (vv. 6–8). **1:** *God of our fathers*, Ex.3.15–16; Dan.2.23; Acts 3.13. **2:** *All their order*, splendor and orderly array. **3:** *Shackled the sea*, Job 38.8–11. **7:** The second part of this verse (*Thou, O Lord . . . may be saved*) is preserved in the later Greek manuscripts and in the Latin and Syriac versions. **8:** *Not . . . for the righteous*, Lk.5.32. *For me . . . a sinner*, Lk.18.13.

9 For the sins I have committed are
more in number than the
sand of the sea;
my transgressions are multiplied,
O Lord, they are multiplied!
I am unworthy to look up and see
the height of heaven
because of the multitude of my
iniquities.
10 I am weighted down with many
an iron fetter,
so that I am rejected because of
my sins,
and I have no relief;
for I have provoked thy wrath
and have done what is evil in
thy sight,
setting up abominations and
multiplying offenses.
11 And now I bend the knee of my
heart,
beseeching thee for thy
kindness.
12 I have sinned, O Lord, I have
sinned,
and I know my transgressions.
13 I earnestly beseech thee,
forgive me, O Lord, forgive me!
Do not destroy me with my
transgressions!
Do not be angry with me for ever
or lay up evil for me;
do not condemn me to the
depths of the earth.
For thou, O Lord, art the God of
those who repent,
14 and in me thou wilt manifest
thy goodness;
for, unworthy as I am, thou wilt
save me in thy great mercy,
15 and I will praise thee continually
all the days of my life.
For all the host of heaven sings
thy praise,
and thine is the glory for ever.
Amen.

9–10: Personal confession of sin. For the background see 2 Kg.21.1–18; 2 Chr.33.1–20.

11–15a: Supplication for pardon. 11: *Knee of my heart*, an expression indicating special depth of feeling. **12:** *I know my transgressions*, compare Ps.19.12. **13:** *The depths of the earth*, probably Sheol or Hades is meant (Ps.63.9).

15b: Concluding doxology. *Host of heaven*, multitude of angelic beings (2 Chr.18.18; Lk.2.13).

THE FIRST BOOK OF THE
MACCABEES

First Maccabees has come down to us in Greek, and also in Latin and several other versions derived from the Greek, the original Hebrew having been lost at an early time. The book was probably written shortly after the death of John Hyrcanus I (high priest 134–104 B.C.), since it refers to the chronicles of John's reign (16.23–24). Some scholars, however, think that chs. 14–16 are an addition made not long after A.D. 70, in which case the rest of the book may have been written about 140 B.C.

The author of 1 Maccabees was probably a Palestinian Jew who lived in Jerusalem. He modeled his work on the historical books of the Old Testament, particularly the books of Kings and Chronicles. After an introduction briefly sketching the conquests of Alexander the Great (336–323 B.C.), the division of his empire, and the origin of the Seleucid Empire (1.1–10), he recounts the principal events of Judea's history from the accession of Antiochus IV (175 B.C.) to the reign of John Hyrcanus I, which marked the period of the successful struggle for Jewish independence.

The style of 1 Maccabees is plain and straightforward and the book is generally an excellent historical source, though the order of events frequently differs from that in 2 Maccabees and it is not always certain which is to be preferred. Though the author (unlike the author of 2 Maccabees) records no miraculous interventions from heaven, he obviously sees the hand of God operative in the victories of Judas Maccabeus and his family. The letters of kings and others that are included are essential to the story, and, whether or not they are genuine copies of historical documents, they appear to be based on reliable information. The book also preserves portions of several contemporary poems (e.g. 1.24–28, 36–40; 2.7–13; 3.3–9, 45, 50–53; 14.4–15).

AFTER ALEXANDER SON OF PHILIP,
the Macedonian, who came from
the land of Kittim, had defeated[a]
Darius, king of the Persians and the
Medes, he succeeded him as king. (He
had previously become king of Greece.)
2 He fought many battles, conquered
strongholds, and put to death the
kings of the earth. 3 He advanced to
the ends of the earth, and plundered
many nations. When the earth became
quiet before him, he was exalted,
and his heart was lifted up. 4 He
gathered a very strong army and
ruled over countries, nations, and
princes, and they became tributary to
him.
5 After this he fell sick and perceived that he was dying. 6 So he summoned his most honored officers, who
had been brought up with him from
youth, and divided his kingdom among
them while he was still alive. 7 And
after Alexander had reigned twelve
years, he died.
8 Then his officers began to rule,
each in his own place. 9 They all put
on crowns after his death, and so did
their sons after them for many years;
and they caused many evils on the
earth.
10 From them came forth a sinful
root, Antiochus Epiphanes, son of
Antiochus the king; he had been a
hostage in Rome. He began to reign

a Gk adds *and he defeated*

1.1–10: Introduction. A summary of history from Alexander to Antiochus IV. **1:** *Alexander* the Great (356–323 B.C.), son of Philip of Macedon, who had conquered *Kittim* (Greece), swept through Asia Minor, and *defeated Darius* III at Issus (333 B.C.) and at Gaugamela (331 B.C.). **3:** After taking Egypt, Mesopotamia, and Persia he advanced to the *ends of the earth* (to Bactria and India). *He was exalted*, i.e. he accepted divine honors. **4:** He planned a universal empire dominated by Greek culture. **5:** *He fell sick* in Babylon. **8–9:** By 275 B.C. three dynasties were established, the Antigonids of Macedonia, the Ptolemies of Egypt, and the Seleucids of Syria. **10:** *Sinful root*, Is.11.10; Dan.11.7. *Antiochus* IV, who took the name

in the one hundred and thirty-seventh
year of the kingdom of the Greeks.[b]
11 In those days lawless men came
forth from Israel, and misled many,
saying, "Let us go and make a covenant with the Gentiles round about
us, for since we separated from them
many evils have come upon us."
12 This proposal pleased them, 13 and
some of the people eagerly went to the
king. He authorized them to observe
the ordinances of the Gentiles. 14 So
they built a gymnasium in Jerusalem,
according to Gentile custom, 15 and
removed the marks of circumcision,
and abandoned the holy covenant.
They joined with the Gentiles and sold
themselves to do evil.
16 When Antiochus saw that his
kingdom was established, he determined to become king of the land of
Egypt, that he might reign over both
kingdoms. 17 So he invaded Egypt with
a strong force, with chariots and
elephants and cavalry and with a large
fleet. 18 He engaged Ptolemy king of
Egypt in battle, and Ptolemy turned
and fled before him, and many were
wounded and fell. 19 And they captured the fortified cities in the land of
Egypt, and he plundered the land of
Egypt.
20 After subduing Egypt, Antiochus
returned in the one hundred and
forty-third year.[c] He went up against
Israel and came to Jerusalem with a
strong force. 21 He arrogantly entered
the sanctuary and took the golden
altar, the lampstand for the light, and
all its utensils. 22 He took also the table
for the bread of the Presence, the cups
for drink offerings, the bowls, the
golden censers, the curtain, the crowns,
and the gold decoration on the front
of the temple; he stripped it all off.
23 He took the silver and the gold, and
the costly vessels; he took also the
hidden treasures which he found.
24 Taking them all, he departed to his
own land.

He committed deeds of murder,
and spoke with great arrogance.
25 Israel mourned deeply in every
community,
26 rulers and elders groaned,
maidens and young men became
faint,
the beauty of the women faded.
27 Every bridegroom took up the
lament;
she who sat in the bridal chamber
was mourning.
28 Even the land shook for its
inhabitants,
and all the house of Jacob was
clothed with shame.

29 Two years later the king sent to
the cities of Judah a chief collector of
tribute, and he came to Jerusalem with
a large force. 30 Deceitfully he spoke
peaceable words to them, and they
believed him; but he suddenly fell upon
the city, dealt it a severe blow, and

b 175 B.C. *c* 169 B.C.

Epiphanes ("god manifest"), reigned 175–164 B.C.; he was *son of Antiochus* III the Great (223–187 B.C.), who had wrested Palestine from Egypt at the battle of Paneas in 198 B.C. but lost most of Asia Minor to Rome at Magnesia in 190 B.C. (compare Dan.11.18). Because of this defeat the son *had been a hostage in Rome. One hundred and thirty-seventh year* of the Seleucid era; reckoning of this era varied in different places; dates given in the margin (notes *b, c*, etc.) are approximate.

1.11–15: The paganizing program. Greek culture had penetrated Palestine peacefully, but now enthusiasts introduced Greek religion (2 Macc.4.11–17). **11:** *Lawless men*, willing to abandon Judaism, led by Jason, whom Antiochus appointed in place of his brother Onias III (2 Macc.4.7). *Evils*, loss of business and prestige because relations with Syria were not close. **14:** *A gymnasium*, see 2 Macc.4.9–10 n.

1.16–40: Antiochus invades Egypt and Palestine. Invasion of Egypt is followed by plundering of the temple in Jerusalem (2 Macc.5.1,11–26). **17:** The Syrian army had *elephants*, though the treaty of Apamea with Rome (188 B.C.) had forbidden this. **18:** *Ptolemy* VI Philometor reigned 180–145 B.C. **20:** *Antiochus returned* because the Roman envoy, Popilius Laenas, threatened him with war if he annexed Egypt. **24–28:** Fragment of a contemporary poem. **28:** *The house*

destroyed many people of Israel. [31]He
plundered the city, burned it with fire,
and tore down its houses and its surrounding walls. [32]And they took captive the women and children, and seized
the cattle. [33]Then they fortified the city
of David with a great strong wall and
strong towers, and it became their
citadel. [34]And they stationed there
a sinful people, lawless men. These
strengthened their position; [35]they
stored up arms and food, and collecting
the spoils of Jerusalem they stored
them there, and became a great snare.

[36]It became an ambush against the
    sanctuary,
  an evil adversary of Israel
    continually.
[37]On every side of the sanctuary
    they shed innocent blood;
  they even defiled the sanctuary.
[38]Because of them the residents of
    Jerusalem fled;
  she became a dwelling of
    strangers;
 she became strange to her
    offspring,
  and her children forsook her.
[39]Her sanctuary became desolate as
    a desert;
  her feasts were turned into
    mourning,
 her sabbaths into a reproach,
  her honor into contempt.
[40]Her dishonor now grew as great as
    her glory;
  her exaltation was turned into
    mourning.

41 Then the king wrote to his whole
kingdom that all should be one people,
[42]and that each should give up his customs. [43]All the Gentiles accepted the
command of the king. Many even
from Israel gladly adopted his religion;
they sacrificed to idols and profaned
the sabbath. [44]And the king sent letters
by messengers to Jerusalem and the
cities of Judah; he directed them to
follow customs strange to the land, [45]to
forbid burnt offerings and sacrifices
and drink offerings in the sanctuary, to
profane sabbaths and feasts, [46]to defile
the sanctuary and the priests, [47]to build
altars and sacred precincts and shrines
for idols, to sacrifice swine and unclean
animals, [48]and to leave their sons uncircumcised. They were to make themselves abominable by everything unclean and profane, [49]so that they should
forget the law and change all the ordinances. [50]"And whoever does not obey
the command of the king shall die."

51 In such words he wrote to his
whole kingdom. And he appointed
inspectors over all the people and commanded the cities of Judah to offer
sacrifice, city by city. [52]Many of the
people, every one who forsook the law,
joined them, and they did evil in the
land; [53]they drove Israel into hiding
in every place of refuge they had.

54 Now on the fifteenth day of
Chislev, in the one hundred and forty-
fifth year,[d] they erected a desolating
sacrilege upon the altar of burnt offering. They also built altars in the surrounding cities of Judah, [55]and burned
incense at the doors of the houses and
in the streets. [56]The books of the law
which they found they tore to pieces
and burned with fire. [57]Where the
book of the covenant was found in the
possession of any one, or if any one
adhered to the law, the decree of the
king condemned him to death. [58]They
kept using violence against Israel,
against those found month after month

d 167 B.C.

of Jacob, Israel, the Jewish people. **33:** *City of David*, the Ophel hill south of the temple area (2 Sam.5.7). **34:** The *sinful people* were irreligious Jews. **36–40:** Poetic fragment (compare Pss.74; 79).

1.41–64: Desecration of the temple. The first outright religious persecution of the Jews, which is also reflected in the book of Daniel (compare 2 Macc. 6.1–11). **41–42:** *His whole kingdom*, Syria, Palestine, Mesopotamia, Persia, and parts of Asia Minor. *One people*, unified in language, religion, culture, and even dress; Judaism, with its revealed law and rejection of other gods, opposed this. **47:** Jews had no *idols* and regarded *swine* as *unclean*. **54:** *Chislev*, approximately December. The *desolating sacrilege* (Dan.11.31; 12.11; 2 Macc.6.2) was an altar to

in the cities. 59 And on the twenty-fifth
day of the month they offered sacrifice
on the altar which was upon the altar
of burnt offering. 60 According to the
decree, they put to death the women
who had their children circumcised,
61 and their families and those who circumcised them; and they hung the
infants from their mothers' necks.

62 But many in Israel stood firm and
were resolved in their hearts not to eat
unclean food. 63 They chose to die
rather than to be defiled by food or to
profane the holy covenant; and they
did die. 64 And very great wrath came
upon Israel.

2 In those days Mattathias the son
of John, son of Simeon, a priest of
the sons of Joarib, moved from Jerusalem and settled in Modein. 2 He had
five sons, John surnamed Gaddi,
3 Simon called Thassi, 4 Judas called
Maccabeus, 5 Eleazar called Avaran,
and Jonathan called Apphus. 6 He saw
the blasphemies being committed in
Judah and Jerusalem, 7 and said,

"Alas! Why was I born to see
 this,
the ruin of my people, the ruin
 of the holy city,
and to dwell there when it was
 given over to the enemy,
the sanctuary given over to
 aliens?
8 Her temple has become like a man
 without honor;[e]
9 her glorious vessels have been
 carried into captivity.
Her babes have been killed in her
 streets,
her youths by the sword of the
 foe.
10 What nation has not inherited her
 palaces[f]
and has not seized her spoils?
11 All her adornment has been taken
 away;
no longer free, she has become
 a slave.
12 And behold, our holy place, our
 beauty,
and our glory have been laid
 waste;
the Gentiles have profaned it.
13 Why should we live any longer?"

14 And Mattathias and his sons rent
their clothes, put on sackcloth, and
mourned greatly.

15 Then the king's officers who were
enforcing the apostasy came to the city
of Modein to make them offer sacrifice.
16 Many from Israel came to them; and
Mattathias and his sons were assembled. 17 Then the king's officers
spoke to Mattathias as follows: "You
are a leader, honored and great in this
city, and supported by sons and brothers. 18 Now be the first to come and do
what the king commands, as all the
Gentiles and the men of Judah and
those that are left in Jerusalem have
done. Then you and your sons will be
numbered among the friends of the
king, and you and your sons will be
honored with silver and gold and many
gifts."

19 But Mattathias answered and
said in a loud voice: "Even if all the
nations that live under the rule of the

e The text of this verse is uncertain
f Other authorities read *has not had a part in her kingdom*

Olympian Zeus and perhaps a statue of him. **59:** *Offered sacrifice*, probably of swine (2 Macc. 6.4–5). **60–64:** 2 Macc. chs. 6–7, and 4 Macc. contain stories of martyrdoms. *Chose to die rather than be defiled by food*, compare Dan.3.8–18. *Wrath came upon Israel*, as a punishment for sin (2 Macc.6.12–16).

2.1–48: Revolt of Mattathias. 1: The family of *Mattathias* is known as Hasmoneans (see p. 295), from a traditional ancestor Hashmonia. *Joarib* was first in the list of divisions of priests (1 Chr.24.7; Neh.11.10). *Modein*, on the road to Beth-horon, about seventeen miles northwest of Jerusalem. **2–5:** *Simon*, third of the family to rule (chs. 13–16). *Maccabeus*, probably from a Hebrew word meaning "hammer." The other surnames are of uncertain derivation. *Jonathan*, successor of Judas (chs. 9–12). **7–13:** Poetic fragment; compare Pss.44; 74; 79; and the book of Lamentations. **14:** *Rent their clothes, put on sackcloth*, signs of mourning (Gen.37.34). **18:** *The friends of the king* were a special class of potentates and courtiers who wore distinctive dress

king obey him, and have chosen to do
his commandments, departing each
one from the religion of his fathers,
20 yet I and my sons and my brothers
will live by the covenant of our fathers.
21 Far be it from us to desert the law
and the ordinances. 22 We will not obey
the king's words by turning aside from
our religion to the right hand or to the
left."

23 When he had finished speaking
these words, a Jew came forward in
the sight of all to offer sacrifice upon
the altar in Modein, according to the
king's command. 24 When Mattathias
saw it, he burned with zeal and his
heart was stirred. He gave vent to
righteous anger; he ran and killed him
upon the altar. 25 At the same time he
killed the king's officer who was forcing
them to sacrifice, and he tore down the
altar. 26 Thus he burned with zeal for
the law, as Phinehas did against Zimri
the son of Salu.

27 Then Mattathias cried out in the
city with a loud voice, saying: "Let
every one who is zealous for the law
and supports the covenant come out
with me!" 28 And he and his sons fled
to the hills and left all that they had
in the city.

29 Then many who were seeking
righteousness and justice went down to
the wilderness to dwell there, 30 they,
their sons, their wives, and their cattle,
because evils pressed heavily upon
them. 31 And it was reported to the
king's officers, and to the troops in
Jerusalem the city of David, that men
who had rejected the king's command
had gone down to the hiding places in
the wilderness. 32 Many pursued them,
and overtook them; they encamped
opposite them and prepared for battle
against them on the sabbath day.
33 And they said to them, "Enough of
this! Come out and do what the king
commands, and you will live." 34 But
they said, "We will not come out, nor
will we do what the king commands
and so profane the sabbath day."
35 Then the enemy[g] hastened to attack
them. 36 But they did not answer them
or hurl a stone at them or block up
their hiding places, 37 for they said,
"Let us all die in our innocence; heaven
and earth testify for us that you are
killing us unjustly." 38 So they attacked
them on the sabbath, and they died,
with their wives and children and cattle,
to the number of a thousand persons.

39 When Mattathias and his friends
learned of it, they mourned for them
deeply. 40 And each said to his neighbor: "If we all do as our brethren have
done and refuse to fight with the
Gentiles for our lives and our ordinances, they will quickly destroy us
from the earth." 41 So they made this
decision that day: "Let us fight against
every man who comes to attack us on
the sabbath day; let us not all die as
our brethren died in their hiding
places."

42 Then there united with them a
company of Hasideans, mighty warriors of Israel, every one who offered
himself willingly for the law. 43 And
all who became fugitives to escape their
troubles joined them and reinforced
them. 44 They organized an army, and
struck down sinners in their anger and
lawless men in their wrath; the survivors fled to the Gentiles for safety.
45 And Mattathias and his friends went
about and tore down the altars; 46 they
forcibly circumcised all the uncircumcised boys that they found within the
borders of Israel. 47 They hunted down

g Gk *they*

---

and insignia. **23:** Elsewhere in chs. 1–13, "man of Israel" is used instead of the term *Jew*, which here perhaps means "Judean." **24:** *His heart*, literally "his kidneys," which were considered the seat of deliberation. **26:** *As Phinehas did*, Num.25.6–15. **28:** 2 Macc.5.27. **29–30:** In *the wilderness* of Judea they found *hiding places* in grottoes and caves (Jg.20.47). **37:** 1.63. **41:** The earliest statement of the principle that one may profane one sabbath in order to keep all the others. **42:** *Hasideans*, "the pious," a group not concerned for Jewish nationalism but only for the religious law. At first they resisted passively (1.62–63; 2.37), but now turned to violent action.

the arrogant men, and the work prospered in their hands. 48They rescued
the law out of the hands of the Gentiles and kings, and they never let the
sinner gain the upper hand.
49 Now the days drew near for
Mattathias to die, and he said to his
sons: "Arrogance and reproach have
now become strong; it is a time of ruin
and furious anger. 50Now, my children,
show zeal for the law, and give your
lives for the covenant of our fathers.
51 "Remember the deeds of the
fathers, which they did in their generations; and receive great honor and
an everlasting name. 52Was not
Abraham found faithful when tested,
and it was reckoned to him as righteousness? 53Joseph in the time of his
distress kept the commandment, and
became lord of Egypt. 54Phinehas our
father, because he was deeply zealous,
received the covenant of everlasting
priesthood. 55Joshua, because he fulfilled the command, became a judge in
Israel. 56Caleb, because he testified in
the assembly, received an inheritance in
the land. 57David, because he was
merciful, inherited the throne of the
kingdom for ever. 58Elijah because of
great zeal for the law was taken up into
heaven. 59Hananiah, Azariah, and
Mishael believed and were saved from
the flame. 60Daniel because of his innocence was delivered from the mouth
of the lions.
61 "And so observe, from generation to generation, that none who put
their trust in him will lack strength.
62Do not fear the words of a sinner, for
his splendor will turn into dung and
worms. 63Today he will be exalted,
but tomorrow he will not be found,
because he has returned to the dust,
and his plans will perish. 64My children, be courageous and grow strong
in the law, for by it you will gain
honor.
65 "Now behold, I know that Simeon
your brother is wise in counsel; always
listen to him; he shall be your father.
66Judas Maccabeus has been a mighty
warrior from his youth; he shall command the army for you and fight the
battle against the peoples.[h] 67You shall
rally about you all who observe the
law, and avenge the wrong done to
your people. 68Pay back the Gentiles
in full, and heed what the law commands."
69 Then he blessed them, and was
gathered to his fathers. 70He died in
the one hundred and forty-sixth year[i]
and was buried in the tomb of his
fathers at Modein. And all Israel
mourned for him with great lamentation.

3 Then Judas his son, who was
called Maccabeus, took command
in his place. 2All his brothers and all
who had joined his father helped him;
they gladly fought for Israel.
3He extended the glory of his people.
Like a giant he put on his
breastplate;
he girded on his armor of war and
waged battles,
protecting the host by his sword.
4He was like a lion in his deeds,
like a lion's cub roaring for
prey.
5He searched out and pursued the
lawless;
he burned those who troubled
his people.
6Lawless men shrank back for fear
of him;
all the evildoers were
confounded;

[h] Or *of the people*
[i] 166 B.C.

2.49–70: Death of Mattathias. 52: *Faithful when tested,* Gen.22.15–18. *Reckoned to him,* Gen.15.6; Rom.4.3. **53:** *Joseph,* Gen. chs. 39–45. **54:** *Phinehas,* v. 26. **55–56:** *Joshua . . . Caleb,* Num.13.1–14.12; 26.65; Jos.1.1–9. **57:** *Merciful,* or perhaps "loyal" (2 Sam.7.16; Pss.89.35–37; 132.11–12). **58:** 2 Kg.2.9–12. **59–60:** Dan.3.8–30; 6.1–24. **63:** Ps.37.10, 35–36. **69:** *Gathered to his fathers,* buried with his ancestors (Jg.2.10).

3.1–12: Defeat of Apollonius. 3–9: From a contemporary poem. **4:** *Like a lion,* Hos.5.14.

and deliverance prospered by his
hand.
7 He embittered many kings,
but he made Jacob glad by his
deeds,
and his memory is blessed for
ever.
8 He went through the cities of
Judah;
he destroyed the ungodly out of
the land;[j]
thus he turned away wrath from
Israel.
9 He was renowned to the ends of the
earth;
he gathered in those who were
perishing.

10 But Apollonius gathered together
Gentiles and a large force from Samaria
to fight against Israel. 11 When Judas
learned of it, he went out to meet him,
and he defeated and killed him. Many
were wounded and fell, and the rest
fled. 12 Then they seized their spoils;
and Judas took the sword of Apollonius, and used it in battle the rest of his
life.

13 Now when Seron, the commander
of the Syrian army, heard that Judas
had gathered a large company, including a body of faithful men who stayed
with him and went out to battle, 14 he
said, "I will make a name for myself
and win honor in the kingdom. I will
make war on Judas and his companions, who scorn the king's command."
15 And again a strong army of ungodly
men went up with him to help him,
to take vengeance on the sons of
Israel.

16 When he approached the ascent
of Beth-horon, Judas went out to meet
him with a small company. 17 But when
they saw the army coming to meet
them, they said to Judas, "How can we,
few as we are, fight against so great and
strong a multitude? And we are faint,
for we have eaten nothing today."
18 Judas replied, "It is easy for many
to be hemmed in by few, for in the
sight of Heaven there is no difference
between saving by many or by few.
19 It is not on the size of the army that
victory in battle depends, but strength
comes from Heaven. 20 They come
against us in great pride and lawlessness
to destroy us and our wives and our
children, and to despoil us; 21 but we
fight for our lives and our laws. 22 He
himself will crush them before us; as
for you, do not be afraid of them."

23 When he finished speaking, he
rushed suddenly against Seron and
his army, and they were crushed before him. 24 They pursued them[k] down
the descent of Beth-horon to the plain;
eight hundred of them fell, and the rest
fled into the land of the Philistines.
25 Then Judas and his brothers began
to be feared, and terror fell upon the
Gentiles round about them. 26 His fame
reached the king, and the Gentiles
talked of the battles of Judas.

27 When King Antiochus heard
these reports, he was greatly angered;
and he sent and gathered all the forces
of his kingdom, a very strong army.
28 And he opened his coffers and gave
a year's pay to his forces, and ordered
them to be ready for any need. 29 Then
he saw that the money in the treasury
was exhausted, and that the revenues
from the country were small because
of the dissension and disaster which he
had caused in the land by abolishing
the laws that had existed from the earli-

j Gk *it*
k Other authorities read *him*

8: *He turned away wrath*, i.e. God's punishment, through his exploits (2 Macc.7.38). **10:** *Apollonius*, according to Josephus (*Antiquities*. XII. v. 5; vii.1), was governor of Samaria.

3.13–26: Battle of Beth-horon. This was Judas' first great victory. **16:** *The ascent of Beth-horon* was a route from the coastal plain to the Judean highlands. The town is about twelve miles northwest of Jerusalem. **18:** The word *Heaven* was used to avoid pronouncing God's name (compare "he himself," v. 22, and see Sus.9 n.). *By many or by few*, 1 Sam.14.6. **24:** *Land of the Philistines*, the coastal plain.

3.27–4.35: Campaigns of Lysias. Antiochus IV goes to Persia; Judas defeats Lysias at Emmaus and Beth-zur. **28:** *Any need* implies that Seleucid power was beginning to decline.

est days. 30 He feared that he might
not have such funds as he had before
for his expenses and for the gifts which
he used to give more lavishly than preceding kings. 31 He was greatly perplexed in mind, and determined to go
to Persia and collect the revenues from
those regions and raise a large fund.
32 He left Lysias, a distinguished
man of royal lineage, in charge of the
king's affairs from the river Euphrates
to the borders of Egypt. 33 Lysias was
also to take care of Antiochus his son
until he returned. 34 And he turned
over to Lysias[l] half of his troops and
the elephants, and gave him orders
about all that he wanted done. As for
the residents of Judea and Jerusalem,
35 Lysias was to send a force against
them to wipe out and destroy the
strength of Israel and the remnant of
Jerusalem; he was to banish the
memory of them from the place, 36 settle
aliens in all their territory, and distribute their land. 37 Then the king
took the remaining half of his troops
and departed from Antioch his capital
in the one hundred and forty-seventh
year.[m] He crossed the Euphrates River
and went through the upper provinces.
38 Lysias chose Ptolemy the son of
Dorymenes, and Nicanor and Gorgias,
mighty men among the friends of the
king, 39 and sent with them forty thousand infantry and seven thousand cavalry to go into the land of Judah and
destroy it, as the king had commanded.
40 So they departed with their entire
force, and when they arrived they
encamped near Emmaus in the plain.
41 When the traders of the region heard
what was said of them, they took silver
and gold in immense amounts, and fetters,[n] and went to the camp to get the
sons of Israel for slaves. And forces
from Syria and the land of the Philistines joined with them.
42 Now Judas and his brothers saw
that misfortunes had increased and
that the forces were encamped in their
territory. They also learned what the
king had commanded to do to the
people to cause their final destruction.
43 But they said to one another, "Let us
repair the destruction of our people,
and fight for our people and the sanctuary." 44 And the congregation assembled to be ready for battle, and to
pray and ask for mercy and compassion.

45 Jerusalem was uninhabited like a
  wilderness;
  not one of her children went in
  or out.
The sanctuary was trampled down,
  and the sons of aliens held the
  citadel;
  it was a lodging place for the
  Gentiles.
Joy was taken from Jacob;
  the flute and the harp ceased to
  play.

46 So they assembled and went to
Mizpah, opposite Jerusalem, because
Israel formerly had a place of prayer
in Mizpah. 47 They fasted that day,
put on sackcloth and sprinkled ashes
on their heads, and rent their clothes.
48 And they opened the book of the law
to inquire into those matters about
which the Gentiles were consulting the
images of their idols. 49 They also
brought the garments of the priesthood
and the first fruits and the tithes, and

l Gk *him* *m* 165 B.C.
n Syr: Gk *slaves*

30: Antiochus was noted for his extravagance (see 2 Macc.4.30 n.). **33:** *Antiochus* V Eupator, *his son*, was only nine years old; he reigned 164–162 B.C. **36:** *Settle aliens*, as the Assyrians had done (2 Kg.17.24). **37:** *Antioch*, modern Antakya, was built by Seleucus I in 300 B.C. and expanded by Antiochus IV. *Upper provinces*, Persia. **38:** *Ptolemy*, known as Macron (2 Macc. 10.12). *Nicanor*, 2 Macc.8.9. *Gorgias*, 2 Macc.10.14. **40:** *Emmaus* (not the Emmaus of Lk.24.13), was about twenty-five miles west of Jerusalem. **41:** Some pro-Syrian Jews joined Antiochus' army. **45:** Compare Ps.74; Is.24.8. **46:** *Mizpah*, perhaps en-Nebi Samwil, seven miles north-west of Jerusalem, but sometimes identified with Tell en-Nasbeh, nine miles north of the city. **48:** They expected guidance from *the book of the law*, the Pentateuch, while the Greeks sought oracles from *their idols*. **49:** *Tithes* were brought to Jerusalem and there distributed (Neh.10.35–

they stirred up the Nazirites who had
completed their days; 50 and they cried
aloud to Heaven, saying,

"What shall we do with these?
Where shall we take them?
51 Thy sanctuary is trampled down
and profaned,
and thy priests mourn in
humiliation.
52 And behold, the Gentiles are
assembled against us to
destroy us;
thou knowest what they plot
against us.
53 How will we be able to withstand
them,
if thou dost not help us?"

54 Then they sounded the trumpets
and gave a loud shout. 55 After this
Judas appointed leaders of the people,
in charge of thousands and hundreds
and fifties and tens. 56 And he said to
those who were building houses, or
were betrothed, or were planting vineyards, or were fainthearted, that each
should return to his home, according to
the law. 57 Then the army marched out
and encamped to the south of Emmaus.

58 And Judas said, "Gird yourselves
and be valiant. Be ready early in the
morning to fight with these Gentiles
who have assembled against us to
destroy us and our sanctuary. 59 It is
better for us to die in battle than to see
the misfortunes of our nation and of
the sanctuary. 60 But as his will in
heaven may be, so he will do."

4 Now Gorgias took five thousand
infantry and a thousand picked
cavalry, and this division moved out
by night 2 to fall upon the camp of the
Jews and attack them suddenly. Men
from the citadel were his guides. 3 But
Judas heard of it, and he and his
mighty men moved out to attack the
king's force in Emmaus 4 while the
division was still absent from the camp.
5 When Gorgias entered the camp of
Judas by night, he found no one there,
so he looked for them in the hills, because he said, "These men are fleeing
from us."

6 At daybreak Judas appeared in the
plain with three thousand men, but
they did not have armor and swords
such as they desired. 7 And they saw
the camp of the Gentiles, strong and
fortified, with cavalry round about it;
and these men were trained in war.
8 But Judas said to the men who were
with him, "Do not fear their numbers
or be afraid when they charge. 9 Remember how our fathers were saved at
the Red Sea, when Pharaoh with his
forces pursued them. 10 And now let
us cry to Heaven, to see whether he
will favor us and remember his
covenant with our fathers and crush
this army before us today. 11 Then all
the Gentiles will know that there is one
who redeems and saves Israel."

12 When the foreigners looked up
and saw them coming against them,
13 they went forth from their camp to
battle. Then the men with Judas blew
their trumpets 14 and engaged in battle.
The Gentiles were crushed and fled into
the plain, 15 and all those in the rear fell
by the sword. They pursued them to
Gazara, and to the plains of Idumea,
and to Azotus and Jamnia; and three
thousand of them fell. 16 Then Judas
and his force turned back from pursuing them, 17 and he said to the people,
"Do not be greedy for plunder, for
there is a battle before us; 18 Gorgias
and his force are near us in the hills.
But stand now against our enemies
and fight them, and afterward seize
the plunder boldly."

19 Just as Judas was finishing this
speech, a detachment appeared, com-

---

38). *Nazirites*, Num.6.1–21. **50–53:** V. 45. **54:** *Trumpets*, to summon the army (Num.10.1–10). **55:** In Moses' day such *leaders* assisted in civic administration (Ex.18.25); here, as in the Essene *War Scroll* from Qumran, they have a military function (2 Macc.8.22–23). **56:** Dt.20.5–8. **4.2:** *Men from the citadel*, Jewish refugees opposed to Judas. **9:** Ex.14.21–29. **15:** The pursuit went in all directions. *Gazara*, or Gezer (Jos.21.21; 1 Kg.9.17), was five miles northwest of Emmaus. *Idumea* was far to the south. *Azotus*, or Ashdod, and *Jamnia*, lay west and southwest. **17–18:** Judas maintained discipline (2 Macc.8.26). **19:** *The hills*, the Judean highland.

ing out of the hills. [20]They saw that
their army[o] had been put to flight, and
that the Jews[o] were burning the camp,
for the smoke that was seen showed
what had happened. [21]When they perceived this they were greatly frightened,
and when they also saw the army of
Judas drawn up in the plain for battle,
[22]they all fled into the land of the
Philistines. [23]Then Judas returned to
plunder the camp, and they seized
much gold and silver, and cloth dyed
blue and sea purple, and great riches.
[24]On their return they sang hymns
and praises to Heaven, for he is good,
for his mercy endures for ever. [25]Thus
Israel had a great deliverance that
day.

26 Those of the foreigners who escaped went and reported to Lysias
all that had happened. [27]When he
heard it, he was perplexed and dis-
couraged, for things had not happened to Israel as he had intended,
nor had they turned out as the king
had commanded him. [28]But the next
year he mustered sixty thousand picked
infantrymen and five thousand cavalry
to subdue them. [29]They came into
Idumea and encamped at Beth-zur,
and Judas met them with ten thousand
men.

30 When he saw that the army was
strong, he prayed, saying, "Blessed art
thou, O Savior of Israel, who didst
crush the attack of the mighty warrior
by the hand of thy servant David, and
didst give the camp of the Philistines
into the hands of Jonathan, the son of
Saul, and of the man who carried his
armor. [31]So do thou hem in this army
by the hand of thy people Israel, and
let them be ashamed of their troops
and their cavalry. [32]Fill them with cowardice; melt the boldness of their
strength; let them tremble in their
destruction. [33]Strike them down with
the sword of those who love thee, and
let all who know thy name praise thee
with hymns."

34 Then both sides attacked, and
there fell of the army of Lysias five
thousand men; they fell in action.[p]
[35]And when Lysias saw the rout of his
troops and observed the boldness
which inspired those of Judas, and
how ready they were either to live or
to die nobly, he departed to Antioch and enlisted mercenaries, to invade Judea again with an even larger
army.

36 Then said Judas and his brothers,
"Behold, our enemies are crushed; let
us go up to cleanse the sanctuary and
dedicate it." [37]So all the army assembled and they went up to Mount
Zion. [38]And they saw the sanctuary
desolate, the altar profaned, and the
gates burned. In the courts they saw
bushes sprung up as in a thicket, or as
on one of the mountains. They saw
also the chambers of the priests in
ruins. [39]Then they rent their clothes,
and mourned with great lamentation,
and sprinkled themselves with ashes.
[40]They fell face down on the ground,
and sounded the signal on the trumpets,
and cried out to Heaven. [41]Then Judas
detailed men to fight against those in
the citadel until he had cleansed the
sanctuary.

42 He chose blameless priests devoted to the law, [43]and they cleansed
the sanctuary and removed the defiled
stones to an unclean place. [44]They
deliberated what to do about the altar
of burnt offering, which had been profaned. [45]And they thought it best to
tear it down, lest it bring reproach upon
them, for the Gentiles had defiled it.

o Gk *they*
p Or *and some fell on the opposite side*

24: *Heaven,* see 3.18 n. **26–35:** The account in 2 Macc.11.1–12 puts the rout of Lysias after the death of Timothy. **28:** *The next year,* perhaps as late as autumn, 164 B.C. **29:** *Beth-zur,* about twenty miles south of Jerusalem on the road to Hebron. Lysias decided to attack Jerusalem from the south. **30–35:** The account in 2 Macc.11.6–15 agrees that Judas won the battle, but states that there was a negotiated peace.

4.36–61: Rededication of the temple. 38: *Chambers of the priests* perhaps surrounded the sanctuary on three sides. **41:** *The citadel* (1.33–35) was occupied by a Syrian garrison until the

So they tore down the altar, 46 and
stored the stones in a convenient place
on the temple hill until there should
come a prophet to tell what to do with
them. 47 Then they took unhewn[q]
stones, as the law directs, and built a
new altar like the former one. 48 They
also rebuilt the sanctuary and the interior of the temple, and consecrated
the courts. 49 They made new holy
vessels, and brought the lampstand,
the altar of incense, and the table into
the temple. 50 Then they burned incense
on the altar and lighted the lamps on
the lampstand, and these gave light in
the temple. 51 They placed the bread
on the table and hung up the curtains.
Thus they finished all the work they
had undertaken.

52 Early in the morning on the
twenty-fifth day of the ninth month,
which is the month of Chislev, in the
one hundred and forty-eighth year,[r]
53 they rose and offered sacrifice, as the
law directs, on the new altar of burnt
offering which they had built. 54 At the
very season and on the very day that
the Gentiles had profaned it, it was
dedicated with songs and harps and
lutes and cymbals. 55 All the people fell
on their faces and worshiped and
blessed Heaven, who had prospered
them. 56 So they celebrated the dedication of the altar for eight days, and
offered burnt offerings with gladness;
they offered a sacrifice of deliverance
and praise. 57 They decorated the front
of the temple with golden crowns and
small shields; they restored the gates
and the chambers for the priests, and
furnished them with doors. 58 There
was very great gladness among the
people, and the reproach of the Gentiles
was removed.

59 Then Judas and his brothers and
all the assembly of Israel determined
that every year at that season the days
of the dedication of the altar should be
observed with gladness and joy for
eight days, beginning with the twenty-
fifth day of the month of Chislev.

60 At that time they fortified Mount
Zion with high walls and strong towers
round about, to keep the Gentiles from
coming and trampling them down as
they had done before. 61 And he
stationed a garrison there to hold it.
He also[s] fortified Beth-zur, so that the
people might have a stronghold that
faced Idumea.

5 When the Gentiles round about
heard that the altar had been built
and the sanctuary dedicated as it was
before, they became very angry, 2 and
they determined to destroy the descendants of Jacob who lived among
them. So they began to kill and destroy
among the people. 3 But Judas made
war on the sons of Esau in Idumea, at
Akrabattene, because they kept lying
in wait for Israel. He dealt them a
heavy blow and humbled them and despoiled them. 4 He also remembered
the wickedness of the sons of Baean,
who were a trap and a snare to the
people and ambushed them on the
highways. 5 They were shut up by him
in their towers; and he encamped
against them, vowed their complete

q Gk *whole*
r 164 B.C.
s Gk adds *to hold it*

---

time of Simon (13.49–52). **46:** Malachi was regarded as the last *prophet;* though such men as John Hyrcanus I and John the Baptist were thought to have prophetic gifts, this was not universally recognized. **47:** Ex.20.25; Dt.27.5–6. **50:** *Burned incense . . . lighted the lamps,* Ex.30:7–8. **51:** *The bread,* of the Presence (Ex.25.30). **52–59:** Judas set the rededication of the temple exactly three years after its pollution (1.54) and three and a half years after Antiochus' capture of Jerusalem (Dan.7.25; but see 2 Macc.10.3). The Hanukkah festival, celebrated *for eight days* like Hezekiah's reconsecration (2 Chr.29.17), commemorates this event.

5.1–68: Campaigns in all directions. Judas now attacked Idumea in the south (vv. 3–5, 65), Ammon and Gilead east of the Jordan (vv. 6–13, 24–51), Galilee in the north (vv. 21–23), and the coastal plain. These events may have occurred after the death of Antiochus IV (6.16). **2:** *Descendants of Jacob,* Israelites or Jews. **3:** *Sons of Esau,* Edomites or Idumeans, south of the Dead Sea. *Akrabattene,* perhaps on the border between Idumea and Judea. **4:** *Baean,*

destruction, and burned with fire their[t]
towers and all who were in them. [6]Then
he crossed over to attack the Ammonites, where he found a strong band
and many people with Timothy as
their leader. [7]He engaged in many
battles with them and they were
crushed before him; he struck them
down. [8]He also took Jazer and its
villages; then he returned to Judea.

9 Now the Gentiles in Gilead gathered together against the Israelites who
lived in their territory, and planned to
destroy them. But they fled to the
stronghold of Dathema, [10]and sent to
Judas and his brothers a letter which
said, "The Gentiles around us have
gathered together against us to destroy
us. [11]They are preparing to come and
capture the stronghold to which we
have fled, and Timothy is leading their
forces. [12]Now then come and rescue us
from their hands, for many of us have
fallen, [13]and all our brethren who were
in the land of Tob have been killed;
the enemy[u] have captured their wives
and children and goods, and have
destroyed about a thousand men
there."

14 While the letter was still being
read, behold, other messengers, with
their garments rent, came from Galilee
and made a similar report; [15]they said
that against them had gathered together men of Ptolemais and Tyre and
Sidon, and all Galilee of the Gentiles,[v]
"to annihilate us." [16]When Judas and
the people heard these messages, a
great assembly was called to determine
what they should do for their brethren
who were in distress and were being
attacked by enemies.[w] [17]Then Judas
said to Simon his brother, "Choose
your men and go and rescue your
brethren in Galilee; I and Jonathan my
brother will go to Gilead." [18]But he
left Joseph, the son of Zechariah, and
Azariah, a leader of the people, with
the rest of the forces, in Judea to guard
it; [19]and he gave them this command,
"Take charge of this people, but do
not engage in battle with the Gentiles
until we return." [20]Then three thousand men were assigned to Simon to go
to Galilee, and eight thousand to
Judas for Gilead.

21 So Simon went to Galilee and
fought many battles against the Gentiles, and the Gentiles were crushed
before him. [22]He pursued them to the
gate of Ptolemais, and as many as three
thousand of the Gentiles fell, and he
despoiled them. [23]Then he took the
Jews[x] of Galilee and Arbatta, with
their wives and children, and all they
possessed, and led them to Judea with
great rejoicing.

24 Judas Maccabeus and Jonathan
his brother crossed the Jordan and
went three days' journey into the
wilderness. [25]They encountered the
Nabateans, who met them peaceably
and told them all that had happened
to their brethren in Gilead: [26]"Many
of them have been shut up in Bozrah
and Bosor, in Alema and Chaspho,
Maked and Carnaim"—all these cities
were strong and large—[27]"and some
have been shut up in the other cities of
Gilead; the enemy[y] are getting ready

t Gk *her*
u Gk *they*
v Gk *aliens*
w Gk *them*
x Gk *those*
y Gk *they*

---

probably in Transjordan (Num.32.3). **6:** *Ammonites*, a Semitic people east of the Jordan near the present Amman. **8:** *Jazer*, west of Amman, fifteen miles north of Heshbon (Num.32.3). **9:** *Gilead*, east of the Jordan between the Yarmuk and the Arnon (Jos.22.9). *Dathema*, possibly el-Hosn, in Gilead opposite Beisan; or Ramtha, now near the Syrian border. **13:** *Land of Tob*, possibly Hippos, twelve miles southeast of the Sea of Galilee (Jg.11.3; 2 Macc.12.17). **15:** *Ptolemais*, or Acco (Jg.1.31), now Acre, north of Haifa on the coast. *Tyre and Sidon*, farther north in Lebanon. As yet few Jews lived in *Galilee of the Gentiles* (Is.9.1; Mt.4.15). **23:** *Arbatta*, either near the Sea of Galilee, or the Arabah depression south of the Dead Sea (Dt.1.7; Jos. 11.16). **25:** *Nabateans*, or Nebaioth (Gen.25.13), an Aramaic-speaking people who occupied the desert east of Palestine as far north as Palmyra. **26:** *Bozrah*, southeast of Dera'a (Is.63.1; Jer.48.24). *Bosor*, Bezer in the desert (Dt.4.43). *Alema*, unidentified. *Chaspho* and *Maked*, cities

to attack the strongholds tomorrow
and take and destroy all these men in
one day."
28 Then Judas and his army quickly
turned back by the wilderness road to
Bozrah; and he took the city, and
killed every male by the edge of the
sword; then he seized all its spoils and
burned it with fire. 29 He departed from
there at night, and they went all the
way to the stronghold of Dathema.[z]
30 At dawn they looked up, and behold,
a large company, that could not be
counted, carrying ladders and engines
of war to capture the stronghold, and
attacking the Jews within.[a] 31 So Judas
saw that the battle had begun and that
the cry of the city went up to Heaven
with trumpets and loud shouts, 32 and
he said to the men of his forces, "Fight
today for your brethren!" 33 Then he
came up behind them in three companies, who sounded their trumpets
and cried aloud in prayer. 34 And when
the army of Timothy realized that it
was Maccabeus, they fled before him,
and he dealt them a heavy blow. As
many as eight thousand of them fell
that day.
35 Next he turned aside to Alema,[b]
and fought against it and took it; and
he killed every male in it, plundered it,
and burned it with fire. 36 From there
he marched on and took Chaspho,
Maked, and Bosor, and the other
cities of Gilead.
37 After these things Timothy gathered another army and encamped opposite Raphon, on the other side of the
stream. 38 Judas sent men to spy out
the camp, and they reported to him,
"All the Gentiles around us have
gathered to him; it is a very large force.
39 They also have hired Arabs to help
them, and they are encamped across
the stream, ready to come and fight
against you." And Judas went to
meet them.
40 Now as Judas and his army drew
near to the stream of water, Timothy
said to the officers of his forces, "If
he crosses over to us first, we will not
be able to resist him, for he will surely
defeat us. 41 But if he shows fear and
camps on the other side of the river,
we will cross over to him and defeat
him." 42 When Judas approached the
stream of water, he stationed the scribes
of the people at the stream and gave
them this command, "Permit no man
to encamp, but make them all enter the
battle." 43 Then he crossed over
against them first, and the whole army
followed him. All the Gentiles were
defeated before him, and they threw
away their arms and fled into the sacred
precincts at Carnaim. 44 But he took
the city and burned the sacred precincts with fire, together with all who
were in them. Thus Carnaim was conquered; they could stand before Judas
no longer.
45 Then Judas gathered together all
the Israelites in Gilead, the small and
the great, with their wives and children
and goods, a very large company, to
go to the land of Judah. 46 So they
came to Ephron. This was a large and
very strong city on the road, and they
could not go around it to the right or
to the left; they had to go through it.
47 But the men of the city shut them out
and blocked up the gates with stones.
48 And Judas sent them this friendly
message, "Let us pass through your
land to get to our land. No one will do
you harm; we will simply pass by on
foot." But they refused to open to him.
49 Then Judas ordered proclamation
made to the army that each should

z Gk lacks *of Dathema.* See verse 9
a Gk *and they were attacking them*
b The name is uncertain

---

of Gilead (v. 36). *Carnaim*, Gen.14.5; Am.6.13; 2 Macc.12.21,26. **28:** *Killed every male*, Gen. 34.25. **37:** *The stream*, a tributary of the Yarmuk. **39:** *Arabs* were not usually hostile to the Jews but could be *hired* as mercenaries. **40–41:** Judas heard Timothy's order or decided to make a surprise attack (compare 1 Sam.14.7–10). **43:** *Sacred precincts*, of Atargatis, the Syrian fish goddess (2 Macc.12.26). **46:** *Ephron*, eight miles east of the Jordan, opposite Beth-shan (v. 52), and west of Irbid (Arbela). **48–51:** Num.21.21–24.

encamp where he was. 50So the men
of the forces encamped, and he fought
against the city all that day and all the
night, and the city was delivered into
his hands. 51He destroyed every male
by the edge of the sword, and razed
and plundered the city. Then he passed
through the city over the slain.

52 And they crossed the Jordan into
the large plain before Beth-shan. 53And
Judas kept rallying the laggards and
encouraging the people all the way till
he came to the land of Judah. 54So
they went up to Mount Zion with gladness and joy, and offered burnt offerings, because not one of them had
fallen before they returned in safety.

55 Now while Judas and Jonathan
were in Gilead and Simon his brother
was in Galilee before Ptolemais,
56Joseph, the son of Zechariah, and
Azariah, the commanders of the forces,
heard of their brave deeds and of the
heroic war they had fought. 57So they
said, "Let us also make a name for
ourselves; let us go and make war on
the Gentiles around us." 58And they
issued orders to the men of the forces
that were with them, and they marched
against Jamnia. 59And Gorgias and his
men came out of the city to meet them
in battle. 60Then Joseph and Azariah
were routed, and were pursued to the
borders of Judea; as many as two
thousand of the people of Israel fell
that day. 61Thus the people suffered a
great rout because, thinking to do a
brave deed, they did not listen to Judas
and his brothers. 62But they did not
belong to the family of those men
through whom deliverance was given
to Israel.

63 The man Judas and his brothers
were greatly honored in all Israel and
among all the Gentiles, wherever their
name was heard. 64Men gathered to
them and praised them.

65 Then Judas and his brothers
went forth and fought the sons of
Esau in the land to the south. He
struck Hebron and its villages and tore
down its strongholds and burned its
towers round about. Then he marched
off to go into the land of the Philistines,
and passed through Marisa.[c] 67On that
day some priests, who wished to do a
brave deed, fell in battle, for they went
out to battle unwisely. 68But Judas
turned aside to Azotus in the land of
the Philistines; he tore down their
altars, and the graven images of their
gods he burned with fire; he plundered
the cities and returned to the land of
Judah.

6 King Antiochus was going through
the upper provinces when he heard
that Elymais in Persia was a city famed
for its wealth in silver and gold. 2Its
temple was very rich, containing golden
shields, breastplates, and weapons left
there by Alexander, the son of Philip,
the Macedonian king who first reigned
over the Greeks. 3So he came and tried
to take the city and plunder it, but he
could not, because his plan became
known to the men of the city 4and they
withstood him in battle. So he fled and
in great grief departed from there to
return to Babylon.

5 Then some one came to him in
Persia and reported that the armies
which had gone into the land of Judah
had been routed; 6that Lysias had gone
first with a strong force, but had turned

c Other authorities read *Samaria*

52: *The large plain*, between the Jordan and Mt. Gilboa. *Beth-shan*, Beisan, about eighteen miles south of the Sea of Galilee (Jg.1.27; 1 Kg.4.12). **58:** *Jamnia*, 4.15. **62:** Only *the family* of the Hasmoneans is regarded as divinely chosen to save Israel. **65:** *Sons of Esau*, Edomites. *Hebron*, the old capital of David, twenty miles south of Jerusalem (Gen.23.2; 2 Sam.2.11). **66:** *Marisa*, or Mareshah (Jos.15.44), near Beit-Jibrin (4.15).

6.1–17: Death of Antiochus IV and accession of Antiochus V (2 Macc. ch. 9). **1:** *The upper provinces*, Persia and Mesopotamia (3.31–37). *Elymais*, biblical Elam or Susiana; but according to 2 Macc. 9.2 the incident occurred in Persepolis. **2:** *Its temple* was that of Nanea (2 Macc. 1.13–16), or Anahita, identified with Artemis. **5:** *In Persia*, perhaps at Ecbatana (2 Macc.9.3). According to Polybius (*History*, XXXI. 11) the king took sick and died at Tabae (perhaps Gabae,

and fled before the Jews;[d] that the
Jews[e] had grown strong from the arms,
supplies, and abundant spoils which
they had taken from the armies they
had cut down; 7that they had torn
down the abomination which he had
erected upon the altar in Jerusalem;
and that they had surrounded the
sanctuary with high walls as before,
and also Beth-zur, his city.
8 When the king heard this news, he
was astounded and badly shaken. He
took to his bed and became sick from
grief, because things had not turned
out for him as he had planned. 9He
lay there for many days, because deep
grief continually gripped him, and he
concluded that he was dying. 10So he
called all his friends and said to them,
"Sleep departs from my eyes and I am
downhearted with worry. 11I said to
myself, 'To what distress I have come!
And into what a great flood I now am
plunged! For I was kind and beloved
in my power.' 12But now I remember
the evils I did in Jerusalem. I seized all
her vessels of silver and gold; and I
sent to destroy the inhabitants of Judah
without good reason. 13I know that
it is because of this that these evils have
come upon me; and behold, I am
perishing of deep grief in a strange
land."
14 Then he called for Philip, one of
his friends, and made him ruler over
all his kingdom. 15He gave him the
crown and his robe and the signet, that
he might guide Antiochus his son and
bring him up to be king. 16Thus
Antiochus the king died there in the
one hundred and forty-ninth year.[f]
17And when Lysias learned that the
king was dead, he set up Antiochus the
king's[g] son to reign. Lysias[h] had
brought him up as a boy, and he
named him Eupator.
18 Now the men in the citadel kept
hemming Israel in around the sanctuary. They were trying in every way to
harm them and strengthen the Gentiles.
19So Judas decided to destroy them,
and assembled all the people to besiege
them. 20They gathered together and
besieged the citadel[i] in the one hundred
and fiftieth year;[j] and he built siege
towers and other engines of war. 21But
some of the garrison escaped from the
siege and some of the ungodly Israelites
joined them. 22They went to the king
and said, "How long will you fail to do
justice and to avenge our brethren?
23We were happy to serve your father,
to live by what he said and to follow
his commands. 24For this reason the
sons of our people besieged the citadel[k]
and became hostile to us; moreover,
they have put to death as many of us
as they have caught, and they have
seized our inheritances. 25And not
against us alone have they stretched
out their hands, but also against all the
lands on their borders. 26And behold,
today they have encamped against the
citadel in Jerusalem to take it; they
have fortified both the sanctuary and
Beth-zur; 27and unless you quickly
prevent them, they will do still greater
things, and you will not be able to stop
them."
28 The king was enraged when he
heard this. He assembled all his
friends, the commanders of his forces
and those in authority.[l] 29And mercenary forces came to him from other

d Gk *them* *e* Gk *they*
f 163 B.C. *g* Gk *his*
h Gk *he* *i* Gk *it* *j* 162 B.C.
k The Greek text underlying *the sons . . . the citadel* is uncertain
l Gk *those over the reins*

modern Isfahan). **7:** *The abomination*, statue of a pagan god. **8–9:** *Deep grief*, perhaps insanity; according to 2 Macc.9.5–12 he was stricken with a loathsome physical malady. **12:** *Her vessels*, Dan.5.2. **14–15:** *Philip . . . ruler*, Lysias, satrap in the west, had previously been given this commission (3.32). *The signet*, a symbol of transfer of authority to the regent. **16:** 2 Macc.11.33 implies that Antiochus IV had died before the restoration of the temple at Jerusalem. **17:** The word *Eupator* means "of a good father."

6.18–54: Attack on the citadel and second battle at Beth-zur. The citadel was equally important to the Syrians and to Judas, for without it the Seleucid monarchy could not maintain sovereignty in Palestine. **21:** *Ungodly*, i.e. pro-Greek. **28–30:** Lysias' second campaign is here

kingdoms and from islands of the seas.
30 The number of his forces was a
hundred thousand foot soldiers, twenty
thousand horsemen, and thirty-two
elephants accustomed to war. 31 They
came through Idumea and encamped
against Beth-zur, and for many days
they fought and built engines of war;
but the Jews[m] sallied out and burned
these with fire, and fought manfully.

32 Then Judas marched away from
the citadel and encamped at Beth-
zechariah, opposite the camp of the
king. 33 Early in the morning the king
rose and took his army by a forced
march along the road to Beth-zechariah,
and his troops made ready for battle
and sounded their trumpets. 34 They
showed the elephants the juice of grapes
and mulberries, to arouse them for
battle. 35 And they distributed the
beasts among the phalanxes; with each
elephant they stationed a thousand
men armed with coats of mail, and with
brass helmets on their heads; and five
hundred picked horsemen were assigned to each beast. 36 These took
their position beforehand wherever the
beast was; wherever it went they went
with it, and they never left it. 37 And
upon the elephants[n] were wooden
towers, strong and covered; they were
fastened upon each beast by special
harness, and upon each were four[o]
armed men who fought from there, and
also its Indian driver. 38 The rest of the
horsemen were stationed on either side,
on the two flanks of the army, to harass
the enemy while being themselves protected by the phalanxes. 39 When the
sun shone upon the shields of gold and
brass, the hills were ablaze with them
and gleamed like flaming torches.

40 Now a part of the king's army
was spread out on the high hills, and
some troops were on the plain, and
they advanced steadily and in good
order. 41 All who heard the noise made
by their multitude, by the marching of
the multitude and the clanking of their
arms, trembled, for the army was very
large and strong. 42 But Judas and his
army advanced to the battle, and six
hundred men of the king's army fell.
43 And Eleazar, called Avaran, saw that
one of the beasts was equipped with
royal armor. It was taller than all the
others, and he supposed that the king
was upon it. 44 So he gave his life to
save his people and to win for himself
an everlasting name. 45 He courageously ran into the midst of the
phalanx to reach it; he killed men right
and left, and they parted before him on
both sides. 46 He got under the elephant, stabbed it from beneath, and
killed it; but it fell to the ground upon
him and there he died. 47 And when the
Jews[p] saw the royal might and the
fierce attack of the forces, they turned
away in flight.

48 The soldiers of the king's army
went up to Jerusalem against them,
and the king encamped in Judea and
at Mount Zion. 49 He made peace with
the men of Beth-zur, and they evacuated the city, because they had no
provisions there to withstand a siege,
since it was a sabbatical year for the
land. 50 So the king took Beth-zur and
stationed a guard there to hold it.
51 Then he encamped before the sanctuary for many days. He set up siege
towers, engines of war to throw fire

m Gk *they* *n* Gk *them*
o Cn: Some authorities read *thirty;* others *thirty-two*
p Gk *they*

---

dated 162 B.C. (v. 20), but in 2 Macc.13.1 a year earlier. **31:** Judas had won the first battle at *Beth-zur* (4.29–34) and had fortified it (4.61). **32:** *Beth-zechariah* was six miles from Beth-zur and ten miles southwest of Jerusalem. **34-35:** *The juice* may have been to simulate blood; but *elephants* were sometimes given wine to madden them. Here the animals were used to force an opening in the ranks. *Phalanxes*, the Greek infantry formation, eight to eighteen men deep, highly disciplined and mobile. The Seleucids could muster twenty thousand of such infantry. **43:** *Eleazar*, brother of Judas (2.5). **48:** *Mount Zion*, south of the temple (1.33). **49:** The garrison was promised immunity if it surrendered. Every seventh year the land had to lie fallow (Ex.23.11; Lev.25.3–7). This *sabbatical year* was apparently 162 B.C. (v. 20) or possibly a year earlier.

and stones, machines to shoot arrows, and catapults. 52 The Jews[q] also made engines of war to match theirs, and fought for many days. 53 But they had no food in storage,[r] because it was the seventh year; those who found safety in Judea from the Gentiles had consumed the last of the stores. 54 Few men were left in the sanctuary, because famine had prevailed over the rest and they had been scattered, each to his own place.

55 Then Lysias heard that Philip, whom King Antiochus while still living had appointed to bring up Antiochus his son to be king, 56 had returned from Persia and Media with the forces that had gone with the king, and that he was trying to seize control of the government. 57 So he quickly gave orders to depart, and said to the king, to the commanders of the forces, and to the men, "We daily grow weaker, our food supply is scant, the place against which we are fighting is strong, and the affairs of the kingdom press urgently upon us. 58 Now then let us come to terms with these men, and make peace with them and with all their nation, 59 and agree to let them live by their laws as they did before; for it was on account of their laws which we abolished that they became angry and did all these things."

60 The speech pleased the king and the commanders, and he sent to the Jews[s] an offer of peace, and they accepted it. 61 So the king and the commanders gave them their oath. On these conditions the Jews[t] evacuated the stronghold. 62 But when the king entered Mount Zion and saw what a strong fortress the place was, he broke the oath he had sworn and gave orders to tear down the wall all around. 63 Then he departed with haste and returned to Antioch. He found Philip in control of the city, but he fought against him, and took the city by force.

7 In the one hundred and fifty-first[u] year Demetrius the son of Seleucus set forth from Rome, sailed with a few men to a city by the sea, and there began to reign. 2 As he was entering the royal palace of his fathers, the army seized Antiochus and Lysias to bring them to him. 3 But when this act became known to him, he said, "Do not let me see their faces!" 4 So the army killed them, and Demetrius took his seat upon the throne of his kingdom.

5 Then there came to him all the lawless and ungodly men of Israel; they were led by Alcimus, who wanted to be high priest. 6 And they brought to the king this accusation against the people: "Judas and his brothers have destroyed all your friends, and have driven us out of our land. 7 Now then send a man whom you trust; let him go and see all the ruin which Judas[v] has brought upon us and upon the land of the king, and let him punish them and all who help them."

q Gk *they*
r Other authorities read *in the sanctuary*
s Gk *them* *t* Gk *they*
u 161 B.C. *v* Gk *he*

6.55–63: Lysias makes peace. The return of Philip caused a diversion; Lysias abandoned the siege and restored Jewish religious rights. **55:** *Philip* had received the symbols of sovereignty (v. 15), though Antiochus IV had previously appointed Lysias. **59:** Judea had generally accepted Seleucid rule until Antiochus IV began his program of hellenization, though there was always a faction engaged in intrigue with Egypt. **62:** Judas had also built a citadel on *Mount Zion*; its wall was now destroyed.

7.1–4: Demetrius I becomes king (2 Macc.14.1–2). **1:** *Demetrius* I Soter (reigned 162–150 B.C.) was *son of Seleucus* IV Philopator, elder brother of Antiochus IV. When Rome demanded hostages (1.10), Antiochus IV was sent to Rome; later when Seleucus became king, his son Demetrius replaced Antiochus. On the latter's death, he vainly petitioned the senate to be released. Subsequently he escaped from Rome with a small group of men and landed in Tripolis, *a city by the sea* (2 Macc.14.1). **2:** *Antiochus*, that is, Antiochus V Eupator (6.17). **3:** *Do not let me see their faces*, a signal for the murder.

7.5–25: Alcimus as high priest. Legitimate high priests were descended from a particular

8 So the king chose Bacchides, one
of the king's friends, governor of the
province Beyond the River; he was a
great man in the kingdom and was
faithful to the king. 9And he sent him,
and with him the ungodly Alcimus,
whom he made high priest; and he
commanded him to take vengeance on
the sons of Israel. 10So they marched
away and came with a large force into
the land of Judah; and he sent messengers to Judas and his brothers with
peaceable but treacherous words. 11But
they paid no attention to their words,
for they saw that they had come with a
large force.

12 Then a group of scribes appeared
in a body before Alcimus and Bacchides to ask for just terms. 13The
Hasideans were the first among the
sons of Israel to seek peace from them,
14for they said, "A priest of the line of
Aaron has come with the army, and
he will not harm us." 15And he spoke
peaceable words to them and swore
this oath to them, "We will not seek to
injure you or your friends." 16So they
trusted him; but he seized sixty of them
and killed them in one day, in accordance with the word which was written,
17"The flesh of thy saints and their
   blood
they poured out round about
   Jerusalem,
and there was none to bury them."
18Then the fear and dread of them fell
upon all the people, for they said,
"There is no truth or justice in them,
for they have violated the agreement
and the oath which they swore."

19 Then Bacchides departed from
Jerusalem and encamped in Beth-zaith.
And he sent and seized many of the
men who had deserted to him,[w] and
some of the people, and killed them and
threw them into the great pit. 20He
placed Alcimus in charge of the country
and left with him a force to help him;
then Bacchides went back to the king.

21 Alcimus strove for the high
priesthood, 22and all who were troubling their people joined him. They
gained control of the land of Judah
and did great damage in Israel. 23And
Judas saw all the evil that Alcimus and
those with him had done among the
sons of Israel; it was more than the
Gentiles had done. 24So Judas[x] went
out into all the surrounding parts of
Judea, and took vengeance on the men
who had deserted, and he prevented
those in the city[y] from going out into
the country. 25When Alcimus saw that
Judas and those with him had grown
strong, and realized that he could not
withstand them, he returned to the
king and brought wicked charges
against them.

26 Then the king sent Nicanor, one
of his honored princes, who hated and
detested Israel, and he commanded
him to destroy the people. 27So
Nicanor came to Jerusalem with a large
force, and treacherously sent to Judas
and his brothers this peaceable message, 28"Let there be no fighting between me and you; I shall come with
a few men to see you face to face in

w Or *many of his men who had deserted*
x Gk *he*
y Gk *they were prevented*

family. Antiochus IV appointed Jason in place of his brother Onias III (2 Macc.4.7); Jason was in turn supplanted by Menelaus (2 Macc.4.23–26), who was put to death about 162 B.C., after having officiated for ten years (2 Macc.13.1–8). Either Onias III or his son Onias IV, last legitimate claimant, fled to Egypt and established a temple at Heliopolis (Cairo). *Alcimus*, or Jakim (2 Macc.14.3), was not a member of the high-priestly family; he belonged to the hellenizing faction and was willing to further Demetrius' plans. **8:** *Beyond the River*, the province west of the Euphrates (Ezra 4.11). **12–14:** *The Hasideans* (2.42), probably the same as the *group of scribes*, had no political ambitions and were content to live under Syrian rule if they were permitted to keep the Mosaic law. **17:** Ps.79.2–3. All ancients regarded an unburied dead body with horror, and to leave foes unburied was the ultimate outrage. **19:** *Beth-zaith*, perhaps three miles north of Beth-zur; or Bezetha, north of the temple area in Jerusalem.

7.26–50: Defeat of Nicanor. The last of Judas' great victories (2 Macc.14.12–15.36). **26:** According to Josephus (*Antiquities*, XII. X. 4), *Nicanor* was one of the men who had escaped from

peace." 29So he came to Judas, and
they greeted one another peaceably.
But the enemy were ready to seize
Judas. 30It became known to Judas
that Nicanor[x] had come to him with
treacherous intent, and he was afraid
of him and would not meet him again.
31When Nicanor learned that his plan
had been disclosed, he went out to
meet Judas in battle near Caphar-
salama. 32About five hundred men of
the army of Nicanor fell, and the rest[z]
fled into the city of David.

33 After these events Nicanor went
up to Mount Zion. Some of the priests
came out of the sanctuary, and some
of the elders of the people, to greet him
peaceably and to show him the burnt
offering that was being offered for the
king. 34But he mocked them and
derided them and defiled them and
spoke arrogantly, 35and in anger he
swore this oath, "Unless Judas and his
army are delivered into my hands this
time, then if I return safely I will burn
up this house." And he went out in
great anger. 36Then the priests went in
and stood before the altar and the
temple, and they wept and said,

37"Thou didst choose this house to
 be called by thy name,
 and to be for thy people a house
 of prayer and supplication.
38Take vengeance on this man and
 on his army,
 and let them fall by the sword;
remember their blasphemies,
 and let them live no longer."

39 Now Nicanor went out from
Jerusalem and encamped in Beth-
horon, and the Syrian army joined
him. 40And Judas encamped in Adasa
with three thousand men. Then Judas
prayed and said, 41"When the messengers from the king spoke blasphemy,
thy angel went forth and struck down
one hundred and eighty-five thousand
of the Assyrians.[a] 42So also crush this
army before us today; let the rest learn
that Nicanor[b] has spoken wickedly
against thy sanctuary, and judge him
according to this wickedness." 43So
the armies met in battle on the thirteenth day of the month of Adar. The
army of Nicanor was crushed, and he
himself was the first to fall in the battle.
44When his army saw that Nicanor had
fallen, they threw down their arms and
fled. 45The Jews[c] pursued them a day's
journey, from Adasa as far as Gazara,
and as they followed kept sounding
the battle call on the trumpets. 46And
men came out of all the villages of
Judea round about, and they out-
flanked the enemy[d] and drove them
back to their pursuers,[e] so that they all
fell by the sword; not even one of them
was left. 47Then the Jews[f] seized the
spoils and the plunder, and they cut
off Nicanor's head and the right hand
which he had so arrogantly stretched
out, and brought them and displayed
them just outside of Jerusalem. 48The
people rejoiced greatly and celebrated
that day as a day of great gladness.
49And they decreed that this day
should be celebrated each year on the
thirteenth day of Adar. 50So the land
of Judah had rest for a few days.

8 Now Judas heard of the fame of
the Romans, that they were very

x Gk *he* z Gk *they*
a Gk *of them* b Gk *he* c Gk *they*
d Gk *them* e Gk *these* f Gk *they*

Rome with Demetrius (see 7.1 n.). **30:** Judas never trusted the Syrians (vv. 10–11). **31:** *Caphar-salama,* perhaps Khirbet Deir Sellam, about five miles northeast of Jerusalem. **33:** The Jews customarily offered sacrifices to God for the welfare of their rulers. **37–38:** Compare 1 Kg.8.29,43; Pss.68.16; 87.1–2. **40:** *Adasa,* about seven miles from Beth-horon on the road to Jerusalem. **41:** 2 Kg.19.35. **43:** *Adar,* roughly March, in 161 B.C. (see 2 Macc.15.36 n.). **45:** *Gazara,* Gezer (4.15). **47:** *Head . . . right hand,* in punishment for blasphemy and for raising his hand against the temple (2 Macc.15.32). **49:** 2 Macc.15.36. This festival, which came to be called Nicanor Day, was one of the days on which the Jews prohibited mourning (compare 13.52).

8.1–32: Treaty with Rome. The author of 1 Maccabees emphasizes friendly relations between Rome and the Jews because the Romans checked the ambitions of the Seleucids. After 190 B.C. Rome steadily increased her influence in the Near East and Syrian power declined. **1:** *The*

strong and were well-disposed toward all who made an alliance with them, that they pledged friendship to those who came to them, 2and that they were very strong. Men told him of their wars and of the brave deeds which they were doing among the Gauls, how they had defeated them and forced them to pay tribute, 3and what they had done in the land of Spain to get control of the silver and gold mines there, 4and how they had gained control of the whole region by their planning and patience, even though the place was far distant from them. They also subdued the kings who came against them from the ends of the earth, until they crushed them and inflicted great disaster upon them; the rest paid them tribute every year. 5Philip, and Perseus king of the Macedonians,[g] and the others who rose up against them, they crushed in battle and conquered. 6They also defeated Antiochus the Great, king of Asia, who went to fight against them with a hundred and twenty elephants and with cavalry and chariots and a very large army. He was crushed by them; 7they took him alive and decreed that he and those who should reign after him should pay a heavy tribute and give hostages and surrender some of their best provinces, 8the country of India and Media and Lydia. These they took from him and gave to Eumenes the king. 9The Greeks planned to come and destroy them, 10but this became known to them, and they sent a general against the Greeks[h] and attacked them. Many of them were wounded and fell, and the Romans[i] took captive their wives and children; they plundered them, conquered the land, tore down their strongholds, and enslaved them to this day. 11The remaining kingdoms and islands, as many as ever opposed them, they destroyed and enslaved; 12but with their friends and those who rely on them they have kept friendship. They have subdued kings far and near, and as many as have heard of their fame have feared them. 13Those whom they wish to help and to make kings, they make kings, and those whom they wish they depose; and they have been greatly exalted. 14Yet for all this not one of them has put on a crown or worn purple as a mark of pride, 15but they have built for themselves a senate chamber, and every day three hundred and twenty senators constantly deliberate concerning the people, to govern them well. 16They trust one man each year to rule over them and to control all their land; they all heed the one man, and there is no envy or jealousy among them.

17 So Judas chose Eupolemus the son of John, son of Accos, and Jason the son of Eleazar, and sent them to Rome to establish friendship and alliance, 18and to free themselves from the yoke; for they saw that the kingdom of the Greeks was completely enslaving Israel. 19They went to Rome, a very long journey; and they entered the

g Or *Kittim* *h* Gk *them* *i* Gk *they*

Romans had made *an alliance* with kings in Asia Minor and Egypt. **2:** Two nations of *Gauls* were *defeated*, those of upper Italy in 190 B.C., and the Galatians of Asia Minor in 189 B.C. **3–4:** Rome conquered the Carthaginian colonies of *Spain*, not *the whole region*, in the Second Punic War. **5:** *Philip*, defeated at Cynoscephalae in 197 B.C.; *Perseus*, his son, last Macedonian king, beaten at Pydna in 168 B.C. **6–8:** *Antiochus* was not captured, but had to *give hostages* (7.1). *India* was not part of his domain; he kept *Media*, but he surrendered *Lydia* and other parts of Asia Minor. *Eumenes* II of Pergamum was given much of Seleucid Asia Minor. **9:** *The Greeks*, possibly the Macedonians (v. 5), or the Achaean league somewhat later. **12:** This is the estimate of a partisan; it is not true that they always *kept friendship*. **14:** *A crown*, Rome wanted no king, but magistrates, senators, and knights wore *purple* borders on their garments. **15:** *Every day*, actually senate meetings were held three times a month, and on the festivals. **16:** *One man*, in reality there were two consuls, and *envy and jealousy* were constant. The author of 1 Maccabees idealizes the Romans because their republican institutions were congenial to the Jews. **17:** *Eupolemus*, 2 Macc.4.11. *Accos*, a priestly family (Ezra 2.61).

senate chamber and spoke as follows:
20 “Judas, who is also called Maccabeus,
and his brothers and the people of the
Jews have sent us to you to establish
alliance and peace with you, that we
may be enrolled as your allies and
friends.” 21 The proposal pleased them,
22 and this is a copy of the letter which
they wrote in reply, on bronze tablets,
and sent to Jerusalem to remain with
them there as a memorial of peace and
alliance:

23 “May all go well with the Romans
and with the nation of the Jews at sea
and on land for ever, and may sword
and enemy be far from them. 24 If war
comes first to Rome or to any of their
allies in all their dominion, 25 the nation
of the Jews shall act as their allies
wholeheartedly, as the occasion may
indicate to them. 26 And to the enemy
who makes war they shall not give or
supply grain, arms, money, or ships, as
Rome has decided; and they shall keep
their obligations without receiving any
return. 27 In the same way, if war comes
first to the nation of the Jews, the
Romans shall willingly act as their
allies, as the occasion may indicate to
them. 28 And to the enemy allies shall
be given no grain, arms, money, or
ships, as Rome has decided; and they
shall keep these obligations and do so
without deceit. 29 Thus on these terms
the Romans make a treaty with the
Jewish people. 30 If after these terms
are in effect both parties shall determine to add or delete anything, they
shall do so at their discretion, and any
addition or deletion that they may
make shall be valid.

31 “And concerning the wrongs
which King Demetrius is doing to them
we have written to him as follows,
‘Why have you made your yoke heavy
upon our friends and allies the Jews?
32 If now they appeal again for help
against you, we will defend their rights
and fight you on sea and on land.’ ”

9 When Demetrius heard that Nicanor and his army had fallen in
battle, he sent Bacchides and Alcimus
into the land of Judah a second time,
and with them the right wing of the
army. 2 They went by the road which
leads to Gilgal and encamped against
Mesaloth in Arbela, and they took it
and killed many people. 3 In the first
month of the one hundred and fifty-
second year[j] they encamped against
Jerusalem; 4 then they marched off and
went to Berea with twenty thousand
foot soldiers and two thousand cavalry.

5 Now Judas was encamped in
Elasa, and with him were three thousand picked men. 6 When they saw the
huge number of the enemy forces, they
were greatly frightened, and many
slipped away from the camp, until no
more than eight hundred of them were
left.

7 When Judas saw that his army had
slipped away and the battle was imminent, he was crushed in spirit, for
he had no time to assemble them. 8 He
became faint, but he said to those who
were left, “Let us rise and go up against
our enemies. We may be able to fight
them.” 9 But they tried to dissuade him,
saying, “We are not able. Let us rather

j 160 B.C.

22: Important documents were often inscribed *on bronze tablets.* **23–30:** The treaty letter begins with the conventional formula and is drawn up as though the two parties were equals, and Judea a sovereign state. **31–32:** This postscript was not part of the treaty, and is correctly omitted from it by Josephus (*Antiquities*, XII. x. 6); there is no evidence that the Romans helped Judas against Demetrius.

9.1–22: Death of Judas. Continual Syrian pressure weakened Judas' forces, which were a guerrilla band facing a highly organized army. Judas decided that it was better to fall in battle than to withdraw. **1–2:** *Bacchides*, 7.8. *Alcimus*, see 7.5 n. Josephus (*Antiquities*, XII. xi. 1) says that they started from Antioch, camped at Arbela in Galilee (not *Gilgal*), besieged refugees in the caves, and went on toward Jerusalem. *Mesaloth*, perhaps the Hebrew word for “steps,” i.e. ascents to *Arbela*. **4:** *Berea*, perhaps el-Bireh, opposite Ramallah, ten miles north of Jerusalem. **5:** *Elasa* has not been identified.

save our own lives now, and let us come
back with our brethren and fight them;
we are too few." [10]But Judas said,
"Far be it from us to do such a thing as
to flee from them. If our time has
come, let us die bravely for our
brethren, and leave no cause to question our honor."

11 Then the army of Bacchides[k]
marched out from the camp and took
its stand for the encounter. The cavalry was divided into two companies,
and the slingers and the archers went
ahead of the army, as did all the chief
warriors. [12]Bacchides was on the right
wing. Flanked by the two companies,
the phalanx advanced to the sound of
the trumpets; and the men with Judas
also blew their trumpets. [13]The earth
was shaken by the noise of the armies,
and the battle raged from morning till
evening.

14 Judas saw that Bacchides and the
strength of his army were on the right;
then all the stouthearted men went
with him, [15]and they crushed the right
wing, and he pursued them as far as
Mount Azotus. [16]When those on the
left wing saw that the right wing was
crushed, they turned and followed close
behind Judas and his men. [17]The battle
became desperate, and many on both
sides were wounded and fell. [18]Judas
also fell, and the rest fled.

19 Then Jonathan and Simon took
Judas their brother and buried him in
the tomb of their fathers at Modein,
[20]and wept for him. And all Israel
made great lamentation for him; they
mourned many days and said,
[21]"How is the mighty fallen,
the savior of Israel!"

[22]Now the rest of the acts of Judas,
and his wars and the brave deeds that
he did, and his greatness, have not
been recorded, for they were very
many.

23 After the death of Judas, the lawless emerged in all parts of Israel;
all the doers of injustice appeared.
[24]In those days a very great famine
occurred, and the country deserted
with them to the enemy. [25]And
Bacchides chose the ungodly and put
them in charge of the country. [26]They
sought and searched for the friends of
Judas, and brought them to Bacchides,
and he took vengeance on them and
made sport of them. [27]Thus there was
great distress in Israel, such as had not
been since the time that prophets
ceased to appear among them.

28 Then all the friends of Judas
assembled and said to Jonathan,
[29]"Since the death of your brother
Judas there has been no one like him
to go against our enemies and Bacchides, and to deal with those of our
nation who hate us. [30]So now we have
chosen you today to take his place as
our ruler and leader, to fight our
battle." [31]And Jonathan at that time
accepted the leadership and took the
place of Judas his brother.

32 When Bacchides learned of this,
he tried to kill him. [33]But Jonathan
and Simon his brother and all who were
with him heard of it, and they fled into
the wilderness of Tekoa and camped by
the water of the pool of Asphar. [34]Bac-
chides found this out on the sabbath
day, and he with all his army crossed
the Jordan.

k Gk *the army*

15: *Mount Azotus*, perhaps el-'Asur, six miles northeast of el-Bireh; Ashdod (4.15) is too far away. **19:** *Modein*, 2.1, 70; 13.27–30. **21:** 2 Sam.1.19. **22:** The expression *Now the rest of the acts* imitates the style of Hebrew chronicles (1 Kg.11.41).

9.23–73: Jonathan becomes leader and defeats Bacchides. **23:** *The lawless*, i.e. the pro-Syrian element. **24:** *The country*, the majority of the nation, or perhaps the rural population; resistance now seemed futile. **25:** *The ungodly*, i.e. hellenized Jews. **27:** *Prophets ceased*, see 4.46 n. **31:** *We have chosen you*, Judas was self-appointed, but *Jonathan* was elected by his peers; he became leader about 160 or 159 B.C. and high priest in 152 (10.21). **33:** *Tekoa*, five miles southeast of Bethlehem (Am. 1.1); *the wilderness* reached from here to the Dead Sea. *The pool of Asphar* may be three miles south of Tekoa. **34:** *Bacchides* thought the Jews might be surprised *on the sabbath day*. He apparently came from Jerusalem, *crossed the Jordan*, and camped on the east

35 And Jonathan[l] sent his brother
as leader of the multitude and begged
the Nabateans, who were his friends,
for permission to store with them the
great amount of baggage which they
had. 36But the sons of Jambri from
Medeba came out and seized John and
all that he had, and departed with it.
37 After these things it was reported
to Jonathan and Simon his brother,
"The sons of Jambri are celebrating a
great wedding, and are conducting the
bride, a daughter of one of the great
nobles of Canaan, from Nadabath with
a large escort." 38And they remembered the blood of John their brother,
and went up and hid under cover of the
mountain. 39They raised their eyes and
looked, and saw a tumultuous procession with much baggage; and the
bridegroom came out with his friends
and his brothers to meet them with
tambourines and musicians and many
weapons. 40Then they rushed upon
them from the ambush and began
killing them. Many were wounded and
fell, and the rest fled to the mountain;
and they took all their goods. 41Thus
the wedding was turned into mourning
and the voice of their musicians into a
funeral dirge. 42And when they had
fully avenged the blood of their brother,
they returned to the marshes of the
Jordan.
43 When Bacchides heard of this,
he came with a large force on the sabbath day to the banks of the Jordan.
44And Jonathan said to those with him,
"Let us rise up now and fight for our
lives, for today things are not as they
were before. 45For look! the battle is
in front of us and behind us; the water
of the Jordan is on this side and on
that, with marsh and thicket; there is
no place to turn. 46Cry out now to
Heaven that you may be delivered from
the hands of our enemies." 47So the
battle began, and Jonathan stretched
out his hand to strike Bacchides, but
he eluded him and went to the rear.
48Then Jonathan and the men with him
leaped into the Jordan and swam across
to the other side, and the enemy[m] did
not cross the Jordan to attack them.
49And about one thousand of Bacchides' men fell that day.
50 Bacchides[n] then returned to Jerusalem and built strong cities in Judea:
the fortress in Jericho, and Emmaus,
and Beth-horon, and Bethel, and Timnath, and[o] Pharathon, and Tephon,
with high walls and gates and bars.
51And he placed garrisons in them to
harass Israel. 52He also fortified the
city of Beth-zur, and Gazara, and the
citadel, and in them he put troops and
stores of food. 53And he took the sons
of the leading men of the land as
hostages and put them under guard in
the citadel at Jerusalem.
54 In the one hundred and fifty-
third year,[p] in the second month,
Alcimus gave orders to tear down the
wall of the inner court of the sanctuary.
He tore down the work of the prophets!
55But he only began to tear it down, for
at that time Alcimus was stricken and
his work was hindered; his mouth was
stopped and he was paralyzed, so that
he could no longer say a word or
give commands concerning his house.

l Gk *he*
m Gk *they* *n* Gk *he*
o Some authorities omit *and*
p 159 B.C.

side. **35:** *His brother*, John (v. 36; 2.2). *The Nabateans*, see 5.25 n. **36:** *Sons of Jambri*, evidently a Nabatean tribe. *Medeba* or Madeba, twelve miles southeast of the north end of the Dead Sea. **37:** *Nadabath*, perhaps Nebo, a little north of Medeba (Num.33.47; Dt.32.49). **38:** *Blood of John*, the sequel to v. 36 was the murder of John and all his companions (Josephus, *Antiquities*, XIII. i. 2). **45:** The Jews were apparently on the east side of the Jordan, between the river and the Syrian forces. **50–53:** Bacchides established forces and garrisons to prevent guerrilla operations. *Emmaus*, see 3.40 n. *Beth-horon*, see 3.16 n. *Bethel*, now Beitin, about twelve miles north of Jerusalem. *Timnath*, perhaps twelve miles northwest of Bethel. *Pharathon*, six miles southwest of Shechem or Nablus. *Tephon*, Tappuah, twenty-five miles north of Jerusalem. *Beth-zur*, see 4.29 n. *Gazara*, see 4.15 n. **54:** *The wall of the inner court* separated this part from the rest of the temple mount, which was open to Gentiles. Pagans were now to have access to *the sanctuary*.

56 And Alcimus died at that time in
great agony. 57 When Bacchides saw
that Alcimus was dead, he returned to
the king, and the land of Judah had
rest for two years.
58 Then all the lawless plotted and
said, "See! Jonathan and his men are
living in quiet and confidence. So now
let us bring Bacchides back, and he will
capture them all in one night." 59 And
they went and consulted with him.
60 He started to come with a large force,
and secretly sent letters to all his allies
in Judea, telling them to seize Jonathan
and his men; but they were unable to
do it, because their plan became known.
61 And Jonathan's men[q] seized about
fifty of the men of the country who
were leaders in this treachery, and
killed them.
62 Then Jonathan with his men, and
Simon, withdrew to Bethbasi in the
wilderness; he rebuilt the parts of it
that had been demolished, and they
fortified it. 63 When Bacchides learned
of this, he assembled all his forces, and
sent orders to the men of Judea.
64 Then he came and encamped against
Bethbasi; he fought against it for many
days and made machines of war.
65 But Jonathan left Simon his
brother in the city, while he went out
into the country; and he went with
only a few men. 66 He struck down
Odomera and his brothers and the sons
of Phasiron in their tents. 67 Then he[r]
began to attack and went into battle
with his forces; and Simon and his
men sallied out from the city and set
fire to the machines of war. 68 They
fought with Bacchides, and he was
crushed by them. They distressed him
greatly, for his plan and his expedition
had been in vain. 69 So he was greatly
enraged at the lawless men who had
counseled him to come into the country, and he killed many of them. Then
he decided to depart to his own land.
70 When Jonathan learned of this,
he sent ambassadors to him to make
peace with him and obtain release of
the captives. 71 He agreed, and did as
he said; and he swore to Jonathan[s] that
he would not try to harm him as long
as he lived. 72 He restored to him the
captives whom he had formerly taken
from the land of Judah; then he turned
and departed to his own land, and
came no more into their territory.
73 Thus the sword ceased from Israel.
And Jonathan dwelt in Michmash.
And Jonathan began to judge the
people, and he destroyed the ungodly
out of Israel.

10 In the one hundred and sixtieth
year[t] Alexander Epiphanes, the
son of Antiochus, landed and occupied
Ptolemais. They welcomed him, and
there he began to reign. 2 When
Demetrius the king heard of it, he
assembled a very large army and
marched out to meet him in battle.
3 And Demetrius sent Jonathan a letter
in peaceable words to honor him; 4 for
he said, "Let us act first to make peace
with him[u] before he makes peace with
Alexander against us, 5 for he will re-

q Gk *they* *r* Other authorities read *they*
s Gk *him* *t* 152 B.C.
u Gk *them*

The prophets, Haggai and Zechariah had built the second temple. **56:** *Alcimus* had been high priest for about two years (7.5). **57:** *He returned*, believing that with the fortresses garrisoned the situation was stable; his departure gave Jonathan a free hand. **61:** *Fifty . . . leaders*, probably the hellenizers (see v. 25 n.). **62:** *Bethbasi*, perhaps Khirbet Beit-Bassa, about three miles northeast of Tekoa. **66:** *Odomera . . . sons of Phasiron*, probably bedouin sheikhs. **68:** *He was crushed*, for Simon attacked by surprise and *Bacchides* had depended heavily on the war machines (v. 67). **72:** Josephus says that there was an exchange of prisoners (*Antiquities*, XIII. i. 6). **73:** *Thus the sword ceased*, for about seven years, until the events of 10.69. *Michmash*, now Mukhmas, eight miles northeast of Jerusalem (1 Sam.14.5–23). *To judge the people*, as a natural leader, like Samuel and those in the book of Judges.

10.1–21: Alexander Balas appoints Jonathan high priest. 1: *Alexander* I *Epiphanes*, who came from Ephesus and whose given name was Balas (or Ba'al), posed as *the son of Antiochus* IV. He claimed the kingship from 150 B.C. onward, and reigned until about 145. Attalus II of Perga-

member all the wrongs which we did to
him and to his brothers and his nation."
[6]So Demetrius[v] gave him authority to
recruit troops, to equip them with arms,
and to become his ally; and he commanded that the hostages in the citadel
should be released to him.
7 Then Jonathan came to Jerusalem
and read the letter in the hearing of all
the people and of the men in the citadel. [8]They were greatly alarmed when
they heard that the king had given him
authority to recruit troops. [9]But the
men in the citadel released the hostages
to Jonathan, and he returned them to
their parents.
10 And Jonathan dwelt in Jerusalem
and began to rebuild and restore the
city. [11]He directed those who were
doing the work to build the walls and
encircle Mount Zion with squared
stones, for better fortification; and
they did so.
12 Then the foreigners who were in
the strongholds that Bacchides had
built fled; [13]each left his place and
departed to his own land. [14]Only in
Beth-zur did some remain who had
forsaken the law and the commandments, for it served as a place of
refuge.
15 Now Alexander the king heard
of all the promises which Demetrius
had sent to Jonathan, and men told
him of the battles that Jonathan[w] and
his brothers had fought, of the brave
deeds that they had done, and of the
troubles that they had endured. [16]So
he said, "Shall we find another such
man? Come now, we will make him
our friend and ally." [17]And he wrote a
letter and sent it to him, in the following words:
18 "King Alexander to his brother
Jonathan, greeting. [19]We have heard
about you, that you are a mighty
warrior and worthy to be our friend.
[20]And so we have appointed you today to be the high priest of your nation; you are to be called the king's
friend" (and he sent him a purple robe
and a golden crown) "and you are to
take our side and keep friendship with
us."
21 So Jonathan put on the holy
garments in the seventh month of the
one hundred and sixtieth year,[x] at the
feast of tabernacles, and he recruited
troops and equipped them with arms
in abundance. [22]When Demetrius
heard of these things he was grieved
and said, [23]"What is this that we have
done? Alexander has gotten ahead of
us in forming a friendship with the
Jews to strengthen himself. [24]I also
will write them words of encouragement and promise them honor and
gifts, that I may have their help." [25]So
he sent a message to them in the following words:
"King Demetrius to the nation of
the Jews, greeting. [26]Since you have
kept your agreement with us and have
continued your friendship with us, and
have not sided with our enemies, we
have heard of it and rejoiced. [27]And
now continue still to keep faith with us,
and we will repay you with good for
what you do for us. [28]We will grant
you many immunities and give you
gifts.

v Gk *he* *w* Gk *he* *x* 152 B.C.

---

mum and Ptolemy VI persuaded the Roman senate to recognize him. **6:** *Gave him authority*, as a local prince or governor, but not independence. *The hostages*, 9.53. The Syrians held the citadel at Jerusalem. **10:** *Jonathan* now left Michmash. **11:** Lysias had ordered the wall of the Jewish fortress torn down (6.62). **14:** *Some*, i.e. hellenized Jews opposed to the Hasmoneans. **18–20:** *Alexander*, hearing of Demetrius' letter, decided to outbid him. Until the time of Antiochus IV, the hereditary high priest had been confirmed but not appointed by the ruler; now Alexander appointed Jonathan and made him one of his friends (see 2.18 n.); the Jews had not elected him. **21:** *The holy garments*, Ex.28.1–39; 39:1–26. *Tabernacles*, a seven day festival held in September (Lev.23.33–43), had come to be associated with the hope of victory over the Gentiles (Zech.14.16–19).

10.22–50: Demetrius' offer to the Jews; his defeat. 25: The letter was addressed *to the nation*, ignoring Jonathan. Demetrius thought that he could drive a wedge between leader and people.

29 "And now I free you and exempt
all the Jews from payment of tribute
and salt tax and crown levies, 30 and
instead of collecting the third of the
grain and the half of the fruit of the
trees that I should receive, I release
them from this day and henceforth.
I will not collect them from the land
of Judah or from the three districts
added to it from Samaria and Galilee,
from this day and for all time. 31 And
let Jerusalem and her environs, her
tithes and her revenues, be holy and
free from tax. 32 I release also my control of the citadel in Jerusalem and give
it to the high priest, that he may station
in it men of his own choice to guard it.
33 And every one of the Jews taken as
a captive from the land of Judah into any part of my kingdom, I set free
without payment; and let all officials
cancel also the taxes on their cattle.

34 "And all the feasts and sabbaths
and new moons and appointed days,
and the three days before a feast and
the three after a feast—let them all be
days of immunity and release for all
the Jews who are in my kingdom. 35 No
one shall have authority to exact anything from them or annoy any of them
about any matter.

36 "Let Jews be enrolled in the
king's forces to the number of thirty
thousand men, and let the maintenance
be given them that is due to all the
forces of the king. 37 Let some of them
be stationed in the great strongholds
of the king, and let some of them be
put in positions of trust in the kingdom.
Let their officers and leaders be of their
own number, and let them live by
their own laws, just as the king has
commanded in the land of Judah.

38 "As for the three districts that
have been added to Judea from the
country of Samaria, let them be so
annexed to Judea that they are considered to be under one ruler and obey
no other authority but the high priest.
39 Ptolemais and the land adjoining it
I have given as a gift to the sanctuary
in Jerusalem, to meet the necessary
expenses of the sanctuary. 40 I also
grant fifteen thousand shekels of silver
yearly out of the king's revenues from
appropriate places. 41 And all the additional funds which the government
officials have not paid as they did in
the first years,[y] they shall give from
now on for the service of the temple.[z]
42 Moreover, the five thousand shekels
of silver which my officials[a] have received every year from the income of
the services of the temple, this too is
canceled, because it belongs to the
priests who minister there. 43 And whoever takes refuge at the temple in
Jerusalem, or in any of its precincts,
because he owes money to the king or
has any debt, let him be released and
receive back all his property in my
kingdom.

44 "Let the cost of rebuilding and
restoring the structures of the sanctuary be paid from the revenues of
the king. 45 And let the cost of rebuilding the walls of Jerusalem and
fortifying it round about, and the cost
of rebuilding the walls in Judea, also
be paid from the revenues of the king."

46 When Jonathan and the people
heard these words, they did not believe or accept them, because they
remembered the great wrongs which

y The Greek text of this verse is uncertain
z Gk *house* *a* Gk *they*

29–30: *All the Jews* in the Seleucid realm, not merely in Judea. *Tribute,* direct taxes proportionate to individual wealth. *Salt tax,* on salt from the marshes and the Dead Sea. *Crown levies,* fixed amounts of money. *The three districts* (11.34) that Alexander the Great had transferred from Samaria to Judea and Antiochus IV had reassigned to Samaria were now restored (v. 38). **32:** *Release* of *control of the citadel* would free Jerusalem from military domination. **34:** *Appointed days,* other public festivals. **36–37:** Opening the army and the civil service to Jews might strengthen their loyalty to the crown. **39:** *Ptolemais* was in the hands of Alexander (v. 1). This was an invitation to the Jews to help Demetrius recapture it. **41:** *The additional funds* were grants once made to the temple by Ptolemaic and Seleucid kings, but *not paid* since the time of Antiochus IV. **44–45:** Here Demetrius followed the custom of Persian kings (Ezra 6.8; 7.20).

Demetrius[b] had done in Israel and how
he had greatly oppressed them. 47 They
favored Alexander, because he had
been the first to speak peaceable words
to them, and they remained his allies
all his days.
48 Now Alexander the king assembled large forces and encamped
opposite Demetrius. 49 The two kings
met in battle, and the army of Demetrius fled, and Alexander[c] pursued him
and defeated them. 50 He pressed the
battle strongly until the sun set, and
Demetrius fell on that day.
51 Then Alexander sent ambassadors
to Ptolemy king of Egypt with the
following message: 52 "Since I have
returned to my kingdom and have
taken my seat on the throne of my
fathers, and established my rule—for
I crushed Demetrius and gained control of our country; 53 I met him in
battle, and he and his army were
crushed by us, and we have taken our
seat on the throne of his kingdom—
54 now therefore let us establish friendship with one another; give me now
your daughter as my wife, and I will
become your son-in-law, and will make
gifts to you and to her in keeping with
your position."
55 Ptolemy the king replied and said,
"Happy was the day on which you
returned to the land of your fathers
and took your seat on the throne of
their kingdom. 56 And now I will do
for you as you wrote, but meet me at
Ptolemais, so that we may see one
another, and I will become your father-
in-law, as you have said."
57 So Ptolemy set out from Egypt,
he and Cleopatra his daughter, and
came to Ptolemais in the one hundred
and sixty-second year.[d] 58 Alexander
the king met him, and Ptolemy[e] gave
him Cleopatra his daughter in marriage, and celebrated her wedding at
Ptolemais with great pomp, as kings do.
59 Then Alexander the king wrote
Jonathan to come to meet him. 60 So
he went with pomp to Ptolemais and
met the two kings; he gave them and
their friends silver and gold and many
gifts, and found favor with them. 61 A
group of pestilent men from Israel,
lawless men, gathered together against
him to accuse him; but the king paid
no attention to them. 62 The king gave
orders to take off Jonathan's garments
and to clothe him in purple, and they
did so. 63 The king also seated him at
his side; and he said to his officers,
"Go forth with him into the middle of
the city and proclaim that no one is
to bring charges against him about any
matter, and let no one annoy him for
any reason." 64 And when his accusers
saw the honor that was paid him, in
accordance with the proclamation, and
saw him clothed in purple, they all fled.
65 Thus the king honored him and
enrolled him among his chief friends,
and made him general and governor
of the province. 66 And Jonathan returned to Jerusalem in peace and
gladness.
67 In the one hundred and sixty-
fifth year[f] Demetrius the son of
Demetrius came from Crete to the
land of his fathers. 68 When Alexander
the king heard of it, he was greatly
grieved and returned to Antioch.
69 And Demetrius appointed Apollonius the governor of Coelesyria, and he

b Gk *he*
c Other authorities read *Alexander fled, and Demetrius*
d 150 B.C. *e* Gk *he* *f* 147 B.C.

47: *Alexander* was also recognized as king by the Jews' allies, the Romans. **50:** *Demetrius fell* probably in 150 B.C. (v. 57).

10.51–66: Alexander's relations with Egypt and Judea. 51: *Ptolemy* VI Philometor (1.18). **55:** *Ptolemy* recognized Alexander as legitimate (see 10.1–21 n.). **57:** *Cleopatra* III, who later married her uncle, Ptolemy VIII. **62:** A change of *garments* often signified honor or dishonor (Zech.3.3–5; Mt.22.11–14). **65:** *Chief friends*, see 2.18 n. *General and governor*, with military and civil authority.

10.67–89: Victories of Jonathan. 67: *Demetrius* II *the son of Demetrius* I disputed the throne with Alexander and later with Tryphon and Antiochus VI; in 138 B.C. he was taken captive by the Parthians. He reigned again from 129 till his death in 125 B.C. **69:** *Coelesyria*, meaning

assembled a large force and encamped
against Jamnia. Then he sent the following message to Jonathan the high
priest:
70 "You are the only one to rise up
against us, and I have become a laughingstock and reproach because of you.
Why do you assume authority against
us in the hill country? 71 If you now
have confidence in your forces, come
down to the plain to meet us, and let
us match strength with each other
there, for I have with me the power of
the cities. 72 Ask and learn who I am
and who the others are that are helping
us. Men will tell you that you cannot
stand before us, for your fathers were
twice put to flight in their own land.
73 And now you will not be able to
withstand my cavalry and such an
army in the plain, where there is no
stone or pebble, or place to flee."
74 When Jonathan heard the words
of Apollonius, his spirit was aroused.
He chose ten thousand men and set
out from Jerusalem, and Simon his
brother met him to help him. 75 He
encamped before Joppa, but the men
of the city closed its gates, for Apollonius had a garrison in Joppa. 76 So they
fought against it, and the men of the
city became afraid and opened the
gates, and Jonathan gained possession
of Joppa.
77 When Apollonius heard of it, he
mustered three thousand cavalry and a
large army, and went to Azotus as
though he were going farther. At the
same time he advanced into the plain,
for he had a large troop of cavalry and
put confidence in it. 78 Jonathan[g] pursued him to Azotus, and the armies
engaged in battle. 79 Now Apollonius
had secretly left a thousand cavalry
behind them. 80 Jonathan learned that
there was an ambush behind him, for
they surrounded his army and shot
arrows at his men from early morning
till late afternoon. 81 But his men stood
fast, as Jonathan commanded, and the
enemy's[h] horses grew tired.
82 Then Simon brought forward his
force and engaged the phalanx in
battle (for the cavalry was exhausted);
they were overwhelmed by him and
fled, 83 and the cavalry was dispersed in
the plain. They fled to Azotus and
entered Beth-dagon, the temple of their
idol, for safety. 84 But Jonathan burned
Azotus and the surrounding towns and
plundered them; and the temple of
Dagon, and those who had taken refuge in it he burned with fire. 85 The
number of those who fell by the sword,
with those burned alive, came to eight
thousand men.
86 Then Jonathan departed from
there and encamped against Askalon,
and the men of the city came out to
meet him with great pomp. 87 And
Jonathan and those with him returned
to Jerusalem with much booty. 88 When
Alexander the king heard of these
things, he honored Jonathan still more;
89 and he sent to him a golden buckle,
such as it is the custom to give to the
kinsmen of kings. He also gave him
Ekron and all its environs as his
possession.

11 Then the king of Egypt gathered
great forces, like the sand by the
seashore, and many ships; and he
tried to get possession of Alexander's
kingdom by trickery and add it to his

g Gk *he* *h* Gk *their*

"hollow Syria," originally designated the country between the Lebanon and anti-Lebanon mountains; here it is Palestine and Transjordan, including the coast. *Jamnia*, 4.15. **72:** *Twice put to flight*, 6.54; 9.18. **74:** Jonathan now had forces for more than guerrilla engagements (v. 65); he had troops organized as phalanxes (v. 82). **75:** *Joppa*, now Jaffa, a seaport near Jamnia and forty miles from Jerusalem. **82:** *His force* had been held in reserve and was fresh. **83:** *Beth-dagon*, house of Dagon, the Philistine grain god (Jg.16.23). **86:** *Askalon*, about twelve miles north of Gaza. **89:** *Ekron*, northernmost of the Philistine cities, was given to Jonathan as a personal possession, and its taxes were assigned to him.

11.1–19: Invasion of Ptolemy VI and victory of Demetrius II. 1: Josephus says that Ptolemy came to aid Alexander, his son-in-law, but that the latter plotted against Ptolemy's life (*Antiq-*

own kingdom. 2 He set out for Syria
with peaceable words, and the people
of the cities opened their gates to him
and went to meet him, for Alexander
the king had commanded them to
meet him, since he was Alexander's[i]
father-in-law. 3 But when Ptolemy
entered the cities he stationed forces as
a garrison in each city.

4 When he[j] approached Azotus,
they showed him the temple of Dagon
burned down, and Azotus and its
suburbs destroyed, and the corpses
lying about, and the charred bodies of
those whom Jonathan[k] had burned in
the war, for they had piled them in
heaps along his route. 5 They also told
the king what Jonathan had done, to
throw blame on him; but the king kept
silent. 6 Jonathan met the king at
Joppa with pomp, and they greeted
one another and spent the night there.
7 And Jonathan went with the king as
far as the river called Eleutherus; then
he returned to Jerusalem.

8 So King Ptolemy gained control
of the coastal cities as far as Seleucia
by the sea, and he kept devising evil
designs against Alexander. 9 He sent
envoys to Demetrius the king, saying,
"Come, let us make a covenant with
each other, and I will give you in
marriage my daughter who was Alexander's wife, and you shall reign over
your father's kingdom. 10 For I now
regret that I gave him my daughter, for
he has tried to kill me." 11 He threw
blame on Alexander[l] because he cov-
eted his kingdom. 12 So he took his
daughter away from him and gave her
to Demetrius. He was estranged from
Alexander, and their enmity became
manifest.

13 Then Ptolemy entered Antioch
and put on the crown of Asia. Thus
he put two crowns upon his head, the
crown of Egypt and that of Asia.
14 Now Alexander the king was in
Cilicia at that time, because the people
of that region were in revolt. 15 And
Alexander heard of it and came against
him in battle. Ptolemy marched out
and met him with a strong force, and
put him to flight. 16 So Alexander fled
into Arabia to find protection there,
and King Ptolemy was exalted. 17 And
Zabdiel the Arab cut off the head of
Alexander and sent it to Ptolemy.
18 But King Ptolemy died three days
later, and his troops in the strongholds
were killed by the inhabitants of the
strongholds. 19 So Demetrius became
king in the one hundred and sixty-
seventh year.[m]

20 In those days Jonathan assembled
the men of Judea to attack the citadel
in Jerusalem, and he built many
engines of war to use against it. 21 But
certain lawless men who hated their
nation went to the king and reported
to him that Jonathan was besieging
the citadel. 22 When he heard this he
was angry, and as soon as he heard it
he set out and came to Ptolemais; and
he wrote Jonathan not to continue the
siege, but to meet him for a conference
at Ptolemais as quickly as possible.

i Gk *his*
j Other ancient authorities read *they*
k Gk *he*
l Gk *him*
m 145 B.C.

---

uities, XIII. iv. 5–6). **5:** *Kept silent*, he had not yet broken with Alexander, and was not ready to commit himself. **7:** *Eleutherus*, now Nahr el-Kebir, north of Tripolis. **8:** *Seleucia* in Pieria, the main port for Antioch, near the mouth of the Orontes. **9:** *My daughter*, Cleopatra III (10.57). **13:** According to Josephus, the army proclaimed *Ptolemy* as king, but he persuaded the people of Antioch to support Demetrius. **14:** *Cilicia*, on the south coast of Turkey, always closely related to Syria, and the only section of Asia Minor then part of the Seleucid Empire. **15:** *Ptolemy marched out*, according to Josephus (*Antiquities*, XIII. iv. 8) with his son-in-law, Demetrius, who had already married Cleopatra. **16:** *Arabia* here includes the country east of Aleppo and Damascus. **18:** *Ptolemy died* of wounds suffered in the victory over Alexander. **19:** *Demetrius* had claimed to be *king* since 150 B.C. (see 10.67 n.).

11.20–37: Agreement between Demetrius II and Jonathan. 20: Demetrius I had once promised to turn *the citadel* over to the high priest (10.32), but he refused to recognize Jonathan as such because the latter had supported Alexander. Now Jonathan resolved to attack the citadel and

23 When Jonathan heard this, he
gave orders to continue the siege; and
he chose some of the elders of Israel
and some of the priests, and put himself in danger, [24]for he went to the king
at Ptolemais, taking silver and gold
and clothing and numerous other gifts.
And he won his favor. [25]Although certain lawless men of his nation kept
making complaints against him, [26]the
king treated him as his predecessors
had treated him; he exalted him in the
presence of all his friends. [27]He confirmed him in the high priesthood and
in as many other honors as he had
formerly had, and made him to be
regarded as one of his chief friends.
[28]Then Jonathan asked the king to free
Judea and the three districts of
Samaria[n] from tribute, and promised
him three hundred talents. [29]The king
consented, and wrote a letter to Jonathan about all these things; its contents were as follows:

30 "King Demetrius to Jonathan his
brother and to the nation of the Jews,
greeting. [31]This copy of the letter
which we wrote concerning you to
Lasthenes our kinsman we have written to you also, so that you may know
what it says. [32]'King Demetrius to
Lasthenes his father, greeting. [33]To
the nation of the Jews, who are our
friends and fulfil their obligations to us,
we have determined to do good, because of the good will they show
toward us. [34]We have confirmed as
their possession both the territory of
Judea and the three districts of
Aphairema and Lydda and Rathamin;
the latter, with all the region bordering
them, were added to Judea from
Samaria. To all those who offer sacrifice in Jerusalem, we have granted
release from[o] the royal taxes which the
king formerly received from them each
year, from the crops of the land and
the fruit of the trees. [35]And the other
payments henceforth due to us of the
tithes, and the taxes due to us, and
the salt pits and the crown taxes due
to us—from all these we shall grant
them release. [36]And not one of these
grants shall be canceled from this time
forth for ever. [37]Now therefore take
care to make a copy of this, and let it
be given to Jonathan and put up in a
conspicuous place on the holy mountain.' "

38 Now when Demetrius the king
saw that the land was quiet before him
and that there was no opposition to
him, he dismissed all his troops, each
man to his own place, except the
foreign troops which he had recruited
from the islands of the nations. So all
the troops who had served his fathers
hated him. [39]Now Trypho had
formerly been one of Alexander's supporters. He saw that all the troops
were murmuring against Demetrius.
So he went to Imalkue the Arab, who
was bringing up Antiochus, the young
son of Alexander, [40]and insistently
urged him to hand Antiochus[p] over to
him, to become king in place of his
father. He also reported to Imalkue[p]
what Demetrius had done and told of
the hatred which the troops of Demetrius[p] had for him; and he stayed there
many days.

41 Now Jonathan sent to Demetrius
the king the request that he remove
the troops of the citadel from Jerusalem, and the troops in the strongholds;
for they kept fighting against Israel.
[42]And Demetrius sent this message to

n Cn: Gk *the three districts and Samaria*
o Or *Samaria, for all those who offer sacrifice in Jerusalem, in place of*
p Gk *him*

make Judea independent. **23–24:** Jonathan decided to *continue the siege* so as to negotiate from strength, but his dangerous visit and gifts showed that he was willing to make terms. **27:** 10.20. **30–37:** The letter repeats earlier promises (10.25–45), but says nothing of the citadel. **31:** *Lasthenes*, probably governor of Coelesyria. **34:** *The three districts*, 10.30,38. *Aphairema*, probably et-Taiyibeh, four miles northeast of Bethel, the Ephraim of Jn.11.54. *Lydda*, or Lod, east of Jaffa. *Rathamin*, perhaps Ramathaim-zophim (1 Sam.1.1), the Arimathea of Mk.15.43.

11.38–52: Jonathan's aid to Demetrius. 38: *Demetrius* in overconfidence reduced his army, probably to save money. This made him unpopular. **42–43:** At last Demetrius seemed to agree

Jonathan, "Not only will I do these
things for you and your nation, but I
will confer great honor on you and
your nation, if I find an opportunity.
43 Now then you will do well to send
me men who will help me, for all my
troops have revolted." 44 So Jonathan
sent three thousand stalwart men to
him at Antioch, and when they came
to the king, the king rejoiced at their
arrival.
45 Then the men of the city assembled within the city, to the number
of a hundred and twenty thousand,
and they wanted to kill the king. 46 But
the king fled into the palace. Then the
men of the city seized the main streets
of the city and began to fight. 47 So the
king called the Jews to his aid, and they
all rallied about him and then spread
out through the city; and they killed
on that day as many as a hundred
thousand men. 48 They set fire to the
city and seized much spoil on that
day, and they saved the king. 49 When
the men of the city saw that the Jews
had gained control of the city as they
pleased, their courage failed and they
cried out to the king with this entreaty,
50 "Grant us peace, and make the Jews
stop fighting against us and our city."
51 And they threw down their arms and
made peace. So the Jews gained glory
in the eyes of the king and of all the
people in his kingdom, and they
returned to Jerusalem with much
spoil.
52 So Demetrius the king sat on the
throne of his kingdom, and the land
was quiet before him. 53 But he broke
his word about all that he had promised; and he became estranged from
Jonathan and did not repay the favors
which Jonathan[q] had done him, but
oppressed him greatly.
54 After this Trypho returned, and
with him the young boy Antiochus,
who began to reign and put on the
crown. 55 All the troops that Demetrius had cast off gathered around him,
and they fought against Demetrius,[r]
and he fled and was routed. 56 And
Trypho captured the elephants[s] and
gained control of Antioch. 57 Then the
young Antiochus wrote to Jonathan,
saying, "I confirm you in the high
priesthood and set you over the four
districts and make you one of the
friends of the king." 58 And he sent
him gold plate and a table service, and
granted him the right to drink from
gold cups and dress in purple and wear
a gold buckle. 59 Simon his brother he
made governor from the Ladder of
Tyre to the borders of Egypt.
60 Then Jonathan set forth and
traveled beyond the river and among
the cities, and all the army of Syria
gathered to him as allies. When he
came to Askalon, the people of the
city met him and paid him honor.
61 From there he departed to Gaza, but
the men of Gaza shut him out. So he
besieged it and burned its suburbs with
fire and plundered them. 62 Then the
people of Gaza pleaded with Jonathan,
and he made peace with them, and took
the sons of their rulers as hostages and
sent them to Jerusalem. And he passed
through the country as far as Damascus.
63 Then Jonathan heard that the
officers of Demetrius had come to

q Gk *he* *r* Gk *him* *s* Gk *beasts*

(compare v. 53) to evacuate the citadel and other fortresses. **45–47:** *Men of the city*, a mob, not an army. *Jews*, Judeans (see 2.23 n.).

11.53–74: Estrangement of Demetrius and Jonathan. **53:** Josephus says that Demetrius now demanded tribute as before (*Antiquities*, XIII. v. 3). **54:** *Antiochus* VI Epiphanes, son of Alexander Balas, reigned nominally from about 145 to 142 B.C. **55:** *All the troops*, v. 38. **57:** *The four districts*, the three of v. 34 and probably Ekron (10.89). **58:** *Gold cups*, Est.1.7. *Gold buckle*, sign of being a friend of the king (see 2.18 n.). **59:** *The Ladder of Tyre*, the coastline between Ptolemais and Tyre. *The borders of Egypt*, probably Wadi el-Arish. **60:** *The river*, Jordan. **61:** *Gaza*, southernmost of the Philistine cities, near the Egyptian border (Jg.16.1). **62:** *Damascus*, outside Jonathan's control, but his influence extended nearly that far. **63:** *Kadesh*, northwest of Lake Huleh or Merom (Jg.4.9).

Kadesh in Galilee with a large army,
intending to remove him from office.
64 He went to meet them, but left his
brother Simon in the country. 65 Simon
encamped before Beth-zur and fought
against it for many days and hemmed
it in. 66 Then they asked him to grant
them terms of peace, and he did so. He
removed them from there, took possession of the city, and set a garrison
over it.
67 Jonathan and his army encamped
by the waters of Gennesaret. Early in
the morning they marched to the plain
of Hazor, 68 and behold, the army of the
foreigners met him in the plain; they
had set an ambush against him in the
mountains, but they themselves met
him face to face. 69 Then the men in
ambush emerged from their places and
joined battle. 70 All the men with
Jonathan fled; not one of them was
left except Mattathias the son of
Absalom and Judas the son of Chalphi,
commanders of the forces of the army.
71 Jonathan rent his garments and put
dust on his head, and prayed. 72 Then
he turned back to the battle against
the enemy[t] and routed them, and they
fled. 73 When his men who were fleeing
saw this, they returned to him and
joined him in the pursuit as far as
Kadesh, to their camp, and there
they encamped. 74 As many as three
thousand of the foreigners fell that
day. And Jonathan returned to Jerusalem.

12 Now when Jonathan saw that
the time was favorable for him,
he chose men and sent them to Rome
to confirm and renew the friendship
with them. 2 He also sent letters to the
same effect to the Spartans and to other
places. 3 So they went to Rome and
entered the senate chamber and said,
"Jonathan the high priest and the
Jewish nation have sent us to renew the
former friendship and alliance with
them." 4 And the Romans[u] gave them
letters to the people in every place,
asking them to provide for the envoys[v]
safe conduct to the land of Judah.
5 This is a copy of the letter which
Jonathan wrote to the Spartans:
6 "Jonathan the high priest, the senate
of the nation, the priests, and the rest
of the Jewish people to their brethren
the Spartans, greeting. 7 Already in
time past a letter was sent to Onias the
high priest from Arius,[w] who was king
among you, stating that you are our
brethren, as the appended copy shows.
8 Onias welcomed the envoy with honor,
and received the letter, which contained
a clear declaration of alliance and
friendship. 9 Therefore, though we
have no need of these things, since we
have as encouragement the holy books
which are in our hands, 10 we have
undertaken to send to renew our
brotherhood and friendship with you,
so that we may not become estranged
from you, for considerable time has
passed since you sent your letter to us.
11 We therefore remember you constantly on every occasion, both in our
feasts and on other appropriate days,
at the sacrifices which we offer and in
our prayers, as it is right and proper to
remember brethren. 12 And we rejoice
in your glory. 13 But as for ourselves,
many afflictions and many wars have
encircled us; the kings round about us
have waged war against us. 14 We were
unwilling to annoy you and our other
allies and friends with these wars, 15 for
we have the help which comes from
Heaven for our aid; and we were delivered from our enemies and our
enemies were humbled. 16 We there-

t Gk *them*
u Gk *they*
v Gk *them*
w Vg Compare verse 20: Gk *Darius*

67: *The waters of Gennesaret*, the Sea of Galilee. *Hazor*, southwest of Lake Huleh (Jos.11.1).
12.1–23: Alliances with the Romans and Spartans (compare ch. 8). **2:** *The Spartans* had not joined the Achaean league against Rome. **4:** *The Romans* continued the old alliance in order to keep Syria weak. **6:** *The senate*, over which the high priest presided; it corresponds to the later council or Sanhedrin (Mk.14.55). **7:** *Onias* I, high priest 320–290 B.C. *Arius*, king of Sparta

fore have chosen Numenius the son of
Antiochus and Antipater the son of
Jason, and have sent them to Rome to
renew our former friendship and alliance with them. 17 We have commanded them to go also to you and
greet you and deliver to you this letter
from us concerning the renewal of our
brotherhood. 18 And now please send
us a reply to this."

19 This is a copy of the letter which
they sent to Onias: 20 "Arius, king of
the Spartans, to Onias the high priest,
greeting. 21 It has been found in writing
concerning the Spartans and the Jews
that they are brethren and are of the
family of Abraham. 22 And now that
we have learned this, please write us
concerning your welfare; 23 we on our
part write to you that your cattle and
your property belong to us, and ours
belong to you. We therefore command
that our envoys[x] report to you accordingly."

24 Now Jonathan heard that the
commanders of Demetrius had returned, with a larger force than before,
to wage war against him. 25 So he
marched away from Jerusalem and
met them in the region of Hamath,
for he gave them no opportunity to
invade his own country. 26 He sent
spies to their camp, and they returned
and reported to him that the enemy[y]
were being drawn up in formation to
fall upon the Jews[z] by night. 27 So
when the sun set, Jonathan commanded his men to be alert and to keep
their arms at hand so as to be ready all
night for battle, and he stationed out-
posts around the camp. 28 When the
enemy heard that Jonathan and his men
were prepared for battle, they were
afraid and were terrified at heart; so
they kindled fires in their camp and
withdrew.[a] 29 But Jonathan and his
men did not know it until morning, for they saw the fires burning.
30 Then Jonathan pursued them, but he
did not overtake them, for they had
crossed the Eleutherus River. 31 So
Jonathan turned aside against the
Arabs who are called Zabadeans, and
he crushed them and plundered them.
32 Then he broke camp and went to
Damascus, and marched through all
that region.

33 Simon also went forth and
marched through the country as far
as Askalon and the neighboring strongholds. He turned aside to Joppa and
took it by surprise, 34 for he had heard
that they were ready to hand over the
stronghold to the men whom Demetrius had sent. And he stationed a
garrison there to guard it.

35 When Jonathan returned he con-
vened the elders of the people and
planned with them to build strongholds
in Judea, 36 to build the walls of Jerusalem still higher, and to erect a high
barrier between the citadel and the city
to separate it from the city, in order to
isolate it so that its garrison[b] could
neither buy nor sell. 37 So they gathered
together to build up the city; part of the
wall on the valley to the east had fallen,
and he repaired the section called
Chaphenatha. 38 And Simon built
Adida in the Shephelah; he fortified it
and installed gates with bolts.

39 Then Trypho attempted to become king of Asia and put on the
crown, and to raise his hand against

x Gk *they*
y Gk *they*
z Gk *them*
a Other ancient authorities omit *and withdrew*
b Gk *they*

309–265 B.C. **21:** *Brethren . . . of the family of Abraham*, compare v. 7; such a tradition was evidently current in the East.

12.24–53: Jonathan captured by Trypho. 24–25: Jonathan met the Syrians at the border of Judea to prevent an invasion. *Hamath*, on the Orontes, modern Hama in Syria. **28:** *Kindled fires*, so that Jonathan would think they were still in camp. **30:** *The Eleutherus* is too far north (see 11.7 n.); perhaps the Orontes. **31:** *Zabadeans*, perhaps people northwest of Damascus. **36:** The purpose was to starve out the garrison. **37:** *The valley to the east*, the Kidron (1 Kg.2.37; Jn.18.1); here the slope was sometimes steep. The location of *Chaphenatha* is unknown. **38:** *Adida*, about three miles east of Lydda (Ezra 2.33; Neh.7.37). *Shephelah*, the foothill country

Antiochus the king. 40He feared that
Jonathan might not permit him to do
so, but might make war on him, so
he kept seeking to seize and kill him,
and he marched forth and came to
Beth-shan. 41Jonathan went out to
meet him with forty thousand picked
fighting men, and he came to Beth-shan.
42When Trypho saw that he had come
with a large army, he was afraid to
raise his hand against him. 43So he
received him with honor and commended him to all his friends, and he
gave him gifts and commanded his
friends and his troops to obey him as
they would himself. 44Then he said to
Jonathan, "Why have you wearied all
these people when we are not at war?
45Dismiss them now to their homes and
choose for yourself a few men to stay
with you, and come with me to Ptolemais. I will hand it over to you as well
as the other strongholds and the remaining troops and all the officials, and
will turn around and go home. For
that is why I am here."

46 Jonathan[c] trusted him and did
as he said; he sent away the troops,
and they returned to the land of Judah.
47He kept with himself three thousand
men, two thousand of whom he left in
Galilee, while a thousand accompanied him. 48But when Jonathan
entered Ptolemais, the men of Ptolemais closed the gates and seized him,
and all who had entered with him they
killed with the sword.

49 Then Trypho sent troops and
cavalry into Galilee and the Great
Plain to destroy all of Jonathan's
soldiers. 50But they realized that
Jonathan[c] had been seized and had
perished along with his men, and they
encouraged one another and kept
marching in close formation, ready for
battle. 51When their pursuers saw that
they would fight for their lives, they
turned back. 52So they all reached the
land of Judah safely, and they mourned
for Jonathan and his companions and
were in great fear; and all Israel
mourned deeply. 53And all the nations
round about them tried to destroy
them, for they said, "They have no
leader or helper. Now therefore let
us make war on them and blot out
the memory of them from among
men."

13 Simon heard that Trypho had
assembled a large army to invade
the land of Judah and destroy it, 2and
he saw that the people were trembling
and fearful. So he went up to Jerusalem, and gathering the people together
3he encouraged them, saying to them,
"You yourselves know what great
things I and my brothers and the house
of my father have done for the laws
and the sanctuary; you know also the
wars and the difficulties which we have
seen. 4By reason of this all my brothers
have perished for the sake of Israel,
and I alone am left. 5And now, far be
it from me to spare my life in any time
of distress, for I am not better than my
brothers. 6But I will avenge my nation
and the sanctuary and your wives and
children, for all the nations have
gathered together out of hatred to
destroy us."

7 The spirit of the people was re-
kindled when they heard these words,
8and they answered in a loud voice,
"You are our leader in place of Judas
and Jonathan your brother. 9Fight our
battles, and all that you say to us we
will do." 10So he assembled all the
warriors and hastened to complete the
walls of Jerusalem, and he fortified it
on every side. 11He sent Jonathan the
son of Absalom to Joppa, and with him

c Gk *he*

between the coastal plain and the central highlands. **40:** *Beth-shan*, see 5.52 n. **45:** *The other strongholds*, probably along the coast. **52:** *They mourned*, because of the supposition that Jonathan had been slain; but see 13.23.

13.1–30: Simon becomes leader; death of Jonathan. **1:** *Simon* (2.3) was governor of the coastal area (11.59). **4:** Eleazar, Judah, and John had died (6.46; 9.18,42), and Simon supposed that Jonathan had been slain. **7–8:** Jonathan had been chosen by his friends (9.28–30); *the people* now elected Simon *leader*, but not yet high priest (compare 14.41). **11:** *Jonathan the son of*

a considerable army; he drove out its
occupants and remained there.
12 Then Trypho departed from
Ptolemais with a large army to invade
the land of Judah, and Jonathan was
with him under guard. 13And Simon
encamped in Adida, facing the plain.
14Trypho learned that Simon had risen
up in place of Jonathan his brother,
and that he was about to join battle
with him, so he sent envoys to him and
said, 15"It is for the money that
Jonathan your brother owed the royal
treasury, in connection with the offices
he held, that we are detaining him.
16Send now a hundred talents of silver
and two of his sons as hostages, so that
when released he will not revolt against
us, and we will release him."
17 Simon knew that they were speaking deceitfully to him, but he sent to
get the money and the sons, lest he
arouse great hostility among the people,
who might say, 18"Because Simon[d] did
not send him the money and the sons,
he perished." 19So he sent the sons and
the hundred talents, but Trypho[e] broke
his word and did not release Jonathan.
20 After this Trypho came to invade
the country and destroy it, and he
circled around by the way to Adora.
But Simon and his army kept marching
along opposite him to every place he
went. 21Now the men in the citadel
kept sending envoys to Trypho urging
him to come to them by way of the
wilderness and to send them food. 22So
Trypho got all his cavalry ready to go,
but that night a very heavy snow fell,
and he did not go because of the snow.
He marched off and went into the land
of Gilead. 23When he approached
Baskama, he killed Jonathan, and he
was buried there. 24Then Trypho
turned back and departed to his own
land.
25 And Simon sent and took the
bones of Jonathan his brother, and
buried him in Modein, the city of his
fathers. 26All Israel bewailed him with
great lamentation, and mourned for
him many days. 27And Simon built a
monument over the tomb of his father
and his brothers; he made it high that
it might be seen, with polished stone in
front and back. 28He also erected
seven pyramids, opposite one another,
for his father and mother and four
brothers. 29And for the pyramids[f] he
devised an elaborate setting, erecting
about them great columns, and upon
the columns he put suits of armor for
a permanent memorial, and beside the
suits of armor carved ships, so that they
could be seen by all who sail the sea.
30This is the tomb which he built in
Modein; it remains to this day.
31 Trypho dealt treacherously with
the young king Antiochus; he killed
him 32and became king in his place,
putting on the crown of Asia; and he
brought great calamity upon the land.
33But Simon built up the strongholds
of Judea and walled them all around,
with high towers and great walls and
gates and bolts, and he stored food in
the strongholds. 34Simon also chose
men and sent them to Demetrius the
king with a request to grant relief to
the country, for all that Trypho did
was to plunder. 35Demetrius the king
sent him a favorable reply to this request, and wrote him a letter as follows,
36"King Demetrius to Simon, the high

d Gk *I* *e* Gk *he*
f Gk *for these*

Absalom, perhaps a brother of Mattathias (11.70). **15–16:** He regarded *Jonathan* as a vassal of Syria who had to pay for *the offices he held* (11.57). **20:** *Adora*, or Adoraim, now Dura, five miles southwest of Hebron (2 Chr.11.9). **22–23:** *He marched off*, south of the Dead Sea. *Baskama*, possibly northeast of the Sea of Galilee. *He killed Jonathan*, late in 143 or early in 142 B.C. **25:** *Modein*, 2.2; 9.19. **28:** *Pyramids*, following Egyptian fashion. **29:** *Carved ships*, symbols claiming domination of the sea, found also on coins of Herod and Archelaus.

13.31–53: Simon makes Judea independent. 31–32: *He killed him*, probably in 142 B.C. *Antiochus* VI was about seven years old and had reigned since 145 (11.54). *Became king*, about 142 or 141 B.C. **34:** *Demetrius* II (see 10.67 n.) now disputed the throne with Trypho. **36–40:** The letter, addressed to *the elders and nation* and to *Simon* as head of a priestly state, recognizes

priest and friend of kings, and to the
elders and nation of the Jews, greeting.
37We have received the gold crown and
the palm branch which you[g] sent, and
we are ready to make a general peace
with you and to write to our officials to
grant you release from tribute. 38All
the grants that we have made to you
remain valid, and let the strongholds
that you have built be your possession.
39We pardon any errors and offenses
committed to this day, and cancel the
crown tax which you owe; and whatever other tax has been collected in
Jerusalem shall be collected no longer.
40And if any of you are qualified to be
enrolled in our bodyguard,[h] let them
be enrolled, and let there be peace
between us."

41 In the one hundred and seven-
tieth year[i] the yoke of the Gentiles
was removed from Israel, 42and the
people began to write in their documents and contracts, "In the first
year of Simon the great high priest
and commander and leader of the
Jews."

43 In those days Simon[j] encamped
against Gazara[k] and surrounded it
with troops. He made a siege engine,
brought it up to the city, and battered
and captured one tower. 44The men in
the siege engine leaped out into the
city, and a great tumult arose in the
city. 45The men in the city, with their
wives and children, went up on the
wall with their clothes rent, and they
cried out with a loud voice, asking
Simon to make peace with them;
46they said, "Do not treat us according
to our wicked acts but according to
your mercy." 47So Simon reached an
agreement with them and stopped
fighting against them. But he expelled
them from the city and cleansed the
houses in which the idols were, and
then entered it with hymns and praise.
48He cast out of it all uncleanness,
and settled in it men who observed the
law. He also strengthened its fortifica-
tions and built in it a house for himself.

49 The men in the citadel at Jerusalem were prevented from going out
to the country and back to buy and
sell. So they were very hungry, and
many of them perished from famine.
50Then they cried to Simon to make
peace with them, and he did so. But
he expelled them from there and
cleansed the citadel from its pollutions.
51On the twenty-third day of the
second month, in the one hundred and
seventy-first year,[l] the Jews[m] entered it
with praise and palm branches, and
with harps and cymbals and stringed
instruments, and with hymns and
songs, because a great enemy had been
crushed and removed from Israel.
52And Simon[n] decreed that every year
they should celebrate this day with
rejoicing. He strengthened the forti-
fications of the temple hill alongside
the citadel, and he and his men dwelt
there. 53And Simon saw that John his
son had reached manhood, so he made
him commander of all the forces, and
he dwelt in Gazara.

14 In the one hundred and seventy-
second year[o] Demetrius the
king assembled his forces and marched
into Media to secure help, so that he
could make war against Trypho.

g The word *you* in verses 37–40 is plural
h Or *court*
i 142 B.C.
j Gk *he*
k Cn: Gk *Gaza*
l 141 B.C.
m Gk *they*
n Gk *he*
o 140 B.C.

---

sovereignty (compare v. 42). The weakness of Demetrius II made possible a great diplomatic victory. **42:** The new era, replacing the Seleucid era, is a mark of sovereignty. It is debated whether Simon was the first of the Hasmoneans to strike coins. **43:** A Greek inscription hostile to Simon has been found at *Gazara*. **47–48:** The later Hasmoneans continued the policy of settling Jews in strategic places. **49–50:** *The men in the citadel*, probably Trypho's men, did not surrender until starved out. **51:** *The second month*, Iyyar or May. *Palm branches* symbolized victory (2 Macc.10.7). **52:** *Celebrate this day*, see 7.49 n. **53:** *John* Hyrcanus reigned as high priest 134–104 B.C.

14.1–24: Capture of Demetrius II. 1: Other historians date this invasion in 138 B.C., the year

2When Arsaces the king of Persia and
Media heard that Demetrius had invaded his territory, he sent one of his
commanders to take him alive. 3And
he went and defeated the army of
Demetrius, and seized him and took
him to Arsaces, who put him under
guard.

4The land[p] had rest all the days of
Simon.
He sought the good of his
nation;
his rule was pleasing to them,
as was the honor shown him, all
his days.
5To crown all his honors he took
Joppa for a harbor,
and opened a way to the isles of
the sea.
6He extended the borders of his
nation,
and gained full control of the
country.
7He gathered a host of captives;
he ruled over Gazara and
Beth-zur and the citadel,
and he removed its uncleanness
from it;
and there was none to oppose
him.
8They tilled their land in peace;
the ground gave its increase,
and the trees of the plains their
fruit.
9Old men sat in the streets;
they all talked together of good
things;
and the youths donned the
glories and garments of war.
10He supplied the cities with food,
and furnished them with the
means of defense,
till his renown spread to the ends
of the earth.
11He established peace in the land,
and Israel rejoiced with great joy.
12Each man sat under his vine and
his fig tree,
and there was none to make
them afraid.
13No one was left in the land to fight
them,
and the kings were crushed in
those days.
14He strengthened all the humble of
his people;
he sought out the law,
and did away with every lawless
and wicked man.
15He made the sanctuary glorious,
and added to the vessels of the
sanctuary.

16 It was heard in Rome, and as far
away as Sparta, that Jonathan had
died, and they were deeply grieved.
17When they heard that Simon his
brother had become high priest in
his place, and that he was ruling over
the country and the cities in it, 18they
wrote to him on bronze tablets to
renew with him the friendship and
alliance which they had established
with Judas and Jonathan his brothers.
19And these were read before the assembly in Jerusalem.

20 This is a copy of the letter which
the Spartans sent: "The rulers and the
city of the Spartans to Simon the high
priest and to the elders and the priests
and the rest of the Jewish people, our
brethren, greeting. 21The envoys who
were sent to our people have told us
about your glory and honor, and we
rejoiced at their coming. 22And what
they said we have recorded in our
public decrees, as follows, 'Numenius
the son of Antiochus and Antipater the

p Other authorities add *of Judah*

---

in which he was captured. *Media*, lying west of Tehran, was still claimed by the Seleucids. **2–3:** *Arsaces* VI Mithradates I (171–138 B.C.), founder of the Parthian Empire, treated Demetrius kindly and later married him to his sister.

14.4–15: A contemporary poem of rejoicing. **5–7:** 13.41–53. *A harbor*, important for trade connections with the sea (13.11). *The isles of the sea*, Cyprus, Rhodes, and Crete. **12:** 1 Kg.4.25; Mic.4.4.

14.16–24: Alliances with Rome and Sparta. Simon was perhaps the first high priest recognized by the Roman senate as ruler of the Jews. **19:** *The assembly*, the people as a whole. **22:** *Numenius* and *Antipater*, 12.16.

son of Jason, envoys of the Jews, have
come to us to renew their friendship
with us. 23It has pleased our people to
receive these men with honor and to
put a copy of their words in the public
archives, so that the people of the
Spartans may have a record of them.
And they have sent a copy of this to
Simon the high priest.' "

24 After this Simon sent Numenius
to Rome with a large gold shield
weighing a thousand minas, to confirm
the alliance with the Romans.[q]

25 When the people heard these
things they said, "How shall we thank
Simon and his sons? 26For he and his
brothers and the house of his father
have stood firm; they have fought and
repulsed Israel's enemies and established its freedom." 27So they made a
record on bronze tablets and put it
upon pillars on Mount Zion.

This is a copy of what they wrote:
"On the eighteenth day of Elul, in the
one hundred and seventy-second year,[r]
which is the third year of Simon the
great high priest, 28in Asaramel,[s] in the
great assembly of the priests and the
people and the rulers of the nation and
the elders of the country, the following
was proclaimed to us:

29 "Since wars often occurred in
the country, Simon the son of Mattathias, a priest of the sons[t] of Joarib,
and his brothers, exposed themselves
to danger and resisted the enemies of
their nation, in order that their sanctuary and the law might be preserved;
and they brought great glory to their
nation. 30Jonathan rallied the[u] nation,
and became their high priest, and was
gathered to his people. 31And when
their enemies decided to invade their
country and lay hands on their sanctuary, 32then Simon rose up and fought
for his nation. He spent great sums of
his own money; he armed the men of
his nation's forces and paid them
wages. 33He fortified the cities of
Judea, and Beth-zur on the borders of
Judea, where formerly the arms of the
enemy had been stored, and he placed
there a garrison of Jews. 34He also
fortified Joppa, which is by the sea, and
Gazara, which is on the borders of
Azotus, where the enemy formerly
dwelt. He settled Jews there, and provided in those cities[v] whatever was
necessary for their restoration.

35 "The people saw Simon's faithfulness[w] and the glory which he had
resolved to win for his nation, and
they made him their leader and high
priest, because he had done all these
things and because of the justice and
loyalty which he had maintained toward his nation. He sought in every
way to exalt his people. 36And in his
days things prospered in his hands, so
that the Gentiles were put out of the[x]
country, as were also the men in the
city of David in Jerusalem, who had
built themselves a citadel from which
they used to sally forth and defile the
environs of the sanctuary and do great
damage to its purity. 37He settled Jews
in it, and fortified it for the safety of
the country and of the city, and built
the walls of Jerusalem higher.

38 "In view of these things King
Demetrius confirmed him in the high
priesthood, 39and he made him one of

q Gk *them* r 140 B.C.
s This word resembles the Hebrew words for *the court of the people of God* or *the prince of the people of God*
t The Greek text of this phrase is uncertain
u Gk *their* v Gk *them*
w Other authorities read *conduct* x Gk *their*

24: *Weighing a thousand minas*, an obvious exaggeration; a Greek mina is over 15 ounces (troy).
14.25–49: Simon elected high priest, military commander, and ruler. The formal document of vv. 27–49 served as a constitution for the new state of Judea. **27–28:** *Bronze tablets*, see 8.22 n. *Mount Zion*, 1.33; 4.37. *Elul*, August-September. *Third year*, see 13.42 n. *The great assembly*, or synagogue, represented all "states" or classes. In theory the high priest held his office by divine appointment, indicated by descent from a particular family. Since there was no legitimate claimant, Simon was legitimized by a democratic process (v. 41). **29:** *Sons of Joarib*, see 2.1 n. **30:** The decree recognizes in retrospect the office of *Jonathan*, first Hasmonean *high priest*. **32:** Use of *his own money* had not been previously mentioned. **33–34:** 13.43–48; 14.3–7. **35:** The high priest must have moral responsibility along with his powers. **36–37:** 1.34; 4.41,60;

the king's[y] friends and paid him high
honors. 40 For he had heard that the
Jews were addressed by the Romans
as friends and allies and brethren, and
that the Romans[z] had received the
envoys of Simon with honor.
41 "And[a] the Jews and their priests
decided that Simon should be their
leader and high priest for ever, until a
trustworthy prophet should arise, 42 and
that he should be governor over them
and that he should take charge of the
sanctuary and appoint men over its
tasks and over the country and the
weapons and the strongholds, and that
he should take charge of the sanctuary,
43 and that he should be obeyed by all,
and that all contracts in the country
should be written in his name, and that
he should be clothed in purple and
wear gold.
44 "And none of the people or
priests shall be permitted to nullify
any of these decisions or to oppose
what he says, or to convene an assembly in the country without his permission, or to be clothed in purple or put
on a gold buckle. 45 Whoever acts contrary to these decisions or nullifies any
of them shall be liable to punishment."
46 And all the people agreed to
grant Simon the right to act in accord
with these decisions. 47 So Simon
accepted and agreed to be high priest,
to be commander and ethnarch of the
Jews and priests, and to be protector of
them all.[b] 48 And they gave orders to
inscribe this decree upon bronze tablets, to put them up in a conspicuous
place in the precincts of the sanctuary,
49 and to deposit copies of them in the
treasury, so that Simon and his sons
might have them.

15 Antiochus, the son of Demetrius
the king, sent a letter from the
islands of the sea to Simon, the priest
and ethnarch of the Jews, and to all the
nation; 2 its contents were as follows:
"King Antiochus to Simon the high
priest and ethnarch and to the nation of
the Jews, greeting. 3 Whereas certain
pestilent men have gained control of
the kingdom of our fathers, and I intend to lay claim to the kingdom so
that I may restore it as it formerly was,
and have recruited a host of mercenary
troops and have equipped warships,
4 and intend to make a landing in the
country so that I may proceed against
those who have destroyed our country
and those who have devastated many
cities in my kingdom, 5 now therefore
I confirm to you all the tax remissions
that the kings before me have granted
you, and release from all the other
payments from which they have released you. 6 I permit you to mint
your own coinage as money for your
country, 7 and I grant freedom to Jerusalem and the sanctuary. All the weapons which you have prepared and the
strongholds which you have built and
now hold shall remain yours. 8 Every
debt you owe to the royal treasury
and any such future debts shall be
canceled for you from henceforth and
for all time. 9 When we gain control
of our kingdom, we will bestow
great honor upon you and your nation
and the temple, so that your glory

y Gk *his* *z* Gk *they*
a Gk *honor; and that*
b Or *to preside over them all*

6.18; 13.49–52. **41–43:** The office was to be hereditary in Simon's family, but since this was an act of the nation rather than of God, a *trustworthy prophet* might annul or confirm the decision (see 4.46 n.). *Clothed in purple and wear gold,* like a king or head of state. From Alexander Janneus onwards (103–76 B.C.), the Hasmoneans assumed the title of king. **46–47:** In this social contract, both the people and Simon accept the conditions. *Ethnarch,* civil magistrate. **49:** The *treasury* in the temple served as a national archive.

15.1–14: Arrival of Antiochus VII. 1: *Antiochus* VII (known as Sidetes because reared at Side in Pamphylia), younger brother of Demetrius II, reigned 138–129 B.C. After his brother's capture he married Cleopatra III (10.57–58; 11.12). **3:** *Pestilent men,* Trypho and his faction. **5:** He reaffirms his brother's grants (13.39). **6:** *To mint your own coinage* was legal recognition of independence. When the Seleucids permitted subject cities to coin money, it bore the king's name. **7–8:** 13.38–39.

will become manifest in all the earth."
10 In the one hundred and seventy-
fourth year[c] Antiochus set out and invaded the land of his fathers. All the
troops rallied to him, so that there
were few with Trypho. 11Antiochus
pursued him, and he came in his flight
to Dor, which is by the sea; 12for he
knew that troubles had converged
upon him, and his troops had deserted
him. 13So Antiochus encamped against
Dor, and with him were a hundred and
twenty thousand warriors and eight
thousand cavalry. 14He surrounded
the city, and the ships joined battle
from the sea; he pressed the city hard
from land and sea, and permitted no
one to leave or enter it.
15 Then Numenius and his companions arrived from Rome, with letters to the kings and countries, in
which the following was written:
16"Lucius, consul of the Romans, to
King Ptolemy, greeting. 17The envoys
of the Jews have come to us as our
friends and allies to renew our ancient
friendship and alliance. They had been
sent by Simon the high priest and by
the people of the Jews, 18and have
brought a gold shield weighing a thousand minas. 19We therefore have
decided to write to the kings and
countries that they should not seek
their harm or make war against them
and their cities and their country, or
make alliance with those who war
against them. 20And it has seemed
good to us to accept the shield from
them. 21Therefore if any pestilent
men have fled to you from their
country, hand them over to Simon the
high priest, that he may punish them
according to their law."
22 The consul[d] wrote the same thing
to Demetrius the king and to Attalus
and Ariarathes and Arsaces, 23and to
all the countries, and to Sampsames,[e]
and to the Spartans, and to Delos, and
to Myndos, and to Sicyon, and to
Caria, and to Samos, and to Pamphylia,
and to Lycia, and to Halicarnassus,
and to Rhodes, and to Phaselis, and to
Cos, and to Side, and to Aradus and
Gortyna and Cnidus and Cyprus and
Cyrene. 24They also sent a copy of
these things to Simon the high priest.
25 Antiochus the king besieged Dor
anew,[f] continually throwing his forces
against it and making engines of war;
and he shut Trypho up and kept him
from going out or in. 26And Simon
sent to Antiochus[g] two thousand
picked men, to fight for him, and silver
and gold and much military equip-
ment. 27But he refused to receive them,
and he broke all the agreements he
formerly had made with Simon,[g] and
became estranged from him. 28He sent
to him Athenobius, one of his friends,
to confer with him, saying, "You hold
control of Joppa and Gazara and the
citadel in Jerusalem; they are cities of
my kingdom. 29You have devastated
their territory, you have done great
damage in the land, and you have
taken possession of many places in my
kingdom. 30Now then, hand over the
cities which you have seized and the
tribute money of the places which you
have conquered outside the borders of
Judea; 31or else give me for them five
hundred talents of silver, and for the
destruction that you have caused and

c 138 B.C. *d* Gk *He*
e The name is uncertain
f Or *on the second day*
g Gk *him*

10: He first landed in Seleucia (11.8), where Cleopatra was living. **11:** *Dor*, about nine miles north of Caesarea (Jg.1.27). **13:** The numbers are probably exaggerated.

15.15–24: Renewal of alliance with Rome. 16: If the letter is genuine, this is *Lucius* Calpurnius Piso, consul 140–139 B.C. *Ptolemy* VII Physcon reigned 145–116 B.C. **18:** *Shield*, see 14.24 n. **22–23:** *Demetrius* II was still a prisoner in Parthia; the Romans had not recognized Antiochus VII. *Attalus* II, king of Pergamum 159–138 B.C.; *Ariarathes* V, king of Cappadocia 162–130 B.C. *Delos* in the Cyclades and the other localities were free states in Greece, the Greek islands and Asia Minor. *Cyrene*, capital of Libya.

15.25–16.10: War with Antiochus VII. 27: Josephus says that Antiochus accepted this aid (*Antiquities*, XIII. vii, 2). **28:** *Cities of my kingdom*, this contradicts v. 7. **30:** *Outside . . . Judea*,

the tribute money of the cities, five
hundred talents more. Otherwise we
will come and conquer you."
32 So Athenobius the friend of the
king came to Jerusalem, and when he
saw the splendor of Simon, and the
sideboard with its gold and silver plate,
and his great magnificence, he was
amazed. He reported to him the words
of the king, 33 but Simon gave him this
reply: "We have neither taken foreign
land nor seized foreign property, but
only the inheritance of our fathers,
which at one time had been unjustly
taken by our enemies. 34 Now that we
have the opportunity, we are firmly
holding the inheritance of our fathers.
35 As for Joppa and Gazara, which you
demand, they were causing great
damage among the people and to our
land; for them we will give a hundred
talents." Athenobius[h] did not answer
him a word, 36 but returned in wrath to
the king and reported to him these
words and the splendor of Simon and
all that he had seen. And the king was
greatly angered.
37 Now Trypho embarked on a ship
and escaped to Orthosia. 38 Then the
king made Cendebeus commander-in-
chief of the coastal country, and gave
him troops of infantry and cavalry.
39 He commanded him to encamp
against Judea, and commanded him to
build up Kedron and fortify its gates,
and to make war on the people; but
the king pursued Trypho. 40 So Cendebeus came to Jamnia and began to
provoke the people and invade Judea
and take the people captive and kill
them. 41 He built up Kedron and
stationed there horsemen and troops,
so that they might go out and make
raids along the highways of Judea, as
the king had ordered him.

16 John went up from Gazara and
reported to Simon his father
what Cendebeus had done. 2 And
Simon called in his two older sons
Judas and John, and said to them: "I
and my brothers and the house of my
father have fought the wars of Israel
from our youth until this day, and
things have prospered in our hands so
that we have delivered Israel many
times. 3 But now I have grown old,
and you by His mercy are mature in
years. Take my place and my brother's,
and go out and fight for our nation,
and may the help which comes from
Heaven be with you."
4 So John[i] chose out of the country
twenty thousand warriors and horsemen, and they marched against Cendebeus and camped for the night in
Modein. 5 Early in the morning they
arose and marched into the plain, and
behold, a large force of infantry and
horsemen was coming to meet them;
and a stream lay between them. 6 Then
he and his army lined up against them.
And he saw that the soldiers were
afraid to cross the stream, so he crossed
over first; and when his men saw him,
they crossed over after him. 7 Then he
divided the army and placed the horsemen in the midst of the infantry, for the
cavalry of the enemy were very numerous. 8 And they sounded the
trumpets, and Cendebeus and his
army were put to flight, and many of
them were wounded and fell; the rest
fled into the stronghold. 9 At that
time Judas the brother of John was
wounded, but John pursued them until
Cendebeus[j] reached Kedron, which he
had built. 10 They also fled into the
towers that were in the fields of Azotus,

h Gk *He* *i* Other authorities read *he*
j Gk *he*

---

perhaps the districts of 11.34; but compare v. 8. **33:** The Hasmoneans claimed that all Palestine had always belonged by right to the Jews. **35:** *Joppa and Gazara*, 12.33; 13.43–48. **37:** *Orthosia*, a few miles north of Tripolis; from there Trypho went to Apamea, where he was besieged and slain. **39–40:** *Kedron*, perhaps Gedereth, southwest of Ekron (Jos.15.41). The plan was to control the coastal plain and recover Gazara and Joppa. **16.1:** *John* Hyrcanus I commanded Gazara (13.53). **4:** *Horsemen* are now for the first time part of the Judean army. **7:** The cavalry were unseasoned, and he protected their flanks. *The stronghold*, Kedron (15.39). **10:** *Azotus*, destroyed by Jonathan (10.84).

and John[j] burned it with fire, and about
two thousand of them fell. And he
returned to Judea safely.
11 Now Ptolemy the son of Abubus
had been appointed governor over the
plain of Jericho, and he had much
silver and gold, [12]for he was son-in-law
of the high priest. [13]His heart was
lifted up; he determined to get control
of the country, and made treacherous
plans against Simon and his sons, to
do away with them. [14]Now Simon was
visiting the cities of the country and
attending to their needs, and he went
down to Jericho with Mattathias and
Judas his sons, in the one hundred and
seventy-seventh year,[k] in the eleventh
month, which is the month of Shebat.
[15]The son of Abubus received them
treacherously in the little stronghold
called Dok, which he had built; he gave
them a great banquet, and hid men
there. [16]When Simon and his sons
were drunk, Ptolemy and his men rose
up, took their weapons, and rushed in
against Simon in the banquet hall, and
they killed him and his two sons and
some of his servants. [17]So he committed an act of great treachery and
returned evil for good.
18 Then Ptolemy wrote a report
about these things and sent it to the
king, asking him to send troops to aid
him and to turn over to him the cities
and the country. [19]He sent other men
to Gazara to do away with John; he
sent letters to the captains asking them
to come to him so that he might give
them silver and gold and gifts; [20]and he
sent other men to take possession of
Jerusalem and the temple hill. [21]But
some one ran ahead and reported to
John at Gazara that his father and
brothers had perished, and that "he
has sent men to kill you also." [22]When
he heard this, he was greatly shocked;
and he seized the men who came to
destroy him and killed them, for he had
found out that they were seeking to
destroy him.
23 The rest of the acts of John and
his wars and the brave deeds which he
did, and the building of the walls
which he built, and his achievements,
[24]behold, they are written in the
chronicles of his high priesthood, from
the time that he became high priest
after his father.

j Gk *he*
k 134 B.C.

16.11–24: Death of Simon and accession of John Hyrcanus I. 11: *Plain of Jericho*, the fertile region north of the Dead Sea. **12:** *The high priest*, Simon. **14:** *Shebat*, February-March. **15:** *Dok*, 'Ain Duq, three miles northwest of Jericho. **18:** *The king*, Antiochus VII. **23:** *John* was high priest 134–104 B.C. When Antiochus later besieged Jerusalem, John was defeated but made peace and accompanied the king on an expedition to Parthia, where Antiochus was killed. Afterward he gained control of most of Palestine, and forced the Idumeans to adopt Judaism. Late in his reign the Pharisees turned against him and demanded that he give up the high priesthood. **24:** *The chronicles* have been lost.

THE SECOND BOOK OF THE

MACCABEES

Second Maccabees is an epitome or abridgment (2.23–28) of a five volume history, now lost, written by a certain Jason of Cyrene. Both Jason's work and 2 Maccabees were evidently composed in Greek, in which language the latter has been preserved. Jason narrated the events of Jewish history from the time of the high priest Onias III and the Syrian king Seleucus IV to the defeat of Nicanor's army (from about 180 to 161 B.C.), thus paralleling 1 Macc.1.10–7.50.

The purpose of Jason was to interpret history theologically. One of his favorite themes is the sanctity of the temple. He is the first writer known to us who celebrates the deeds of the martyrs, though there is a foreshadowing of such an interest in the book of Daniel. He also seems to be the first to teach clearly that the world was created out of nothing (7.28). He believed that the saints in heaven interceded for men on earth (15.11–16), and that the living might pray and offer sacrifices for the dead (12.43–45). His book includes accounts of marvelous portents and the miraculous intervention of angels. Jason seems not to have been a Pharisee; he may reflect the ideas of Jews at Antioch or possibly Alexandria.

The epitomist added chs. 1–2, 15.37–39, and several pretentious comments elsewhere. Sometimes there are signs of careless abbreviation, and he may have rearranged some incidents. Jason's history was probably not written before 110 B.C., and 2 Maccabees, as we have it, may have been composed some time during the first century B.C. It often supplements the information contained in 1 Maccabees, but its historical veracity is, on the whole, less trustworthy than that of 1 Maccabees.

THE JEWISH BRETHREN IN JERUSALEM
and those in the land of Judea,
To their Jewish brethren in Egypt,
Greeting, and good peace.
2 May God do good to you, and may
he remember his covenant with Abraham and Isaac and Jacob, his faithful
servants. 3 May he give you all a heart
to worship him and to do his will with
a strong heart and a willing spirit.
4 May he open your heart to his law
and his commandments, and may he
bring peace. 5 May he hear your prayers
and be reconciled to you, and may he
not forsake you in time of evil. 6 We
are now praying for you here.
7 In the reign of Demetrius, in the
one hundred and sixty-ninth year,[a] we
Jews wrote to you, in the critical distress which came upon us in those years
after Jason and his company revolted
from the holy land and the kingdom
8 and burned the gate and shed innocent
blood. We besought the Lord and we
were heard, and we offered sacrifice and
cereal offering, and we lighted the
lamps and we set out the loaves. 9 And
now see that you keep the feast of
booths in the month of Chislev, in the
one hundred and eighty-eighth year.[b]

a 143 B.C.
b 124 B.C.

1.1–9: Letter to the Jews in Egypt. The epitomist, who abridged the history of Jason of Cyrene (2.23), includes two letters urging that the new festival be kept (v. 9). The first is addressed to the large Jewish community that had lived in Egypt since Alexander the Great (1 Macc.1.1). **1:** Greek letters usually began with the word *greeting*, and Jewish ones with *peace* (Rom.1.7). **2:** Gen.15.18; 26.3; 35.12; Lev.26.27–45. **5:** To live outside Judea was thought of as divine punishment. **7:** The previous letter was in the reign of Demetrius II (see 1 Macc. 10.67 n.). *The critical distress* was the capture and murder of the high priest Jonathan (1 Macc. 12.48; see 13.23 n.). *Jason and his company*, 4.7–22. *The kingdom*, rule of the legitimate high priests. **8:** *Burned the gate*, 1 Macc.4.38. *Shed innocent blood*, 1 Macc.1.60–61. *We were heard*, i.e. by God, when Simon made Judea independent (1 Macc.13.1–42). **9:** *The feast of booths* would properly be kept in September (Lev.23.33–43). This refers to Hanukkah, celebrated on the 25th of *Chislev* (November-December), commemorating Judas Maccabeus' restoration of the temple (10.1–8; 1 Macc.4.59). Palestinian Jews now wished the Egyptian Jews to observe the feast in 124 B.C., when they wrote.

10 Those in Jerusalem and those in
Judea and the senate and Judas,

To Aristobulus, who is of the family
of the anointed priests, teacher of
Ptolemy the king, and to the Jews in
Egypt,

Greeting, and good health.

11 Having been saved by God out
of grave dangers we thank him greatly
for taking our side against the king.[c]
12 For he drove out those who fought
against the holy city. 13 For when the
leader reached Persia with a force that
seemed irresistible, they were cut to
pieces in the temple of Nanea by a
deception employed by the priests of
Nanea. 14 For under pretext of intending to marry her, Antiochus came to
the place together with his friends, to
secure most of its treasures as a dowry.
15 When the priests of the temple of
Nanea had set out the treasures and
Antiochus had come with a few men
inside the wall of the sacred precinct,
they closed the temple as soon as he
entered it. 16 Opening the secret door
in the ceiling, they threw stones and
struck down the leader and his men,
and dismembered them and cut off
their heads and threw them to the
people outside. 17 Blessed in every way
be our God, who has brought judgment
upon those who have behaved impiously.

18 Since on the twenty-fifth day of
Chislev we shall celebrate the purification of the temple, we thought it necessary to notify you, in order that you
also may celebrate the feast of booths
and the feast of the fire given when
Nehemiah, who built the temple and
the altar, offered sacrifices.

19 For when our fathers were being
led captive to Persia, the pious priests
of that time took some of the fire of
the altar and secretly hid it in the hollow of a dry cistern, where they took
such precautions that the place was
unknown to any one. 20 But after many
years had passed, when it pleased God,
Nehemiah, having been commissioned
by the king of Persia, sent the descendants of the priests who had hidden the
fire to get it. And when they reported
to us that they had not found fire but
thick liquid, he ordered them to dip it
out and bring it. 21 And when the
materials for the sacrifices were presented, Nehemiah ordered the priests
to sprinkle the liquid on the wood and
what was laid upon it. 22 When this was
done and some time had passed and
the sun, which had been clouded over,
shone out, a great fire blazed up, so
that all marveled. 23 And while the
sacrifice was being consumed, the
priests offered prayer—the priests and
every one. Jonathan led, and the rest
responded, as did Nehemiah. 24 The
prayer was to this effect:

"O Lord, Lord God, Creator of all
things, who art awe-inspiring and
strong and just and merciful, who alone
art King and art kind, 25 who alone art
bountiful, who alone art just and al-

c Cn: Gk *as those who array themselves against a king*

1.10–2.18: Letter to Aristobulus. The purpose of the letter is to show why the new eight day festival should be kept, though it had not been prescribed by the Mosaic law. Nehemiah's rededication of the temple was a precedent (1.18–36). **10:** *The senate*, see 1 Macc.12.6 n. *The anointed priests*, descendants of Zadok (2 Chr.31.10), from whom high priests were chosen. One branch of these came to Egypt with Ptolemy I. *The king*, Ptolemy VII Physcon, who reigned 145–116 B.C. **11:** *Grave dangers*, in the time of king Antiochus IV (4.7). **13:** *The leader*, Antiochus IV, died later; his forces *were cut to pieces* (9.1–4; 1 Macc.6.1–4). *Nanea*, a Syrian goddess equated with Artemis or Aphrodite and the Persian Anahita. **14:** *Marry her*, the goddess, so as to obtain a large *dowry* from the treasures at her temple (compare 9.2; 1 Macc.6.1–4). **18:** *The feast of booths*, compare 1 Macc.10.21; 1 Kg.8.2; Neh.8.13–18. *The feast of the fire*, vv. 19–36. Fire and light are associated with Hanukkah, which is celebrated with a nine-branched candlestick. A Talmudic tradition tells of a small amount of oil that burned miraculously for a long time till new oil could be consecrated. **19:** *Persia*, actually Babylonia (2 Kg.24.14), later part of the Persian empire. **20:** *Nehemiah . . . commissioned*, Neh.2.7–8; his book does not contain the legend of the fire. *Thick liquid*, naphtha or petroleum (v. 36). **22:** 1 Kg.18.33–38.

mighty and eternal, who dost rescue
Israel from every evil, who didst choose
the fathers and consecrate them, 26ac-
cept this sacrifice on behalf of all thy
people Israel and preserve thy portion
and make it holy. 27Gather together
our scattered people, set free those who
are slaves among the Gentiles, look
upon those who are rejected and despised, and let the Gentiles know that
thou art our God. 28Afflict those who
oppress and are insolent with pride.
29Plant thy people in thy holy place, as
Moses said."

30 Then the priests sang the hymns.
31And when the materials of the sacrifice were consumed, Nehemiah ordered
that the liquid that was left should be
poured upon large stones. 32When
this was done, a flame blazed up; but
when the light from the altar shone
back, it went out. 33When this matter
became known, and it was reported to
the king of the Persians that, in the
place where the exiled priests had
hidden the fire, the liquid had appeared with which Nehemiah and his
associates had burned the materials of
the sacrifice, 34the king investigated the
matter, and enclosed the place and
made it sacred. 35And with those
persons whom the king favored he
exchanged many excellent gifts. 36Ne-
hemiah and his associates called this
"nephthar," which means purification,
but by most people it is called naphtha.[d]

2 One finds in the records that Jeremiah the prophet ordered those
who were being deported to take some
of the fire, as has been told, 2and that
the prophet after giving them the law
instructed those who were being deported not to forget the commandments of the Lord, nor to be led astray
in their thoughts upon seeing the gold
and silver statues and their adornment.
3And with other similar words he exhorted them that the law should not
depart from their hearts.

4 It was also in the writing that the
prophet, having received an oracle,
ordered that the tent and the ark should
follow with him, and that he went out
to the mountain where Moses had
gone up and had seen the inheritance of
God. 5And Jeremiah came and found
a cave, and he brought there the tent
and the ark and the altar of incense,
and he sealed up the entrance. 6Some
of those who followed him came up to
mark the way, but could not find it.
7When Jeremiah learned of it, he
rebuked them and declared: "The
place shall be unknown until God
gathers his people together again and
shows his mercy. 8And then the Lord
will disclose these things, and the glory
of the Lord and the cloud will appear,
as they were shown in the case of
Moses, and as Solomon asked that
the place should be specially consecrated."

9 It was also made clear that being
possessed of wisdom Solomon[e] offered
sacrifice for the dedication and completion of the temple. 10Just as Moses
prayed to the Lord, and fire came down
from heaven and devoured the sacrifices, so also Solomon prayed, and the
fire came down and consumed the
whole burnt offerings. 11And Moses
said, "They were consumed because
the sin offering had not been eaten."

d Gk *nephthai* *e* Gk *he*

25: *Who didst choose*, Gen.12.1–3; 22.15–18; Dt.14.2; Mal.1.2. **26:** *Thy portion*, Israel (Dt.32.9). *Holy*, Lev.19.2. **27:** *Gather together*, Ps.147.2; Jer.23.8; Sir.36.11; Bar.5.6. **28:** *Afflict . . . insolent*, 1 Sam.2.3–4; Lk.1.51–52. **29:** *As Moses said*, Dt.30.5. **34:** Localities where miracles occurred were *enclosed* as *sacred*. The Persians considered fire holy. **36:** *Nephthar* is an otherwise unknown word. **2.1:** No such *records* are known. *Jeremiah* remained in Judea after the exile (Jer.29.1–23; 40.1–42.7). **4:** Solomon brought the *tent* to Jerusalem with the ark (1 Kg.8.4). There is no further record in the Old Testament of the tent, but the ark was kept in the first temple; according to a later tradition Jeremiah concealed the ark after the temple was destroyed in 587–6 B.C. *The mountain*, Nebo (Dt.32.49). **8:** *The glory* and *the cloud* indicate God's direct presence (Ex.16.10; Mk.9.2–8). *Solomon*, 1 Kg.8.11. **9:** Solomon's *wisdom*, 1 Kg. 3.3–28; 4.29–34. *Offered sacrifice*, 1 Kg.8.62–64. **10:** *Moses prayed*, Lev.9.24. *Solomon*, 2 Chr.

12 Likewise Solomon also kept the
eight days.
13 The same things are reported in
the records and in the memoirs of
Nehemiah, and also that he founded
a library and collected the books about
the kings and prophets, and the writings of David, and letters of kings
about votive offerings. 14 In the same
way Judas also collected all the books
that had been lost on account of the
war which had come upon us, and
they are in our possession. 15 So if you
have need of them, send people to get
them for you.
16 Since, therefore, we are about to
celebrate the purification, we write to
you. Will you therefore please keep
the days. 17 It is God who has saved
all his people, and has returned the
inheritance to all, and the kingship
and priesthood and consecration, 18 as
he promised through the law. For we
have hope in God that he will soon
have mercy upon us and will gather us
from everywhere under heaven into
his holy place, for he has rescued us
from great evils and has purified the
place.

19 The story of Judas Maccabeus
and his brothers, and the purification
of the great temple, and the dedication
of the altar, 20 and further the wars
against Antiochus Epiphanes and his
son Eupator, 21 and the appearances
which came from heaven to those who
strove zealously on behalf of Judaism,
so that though few in number they
seized the whole land and pursued the
barbarian hordes, 22 and recovered the
temple famous throughout the world
and freed the city and restored the laws
that were about to be abolished, while
the Lord with great kindness became
gracious to them— 23 all this, which has
been set forth by Jason of Cyrene in
five volumes, we shall attempt to con-
dense into a single book. 24 For considering the flood of numbers involved
and the difficulty there is for those who
wish to enter upon the narratives of
history because of the mass of material,
25 we have aimed to please those who
wish to read, to make it easy for those
who are inclined to memorize, and to
profit all readers. 26 For us who have
undertaken the toil of abbreviating, it
is no light matter but calls for sweat
and loss of sleep, 27 just as it is not easy
for one who prepares a banquet and
seeks the benefit of others. However,
to secure the gratitude of many we will
gladly endure the uncomfortable toil,
28 leaving the responsibility for exact
details to the compiler, while devoting
our effort to arriving at the outlines of
the condensation. 29 For as the master
builder of a new house must be concerned with the whole construction,
while the one who undertakes its painting and decoration has to consider only
what is suitable for its adornment, such
in my judgment is the case with us.
30 It is the duty of the original historian
to occupy the ground and to discuss
matters from every side and to take
trouble with details, 31 but the one who

7.1. **11:** The meaning is obscure, but see Lev.10.16–19. **12:** *Eight days*, 1 Kg.8.65; 2 Chr.7.9. **13:** *The memoirs of Nehemiah*, Neh. ch. 8. There is no record that *he founded a library*, but the Pentateuch was canonized in his time, and part of *the books . . . and the writings of David* were perhaps collected then. *Votive offerings*, made to the temple (Ezra 7.15–20). **14:** *Judas* Maccabeus may have *collected all the books* remaining after the destruction in the time of Antiochus IV (1 Macc.1.56–57). **16:** 1.18. **17:** *The kingship*, independence; the Hasmoneans were not yet called kings. **18:** 1.27; Dt.30.3.

2.19–32: The epitomist's preface. This is like Polonius' long speech in *Hamlet:* "Since brevity is the soul of wit . . . I will be brief" (compare v. 31). He summarizes parts of the book (vv. 19–22): *wars against Antiochus* IV (4.7–10.9) and *his son* Antiochus V *Eupator* (10.10–13.26) and explains that he is condensing the work of *Jason* (vv. 23–24; see the Introduction to 2 Maccabees). **20–21:** *Appearances*, (Gr. *epiphaneiai*), true divine manifestations, in contrast to Antiochus' boastful title *Epiphanes*, "god manifest." *Judaism*, first known use of this term for the religion, in contrast to Hellenism (4.13).

recasts the narrative should be allowed
to strive for brevity of expression and
to forego exhaustive treatment. 32At
this point therefore let us begin our
narrative, adding only so much to what
has already been said; for it is foolish
to lengthen the preface while cutting
short the history itself.

3 While the holy city was inhabited
in unbroken peace and the laws
were very well observed because of the
piety of the high priest Onias and his
hatred of wickedness, 2it came about
that the kings themselves honored the
place and glorified the temple with the
finest presents, 3so that even Seleucus,
the king of Asia, defrayed from his own
revenues all the expenses connected
with the service of the sacrifices. 4But a
man named Simon, of the tribe of
Benjamin, who had been made captain
of the temple, had a disagreement with
the high priest about the administration
of the city market; 5and when he could
not prevail over Onias he went to
Apollonius of Tarsus,[f] who at that time
was governor of Coelesyria and Phoenicia. 6He reported to him that the
treasury in Jerusalem was full of untold
sums of money, so that the amount of
the funds could not be reckoned, and
that they did not belong to the account
of the sacrifices, but that it was possible
for them to fall under the control of the
king. 7When Apollonius met the king,
he told him of the money about which
he had been informed. The king[g] chose
Heliodorus, who was in charge of his
affairs, and sent him with commands
to effect the removal of the aforesaid
money. 8Heliodorus at once set out on
his journey, ostensibly to make a tour
of inspection of the cities of Coelesyria
and Phoenicia, but in fact to carry out
the king's purpose.

9 When he had arrived at Jerusalem
and had been kindly welcomed by the
high priest of[h] the city, he told about
the disclosure that had been made and
stated why he had come, and he inquired whether this really was the situation. 10The high priest explained that
there were some deposits belonging to
widows and orphans, 11and also some
money of Hyrcanus, son of Tobias, a
man of very prominent position, and
that it totaled in all four hundred
talents of silver and two hundred of
gold. To such an extent the impious
Simon had misrepresented the facts.
12And he said that it was utterly impossible that wrong should be done to
those people who had trusted in the
holiness of the place and in the sanctity
and inviolability of the temple which is
honored throughout the whole world.
13But Heliodorus, because of the king's
commands which he had, said that this
money must in any case be confiscated
for the king's treasury. 14So he set a
day and went in to direct the inspection
of these funds.

There was no little distress through-

f Gk *Apollonius son of Tharseas*
g Gk *He*
h Some authorities read *and*

3.1–4.6: Simon's plot against Onias. **1:** Jerusalem was not *in unbroken peace,* though quieter than in later years. *The high priest Onias* III, son of Simon the Just (Sir.50.1–21), ruled before 175 B.C. He turned against Syria and collaborated with Egypt, while his cousins, the family of Tobias, to which Simon (v. 4) belonged, were pro-Syrian. **2:** *The kings,* i.e. the Ptolemies of Egypt and Antiochus III the Great (reigned 233–187 B.C.). **3:** *Seleucus* IV Philopator, son of Antiochus III, reigned 187–175 B.C. The events of 3.1–4.6 were in his reign. He was assassinated by Heliodorus (v. 7). **4:** *Simon* was a grandson of Tobias, who married a sister of Onias II. When Onias II refused to pay tribute to Egypt, Ptolemy III took away his civil authority and appointed Joseph, son of Tobias, *captain of the temple.* His son Simon succeeded him. **5:** *Tarsus,* capital of Cilicia (Acts 9.11), then part of the Seleucid empire. *Coelesyria,* see 1 Macc. 10.69 n. *Apollonius* was removed from office at the death of Seleucus IV in 175 B.C. **7:** *Heliodorus,* see v. 3 n. **9:** *The high priest,* Onias III. **11:** *Hyrcanus,* actually son of Joseph and half-brother of Simon (v. 4), was pro-Egyptian. He fled east of the Jordan after 198 B.C. and built the fortress of 'Araq el-Emir. He committed suicide on the accession of Antiochus IV in 175 B.C. *Simon had misrepresented the facts* only in part; Onias and Hyrcanus probably withheld tribute.

out the whole city. 15The priests prostrated themselves before the altar in
their priestly garments and called toward heaven upon him who had given
the law about deposits, that he should
keep them safe for those who had
deposited them. 16To see the appearance of the high priest was to be
wounded at heart, for his face and the
change in his color disclosed the
anguish of his soul. 17For terror and
bodily trembling had come over the
man, which plainly showed to those
who looked at him the pain lodged in
his heart. 18People also hurried out of
their houses in crowds to make a
general supplication because the holy
place was about to be brought into
contempt. 19Women, girded with sackcloth under their breasts, thronged the
streets. Some of the maidens who were
kept indoors ran together to the gates,
and some to the walls, while others
peered out of the windows. 20And
holding up their hands to heaven, they
all made entreaty. 21There was something pitiable in the prostration of the
whole populace and the anxiety of the
high priest in his great anguish.

22 While they were calling upon the
Almighty Lord that he would keep
what had been entrusted safe and
secure for those who had entrusted it,
23Heliodorus went on with what had
been decided. 24But when he arrived
at the treasury with his bodyguard,
then and there the Sovereign of spirits
and of all authority caused so great a
manifestation that all who had been so
bold as to accompany him were astounded by the power of God, and
became faint with terror. 25For there
appeared to them a magnificently
caparisoned horse, with a rider of
frightening mien, and it rushed furiously at Heliodorus and struck at him
with its front hoofs. Its rider was seen
to have armor and weapons of gold.
26Two young men also appeared to
him, remarkably strong, gloriously
beautiful and splendidly dressed, who
stood on each side of him and scourged
him continuously, inflicting many
blows on him. 27When he suddenly
fell to the ground and deep darkness
came over him, his men took him up
and put him on a stretcher 28and
carried him away, this man who had
just entered the aforesaid treasury with
a great retinue and all his bodyguard
but was now unable to help himself;
and they recognized clearly the sovereign power of God. 29While he lay
prostrate, speechless because of the
divine intervention and deprived of any
hope of recovery, 30they praised the
Lord who had acted marvelously for
his own place. And the temple, which
a little while before was full of fear and
disturbance, was filled with joy and
gladness, now that the Almighty Lord
had appeared.

31 Quickly some of Heliodorus'
friends asked Onias to call upon the
Most High and to grant life to one who
was lying quite at his last breath. 32And
the high priest, fearing that the king
might get the notion that some foul
play had been perpetrated by the Jews
with regard to Heliodorus, offered
sacrifice for the man's recovery.
33While the high priest was making
the offering of atonement, the same
young men appeared again to Heliodorus, dressed in the same clothing,
and they stood and said, "Be very
grateful to Onias the high priest, since
for his sake the Lord has granted you
your life. 34And see that you, who have
been scourged by heaven, report to all
men the majestic power of God."
Having said this they vanished.

35 Then Heliodorus offered sacrifice
to the Lord and made very great vows
to the Savior of his life, and having
bidden Onias farewell, he marched off

18: Temples, whether pagan or Jewish, were considered inviolate. **19:** *Sackcloth*, a sign of mourning and penitence. *Maidens* were usually *kept indoors* until their marriage. **20:** *Holding up their hands*, the ancient gesture of prayer (1 Kg.8.54; 1 Tim.2.8). **24:** *Manifestation*, see 2.21 n. **29:** *Speechless*, Lk.1.20. **31:** *The Most High* (Gen.14.18), a title often used by non-Jews

with his forces to the king. 36 And he
bore testimony to all men of the deeds
of the supreme God, which he had
seen with his own eyes. 37 When the
king asked Heliodorus what sort of
person would be suitable to send on
another mission to Jerusalem, he replied, 38 "If you have any enemy or
plotter against your government, send
him there, for you will get him back
thoroughly scourged, if he escapes at
all, for there certainly is about the place
some power of God. 39 For he who has
his dwelling in heaven watches over
that place himself and brings it aid, and
he strikes and destroys those who come
to do it injury." 40 This was the outcome of the episode of Heliodorus and
the protection of the treasury.

4 The previously mentioned Simon,
who had informed about the
money against[i] his own country,
slandered Onias, saying that it was he
who had incited Heliodorus and had
been the real cause of the misfortune.
2 He dared to designate as a plotter
against the government the man who
was the benefactor of the city, the protector of his fellow countrymen, and a
zealot for the laws. 3 When his hatred
progressed to such a degree that even
murders were committed by one of
Simon's approved agents, 4 Onias recognized that the rivalry was serious and
that Apollonius, the son of Menestheus[j]
and governor of Coelesyria and Phoenicia, was intensifying the malice of
Simon. 5 So he betook himself to the
king, not accusing his fellow citizens
but having in view the welfare, both
public and private, of all the people.
6 For he saw that without the king's
attention public affairs could not again
reach a peaceful settlement, and that
Simon would not stop his folly.

7 When Seleucus died and Antiochus
who was called Epiphanes succeeded
to the kingdom, Jason the brother of
Onias obtained the high priesthood by
corruption, 8 promising the king at an
interview[k] three hundred and sixty
talents of silver and, from another
source of revenue, eighty talents. 9 In
addition to this he promised to pay one
hundred and fifty more if permission
were given to establish by his authority
a gymnasium and a body of youth for
it, and to enrol the men of Jerusalem
as citizens of Antioch. 10 When the
king assented and Jason[l] came to
office, he at once shifted his countrymen over to the Greek way of life. 11 He
set aside the existing royal concessions
to the Jews, secured through John the
father of Eupolemus, who went on the
mission to establish friendship and
alliance with the Romans; and he
destroyed the lawful ways of living and
introduced new customs contrary to
the law. 12 For with alacrity he founded
a gymnasium right under the citadel,
and he induced the noblest of the

i Gk *and*
j Vg Compare verse 21: Gk uncertain
k Or *by a petition* *l* Gk *he*

(Dan.3.26; Mk.5.7). **4.1–6:** Intrigues concerning the high priesthood. *Simon* (see 3.4 n.) was disturbed because *Onias* and *Heliodorus* were now friends. The latter may already have planned to kill Seleucus IV and wanted the high priest's good will. *Apollonius*, in favor with Seleucus, continued to support Simon. **5:** Before Onias arrived in Antioch, Seleucus had already been assassinated by Heliodorus (175 B.C.).

4.7–22: Jason as high priest. 7: *Antiochus* IV *Epiphanes*, "god manifest," called Epimanes, "madman," by his enemies, was brother of Seleucus IV, and *succeeded to the kingdom* despite Heliodorus' attempt at revolution. He reigned 175–164 B.C. He had great ability but intense passion and pride (1 Macc.1.1–10). *Jason the brother of Onias* III (3.1), originally named Joshua, took a Greek name. **9–10:** Like Alexander the Great and his successors, Antiochus promoted *the Greek way of life* in order to strengthen his kingdom through cultural unity; this involved worship of other gods. *A gymnasium and a body of youth for it* were necessary *to enrol the men of Jerusalem as citizens of Antioch*, so that the city could coin money and have honors and commercial advantages. **11:** *Royal concessions*, granted by Antiochus III (3.2) The mission of *Eupolemus* (1 Macc.8.17) was later. *Destroyed*, 1 Macc.1.15,44–50. **12:** The broad-brimmed *Greek hat* was worn by the god Hermes; headgear has usually had national or

young men[m] to wear the Greek hat.
13There was such an extreme of Hellenization and increase in the adoption of
foreign ways because of the surpassing
wickedness of Jason, who was ungodly
and no high priest, 14that the priests
were no longer intent upon their service at the altar. Despising the sanctuary and neglecting the sacrifices, they
hastened to take part in the unlawful
proceedings in the wrestling arena after
the call to the discus, 15disdaining the
honors prized by their fathers and
putting the highest value upon Greek
forms of prestige. 16For this reason
heavy disaster overtook them, and
those whose ways of living they admired and wished to imitate completely
became their enemies and punished
them. 17For it is no light thing to show
irreverence to the divine laws—a fact
which later events will make clear.

18 When the quadrennial games
were being held at Tyre and the king
was present, 19the vile Jason sent
envoys, chosen as being Antiochian
citizens from Jerusalem, to carry three
hundred silver drachmas for the sacrifice to Hercules. Those who carried
the money, however, thought best not
to use it for sacrifice, because that was
inappropriate, but to expend it for
another purpose. 20So this money was
intended by the sender for the sacrifice
to Hercules, but by the decision of its
carriers it was applied to the construction of triremes.

21 When Apollonius the son of
Menestheus was sent to Egypt for the
coronation[n] of Philometor as king,
Antiochus learned that Philometor[o]
had become hostile to his government,
and he took measures for his own
security. Therefore upon arriving at
Joppa he proceeded to Jerusalem. 22He
was welcomed magnificently by Jason
and the city, and ushered in with a
blaze of torches and with shouts. Then
he marched into Phoenicia.

23 After a period of three years
Jason sent Menelaus, the brother of
the previously mentioned Simon, to
carry the money to the king and to
complete the records of essential business. 24But he, when presented to the
king, extolled him with an air of
authority, and secured the high priesthood for himself, outbidding Jason by
three hundred talents of silver. 25After
receiving the king's orders he returned,
possessing no qualification for the high
priesthood, but having the hot temper
of a cruel tyrant and the rage of a
savage wild beast. 26So Jason, who
after supplanting his own brother was
supplanted by another man, was driven
as a fugitive into the land of Ammon.
27And Menelaus held the office, but
he did not pay regularly any of the
money promised to the king. 28When
Sostratus the captain of the citadel
kept requesting payment, for the collection of the revenue was his responsibility, the two of them were summoned
by the king on account of this issue.
29Menelaus left his own brother Lysimachus as deputy in the high priesthood,
while Sostratus left Crates, the commander of the Cyprian troops.

30 While such was the state of

m Some authorities add *subjecting them*
n The exact meaning of the Greek word is uncertain
o Gk *he*

religious significance in the East. **13:** *Hellenization*, Greek religion and culture (see vv. 9–10 n.). *No high priest*, because he got the office by bribery and did not keep the Mosaic law. **18:** *Tyre*, an important port north of Palestine (Jos.19.29; 1 Kg.7.13); *quadrennial games* had been held there as early as the time of Alexander the Great. **19:** *Hercules*, the Greek name of the god Melkart of Tyre. **20:** *Triremes*, war vessels manned by three benches of rowers. **21:** *Apollonius*, v. 4. *The coronation* of Ptolemy VI *Philometor* occurred about 172 B.C., some time after the death of his mother, Cleopatra I, and he ruled until 146 or 145 B.C. His advisers abandoned Cleopatra's policy, became *hostile* to Syria, and claimed Palestine. *Joppa*, the port forty miles from Jerusalem. **22:** *Phoenicia*, the coastal plain.

4.23–50: Menelaus as high priest. **23:** *Menelaus* reigned from about 172 to 162 B.C., when he was executed (13.3–8) and replaced by Alcimus (14.3–14). **26:** *Land of Ammon*, east of the Jordan, near the present Amman. **29:** *The Cyprian troops* were mercenaries. **30:** *Mallus* was

affairs, it happened that the people of
Tarsus and of Mallus revolted because
their cities had been given as a present
to Antiochis, the king's concubine.
31 So the king went hastily to settle the
trouble, leaving Andronicus, a man of
high rank, to act as his deputy. 32 But
Menelaus, thinking he had obtained a
suitable opportunity, stole some of the
gold vessels of the temple and gave
them to Andronicus; other vessels, as
it happened, he had sold to Tyre and
the neighboring cities. 33 When Onias
became fully aware of these acts he
publicly exposed them, having first
withdrawn to a place of sanctuary at
Daphne near Antioch. 34 Therefore
Menelaus, taking Andronicus aside,
urged him to kill Onias. Andronicus[p]
came to Onias, and resorting to
treachery offered him sworn pledges
and gave him his right hand, and in
spite of his suspicion persuaded Onias[q]
to come out from the place of sanctuary; then, with no regard for justice,
he immediately put him out of the way.
35 For this reason not only Jews, but
many also of other nations, were
grieved and displeased at the unjust
murder of the man. 36 When the king
returned from the region of Cilicia, the
Jews in the city[r] appealed to him with
regard to the unreasonable murder of
Onias, and the Greeks shared their
hatred of the crime. 37 Therefore
Antiochus was grieved at heart and
filled with pity, and wept because of
the moderation and good conduct of
the deceased; 38 and inflamed with
anger, he immediately stripped off the
purple robe from Andronicus, tore off
his garments, and led him about the
whole city to that very place where he
had committed the outrage against
Onias, and there he dispatched the
bloodthirsty fellow. The Lord thus
repaid him with the punishment he
deserved.

39 When many acts of sacrilege had
been committed in the city by Lysimachus with the connivance of Menelaus, and when report of them had
spread abroad, the populace gathered
against Lysimachus, because many of
the gold vessels had already been
stolen. 40 And since the crowds were
becoming aroused and filled with anger,
Lysimachus armed about three thousand men and launched an unjust attack, under the leadership of a certain
Auranus, a man advanced in years and
no less advanced in folly. 41 But when
the Jews[s] became aware of Lysimachus' attack, some picked up stones,
some blocks of wood, and others took
handfuls of the ashes that were lying
about, and threw them in wild confusion at Lysimachus and his men. 42 As
a result, they wounded many of them,
and killed some, and put them all to
flight; and the temple robber himself
they killed close by the treasury.

43 Charges were brought against
Menelaus about this incident. 44 When
the king came to Tyre, three men sent
by the senate presented the case before
him. 45 But Menelaus, already as good
as beaten, promised a substantial bribe
to Ptolemy son of Dorymenes to win
over the king. 46 Therefore Ptolemy,
taking the king aside into a colonnade
as if for refreshment, induced the king
to change his mind. 47 Menelaus, the

p Gk *He* *q* Gk *him*
r Or *in each city*
s Gk *they*

on the Pyramus river east of *Tarsus* (3.5). Hellenistic kings often provided a wife or *concubine* with a regular income by giving her a city. Antiochus, being extravagant (see 1 Macc.3.30 n.), was often in need of money. **32:** *Gave them*, either to pay tribute or as a bribe. **33:** *Daphne*, about five miles from *Antioch*, had a *place of sanctuary* to Apollo and Artemis. **35:** *Unjust murder*, he had been lured from a place protected by the gods. **38:** *Stripped off the purple robe*, degrading him before execution. **39:** *The city*, Jerusalem. *Menelaus* was still in Antioch. **42:** *The temple robber*, Lysimachus. **44:** *The senate*, see 1 Macc.12.6 n. **45:** *Dorymenes* had fought for Ptolemy IV against Antiochus III; his son *Ptolemy* had been governor of Cyprus and deserted to Antiochus IV (see 10.12–13 n.). **47:** The *Scythians* (Col.3.11) lived in what is now southern Russia and were proverbial for their brutality.

cause of all the evil, he acquitted of the charges against him, while he sentenced to death those unfortunate men, who would have been freed uncondemned if they had pleaded even before Scythians. [48]And so those who had spoken for the city and the villages[t] and the holy vessels quickly suffered the unjust penalty. [49]Therefore even the Tyrians, showing their hatred of the crime, provided magnificently for their funeral. [50]But Menelaus, because of the cupidity of those in power, remained in office, growing in wickedness, having become the chief plotter against his fellow citizens.

5 About this time Antiochus made his second invasion of Egypt. [2]And it happened that over all the city, for almost forty days, there appeared golden-clad horsemen charging through the air, in companies fully armed with lances and drawn swords—[3]troops of horsemen drawn up, attacks and counterattacks made on this side and on that, brandishing of shields, massing of spears, hurling of missiles, the flash of golden trappings, and armor of all sorts. [4]Therefore all men prayed that the apparition might prove to have been a good omen.

5 When a false rumor arose that Antiochus was dead, Jason took no less than a thousand men and suddenly made an assault upon the city. When the troops upon the wall had been forced back and at last the city was being taken, Menelaus took refuge in the citadel. [6]But Jason kept relentlessly slaughtering his fellow citizens, not realizing that success at the cost of one's kindred is the greatest misfortune, but imagining that he was setting up trophies of victory over enemies and not over fellow countrymen. [7]He did not gain control of the government, however; and in the end got only disgrace from his conspiracy, and fled again into the country of the Ammonites. [8]Finally he met a miserable end. Accused[u] before Aretas the ruler of the Arabs, fleeing from city to city, pursued by all men, hated as a rebel against the laws, and abhorred as the executioner of his country and his fellow citizens, he was cast ashore in Egypt; [9]and he who had driven many from their own country into exile died in exile, having embarked to go to the Lacedaemonians in hope of finding protection because of their kinship. [10]He who had cast out many to lie unburied had no one to mourn for him; he had no funeral of any sort and no place in the tomb of his fathers.

11 When news of what had happened reached the king, he took it to mean that Judea was in revolt. So, raging inwardly, he left Egypt and took the city by storm. [12]And he commanded his soldiers to cut down relentlessly every one they met and to slay those who went into the houses. [13]Then there was killing of young and old, destruction of boys, women, and children, and slaughter of virgins and infants. [14]Within the total of three days eighty thousand were destroyed, forty thousand in hand-to-hand fight-

t Other authorities read *the people*
u Cn: Gk *Imprisoned*

5.1–27: Antiochus IV desecrates the temple. 1: *Second invasion*, in 169 B.C.; perhaps the writer regards the coming of the Seleucid army into Palestine in 171 B.C. (4.21–22) as the first invasion. We would speak of them as the first and second phases of the invasion (compare 1 Macc.1.16–19). **2–4:** 3.25–26. *The city*, Jerusalem. **5–8:** *Jason* was an Oniad and pro-Egyptian (see 3.1 n.). Thinking *that Antiochus was dead*, he planned, with Egyptian help, to recover the high priesthood. He was opposed by *Menelaus* the Tobiad (4.23) and also by the Jews loyal to Judaism; he massacred people of both factions. *Ammonites*, 4.26. *Aretas*, king of Nabatean Arabia, south and east of Palestine; his capital was at Petra. **9–10:** Rejected in Egypt, Jason fled to Sparta (1 Macc.12.7). *Unburied*, see 1 Macc.7.17 n.; 1 Kg.13.22. **11–14:** So confused was the situation that Antiochus thought all *Judea was in revolt*. He was *raging inwardly* because the Romans had forced him out of Egypt (see 1 Macc.1.20 n.); both his foreign and his domestic programs were collapsing. **11:** *The city*, Jerusalem.

ing; and as many were sold into
slavery as were slain.
15 Not content with this, Antiochus[v] dared to enter the most holy
temple in all the world, guided by
Menelaus, who had become a traitor
both to the laws and to his country.
16 He took the holy vessels with his
polluted hands, and swept away with
profane hands the votive offerings
which other kings had made to en-
hance the glory and honor of the place.
17 Antiochus was elated in spirit, and
did not perceive that the Lord was
angered for a little while because of the
sins of those who dwelt in the city, and
that therefore he was disregarding the
holy place. 18 But if it had not happened that they were involved in many
sins, this man would have been
scourged and turned back from his
rash act as soon as he came forward,
just as Heliodorus was, whom Seleucus
the king sent to inspect the treasury.
19 But the Lord did not choose the
nation for the sake of the holy place,
but the place for the sake of the nation.
20 Therefore the place itself shared in
the misfortunes that befell the nation
and afterward participated in its benefits; and what was forsaken in the
wrath of the Almighty was restored
again in all its glory when the great
Lord became reconciled.
21 So Antiochus carried off eighteen
hundred talents from the temple, and
hurried away to Antioch, thinking in
his arrogance that he could sail on the
land and walk on the sea, because his
mind was elated. 22 And he left governors to afflict the people: at Jerusalem,
Philip, by birth a Phrygian and in
character more barbarous than the
man who appointed him; 23 and at
Gerizim, Andronicus; and besides
these Menelaus, who lorded it over his
fellow citizens worse than the others
did. In his malice toward the Jewish
citizens,[w] 24 Antiochus[x] sent Apollonius, the captain of the Mysians, with
an army of twenty-two thousand, and
commanded him to slay all the grown
men and to sell the women and boys
as slaves. 25 When this man arrived in
Jerusalem, he pretended to be peaceably disposed and waited until the holy
sabbath day; then, finding the Jews not
at work, he ordered his men to parade
under arms. 26 He put to the sword all
those who came out to see them, then
rushed into the city with his armed
men and killed great numbers of
people.
27 But Judas Maccabeus, with about
nine others, got away to the wilderness,
and kept himself and his companions
alive in the mountains as wild animals
do; they continued to live on what
grew wild, so that they might not share
in the defilement.

6 Not long after this, the king sent
an Athenian[y] senator[z] to compel
the Jews to forsake the laws of their
fathers and cease to live by the laws of
God, 2 and also to pollute the temple in
Jerusalem and call it the temple of
Olympian Zeus, and to call the one in
Gerizim the temple of Zeus the Friend
of Strangers, as did the people who
dwelt in that place.

v Gk *he*
w Or *worse than the others did in his malice toward the Jewish citizens.* *x* Gk *he*
y Some authorities read *Antiochian*
z Or *Geron an Athenian*

15–23a: The temple had been pillaged after the first Egyptian invasion (1 Macc.1.21–28). *Angered for a little while,* not permanently (compare 6.12–16). **21:** *His arrogance* was that of a god manifest (see 4.7 n.). **22–23:** *Philip,* probably not the later regent (9.29). *Andronicus* (4.31) was now made governor of Samaria. **24–26:** *Antiochus sent Apollonius* about two years after the events of vv. 15–23 (see 1 Macc.1.29). Loyal Jews did not yet fight on the *sabbath* (1 Macc.2.32–41). **27:** *Judas Maccabeus,* the third son of Mattathias, of the Hasmonean family (1 Macc.2.1–28). *The defilement,* 4.11; 1 Macc.1.48, 63.

6.1–6: Campaign against Judaism. What had been voluntary (4.9–17) was now enforced (see 1 Macc.1.41–64 n.). **2:** *Olympian Zeus* was now identified with the God of Israel and probably with Antiochus. *To pollute the temple,* they set up a statue or pagan altar (1 Macc.1.54). The Samaritans, descendants of the ten northern tribes and Assyrian settlers (2 Kg.17.6,24), had

3 Harsh and utterly grievous was
the onslaught of evil. [4]For the temple
was filled with debauchery and reveling
by the Gentiles, who dallied with harlots and had intercourse with women
within the sacred precincts, and besides
brought in things for sacrifice that were
unfit. [5]The altar was covered with
abominable offerings which were forbidden by the laws. [6]A man could
neither keep the sabbath, nor observe
the feasts of his fathers, nor so much as
confess himself to be a Jew.

7 On the monthly celebration of the
king's birthday, the Jews[a] were taken,
under bitter constraint, to partake of
the sacrifices; and when the feast of
Dionysus came, they were compelled
to walk in the procession in honor of
Dionysus, wearing wreaths of ivy. [8]At
the suggestion of Ptolemy a decree was
issued to the neighboring Greek cities,
that they should adopt the same policy
toward the Jews and make them partake of the sacrifices, [9]and should slay
those who did not choose to change
over to Greek customs. One could see,
therefore, the misery that had come
upon them. [10]For example, two
women were brought in for having circumcised their children. These women
they publicly paraded about the city,
with their babies hung at their breasts,
then hurled them down headlong from
the wall. [11]Others who had assembled
in the caves near by, to observe the
seventh day secretly, were betrayed to
Philip and were all burned together,
because their piety kept them from
defending themselves, in view of their
regard for that most holy day.

12 Now I urge those who read this
book not to be depressed by such
calamities, but to recognize that these
punishments were designed not to
destroy but to discipline our people.
[13]In fact, not to let the impious alone
for long, but to punish them immediately, is a sign of great kindness.
[14]For in the case of the other nations
the Lord waits patiently to punish
them until they have reached the full
measure of their sins; but he does not
deal in this way with us, [15]in order that
he may not take vengeance on us afterward when our sins have reached their
height. [16]Therefore he never with-
draws his mercy from us. Though
he disciplines us with calamities, he
does not forsake his own people.
[17]Let what we have said serve as a
reminder; we must go on briefly with
the story.

18 Eleazar, one of the scribes in
high position, a man now advanced in
age and of noble presence, was being
forced to open his mouth to eat swine's
flesh. [19]But he, welcoming death with
honor rather than life with pollution,
went up to the rack of his own accord,
spitting out the flesh, [20]as men ought
to go who have the courage to refuse
things that it is not right to taste, even
for the natural love of life.

21 Those who were in charge of that
unlawful sacrifice took the man aside,
because of their long acquaintance
with him, and privately urged him to
bring meat of his own providing,
proper for him to use, and pretend that
he was eating the flesh of the sacrificial
meal which had been commanded by
the king, [22]so that by doing this he
might be saved from death, and be
treated kindly on account of his old

a Gk *they*

---

built the temple on Mount *Gerizim.* **4:** *Intercourse . . . sacred precincts*, as in Syrian fertility cults (see Let. Jer.6.11 n. and 6.43 n.). *Things unfit*, swine (Lev.11.7; 1 Macc.1.47). **6:** 1 Macc. 1.45–51. *Jew*, originally "Judean"; here "one loyal to the religion" (Judaism, 2.21).

6.7–17: The first martyrdoms. Chs. 6–7 are the earliest martyrologies, a type of writing popular subsequently in Christianity, designed to encourage the faithful when persecuted. **7:** *Dionysus*, god of wine and the grape harvest; *ivy* was one of his symbols. **8:** *Ptolemy*, see 4.45 n. *The same policy toward the Jews* outside Judea. **12–17:** The victories of Israel's enemies are explained as God's corrective punishment, always followed by mercy (compare Is.54.7–8).

6.18–31: Martyrdom of Eleazar. The story is told more elaborately in 4 Maccabees. **18:** *Scribes*, scholars learned in the Mosaic law, not necessarily priests. **19:** *Of his own accord*, like

friendship with them. 23But making a
high resolve, worthy of his years and
the dignity of his old age and the gray
hairs which he had reached with distinction and his excellent life even from
childhood, and moreover according
to the holy God-given law, he declared
himself quickly, telling them to send
him to Hades.
24 "Such pretense is not worthy of
our time of life," he said, "lest many
of the young should suppose that
Eleazar in his ninetieth year has gone
over to an alien religion, 25and through
my pretense, for the sake of living a
brief moment longer, they should be led
astray because of me, while I defile and
disgrace my old age. 26For even if for
the present I should avoid the punishment of men, yet whether I live or die
I shall not escape the hands of the
Almighty. 27Therefore, by manfully
giving up my life now, I will show myself worthy of my old age 28and leave
to the young a noble example of how
to die a good death willingly and nobly
for the revered and holy laws."
When he had said this, he went[b] at
once to the rack. 29And those who a
little before had acted toward him with
good will now changed to ill will,
because the words he had uttered were
in their opinion sheer madness.[c]
30When he was about to die under the
blows, he groaned aloud and said: "It
is clear to the Lord in his holy knowledge that, though I might have been
saved from death, I am enduring terrible sufferings in my body under this
beating, but in my soul I am glad
to suffer these things because I fear
him."
31 So in this way he died, leaving in
his death an example of nobility and a
memorial of courage, not only to the
young but to the great body of his
nation.

7 It happened also that seven brothers and their mother were arrested
and were being compelled by the king,
under torture with whips and cords, to
partake of unlawful swine's flesh.
2One of them, acting as their spokesman, said, "What do you intend to
ask and learn from us? For we are
ready to die rather than transgress the
laws of our fathers."
3 The king fell into a rage, and gave
orders that pans and caldrons be
heated. 4These were heated immediately, and he commanded that the
tongue of their spokesman be cut out
and that they scalp him and cut off his
hands and feet, while the rest of the
brothers and the mother looked on.
5When he was utterly helpless, the
king[d] ordered them to take him to the
fire, still breathing, and to fry him in a
pan. The smoke from the pan spread
widely, but the brothers[e] and their
mother encouraged one another to die
nobly, saying, 6"The Lord God is
watching over us and in truth has compassion on us, as Moses declared in his
song which bore witness against the
people to their faces, when he said,
'And he will have compassion on his
servants.'"
7 After the first brother had died in
this way, they brought forward the
second for their sport. They tore off
the skin of his head with the hair, and
asked him, "Will you eat rather than
have your body punished limb by
limb?" 8He replied in the language of
his fathers, and said to them, "No."
Therefore he in turn underwent tortures as the first brother had done.
9And when he was at his last breath,
he said, "You accursed wretch, you
dismiss us from this present life, but
the King of the universe will raise us

b Other authorities read *was dragged*
c The Greek text of this verse is uncertain
d Gk *he* *e* Gk *they*

many later martyrs. **29:** Pagans often regarded the martyrs as deluded fanatics. **30:** *Fear*, revere (Job 28.28; Ps.19.9).

7.1–42: Martyrdom of seven brothers and their mother. This story is the principal subject of 4 Maccabees. **2:** Dan.3.16–18. **6:** Dt.32.36. **7:** *Their sport*, Mk.15.17–20; Jn.19.2–3; Heb.11.36. **9:** God is often addressed in Jewish prayer as *King of the universe*. The doctrine of resurrection

up to an everlasting renewal of life,
because we have died for his laws."

10 After him, the third was the victim of their sport. When it was demanded, he quickly put out his tongue
and courageously stretched forth his
hands, 11 and said nobly, "I got these
from Heaven, and because of his laws
I disdain them, and from him I hope
to get them back again." 12 As a result
the king himself and those with him
were astonished at the young man's
spirit, for he regarded his sufferings as
nothing.

13 When he too had died, they maltreated and tortured the fourth in the
same way. 14 And when he was near
death, he said, "One cannot but choose
to die at the hands of men and to
cherish the hope that God gives of
being raised again by him. But for you
there will be no resurrection to life!"

15 Next they brought forward the
fifth and maltreated him. 16 But he
looked at the king,[f] and said, "Because
you have authority among men, mortal
though you are, you do what you
please. But do not think that God has
forsaken our people. 17 Keep on, and
see how his mighty power will torture
you and your descendants!"

18 After him they brought forward
the sixth. And when he was about to
die, he said, "Do not deceive yourself
in vain. For we are suffering these
things on our own account, because of
our sins against our own God. Therefore[g] astounding things have happened.
19 But do not think that you will go unpunished for having tried to fight
against God!"

20 The mother was especially ad-
mirable and worthy of honorable
memory. Though she saw her seven
sons perish within a single day, she
bore it with good courage because of
her hope in the Lord. 21 She encouraged
each of them in the language of their
fathers. Filled with a noble spirit, she
fired her woman's reasoning with a
man's courage, and said to them, 22 "I
do not know how you came into being
in my womb. It was not I who gave
you life and breath, nor I who set in
order the elements within each of you.
23 Therefore the Creator of the world,
who shaped the beginning of man and
devised the origin of all things, will in
his mercy give life and breath back to
you again, since you now forget yourselves for the sake of his laws."

24 Antiochus felt that he was being
treated with contempt, and he was
suspicious of her reproachful tone.
The youngest brother being still alive,
Antiochus[h] not only appealed to him
in words, but promised with oaths that
he would make him rich and enviable
if he would turn from the ways of his
fathers, and that he would take him for
his friend and entrust him with public
affairs. 25 Since the young man would
not listen to him at all, the king called
the mother to him and urged her to
advise the youth to save himself.
26 After much urging on his part, she
undertook to persuade her son. 27 But,
leaning close to him, she spoke in their
native tongue as follows, deriding the
cruel tyrant: "My son, have pity on
me. I carried you nine months in my
womb, and nursed you for three years,
and have reared you and brought you
up to this point in your life, and have
taken care of you.[i] 28 I beseech you, my
child, to look at the heaven and the
earth and see everything that is in
them, and recognize that God did not
make them out of things that existed.[j]

f Gk *him*
g Lat: other authorities omit *Therefore*
h Gk *he*
i Or *have borne the burden of your education*
j Or *God made them out of things that did not exist*

---

is now clearly stated (Dan.12.2; Mt.19.29; Lk.18.30). **11:** The whole body will be restored (Rom.8.23). **14:** The wicked will have *no resurrection to life* (Dan.12.2; Rev.20.14–15). **17:** Antiochus IV died in misery and his son was murdered (9.5–28). **18–19:** 6.12–16. **21:** *The language of their fathers,* Aramaic or possibly Hebrew. **22–23:** The hope of resurrection depends entirely on *the Creator* and his mercy. **27:** Children were often *nursed . . . for three years.* **28:** God made all things out of nothing, by his will and creative power, not from previously

Thus also mankind comes into being. 29 Do not fear this butcher, but prove worthy of your brothers. Accept death, so that in God's mercy I may get you back again with your brothers."

30 While she was still speaking, the young man said, "What are you[k] waiting for? I will not obey the king's command, but I obey the command of the law that was given to our fathers through Moses. 31 But you,[l] who have contrived all sorts of evil against the Hebrews, will certainly not escape the hands of God. 32 For we are suffering because of our own sins. 33 And if our living Lord is angry for a little while, to rebuke and discipline us, he will again be reconciled with his own servants. 34 But you, unholy wretch, you most defiled of all men, do not be elated in vain and puffed up by uncertain hopes, when you raise your hand against the children of heaven. 35 You have not yet escaped the judgment of the almighty, all-seeing God. 36 For our brothers after enduring a brief suffering have drunk[m] of everflowing life under God's covenant; but you, by the judgment of God, will receive just punishment for your arrogance. 37 I, like my brothers, give up body and life for the laws of our fathers, appealing to God to show mercy soon to our nation and by afflictions and plagues to make you confess that he alone is God, 38 and through me and my brothers to bring to an end the wrath of the Almighty which has justly fallen on our whole nation."

39 The king fell into a rage, and handled him worse than the others, being exasperated at his scorn. 40 So he died in his integrity, putting his whole trust in the Lord.

41 Last of all, the mother died, after her sons.

42 Let this be enough, then, about the eating of sacrifices and the extreme tortures.

8 But Judas, who was also called Maccabeus, and his companions secretly entered the villages and summoned their kinsmen and enlisted those who had continued in the Jewish faith, and so they gathered about six thousand men. 2 They besought the Lord to look upon the people who were oppressed by all, and to have pity on the temple which had been profaned by ungodly men, 3 and to have mercy on the city which was being destroyed and about to be leveled to the ground, and to hearken to the blood that cried out to him, 4 and to remember also the lawless destruction of the innocent babies and the blasphemies committed against his name, and to show his hatred of evil.

5 As soon as Maccabeus got his army organized, the Gentiles could not withstand him, for the wrath of the Lord had turned to mercy. 6 Coming without warning, he would set fire to towns and villages. He captured strategic positions and put to flight not a few of the enemy. 7 He found the nights most advantageous for such attacks. And talk of his valor spread everywhere.

8 When Philip saw that the man was gaining ground little by little, and that he was pushing ahead with more frequent successes, he wrote to Ptolemy, the governor of Coelesyria and Phoenicia, for aid to the king's government. 9 And Ptolemy[n] promptly ap-

k The Greek here for *you* is plural
l The Greek word here for *you* is singular
m Cn: Gk *fallen* *n* Gk *he*

---

existing matter (Heb.11.3). **31:** The Jews of Antioch called themselves *Hebrews*. **33:** 5.17; 6.12–16. **36:** The martyrs already enjoy *life*. *God's covenant* with Abraham (Gen.12.1–3; 15.5–6; 17.4–8) is believed to guarantee the resurrection of his descendants (compare Mk.12.26–27). **37:** Martyrs often prayed that their enemies would *confess that he alone is God* (compare 9.12).

8.1–7: Judas begins the revolt; after prayer (vv. 2–4) he begins guerrilla warfare (vv. 5–7).

8.8–29: First victory over Nicanor. Judas assembled his forces at Mizpah and attacked Gorgias' army at Emmaus (see 1 Macc.3.40 n.). **8:** *Philip*, see 5.22 n. *Ptolemy* (see 4.45 n.), appointed by Lysias after Antiochus had left for Persia (1 Macc.3.38). **9:** *Gorgias*, not Nicanor,

pointed Nicanor the son of Patroclus,
one of the king's chief friends, and sent
him, in command of no fewer than
twenty thousand Gentiles of all nations,
to wipe out the whole race of Judea.
He associated with him Gorgias, a
general and a man of experience in
military service. [10]Nicanor determined
to make up for the king the tribute due
to the Romans, two thousand talents,
by selling the captured Jews into
slavery. [11]And he immediately sent to
the cities on the seacoast, inviting them
to buy Jewish slaves and promising to
hand over ninety slaves for a talent,
not expecting the judgment from the
Almighty that was about to overtake
him.
12 Word came to Judas concerning
Nicanor's invasion; and when he told
his companions of the arrival of the
army, [13]those who were cowardly and
distrustful of God's justice ran off and
got away. [14]Others sold all their remaining property, and at the same time
besought the Lord to rescue those who
had been sold by the ungodly Nicanor
before he ever met them, [15]if not for
their own sake, yet for the sake of the
covenants made with their fathers, and
because he had called them by his holy
and glorious name. [16]But Maccabeus
gathered his men together, to the
number of six thousand, and exhorted
them not to be frightened by the enemy
and not to fear the great multitude of
Gentiles who were wickedly coming
against them, but to fight nobly,
[17]keeping before their eyes the lawless
outrage which the Gentiles[o] had committed against the holy place, and the
torture of the derided city, and besides,
the overthrow of their ancestral way of
life. [18]"For they trust to arms and acts
of daring," he said, "but we trust in
the Almighty God, who is able with a
single nod to strike down those who
are coming against us and even the
whole world."
19 Moreover he told them of the
times when help came to their ancestors; both the time of Sennacherib,
when one hundred and eighty-five thousand perished, [20]and the time of the
battle with the Galatians that took
place in Babylonia, when eight thousand in all went into the affair, with
four thousand Macedonians; and when
the Macedonians were hard pressed,
the eight thousand, by the help that
came to them from heaven, destroyed
one hundred and twenty thousand and
took much booty.
21 With these words he filled them
with good courage and made them
ready to die for their laws and their
country; then he divided his army into
four parts. [22]He appointed his brothers
also, Simon and Joseph and Jonathan,
each to command a division, putting
fifteen hundred men under each. [23]Be-
sides, he appointed Eleazar to read
aloud[p] from the holy book, and gave
the watchword, "God's help"; then,
leading the first division himself, he
joined battle with Nicanor.
24 With the Almighty as their ally,
they slew more than nine thousand of
the enemy, and wounded and disabled
most of Nicanor's army, and forced
them all to flee. [25]They captured the
money of those who had come to buy

o Gk *they*
p The Greek text of this clause is uncertain

---

is the principal figure in 1 Macc.3.38–4.25. **10:** Since the battle of Magnesia (see 1 Macc.1.10 n.) the Seleucids had been forced to pay *tribute;* perhaps the *two thousand talents* represented the last instalment. **11:** Slave traders accompanied the expedition (compare 8.34 and 1 Macc.3.41). **13:** Compare 1 Macc.3.56. **14:** They *sold . . . property* so as to escape and join Judas' army. **15:** *Covenants,* with the patriarchs and at Sinai (see 1.24–29 n.; Ex.19.5–6). *Called them by his . . . name,* as God's people (Dt.28.10). **17:** *Lawless outrage,* 5.15–16. *Ancestral way of life,* or government under true high priests. **19:** 2 Kg.19.35. **20:** *The Galatians* from Asia Minor often served as mercenaries. Jewish forces evidently aided Antiochus III and *the Macedonians.* **22:** *Simon,* high priest 142–134 B.C., and *Jonathan,* from 160 to 143 or 142 B.C. *Joseph,* called John in 1 Macc.2.2; 9.36. **23:** *Eleazar,* another brother, was killed at Beth-zechariah (1 Macc. 2.5; 6.43–46). The motto "*God's help*" is prescribed by the Qumran *War Scroll* for one of the

them as slaves. After pursuing them
for some distance, they were obliged to
return because the hour was late. 26For
it was the day before the sabbath, and
for that reason they did not continue
their pursuit. 27And when they had
collected the arms of the enemy and
stripped them of their spoils, they kept
the sabbath, giving great praise and
thanks to the Lord, who had preserved
them for that day and allotted it to
them as the beginning of mercy.
28After the sabbath they gave some of
the spoils to those who had been tortured and to the widows and orphans,
and distributed the rest among themselves and their children. 29When they
had done this, they made common supplication and besought the merciful
Lord to be wholly reconciled with his
servants.

30 In encounters with the forces of
Timothy and Bacchides they killed
more than twenty thousand of them
and got possession of some exceedingly
high strongholds, and they divided very
much plunder, giving to those who had
been tortured and to the orphans and
widows, and also to the aged, shares
equal to their own. 31Collecting the
arms of the enemy,[q] they stored them
all carefully in strategic places, and
carried the rest of the spoils to Jerusalem. 32They killed the commander of
Timothy's forces, a most unholy man,
and one who had greatly troubled the
Jews. 33While they were celebrating
the victory in the city of their fathers,
they burned those who had set fire to
the sacred gates, Callisthenes and some
others, who had fled into one little
house; so these received the proper
recompense for their impiety.[r]

34 The thrice-accursed Nicanor, who
had brought the thousand merchants
to buy the Jews, 35having been humbled
with the help of the Lord by opponents
whom he regarded as of the least account, took off his splendid uniform
and made his way alone like a runaway
slave across the country till he reached
Antioch, having succeeded chiefly in
the destruction of his own army!
36Thus he who had undertaken to
secure tribute for the Romans by the
capture of the people of Jerusalem
proclaimed that the Jews had a Defender, and that therefore the Jews were
invulnerable, because they followed the
laws ordained by him.

9 About that time, as it happened,
Antiochus had retreated in disorder from the region of Persia. 2For
he had entered the city called Persepolis, and attempted to rob the temples
and control the city. Therefore the
people rushed to the rescue with arms,
and Antiochus and his men were
defeated,[s] with the result that Antiochus was put to flight by the inhabitants and beat a shameful retreat.
3While he was in Ecbatana, news came
to him of what had happened to
Nicanor and the forces of Timothy.
4Transported with rage, he conceived
the idea of turning upon the Jews the
injury done by those who had put him
to flight; so he ordered his charioteer
to drive without stopping until he com-

q Gk *their arms*
r The Greek text of this verse is uncertain
s Gk *they were defeated*

banners of the army returning from battle. **25:** *Slaves*, vv. 11, 34. **26:** Gorgias and his army were in the hills (1 Macc.4.16–18). **27–29:** The victory was a sign of God's favor, but the campaign had not yet been won (6.12–16; 1 Macc.4.19–25).

8.30–36: Other victories (1 Macc.5.37–44 tells of a battle against *Timothy* at Raphon). **30:** *Bacchides*, 1 Macc.7.8. **33:** *City of their fathers*, Jerusalem, with its *sacred gates*, Judas' ancestral home (1 Macc.2.1). **34:** *Thrice-accursed*, 15.3; Ad. Est.16.15.

9.1–12: Antiochus' illness (1 Macc.6.1–16). Here this story is placed before the purification of the temple (10.1–8; 1 Macc.4.36–61), Judas' southern campaigns (10.14–38; 1 Macc. ch. 5), and Lysias' first expedition (11.1–15; 1 Macc.4.26–35). **1:** *Antiochus* went to *Persia* to strengthen his authority there and to get funds. **2:** *Persepolis*, near Shiraz, the capital of Persia, founded by Darius I. **3:** Antiochus was on his way to Babylon (1 Macc.6.4) but went north by way of *Ecbatana*, Hamadan. **4:** 5.11; 7.3.

pleted the journey. But the judgment
of heaven rode with him! For in his
arrogance he said, "When I get there I
will make Jerusalem a cemetery of
Jews."
5 But the all-seeing Lord, the God
of Israel, struck him an incurable and
unseen blow. As soon as he ceased
speaking he was seized with a pain in
his bowels for which there was no relief and with sharp internal tortures
—6and that very justly, for he had
tortured the bowels of others with
many and strange inflictions. 7Yet he
did not in any way stop his insolence,
but was even more filled with arrogance, breathing fire in his rage against
the Jews, and giving orders to hasten
the journey. And so it came about that
he fell out of his chariot as it was rushing along, and the fall was so hard as to
torture every limb of his body. 8Thus
he who had just been thinking that he
could command the waves of the sea,
in his superhuman arrogance, and
imagining that he could weigh the high
mountains in a balance, was brought
down to earth and carried in a litter,
making the power of God manifest
to all. 9And so the ungodly man's
body swarmed with worms, and while
he was still living in anguish and pain,
his flesh rotted away, and because of
his stench the whole army felt revul-
sion at his decay. 10Because of his
intolerable stench no one was able to
carry the man who a little while before
had thought that he could touch the
stars of heaven. 11Then it was that,
broken in spirit, he began to lose much
of his arrogance and to come to his
senses under the scourge of God, for
he was tortured with pain every moment. 12And when he could not endure
his own stench, he uttered these words:
"It is right to be subject to God, and
no mortal should think that he is equal
to God."[t]
13 Then the abominable fellow made
a vow to the Lord, who would no
longer have mercy on him, stating
14that the holy city, which he was
hastening to level to the ground and
to make a cemetery, he was now declaring to be free; 15and the Jews,
whom he had not considered worth
burying but had planned to throw out
with their children to the beasts, for
the birds to pick, he would make, all
of them, equal to citizens of Athens;
16and the holy sanctuary, which he had
formerly plundered, he would adorn
with the finest offerings; and the holy
vessels he would give back, all of them,
many times over; and the expenses in-
curred for the sacrifices he would provide from his own revenues; 17and in
addition to all this he also would become
a Jew and would visit every inhabited
place to proclaim the power of God.
18But when his sufferings did not in
any way abate, for the judgment of God
had justly come upon him, he gave up
all hope for himself and wrote to the
Jews the following letter, in the form of
a supplication. This was its content:
19 "To his worthy Jewish citizens,
Antiochus their king and general sends
hearty greetings and good wishes for
their health and prosperity. 20If you
and your children are well and your
affairs are as you wish, I am glad. As
my hope is in heaven, 21I remember
with affection your esteem and good
will. On my way back from the region
of Persia I suffered an annoying illness,
and I have deemed it necessary to take
thought for the general security of all.
22I do not despair of my condition, for
I have good hope of recovering from
my illness, 23but I observed that my fa-

t Or *think thoughts proper only to God*

5: See 1 Macc.6.9 n. **8:** *Command the waves*, like Xerxes invading Greece. *Weigh the high mountains*, like God (see 5.21 n.; Is.40.12). **9:** *Worms*, Acts 12.23.

9.13–29: Repentance and death of Antiochus. **15:** *Citizens of Athens* were proud of their heritage, though the city no longer had actual power. **16:** 5.16. **17:** 7.37; Dan.4.31–35. **19–27:** The letter is no supplication (v. 18); it is addressed to Jews loyal to the king and bids them support his *son Antiochus* V (vv. 25–27). **23:** *My father*, Antiochus III (see 3.3 n.), who *appointed*

ther, on the occasions when he made expeditions into the upper country, appointed his successor, [24]so that, if anything unexpected happened or any unwelcome news came, the people throughout the realm would not be troubled, for they would know to whom the government was left. [25]Moreover, I understand how the princes along the borders and the neighbors to my kingdom keep watching for opportunities and waiting to see what will happen. So I have appointed my son Antiochus to be king, whom I have often entrusted and commended to most of you when I hastened off to the upper provinces; and I have written to him what is written here. [26]I therefore urge and beseech you to remember the public and private services rendered to you and to maintain your present good will, each of you, toward me and my son. [27]For I am sure that he will follow my policy and will treat you with moderation and kindness."

28 So the murderer and blasphemer, having endured the most intense suffering, such as he had inflicted on others, came to the end of his life by a most pitiable fate, among the mountains in a strange land. [29]And Philip, one of his courtiers, took his body home; then, fearing the son of Antiochus, he betook himself to Ptolemy Philometor in Egypt.

10 Now Maccabeus and his followers, the Lord leading them on, recovered the temple and the city; [2]and they tore down the altars which had been built in the public square by the foreigners, and also destroyed the sacred precincts. [3]They purified the sanctuary, and made another altar of sacrifice; then, striking fire out of flint, they offered sacrifices, after a lapse of two years, and they burned incense and lighted lamps and set out the bread of the Presence. [4]And when they had done this, they fell prostrate and besought the Lord that they might never again fall into such misfortunes, but that, if they should ever sin, they might be disciplined by him with forbearance and not be handed over to blasphemous and barbarous nations. [5]It happened that on the same day on which the sanctuary had been profaned by the foreigners, the purification of the sanctuary took place, that is, on the twenty-fifth day of the same month, which was Chislev. [6]And they celebrated it for eight days with rejoicing, in the manner of the feast of booths, remembering how not long before, during the feast of booths, they had been wandering in the mountains and caves like wild animals. [7]Therefore bearing ivy-wreathed wands and beautiful branches and also fronds of palm, they offered hymns of thanksgiving to him who had given success to the purifying of his own holy place. [8]They decreed by public ordinance and vote that the whole nation of the Jews should observe these days every year.

Seleucus IV as *his successor. The upper country,* Babylonia and Persia (1 Macc.3.37). **28:** Antiochus IV *died among the mountains,* perhaps at Gabae or Isfahan (see 1 Macc.6.5 n.). **29:** *Philip* was perhaps Antiochus V's guardian (see 1 Macc.6.14–15 n.). *Fearing* Lysias, viceroy in the west, rather than *the son of Antiochus,* who was a child, he went over to Syria's enemy, *Ptolemy* VI (see 4.21 n.). Josephus says that Philip took over the Seleucid government and was later killed (*Antiquities,* XII. ix. 7).

10.1–9: Purification of the temple (compare 1 Macc.4.36–61). **1:** They *recovered the temple,* desecrated by Antiochus (4.11; 1 Macc.1.54), *and the city,* except for the citadel (1 Macc.4.60; 6.18). **2:** *The altars* had been used for pagan worship. **3:** They *purified the sanctuary* by removing the desecrated stones (1 Macc.1.44–46). The reference to *striking fire out of flint* ignores the legends of 1.19–2.1. *Two years,* according to 1 Macc.1.54 and 4.52 it was three years. The *incense, lamps,* and *bread of the Presence,* prescribed by Ex.30.7–8; 25.30. **4:** 5.17–20; 6.12–16. **5–6:** *Chislev,* December, 164 B.C. (see 1 Macc.4.52–59 n.). At the normal time of *the feast of booths,* in September, *they had been wandering* like their ancestors (Lev.23.43) and could not celebrate it. **7:** *Ivy-wreathed wands,* here in honor of God (compare 6.7). *Branches* were carried

9 Such then was the end of Antiochus, who was called Epiphanes.

10 Now we will tell what took place
under Antiochus Eupator, who was
the son of that ungodly man, and will
give a brief summary of the principal
calamities of the wars. 11This man,
when he succeeded to the kingdom,
appointed one Lysias to have charge
of the government and to be chief
governor of Coelesyria and Phoenicia.
12Ptolemy, who was called Macron,
took the lead in showing justice to the
Jews because of the wrong that had
been done to them, and attempted to
maintain peaceful relations with them.
13As a result he was accused before
Eupator by the king's friends. He
heard himself called a traitor at every
turn, because he had abandoned
Cyprus, which Philometor had entrusted to him, and had gone over to
Antiochus Epiphanes. Unable to command the respect due his office,[u] he
took poison and ended his life.

14 When Gorgias became governor
of the region, he maintained a force of
mercenaries, and at every turn kept on
warring against the Jews. 15Besides
this, the Idumeans, who had control of
important strongholds, were harassing
the Jews; they received those who were
banished from Jerusalem, and en-
deavored to keep up the war. 16But
Maccabeus and his men, after making
solemn supplication and beseeching
God to fight on their side, rushed to
the strongholds of the Idumeans. 17At-
tacking them vigorously, they gained
possession of the places, and beat off
all who fought upon the wall, and
slew those whom they encountered,
killing no fewer than twenty thousand.

18 When no less than nine thousand
took refuge in two very strong towers
well equipped to withstand a siege,
19Maccabeus left Simon and Joseph,
and also Zacchaeus and his men, a
force sufficient to besiege them; and he
himself set off for places where he was
more urgently needed. 20But the men
with Simon, who were money-hungry,
were bribed by some of those who were
in the towers, and on receiving seventy
thousand drachmas let some of them
slip away. 21When word of what had
happened came to Maccabeus, he
gathered the leaders of the people,
and accused these men of having sold
their brethren for money by setting
their enemies free to fight against
them. 22Then he slew these men who
had turned traitor, and immediately
captured the two towers. 23Having
success at arms in everything he undertook, he destroyed more than twenty
thousand in the two strongholds.

24 Now Timothy, who had been defeated by the Jews before, gathered a
tremendous force of mercenaries and
collected the cavalry from Asia in no
small number. He came on, intending
to take Judea by storm. 25As he drew
near, Maccabeus and his men sprinkled
dust upon their heads and girded their
loins with sackcloth, in supplication to
God. 26Falling upon the steps before
the altar, they besought him to be gracious to them and to be an enemy to
their enemies and an adversary to their

u Cn: the Greek text here is uncertain

in procession at the feast of booths. *Fronds of palm* symbolize victory (1 Macc.13.51; Jn.12.13).

10.10–13: Antiochus V and Ptolemy Macron. 10–11: *Antiochus* V *Eupator* (9.25), son of Antiochus IV, reigned from 164 to 162 B.C., when he was murdered by order of Demetrius I. He was about nine years old; his father had *appointed . . . Lysias* as regent (1 Macc.3.32–33). **12–13:** *Ptolemy* had changed allegiance from Egypt to Syria (see 4.45 n.; 6.8); now he was friendly *to the Jews.*

10.14–23: Attacks on the Idumeans (1 Macc.5.1–3,9–54). **14:** *Gorgias* succeeded Ptolemy. **15:** *Idumeans,* or Edomites (see 1 Macc.5.3 n.); John Hyrcanus later forced them to adopt Judaism. *Those . . . banished,* supporters of Menelaus. **19:** *Urgently needed,* perhaps in Ammon and Gilead (1 Macc.5.6–13).

10.24–38: Victory over Timothy. 24: They met *Timothy* (8.30) *at dawn* (v. 28) at Dathema east of the Jordan (1 Macc.5.28–34). **26:** Ex.23.22.

adversaries, as the law declares. 27And
rising from their prayer they took up
their arms and advanced a considerable
distance from the city; and when they
came near to the enemy they halted.
28Just as dawn was breaking, the two
armies joined battle, the one having as
pledge of success and victory not only
their valor but their reliance upon the
Lord, while the other made rage their
leader in the fight.
29 When the battle became fierce,
there appeared to the enemy from
heaven five resplendent men on horses
with golden bridles, and they were
leading the Jews. 30Surrounding Maccabeus and protecting him with their
own armor and weapons, they kept
him from being wounded. And they
showered arrows and thunderbolts
upon the enemy, so that, confused and
blinded, they were thrown into disorder
and cut to pieces. 31Twenty thousand
five hundred were slaughtered, besides
six hundred horsemen.
32 Timothy himself fled to a stronghold called Gazara, especially well
garrisoned, where Chaereas was commander. 33Then Maccabeus and his
men were glad, and they besieged the
fort for four days. 34The men within,
relying on the strength of the place,
blasphemed terribly and hurled out
wicked words. 35But at dawn of the
fifth day, twenty young men in the
army of Maccabeus, fired with anger
because of the blasphemies, bravely
stormed the wall and with savage fury
cut down every one they met. 36Others
who came up in the same way wheeled
around against the defenders and set
fire to the towers; they kindled fires
and burned the blasphemers alive.
Others broke open the gates and let in
the rest of the force, and they occupied
the city. 37They killed Timothy, who
was hidden in a cistern, and his brother
Chaereas, and Apollophanes. 38When
they had accomplished these things,
with hymns and thanksgivings they
blessed the Lord who shows great kindness to Israel and gives them the
victory.

11 Very soon after this, Lysias, the
king's guardian and kinsman, who
was in charge of the government, being
vexed at what had happened, 2gathered
about eighty thousand men and all his
cavalry and came against the Jews. He
intended to make the city a home for
Greeks, 3and to levy tribute on the
temple as he did on the sacred places
of the other nations, and to put up the
high priesthood for sale every year. 4He
took no account whatever of the power
of God, but was elated with his ten
thousands of infantry, and his thousands of cavalry, and his eighty
elephants. 5Invading Judea, he approached Beth-zur, which was a fortified place about five leagues[v] from
Jerusalem, and pressed it hard.
6 When Maccabeus and his men got
word that Lysias[w] was besieging the
strongholds, they and all the people,
with lamentations and tears, besought
the Lord to send a good angel to save
Israel. 7Maccabeus himself was the
first to take up arms, and he urged the
others to risk their lives with him to aid
their brethren. Then they eagerly
rushed off together. 8And there, while
they were still near Jerusalem, a horse-
man appeared at their head, clothed in
white and brandishing weapons of gold.
9And they all together praised the

v About twenty miles. The text is uncertain here
w Gk *he*

29: 3.24–26. **31:** *Twenty thousand five hundred*, compare the number of fatalities mentioned in 8.30; 10.17,23. **32–38:** The fort of *Gazara* (1 Macc.4.15; 7.45) was well garrisoned; Simon captured it much later (1 Macc.13.43–48). **37:** *They killed Timothy;* but a Timothy reappears in 12.2, 18–25 (compare 1 Macc.5.11–40).

11.1–15: Victory over Lysias at Beth-zur. This probably occurred before the dedication of the temple (1 Macc.4.26–35). **1:** *Lysias*, see 10.10–13 n. **3:** In many Greek cults the *priesthood* was *for sale every year;* Antiochus IV had twice disposed of the Jewish high priesthood (4.7,24). **4:** *Elephants*, see 1 Macc.1.17 n.; 6.34–35 n. **5:** *Beth-zur*, about twenty miles south of Jerusalem on the road to Hebron. **6:** *Good angel*, Ex.23.20; Jos.5.13–15; Jg.6.11; 2 Kg.19.35.

merciful God, and were strengthened
in heart, ready to assail not only men
but the wildest beasts or walls of iron.
10They advanced in battle order, having
their heavenly ally, for the Lord had
mercy on them. 11They hurled themselves like lions against the enemy, and
slew eleven thousand of them and
sixteen hundred horsemen, and forced
all the rest to flee. 12Most of them got
away stripped and wounded, and
Lysias himself escaped by disgraceful
flight. 13And as he was not without
intelligence, he pondered over the defeat which had befallen him, and
realized that the Hebrews were invincible because the mighty God fought
on their side. So he sent to them 14and
persuaded them to settle everything on
just terms, promising that he would
persuade the king, constraining him to
be their friend.[x] 15Maccabeus, having
regard for the common good, agreed to
all that Lysias urged. For the king
granted every request in behalf of the
Jews which Maccabeus delivered to
Lysias in writing.

16 The letter written to the Jews by
Lysias was to this effect:

"Lysias to the people of the Jews,
greeting. 17John and Absalom, who
were sent by you, have delivered your
signed communication and have asked
about the matters indicated therein.
18I have informed the king of everything that needed to be brought before
him, and he has agreed to what was
possible. 19If you will maintain your
good will toward the government, I
will endeavor for the future to help
promote your welfare. 20And concerning these matters and their details,
I have ordered these men and my
representatives to confer with you.
21Farewell. The one hundred and
forty-eighth year,[y] Dioscorinthius
twenty-fourth."

22 The king's letter ran thus:

"King Antiochus to his brother
Lysias, greeting. 23Now that our
father has gone on to the gods, we
desire that the subjects of the kingdom be undisturbed in caring for their
own affairs. 24We have heard that the
Jews do not consent to our father's
change to Greek customs but prefer
their own way of living and ask that
their own customs be allowed them.
25Accordingly, since we choose that
this nation also be free from disturbance, our decision is that their temple
be restored to them and that they live
according to the customs of their
ancestors. 26You will do well, therefore, to send word to them and give
them pledges of friendship, so that they
may know our policy and be of good
cheer and go on happily in the conduct
of their own affairs."

27 To the nation the king's letter
was as follows:

"King Antiochus to the senate of
the Jews and to the other Jews, greeting. 28If you are well, it is as we desire.
We also are in good health. 29Mene-
laus has informed us that you wish to
return home and look after your own
affairs. 30Therefore those who go
home by the thirtieth day of Xanthicus
will have our pledge of friendship and
full permission 31for the Jews to enjoy

x The Greek text here is corrupt *y* 164 B.C.

13–15: According to 1 Macc.4.35 no peace was made, but Lysias returned to Antioch for reinforcements. He may have heard of Antiochus' death and hastened home to take control.

11.16–38: Letters of Lysias, Antiochus V, and the Romans. If Lysias heard of Philip's plot (see 9.29 n.), he may have wished to gain time through friendly gestures to the Jews. **16:** He wrote *to the people;* he did not recognize Judas' authority. **19:** Part of the Jews had *good will toward the government.* **21:** The date is early December, 164 B.C., before Judas rededicated the temple (1 Macc.4.52). **23:** *Our father*, Antiochus IV, *has gone on to the gods;* in his lifetime he had been worshiped. **25:** 1 Macc.4.36–61 says nothing of this, but Lysias may have instructed the citadel garrison not to interfere with the temple. **27:** The letter *to the senate* (1.10) and people ignores Judas (compare vv. 16–21). **29:** *Menelaus* had gone to Antioch and advised the king to let the Jews *return* to Jerusalem. He was now sent back (v. 32), hoping to regain the high priesthood. **30:** *Xanthicus*, March-April. **31:** *Their own food and laws,* 1 Macc.1.47–49. The

their own food and laws, just as formerly, and none of them shall be
molested in any way for what he may
have done in ignorance. 32 And I have
also sent Menelaus to encourage you.
33 Farewell. The one hundred and
forty-eighth year,[z] Xanthicus fifteenth."
34 The Romans also sent them a
letter, which read thus:
"Quintus Memmius and Titus
Manius, envoys of the Romans, to
the people of the Jews, greeting. 35 With
regard to what Lysias the kinsman of
the king has granted you, we also give
consent. 36 But as to the matters which
he decided are to be referred to the
king, as soon as you have considered
them, send some one promptly, so that
we may make proposals appropriate
for you. For we are on our way to
Antioch. 37 Therefore make haste and
send some men, so that we may have
your judgment. 38 Farewell. The one
hundred and forty-eighth year,[a] Xanthicus fifteenth."

12 When this agreement had been
reached, Lysias returned to the
king, and the Jews went about their
farming.
2 But some of the governors in
various places, Timothy and Apollonius the son of Gennaeus, as well
as Hieronymus and Demophon, and
in addition to these Nicanor the governor of Cyprus, would not let them
live quietly and in peace. 3 And some
men of Joppa did so ungodly a deed
as this: they invited the Jews who
lived among them to embark, with
their wives and children, on boats
which they had provided, as though
there were no ill will to the Jews;[b]
4 and this was done by public vote of
the city. And when they accepted,
because they wished to live peaceably
and suspected nothing, the men of
Joppa[c] took them out to sea and
drowned them, not less than two hundred. 5 When Judas heard of the
cruelty visited on his countrymen, he
gave orders to his men 6 and, calling
upon God the righteous Judge, attacked the murderers of his brethren.
He set fire to the harbor by night, and
burned the boats, and massacred those
who had taken refuge there. 7 Then,
because the city's gates were closed, he
withdrew, intending to come again and
root out the whole community of
Joppa. 8 But learning that the men in
Jamnia meant in the same way to wipe
out the Jews who were living among
them, 9 he attacked the people of
Jamnia by night and set fire to the
harbor and the fleet, so that the glow
of the light was seen in Jerusalem,
thirty miles[d] distant.
10 When they had gone more than a
mile[e] from there, on their march
against Timothy, not less than five
thousand Arabs with five hundred
horsemen attacked them. 11 After a
hard fight Judas and his men won the
victory, by the help of God. The
defeated nomads besought Judas to
grant them pledges of friendship,
promising to give him cattle and to help
his people[f] in all other ways. 12 Judas,
thinking that they might really be useful in many ways, agreed to make peace
with them; and after receiving his
pledges they departed to their tents.
13 He also attacked a certain city
which was strongly fortified with

z 164 B.C. *a* 164 B.C.
b Gk *them* *c* Gk *they*
d Gk *two hundred and forty stadia*
e Gk *nine stadia* *f* Gk *them*

---

words *in ignorance* imply that the king still maintained his claims and merely granted pardon (1 Macc.13.39). **34–37:** The *envoys* acted as intermediaries in *matters . . . referred to the king* that were still under negotiation.

12.1–16: Attacks on Joppa, Jamnia, and Caspin (the section 11.1–12.1 is out of place, and 12.2 resumes the narrative of 10.31). **1:** Palestinian Jews lived by *farming*. **2:** *Timothy*, 8.30–33; 10.24–37. *Apollonius*, not the Apollonius of 4.21. *Nicanor* is called *governor of Cyprus;* it was under Egypt's rule till 58 B.C., but Syria may have claimed it after the defection of Ptolemy Macron (10.13). There may have been two Nicanors (see 14.12 n.). **8:** *Jamnia*, about twelve miles south of Joppa. **13:** *Caspin*, perhaps Chaspho (1 Macc.5.36). **15:** Jos.6.1–21.

earthworks[g] and walls, and inhabited
by all sorts of Gentiles. Its name was
Caspin. 14And those who were within,
relying on the strength of the walls
and on their supply of provisions,
behaved most insolently toward Judas
and his men, railing at them and even
blaspheming and saying unholy things.
15But Judas and his men, calling upon
the great Sovereign of the world, who
without battering-rams or engines of
war overthrew Jericho in the days of
Joshua, rushed furiously upon the
walls. 16They took the city by the will
of God, and slaughtered untold numbers, so that the adjoining lake, a
quarter of a mile[h] wide, appeared to be
running over with blood.

17 When they had gone ninety-five
miles[i] from there, they came to
Charax, to the Jews who are called
Toubiani. 18They did not find Timothy in that region, for he had by then
departed from the region without
accomplishing anything, though in one
place he had left a very strong garrison.
19Dositheus and Sosipater, who were
captains under Maccabeus, marched
out and destroyed those whom Timothy
had left in the stronghold, more than
ten thousand men. 20But Maccabeus
arranged his army in divisions, set
men[j] in command of the divisions, and
hastened after Timothy, who had with
him a hundred and twenty thousand
infantry and two thousand five hundred
cavalry. 21When Timothy learned of
the approach of Judas, he sent off the
women and the children and also the
baggage to a place called Carnaim; for
that place was hard to besiege and
difflcult of access because of the nar-
rowness of all the approaches. 22But
when Judas' first division appeared,
terror and fear came over the enemy
at the manifestation to them of him
who sees all things; and they rushed
off in flight and were swept on, this
way and that, so that often they were
injured by their own men and pierced
by the points of their swords. 23And
Judas pressed the pursuit with the utmost vigor, putting the sinners to the
sword, and destroyed as many as
thirty thousand men.

24 Timothy himself fell into the
hands of Dositheus and Sosipater and
their men. With great guile he besought
them to let him go in safety, because
he held the parents of most of them and
the brothers of some and no consideration would be shown them. 25And
when with many words he had confirmed his solemn promise to restore
them unharmed, they let him go, for
the sake of saving their brethren.

26 Then Judas[k] marched against
Carnaim and the temple of Atargatis,
and slaughtered twenty-five thousand
people. 27After the rout and destruction of these, he marched also against
Ephron, a fortified city where Lysias
dwelt with multitudes of people of all
nationalities.[l] Stalwart young men
took their stand before the walls and
made a vigorous defense; and great
stores of war engines and missiles were
there. 28But the Jews[m] called upon the
Sovereign who with power shatters the
might of his enemies, and they got the
city into their hands, and killed as
many as twenty-five thousand of those
who were within it.

29 Setting out from there, they
hastened to Scythopolis, which is
seventy-five miles[n] from Jerusalem.
30But when the Jews who dwelt there
bore witness to the good will which
the people of Scythopolis had shown
them and their kind treatment of them

g The Greek text here is uncertain
h Gk *two stadia*
i Gk *seven hundred and fifty stadia*
j Gk *them* *k* Gk *he*
l The Greek text of this sentence is uncertain
m Gk *they* *n* Gk *six hundred stadia*

12.17–31: Battles in the northeast (the account supplements 1 Macc.5.9–32). **17:** *Toubiani,* perhaps men of Tob (1 Macc.5.13). **18:** *One place,* perhaps Bozrah, southeast of Tob (1 Macc. 5.28). **21:** *Carnaim,* a little north of Dera'a in Syria (Gen.14.5; 1 Macc.5.26). **26:** *Atargatis,* the Syrian goddess to whom fish were sacred. **27:** He *marched* south *against Ephron,* eight miles east of the Jordan, opposite Scythopolis (v. 29; 1 Macc.5.46–51). **29:** *Scythopolis,* ancient

in times of misfortune, [31]they thanked
them and exhorted them to be well disposed to their race in the future
also. Then they went up to Jerusalem, as the feast of weeks was close
at hand.

32 After the feast called Pentecost,
they hastened against Gorgias, the
governor of Idumea. [33]And he came
out with three thousand infantry and
four hundred cavalry. [34]When they
joined battle, it happened that a few
of the Jews fell. [35]But a certain
Dositheus, one of Bacenor's men, who
was on horseback and was a strong
man, caught hold of Gorgias, and
grasping his cloak was dragging him
off by main strength, wishing to take
the accursed man alive, when one of
the Thracian horsemen bore down
upon him and cut off his arm; so
Gorgias escaped and reached Marisa.

36 As Esdris and his men had been
fighting for a long time and were
weary, Judas called upon the Lord to
show himself their ally and leader in
the battle. [37]In the language of their
fathers he raised the battle cry, with
hymns; then he charged against Gorgias' men when they were not expecting it, and put them to flight.

38 Then Judas assembled his army
and went to the city of Adullam. As
the seventh day was coming on, they
purified themselves according to the
custom, and they kept the sabbath
there.

39 On the next day, as by that time
it had become necessary, Judas and
his men went to take up the bodies of
the fallen and to bring them back to lie
with their kinsmen in the sepulchres of
their fathers. [40]Then under the tunic
of every one of the dead they found
sacred tokens of the idols of Jamnia,
which the law forbids the Jews to wear.
And it became clear to all that this was
why these men had fallen. [41]So they
all blessed the ways of the Lord, the
righteous Judge, who reveals the things
that are hidden; [42]and they turned to
prayer, beseeching that the sin which
had been committed might be wholly
blotted out. And the noble Judas exhorted the people to keep themselves
free from sin, for they had seen with
their own eyes what had happened
because of the sin of those who had
fallen. [43]He also took up a collection,
man by man, to the amount of two
thousand drachmas of silver, and sent
it to Jerusalem to provide for a sin
offering. In doing this he acted very
well and honorably, taking account of
the resurrection. [44]For if he were not
expecting that those who had fallen
would rise again, it would have been
superfluous and foolish to pray for the
dead. [45]But if he was looking to the
splendid reward that is laid up for those
who fall asleep in godliness, it was a
holy and pious thought. Therefore he
made atonement for the dead, that
they might be delivered from their sin.

13 In the one hundred and forty-
ninth year[o] word came to Judas

o 163 B.C.

Beth-shan, then and later an important city (see 1 Macc.5.52 n.). **31:** The *feast of weeks* or Pentecost was at the time of the wheat harvest, seven weeks after Passover, and was celebrated in Jerusalem (Ex.34.22–24; Dt.16.9–12).

12.32–38: Battle with Gorgias. 35: *Marisa*, in the foothills southwest of Jerusalem near Beit-Jibrin (see 1 Macc.5.66 n.). **36:** *Esdris*, evidently a division leader (v. 20); the author of 2 Maccabees has abbreviated his source. **38:** *City of Adullam*, northeast of Marisa (Jos.12.15; 15.35). *They kept the sabbath*, when it was not necessary to fight (8.27; see 1 Macc.2.41 n.).

12.39–45: Burial of the dead. The author believed that many had been killed because they wore *sacred tokens* of pagan gods *which the law forbids* (v. 40; Dt.7.25–26), but Josephus says (*Antiquities*, XII. viii. 6) this reverse befell them because they had disobeyed Judas' instructions not to join battle before his arrival. This is the first known statement of the doctrine that a *sin offering* and prayer make *atonement* for the sins of *the dead* (v. 45), and it is justified by the hope that *those who had fallen would rise again* (vv. 43–44; 7.11; 14.46). *Fall asleep*, die (1 Cor.15.20).

13.1–8: Death of Menelaus. 1–2: *Antiochus* and *Lysias*, see 10.10–11 n. *Chariots armed with*

and his men that Antiochus Eupator
was coming with a great army against
Judea, 2and with him Lysias, his
guardian, who had charge of the government. Each of them had a Greek
force of one hundred and ten thousand
infantry, five thousand three hundred
cavalry, twenty-two elephants, and
three hundred chariots armed with
scythes.

3 Menelaus also joined them and
with utter hypocrisy urged Antiochus
on, not for the sake of his country's
welfare, but because he thought that
he would be established in office. 4But
the King of kings aroused the anger of
Antiochus against the scoundrel; and
when Lysias informed him that this
man was to blame for all the trouble,
he ordered them to take him to Beroea
and to put him to death by the method
which is the custom in that place. 5For
there is a tower in that place, fifty
cubits high, full of ashes, and it has a
rim running around it which on all
sides inclines precipitously into the
ashes. 6There they all push to destruction any man guilty of sacrilege or
notorious for other crimes. 7By such a
fate it came about that Menelaus the
lawbreaker died, without even burial
in the earth. 8And this was eminently
just; because he had committed many
sins against the altar whose fire and
ashes were holy, he met his death in
ashes.

9 The king with barbarous arrogance
was coming to show to the Jews things
far worse than those that had been
done[p] in his father's time. 10But when
Judas heard of this, he ordered the
people to call upon the Lord day and
night, now if ever to help those who
were on the point of being deprived of
the law and their country and the holy
temple, 11and not to let the people who
had just begun to revive fall into the
hands of the blasphemous Gentiles.
12When they had all joined in the same
petition and had besought the merciful Lord with weeping and fasting
and lying prostrate for three days
without ceasing, Judas exhorted
them and ordered them to stand
ready.

13 After consulting privately with
the elders, he determined to march out
and decide the matter by the help of
God before the king's army could enter
Judea and get possession of the city.
14So, committing the decision to the
Creator of the world and exhorting his
men to fight nobly to the death for the
laws, temple, city, country, and com-
monwealth, he pitched his camp near
Modein. 15He gave his men the watchword, "God's victory," and with a
picked force of the bravest young men,
he attacked the king's pavilion at night
and slew as many as two thousand men
in the camp. He stabbed[q] the leading
elephant and its rider. 16In the end
they filled the camp with terror and
confusion and withdrew in triumph.
17This happened, just as day was dawning, because the Lord's help protected
him.

18 The king, having had a taste of
the daring of the Jews, tried strategy in
attacking their positions. 19He advanced against Beth-zur, a strong
fortress of the Jews, was turned back,
attacked again,[r] and was defeated.
20Judas sent in to the garrison what-

p Or *the worst of the things that had been done*
q The Greek text here is uncertain
r Or *faltered*

---

scythes to cut down foot soldiers had been used since the days of the Persian Empire. **4:** *The King of kings*, God (Rev.19.16). What *aroused* his *anger* is not known (but see 4.27). *Beroea*, now Aleppo in northern Syria. *The method* of execution (vv. 5–6) was Persian.

13.9–17: Preliminary skirmish. 12: Jews employed such acts of penitence particularly when there was danger of sacrilege (3.15; 10.4; 1 Macc.4.40). **14:** The Syrian army had invaded Judea from the south, through Idumea (1 Macc.6.31). Judas first *pitched his camp near Modein* to watch the Syrian line along the coast. The first battle occurred at Beth-zechariah (1 Macc.6.32–47). **15:** "*God's victory*," see 8.23 n. Eleazar *stabbed the leading elephant* (1 Macc.6.43–46). **16:** According to 1 Macc.6.47 the Jews fled.

13.18–26: Attack on Beth-zur. 19: The Syrians were defeated in the first attempt (1 Macc.

ever was necessary. [21]But Rhodocus, a man from the ranks of the Jews, gave secret information to the enemy; he was sought for, caught, and put in prison. [22]The king negotiated a second time with the people in Beth-zur, gave pledges, received theirs, withdrew, attacked Judas and his men, was defeated; [23]he got word that Philip, who had been left in charge of the government, had revolted in Antioch; he was dismayed, called in the Jews, yielded and swore to observe all their rights, settled with them and offered sacrifice, honored the sanctuary and showed generosity to the holy place. [24]He received Maccabeus, left Hegemonides as governor from Ptolemais to Gerar, [25]and went to Ptolemais. The people of Ptolemais were indignant over the treaty; in fact they were so angry that they wanted to annul its terms.[s] [26]Lysias took the public platform, made the best possible defense, convinced them, appeased them, gained their good will, and set out for Antioch. This is how the king's attack and withdrawal turned out.

14 Three years later, word came to Judas and his men that Demetrius, the son of Seleucus, had sailed into the harbor of Tripolis with a strong army and a fleet, [2]and had taken possession of the country, having made away with Antiochus and his guardian Lysias.

3 Now a certain Alcimus, who had formerly been high priest but had wilfully defiled himself in the times of separation, realized that there was no way for him to be safe or to have access again to the holy altar, [4]and went to King Demetrius in about the one hundred and fifty-first year,[t] presenting to him a crown of gold and a palm, and besides these some of the customary olive branches from the temple. During that day he kept quiet. [5]But he found an opportunity that furthered his mad purpose when he was invited by Demetrius to a meeting of the council and was asked about the disposition and intentions of the Jews. He answered:

6 "Those of the Jews who are called Hasideans, whose leader is Judas Maccabeus, are keeping up war and stirring up sedition, and will not let the kingdom attain tranquillity. [7]Therefore I have laid aside my ancestral glory—I mean the high priesthood—and have now come here, [8]first because I am genuinely concerned for the interests of the king, and second because I have regard also for my fellow citizens. For through the folly of those whom I have mentioned our whole nation is now in no small misfortune. [9]Since you are acquainted, O king, with the details of this matter, deign to take thought for our country and our hard-pressed nation with the gracious kindness which you show to all. [10]For as long as Judas lives, it is impossible for the government to find peace."

11 When he had said this, the rest of the king's friends, who were hostile to Judas, quickly inflamed Demetrius still more. [12]And he immediately chose Nicanor, who had been in command of

s The Greek text of this clause is uncertain
t 161 B.C.

6.31). **21–22:** The garrison surrendered because of lack of food (1 Macc.6.49); possibly this was the *secret information.* **23:** *Philip*, see 9.29 n.; 1 Macc.6.14–15,55–56. **24:** *Gerar*, south of Gaza on the coastal plain. **26:** 1 Macc.6.63.

14.1–10: Accession of Demetrius I (1 Macc.7.1–7). **1:** *Three years later*, about 161 B.C. *Demetrius* I Soter, *the son of Seleucus* IV, reigned 162–150. *Tripolis*, see 1 Macc.7.1 n. **2:** *Antiochus . . . Lysias*, 1 Macc.7.3–4. **3:** *Alcimus* may not have *been high priest*. *Defiled*, 4.11–15. **4:** 1 Macc.7.5–7 may record an earlier visit. *Crown*, emblem of sovereignty; the *palm*, victory. **6:** *Hasideans*, see 1 Macc.2.42 n. **7:** *Ancestral glory*, he claimed legitimate succession. **8:** See 1 Macc.1.11 n.

14.11–14: Appointment of Nicanor and Alcimus. This story omits the expedition of Bacchides (1 Macc.7.8–25). Josephus says that *Nicanor* had escaped from Rome with Demetrius (*Antiqui-*

the elephants, appointed him governor
of Judea, and sent him off 13with orders
to kill Judas and scatter his men, and
to set up Alcimus as high priest of the
greatest temple. 14And the Gentiles
throughout Judea, who had fled before[u] Judas, flocked to join Nicanor,
thinking that the misfortunes and
calamities of the Jews would mean
prosperity for themselves.

15 When the Jews[v] heard of Nicanor's coming and the gathering of the
Gentiles, they sprinkled dust upon
their heads and prayed to him who
established his own people for ever
and always upholds his own heritage
by manifesting himself. 16At the command of the leader, they[w] set out from
there immediately and engaged them
in battle at a village called Dessau.[x]
17Simon, the brother of Judas, had
encountered Nicanor, but had been
temporarily[y] checked because of the
sudden consternation created by the
enemy.

18 Nevertheless Nicanor, hearing of
the valor of Judas and his men and
their courage in battle for their country, shrank from deciding the issue by
bloodshed. 19Therefore he sent Posi-
donius and Theodotus and Mattathias
to give and receive pledges of friendship. 20When the terms had been fully
considered, and the leader had informed the people, and it appeared
that they were of one mind, they agreed
to the covenant. 21And the leaders[z]
set a day on which to meet by themselves. A chariot came forward from
each army; seats of honor were set in
place; 22Judas posted armed men in
readiness at key places to prevent sudden treachery on the part of the enemy;
they held the proper conference.

23 Nicanor stayed on in Jerusalem
and did nothing out of the way, but
dismissed the flocks of people that had
gathered. 24And he kept Judas always
in his presence; he was warmly attached to the man. 25And he urged
him to marry and have children; so
he married, settled down, and shared
the common life.

26 But when Alcimus noticed their
good will for one another, he took the
covenant that had been made and went
to Demetrius. He told him that Nicanor was disloyal to the government, for
he had appointed that conspirator
against the kingdom, Judas, to be his
successor. 27The king became excited
and, provoked by the false accusations
of that depraved man, wrote to Nicanor, stating that he was displeased with
the covenant and commanding him to
send Maccabeus to Antioch as a
prisoner without delay.

28 When this message came to Nicanor, he was troubled and grieved that
he had to annul their agreement when
the man had done no wrong. 29Since
it was not possible to oppose the king,
he watched for an opportunity to
accomplish this by a stratagem. 30But
Maccabeus, noticing that Nicanor was
more austere in his dealings with him
and was meeting him more rudely than
had been his custom, concluded that
this austerity did not spring from the
best motives. So he gathered not a few
of his men, and went into hiding from
Nicanor.

31 When the latter became aware
that he had been cleverly outwitted by
the man, he went to the great[a] and holy
temple while the priests were offering
the customary sacrifices, and com-

u The Greek text is uncertain
v Gk *they*
w Gk *he*
x The name is uncertain
y Other authorities read *slowly*
z Gk *they*
a Gk *greatest*

---

ties, XII. x. 4); if he is the person in 8.9–36 he must have gone from Syria to Rome to assist the escape.

14.15–36: Nicanor seeks friendship with Judas. 15: *Sprinkled dust*, Jos.7.6. **16:** *The leader*, Judas, or possibly Nicanor. *Dessau*, perhaps Adasa (1 Macc.7.40–45). **20–21:** *The leader*, Nicanor. *The people*, his army. Afterward *the leaders*, Nicanor and Judas, met. **22:** 1 Macc.7.12–18. **24:** *Warmly attached* only so long as things went well (compare vv. 31–33). **26:** *Alcimus* failed to get civil power and feared that *Judas* would be made his *successor* as high priest.

manded them to hand the man over. 32And when they declared on oath that they did not know where the man was whom he sought, 33he stretched out his right hand toward the sanctuary, and swore this oath: "If you do not hand Judas over to me as a prisoner, I will level this precinct of God to the ground and tear down the altar, and I will build here a splendid temple to Dionysus."

34 Having said this, he went away. Then the priests stretched forth their hands toward heaven and called upon the constant Defender of our nation, in these words: 35"O Lord of all, who hast need of nothing, thou wast pleased that there be a temple for thy habitation among us; 36so now, O holy One, Lord of all holiness, keep undefiled for ever this house that has been so recently purified."

37 A certain Razis, one of the elders of Jerusalem, was denounced to Nicanor as a man who loved his fellow citizens and was very well thought of and for his good will was called father of the Jews. 38For in former times, when there was no mingling with the Gentiles, he had been accused of Judaism, and for Judaism he had with all zeal risked body and life. 39Nicanor, wishing to exhibit the enmity which he had for the Jews, sent more than five hundred soldiers to arrest him; 40for he thought that by arresting[b] him he would do them an injury. 41When the troops were about to capture the tower and were forcing the door of the courtyard, they ordered that fire be brought and the doors burned. Being surrounded, Razis[c] fell upon his own sword, 42preferring to die nobly rather than to fall into the hands of sinners and suffer outrages unworthy of his noble birth. 43But in the heat of the struggle he did not hit exactly, and the crowd was now rushing in through the doors. He bravely ran up on the wall, and manfully threw himself down into the crowd. 44But as they quickly drew back, a space opened and he fell in the middle of the empty space. 45Still alive and aflame with anger, he rose, and though his blood gushed forth and his wounds were severe he ran through the crowd; and standing upon a steep rock, 46with his blood now completely drained from him, he tore out his entrails, took them with both hands and hurled them at the crowd, calling upon the Lord of life and spirit to give them back to him again. This was the manner of his death.

15 When Nicanor heard that Judas and his men were in the region of Samaria, he made plans to attack them with complete safety on the day of rest. 2And when the Jews who were compelled to follow him said, "Do not destroy so savagely and barbarously, but show respect for the day which he who sees all things has honored and hallowed above other days," 3the thrice-accursed wretch asked if there were a sovereign in heaven who had commanded the keeping of the sabbath day. 4And when they declared, "It is the living Lord himself, the Sovereign in heaven, who ordered us to observe the seventh day," 5he replied, "And I am a sovere gn also, on earth, and I command you to take up arms and finish the king's business." Nevertheless, he did not succeed in carrying out his abominable design.

6 This Nicanor in his utter boastfulness and arrogance had determined to erect a public monument of victory

b The Greek text here is uncertain
c Gk *he*

33: *Stretched out his right hand . . . and swore*, 15.32–33. *Dionysus*, 6.7. **35–36:** 1 Kg.8.27–30. *Purified*, 10.1–8.

14.37–46: Death of Razis. A martyrology in the style of 6.18–7.42. **37:** *Elders*, 13.13. **46:** He expected his body to be restored in the resurrection (7.11).

15.1–36: Death of Nicanor (1 Macc.7.39–50). **1:** *Nicanor* camped at Beth-horon, and *Judas* was at Adasa, between Beth-horon and Jerusalem. **2:** *The Jews* in Nicanor's army wished to honor the sabbath. **3:** *Thrice-accursed*, 8.34. **4–5:** Ex.20.8–11; Dan.3.16–18.

over Judas and his men. [7]But Maccabeus did not cease to trust with all confidence that he would get help from the Lord. [8]And he exhorted his men not to fear the attack of the Gentiles, but to keep in mind the former times when help had come to them from heaven, and now to look for the victory which the Almighty would give them. [9]Encouraging them from the law and the prophets, and reminding them also of the struggles they had won, he made them the more eager. [10]And when he had aroused their courage, he gave his orders, at the same time pointing out the perfidy of the Gentiles and their violation of oaths. [11]He armed each of them not so much with confidence in shields and spears as with the inspiration of brave words, and he cheered them all by relating a dream, a sort of vision,[d] which was worthy of belief.

12 What he saw was this: Onias, who had been high priest, a noble and good man, of modest bearing and gentle manner, one who spoke fittingly and had been trained from childhood in all that belongs to excellence, was praying with outstretched hands for the whole body of the Jews. [13]Then likewise a man appeared, distinguished by his gray hair and dignity, and of marvelous majesty and authority. [14]And Onias spoke, saying, "This is a man who loves the brethren and prays much for the people and the holy city, Jeremiah, the prophet of God." [15]Jeremiah stretched out his right hand and gave to Judas a golden sword, and as he gave it he addressed him thus: [16]"Take this holy sword, a gift from God, with which you will strike down your adversaries."

17 Encouraged by the words of Judas, so noble and so effective in arousing valor and awaking manliness in the souls of the young, they determined not to carry on a campaign but to attack bravely, and to decide the matter, by fighting hand to hand with all courage, because the city and the sanctuary and the temple were in danger. [18]Their concern for wives and children, and also for brethren and relatives, lay upon them less heavily; their greatest and first fear was for the consecrated sanctuary. [19]And those who had to remain in the city were in no little distress, being anxious over the encounter in the open country.

20 When all were now looking forward to the coming decision, and the enemy was already close at hand with their army drawn up for battle, the elephants[e] strategically stationed and the cavalry deployed on the flanks, [21]Maccabeus, perceiving the hosts that were before him and the varied supply of arms and the savagery of the elephants,[e] stretched out his hands toward heaven and called upon the Lord who works wonders; for he knew that it is not by arms, but as the Lord[f] decides, that he gains the victory for those who deserve it. [22]And he called upon him in these words: "O Lord, thou didst send thy angel in the time of Hezekiah king of Judea, and he slew fully a hundred and eighty-five thousand in the camp of Sennacherib. [23]So now, O Sovereign of the heavens, send a good angel to carry terror and trembling before us. [24]By the might of thy arm may these blasphemers who come against thy holy people be struck down." With these words he ended his prayer.

d The Greek text here is uncertain
e Gk *beasts*
f Gk *he*

8: 1 Macc.7.41. **9:** *The law and the prophets*, the first two major divisions of the Old Testament, were now regarded as scripture (compare the Prologue to Sirach; see 2 Esd.14.45 n.); not all the other books had been collected. **10:** *Violation of oaths*, 11.27–32; 14.20–28. **12:** *Onias*, 3.1–40. **14:** The writer believed that saints like *Jeremiah* were alive even before the resurrection. **15–16:** The *golden sword* was a sign that God approved the Jews' self-defense on the sabbath. **18:** *First fear*, compare 14.33. **20:** *Elephants*, to break through the Jewish infantry; the *cavalry* protected the *flanks* of the Syrian infantry. **22–23:** See 11.6 n.; 2 Kg.19.35.

25 Nicanor and his men advanced
with trumpets and battle songs; [26]and
Judas and his men met the enemy in
battle with invocation to God and
prayers. [27]So, fighting with their hands
and praying to God in their hearts, they
laid low no less than thirty-five thousand men, and were greatly gladdened
by God's manifestation.

28 When the action was over and
they were returning with joy, they
recognized Nicanor, lying dead, in full
armor. [29]Then there was shouting and
tumult, and they blessed the Sovereign
Lord in the language of their fathers.
[30]And the man who was ever in body
and soul the defender of his fellow
citizens, the man who maintained his
youthful good will toward his countrymen, ordered them to cut off Nicanor's
head and arm and carry them to Jerusalem. [31]And when he arrived there
and had called his countrymen together
and stationed the priests before the
altar, he sent for those who were in the
citadel. [32]He showed them the vile
Nicanor's head and that profane man's
arm, which had been boastfully
stretched out against the holy house of
the Almighty; [33]and he cut out the
tongue of the ungodly Nicanor and
said that he would give it piecemeal to
the birds and hang up these rewards of
his folly opposite the sanctuary. [34]And
they all, looking to heaven, blessed the
Lord who had manifested himself,
saying, "Blessed is he who has kept
his own place undefiled." [35]And he
hung Nicanor's head from the citadel,
a clear and conspicuous sign to every
one of the help of the Lord. [36]And
they all decreed by public vote never to
let this day go unobserved, but to celebrate the thirteenth day of the twelfth
month—which is called Adar in the
Syrian language—the day before Mordecai's day.

37 This, then, is how matters turned
out with Nicanor. And from that time
the city has been in the possession of
the Hebrews. So I too will here end my
story. [38]If it is well told and to the
point, that is what I myself desired;
if it is poorly done and mediocre, that
was the best I could do. [39]For just as
it is harmful to drink wine alone, or,
again, to drink water alone, while wine
mixed with water is sweet and delicious
and enhances one's enjoyment, so
also the style of the story delights the
ears of those who read the work. And
here will be the end.

25: *Battle songs*, such as Pss.68.1–3; 83. **29:** *Language of their fathers*, Hebrew or Aramaic. **31:** *The citadel* on the Ophel hill was held by Syrians (1 Macc.1.33; 6.18); but the Jews had built another fort (1 Macc.4.60). **32:** *Head . . . arm*, 14.33. **35:** 1 Sam.31.9; Jdt.14.1; 1 Macc.7.47. **36:** The *twelfth month* (February-March) was *called Adar in the Syrian language* (that is, in Aramaic) and also in Hebrew. If there was but one month of Adar in this year (probably 161 B.C.), it was *the day before Mordecai's day*, but in some years a second month of Adar was intercalated to harmonize the calendar. Nicanor's day was observed up to A.D. 70 (see 1 Macc.7.49 n.).

15.37–39: Conclusion. The epitomist wrote some time before the Jewish war (A.D. 66–70), when Jerusalem was still in Jewish hands. **37:** *Hebrews*, see 7.31 n. **39:** To *drink wine alone* was a mark of the drunkard or spendthrift. *Water alone* was the drink of the poor, or of certain Greek philosophers, or those who like the Rechabites were forbidden wine (Jer.35.5–10). *The style* will delight *the ears of those who read*, because in antiquity it was the custom to read literary works aloud, even to oneself.

CHRONOLOGICAL TABLES OF RULERS

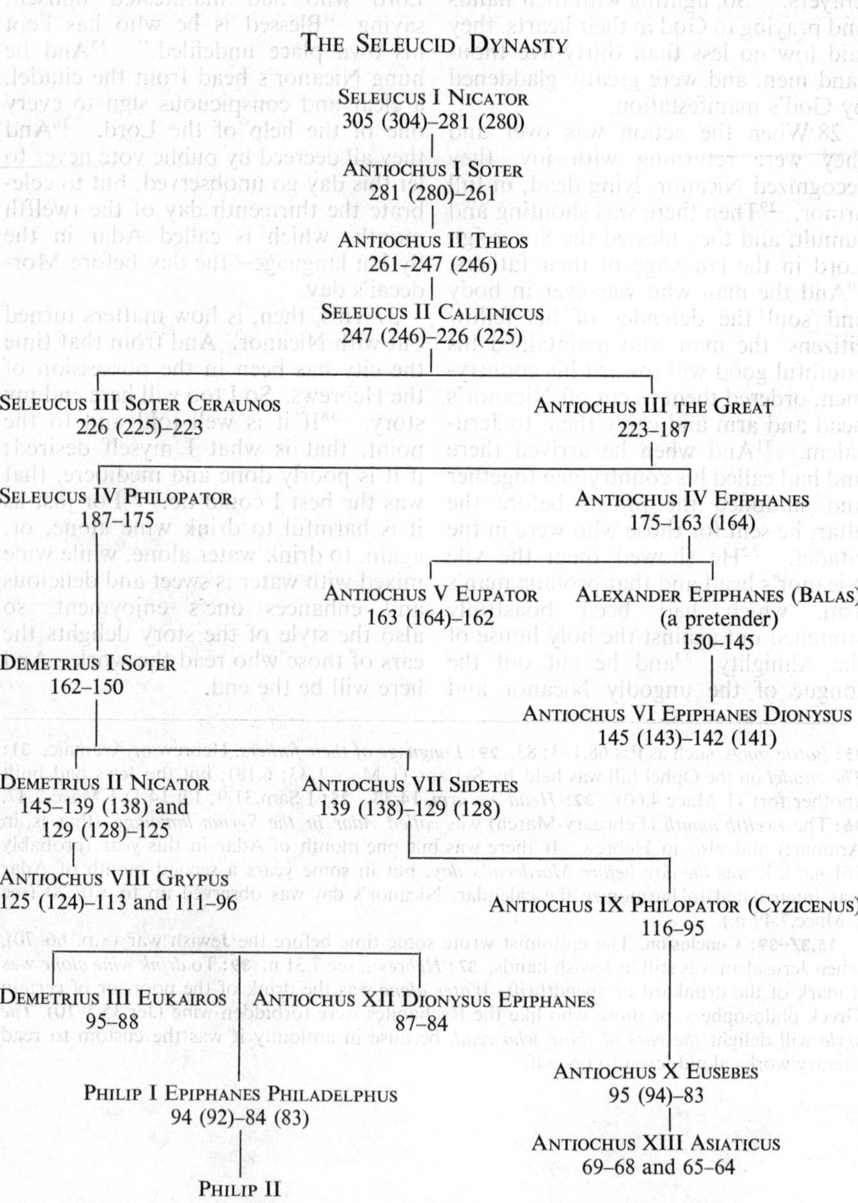

The House of the Maccabees (Hasmoneans)

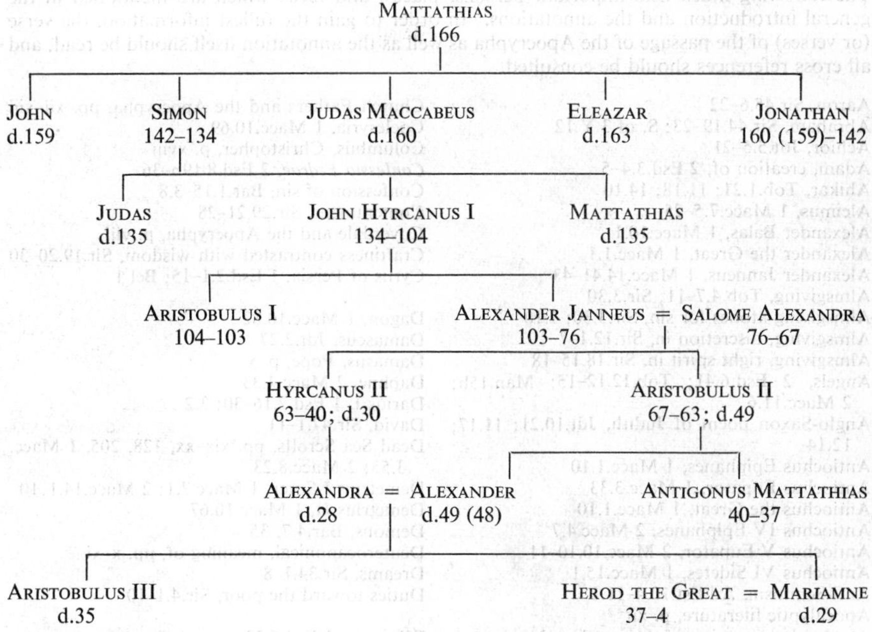

These two family trees include the names of the more important rulers. The presence of short parallel lines between two names indicates marriage. The date of an individual's death or the dates of his rule are in some cases disputed, and alternative possibilities are given within parentheses. All the dates are B.C. Besides the standard works on the chronology of the inter-testamental period, special mention should be made of F. M. Heichelheim's "Chronological Table from 323–30 B.C." in *Proceedings of the IX International Congress of Papyrology*, Oslo, 1958, pp. 163–182 (also published separately by the Norwegian Universities Press). Seleucus I became king in the seventh year of the Seleucid era; see A. J. Sachs and D. J. Wiseman, "A Babylonian King List of the Hellenistic Period," *Iraq*, xvi (1954), p. 205. Syria became a Roman province in 64 B.C., and Pompey conquered Jerusalem in 63 B.C.

INDEX TO THE ANNOTATIONS

The following index lists important persons, places, and ideas which are mentioned in the general introduction and the annotations. In order to gain the fullest information, the verse (or verses) of the passage of the Apocrypha as well as the annotation itself should be read, and all cross references should be consulted.